lonely planet

USA'S BEST TRIPS

52 AMAZING ROAD TRIPS

This edition written and researched by

**Sara Benson,
Amy C Balfour, Michael Benanav, Greg Benchwick,
Lisa Dunford, Michael Grosberg, Adam Karlin,
Mariella Krause, Carolyn McCarthy, Christopher Pitts,
Adam Skolnick, Ryan Ver Berkmoes, Mara Vorhees,
Karla Zimmerman**

SYMBOLS IN THIS BOOK

 Top Tips

History & Culture

 Essential Photo

Link Your Trips

 Family

Walking Tour

Tips from Locals

Food & Drink

Eating

Trip Detour

Outdoors

Sleeping

☎ Telephone Number

@ Internet Access

🄳 English-Language Menu

⊘ Opening Hours

🛜 Wi-Fi Access

👪 Family-Friendly

ⓟ Parking

✏ Vegetarian Selection

😺 Pet-Friendly

⊖ Nonsmoking

🏊 Swimming Pool

❄ Air-Conditioning

MAP LEGEND

Routes
- Trip Route
- Trip Detour
- Linked Trip
- Walk Route
- Tollway
- Freeway
- Primary
- Secondary
- Tertiary
- Lane
- Unsealed Road
- Plaza/Mall
- Steps
- Tunnel
- Pedestrian Overpass
- Walk Track/Path

Boundaries
- International
- State/Province
- Cliff

Population
- ✪ Capital (National)
- ◎ Capital (State/Province)
- ● City/Large Town
- ○ Town/Village

Transport
- ✈ Airport
- Cable Car/Funicular
- ⓟ Parking
- Train/Railway
- Tram
- Ⓜ Underground Train Station

Trips
- **1** Trip Numbers
- **9** Trip Stop
- Walking tour
- Trip Detour

Highway Route Markers
- [97] US National Hwy
- [5] US Interstate Hwy
- [44] State Hwy
- [99] California State Hwy

Hydrography
- River/Creek
- Intermittent River
- Swamp/Mangrove
- Canal
- Water
- Dry/Salt/Intermittent Lake
- Glacier

Areas
- Beach
- Cemetery (Christian)
- Cemetery (Other)
- Park
- Forest
- Reservation
- Urban Area
- Sportsground

PLAN YOUR TRIPS

ON THE ROAD

CONTENTS

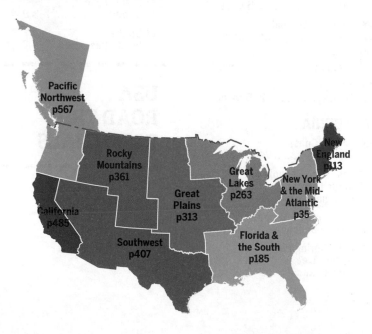

Pacific
Northwest
p567

Rocky
Mountains
p361

Great
Lakes
p263

New
England
p113

New York
& the Mid-
Atlantic
p35

Great
Plains
p313

California
p485

Great
Plains
p313

Southwest
p407

Florida &
the South
p185

Contents cont.

USA ROAD TRIP ESSENTIALS

Classic Trips

**Look out for the Classic Trips stamp
on our favorite routes in this book.**

Statue of Liberty New York City

WELCOME TO
THE USA

Fill up the gas tank and buckle up – the USA is an unforgettably crazy trip. And there's no better way to get to know this enormous, energetic and engaging country than by hitting the road, Jack.

With this book as your travel companion, you can drive up, down, across or straight through every state on the continental map. If you're on the hunt for that perfect California seafood shack, Texas hill country swimming hole or New England ivy-clad college town, we've got you covered.

Whether you want to dive into the wildest terrain or connect the dots between the USA's brightest, most buzzing cities, you'll find a trip designed just for you in this book. And if you've only got time for one journey, pick from our 10 Classic Trips, which take you on a tour of the very best of the USA. Turn the page for more.

USA
Classic Trips

8

What Is A Classic Trip?

All the trips in this book show you the best of the USA, but we've chosen 15 as our all-time favorites. These are our Classic Trips – the ones that lead you to the best of the iconic sights, the top activities and the unique USA experiences. Turn the page to see the map, and look out for the Classic Trip stamp throughout the book.

14 **Highway 1** Follow miles and miles of beach all the way down the Florida coast.

8 **Fall Foliage Tour** Bask in the Vermont countryside – at its best during the fall.

39 **Pacific Coast Highways** Cruise the cliffs along California's Big Sur coast.

39

USA
Classic Trips

BRITISH COLUMBIA

46 **Cascade Drive** Wild West towns, Bavarian villages and moody mountains. **4–5 DAYS**

28 **Grand Teton to Yellowstone** Outstanding wildlife, gushing geysers and alpine scenery. **7 DAYS**

SASKATCHEWAN

Vancouver
Kelowna
ALBERTA
Regina

Victoria
Seattle
CANADA

Olympia
WASHINGTON
Lolo National Forest
MONTANA
Helena
NORTH DAKOTA

49 **Highway 101 Oregon Coast** Diversions include whale-watching, lighthouses and seafood. **7 DAYS**

Salem
OREGON
Boise National Forest
Mammoth
Bismarck

Boise
IDAHO
Yellowstone National Park
Jackson
Rapid City
SOUTH DAKOTA
Pierre

PACIFIC OCEAN

Carson City
Elko
WYOMING
Cheyenne
NEBRASKA

San Francisco
Sacramento
NEVADA
Salt Lake City
Denver

39 **Pacific Coast Highways** The ultimate coastal road trip takes in beaches, redwood forests and more. **7–10 DAYS**

Fresno
Death Valley National Park
UTAH
Grand Junction
COLORADO

Las Vegas
CALIFORNIA
Navajo Nation

Los Angeles
Prescott
Santa Fe
Albuquerque

San Diego
Mexicali
Phoenix
ARIZONA
NEW MEXICO

32 **Four Corners Cruise** Loop past the Southwest's biggest and boldest parks and sights. **10 DAYS**

40 **Yosemite, Sequoia & Kings Canyon** Be awed by peaks, wildflowers, sequoias and waterfalls. **5–7 DAYS**

33 **Fantastic Canyon Voyage** Cowboy up in Wickenburg, then applaud the Grand Canyon. **4–5 DAYS**

MEXICO

MEXICO CITY

8 Fall Foliage Tour
The ultimate fall foliage trip, featuring dappled trails and awesome views. **5–7 DAYS**

7 Coastal New England
The ultimate coastal drive connects fishing villages and trading ports. **6–8 DAYS**

26 Black Hills Loop
Icons, beauty and fun combine for the perfect driving loop. **2–3 DAYS**

1 Finger Lakes Loop
Lakeside roads lead past vineyards to deep gorges and ravines for hiking. **3 DAYS**

5 The Civil War Tour
See preserved battlefields and 19th-century countryside. **3 DAYS**

20 Route 66
America's 'Mother Road' offers a time-warped journey from Chicago to LA. **14 DAYS**

14 Highway 1
Embark on an adventure that runs the length of the Atlantic Coast. **6 DAYS**

18 Blue Ridge Parkway
The beloved byway explores the craggy, misty depths of the Appalachians. **5 DAYS**

MANITOBA

ONTARIO

Winnipeg

Québec City

Fredericton

Halifax

Montréal

MAINE

NEW HAMPSHIRE

OTTAWA

Augusta

VERMONT

Montpelier

Concord

MASSACHUSETTS

Albany

Boston

RHODE ISLAND

WISCONSIN

NEW YORK

Toronto

Providence

CONNECTICUT

MINNESOTA

Madison

Lansing

PENNSYLVANIA

Corning

IOWA

Chicago

MICHIGAN

New York

NEW JERSEY

Des Moines

ILLINOIS

OHIO

Harrisburg

Trenton

Lincoln

INDIANA

Columbus

Dover

DELAWARE

Springfield

WEST VIRGINIA

WASHINGTON DC

MARYLAND

Jefferson City

Indianapolis

St Louis

Frankfort

Richmond

Topeka

KANSAS

MISSOURI

KENTUCKY

VIRGINIA

Boone

NORTH CAROLINA

OKLAHOMA

ARKANSAS

TENNESSEE

Nashville

Oklahoma City

Little Rock

Columbia

SOUTH CAROLINA

MISSISSIPPI

Atlanta

Dallas

Jackson

ALABAMA

GEORGIA

TEXAS

LOUISIANA

Jacksonville

Austin

Baton Rouge

New Orleans

FLORIDA

Orlando

ATLANTIC OCEAN

Tampa

Gulf of Mexico

Miami

CUBA

Chetumal

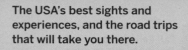
The USA's best sights and experiences, and the road trips that will take you there.

USA
HIGHLIGHTS

Route 66

No US road trip is more classic than Route 66, America's 'Mother Road.' Running over 2400 miles between windy Chicago and sunny Los Angeles, this mostly two-lane ribbon of concrete passes neon-signed motor courts, old-fashioned diners that dish up pie, and drive-in theaters under the stars. Meet genuinely friendly, small-town Americans on **Trip 20: Route 66**.

TRIPS    20 22 24 32

Route 66 Mother of all classic drives

Pacific Coast Highways San Francisco's Golden Gate Bridge

Pacific Coast Highways

Stretching from Mexico to Canada, the West Coast's ocean-view highways snake past dizzying beach cliffs and dozens of beach towns, all with their own idiosyncratic personalities. On **Trip 39: Pacific Coast Highways**, you'll uncover hidden strands, ancient redwood forests, seafood shacks and creaky old wooden piers for watching glorious sunsets.

TRIPS

Great Smokies

Welcoming more visitors annually than any other US national park, this 800-sq-mi pocket of southern Appalachian woodland is ribbed by forested ridges, where bears, deer, wild turkeys and more than 1600 different kinds of wildflowers all find refuge. Take an unforgettable trip amid gold, orange and flame-colored autumn foliage on **Trip 19: The Great Smokies**.

TRIP

Great Lakes

Like huge inland seas, the gorgeous Great Lakes are freckled with beaches, sand dunes and lighthouses on rocky shores, as you'll discover on **Trip 21: Michigan's Gold Coast**. Ready for a bigger adventure? Meander south down by the Mississippi River, motor west along retro Route 66 or make your way north to the Canadian border.

TRIPS

14

Rocky Mountains Grand Teton National Park

BEST ROADS FOR DRIVING

US 101 Panoramic views from the West Coast.
Trips 39 47 49

Blue Ridge Parkway Roll alongside Appalachian
hills. **Trips** 18 19

Going-to-the-Sun Road Glimpse glaciers
before they vanish. **Trip** 29

Route 66 A nostalgic journey back in time.
Trip 20

Route 100 Wind through Vermont's green
mountains. **Trip** 11

Rocky Mountains

Wildflower-strewn
meadows, saw-toothed
peaks and placid lakes
along the jagged spine
of the Continental
Divide call to outdoor
adventurers. Equally
rich in wildlife, pioneer
history and Native
American traditions,
the Rocky Mountains
embody the American
frontier spirit. Be
haunted by Old West
ghost towns on **Trip 30:
Top of the Rockies**.

TRIPS   28 29 30 31

HIGHLIGHTS ★

Grand Canyon North Rim view

CAROL POLICH PHOTO WORKSHOPS / GETTY IMAGES ©

Grand Canyon

Protected by a national park and Native American tribal lands, this canyon, cut by the Colorado River, is an eye-popping spectacle of colorful rock strata. Its spiring buttes, sculpted cliffs and waterfall springs make up an ever-changing landscape that shifts moods with the weather and seasons. Be awed by Mother Nature's showstopper on **Trip 33: Fantastic Canyon Voyage**.

TRIPS 32 33

BEST NATIVE AMERICAN PLACES

- - - - - - - - - - - - - - - - - - - -

Monument Valley Preserved inside the Navajo Nation.
Trips 32 35

- - - - - - - - - - - - - - - - - - - -

Mesa Verde Visit Ancestral Puebloan cliff dwellings.
Trip 32

- - - - - - - - - - - - - - - - - - - -

Grand Canyon Sacred to tribes across the Southwest.
Trips 32 33

- - - - - - - - - - - - - - - - - - - -

Natchez Trace Parkway Follow the footsteps of indigenous peoples. **Trip** 17

- - - - - - - - - - - - - - - - - - - -

Anadarko A Great Plains tribal center. **Trip** 24

National Mall Washington Monument

Yellowstone National Park Grand Prismatic Spring

National Mall

Kick off **Trip 5: The Civil War Tour** in Washington, DC, the USA's capital. Along the National Mall stand iconic monuments styled like ancient Greek and Roman temples, moving memorials to wars and civic heroes, and the Smithsonian Institution's immense museums. There's no better place to take the country's pulse than on the long, grassy lawn, where Americans gather in protest and celebration.

TRIP 5

Yellowstone National Park

The country's oldest national park never fails to amaze with its spouting geysers, rainbow-colored hot springs and heart-stopping megafauna – grizzly bears, bison, elk, wolves, moose and more – that range across North America's largest intact ecosystem. Trek into some of the West's wildest wonderlands on **Trip 28: Grand Teton to Yellowstone**.

TRIP 28

Acadia National Park

It's a weather-beaten New England tradition to witness the first sunrise of the year from atop Cadillac Mountain, the highest peak on the USA's eastern seaboard. But if a winter sojourn sounds too chilly, then show up during the sun-kissed summer instead to explore these end-of-the-world islands tossed along rocky North Atlantic shores on **Trip 13: Acadia Byway**.

TRIP 13

Blue Ridge Parkway

Traversing rural Appalachia from Shenandoah National Park to the Great Smoky Mountains, the Blue Ridge Parkway is the nation's most popular scenic drive. Each year more than 15 million people drive over its rolling hills and through pastoral valleys, touring historic battlegrounds and listening to bluegrass music. Join the parade on **Trip 18: Blue Ridge Parkway**.

TRIPS 18 19

Cajun Country

Down by the bayou in the swamplands of southern Louisiana, delve into a gumbo mix of Creole, French Canadian, Native American and African American folk culture. Step inside ramshackle roadside taverns, where fresh crawfish boil in big pots and zydeco musicians jam all night long. *Allons danser* ('Let's dance!') on **Trip 15: Cajun Country**.

TRIP 15

(left) **Blue Ridge Parkway** Linn Cove Viaduct;
(below) **Florida's beaches** South Beach, Miami

Florida's Beaches

Blessed with almost year-round sunshine, Florida is a beautiful, sexy, semitropical peninsula edged by bone-white sand, lapped by aquamarine waters, and drenched in lurid, neon sunsets. Florida's beaches are its calling card: you could hit a different one every day for a year. Track down some of the very best on **Trip 14: Highway 1.**

TRIP

BEST ODDBALL ROADSIDE SIGHTS

Gemini Giant Ready to rocket down Route 66. **Trip** 20

Wall Drug The USA's most shameless tourist trap. **Trip** 26

Tunnel Log Drive through a fallen giant sequoia tree. **Trip** 40

Marfa Lights Watch for otherworldly apparitions in West Texas. **Trip** 37

Salvation Mountain A folk-art monument to religious fervor. **Trip** 42

21

IF YOU LIKE...

Family fun Pacific Park Ferris wheel (Trip 20)

Outdoor Adventures

Towering forests, deep canyons, alpine lakes, chiseled peaks, alien-looking deserts and unspoiled beaches – there's no shortage of spectacular landscapes unscrolling before your windshield in the USA. Hop out of the car for an afternoon hike, morning paddle or all-day communion with nature.

8 Fall Foliage Tour Breathe in New England's natural beauty during its showiest season.

28 Grand Teton to Yellowstone Quintessential Western national parks in the Rocky Mountains.

32 Four Corners Cruise See the Southwest's canyon country from rim to rim.

40 Yosemite, Sequoia & Kings Canyon National Parks Drive across the Sierra Nevada's highlands.

History

Start on the East Coast, home of America's revolutionary 13 colonies. Go west, following scouts' trails across the Great Plains and over the Continental Divide to Pacific shores. Dig up the country's Spanish colonial roots mixed with indigenous traditions across the Southwest.

5 The Civil War Tour Follow in the wake of men and women who fought in the USA's bloodiest conflict.

25 On the Pioneer Trails Where homesteaders once rolled their 'prairie schooners' and daring Pony Express riders galloped.

45 Highway 49 Through Gold Country Ramble the hurly-burly boomtowns of California's 19th-century gold rush.

48 On the Trail of Lewis & Clark America's original cross-country trip.

Family Travel

Coast to coast, there's endless fun for anyone traveling with kids, including eye-popping theme parks, hands-on science museums, zoos and aquariums. Or focus your road trip on the great outdoors: beaches and national parks rank among the most popular destinations for families.

13 Acadia Byway An island idyll in New England, most bewitching in summer.

19 The Great Smokies Wildlife spotting, historical train rides, waterfall hikes and kitschy Dollywood.

26 Black Hills Loop A summer-vacation rite of passage for uncountable American kids.

41 Disneyland & Orange County Beaches Mickey's 'Magic Kingdom' is a short drive from SoCal's cinematic coast.

Local seafood Fresh from the Pacific (Trip 44)

Beaches

With 5000-plus miles of coastline along two oceans and the Gulf of Mexico, there's enough sand to satisfy all kinds of beach lovers here, from the rugged and wild shores of New England to the sunny, surfable strands of Florida and Southern California.

2 The Jersey Shore
It's a nonstop party with Atlantic boardwalks, carnival fun and funnel cake.

14 Highway 1 Spring-break beaches and peaceful islands and inlets down in the Sunshine State.

39 Pacific Coast Highways Kick back in quirky beach towns on California's coast, equal parts sunshine and rainbow mist.

49 Highway 101 Oregon Coast For lighthouses, rocky bluffs, jewel-like beaches and Pacific horizons.

Urban Exploration

In the USA's biggest, most diverse cities, high and low culture collide in a heady blow-up of sights, sounds and tastes: star chefs' kitchens to food trucks, symphony halls to underground punk clubs, museums to graffiti-art murals, and much more.

7 Coastal New England
Bop through Boston on this seaboard drive – it's not too much of a detour from NYC either.

20 Route 66 Link the skyscrapers of Chicago and glamorous Los Angeles with a chain of other great American cities.

39 Pacific Coast Highways Cruise up the West Coast from San Diego to Los Angeles, San Francisco and beyond, where Portland and Seattle await.

Regional Food

Down-home cooking is the cherry on top of any classic American road trip. Make a mess at a Maine lobster shack, plow through BBQ in Texas, order 'Christmas-style' enchiladas at a New Mexico diner or find farm-to-table goodness in the Midwest. What's for dessert? Pie, oh my.

3 Pennsylvania Dutch Country Amish bakeries, all-you-can-eat suppers, and pretzel and chocolate factories.

11 Vermont's Spine: Route 100 Roadside apple orchards, dairy cows and microbreweries.

15 Cajun Country Where rustic Cajun spice mixes with sophisticated Creole cooking.

44 San Francisco, Marin & Napa Loop California's locavore heaven, with famous wineries, green farms and fresh seafood.

NEED TO KNOW

CELL PHONES
The only foreign phones that work in the USA are GSM tri- or quad-band models. Buy pay-as-you-go cell phones from electronics stores or rent them at major airports.

INTERNET ACCESS
Wi-fi is available at most accommodations and coffee shops. Average rates at city cybercafes are $6 to $12 per hour. Internet access at public libraries is usually free.

FUEL
Gas stations are everywhere, except in some remote desert and mountain areas and national parks. Expect to pay $3.15 to $4.25 per gallon.

RENTAL CARS
Alamo (www.alamo.com)

Car Rental Express (www.carrentalexpress.com)

Enterprise (www.enterprise.com)

Rent-a-Wreck (www.rentawreck.com)

IMPORTANT NUMBERS
AAA (☎ 800-222-4357) Roadside assistance for auto-club members.

Emergency (☎ 911)

Directory Assistance (☎ 411)

Operator (☎ 0)

Climate

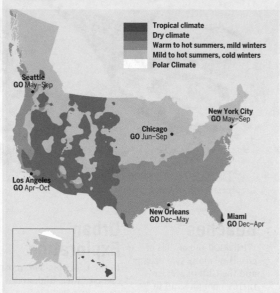

Tropical climate
Dry climate
Warm to hot summers, mild winters
Mild to hot summers, cold winters
Polar Climate

Seattle
GO May–Sep

New York City
GO May–Sep

Chicago
GO Jun–Sep

Los Angeles
GO Apr–Oct

New Orleans
GO Dec–May

Miami
GO Dec–Apr

When to Go

High Season (Jun–Aug)
» Warm days nationwide, with generally high temperatures.

» Busy travel season brings huge crowds and higher prices.

» Tourism slows in hot deserts; very humid in southeastern US.

Shoulder Seasons (Apr–May & Sep–Oct)
» Milder temperatures; hurricane season peaks (Aug–Nov) on Gulf and Atlantic coasts.

» Fewer crowds, discounted accommodations and airfares.

» Spring wildflowers (Apr–May) and autumn foliage (Sep–Oct) in many areas.

Low Season (Nov–Mar)
» Colder wintry days, with snowfall and heavy rainstorms in many regions.

» Lowest prices on lodgings, except at ski resorts and warm, sunny destinations, such as Florida.

Daily Costs

Budget: Less than $100

» Hostel dorm bed: $25–40; campsite: $10–40; cheap motel room: $50–100

» Roadside diner or take-out meal: $10–15

» Hit the beach, find a park and keep an eye out for discount days at museums

Midrange: $100–$200

» Two-star hotel room: $100–200

» Casual sit-down restaurant meal: $25–40

» Rental car: from $30 per day, excluding insurance and gas

» State and national park entry: $5–25 (some free)

Top End: Over $200

» Resort hotel room: from $250

» Three-course meal in top restaurant: $75–100

» Theme-park entry: $40–100

Eating

Diners, drive-ins & cafes Cheap, simple and occasionally with homemade food.

Seafood shacks Casual waterfront kitchens.

Brewpubs & gastropubs Regional craft beers and wines, 'pub grub' from hearty to high-end cuisine.

Vegetarians & other diets Can often be catered for, especially in cities.

Eating price indicators represent the cost of a main course:

$	less than $10
$$	$10–20
$$$	more than $20

Sleeping

Camping Ranging from amenity-rich RV parks to primitive wilderness sites.

Motels Everywhere along highways, around cities and in heavily touristed spots.

Hotels & hostels Common in metro areas and popular tourist destinations.

B&Bs Smaller, often historic and romantic, but pricey.

Sleeping price indicators represent the cost of a room with private bathroom, excluding taxes:

$	less than $100
$$	$100–200
$$$	more than $200

Arriving in the USA

Major US airports offer free inter-terminal transportation and car-rental shuttles.

Los Angeles International Airport (LAX)

Taxis $30–55; 30 to 60 minutes.

Door-to-door shuttles Around $16–$25.

Public transportation Shuttle C (free) to LAX City Bus Center or Shuttle G (free) to Metrorail's Aviation Station; LAX FlyAway Bus to downtown Union Station ($7; 30 to 50 minutes).

John F Kennedy International Airport (JFK, New York)

Taxis $45–65; 35 to 90 minutes.

Door-to-door shuttles Around $16–24.

Public transportation AirTrain ($5) to Jamaica Station for MTA subway and bus connections ($2.50; 50 to 75 minutes) or LIRR trains ($10.50; 35 minutes) into Manhattan.

Money

ATMs are practically everywhere. Credit cards are almost universally accepted and often required for making reservations (debit cards are sometimes OK).

Tipping

Tipping is expected, not optional: 15% to 20% at restaurants, 10% to 15% for bartenders and taxi drivers, and $2 per bag for porters.

Opening Hours

Opening hours may be shorter in winter (November to March).

Restaurants ⏲7–10:30am, 11:30am–2:30pm and 5–9pm daily, some later Friday and Saturday

Shops ⏲10am–6pm Monday to Saturday, noon–5pm Sunday (malls close later)

Useful Websites

Lonely Planet (www.lonelyplanet.com/usa) Destination information, hotel and hostel bookings, traveler forums and more.

Festivals.com (www.festivals.com) Fun celebrations of music, food, drink and dance.

Roadside America (www.roadsideamerica.com) For everything weird and wacky.

For more, see the Driving Guide (p645).

CITY GUIDE

NEW YORK CITY

Surely, if anything justifies all that East Coast braggadocio, it's NYC. Bold and brash, the city sparks with electric energy. See it on the run, just as the locals do: ride the subway to dive into culturally edgy and ethnically diverse neighborhoods, each with its own personality and irresistible gravitational pull.

New York City View of the Empire State Building from Rockefeller Center

Getting Around

Only the brave, desperate or foolish drive in NYC. With a comprehensive subway, bus, train and bike-sharing system, there's simply no need. For drivers, turning right on red is illegal except where posted.

Parking

In Manhattan, metered on-street parking is limited and garages are expensive. It's cheaper and easier to park near an Outer Borough subway stop or at a suburban train station, then ride into the city.

Discover the Tastes of NYC

NYC's neighborhoods offer up a global buffet of ethnic tastes, starting in Chinatown. Foodies prowl the halls of Chelsea Market and Manhattan's East and West Villages, Nolita and Tribeca. Uncover break-out restaurants in Brooklyn (hello, Williamsburg, Park Slope and Red Hook).

Live Like a Local

In Manhattan, Midtown's high-rise hotels are convenient for sightseeing, while stylish boutique and luxury properties lie further south, including in fashion-forward SoHo and Chelsea, and north around Central Park on the Upper West and East Sides.

Useful Websites

Official NYC Guide (www.nycgo.com) Trip planning info, events, freebies and deals.

Lonely Planet (www.lonelyplanet.com/usa) Travel tips, videos, accommodations and traveler forums.

Trips Around NYC see New York & the Mid-Atlantic Trips p35

For more, check out our city and country guides.
www.lonelyplanet.com

TOP EXPERIENCES

➡ Meet the Metropolitan Museum of Art
You could spend a whole day inside this storehouse of artistic treasures from around the world and still not see it all.

➡ Escape into Central Park
Meandering paths, grassy meadows and marshy ponds make a respite from Manhattan's concrete jungle. Show up in summer and rent a rowboat or catch an outdoor concert.

➡ Brooklyn Bridge at Night
For NYC's most romantic views, amble hand-in-hand across this arched, neo-Gothic suspension bridge, now a National Historic Landmark.

➡ See a Show
Pick a splashy Broadway musical near Times Square, an experimental off-Broadway play, big-name players at Carnegie Hall or indie rock, experimental jazz and stand-up comedy shows in the East and West Villages.

➡ Top of the Rock
Even if you don't take a backstage tour of the Rockefeller Center's art-deco Radio City Music Hall or modern NBC Studios, zoom up to the 360-degree observation deck for sweeping cityscapes.

➡ Climb the Statue of Liberty
More than 12 million immigrants who passed through nearby Ellis Island saw this copper statue as a beacon of new-world hopes. Reserve far ahead for a ticket to reach the crown.

➡ Walk the High Line
Reclaimed from an elevated train line, this kid-friendly urban green space opens up new perspectives on Manhattan and the Hudson River.

Chicago The Chicago River from the Wells St Bridge

CHICAGO

The Windy City will blow you away with its cloud-scraping architecture and lakefront beaches. High and low culture comfortably coexist without any taint of pretension. Take in world-class museums and landmark theater stages, or drop by divey blues clubs and graffiti-scrawled pizzerias – they're all equally beloved in 'Chi-town.'

Getting Around

Driving Chicago's well-laid-out street grid is slow, but not too difficult, except around the Loop. If you're exploring downtown and other neighborhoods served by 'El' lines, ditch your car for the day and get around on foot and by train (or bus) instead.

Parking

Overnight hotel parking and city parking garages are expensive. Metered on-street parking is easier to find in outlying neighborhoods than around downtown, but it's not necessarily cheap (occasionally it's free in residential areas).

Discover the Tastes of Chicago

Essential eats include Chicago-style hot dogs, Italian beef sandwiches and deep-dish pizza. Star chefs run restaurants in the West Loop and on the North Side. For an eclectic mix of cafes, bistros, gastropubs and more, nose around Wicker Park, Bucktown and Andersonville.

Live Like a Local

Base yourself in the Loop for convenient 'El' train stops, seek luxury on the Gold Coast or look for deals at the Near North's boutique and high-rise hotels. For more personalized stays, book a B&B in a trendy neighborhood such as Wicker Park.

Useful Websites

Choose Chicago (www.choosechicago.com) Official tourist information site.

CTA (www.transitchicago.com) Bus and train maps, schedules and fares

Chicago Reader (www.chicagoreader.com) Alternative weekly covering events, arts and entertainment.

Trips Around Chicago see the Great Lakes Trips p263

Los Angeles Downtown at dusk

LOS ANGELES

If you think you've already got LA figured out – celebrity culture, smog, traffic, bikini babes and reality TV – think again. Dozens of independent mini cities, where over 90 languages are spoken, comprise the West's biggest, most provocative metropolis, home of Hollywood stars, boundary-breaking artists and musicians, and other cultural icons.

Getting Around

Most people get around by car, despite jammed freeways and slow surface streets. Metro rail lines and a network of local buses connect many of the neighborhoods that are popular with visitors.

Parking

Valet parking is widely available at hotels, restaurants, night spots etc; fees vary (a tip is expected). Metered on-street parking is limited but inexpensive. In downtown LA, parking lots and garages are plentiful but pricey – the cheapest are in Chinatown.

Discover the Tastes of LA

LA's creative culinary scene embraces TV chefs, food trucks and farmers markets. With some 140 nationalities living here, there's an abundance of immigrant neighborhoods with good eats including downtown's Little Tokyo, Thai Town near Hollywood and East LA for Mexican flavors.

Live Like a Local

For seaside life, book a motel or hotel in Santa Monica, Venice or Long Beach. Cool-hunters and party people will be happy at boutique and luxury hotels in Hollywood, West Hollywood and Beverly Hills. Culture vultures descend on downtown LA's high-rise hotels.

Useful Websites

Discover Los Angeles (www.discoverlosangeles.com) Official tourist information site.

Metro (www.metro.net) Bus and rail maps, schedules and fares.

LA Weekly (www.laweekly.com) Alternative tabloid covering food, film, music, nightlife and more.

Trips Around Los Angeles see California Trips p485

WASHINGTON DC

No stranger to the world's gaze, the nation's capital is complicated and controversial, a place of politics and protests. Yet it's also a proud city of grand boulevards, illustrious monuments and postcard vistas over the Potomac River. Walk colonial cobblestone streets past unmissable museums, theaters and more.

Getting Around

Driving around Washington DC can be a headache. It's better to leave your car parked for the day, then plan on walking between sights, riding Metrorail trains and taking Metrobus and DC Circulator buses.

Parking

Metered (occasionally free) on-street parking is limited, especially by the National Mall. Public garages and lots are expensive in the city, but more affordable at suburban train stations. Hotels charge steeply for overnight parking.

TOP EXPERIENCES

➡ Lincoln Memorial at Sunset
No other monument on the National Mall evokes the heritage and ideals of the USA more than this one. Snap a photo as the white marble of this Greek-style temple lights up for night time.

➡ Size up the Smithsonian
Be astonished by the renowned collections housed inside 19 different museums and galleries, plus the national zoo.

➡ Stroll Tidal Basin in Spring
Around this picturesque reservoir, capture panoramic views of famous DC landmarks, best when framed by delicate pink cherry blossoms.

➡ Tour the White House
Request permission many months in advance to visit the most famous address in the country, only a short walk from Capitol Hill.

Washington DC Washington Monument

Discover the Tastes of DC

Make a beeline for Capitol Hill's Eastern Market, then check out rave-reviewed restaurants along the 14th St corridor and downtown's Penn Quarter. For a big array of dining and drinking options, wander U Street, Dupont Circle, Adams Morgan, the West End or Georgetown.

Live Like a Local

Downtown claims the bulk of DC's historic and high-rise hotels. Conveniently located, busy Dupont Circle has historical inns, B&Bs and boutique and luxury hotels. Save money at hotels just across the river in Arlington, VA.

Useful Websites

Washington DC (http://washington.org) Official tourist information site.

goDCgo (http://godcgo.com) Comprehensive local transportation and parking guide.

Washington City Paper (www.washingtoncitypaper.com) Alternative weekly covering news, dining and the performing arts.

Trips Around Washington DC see New York & the Mid-Atlantic Trips p35

USA BY REGION

Everyone knows that road-tripping is the ultimate way to experience the USA, from twisting coastal highways to big-sky mountain roads. Here's your guide to what each region has to offer and the best road trips to experience it for yourself.

Rocky Mountains (p361)

Gasp at postcard views from high-country byways, then drive around pristine lakes, natural geysers, celebrity ski resorts and wild national parks.

Climb to cliff dwellings on Trip 30

Pacific Northwest (p567)

Lose yourself amid snow-topped volcanoes, bubbling hot springs, wind-whipped beaches and deep coastal rainforest, or trace pioneer trails beside the Columbia River.

Board a ferry to Alaska on Trip 51

California (p485)

Cruise by surf-tossed strands on the famous Pacific Coast Highway and reach for the sky in the Sierra Nevada.

Try world-class wines on Trip 43

Southwest (p407)

Gaze out at boundless horizons from the Grand Canyon, between Monument Valley's buttes or the banks of the Rio Grande.

Marvel at the canyon on Trip 33

Great Plains (p313)

Tales of Wild West outlaws and cowboys, Native American tribal traditions and endless miles of golden prairie unroll through America's heartland.

Go where buffalo roam on Trip 25

Great Lakes (p263)

Motor from Chicago's skyscrapers down Route 66, America's 'Mother Road,' then wind beside the mighty Mississippi River or past lakefront beaches and lighthouses.

Spy moose on Trip 22

New England (p113)

Craggy coastlines strung with fishing villages, ivy-covered colleges and brilliant fall foliage along country roads beckon drivers to this lauded literary landscape.

Eat lobster on Trip 6

New York & the Mid-Atlantic (p35)

Americana abounds, from Amish farms and Civil War battlefields to Maryland's historic roads. Spot waterfalls on Skyline Drive and around the Finger Lakes.

Party on Jersey Shore on Trip 2

Florida & the South (p185)

Natural beauty is always nearby, whether you're lazing on the breezy Gulf and Atlantic coasts or rolling inland through rural Appalachia and Cajun country.

Sing the blues on Trip 16

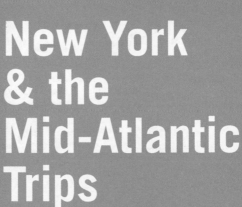

New York & the Mid-Atlantic Trips

ALONG THE EAST COAST, SANDWICHED BETWEEN THE PICTURESQUE HAMLETS of New England and the gracious plantations of the South, you'll find the Northeast Corridor. Stretching from Washington DC to Boston, this scenic strip includes America's most dynamic, cosmopolitan metropolis: New York. But there is so much more to be discovered in this beautiful and remarkably diverse area.

After 48 unforgettable hours in Manhattan, seek out the Jersey Shore or Pennsylvania's backroads. Further south, Appalachian landscapes await on Virginia's Skyline Drive, while waterfalls and vineyards provide food for the soul around the Finger Lakes. No matter where you find yourself, you're guaranteed to find something unexpected and delightful.

Taughannock Falls Among stunning fall color (Trip 1)
RON WATTS / CORBIS ©

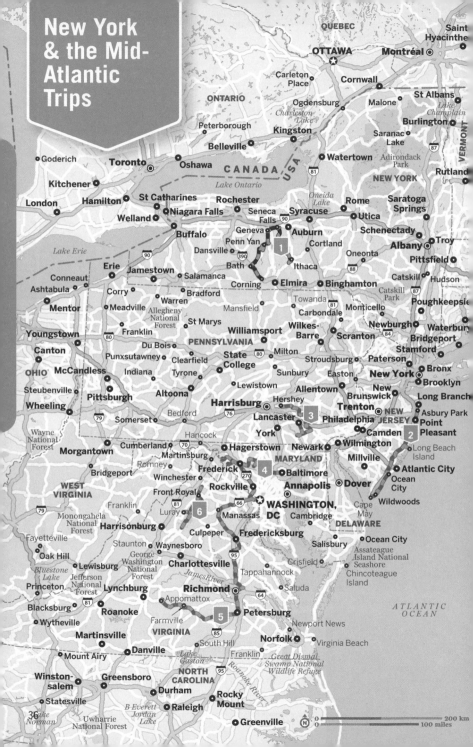

New York & the Mid-Atlantic Trips

Classic Trip

1 Finger Lakes Loop 3 Days
Lakeside roads lead past dozens of vineyards to deep gorges and ravines for hiking. (p39)

2 The Jersey Shore 3–7 Days
Boardwalks and beaches galore line the Atlantic for classic summertime fun. (p49)

3 Pennsylvania Dutch Country 3–4 Days
Back roads snake their way past farmers markets through Amish countryside. (p61)

4 Maryland's National Historic Road 2 Days
Drive from Baltimore's docks to the tiny villages of the Catoctin Mountains. (p73)

Classic Trip

5 The Civil War Tour 3 Days
See preserved battlefields, 19th-century countryside, museums a-plenty and Southern small towns. (p83)

6 Skyline Drive 3 Days
Cross the Commonwealth's high-altitude spine in the green Shenandoah Valley. (p95)

✔ DON'T MISS

The Music Man
Vaudeville-style performances at an ice-cream theatre encapsulate the Jersey Shore culture. Stop by for a taste on Trip **2**

Urban Exploration
Cities like Baltimore and Frederick are steeped in history, good eats and hot nightlife. See them on Trip **4**

Trail Trekking
Many trails arc along Skyline Drive, plunging past forests, white waterfalls and lonely mountains. Get your boots on for Trip **6**

Strasburg Railroad
Board a beautifully restored steam-driven locomotive for a slow roll through the lush Amish countryside. Ride the rails on Trip **3**

Taughannock Falls State Park
A short hike takes you to this narrow cascade, higher than Niagara and in a majestic amphitheater-like setting. Hike to the falls on Trip **1**

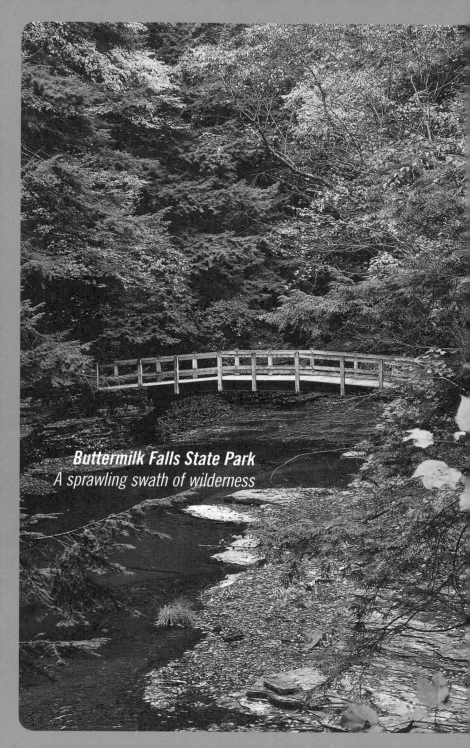

Buttermilk Falls State Park
A sprawling swath of wilderness

Classic Trip

Finger Lakes Loop

1

'Ithaca is Gorges' T-shirts don't lie. Cornell's Ivy League campus has them, but there are dozens more in the area with gorgeous waterfalls, plus lakeside vineyards producing top wines.

TRIP HIGHLIGHTS

92 miles

Rte 54, Keuka Lake
Picturesque vineyards on bluffs overlooking the lake

1 mile

Ithaca
Dramatic gorges run through college town's campus

Seneca Falls

Geneva

Cayuga Lake

Seneca Lake

6

Keuka Lake

1 START

2

Hammondsport

8 FINISH

Corning
One of the world's finest collections of glass

144 miles

Buttermilk Falls & Robert H Treman State Parks
A dazzling variety of falls and swimming holes

5 miles

3 DAYS
144 MILES / 231KM

GREAT FOR...

BEST TIME TO GO
May to October for farmers markets and glorious sunny vistas.

ESSENTIAL PHOTO
The full height of Taughannock Falls.

BEST FOR OENOPHILES
With more than 65 vineyards, a designated driver is needed.

Classic Trip

1 Finger Lakes Loop

A bird's-eye view of this region of rolling hills and 11 long narrow lakes – the eponymous fingers – reveals an outdoor paradise stretching all the way from Albany to far-western New York. Of course there's boating, fishing, cycling, hiking and cross-country skiing, but this is also the state's premier wine-growing region, with enough variety for the most discerning oenophile, and palate-cleansing whites and reds available just about every few miles.

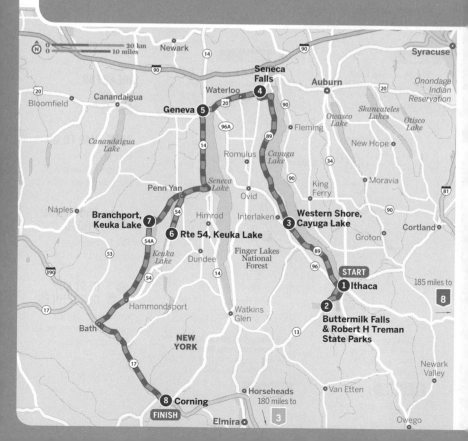

❶ Ithaca

An idyllic home for college students and older hippies who cherish elements of the traditional collegiate lifestyle – laid-back vibe, cafe poetry readings, art-house cinemas, good eats – Ithaca is perched above Cayuga Lake.

Founded in 1865, Cornell University boasts a lovely campus, mixing traditional and contemporary architecture. The modern **Johnson Museum of Art** (☏607-255-6464; www.museum.cornell.edu; University Ave; ⏰10am-5pm Tue- Sun) **FREE**, designed by IM Pei, has a major Asian collection, plus pre-Columbian, American

and European exhibits. Just east of the center of the campus is **Cornell Plantations** (☏607-255-2400; www.cornellplantations.org; Plantations Rd; ⏰10am-5pm, closed Mon) **FREE**, an expertly curated herb and flower garden and arboretum. Kids can go interactive-wild at **Sciencenter** (☏607-272-0600; www.sciencenter.org; 601 First St; adult/child $8/6; ⏰10am-5pm Tue-Sat, from noon Sun; 👶).

The area around Ithaca is known for its waterfalls, gorges and gorgeous parks. However, downtown has its very own, **Cascadilla Gorge**, starting several blocks from Ithaca Commons and ending, after a steep and stunning vertical climb, at the Performing Arts Center of Cornell.

🍴 🛏 p46

The Drive » It's only 2 miles south on Rte 13 to Buttermilk Falls State Park.

❷ Buttermilk Falls & Robert H Treman State Parks

A sprawling swath of wilderness, **Buttermilk Falls State Park** (☏607-273-5761; Rte 13) has something for everyone – a beach, cabins, fishing, hiking, recreational fields and camping. The big draw, however, is the waterfalls. There's more than 10, with some

sending water tumbling as far as 500ft below into clear pools. Hikers like the raggedy Gorge Trail that brings them up to all the best cliffs. It parallels Buttermilk Creek, winding up about 500ft. On the other side of the falls is the equally popular Rim Trail, a loop of about 1.5 miles around the waterfalls from a different vantage point. Both feed into Bear Trail, which will take you to neighboring Treman Falls.

It's a trek of about 3 miles to Treman, or you can pop back in the car and drive the 3 miles south to **Robert H Treman State Park** (☏607-273-3440; 105 Enfield Falls Rd), still on bucolic Rte 13. Also renowned for cascading falls, Treman's gorge trail passes a stunning 12 waterfalls in less than 3 miles. The two biggies you don't want to miss are Devil's Kitchen and Lucifer Falls, a multi-tiered wonder that spills Enfield Creek over rocks for about 100ft. At the bottom of yet another watery gorge – Lower Falls – there's a natural swimming hole; it's a deep, dark, refreshing pool of river water that's impossible to resist on hot summer days.

The Drive » Take Rte 13 back into Ithaca to connect with Rte 89, which hugs Cayuga Lake shore for 10 miles. The entrance to Taughannock Falls State Park is just after crossing the river gorge.

LINK YOUR TRIP

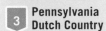

3 Pennsylvania Dutch Country

Journey south through Scranton and Allentown to southern PA to reach these tranquil country roads.

8 Fall Foliage Tour

Make your way east from Ithaca through Albany to the Berkshires to experience legendary New England colors.

Classic Trip

③ Western Shore, Cayuga Lake

Trumansburg, a one-street town about 15 miles north of Ithaca, is the gateway to **Taughannock Falls State Park** (☎607-387-6739; www.nysparks.com; 2221 Taughannock Rd, Trumansburg). At 215ft, the falls of the same name are 30ft higher than Niagara Falls. There are 5 miles of hiking trails, most of which wind their way around the slippery parts to bring you safely to the lookout spots at the top. One trail follows the stream bed to the falls.

A little further along on Rte 89, near the village of Interlaken, is the **Creamery** (◷11am-8pm), a roadside restaurant that, in addition to ice-cream sundaes, serves buzz-inducing wine-infused sorbets. Just past here

is **Lucas Vineyards** (☎607-532-4825; www.lucasvineyards.com; 3862 County Rd 150, Interlaken; ◷10:30am-5:30pm), one of the pioneers of Cayuga wineries. A little further north, by the lake shore and a small community of modest but charming summer homes, is **Sheldrake Point Winery** (☎607-532-9401; www.sheldrakepoint.com; 7448 County Rd; ◷11am-5pm Fri-Mon Jan-Mar, 10am-5:30pm daily Apr-Dec), which has stunning views and award-winning whites. **Knapp Winery & Restaurant** (☎607-869-9271; www.knappwine.com; 2770 Ernsberger Rd, Romulus; ◷10am-5:30pm Apr-Nov, 11am-5pm Dec-Mar) has a wide lawn surrounded by gnarly roots and rioting wildflowers; you can look out over the trellis-covered vineyards while sampling homemade wines, grappas and limoncellos.

🍴 🛏 p46

> ✓ **TOP TIP:**
> **SAPSUCKER WOODS SANCTUARY**
>
> Only a few miles northeast of Ithaca is Cornell University's **Sapsucker Woods** (☎800-843-2473; www.birds.cornell.edu; 159 Sapsucker Woods Rd), a bird-feeding garden and 10-acre pond full of ducks, geese and other wildlife. The 4 miles of trails, open from dawn to dusk, are teeming with birds and butterflies. Also look out for *Stone Egg*, a huge cairn built from local stone by internationally acclaimed environmental artist Andy Goldsworthy and students from Cornell.

The Drive » Rte 89 continues along the lake shore and passes Cayuga Lake State Park, which has beach access and picnic tables, a few miles before you turn left onto County Rd 116 east.

---

④ Seneca Falls

This small, sleepy town is where the country's organized women's rights movement was born. After being excluded from an anti-slavery meeting, Elizabeth Cady Stanton and her friends drafted an 1848 declaration asserting that 'all men and women are created equal.' The inspirational **Women's Rights National Historical Park** (☎315-568-2991; www.nps.gov/wori; 136 Fall St; ◷9am-5pm) **FREE** has a small but impressive museum with an informative film, plus a visitor center offering tours of Cady Stanton's house. The surprisingly tiny **National Women's Hall of Fame** (☎315-568-8060; www.greatwomen.org; 76 Fall St; adult/child $3/free; ◷10am-4pm Wed-Sat year-round, from noon Sun Jun-Aug) honors American women such as First Lady Abigail Adams, American Red Cross founder Clara Barton and civil-rights activist Rosa Parks.

🛏 p46

The Drive » The 10 miles on NY-20 west to Geneva pass through strip mall-lined Waterloo; Mac's Drive-In, a classic 1950s-style burger joint, is worth a stop.

5 Geneva

Geneva, one of the larger towns on this route, has interesting, historic architecture and a lively vibe with both Hobart and William Smith colleges calling it home. South Main St is lined with turn-of-the-century Italianate, Federal and Greek Revival homes in immaculate condition, products of its former status as the region's commercial hub. The restored 1894 **Smith Opera House** (☎315-781-5483; www.thesmith.org; 82 Seneca St) is the place to go for theater, concerts and performing arts in the area. Stop by **Microclimate** (38 Linden St, Geneva; ◷6pm-midnight Mon, 4:30pm-1am Thu-Sun), a cool little wine bar offering wine flights where you can compare locally produced varietals with their international counterparts.

🛏 p47

The Drive ≫ On your way south on Rte 14 you pass Red Tail Ridge winery, a gold Leadership in Energy & Environmental Design (LEED) certified place on Seneca Lake. Then turn right on Rte 54 to Penn Yan.

TRIP HIGHLIGHT

6 Route 54, Keuka Lake

Y-shaped Keuka is about 20 miles long and in some parts up to 2 miles wide, its lush vegetation uninterrupted except for neat patches of vineyards. Keuka is surrounded on both sides by two small state parks that keep it relatively pristine. One of its old canals has been converted into a rustic bike path, and it's a favorite lake for trout fishers.

Just south of Penn Yan, the largest village on Keuka Lake's shores, you come to **Keuka Spring Vineyards** (☎315-536-3147; www.keukaspringwinery. com; 54 E Lake Rd, Penn Yan; ◷10am-5pm Mon-Sat, from 11am Sun summer, weekends other months) and then **Rooster Hill Vineyards** (☎315-536-4773; www. roosterhill.com; 489 Rte 54, Penn Yan; ◷10am-5pm Mon-Sat, from 11am Sun) – two local favorites that offer tastings and tours. Keuka Spring has won many awards for its oaky Cabernet Franc and Rooster Hill's fine whites spark a buzz among wine aficionados. A few miles further south along Rte 54 brings you to **Barrington Cellars** (☎315-536-9686; www. barringtoncellars.com; 2690 Gray Rd, Penn Yan; ◷10:30am-5pm Mon-Sat, from noon Sun summer, Fri-Sun spring, Sat winter), flush with Labrusca and Vinifera wines made from local grapes. Barrington's deck is a favorite place to stop for a drink.

On Saturdays in summer everyone flocks to the **Windmill Farm & Craft Market** (◷8am-4:30pm) just outside Penn Yan. Check out Amish and Mennonite goods, from hand-carved wooden rockers to homegrown veggies and flowers.

The Drive ≫ After about 5.5 miles on Rte 54A take a detour south onto Skyline Dr, which runs down the middle of 800ft Bluff Point, for outstanding views. Backtrack to Rte 54A and Branchport is only a few miles further along.

7 Branchport, Keuka Lake

As you pass through the tiny village of Branchport at the tip of Keuka's left fork in its Y, keep an eye out for **Hunt Country Vineyards** (☎315-595-2812; www.huntwine.com; 4021 County Rd 32, Branchport; ◷10am-6pm Mon-Sat, from 11am Sun summer) and **Stever Hill Vineyards** (☎315-595-2230; 3962 Stever Hill Rd, Branchport; ◷11am-6pm daily summer), the latter of which has its tasting room in a restored old barn. Both wineries are family run and edging into their sixth generation. On top of tastings there are tours of the grape-growing facilities and snacks from the vineyards' own kitchens.

🍴🛏 p47

The Drive ≫ Rte 54A along the west branch of Keuka passes by the Taylor Wine Museum just north of Hammondsport. Carry on to Bath where you connect with I-86 east/NY-17 east for another 19 miles to Corning.

Classic Trip

SHOBEIR ANSARI/GETTY IMAGES ©

EDUCATION IMAGES/UIG/GETTY IMAGES ©

LOCAL KNOWLEDGE
DAVE BREEDEN,
WINEMAKER,
SHELDRAKE POINT

There's a burgeoning new food and wine economy. New distilleries, microbreweries, bakeries, cheese shops and community-supported agriculture ventures. And everyone is collegial, we borrow things when needed and of course taste each other's wines. If you come in the spring you'll likely be able to interact more with winemakers, while harvest time in the autumn is beautiful because of the fall foliage.

Top: Buttermilk Falls State Park
Left: Vineyard, Lake Keuka
Right: Cornell University, Ithaca

GLENN VAN DER KNIJFF/GETTY IMAGES ©

TRIP HIGHLIGHT

⑧ Corning

The massive **Corning Museum of Glass** (☎800-732-6845; www.cmog.org; 1 Museum Way; adult/child $15/free; ⊙9am-5pm, to 8pm Memorial Day-Labor Day; ⛹) is home to fascinating exhibits on glass-making arts, with demonstrations and interactive items for kids and adults. It's possibly the world's finest collection, both in terms of its historic breadth – which spans 35 centuries – and its sculptural pieces. Also stop by **Vitrix Hot Glass Studio** (www.vitrixhotglass.com; 77 W Market St; ⊙9am-8pm Mon-Fri, from 10am Sat, noon-5pm Sun) to take a gander at museum-quality glass pieces ranging from functional bowls to organic-shaped sculptures.

Housed in the former City Hall, a Romanesque Revival building c 1893, the **Rockwell Museum of Western Art** (☎607-937-5386; www.rockwellmuseum.org; 111 Cedar St; adult/child $8/free; ⊙9am-5pm, to 8pm summer; ⛹) has the largest collection of art of the American West including great works by Albert Bierstadt, Charles M Russell and Frederic Remington. Native American arts and crafts are also well represented and there's a room designed and decorated like a great western lodge.

✗ p47

Classic Trip

Eating & Sleeping

Ithaca ❶

✖ Glenwood Pines   Burgers $

(1213 Taughannock Blvd; burgers $6; ⏰11am-10pm) According to locals in the know this modest roadside restaurant, overlooking Lake Cayuga on Rte 89 and 4 miles north of Ithaca, serves the best burgers.

✖ Moosewood Restaurant   Vegetarian $$

(www.moosewoodcooks.com; 215 N Cayuga St; mains $8-18; ⏰11:30am-8:30pm Mon-Sat, 5:30-9pm Sun; 🖋) Famous for its creative and constantly changing vegetarian menu and recipe books by founder Mollie Katzen. Meat eaters should be able to find something to their liking, such as fish or Szechuan eggplant.

✖ Yerba Maté Factor Café & Juice Bar   Sandwiches $

(143 The Commons; mains $8; ⏰9am-9pm Mon-Thu, to 3pm Fri, from noon Sun) Run by members of a fairly obscure religious organization, this large restaurant, housed in a converted historic building on the Ithaca commons, is good for Belgian waffles, sandwiches and coffee.

⌁ Inn on Columbia   Inn $$

(📞607-272-0204; www.columbiabb.com; 228 Columbia St, Ithaca; r incl breakfast $175-225; ❄🛜🐾) This modern, contemporary inn on a quiet residential street is the kind of place that appeals to those who have fantasies of living as a tenured professor. Restored by its architect-owner, the inn is suffused with light and sophistication.

⌁ William Henry Miller Inn   B&B $$

(📞607-256-4553; www.millerinn.com; 303 N Aurora St, Ithaca; r incl breakfast $115-215;

❄🛜🐾) Gracious, grand and only a few steps from the commons, this completely restored historic home features luxuriously designed rooms – three have Jacuzzis – and gourmet breakfasts.

Cayuga Lake ❸

✖ Hazelnut Kitchen   Modern American $$

(📞607-387-4433; 53 East Main St, Trumansburg; mains $14-23; ⏰5-9pm Thu-Mon) The new owners, a young couple from Chicago interested in collaborating with area farmers, have maintained Hazelnut's status as arguably the finest restaurant in the region. Local ingredients of course, seasonally inspired menu and *au courant* interesting meat dishes such as pig-face torchon.

⌁ Buttonwood Grove Winery   Cabin $$

(📞607-869-9760; www.buttonwoodgrove.com; 5986 Rte 89; r $135; 🐾) Has four fully furnished log cabins nestled in the hills above Lake Cayuga (open April to December); free wine tasting included.

Seneca Falls ❹

⌁ Hotel Clarence   Boutique Hotel $$

(📞315-712-4000; www.hotelclarence.com; 108 Fall St, Seneca Falls; r $140; ❄🛜🐾) Originally a 1920s-era hotel, the downtown building housing the Clarence has undergone a stylish renovation with a nod to the past – the mahogany bar comes from an old Seneca Falls saloon and there's a projection of Frank Capra's film *It's a Wonderful Life* on the lobby wall. The standard rooms are small but the Kitchen, an upscale restaurant, is the best in town.

Geneva ➎

🛏 Belhurst Castle   Inn **$$**

(☎315-781-0201; www.belhurst.com; 4069 Rte
14 S, Geneva; ❄ 📶) Even if you're not planning
a wedding, this fairy-tale castle overlooking
Lake Seneca might inspire you to take the
plunge. The huge back lawn is so picturesque it
feels cinematic. Check out the three separate
properties with a variety of room types. There's
also two restaurants: the casual Stone Cutters,
with live music on weekends, and the more
formal Edgar's.

Keuka Lake ➏

✖ Switz Inn   American, Seafood **$$**

(www.theswitz.com; 14109 Keuka Village Rd;
mains $8-16; ⏱11am-10pm) A rowdy, outdoorsy
burger joint that also serves up all-you-can-eat
crab legs and a weekend fish fry. On hot days
you can dive off the dock into the lake.

🛏 Gone with the Wind B&B   B&B **$$**

(☎607-868-4603; www.gonewiththewindon
keukalake.com; 14905 West Lake Rd, Branchport;
r incl breakfast $110-200; ❄) This lakeside
B&B is every bit as beautiful as Tara and has a
sweeping deck with great views. There are two
accommodation choices – the original stone
mansion and a log lodge annex – though both
have generally homey furnishings.

Corning ➑

✖ Gaffer Grill & Tap Room   Steakhouse **$$**

(www.gaffergrillandtaproom.com; 58 W Market
St; mains $10-35; ⏱11:30am-10:30pm Mon-
Thu, from 4:30pm Sat & Sun) An old-school
steakhouse with a contemporary dedication to
sourcing meat only from local organic farms.
The biggies including New York strip, Delmonico
and ribs are on the menu as are brisket
sandwiches and pasta, fish and chicken dishes.
An inn is attached.

Asbury Park Rock out in the town immortalized by Bruce Springsteen

The Jersey Shore

2

Jersey girls in bikinis, tatted-up guidos, mile-long boardwalks, neon-lit Ferris wheels, steamed crabs, sweaty beers and 127 miles of Atlantic Ocean coast. Pack the car and hit the shore.

TRIP HIGHLIGHTS

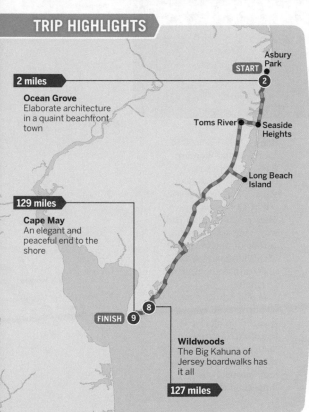

2 miles

Ocean Grove
Elaborate architecture in a quaint beachfront town

129 miles

Cape May
An elegant and peaceful end to the shore

START

Asbury Park

Toms River • Seaside Heights

Long Beach Island

FINISH 9

8

Wildwoods
The Big Kahuna of Jersey boardwalks has it all

127 miles

3–7 DAYS
120 MILES / 193KM

GREAT FOR ...

BEST TIME TO GO
Midweek in June – crowds are smaller and rooms cheaper than in the high season.

 ESSENTIAL PHOTO
Wildwood boardwalk roller coaster.

 BEST TWO DAYS
Polar opposites, Wildwood and Cape May: both classics.

49

2 The Jersey Shore

The New Jersey coastline is studded with resort towns from classy to tacky that fulfill the Platonic ideal of how a long summer day should be spent. Super-sized raucous boardwalks – where singles more than mingle – are a short drive from old-fashioned inter-generational family retreats. When the temperature rises, the entire state tips eastward and rushes to the beach to create memories that they'll view later with nostalgia or perhaps some regret.

❶ Asbury Park

Let's start with the town that Bruce Springsteen, the most famous of a group of musicians who developed the Asbury Sound in the 1970s, immortalized in song. Several of these musicians – such as Steve Van Zandt, Garry Tallent, Danny Federici and Clarence Clemmons – formed Springsteen's supporting E Street Band. The main venues to check out are the still-grungy, seen-it-all club the **Stone**

Pony (☎732-502-0600; 913 Ocean Ave) and **Wonder Bar** (1213 Ocean Ave); the latter is across the street from the majestic red-brick Paramount Theatre/Convention Hall where big acts perform (although the future of this landmark was uncertain at the time of research).

Led by wealthy gay men from NYC who snapped up blocks of forgotten Victorian homes and storefronts to refurbish, the **downtown** area (probably the hippest on the shore)

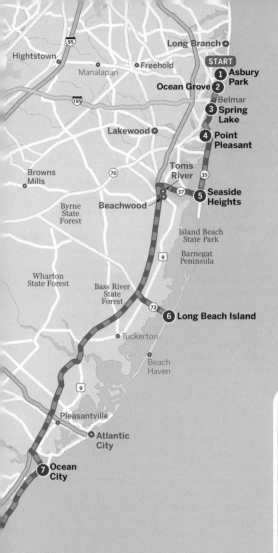

includes several blocks of Cookman and Bangs Aves, lined with charming shops, bars, cafes, restaurants and a restored art-house cinema.

The **boardwalk** itself is short and unspectacular by Jersey standards: at one end is the gorgeous but empty shell of a 1920s-era carousel and casino building, the Paramount Theatre is near the other end and there's an attractive, well-cared-for stretch of sand in front. Asbury Park's amusements tend to be more for adults than children: its clubs and bars rock late into the night, it has decent surf, and it has the shore's liveliest gay scene.

LINK YOUR TRIP

3 Pennsylvania Dutch Country

From Atlantic City, head northwest through Philadelphia and make your way west to US-30 for the rural byways of Amish country.

4 Maryland's National Historic Road

Take the Alantic City Expwy north toward Camden and connect with I-95 south to Baltimore to take in the diversity of this bay-to-mountains trip.

p58

The Drive » There's no beachfront road to Ocean Grove – the two towns are separated by narrow Wesley Lake. Take the generically commercial Main St/Rte 71 and turn left on Ocean Grove's own Main Ave. However, it might be worthwhile to first head north on Rte 71 for a few miles to take a gander at the impressively grand homes in the community of Deal.

- - - - - - - - - - - - - -

TRIP HIGHLIGHT

❷ Ocean Grove

Next to Asbury Park is Ocean Grove, one of the cutest Victorian seaside towns anywhere, with a boardwalk boasting not a single business to disturb the peace and quiet. Known as 'God's Square Mile at the Jersey Shore,' Ocean Grove

is perfectly coifed, sober, conservative and quaint. Founded by Methodists in the 19th century, the place retains what's left of a post–Civil War **Tent City** revival camp – now a historic site with 114 cottage-like canvas tents clustered together that are used for summer homes.

Towering over the tents, the 1894 mustard-yellow **Great Auditorium** (📞 732-775-0035, tickets 800-965-9324; www.oceangrove. org; Pilgrim Pathway; recitals free, concerts $13; ⏰ recitals 7:30pm Wed, 10am or noon Sat; 🖕) shouldn't be missed: its vaulted interior, amazing acoustics and historic organ recall Utah's Mormon Tabernacle. Make sure to catch a recital or concert or one of the

open-air services held in a boardwalk pavilion.

 p58

The Drive » Follow Rte 71 south through a string of relatively sleepy towns (Bradley Beach, Belmar) for just over 5 miles to reach Spring Lake.

- - - - - - - - - - - - - -

❸ Spring Lake

The quiet streets of this prosperous community, once known as the 'Irish Riviera,' are lined with grand oceanfront Victorian houses set in meticulously manicured lawns. As a result of Hurricane Sandy, the gorgeous beach was extremely narrow at high tide. If you're interested in a low-key quiet base, a stay here is about as far

HURRICANE SANDY

In late October 2012 Hurricane Sandy devastated much of the New York and New Jersey coastline, destroying homes, breaching barrier islands, ripping away boardwalks and washing away entire waterfront communities. In New York, Staten Island, the Rockaways and Red Hook were the hardest hit, while the Jersey Shore from Sandy Hook to Atlantic City suffered the brunt of the hurricane's impact. The dimensions and profiles of many beaches were diminished and it remains to be seen whether rebuilding efforts will add dunes and other storm surge impediments where none existed before.

More than six months later, there are still significant pockets of desolation: piles of debris rise higher than sand dunes; entire sides of houses are ripped away, others teeter precariously at gravity-defying angles. While a new boardwalk was being built in Seaside Heights for the 2013 summer season, the *Star Jet* roller coaster, in perhaps the most dramatically symbolic posture of displacement, still remained perched in the ocean like a remnant of an antedeluvian civilization. This book was researched just prior to the start of the 2013 summer season when state officials and locals alike were promising to be ready to welcome sun-worshipping throngs with open arms.

from the typical shore boardwalk experience as you can get.

Only 5 miles inland from Spring Lake is the quirky **Historic Village at Allaire** (☑732-919-3500; www.allairevillage.org; adult/child $3/2; ◷noon-4pm Wed-Sun late May-early Sep, noon-4pm Sat & Sun Nov-May), the remains of what was a thriving 19th-century village called Howell Works. You can still visit various 'shops' in this living history museum, all run by folks in period costume.

🛏 p58

The Drive » For a slow but pleasant drive, take Ocean Ave south – at Wreck Pond you turn inland before heading south again. At Crescent Park in the town of Sea Girt (the boardwalk has a couple casual restaurants), Washington Ave connects back to Union Ave/Rte 71 which leads into Rte 35 and over the Manasquan Inlet. The first exit for Broadway takes you past several marina-side restaurants.

- - - - - - - - - - - - - - -

❹ Point Pleasant

Point Pleasant is the first of five quintessential bumper-car-and-Skee-Ball boardwalks. On a July weekend, Point Pleasant's long beach is jam-packed: squint, cover up all that nearly naked flesh with striped unitards, and it could be the 1920s, with umbrellas shading every inch of sand and the surf clogged with bodies and bobbing heads.

Families with young kids love Point Pleasant,

TOP TIP: PLAN AHEAD

We love the shore but let's be honest, in summer months, the traffic's a nightmare, parking's impossible and the beaches are overflowing. Pack the car – the night before. Leave at dawn, or soon thereafter. If at all possible, come midweek. If you want to stay, make reservations. And if you want something besides a run-down, sun-bleached, musty, three-blocks-from-the-water, sand-crusted flea box to stay in, make reservations six months to a year in advance.

as the boardwalk is big but not overwhelming, and the squeaky-clean amusement rides, fun house and small aquarium – all run by **Jenkinson's** (☑732-295-4334, aquarium 732-899-1659; www.jenkinsons.com; 300 Ocean Ave; aquarium adult/child $10/6; ◷rides noon-11pm, aquarium 10am-10pm, hours vary off-season; ♿) – are geared to the height and delight of the 10-and-under set. That's not to say Point Pleasant is only for little ones. **Martell's Tiki Bar** (☑732-892-0131; www.tikibar. com; Boardwalk; mains $5-30; ◷11am-11pm, to 12:30am Fri & Sat), a place margarita pitchers go to die, makes sure of that: look for the neon-orange palm trees and listen for the live bands.

The Drive » Head south on Rte 35 past several residential communities laid out on a long barrier island only a block or two wide in parts – Seaside Heights is where it's at its widest on this 11-mile trip.

❺ Seaside Heights

Coming from the north, Seaside Heights has the first of the truly overwhelming boardwalks: a sky ride and two rollicking amusement piers with double corridors of arcade games and adult-size, adrenaline-pumping rides, roller coasters, and various iterations of the vomit-inducing 10-story drop. During the day, it's as family-friendly as Point Pleasant, but once darkness falls Seaside Heights becomes a scene of such hedonistic mating rituals that an evangelical church has felt the need for a permanent booth on the pier. Packs of young men – caps askew, tatts gleaming – check out packs of young women in micro-dresses as everyone rotates among the string of loud bars with live bands playing Eagles tunes. It's pure Jersey.

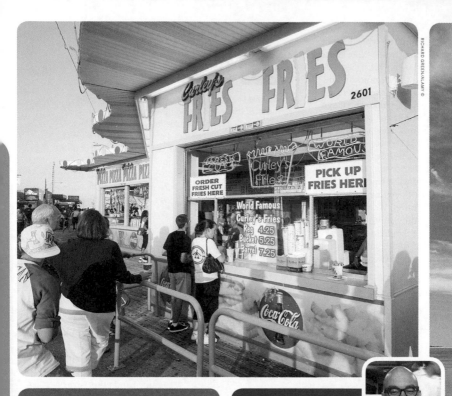

LOCAL KNOWLEDGE
DAVE POWITZ
OWNER, SKIPPER
DIPPER ICE CREAM

The Barnegat Lighthouse is beautiful from nearly every angle, but I think it looks best from the water. Don't have access to a boat? A great view is from the beach in the neighborhood of High Bar Harbor. Drive to the end of Sunset Blvd, and look across Barnegat Bay to enjoy the best view on the island.

Top: Snack time at the beach
Left: Wildwoods boardwalk sign
Right: Barnegat Lighthouse

GEORGE OZE/ALAMY ©

Detour south on Rte 35 to the 10-mile-long **Island Beach State Park** (weekday/weekend summer $12/20; ⊙8am-8pm), a completely undeveloped barrier island backed by dunes and tall grasses separating the bay from the ocean.

✗ p58

The Drive ≫ To reach the mainland, take Rte 37 from Seaside Heights; you cross a long bridge over Barnegat Bay before reaching the strip-mall-filled sprawl of Tom's River. Hop on the Garden State Pkwy south, then Rte 72 and the bridge over Manahawkin Bay.

- - - - - - - - - - - -

❻ Long Beach Island

Only a very narrow inlet separates this long sliver of an island, with its beautiful beaches and impressive summer homes, from the very southern tip of Island Beach State Park and northern shore towns. Within throwing distance of the park is the landmark **Barnegat Lighthouse** (☎609-494-2016; www.njparksandforests.org; off Long Beach Blvd; ⊙8am-4pm) which offers panoramic views at the top. Fishermen cast off from a jetty extending 2000ft along the Atlantic Ocean, and a short nature trail begins just in front of a visitor center with small history and photography displays.

Nearly every morning practically half the island is jogging, walking, blading or biking on Beach Ave, the 7.5-mile stretch of asphalt that stretches from Ship Bottom to Beach Haven (south of the bridge); it's a great time to exercise, enjoy the sun and people-watch. Tucked down a residential street is **Hudson House** (13th St, Beach Haven), a nearly locals-only dive bar about as worn and comfortable as an old pair of flip-flops. Don't be intimidated by the fact that it looks like a crumbling biker bar – it is.

The Drive » The only way in and out of Long Beach Island is via the bridge between Ship Bottom and Beach Haven West. The Garden State Pkwy heads south past the marshy pinelands area and Atlantic City. Take exit 30 for Somers Point; Laurel Dr turns into Mac

Arthur Blvd/Rte 52 and then a long causeway crosses Great Egg Harbor Bay. All up, this is a 48-mile drive.

- - - - - - - - - - - - -

❼ Ocean City

An almost heavenly amalgam of Ocean Grove and Point Pleasant, Ocean City is a dry town with a roomy boardwalk packed with genuine family fun and facing an exceedingly pretty beach. There's a small water park, and Gillian's Wonderland has a heart-thumpingly tall Ferris wheel, a beautifully restored merry-go-round, kiddie rides galore – and no microphoned teens hawking carnie games. The mood is light and friendly (a lack of alcohol will do that).

Minigolf aficionados: dingdingdingding! You hit the jackpot. Pint-size duffers can play through on a three-masted

schooner, around great white sharks and giant octopus, under reggae monkeys piloting a helicopter and even in black light. If you haven't yet, beat the heat with a delicious Kohr's soft-serve frozen custard, plain or dipped. While saltwater taffy is offered in many places, **Shriver's Taffy** (☎877-668-2339, 609-399-0100; www.shrivers.com; 9th & Boardwalk; ☉9am-midnight, shorter hours off-season; 🚻) is, in our humble opinion, the best: watch machines stretch and wrap it, and then fill a bag with two dozen or more flavors.

🛏 p59

The Drive » If time isn't a factor, cruise down local streets and several small bridges over inlets and channels ($1.50 toll on two of the four in each direction; no E-Z Pass) through the beachfront communities of Strathmere, Sea Isle City, Avalon and Stone Harbor; this is roughly a 26-mile drive. Otherwise, head back to the Garden State Pkwy and get off at one of two exits for the Wildwoods on a 30-mile drive.

- - - - - - - - - - - -

❽ Wildwoods

A party town popular with teens, 20-somethings and the young, primarily Eastern Europeans who staff the restaurants and shops, Wildwood is the main social focus here (North Wildwood and Wildwood Crest are

WE'RE HAVIN' A PARTY

Yes, in summer, every day is a party at the Jersey Shore. But here are some events not to miss:

» Gay Pride Parade, Asbury Park, early June (www.gayasburypark.com)

» Polka Spree by the Sea, Wildwood, late June (www.northwild.com/events.asp)

» New Jersey Sandcastle Contest, Belmar, July (www.njsandcastle.com)

» New Jersey State Barbecue Championship, Wildwood, mid-July (www.njbbq.com)

» Ocean City Baby Parade, Ocean City, early August (www.ocnj.us)

to the north and south respectively). Access to all three beaches is free, and the width of the beach – more than 1000ft in parts, making it the widest in New Jersey – means there's never a lack of space. Several massive piers are host to water parks and amusement parks – easily the rival of any Six Flags Great Adventure – with roller coasters and rides best suited to aspiring astronauts anchoring the 2-mile-long Grand Daddy of Jersey Shore boardwalks. Glow-in-the-dark 3D minigolf is a good example of the Wildwood boardwalk ethos – take it far, then one step further. Maybe the best ride of all, and one that doesn't induce nausea, is the tram running the length of the boardwalk from Wildwood Crest to North Wildwood. There's always a line for a table at Jersey Shore staple pizzeria **Mack & Manco's** on the boardwalk (it also has other shore boardwalk locations).

Wildwood Crest is an archaeological find, a kitschy slice of 1950s Americana – whitewashed motels with flashing neon signs, turquoise curtains and pink doors. Check out eye-catching motel signs such as the **Lollipop** at 23rd and Atlantic Aves.

🛏 p59

Cape May Victorian architecture

The Drive » Take local roads: south on Pacific Ave to Ocean Dr, which passes over a toll bridge over an estuary area separating Jarvis Sound from Cape May Harbor. Then left on NJ-109 over the Cape May harbor itself. You can turn left anywhere from here, depending on whether you want to head to town or the beach.

- - - - - - - - - -

TRIP HIGHLIGHT

❾ Cape May

Founded in 1620, Cape May – the only place in the state where the sun both rises and sets over the water – is on the state's southern tip and is the country's oldest seashore resort. Its sweeping beaches get crowded in summer, but the stunning Victorian architecture is attractive year-round.

In addition to 600 gingerbread-style houses, the city boasts antique shops and places for dolphin-, whale- (May to December) and bird-watching, and is just

outside the **Cape May Point State Park** (www.state.nj.us/dep/parksandforests; 707 E Lake Dr; ⏱8am-4pm) and its 157ft **Cape May Lighthouse** (adult/child $7/3) (there's 199 steps to the observation deck at the top); there's an excellent visitor center and museum with exhibits on wildlife in the area as well as trails to ponds, dunes and marshes. A mile-long loop of the nearby **Cape May Bird Observatory** (☎609-898-2473, 609-861-0700; www.birdcapemay.org; 701 East Lake Dr; ⏱9am-4:30pm) is a pleasant stroll through preserved wetlands. The wide sandy beach at the park (free) and the one in town are the main attractions in summer months. **Aqua Trails** (☎609-884-5600; www.aquatrails.com; from single/double $40/70) offers kayak tours of the coastal wetlands.

🍴 🛏 p59

Eating & Sleeping

Asbury Park ❶

✖ Sunset Landing   Cafe $

(☎732-776-9732; 1215 Sunset Ave; mains $5-8; ⏱7am-2pm Tue-Sun; 🖐) On Deal Lake, about 10 blocks from the beach, Sunset Landing is like a Hawaiian surf shack transported to a suburban Asbury lakeside. Vintage longboards crowd the wooden rafters, cheesy omelets are super-fresh, and delicious specialty pancakes come with cranberries, cinnamon, coconut, macadamia nuts and other island flavors. Cash only.

Ocean Grove ❷

✖ Moonstruck   Italian $$$

(☎732-988-0123; www.moonstrucknj.com; 517 Lake Ave; mains $16-30; ⏱5-10pm Wed,Thu & Sun, to 11pm Fri & Sat) There's nothing staid or proper about this bustling, popular restaurant housed in a striking Victorian building with tables on the wraparound porches. The menu is eclectic, though it leans towards Italian with a good selection of pastas; the meat and fish dishes have varied ethnic influences.

✖ Starving Artist   Cafe $

(☎732-988-1007; 47 Olin St; mains $3-9; ⏱8am-3pm Mon-Sat, to 2pm Sun, closed Wed; 🖐) The menu at this adorable eatery with a large outdoor patio highlights breakfast, the grill, and fried seafood; tasty ice cream is served at the adjacent shop.

🛏 Quaker Inn   Inn $$

(☎732-775-7525; www.quakerinn.com; 39 Main St; r $90-150; 🖐) The 135-year-old inn has 29 small, well-priced rooms, all with air-con and TV, and some with balconies. Open year-round; no breakfast.

Spring Lake ❸

🛏 Grand Victorian at
Spring Lake   Inn $$

(☎732-449-5237; www.grandvictorian springlake.com; 1505 Ocean Ave; r with shared/ private bath including breakfast from $100/150; ❄🛜) A stay at this bright and airy Victorian directly across the street from the beach is about as far from the TV version of a shore break as you can get. Rooms are simple and tastefully done and a wraparound porch and excellent attached restaurant add to the general air of oceanfront elegance.

Seaside Heights ❺

✖ Music Man   Ice Cream $

(☎732-854-2779; www.njmusicman.com; 2305 Grand Central Ave (Rte 35), Lavallette; mains $3-8; ⏱takeout 6am-midnight, shows 6pm-midnight; 🖐) Stop in Lavallette for an ice cream at this true crowd-pleaser where every evening is 'dessert theater,' with servers belting out Broadway show tunes tableside. Go on, order a sundae; you'll smile all the way home.

✖ Shut Up and Eat!   Breakfast $

(☎732-349-4544; 213 Rte 37 East) About 6 miles west of Seaside Heights, tucked away in the Kmart shopping plaza in Tom's River, this sarcastically named place could be the silliest breakfast joint ever: there are waitresses in pajamas (wear yours for a 13% discount), snappy repartee, mismatched furniture and a cornucopia of kitsch. The food's even better: try stuffed French toast with real maple syrup, plus top-quality omelets, pancakes and more.

Ocean City ❼

🛏 Flanders Hotel   Hotel $$$

(📞609-399-1000; www.flandershotel.com; 719
E 11th St; r $260-440; 🏊) Shake off those sandy
motel blues at Ocean City's Flanders Hotel:
every room is a modern, immaculate, 650-sq-ft
(or larger) suite with full kitchen, and the blue-
and-yellow decor evokes a pleasantly low-key
seaside feel.

Wildwoods ❽

🛏 Heart of Wildwood   Hotel $$

(📞609-522-4090; www.heartofwildwood.com;
Ocean & Spencer Aves, Wildwood; r $125-245;
🏊) If you're here for waterslides and roller
coasters, book a room at Heart of Wildwood,
facing the amusement piers. It's not fancy, but
gets high marks for cleanliness (the tile floors
help), and from the heated rooftop pool you can
watch the big wheel go round and round.

🛏 Starlux   Hotel $$

(📞609-522-7412; www.thestarlux.com; Rio
Grande & Atlantic Aves, Wildwood; r $130-310; 🏊)
The sea-green-and-white Starlux has the soaring
profile, the lava lamps, the boomerang-decorated
bedspreads and the sailboat-shaped mirrors, plus
it's clean as a whistle. Even more authentically
retro are its two chrome-sided Airstream trailers.

🛏 Summer Nites B&B   B&B $$

(📞609-846-1955; www.summernites.com;
2110 Atlantic Ave, Wildwood; r $145-275) North

of the noise and lights, in an unassuming white
house, is the coolest vintage experience of all:
real jukeboxes play 45s; the breakfast room is a
perfectly re-created diner and the eight themed
rooms are dominated by wall-size murals and
framed, signed memorabilia.

Cape May ❾

🍴 Lobster House   Seafood $$

(906 Schellengers Landing Rd, Fisherman's
Wharf; mains $12-27; ⏱11:30am-3pm &
4:30-10pm Apr-Dec, to 9pm other times) Talk
about locally sourced...You know the fish is
fresh at this classic surf and turf because the
restaurant's own boats haul the day's catch in.
There are no reservations which means very
long waits are a possibility; in that case try to
grab a seat at the dockside raw-seafood bar.

🍴 Uncle Bill's
Pancake House   American $

(Beach Ave at Perry St; mains $7; ⏱6:30am-
2pm) The size (and decor) of a high-school
cafeteria from the 1950s, Uncle Bill's has been
drawing in crowds for its flapjacks for 50 years.

🛏 Congress Hall   Hotel $$

(📞609-884-8421; www.congresshall.com;
251 Beach Ave; r $100-465) The classic and
regal-looking Congress Hall has a range of
beautiful quarters to suit various budgets, plus
a long, oceanfront porch lined with rocking
chairs. An ideal location, on-site restaurant and
downstairs bar called the Boiler Room (with live
music some nights) make this hard to beat.

Lancaster Lush farmland produces gastronomic delights

Pennsylvania Dutch Country

3

This fairly compact trip takes you to rural Amish communities where farmers markets and roadside stalls offer homemade goods, and traditions and history are preserved in everyday life.

TRIP HIGHLIGHTS

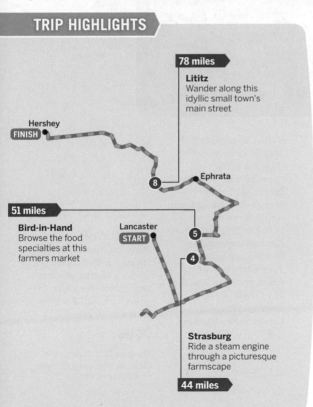

78 miles

Lititz
Wander along this idyllic small town's main street

Hershey
FINISH

Ephrata

8

51 miles

Bird-in-Hand
Browse the food specialties at this farmers market

Lancaster
START

5

4

Strasburg
Ride a steam engine through a picturesque farmscape

44 miles

3–4 DAYS
102 MILES / 164KM

GREAT FOR...

BEST TIME TO GO
Less crowded in early Spring or September.

 ESSENTIAL PHOTO

A windmill or grain silo with a horse-drawn plow in the foreground.

 BEST FOR FOODIES

Almost everything can be jarred at the Intercourse Canning Co.

FINISH
Hershey **9**
322

283

Elizabethtown

Susquehanna River

28 miles to
Gettysburg

30

p65
York

72 miles to
4

3 Pennsylvania Dutch Country

The Amish really do drive buggies and plow their fields by hand. In Dutch Country, the pace is slower, and it's no costumed reenactment. For the most evocative Dutch Country experience, go driving along the winding, narrow lanes between the thruways – past rolling green fields of alfalfa, asparagus and corn, past pungent working barnyards and manicured lawns, waving to Amish families in buggies and straw-hatted teens on scooters.

❶ Lancaster

A good place to start is Lancaster's (LANK-uh-stir) walkable, red-brick historic district, just off Penn Sq. The Romanesque Revival-style **Central Market** (www.centralmarketlancaster. com; 23 N Market St; ☺6am-4pm Tue & Fri, to 2pm Sat), has regional gastronomic delicacies – fresh horseradish, whoopie pies, soft pretzels, sub sandwiches stuffed with cured meats and dripping with oil – as well as Spanish and Middle Eastern food. Plus, the market is crowded with handicraft booths staffed by bonneted, plain-dressed Amish women.

In the 18th century, German immigrants flooded southeastern Pennsylvania, and only some were Amish. Most lived like the costumed docents at the **Landis Valley Museum** (☎717-569-0401; www. landisvalleymuseum.org; 2451 Kissel Hill Rd; adult/child $12/8; ☺9am-5pm, from noon Sun), a re-creation of Pennsylvania German village life that includes a working smithy, weavers and stables. It's a few miles north of Lancaster off Rte 272/Oregon Pike.

✖ 🛏 p70

The Drive ⟩⟩ From downtown Lancaster head south on Prince St, which turns into Rte 222

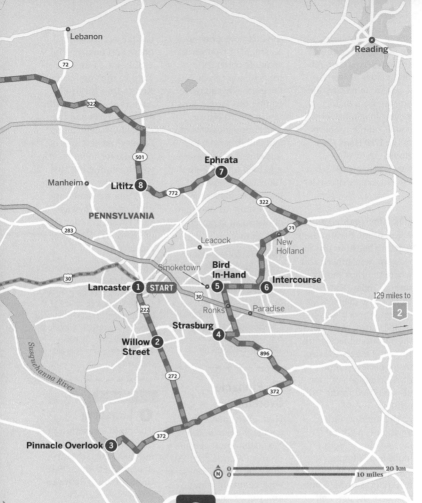

Lebanon

Reading

72

322

501

Ephrata
7

Manheim Lititz **8** 772

PENNSYLVANIA

283

Leacock

New Holland

322

23

Smoketown

Bird In-Hand

Lancaster ① START

Intercourse

5

6

30

222

Ronks Paradise

Strasburg

129 miles to

2

Willow Street **2**

4

272

896

372

Pinnacle Overlook ③

372

0   20 km
0   10 miles

and then Rte 272 all the way to Willow Street.

 LINK YOUR TRIP

② Willow Street

Prior to the arrival of European émigrés, Coney, Lenape, Mohawk, Seneca and other Native Americans lived in the area. However, Pennsylvania remains

2 **The Jersey Shore**

Head east to Philadelphia where you can connect to a number of routes that will transport you to the boardwalks of Jersey Shore towns.

4 **Maryland's National Historic Road**

Continue on US 30 west to York and then head south to Baltimore for a journey through this state's defining small towns.

NEW YORK & THE MID-ATLANTIC TRIPS **3** PENNSYLVANIA DUTCH COUNTRY

one of the few states with no officially recognized tribal reserves – or, for that matter, tribes. In a gesture to rectify this erasure from history, a replica longhouse now stands on the property of the **1719 Hans Herr House** (717-464-4438; www.hansherr.org; 1849 Hans Herr Dr; combined guided tour adult/child $15/7; 9am-4pm Mon-Sat Apr 1-Nov 30), generally regarded as the oldest original Mennonite meeting house in the western hemisphere and where the Herr family settled. Today, Hans Herr House displays colonial-era artifacts in period- furnished rooms; there's also a blacksmith shop and a barn. 'Living history interpreters' provide an idea of how life was lived in the 18th century.

The interior of the longhouse, a typical narrow, single room, multi-family home built only from natural materials, is divided into two sections: pre- and post-European contact. They are decorated and furnished with artifacts typical of each era. The primary mission is to teach visitors about the history of Native American life in Lancaster County from around 1570 to 1770 when for all intents and purposes they ceased to exist as distinctive groups in the area. And this includes

the infamous Conestoga Massacre of 1763 when vigilante colonists from Paxton (given the curiously anodyne epithet the 'Paxton Boys') murdered 20 Native American men, women and children from the settlement of Conestoga. A guided tour of both the Hans Herr House and the longhouse makes for an interesting juxtaposition of historical perspectives and culture.

The Drive » The simplest route is Rte 272 south to Rte 372 west. However, if you have time head west on Long Ln or W Penn Grant Rd, then right on River Rd, a pretty but hard-to-follow backcountry road. You'll pass by Tucquan Glen Nature Preserve – park and hike to the river.

- - - - - - - - - - - -

❸ Pinnacle Overlook

High over Lake Aldred, a wide portion of the Susquehanna River just up from a large dam, is this **overlook** (8am-9pm) with beautiful views and eagles and other raptors soaring overhead. This and the adjoining Holtwood Environmental Preserve are parts of a large swath of riverfront property maintained by the Pennsylvania Power & Light Co (PPL). But electrical plant infrastructure and truck traffic is largely kept at bay, making this a popular spot for locals, non-Amish, that is (it's

too far to travel by horse and buggy). The 4-mile-long Fire Line Trail to the adjoining Kelly's Run Natural Area is challenging and steep in parts and the rugged Conestoga Trail follows the east side of the lake for 15 miles. It's worth coming out this way if only to see more rough-hewn landscape and the rural byways that reveal another facet of Lancaster County's character.

The Drive » You could retrace your route back to Willow St and then head to Strasburg, but to make a scenic loop, take Rte 372 east, passing agrarian scenes, to the small hamlet of Georgetown. Make a left onto Rte 896 – vistas open up on either side of the road.

- - - - - - - - - - - -

TRIP HIGHLIGHT

❹ Strasburg

The main attraction in Strasburg is trains – the old-fashioned, steam-driven kind. Since 1832, the **Strasburg Railroad** (717-687-7522; www. strasburgrailroad.com; Rte 741; coach class adult/child $14/8; multiple trips daily, times vary by season;) has run the same route (and speed) to Paradise and back that it does today, and wooden train cars are gorgeously restored with stained glass, shiny brass lamps and plush burgundy seats. Several classes of seats are offered including the private President's Car; there's also a wine and cheese option.

The **Railroad Museum of Pennsylvania** (☎717-687-8628; www.rrmuseumpa.org; Rte 741; adult/child $10/8; ☺9am 5pm Mon-Sat, noon-5pm Sun, closed Sun Nov-Mar; ♿) has 100 gigantic mechanical marvels to climb around and admire, but even more delightful is the HO-scale **National Toy Train Museum** (☎717-687-8976; www.nttmuseum.org; 300 Paradise Lane; adult/child $6/3; ☺10am-5pm May-Oct, call for hours off-season; ♿). The push-button interactive dioramas are so up-to-date and clever (such as a 'drive-in movie' that's a live video of kids working the trains), and the walls are packed with so many gleaming railcars, that you can't help but feel a bit of that childlike Christmas-morning wonder. Stop at the Red Caboose Motel next to the museum – you can climb the silo in back for wonderful views ($0.50) and kids can enjoy a small petting zoo.

🛏 p71

The Drive ›› Continue north on S Ronks Rd past farmland scenery in Ronks (p71), cross busy Rte 30 and carry on for 2 miles to Bird-in-Hand. Hungry? Smoketown's Good 'N Plenty Restaurant (p70) is a mile west of Bird-in-Hand on Rte 340 at the intersection with Rte 896.

- - - - - - - - - - - - -

TRIP HIGHLIGHT

❺ Bird-in-Hand

The primary reason to make your way to this

DETOUR: GETTYSBURG

Start: ❶ Lancaster

Take US 30 west (also called Lincoln Hwy) for 55 miles into downtown Gettysburg. This tranquil, compact and memorial-laden town saw one of the Civil War's most decisive and bloody battles for three days in July, 1863. It's also where, four months later, Lincoln delivered his Gettysburg Address consecrating, eulogizing and declaring the mission unfinished. At only 200-plus words, it's one of the most defining and effective rhetorical examples in US history. Much of the ground where Robert E Lee's Army of Northern Virginia and Major General Joseph Hooker's Union Army of the Potomac fought can be explored – either in your own car with a map and guide, on an audio CD tour, a bus tour or a two-hour guided ranger tour ($65 per vehicle). The latter is most highly recommended but if you're short on time it's still worth driving the narrow lanes past fields with dozens of monuments marking significant sites and moments on the battle.

Don't miss the massive new **Gettysburg National Military Park Museum & Visitor Center** (☎717-334-1124; www.gettysburgfoundation.org; 1195 Baltimore Pike; adult/child $12.50/8.50; ☺8am-5pm Nov-Mar, to 6pm Apr-Oct) several miles south of town, which houses a fairly incredible museum filled with artifacts and displays exploring every nuance of the battle; a film explaining Gettysburg's context and why it's considered a turning point in the war; and Paul Philippoteaux's 377ft cyclorama painting of Pickett's Charge. The aforementioned bus tours and ranger-led tours are booked here. While overwhelming, in the very least, it's a foundation for understanding the Civil War's primacy and lingering impact in the nation's evolution.

The annual Civil War Heritage Days festival, held from the last weekend of June to the first weekend of July, features living history encampments, battle re-enactments, a lecture series and book fair that draws war reenactment aficionados from near and wide. You can find re-enactments throughout the year as well.

PENNSYLVANIA DUTCH COUNTRY
MICHAEL GROSBERG, AUTHOR

One of the best things about eating Pennsylvania Dutch food – it's certainly not its nutritional content – is how it's eaten: communally, at long tables where you actually have to sit next to and converse with strangers. You won't be strained for conversation, as the massive offerings give you plenty to chat about – the food keeps coming until you can't take another bite.

Top: A horse-drawn buggy drives towards a farm
Left: An Amish girl makes handicrafts at the Bird-in-Hand Farmers Market
Right: Cranberry harvest

delightfully named Amish town is the **Bird-in-Hand Farmers Market** (717-393-9674; 2710 Old Philadelphia Pike; 8:30am-5:30pm Wed-Sat Jul-Oct, call for other times of year), which is pretty much a one-stop shop of Dutch Country highlights. There's fudge, quilts and crafts, and you can buy scrapple (pork scraps mixed with cornmeal and wheat flour, shaped into a loaf and fried), homemade jam and shoofly pie (molasses pie sprinkled with a crumbly mix of brown sugar, flour and butter). Two lunch counters sell cheap sandwiches, homemade pretzels and healthy juices and smoothies. It's worth bringing a cooler to stock up for the drive home.

The Drive » It's less than 4 miles east on Old Philadelphia Pike/Rte 340 but traffic can back up, in part because it's a popular route for tourist horse and buggy rides.

- - - - - - - - - - - -

6 Intercourse

Named for the crossroads, not the act, Intercourse is a little more amenable to walking than Bird-in-Hand. The **horse-drawn buggy rides** (717-391-9500; www.aaabuggyrides.com; 3529 Old Philadelphia Pike; adult/child $12/6; 9am-7pm Mon-Sat;) on offer can also be fun. How much fun depends largely on your driver: some Amish are strict, some liberal, and Mennonites are different again. All drivers strive to present Amish culture to the 'English' (the Amish term for non-Amish, whether English or not), but some are more openly personal than others.

Kitchen Kettle Village, essentially an open-air mall for tourists with stores selling smoked meats, jams, pretzels and tchotchkes, feels like a Disneyfied version of the Bird-in-Hand Farmers Market. It offers the commercialized 'PA Dutch Country experience' which means your perception of it will depend on your attitude toward a parking lot jammed with tour buses.

The **Quilt Museum at the Old Country Store** (www.ocsquiltmuseum.com; 3510 Old Philadelphia Pike; ⊙9am-5pm, closed Sun) displays museum-quality artisan quilts, and the **Intercourse Canning**

Company (13 Center St; ⊙9:30am-5pm Mon-Sat) shows that almost anything can be pickled and put in a mason jar.

 p71

The Drive >> Head north on Rte 722 and make your first right onto Centerville Rd, a country lane that takes you to Rte 23. Turn right here and it's a few miles to Blue Ball – which has a restaurant and country store or two – and then left on the busier Rte 322 all the way to Ephrata.

- - - - - - - - - - - - - -

⑦ Ephrata

One of the country's earliest religious communities was founded in 1732 by Conrad Beissel, an émigré escaping religious persecution in his native Germany. Beissel, like others throughout human history dissatisfied with worldly ways and distractions (difficult to imagine what

these were in his pre-pre-pre digital age), sought a mystical, personal relationship with God. At its peak there were close to 300 members including two celibate orders of brothers and sisters, known collectively as 'the Solitary,' who patterned their dress after Roman Catholic monks (the last of these passed away in 1813), as well as married 'households' who were less all-in, if you will.

Today, the collection of austere, almost medieval-style buildings of the **Ephrata Cloister** (☎717-733-6600; www.ephratacloister.org; 632 W Main St; adult/child $10/6; ⊙9am-5pm Mon-Sat, from noon Sun) have been preserved and are open to visitors; guided tours are offered or take an audio cell-phone tour on your own. There's a small museum and a short film in the visitor

THE AMISH

The Amish (Ah-mish), Mennonite and Brethren religious communities are collectively known as the 'Plain People.' All are Anabaptist sects (only those who choose the faith are baptized) who were persecuted in their native Switzerland, and from the early 1700s settled in tolerant Pennsylvania. Speaking German dialects, they became known as 'Dutch' (from 'Deutsch'). Most Pennsylvania Dutch live on farms and their beliefs vary from sect to sect. Many do not use electricity, and most opt for horse-drawn buggies – a delightful sight in the area. The strictest believers, the Old Order Amish who make up nearly 90% of Lancaster County's Amish, wear dark, plain clothing (no zippers, only buttons, snaps and safety pins) and live a simple, Bible-centered life – but have, ironically, become a major tourist attraction, thus bringing busloads of gawkers and the requisite strip malls, chain restaurants and hotels that lend this entire area an oxymoronic quality. Because there is so much commercial development – fast-food restaurants, mini-malls, big-box chain stores, tract housing – continually encroaching on multigenerational family farms, it takes some doing to appreciate the unique nature of the area.

center that tells the story of Ephrata's founding and demise – if the narrator's tone and rather somber *mise-en-scène* are any indication, not to mention the extremely spartan sleeping quarters, it was a demanding existence. No doubt Beissel would disapprove of today's Ephrata, whose commercial Main Street is anchored by a Walmart.

If you're around on a Friday, be sure to check out the **Green Dragon Farmers Market** (www. greendragonmarket.com; 955 N State St; ⊙9am-9pm Fri).

The Drive » This is a simple 8.5 mile drive; for the most part, Rte 772/Rothsville Rd between Ephrata and Lititz is an ordinary commercial strip.

TRIP HIGHLIGHT

8 Lititz

Like other towns in Pennsylvania Dutch Country, Lititz was founded by a religious community from Europe, in this case Moravians who settled here in the 1740s. But unlike Ephrata, Lititz was more outward looking and integrated with the world beyond its historic center. Many of its original handsome stone and wood buildings still line its streets. Take a stroll down E Main St from the **Sturgis Pretzel House** (☏717-626-4354; www. juliussturgis.com; 219 E Main St; admission $3; ⊙9am-5pm Mon-Sat; ⊕), the first pretzel

TOP TIP: FARM STAY

If you like your vacations to be working ones, check out **A Farm Stay** (www.afarmstay.com; r from $60-180) which represents several dozen farm stays that range from stereotypical B&Bs to Amish farms. Most include breakfast, private bathrooms and some activity such as milking cows, gathering eggs or simply petting a goat.

factory in the country – you can try rolling and twisting the dough. Across the street is the Moravian Church (c 1787); then head to the intersection with S Broad. Rather than feeling sealed in amber, the small shops, which do seem to relish their small-town quality, are the type that sophisticated urbanites cherish. There's an unusual effortlessness to this vibe, from the Bulls Head Public House, an English-style pub with an expertly curated beer menu, to Greco's Italian Ices, a little ground-floor hole-in-the-wall where local teens and families head on weekend nights for delicious homemade ice cream.

✕ ⌁ p71

The Drive » It's an easy 27 miles on Rte 501 to US 322. Both pass through a combination of farmland and suburban areas.

9 Hershey

Hershey is home to a collection of attractions that detail, hype and, of course, hawk the many trappings of Milton

Hershey's chocolate empire. The pièce de résistance is **Hersheypark** (☏800-437-7439; www. hersheypark.com; 100 W Hersheypark Dr; adult/child $52/31; ⊙10am-10pm Jun-Aug, 9am-6pm or 8pm Sep-May), an amusement park with more than 60 thrill rides, a zoo and a water park plus various performances and frequent fireworks displays. Don a hairnet and apron, punch in a few choices on a computer screen and voilà, watch your very own chocolate bar roll down a conveyor belt at the Create Your Own Candy Bar ($15) attraction. This forms part of Hershey's Chocolate World, a mock factory and massive candy store with over-stimulating features including singing characters and free chocolate galore. For a more informative visit, try the **Hershey Story**, The **Museum on Chocolate Avenue**, which explores the life and fascinating legacy of Mr Hershey through interactive history exhibits; try molding your own candy in the hands-on Chocolate Lab.

Eating & Sleeping

Lancaster ❶

✖ Bube's
Brewery   Continental, Brewery **$$**

(www.bubesbrewery.com; 102 North Market St, Mt Joy) This well-preserved 19th-century German brewery-cum-restaurant complex is in Mt Joy, 15 miles northwest of Lancaster off Rte 283. It contains several atmospheric bars and four separate dining rooms (one underground), hosts costumed 'feasts' and, naturally, brews its own beer.

✖ Lancaster
Brewing Co   American, Brewery **$$**

(302 N Plum St; mains $9-22; ⊙11:30am-10pm) Just around the corner from the Cork Factory hotel, the bar here draws young neighborhood regulars and the menu is a big step-up from standard pub fare – rack of wild boar and cranberry sausage is an example. But you can't beat specials like 35¢-wing night.

✖ Ma(i)son   French, Italian **$$$**

(☎717-293-5060; www.maisonlancaster.com; 230 N Prince St; mains $25 ; ⊙5-11pm Wed-Sat) Every worthy current trend of the slow-food, farm-to-table culinary movement is embodied in this sophisticated, though of course rustically furnished, Lancaster restaurant. It's run by a husband-and-wife team who like to keep things local; they value the bounty from the area's farms and live above the restaurant. Expect the menu to change with the seasons – it may include meticulously prepared mains such as Madeira-braised veal and wild nettle sausage pasta. BYOB and reservations recommended.

🛏 Cork Factory   Boutique Hotel **$$**

(☎717-735-2075; www.corkfactoryhotel.com; 480 New Holland Ave; r incl breakfast from $125; ❄🛜) An abandoned-brick behemoth now houses a stylishly up-to-date hotel only a few miles northeast of the Lancaster city center. Sunday brunch at the hotel's restaurant is a fusion of seasonal new American and down-home comfort cooking.

🛏 Lancaster Arts Hotel   Hotel **$$**

(☎866-720-2787; www.lancasterartshotel.com; 300 Harrisburg Ave; r from $180; P❄🛜) For a refreshingly hip and urban experience, make a beeline to the snazzy Lancaster Arts Hotel, housed in an old brick tobacco warehouse and featuring a groovy boutique-hotel ambience.

🛏 Landis Farm   Guest House **$$**

(☎717-898-7028; www.landisfarm.com; 2048 Gochlan Rd, Manheim; d incl breakfast $125; 🛜) A slightly upscale and modern (complete with cable TV and wi-fi) homestay farm experience can be had here, a 200-year-old stone home with pinewood floors.

Smoketown

✖ Good 'N Plenty
Restaurant   American **$$**

(Intersection Rte 896 & Rte 340; mains $11; ⊙11:30am-8pm Mon-Sat, closed Jan; ♿) Sure, you'll be dining with busloads of tourists and your cardiologist might not approve, but hunkering down at one of the picnic tables here for a family-style meal ($21) is a lot of fun. Besides the main dining room, which is the size of a football field, there are a couple of other mini-areas where you can order from an à la carte menu.

🛏 Fulton Steamboat Inn   Hotel **$$**

(☎717-299-9999; 1 Hartman Bridge Rd; r from $100; ❄🛜🏊) A nautically themed hotel in landlocked Amish country seems like a gimmick even if the inventor of the steamboat was born nearby. The slight kitsch works, however – shiny brass old-timey light fixtures and painterly wallpaper, the hotel's interior is rather elegant and rooms are spacious and comfy. It's located at a crossroads convenient for trips to farm country or Lancaster.

Ronks

✕ Miller's Smorgasbord   Buffet $

(2811 Lincoln Hwy; mains from $8; ⏰11:30am-8pm Mon-Fri, 7:30am-8pm Sat & Sun; ♿) To smorgasbord ($23) or not to smorgasbord – there's no question. Otherwise, the alternative menu of diner-style dishes is fairly ordinary. The anchor of a touristy complex of shops, this pavilion-size restaurant draws crowds for the buffet featuring Amish-style entrees and desserts.

🛏 Red Caboose Motel & Restaurant   Motel $$

(☎888-687-5005; www.redcaboosemotel.com; 312 Paradise Lane; r from $120; ❄🛜) There's nothing very hobo-esque about a night's sleep in one of these 25-ton cabooses – TVs and mini-fridges included – though the basic furnishings aren't the draw. Spaces are narrow – the width of a train car – but the setting, on a rural lane surrounded by picturesque countryside, is beautiful.

Intercourse

✕ Stoltzfus Farm Restaurant   Diner $$

(☎768-8156; www.stoltzfusmeats.com; 3718 E Newport Rd; ⏰11:30am-8pm Mon-Sat Apr-Oct, Fri & Sat only in Nov) An all-you-can-eat,

family-style Dutch restaurant with chow-chow (a sweet pickled relish made from a combination of vegetables), pepper cabbage, fried chicken, homemade sausage, shoofly pie and more. It's just country cooking, plain and plentiful, but served by waitresses so preternaturally friendly you wonder for your own hardened soul.

Lititz ❽

✕ Tomato Pie Cafe   Sandwiches $

(23 N Broad St; mains $6; ⏰7am-9pm Mon-Sat; 🛜) Housed in a charming yellow and green home just around the corner from Main St, this cafe gets crowded, especially at lunchtime on weekends. Besides the signature tomato pie, the menu has salads and sandwiches including a peanut butter, Nutella and banana panini, excellent breakfasts and baristas who take their coffee seriously.

🛏 General Sutter Inn   Inn $

(☎717-626-2115; www.generalsutterinn.com; 14 East Main St; r from $70; ❄🛜) The bones of this atmospheric and charming inn anchoring one end of Lititz's Main St date to 1764. Ten wood-floored and cheerful rooms are tastefully furnished with antiques. A new top-floor annex called the Rock Lititz Penthouse has six decidedly modern suites with a playful rock 'n' roll theme. Attached is the extremely popular craft-beer-centric Bull's Head Pub.

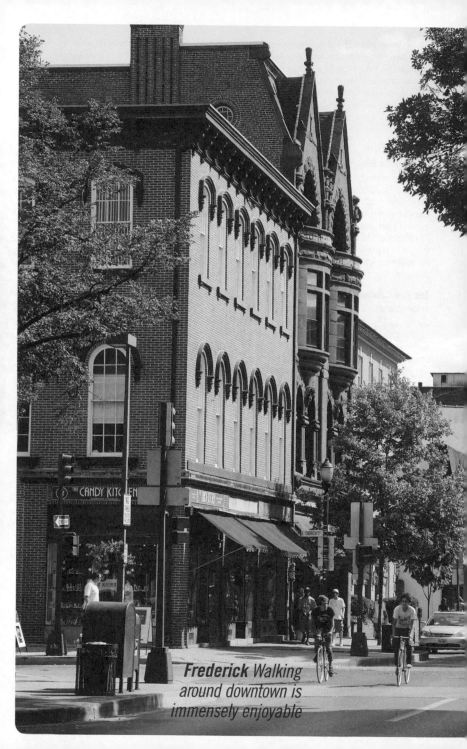

Frederick *Walking around downtown is immensely enjoyable*

Maryland's National Historic Road

4

From Baltimore's salty docks to the forested foothills around old Frederick, delve into the past of one of the most diverse states in the country.

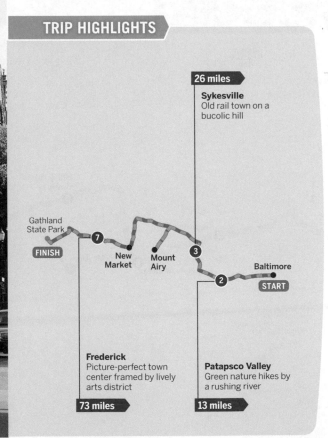

26 miles

Sykesville
Old rail town on a bucolic hill

Gathland State Park

7

FINISH

New Market

Mount Airy

3

2

Baltimore

START

Frederick
Picture-perfect town center framed by lively arts district

73 miles

Patapsco Valley
Green nature hikes by a rushing river

13 miles

2 DAYS
92 MILES / 150KM

GREAT FOR...

BEST TIME TO GO
April to June to soak up late spring's sunniness and warmth.

 ESSENTIAL PHOTO

The historic buildings lining New Market, MD.

 BEST FOR OUTDOORS

Hiking along the bottom of Patapsco Valley.

WILLIAM S KUTA/ALAMY ©

73

Maryland's National Historic Road

4

For such a small state, Maryland has a staggering array of landscapes and citizens, and this trip engages both of these elements of the Old Line State. Move from Chesapeake Bay and Baltimore, a port that mixes bohemians with blue-collar workers, through the picturesque small towns of the Maryland hill country, into the stately cities that mark the lower slopes of the looming Catoctin Mountains.

❶ Baltimore

Maryland's largest city is one of the most important ports in the country, a center for the arts and culture and an entrepôt of immigrants from Greece, El Salvador, East Africa, the Caribbean and elsewhere. These streams combine into an idiosyncratic culture that, in many ways, encapsulates Maryland's depth of history and prominent diversity – not just of race, but creed and socioeconomic status.

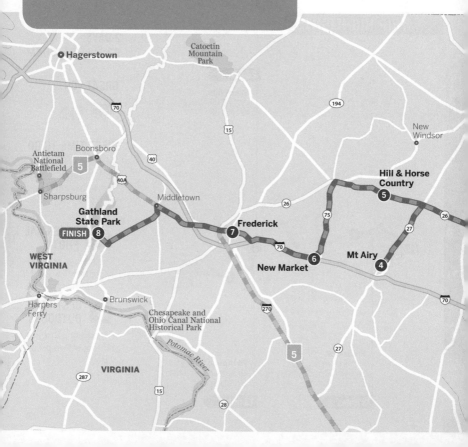

Baltimore was a notable hold-out against the British military during the War of 1812, even after Washington DC fell. The morning after an intense shelling, staring 'through the rockets' red glare,' local lawyer Francis Scott Key saw that 'our flag was still there' and wrote 'The Star-Spangled Banner'. The history of that battle and the national anthem are explored at **Fort McHenry** (☏410-962-4290; 2400 E Fort Ave; adult/child $7/free; ☺8am-5pm), located in South Baltimore.

Have a wander through nearby **Federal Hill Park** (300 Key Hwy), a 70-acre hill that rises above the city, and admire the view out over the harbor.

✖ 🛏 p81

The Drive ›› Get on US 40 (Baltimore National Pike – and the basis of the National Historic Road this trip is named for) westbound in Baltimore. The easiest place to access it is at Charles and Franklin St. Franklin becomes US 40/the Pike as you head west out of downtown Baltimore, into the woods that mark the edges of the Patapsco Valley. The whole drive takes about 30 minutes in traffic.

- - - - - - - - - - - -

TRIP HIGHLIGHT

➋ Patapsco Valley

The Patapsco river and river valley are the defining geographic features of the region, running through Central Maryland to Chesapeake Bay. To explore the area, head to **Patapsco Valley State Park** (☏410-461-5005; 8020 Baltimore National Pike, Ellicott City; ☺9am-sunset), an enormous protected area – one of the oldest in the state – that runs for 32 miles along a whopping 170 miles of trails. The main visitor center provides insight into the settled history of the area, from Native Americans to the present, and is housed in a 19th-century stone cottage that looks as though it were plucked from a CS Lewis bedtime story.

LINK YOUR TRIP

3 Pennsylvania Dutch Country

Take I-95 north from Baltimore and then MD-222 towards Lancaster to begin exploring this patch of bucolic farmland.

5 The Civil War Tour

In Gathland State Park, head 10 miles west to Antietam to begin exploring America's seminal internal conflict.

NEW YORK & THE MID-ATLANTIC TRIPS **4** MARYLAND'S NATIONAL HISTORIC ROAD

The Drive ≫ Get back on the Pike/US 40 westbound until you see signs to merge onto I-70W, which is the main connecting road between Baltimore and Central and Western Maryland. Get on 70, then take exit 80 to get onto MD-32 (Sykesville Rd). Follow for about 5 miles into Sykesville proper.

TRIP HIGHLIGHT

❸ Sykesville

Like many of the towns in the Central Maryland hill country between Baltimore and Frederick, Sykesville has a **historic center** that looks and feels picture perfect. **Main Street**, between Springfield Ave and Sandosky Rd, is filled with structures built between the 1850s and 1930s, and almost looks like an advertisement for small-town America.

The old Baltimore & Ohio (B&O) train station, now **Baldwin's** restaurant (7618 Main St), was built in 1883 in the Queen Anne style. The station was the brainchild of E Francis Baldwin, a Baltimore architect who designed many B&O stations, giving that rail line a satisfying aesthetic uniformity along its extent.

Fun fact: Sykesville was founded on land James Sykes bought from George Patterson. Patterson was the son of Elizabeth Patterson and Jerome Bonaparte, brother of Napoleon. The French emperor insisted his brother marry royalty and never let his sister-in-law (the daughter of a merchant) in to France; her family estate (which formed the original parcel of land that the town grew from) is the grounds of Sykesville proper.

✕ p81

The Drive ≫ Although this trip is largely based on US 40 – the actual National Historic Road – detour up to Liberty Rd (MD-26) and take that west 8 miles to Ridge Rd (MD-27). Take Ridge Rd/27 south for 5.5 miles to reach Mt Airy.

-----

❹ Mt Airy

Mt Airy is the next major (we use that term with a grain of salt) town along the B&O railroad and US 40/National Historic Road. Like Sykesville, it's a handsome town, with a stately center that benefited from the commerce the railway brought westward from Baltimore. When the railway was replaced by the highway, Mt Airy, unlike other towns, still retained much of its prosperity thanks to the proximity of jobs in cities including DC and Baltimore.

Today the town centers on a **historic district** of 19th- and early-20th-century buildings, many of which can be found around Main St. The posher historical homes near 'downtown' Mt Airy

DETOUR: CALVERT CLIFFS

Start: ❶ Baltimore

In Southern Maryland, 75 miles south of Baltimore via US 301 and MD-4, skinny Calvert County scratches at Chesapeake Bay and the Patuxent River. This is a gentle landscape ('user-friendly' as a local ranger puts it) of low-lying forests, estuarine marshes and placid waters, but there is one rugged feature: the Calvert Cliffs. These burnt umber pillars stretch along the coast for some 24 miles, and form the seminal landscape feature of **Calvert Cliffs State Park** (📞301-743-7613; 9500 H. G. Trueman Road, Lusby; 🕐sunrise-sunset; 🅿🚻🐾), where they front the water and a pebbly, honey-sand beach scattered with driftwood and drying beds of kelp.

Back in the day (10 to 20 million years ago), this area sat submerged under a warm sea. Eventually, that sea receded and left the fossilized remains of thousands of prehistoric creatures embedded in the cliffs. Fast forward to the 21st century, and one of the favorite activities of Southern Maryland families is coming to this park, strolling across the sand and plucking out fossils and sharks' teeth from the pebbly debris at the base of the cliffs. Over 600 species of fossils have been identified at the park. In addition, a full 1079 acres and 13 miles of the park are set aside for trails and hiking and biking.

While this spot is pet- and family-friendly, fair warning: it's a 1.8 mile walk from the parking lot to the open beach and the cliffs, so this may not be the best spot to go fossil hunting with very small children unless they can handle the walk. Also: don't climb the cliffs as erosion makes this an unstable and unsafe prospect.

were built in the Second Empire, Queen Anne and Colonial Revival styles, while most 'regular' homes are two-story, center gable 'I-houses,' once one of the most common housing styles in rural America in the 19th century, now largely displaced in this region by modern split-levels.

The Drive » Take Ridge Rd/MD-27 back to Liberty Rd/MD-26. Turn left and proceed along for 10 miles to reach Elk Run.

❺ Hill & Horse Country

Much of Frederick, Carroll, Baltimore and Hartford counties consist of trimmed, rolling grassy hills intersected by copses of pine and broadleaf woods and tangled hedgerows; it's the sort of landscape that could put you in mind of the bocage country of northern France or rural England. A mix of working farmers and wealthy city folks live out here, and horse breeding and raising is a big industry.

It can be pretty enchanting just driving around and getting lost on some of the local back roads, but if you want a solid destination, it's tough to go wrong

with **Elk Run Vineyards** (📞410-775-2513; www.elkrun.com; 15113 Liberty Rd, Mt Airy; tastings from $5, tours free; 🕐10am-5pm Tue-Sat, 1-5pm Sun), almost exactly halfway between Mt Airy and New Market. Free tours are offered at 1pm and 3pm, and tastings can be arranged without reservations for at least two people.

The Drive » Continue west on Liberty Rd/MD-26 for 6 miles, then turn left (southbound) onto MD-75/Green Valley Rd. After about 7 miles, take a right onto Old New Market Road to reach New Market's Main St.

6 New Market

Pretty New Market is the smallest and best preserved of the historical towns that lies between Baltimore and Frederick. **Main Street**, full of antique shops, is lined with Federal and Greek Revival houses. More than 90% of the structures are of brick or frame construction, as opposed to modern vinyl, sheet rock and/ or dry wall; the National Register of Historical places deems central New Market 'in appearance, the quintessence of the c[irca] 1800 small town in western central Maryland.'

The Drive » Frederick is about 7 miles west of New Market via I-70. Take exit 56 for MD-144 to reach the city center.

TRIP HIGHLIGHT

7 Frederick

Frederick boasts a historically preserved center, but unlike the previously listed small towns, this is a mid-sized city, an important commuter base for thousands of federal government employees and a biotechnology hub in its own right.

Central Frederick is, well, perfect. For a city of its size (around 65,000), what more could you want? A historic, pedestrian-friendly center of red-brick rowhouses with a large, diverse array of restaurants usually found in a larger town; an engaged, cultured arts community anchored by the excellent events calender at the **Weinberg Center for the Arts** (📞301-600-2828; www.weinbergcenter. org; 20 West Patrick St); and meandering Carroll Creek running through the center of

DETOUR: WASHINGTON DC

Start: ❶ Baltimore

A natural complement to your historical tour is the nation's capital, just 40 miles south of Baltimore on the BWI Parkway. The **National Mall**, part of which is covered in our Stretch Your Legs tour (p108) is the site of some of the nation's most iconic protests, from Martin Luther King's March on Washington to recent rallies for the legalization of gay marriage.

The east end of the Mall is filled with the (free!) museums of the **Smithsonian Institution**. All are worth your time. We could easily get lost amid the silk screens, Japanese prints and sculpture of the often-bypassed **Sackler & Freer Gallery** (1050 Independence Ave SW).

On the other side of the Mall is a cluster of memorials and monuments. The most famous is the back of the penny: the **Lincoln Memorial** (🕐24hr). The view over the reflecting pool to the Washington Monument is as spectacular as you've imagined. The **Roosevelt Memorial** (www.nps.gov/fdrm; W Basin Dr SW; 🕐24hr) is notable for its layout, which explores the entire term of America's longest-serving president.

On the north flank of the Lincoln Memorial (left if you're facing the pool) is the immensely powerful **Vietnam Veterans Memorial** (Constitution Gardens; 🕐24hr), a black granite 'V' cut into the soil inscribed with names of the American war dead of that conflict. Search for the nearby but rarely visited **Constitution Gardens** (🕐24hr), featuring a tranquil, landscaped pond and artificial island inscribed with the names of the signatories of the Constitution.

SOME MORE OF BALTIMORE'S BEST

Everyone knows DC is chock-a-block replete with museums, but the capital's scruffier, funkier neighbor to the northeast gives Washington a run for its money in the museum department.

Out by the Baltimore waterfront is a strange building, seemingly half enormous warehouse, half explosion of intense artsy angles, multicolored windmills and rainbow-reflecting murals, like someone had bent the illustrations of a Dr Seuss book through a funky mirror. This is quite possibly the coolest art museum in the country: the **American Visionary Art Museum** (☏410-244-1900; www.avam. org; 800 Key Hwy; adult/child $16/10; ⊙10am-6pm Tue-Sun). It's a showcase for self-taught (or 'outsider' art), which is to say, art made by people who aren't formally trained artists. It's a celebration of unbridled creativity utterly free of arts-scene pretension. Some of the work comes from asylums, others are created by self-inspired visionaries, but it's all rather captivating and well worth a long afternoon.

The Baltimore & Ohio railway was (arguably) the first passenger train in America, and the **B&O Railroad Museum** (☏410-752-2490; www.borail.org; 901 W Pratt St; adult/child $16/10; ⊙10am-4pm Mon-Sat, 11am-4pm Sun; ♿) is a loving testament to both that line and American railroading in general. Train spotters will be in heaven among more than 150 different locomotives. Train rides cost an extra $3; call for the schedule.

If you're traveling with a family, or if you just love science and science education, come by the **Maryland Science Center** (☏410-685-5225; www.mdsci.org; 601 Light St; adult/child $17/14, IMAX film only $8; ⊙10am-5pm Mon-Fri, 10am-6pm Sat, 11am-5pm Sun winter; 10am-6pm Sun-Thu, to 8pm Fri & Sat summer). This awesome center features a three-story atrium, tons of interactive exhibits on dinosaurs, outer space and the human body, and the requisite IMAX theater.

---

it all. Walking around downtown is immensely enjoyable.

Said creek is crossed by a lovely bit of community art: the mural on **Frederick Bridge**, at S Carroll St between E Patrick & E All Saints. The trompe l'oeil–style art essentially transforms a drab concrete span into an old, ivy-covered stone bridge from Tuscany.

✕ 🛏 p81

The Drive ≫ Head west on old National Pike (US 40A) and then, after about 6.5 miles, get on MD-17 southbound/ Burkittsville Rd. Turn right on Gapland Rd after 6 miles and follow it for 1.5 miles to Gathland.

- - - - - - - - - - - - -

❽ Gathland State Park

This tiny **park** (☏301-791-4767; ⊙8am-sunset) **FREE** is a fascinating tribute to a profession that doesn't lend itself to many memorials: war correspondents. Civil War correspondent and man of letters George Alfred Townsend fell in love with these mountains and built an impressive arch decorated with classical Greek mythological features and quotes that emphasize the necessary qualities of a good war correspondent.

Sleeping & Eating

Baltimore ❶

✖ Chaps   American
(☎410-483-2379; 5801 Pulaski Hwy; mains under $10; ⏱10:30am-10pm, to midnight Fri & Sat) This is the go-to stop for pit beef, Baltimore's take on barbeque – thinly sliced top round grilled over charcoal. Park and follow your nose to smoky mouth-watering goodness, and get that beef like a local: shaved onto a kaiser roll with a raw onion slice on top, smothered in tiger sauce (a creamy blend of horseradish and mayonnaise).

✖ Dukem   Ethiopian $$
(☎410-385-0318; 1100 Maryland Ave; mains $13-22; ⏱11am-10:30pm) Dukem is a standout among Baltimore's many Ethiopian places. Delicious mains, including spicy chicken, lamb and vegetarian dishes, all sopped up with spongy flatbread.

✖ PaperMoon Diner   Diner $$
(227 W 29th St; mains $7-16; ⏱7am-midnight Sun-Thu, to 2am Fri & Sat) Like a kaleidoscopic dream, this brightly colored, quintessential Baltimore diner is decorated with thousands of old toys, creepy mannequins and other quirky knickknacks. The real draw here is the anytime breakfast – fluffy French toast, crispy bacon and bagels with lox.

✖ Vaccaro's Pastry   Italian $
(222 Albemarle St; desserts $7; ⏱9am-10pm Sun-Thu, to midnight Fri & Sat) Vacarro's serves some of the best desserts and coffee in town. The cannoli are legendary, and the gelato and tiramisu are also quite good.

🛏 Peabody Court   Hotel $$
(☎410-727-7101; www.peabodycourthotel.com; 612 Cathedral St; r from $120; 🅿❄🛜) Smack dab in the middle of Mt Vernon, this upscale larger hotel with a boutique feel has large, handsomely appointed guest rooms with all-marble bathrooms and top-notch service. Often has great-rate deals online.

Sykesville ❸

✖ E.W. Beck's   Pub $
(☎410-795-1001; 7565 Main St; mains $9-15; ⏱11:30am-10pm, bar to 1am) In the middle of Sykesville's historic district, Beck's feels like a traditional pub, with wooden furnishings, soused regulars and serviceable pub grub.

Frederick ❼

✖ Brewer's Alley   Gastropub $$
(☎301-631-0089; 124 N Market St; burgers $9-13, mains $18-29; ⏱11:30am-11:30pm Mon & Tue, to midnight Wed & Thu, to 12:30am Fri & Sat, noon-11:30pm Sun; 🛜) This bouncy brewpub is one of our favorite places in Frederick, for several reasons. First, the beer: homemade, plenty of variety, delicious. Second, the burgers: enormous, half-pound monstrosities of staggeringly yummy proportions. Third, the rest of the menu: excellent Chesapeake seafood and Frederick county farm produce and meats. Finally: the beer. Again. The beer.

✖ Cacique   Latin $$
(☎301-695-2756; 26 N Market St; $11-29; ⏱11:30am-10pm Sun-Thu, to 1:30pm Fri & Sat) This interesting spot mixes up a menu of Spanish favorites such as paella and tapas with Latin American gut busters including enchiladas ceviche. That said, the focus and the expertise seem bent more towards the Iberian side of the menu; the shrimp sauteed in garlic and olive oil is wonderful.

🛏 Hollerstown Hill B&B   B&B $$
(☎301-228-3630; www.hollerstownhill.com; 4 Clarke Pl; r $135-145; 🅿❄🛜) The elegant, friendly Hollerstown has four pattern-heavy rooms, two resident terriers and an elegant billiards room. It's right in the middle of the historic downtown area of Frederick, so you're within easy walking distance of all the goodness.

Fredericksburg *Locals reenact Civil War battles*

Classic Trip

The Civil War Tour

5

Virginia and Maryland pack many of the seminal sites of America's bloodiest war into a space that includes some of the Eastern seaboard's most attractive countryside.

TRIP HIGHLIGHTS

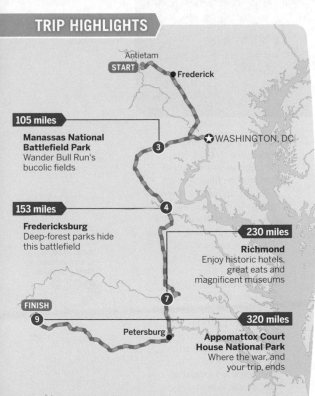

Antietam
START
● Frederick

105 miles
Manassas National Battlefield Park
Wander Bull Run's bucolic fields
3

 WASHINGTON, DC

153 miles
Fredericksburg
Deep-forest parks hide this battlefield
4

230 miles
Richmond
Enjoy historic hotels, great eats and magnificent museums

7

FINISH
9
Petersburg

320 miles
Appomattox Court House National Park
Where the war, and your trip, ends

---

3 DAYS
320 MILES / 515KM

GREAT FOR...

BEST TIME TO GO
September to November for sunny skies and autumnal color shows at preserved battlefields.

 ESSENTIAL PHOTO
The fences and fields of Antietam at sunset.

 BEST FOR FOODIES
Lamb burgers at Richmond's Burger Bach.

Classic Trip

5 The Civil War Tour

The Civil War was fought from 1861–1865 in the nation's backyards, and many of those backyards are between Washington, DC and Richmond. On this trip you will cross battlefields where over 100,000 Americans perished and are buried, foe next to foe. Amid rolling farmlands, sunny hills and deep forests, you'll discover a jarring juxtaposition of bloody legacy and bucolic scenery, and along the way, the places where America forged its identity.

❶ Antietam

While most of this trip takes place in Virginia, there is Civil War ground to be covered in neighboring Maryland, a border state officially allied with the Union yet close enough to the South to have Southern sympathies. Confederate General Robert E Lee, hoping to capitalize on a friendly populace, tried to invade Maryland early in the conflict. The subsequent Battle of Antietam, fought in Sharpsburg, MD, on September 17, 1862, has the dubious distinction of marking the bloodiest day in American history. The battle site is preserved at **Antietam National Battlefield** (☏301-432-5124; www.nps.gov/anti; 5831 Dunker Church Rd, Sharpsburg; ⏱8:30am-around 6pm) in the corn-and-hill country of north-central Maryland.

As befits an engagement that claimed 22,000 casualties in the course of a single, nightmarish day, even the local geographic nomenclature has become violent. An

area known as the Sunken Road turned into 'Bloody Lane' after bodies were stacked there. In the park's cemetery, many of the Union gravestones bear the names of Irish and German immigrants who died in a country they had only recently adopted.

The Drive » Take MD-65 south out of Antietam to the town of Sharpsburg. From here, take MD-34 east for 6 miles, then turn right onto US 40A (eastbound). Take US 40A for 11 miles, then merge onto US 70 south, followed 3 miles later by US 270 (bypassing Frederick). Take US 270 south to the Beltway (I-495); access exit 45B to get to I-66 east, which will eventually lead you to the National Mall, where the next stops are located.

② Washington, DC

Washington, DC, was the capital of the Union during the Civil War, just as it is the capital of the

LINK YOUR TRIP

4 Maryland's National Historic Road

For another look into the past, go east from Antietam to the picturesque and historic Frederick.

6 Skyline Drive

Travel west from Fredericksburg through Culpeper to this trip along one of the nation's most scenic roadways.

Classic Trip

country today. While the city was never invaded by the Confederacy, thousands of Union soldiers passed through, trained and drilled inside of the city; indeed, the official name of the North's main fighting force was the Army of the Potomac.

The **National Museum of American History** (www.americanhistory.si.edu; cnr 14th St & Constitution Ave NW; ⊙10am-5:30pm, to 7:30pm Jun-Aug; 🖼), located directly on the National Mall, has good permanent exhibitions on the Civil War. Perhaps more importantly, it provides visitors with the context for understanding why the war happened.

Following the war, a grateful nation erected many monuments to Union generals. A statue worth visiting is the **African American Civil War Memorial** (www.afroamcivilwar.

org; cnr U St & Vermont Ave NW; underground rail U St-Cardozo), next to the eastern exit of the U St metro stop, inscribed with the names of soldiers of color who served in the Union army.

The Drive » From Washington, DC, it takes about an hour driving along I-66W to reach Manassas.

TRIP HIGHLIGHT

❸ Manassas National Battlefield Park (Bull Run)

The site of the first major pitched battle of the Civil War is mere minutes from the strip malls of Northern Virginia. NPS-run **Manassas National Battlefield Park** (📞703-361-1339; www.nps.gov/mana; 12521 Lee Hwy; adult/child $3/free, film $3; ⊙8:30am-5pm, tours 11:15am, 12:15pm, 2:15pm Jun-Aug) occupies the site where, in 1861, 35,000 Union soldiers and 32,500 Confederates saw the view you have today: a stretch of gorgeous countryside that has miraculously survived the predations

of the Army of Northern Virginia real-estate developers.

This is as close as many will come to 19th-century rural America; distant hills, dark, brooding tree lines, low curving fields and the soft hump of overgrown trench works.

Following the battle, both sides realized a long war was at hand. Europe watched nervously; in a matter of weeks, the largest army in the world was the Union Army of the Potomac. The second biggest was the Confederate States of America Army. A year later, at the Battle of Shiloh, 24,000 men were listed as casualties – more than all the accumulated casualties of every previous American war combined.

🍴 p92

The Drive » In Manassas, take US 29N for 13 miles and then turn left onto US 17S (Marsh Rd). Follow it south for about 35 miles to get to downtown Fredericksburg.

TRIP HIGHLIGHT

❹ Fredericksburg

If battlefields preserve rural America, Fredericks-burg is an example of what the nation's main streets once looked like: orderly grids, touches of green and friendly storefronts. But for all its cuteness, this is the site of one of the worst blunders in American military

---

WHAT'S IN A NAME, PART 1?

Although the Civil War is the widely accepted label for the conflict covered in this trip, you'll still hear die-hard Southern boosters refer to the period as the 'War Between the States.' What's the difference? Well, a Civil War implies an armed insurrection against a ruling power that never lost its privilege to govern, whereas the name 'War Between the States' suggests said states always had (and still have) a right to secession from the Republic.

DETOUR:
GETTYSBURG NATIONAL MILITARY PARK

Start: ❶ Antietam

The Battle of Gettysburg, fought in Gettysburg, PA, in July of 1863, marked the turning point of the war and the high-water mark of the Confederacy's attempted rebellion. Lee never made a gambit as bold as this invasion of the North, and his army (arguably) never recovered from the defeat it suffered here.

Gettysburg National Military Park (☎717-334-1124; www.nps.gov/gett; incl museum & visitor center, adult/child/senior $12.50/8.50/11.50; ⊗park 6am-10pm Apr-Oct, to 7pm Nov-Mar, museum 8am-6pm Apr-Oct, to 5pm Nov-Mar) does an excellent job of explaining the course and context of the combat. Look for Little Round Top Hill, where a Union unit checked a Southern flanking maneuver, and the field of Pickett's Charge, where the Confederacy suffered its most crushing defeat up to that point. Following the battle Abraham Lincoln gave his Gettysburg Address here to mark the victory and the 'new birth of the nation' on said country's birthday: July 4.

You can easily lose a day here just soaking up the scenery – a gorgeous swath of rolling hills and lush forest interspersed with hollows, rock formations and farmland. To get here, jump on US 15 northbound in Frederick, MD during the drive between Antietam and Washington, DC. Follow 15 north for 35 miles to Gettysburg.

history. In 1862, when the Northern Army attempted a massed charge against an entrenched Confederate position, a Southern artilleryman looked at the bare slope that Union forces had to cross and told a commanding officer, 'A chicken could not live on that field when we open on it.' Sixteen charges resulted in an estimated 6000 to 8000 Union casualties.

Fredericksburg & Spotsylvania National Military Park (adult/child $32/10) is not as immediately compelling as Manassas because of the thick forest that still covers the battlefields, but the woods themselves are a sylvan wonder. Again, the pretty nature

of...well, nature, grows over graves; the nearby Battle of the Wilderness was named for these thick woods, which caught fire and killed hundreds of wounded soldiers after the shooting was finished.

✗ ⊨ p92

The Drive » From Fredericksburg, take US 17 south for 5 miles, after which 17 becomes VA-2 (also known as Sandy Lane Dr and Fredericksburg Turnpike). Follow this road for 5 more miles, then turn right onto Stonewall Jackson Rd (State Rd 606).

- - - - - - - - - -

❺ Stonewall Jackson Shrine

In Chancellorsville, Robert E Lee, outnumbered two to

one, split his forces and attacked both flanks of the Union army. The audacity of the move caused the Northern force to crumble and flee across the Potomac River, but the victory was costly; in the course of the fighting, Lee's ablest general, Stonewall Jackson, had his arm shot off by a nervous Confederate sentry (the arm is buried near the Fredericksburg National Park visitor center; ask a ranger for directions there).

The wound was patched, but Jackson went on to contract a fatal dose of pneumonia. He was taken to what is now the next stop on this tour: the **Stonewall Jackson Shrine** (☎804-633-6076;

Classic Trip

WHY THIS IS A CLASSIC TRIP
ADAM KARLIN, AUTHOR

Want to see some of the finest countryside left in the Eastern seaboard, while simultaneously exploring the contradictions, struggles and triumphs at the root of the American experiment? Yeah, we thought so. The Civil War Tour allows travelers to access the formative spaces of the nation, all set against a backdrop of lush fields, dark forests, dirt-rutted country lanes and the immense weight of history.

Top: Visitors at Manassas National Battlefield Park
Left: Walking a trail at Manassas
Right: American Civil War Center, Richmond

12019 Stonewall Jackson Rd, Woodford; 9am-5pm) in nearby Guinea Station. In a small white cabin set against attractive Virginia horse-country, overrun with sprays of purple flowers and daisy fields, Jackson uttered a series of prolonged ramblings. Then he fell silent, whispered, 'Let us cross over the river and rest in the shade of the trees,' and died.

The Drive » You can get here via I-95, which you take to I-295S (then take exit 34A), which takes 50 minutes. Or, for a back road experience (one hour, 10 minutes), take VA-2S south for 35 miles until it connects to VA-643/Rural Point Rd. Stay on VA-643 until it becomes VA-156/ Cold Harbor Rd, which leads to the battlefield.

- - - - - - - - - -

6 Cold Harbor Battlefield

By 1864, Union General Ulysses Grant was ready to take the battle into Virginia. His subsequent invasion, dubbed the Overland (or Wilderness) Campaign, was one of the bloodiest of the war. It reached a violent climax at Cold Harbor, just north of Richmond.

At the site now known as **Cold Harbor Battlefield** (804-226-1981; www.nps. gov/rich; 5515 Anderson-Wright Dr, Mechanicsville, VA; sunrise-sunset, visitor center 9am-4:30pm), Grant threw his men into a full frontal assault; the resultant casualties

Classic Trip

were horrendous, and a precursor to WWI trench warfare.

The area has reverted to a forest and field checkerboard overseen by the National Park Service. Ask a ranger to direct you to the third turnout, a series of Union earthworks from where you can look out at the most preserved section of the battlefield: the long, low field northern soldiers charged across. This landscape has essentially not changed in over 150 years.

The Drive » From Cold Harbor, head north on VA-156/ Cold Harbor Rd for about 3 miles until it intersects Creighton Rd. Turn left on Creighton and follow it for 6 miles into Richmond.

TRIP HIGHLIGHT

❼ Richmond

There are two Civil War museums in the former capital of the Confederacy, and they make for an interesting study in contrasts. The **Museum of the Confederacy** (MOC; ☎804-649-1861; www.moc. org; 1201 E Clay St; admission $8; ⏰10am-5pm Mon-Sat, from noon Sun) was once a shrine to the Southern 'Lost Cause,' and still attracts a fair degree of neo-Confederate types. But the MOC has also graduated into a respected educational institution, and its collection of Confederate artifacts is probably the best in the country. The optional tour of the Confederate White House is recommended for its quirky insights (did you know the second-most powerful man in the Confederacy may have been a gay Jew?).

On the other hand, the **American Civil War Center** (☎804-780-1865; www.tredegar.org; 490 Tredegar St; adult/student/ child 7-12 $8/6/2; ⏰9am-5pm; 🖕), located in the old Tredegar ironworks (the main armament producer for the Confederacy), presents the war from three perspectives: Northern, Southern and African American. Exhibits are well presented and insightful. The effect is clearly powerful and occasionally divisive, a testament to the conflict's lasting impact.

✕ 🛏 p92

The Drive » Take Rte 95 southbound for about 23 miles and get on exit 52. Get onto 301 (Wythe St) and follow until it becomes Washington St, and eventually VA-35/Oaklawn Dr. Look for signs to the battlefield park from here.

❽ Petersburg

Petersburg, just south of Richmond, is the blue-collar sibling city to the Virginia capital, its center gutted by white flight following desegregation. **Petersburg National Battlefield Park** (US 36; vehicle/pedestrian $5/3; ⏰9am-5pm) marks the spot where Northern and Southern soldiers spent almost a quarter of the war in a protracted, trench-induced stand-off. The Battle of the Crater, made well-known in Charles Frazier's *Cold Mountain*, was an attempt by Union soldiers to break this stalemate by tunneling under the Confederate lines and blowing up their fortifications; the end result was Union soldiers caught in the hole wrought by their own sabotage, killed like fish in a barrel.

WHAT'S IN A NAME, PART 2?

One of the more annoying naming conventions of the war goes thus: while the North preferred to name battles for defining geographic terms (Bull Run, Antietam), Southern officers named them for nearby towns (Manassas, Sharpsburg). Although most Americans refer to battles by their Northern names, in some areas folks simply know Manassas as the Battle Of, not as the strip mall with a good Waffle House.

LOCAL KNOWLEDGE: CIVIL WAR BATTLEFIELDS

What is the appeal of Civil War battlefields?
Civil War battlefields are the touchstone of the not-too-distant past. They are the physical manifestation of the great eruptive moments in American history that defined America for the last 150 years. Large events on a large landscape compel us to think in big terms about big issues.

The Civil War battlefields appeal to visitors because they allow us to walk in the virtual footsteps of great men and women who lived and died fighting for their convictions. Their actions transformed nondescript places into hallmarks of history. The Civil War converted sleepy towns and villages into national shrines based on a moment of intense belief and action. The battlefields literally focus our understanding of the American character.

I linger longest on the battlefields that are best preserved, like Antietam and Gettysburg, because they paint the best context for revealing why things happen the way they do, where they do. Walking where they walked, and seeing the ground they saw, makes these battlefields the ultimate outdoor classrooms in the world!

Why is Virginia such a hot bed for Civil War tourism?
Virginia paid a terrible price during the Civil War. Hosting the capital of the Confederacy only 100 miles from the capital of the United States made sure that the ground between and around the two opposing capitals would be a relentless nightmare of fighting and bloodshed. People can visit individual, isolated battlefields all across America – but people come to Virginia to visit several, many, if not all of them. Unlike anywhere else, Virginia offers a Civil War immersion. It gives visitors a sense of how pervasive the Civil War was – it touched every place and everyone. Around the country, people may seek out the Civil War; but in Virginia, it finds you.

Frank O'Reilly, Historian and Interpretive Ranger with the National Park Service

The Drive » Drive south of Petersburg, then west through back roads to follow Lee's last retreat. There's an excellent map available at www.civilwartraveler.com; we prefer taking VA-460 west from Petersburg, then connecting to VA-635, which leads to Appomattox via VA-24, near Farmville.

TRIP HIGHLIGHT

❾ Appomattox Court House National Park

About 92 miles west of Petersburg is **Appomattox Court House National Park** (📞434-352-8987; www.nps.gov/apco; admission $4, Sep-May $3; ⊘8:30am-5pm), where the Confederacy finally surrendered. The park itself is wide and lovely, and the ranger staff are extremely helpful.

There are several marker stones dedicated to the surrendering Confederates; the most touching one marks the spot where Robert E Lee rode back from Appomattox after surrendering to Union General Ulysses Grant. Lee's soldiers stood on either side of the field waiting for the return of their commander. When Lee rode into sight he doffed his hat; the troops surged toward him, some saying goodbye while others, too overcome to speak, passed their hands over the flanks of Lee's horse. The spot's dedicated to defeat, humility and reconciliation, and the imperfect realization of all those qualities is the character of the America you've been driving through.

🛏 p93

Classic Trip

Eating & Sleeping

Manassas ③

✕ Tandoori Village　　Indian $$

(☎703-369-6526; 7607 Centreville Rd; mains $8-19; ⊙11am-2:30pm & 5-10pm, Mon-Fri, 11am-10pm Sat & Sun) Tandoori Village serves up solid Punjabi cuisine, offering a welcome dash of spice and flavor complexity to an area that's pretty rife with fast-food chains. No menu shockers here, but all the standards, including butter chicken, dal, paneer and the rest, are executed with competence.

Fredericksburg ④

✕ Bistro Bethem　　American $$$

(☎540-371-9999; 309 William St; mains $15-34; ⊙11:30am-2:30pm & 5-10pm Tues-Sat, to 9pm Sun) The New American menu, seasonal ingredients and down-to-earth but dedicated foodie vibe here all equal gastronomic bliss. On any given day duck confit and quinoa may share the table with a roasted beet salad and local clams.

✕ Foode　　American $$

(☎540-479-1370; 1006 C Caroline Street; mains $13-24; ⊙11am-3pm & 4:30pm-8pm Tue-Thu, to 9pm Fri, 10am-2:30pm & 4:30-9pm Sat, 10am-2pm Sun; ✈) Foode takes all the feel-good restaurant trends of the late noughties/early teens – fresh, local, free range, organic, casual-artsy-rustic-chic decor over white tablecloths and dark lighting – and runs with the above all the way to pretty delicious results.

✕ Sammy T's　　American $

(☎540-371-2008; 801 Caroline St; mains $6-14; ⊙11:30am-9:30pm; ☎✈) Sammy T's wins points off the bat for its attractive location: a cute brick building constructed circa 1805 in

the heart of historic Fredericksburg. The food isn't bad either, mainly consisting of soup and sandwich, pub-like fare, with an admirable mix of vegetarian options such as a local take on lasagna and black-bean quesadillas. There's a good beer selection, too.

🛏 Richard Johnston Inn　　B&B $$

(☎540-899-7606; www.therichardjohnstoninn. com; 711 Caroline St; r $125-200; P ❄ ☎) Another B&B that's pretty much as cute, friendly and historically evocative as surrounding Fredericksburg itself. There are nine rooms to pick from; the Old Town features red-brick walls and exposed beams, while the Canopy is lacy and filigreed from the floor to the ceiling.

🛏 Schooler House　　B&B $$

(☎540-374-5258; www.theschoolerhouse.com; 1301 Caroline St; r $160-175; P ❄) Two lacy bedrooms in a watermelon-colored house with a gorgeous patio and backyard set the scene in this excellent Victorian B&B. Owners Andi and Paul are warm and welcoming, and Andi cooks a mean breakfast to boot. Service is personalized – you feel like these folks really care about your holiday.

Richmond ⑦

✕ Burger Bach　　Gastropub $

(☎804-359-1305; 10 S Thompson St; mains $7-12; ⊙11am-10pm Sun-Thu, to 11pm Fri & Sat; ✈ 👶) We give Burger Bach credit for being the only restaurant found in the area that self-classifies as a New Zealand–inspired burger joint. And that said, why yes, they do serve excellent lamb burgers here, although the locally sourced beef (and vegetarian) options are awesome as well. You should really go crazy with the 14 different sauces available for the thick-cut fries.

Croaker's Spot
Seafood $$

(📞804-269-0464; 1020 Hull St; mains $8-17; ⏰11am-9pm Mon, Tue & Thu, to midnight Wed, to 11pm Fri, noon-11pm Sat, noon-9pm Sun; P) Croaker's is an institution in these parts, a backbone of the African American dining scene. Richmond's most famous rendition of refined soul food is comforting, delicious and sits in your stomach like a brick. Beware the intimidating Fish Boat: fried catfish, cornbread and mac 'n' cheese.

Edo's Squid
Italian $$$

(📞804-864-5488; 411 N Harrison St; mains $12-30) One of the best Italian restaurants in Richmond, Edo's serves up mouth-watering, authentic cuisine such as eggplant parmesan, spicy shrimp diavolo pasta, daily specials and, of course, squid.

Julep's
Modern American $$$

(📞804-377-3968; 1719 E Franklin St; mains $18-32; ⏰5:30-10pm Mon-Sat; P) This is where classy, old-school Southern aristocrats like to meet and eat, drawn by the fresh experimentation of an innovative kitchen. We're a fan of the wild boar and lamb stew, but vegetarian options abound, and the salad menu is particularly noteworthy and creative.

Jefferson Hotel
Luxury Hotel $$$

(📞804-788-8000; www.jeffersonhotel.com; 101 W Franklin St; r from $250; P ✳ 🛜 ⛴) There's an almost imperial sense of tradition at this most famed of Richmond hotels, which comes off as a modern execution of the moonlight-and-magnolia cliché. With that said, the effect isn't put upon: service is warm without becoming obtrusive. The grand appearance of the place could put you in mind of a fairy-tale castle.

Linden Row Inn
Boutique Hotel $$

(📞804-783-7000; www.lindenrowinn.com; 100 E Franklin St; r incl breakfast $120-170, ste $250; P ✳ @ 🛜) This antebellum gem has attractive rooms (with period Victorian furnishings) spread among neighboring Greek Revival townhouses in an excellent downtown location. Friendly southern hospitality and thoughtful extras (free passes to the YMCA, free around-town shuttle service) sweeten the deal.

Massad House Hotel
Motel $

(📞804-648-2893; www.massadhousehotel.com; 11 N 4th St; r $75-110) Massad's great by any standard, but excellent rates and a supreme location near the heart of Richmond's best attractions give it a special place in our hearts. The design will put you in mind of a cozy study in Tudor-style budget bliss.

Appomattox Court House National Park ❾

Longacre
B&B $$

(📞800-758-7730; www.longacreva.com; 1670 Church St; r from $105, ste $275; P ✳) Longacre looks like it got lost somewhere in the English countryside and decided to set up shop in Virginia. Seriously, there might be rooms here where children disappear into magical kingdoms after slipping through wardrobes. There are lovely grounds replete with a shady magnolia tree, plus six elegantly furnished rooms scattered throughout the impressive building.

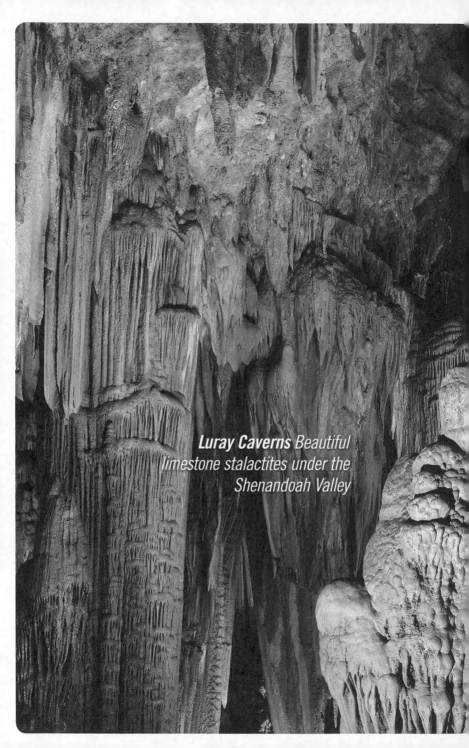

Luray Caverns *Beautiful limestone stalactites under the Shenandoah Valley*

Skyline Drive

6

Skyline Drive is one of America's classic road trips. Befittingly, it comes studded like a leather belt with natural wonders and stunning scenery.

TRIP HIGHLIGHTS

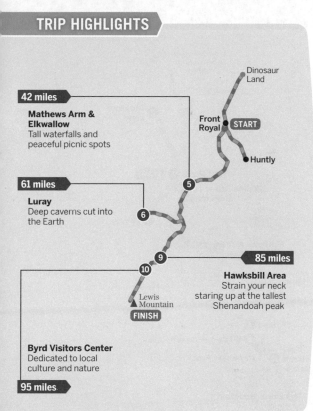

42 miles

Mathews Arm & Elkwallow
Tall waterfalls and peaceful picnic spots

61 miles

Luray
Deep caverns cut into the Earth

Dinosaur Land

Front Royal **START**

Huntly

5

6

9

10

Lewis Mountain
FINISH

85 miles

Hawksbill Area
Strain your neck staring up at the tallest Shenandoah peak

Byrd Visitors Center
Dedicated to local culture and nature

95 miles

3 DAYS
150 MILES / 240KM

GREAT FOR...

BEST TIME TO GO
May to November for great weather, open facilities and top views.

 ESSENTIAL PHOTO

The fabulous 360-degree horizon at the top of Bearfence Rock Scramble.

 BEST FOR CULTURE

Byrd Visitors Center offers an illuminating peek into Appalachian folkways.

6 Skyline Drive

The centerpiece of the ribbon-thin Shenandoah National Park is the jaw-dropping beauty of Skyline Drive, which runs for just over 100 miles atop the Blue Ridge Mountains. Unlike the massive acreage of western parks like Yellowstone or Yosemite, Shenandoah is at times only a mile wide. That may seem to narrow the park's scope, yet it makes it a perfect space for traversing and road-tripping goodness.

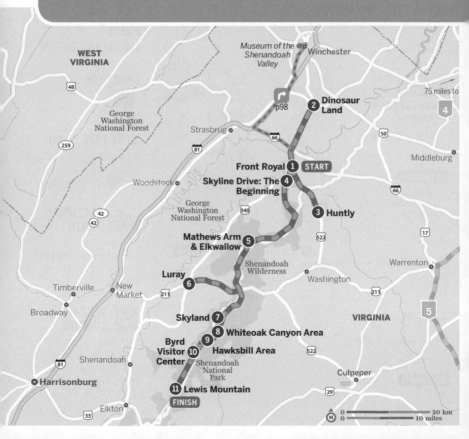

❶ Front Royal

Straddling the northern entrance to the park is the tiny city of Front Royal. Although it's not among Virginia's fanciest ports-of-call, this lush riverside town offers all the urban amenities one might need before a camping or hiking trip up in the mountains.

If you need to gather your bearings, an obvious place to start is the **Front Royal Visitor Center** (☎800-338-2576; 414 E Main St; ⏰9am-5pm). Friendly staff are on hand to overwhelm you with information about what to do in the area.

For a summer night under the stars

LINK YOUR TRIP

4 Maryland's National Historic Road

US-340 takes you north from Front Royal to historic Frederick, the gateway to a region of quintessential stately small towns.

5 The Civil War Tour

From the Luray Caverns head southeast past the town of Culpeper to Fredericksburg to begin traversing the battlefields where the nation's identity was forged.

TOP TIP: MILEPOSTS

Handy stone mileposts (MP or Mile) are still the best means of figuring out just where you are on Skyline Drive. They begin at MP 0 near Front Royal, and end at MP 105 at the park's southern entrance near Rockfish Gap.

with endangered species, check out the Smithsonian Conservation Biology Institute (p102).

🍴 🛏 p104

The Drive ❯❯ Dinosaur Land is 10 miles north of Front Royal, towards Winchester, via US 340 (Stonewall Jackson Highway).

❷ Dinosaur Land

Before you head into the national park and its stunning natural beauty, visit **Dinosaur Land** (☎540-869-2222; www.dinosaurland.com; 3848 Stonewall Jackson Hwy, White Post; adult/child $6/5; ⏰9:30am-5:30pm Mar-May, to 6:30pm in summer, to 5pm Sep-Dec; ♿) for some fantastic man-made tackiness. This spectacularly low-brow shrine-to-concrete sculpture is not to be missed. Although it's an 'educational prehistoric forest,' with more than 50 life-size dinosaurs (and a King Kong for good measure), you'd probably learn more about the tenants by fast-forwarding through *Jurassic Park 3*. But that's not why you've

stopped here, so grab your camera and sidle up to the triceratops for memories that will last a millennium.

The Drive ❯❯ Head back to Front Royal, then go south on US 522 (Remount Rd) for about 9 miles to reach Huntly.

❸ Huntly

Huntly is a smallish town nestled in the green foothills of the Shenandoahs, lying just in the southern shadows of Front Royal. It's a good spot to refuel on some cosmopolitan culture and foodie deliciousness in the form of **Rappahannock Cellars** (☎540-635-9398; www.rappahannockcellars.com; 14437 Hume Road; tasting $8; ⏰11:30am-5pm, to 6pm Sat), one of the nicer wineries of north-central Virginia. Frankly, you get a lot of wine for your buck here, although the real draw is the vineyard-covered hills shadowing the horizon, like some slice of Northern Italian pastoral prettiness that got lost somewhere in the upcountry of the Old Dominion. Give the port a whirl (well, maybe not if you're driving).

The Drive » Head back to Front Royal, as you'll enter Skyline Drive from there. From the beginning of Skyline Drive, it's 5.5 miles to Dickey Ridge.

- - - - - - - - - - - - -

❹ Skyline Drive: The Beginning

Skyline Drive (📞540-999-3500; www.nps.gov/shen; north entrance at Front Royal; car $10; ♿) is the scenic drive to end all scenic drives. The 75 overlooks, with views into the Shenandoah Valley and the Piedmont, are all breathtaking. In spring and summer, endless variations on the color green are sure to enchant, just as the vibrant reds and yellows will amaze you in autumn. This might be your chance to finally hike a section of the Appalachian Trail, which crosses Skyline Drive at 32 places.

The logical first stop on an exploration of Skyline and Shenandoah National Park is the **Dickey Ridge Visitors Center** (📞540-635-3566; Skyline Dr, Mile 4.6; ⏱9am-5pm Apr-Nov). It's not just an informative leaping-off point; it's a building with a fascinating history all of its own. This spot originally operated as a 'wild' dining hall in 1908 (back then, that simply meant it had a terrace for dancing). However, it closed during WWII and didn't reopen until 1958, when it became a visitor center. Now it's one of the park's two main information centers and contains a little bit of everything you'll need to get started on your trip along Skyline Drive.

The Drive » It's a twisty 19 more miles along Skyline Drive to Mathews Arm.

- - - - - - - - - - - - -

TRIP HIGHLIGHT

❺ Mathews Arm & Elkwallow

Mathews Arm is the first major section of Shenandoah National Park you encounter after leaving Dickey's Ridge. Before you get there, you can stop at a pullover at MP 19.4 and embark on a 4.8-mile loop hike to **Little Devils Stairs**. Getting through this narrow gorge is as tough as the name suggests; expect hand-over-hand climbing for some portions.

At Mathews Arm there's a campground as well as an amphitheater, and some nice breezes; early on in your drive, you're already at a 2750ft altitude.

From the amphitheater, it's a 6.5-mile moderately taxing hike to lovely **Overall Run Falls**, the tallest in the national park (93ft). There's plenty of rock

DETOUR: MUSEUM OF THE SHENANDOAH VALLEY

Start: ❶ Front Royal

Of all the places where you can begin your journey into Shenandoah National Park, none seem to make quite as much sense as the **Museum of the Shenandoah Valley** (📞540-662-1473, 888-556-5799; www.shenandoahmuseum.org; 901 Amherst St; adult/student $10/8; ⏱10am-4pm Tue-Sun), an institution dedicated to its namesake. Located in the town of Winchester, some 25 miles north of Front Royal, the museum is an exhaustive repository of information on the valley, Appalachian culture and its associated folkways, some of the most unique in the USA. Exhibits are divided into four galleries, accompanied by the restored Glen Burnie historical home (closed until 2014) and 6 acres of gardens.

To get there, take I-66 west from Front Royal to I-81 and head north for 25 miles. In Winchester, follow signs to the museum, which is on the outskirts of town.

Shenandoah Valley Colorful Virginian town in the valley

ledges where you can enjoy the view and snap a picture, but be warned that the falls sometimes dry out in the summer.

Elkwallow Wayside, which includes a nice picnic area and lookout, is at MP 24, just past Mathews Arm.

The Drive » From Mathews Arm, proceed south along Skyline for about 10 miles, then take the US 211 ramp westbound for about 7 miles to reach Luray.

TRIP HIGHLIGHT

❻ Luray

Luray is a good spot to grab some grub and potentially rest your head if you're not into camping. It's also where you'll find the wonderful **Luray Caverns** (☎540-743-6551; www.luraycaverns.com;

Rte 211; adult/child $21/10; ⏰9am-7pm Jun-Aug, to 6pm Sep-Nov, Apr & May, to 4pm Mon-Fri Dec-Mar), one of the most extensive cavern systems on the East Coast.

Here you can take a one-hour, roughly 1-mile guided tour of these caves, opened to the public more than 100 years ago. The rock formations throughout are quite stunning, and Luray boasts what is surely a one-of-a-kind attraction – the Stalacpipe Organ – in the pit of its belly. This crazy contraption has been banging out melodies on the rock formations for decades. As the guide says, the caves are 400 million years old '*if* you believe in geological

dating' (if the subtext is lost on you, understand this is a conservative part of the country where creationism is widely accepted, if hotly debated). No matter what you believe in, you'll be impressed by the fantastic underground expanses.

✕ 🛏 p105

The Drive » Take US 211 east for 10 miles to get back on Skyline Drive. Then proceed 10 miles south along Skyline to get to Skyland. Along the way you'll drive over the highest point of Skyline Drive (3680ft). At MP 40.5, just before reaching Skyland, you can enjoy amazing views from the parking overlook at Thorofare Mountain (3595ft).

SKYLINE DRIVE
ADAM KARLIN, AUTHOR

Skyline Drive is one of America's original scenic drives. The Shenandoah Valley is a mind-bendingly beautiful combination of two seemingly at odds ecosystems: the rough, forested mountains of the Appalachians on one hand, and the manicured hills of the Virginia Piedmont on the other. We've included plenty of grand hikes and great food to accompany you on your way among the clouds.

Top: Bearfence Mountain
Left: Black bear cub
Right: Dinosaur Land, White Post

FRANCK FOTOS/ALAMY ©

7 Skyland

Horse-fanciers will want to book a trail ride through Shenandoah at **Skyland Stables** (📞540-999-2210; guided group rides 1/2½hr $30/50; ⏰9am-5pm May-Oct). Rides last up to two-and-a-half hours and are a great way to see the wildlife and epic vistas. Pony rides are also available for the wee members of your party. This is a good spot to break up your trip if you're into hiking (and if you're on this trip, we're assuming you are).

You've got great access to local trailheads around here, and the sunsets are fabulous. The accommodations are a little rustic, but in a charming way (the Trout Cabin was built in 1911, and it feels like it, but we mean this in the most complimentary way possible.) The place positively oozes nostalgia, but if you're into amenities, you may find it a little dilapidated.

The Drive » It's only 1.5 miles south on Skyline Drive to get to the Whiteoak parking area.

8 Whiteoak Canyon Area

At MP 42.6, Whiteoak Canyon is another area of Skyline Drive that offers unmatched hiking and exploration opportunities. There are several parking areas that all provide different entry points to the various trails that snake through this ridge- and stream-scape.

Most hikers are attracted to Whiteoak Canyon for its **waterfalls** – there are six in total, with the tallest topping out at 86ft high. At the Whiteoak parking area, you can make the 4.6-mile round-trip hike to these cascades, but beware – it's both a steep climb up and back to your car. To reach the next set of waterfalls, you'll have to add 2.7 miles to the round trip and prepare yourself for a steep (1100ft) elevation shift.

The **Limberlost Trail** and parking area is just south of Whiteoak Canyon. This is a moderately difficult 1.3-mile trek into spruce upcountry thick with hawks, owls and other birds; the boggy ground is home to many salamanders.

The Drive » It's about 3 miles south of Whiteoak Canyon to the Hawksbill area via Skyline Drive.

TRIP HIGHLIGHT

❾ Hawksbill Area

Once you reach MP 45.6, you've reached **Hawksbill**, the name of both this part of Skyline Drive and the tallest peak in Shenandoah National Park. Numerous trails in this area skirt the summits of the mountain.

Pull into the parking area at Hawksbill Gap (MP 45.6). You've got a few hiking options to choose from. The **Lower**

LOCAL KNOWLEDGE: SMITHSONIAN CONSERVATION BIOLOGY INSTITUTE

If you're into wildlife, one of the coolest adventures you can embark upon on the Eastern seaboard is a Conservation Campout with the **Smithsonian Conservation Biology Institute** (SCBI; 202-633-2614, 540-635-6500; http://nationalzoo.si.edu/activitiesandevents/activities/conservationcampout; 1500 Remount Rd, Front Royal; $125; Jun-Aug;) The Smithsonian Institution is a collection of museum and research centers dedicated to 'the increase and diffusion of knowledge'; the SCBI is the umbrella organization for the Smithsonian's conservation work and research.

Based in Front Royal, the SCBI is generally closed to the public. But during the summer months, via the Friends of the National Zoo (FONZ), SCBI hosts overnight trips during the weekends that put you face to face with its conservation efforts. You'll be allowed (under the supervision of SCBI staff) to explore an animal habitat area; some of the species based at the center include maned wolves, cheetahs, black-footed ferrets and clouded leopards. Following this, you'll camp under the stars in four-person tents and have a continental breakfast the next day, along with family-oriented activities throughout your stay.

This activity is aimed at families (a maximum of six people can register per campout), but some campouts are adults only. In addition, children must be aged six or older, and anyone under 18 must be accompanied by a paying adult. With all that said, the experience comes highly recommended; you're having a wildlife encounter with trained, very knowledgeable professionals. Registration for campouts begins in spring (check website for details); register fast, as this is a popular event.

Adam Karlin

Hawksbill Trail is a steep 1.7-mile round trip that circles Hawksbill Mountain's lower slopes; that huff-inducing ascent yields a pretty great view over the park. Another great lookout lies at the end of the **Upper Hawksbill Trail**, a moderately difficult 2.1-mile trip. You can link up with the Appalachian Trail here via a spur called the Salamander Trail.

If you continue south for about 5 miles you'll reach **Fishers Gap Overlook**. The attraction here is the **Rose River Loop**, a 4-mile, moderately strenuous trail that is positively Edenic. Along the way you'll pass by waterfalls, under thick forest canopy and over swift-running streams.

The Drive » From Fishers Gap, head about a mile south to the Byrd Visitors Center, technically located at MP 51.

- - - - - - - - - - -

TRIP HIGHLIGHT

⑩ Byrd Visitors Center

The **Byrd Visitors Center** (☎540-999-3283; Skyline Dr, MP 50; ⊙9am-5pm Apr-Nov) is the central visitor center of Shenandoah National Park, marking (roughly) a halfway point between the two ends of Skyline Drive. It's devoted to explaining the settlement and development of the

Shenandoah Valley via a series of small but well-curated exhibitions; as such, it's a good place to stop and learn about the surrounding culture (and pick up backcountry camping permits).

There's camping and ranger activities in the **Big Meadows** area, located across the road from the visitor center.

The **Story of the Forest** trail is an easy, paved, 1.8-mile loop that's quite pretty; the trailhead connects to the visitor center. You can also explore two nearby waterfalls. **Dark Hollow Falls**, which sounds (and looks) like something out of a Tolkien novel, is a 70ft-high cascade located at the end of quite a steep 1.4-mile trail. **Lewis Falls**, accessed via Big Meadows, is on a moderately difficult 3.3-mile trail that intersects the Appalachian Trail; at one point you'll be scrabbling up a rocky slope.

The Drive » The Lewis Mountain area is about 5 miles south of the Byrd Visitors Center via Skyline Drive. Stop for good overlooks at Milam Gap and Naked Creek (both clearly signposted from the road).

- - - - - - - - - - -

⑪ Lewis Mountain

Lewis Mountain is both the name of one of the major camping areas of Shenandoah National Park and a nearby 3570ft mountain. The trail to the mountain is only about a mile long with a small elevation gain, and leads to a nice overlook. But the best view here is at the **Bearfence Rock Scramble.** That name is no joke; this 1.2-mile hike gets steep and rocky, so don't attempt it during or after rainfall. The reward is one of the best panoramas of the Shenandoahs. After you leave, remember there are still about 50 miles of Skyline Drive between you and the park exit at Rockfish Gap.

Eating & Sleeping

Front Royal ❶

✖ Apartment 2G   Fusion $$$

(☑540-636-9293; 206 S Royal Ave; 5 courses
$50, tapas $6-14; ☺from 6:30pm Sat & 3rd Thu)
The best restaurant in Front Royal is only open
once a week (well, twice if you count the third
Thursday of the month, when it serves tapas).
Owned and operated by a husband-and-wife
team (two chefs from the acclaimed Inn at Little
Washington), the Apartment's culinary philosophy
is simple and wonderful: uncompromisingly fresh
ingredients fashioned into ever-changing five-
course fixed menus.

✖ Element   Fusion $$

(☑540-636-9293; www.jsgourmet.com; 206 S
Royal Ave; mains $12-22; ☺11am-3pm & 5-10pm
Tue-Sat; ✈) Element is the casual-but-gourmet-
quality cousin of Apartment 2G, owned and
operated by that restaurant's proprietors. It's a
superior spot for sandwiches and soup, and the
dinner mains, which revolve around a fusion of
Asia and Appalachia (think quail with shiitake
mushrooms), are excellent. Vegetarian options
(including a righteous avocado sandwich and
vegetables cooked in Caribbean jerk spices) are
plentiful and delicious.

✖ Jalisco's   Mexican $

(☑540-635-7348; 1303 N Royal Ave; mains
$8-15; ☺11am-10pm Mon-Thu, to 11pm Fri &
Sat, to 9:30pm Sun) Jalisco's has pretty good
Mexican food. It's definitely the sort of Mexican
that derives flavor from refried beans and melted
cheese, but that's not such a terrible thing (well,
unless we're talking about your heart). The chili
rellenos go down a treat, as do the margaritas.

✖ Main Street Mill & Tavern   Cafe $

(☑540-636-3123; 500 E Main St; mains $6-15;
☺10:30am-9pm Sun-Thu, to 10pm Fri & Sat; ♿)
This folksy restaurant is located in a spacious
renovated 1880s feed mill. There are no big

surprises when it comes to the cuisine, which
is of the soup and sandwich and salad school of
cookery, but it is filling and satisfying and does
the job.

🛏 Killahevlin B&B   B&B $$

(☑800-847-6132, 540-636-7335; www.
vairish.com; 1401 N Royal Ave; r $155-225, ste
$255-285) This Irish-style B&B is located in
a lovely old building that's on the National
Register of Historic Places. There's free beer
on tap for guests, because clichés sell as well
as quaintness, we suppose. Rooms are quite
flowery and service is friendly.

🛏 Woodward House
on Manor Grade   B&B $$

(☑800-635-7011, 540-635-7010; www.
acountryhome.com; 413 S Royal Ave/US 320;
r $110-155, cottage $225; [P]🔊) This cluttered
B&B has eight bright rooms complemented by
owners who bring a lot of cheerful energy to the
table. Serves as a lovely base for exploring the
northern reaches of Shenandoah National Park.

Shenandoah National Park

The following three accommodation
options are all operated by the same
concessionaire. There are also four
campgrounds (☑877-444-6777; www.
recreation.gov; sites $15-25) in the park if
you're so inclined.

🛏 Big Meadows Lodge   Lodge $$

(☑540-999-2255; www.goshenandoah.com/
Big-Meadows-Lodge.aspx; Skyline Dr, MP 51.2;
r $130-210; ☺late May-Oct; 🔊♿) This *Wonder
Years*–reminiscent lodge and campsite is
located in the heart of Skyline Drive at MP 51.2
(Byrd Visitors Center). The atmosphere here is
very peaceful, as chipmunks and birds go flitting
about the branches. You can stay in either the
1939 stone lodge or one of the rustic cabins that
are the picture of 1950s vacation paradise. Wi-fi

is available in the central buildings of the lodge campus.

⊨ Lewis Mountain Cabins   Cabins $

(📞877-247-9261; www.goshenandoah.com/lewis-mountain-cabins.aspx; Skyline Dr, MP 57.6; cabins $90-100, campsites $16; ⊙Apr-Oct; P🐾) Lewis Mountain has several furnished cabins complete with private baths for a hot shower. The complex also has a campground with a store, a laundry and showers. This is the most rustic accommodation option in the area short of camping. Bear in mind many cabins are attached, although we've never heard our neighbors here.

⊨ Skyland Resort   Resort $$

(📞877-247-9261; www.goshenandoah.com/skyland-resort.aspx; Skyline Dr, MP 41.7; r from $140, incl breakfast $150; ⊙Apr-Oct; P🐴) Founded in 1888, this beautiful resort has fantastic views over the countryside, which is unsurprising as it occupies one of the highest points within Shenandoah National Park (the elevation of the hotel is around 3680ft). You'll find simple, wood-finished rooms and a full-service dining room, and you can arrange horseback rides from here.

Luray ❻

✖ Gathering Grounds Patisserie & Cafe   Bakery $

(📞540-743-1121; 55 E Main St; baked goods under $5, mains $5-7; ⊙7am-6pm Mon-Thu, to 7pm Fri, 8am-7pm Sat, 11am-3pm Sun; 🛜📶) If you need a bit of caffeine or an internet break, Gathering Grounds is the spot to stop by in Luray. The coffee is served strong and the pastries are all tasty, but what really sets this place apart is the interior, a refreshingly innovative, airy space that combines warm artsy-hippie cafe chic with modern hip.

✖ West Main Market   Deli $

(📞540-743-1125; 123 W Main St; mains $5-7; ⊙10am-6pm Tue-Thu, to 7pm Fri & Sat; P📶📶) Exploring Skyline Drive lends itself to picnic lunches, and there are few better places to pick up said lunch than the salad and sandwich counter at West Main. The grilled turkey and avocado is wonderful, while the fresh garden salad kept us rolling all the way down Skyline Drive.

⊨ Yogi Bear's Jellystone Park Campsite   Camping $

(📞800-420-6679; www.campluray.com; 2250 Hwy 211 East; campsites/cabins from $30/85; 📶) Miniature-golf courses, water slides and paddleboats all await inside this fanciful campus. Bargain-basement campsite and cabin prices don't reflect the possibility you might strike it rich while panning for gold at Old Faceful Mining Company. For those interested in passing by and peeking in, there are a few oversized figures of Yogi and Boo Boo that are ready-made photo ops.

STRETCH YOUR LEGS **NEW YORK CITY**

Start/Finish: New Museum of Contemporary Art

Distance: 2.6 miles

Duration: 3 hours

A stroll through these downtown neighborhoods, home to successive waves of immigrants and lively ethnic communities, is a microcosm of how the city blends the old and the new.

New Museum of Contemporary Art

Housed in an architecturally ambitious building, the **New Museum of Contemporary Art** (☎212-219-1222; www.newmuseum.org; 235 Bowery btwn Prince & Rivington Sts; adult/child $14/free, 7-9pm Thu free; ☺11am-6pm Wed & Fri-Sun, to 9pm Thu) towers over this formerly gritty, but now rapidly gentrifying strip of the Lower East Side. The museum's cache of work will dazzle and confuse as much as the building's stacked-box facade; check out the rooftop viewing platform for a unique perspective on the landscape.

The Walk » Head south on the relatively wide Bowery for a block until Spring St. Make a right and in three fashionable blocks you'll reach Mulberry St.

Mulberry Street

Although it feels more like a theme park than an authentic Italian strip, Mulberry St is still the heart of Little Italy. It's home to such landmarks as **Umberto's Clam House** (☎212-431-7545; www.umbertosclamhouse.com; 132 Mulberry St), where mobster Joey Gallo was shot to death in the '70s, and the old-time **Mulberry Street Bar** (☎212-226-9345; 176½ Mulberry St btwn Broome & Grand Sts), one of Frank Sinatra's favorite haunts. Waiters hawk their restaurant's menus as you pass, laying on the Italian shtick as heavily as they lay red sauce on their pastas.

The Walk » In warm weather the restaurants that line Mulberry St set out tables on the sidewalk, making for a very tight fit. Cross over the wide, traffic-clogged Canal St (you'll explore it later) and continue south to Columbus Park.

Columbus Park

This is where outdoor mah-jongg and domino games take place at bridge tables while tai-chi practitioners move through lyrical poses under shady trees. Judo-sparring folks and relaxing families are also common sights in this active communal space originally created in the 1890s.

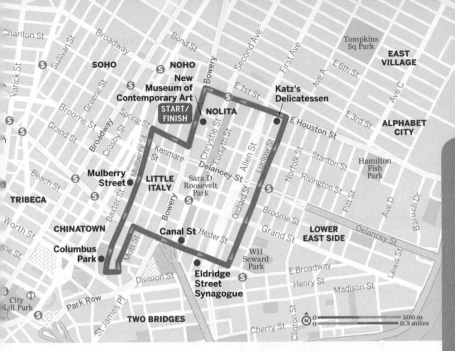

The Walk » Near the southern end of the park is a small alley that leads to Mott St. Follow Mott St back through Chinatown and make a right on Canal St – explore these blocks at your leisure.

Canal Street

This is Chinatown's main artery, where you'll dodge oncoming human traffic as you scurry into back alleys to scout for treasures from the Far East. You'll pass seafood stalls hawking slippery fish; herb shops displaying a witch's cauldron's worth of roots and potions; restaurants with whole roasted ducks hanging in the windows; and street vendors selling every iteration of knock-off designer goods.

The Walk » Walk east on Canal St and navigate the tricky intersection where the Manhattan Bridge on- and off-ramps converge. Continue for another two blocks before making a right on Eldridge St.

Eldridge Street Synagogue

Built in 1887 with Moorish and Romanesque ornamental work, this synagogue was flourishing at the turn of the 20th century but closed in the 1950s because of dwindling

membership. A 20-year restoration project was completed in 2007 and it now holds Friday evening and Saturday morning services; tours of the building are available. Perhaps the most breathtaking aspect of the interior is the massive circular stained-glass window above the ark (where Torahs are kept).

The Walk » Take Orchard St or Ludlow St, both lined with trendy cafes and shops, north to Katz's.

Katz's Delicatessen

One of the few remnants of the classic, old-world Jewish Lower East Side dining scene, this is the restaurant where Meg Ryan famously faked her orgasm in the 1989 flick *When Harry Met Sally*. If you love classic deli grub such as massive pastrami, corned beef, brisket and tongue sandwiches, it might have the same effect on you. Hold on to the ticket you're handed when you walk in and pay cash only.

The Walk » Head west on East Houston St until you reach the Bowery; a left will take you back to the New Museum.

STRETCH YOUR LEGS
WASHINGTON, DC

Start/Finish: Library of Congress

Distance: 3 miles

Duration: 3 hours

Washington, DC, is more than monuments, museums and memorials, but it is still partly defined by these structures. All along the National Mall, you'll find symbols of the American dream, the physical representation of the nation's highest ideals and aspirations.

Take this walk on Trips

Library of Congress

To prove America was just as cultured as the Old World, second US president John Adams established the Library of Congress, now the largest library in the world. The motivation behind the library is simple: 'universality,' the concept that all knowledge is useful. Stunning in scope and design, the building's baroque interior and flourishes are set off by a Main Reading Room that looks like an ant colony constantly harvesting 29 million books.

The Walk ⟩⟩ Head across the street to the underground Capitol Visitor Center.

Capitol Visitor Center

The US Capitol – that would be the big domed building that dominates the eastern end of the National Mall – is the seat of the legislative branch of government, otherwise known as Congress. The underground **Capitol Visitor Center** (www.visitthecapitol.gov; 1st St NE & E Capitol St; ◷8:30am-4:30pm Mon-Sat) is an introduction to the history and architecture of this iconic structure. Use the center's website to book tours of the Capitol itself.

The Walk ⟩⟩ Walk along the edge of the Capitol towards the Washington Monument (the big obelisk in the middle of the Mall). At the traffic circle, walk onto Maryland Ave; the Botanic Garden will be on your right.

United States Botanic Garden

Resembling London's Crystal Palace, the **United States Botanic Garden** (www.usbg.gov; 100 Maryland Ave SW; ◷10am-5pm; ⟨🏃⟩) provides a beautiful setting for displays of exotic and local plants. Check out titan arum, also known as *Amorphophallus titanum* ('giant misshapen penis'). If you're lucky, the plant's 'corpse flower' will be on display. This Sumatran native only blooms every three to five years; when it does, it smells like rotten meat. Mmm!

The Walk ⟩⟩ Continue on Maryland Ave for a little over 500ft; the National Museum of the American

Indian is on your right-hand side. The curving exterior, fashioned from amber kasota limestone, blobs like an amoeba.

National Museum of the American Indian

The **National Museum of the American Indian** (www.americanindian.si.edu; cnr 4th St & Independence Ave SW; ⏰10am-5:30pm; 👪) uses native communities' voices and their own interpretive exhibits to tell respective tribal sagas. The ground-floor **Mitsitam Native Foods Cafe** (www.mitsitamcafe.com; mains $8-18; ⏰11am-5pm) is the best dining option on the Mall.

The Walk » Walk west across the Mall, following Jefferson Ave. After about 2000ft you'll reach the doughnut-shaped Hirshhorn Museum.

Hirshhorn Museum and Sculpture Garden

The **Hirshhorn Museum** (www.hirshhorn. si.edu; cnr 7th St & Independence Ave SW; ⏰10am-5:30pm, sculpture garden 7:30am-dusk; 👪) houses the Smithsonian's modern art collection. Just across Jefferson

Dr, the sunken **Sculpture Garden** feels, on the right day, like a bouncy jaunt through a Lewis Carroll–style Wonderland. Young lovers, lost tourists and serene locals wander by sculptures such as Rodin's *The Burghers of Calais*.

The Walk » Walk up 7th Ave towards Pennsylvania Ave. Turn left on Pennsylvania Ave and you're at the National Archives.

National Archives

It's hard not to feel a little in awe of the big documents in the **National Archives** (www.archives.gov; 700 Constitution Ave NW; ⏰10am-7pm mid-Mar–early Sep, to 5:30pm early Sep–mid-Mar). The Declaration of Independence, the Constitution and the Bill of Rights, plus one of four copies of the Magna Carta: viewed together, it becomes clear just how radical the American experiment was for its time.

The Walk » Getting back to the Library of Congress is easy – just head down Pennsylvania Ave towards the Capitol Building, skirt the Capitol and there you are. But feel free to explore the National Mall while you're down here.

109

STRETCH
YOUR LEGS
PHILADELPHIA

Start/Finish: Rittenhouse Square

Distance: 2.8 miles

Duration: 2.5 hours

Historic Philadelphia, so well-known, lives side by side with contemporary skyscrapers and fashionable squares. This walk takes in the old and the new, which often means regal-looking spaces and structures from centuries past revitalized for a vibrant modern city.

Rittenhouse Square

This elegant square, with its wading pool and fine statues, marks the heart of the prosperous Center City neighborhood. Several excellent restaurants with sidewalk seating in warm weather line the east side of the square – a great spot for people-watching.

The Walk » It's only 10 steps or so from the southeast corner of the square to the next stop.

Philadelphia Art Alliance

Housed in a Gilded Age mansion, one of the few buildings on the square to escape the skyscraper age, is the **Philadelphia Art Alliance** (☎216-646-4302; www.philartalliance.org; 261 S 18th St; adult/child $5/3; ⊙11am-5pm Tue-Fri, from noon Sat & Sun). Its exhibits of modern crafts are always interesting.

The Walk » Walk back through the square and exit on the west side onto Locust St. Turn left on 21st before making a left on Delancey Pl.

Rosenbach Museum & Library

This three-story brick townhouse is an unassuming repository of treasures and a bibliophile's dream. The collection includes 30,000 rare books, drawings by William Blake, James Joyce's original manuscript for *Ulysses* and a re-creation of the modernist poet Marianne Moore's Greenwich Village apartment.

The Walk » Head east on Delancey Pl for three blocks, then left on 17th St and then right on Spruce. The modern Kimmel Center for the Performing Arts is on the right side of the intersection at Broad St.

Avenue of the Arts

Tours of **Kimmel Center for the Performing Arts** (☎215-790-5800; www.kimmelcenter.org; cnr Broad & Spruce Sts), Philadelphia's most active center for fine music, are available at 1pm Tuesday through Saturday. When walking north on Broad St (aka 'the Avenue of the Arts'), look up. The facades of these early incarnations of skyscrapers have signature flourishes such as terracotta roofs and elaborate filigree work

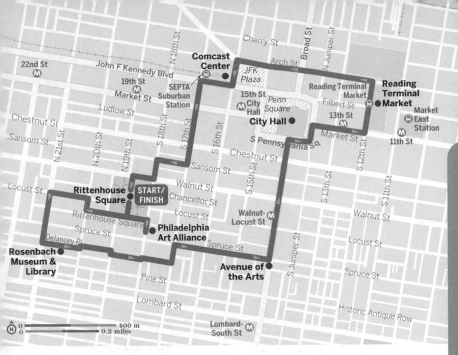

highlighted even more when they're illuminated at night.

The Walk » City Hall is dead center down Broad St; it's visible the entire way. Entering from the south portal, look for the keystone sculpture of Moses.

City Hall

The majestic 548ft tall **City Hall** sits in the center of the original orderly city between the Delaware and Schuykill Rivers. Standing at the intersection of Market and Broad Sts, the avenues shoot out in plumb-straight lines. It was the world's tallest occupied building until 1909 and the tallest in Philly until 1987. Check out the 250 sculptures including a 37ft tall, 27-ton statue of William Penn on the top.

The Walk » Walk through the east-side portal; look for the Benjamin Franklin keystone. Tower and building tours leave from here. The two-block stretch of Market St isn't the prettiest; turn left at 12th.

Reading Terminal Market

Housed in the railroad terminal since 1892 and renovated in the 1990s, the **Reading Terminal Market** (☎215-922-2317; www.readingterminalmarket.org; 51 N 12th St; ☺8am-5:30pm Mon-Sat, 9am-4pm Sun) is a bustling cornucopia of cuisines, crowded with tourists and locals at lunchtime. The market has everything: cheesesteaks, Amish crafts, regional specialties, ethnic eats, top-quality butchers, produce, cheese, flowers, bakeries and more.

The Walk » Head west on Arch until you reach JFK Plaza and Robert Indiana's *LOVE* sculpture. Good food trucks congregate here at lunchtime.

Comcast Center

An entrance to this skyscraper, the tallest in the city, leads into a massive all-glass atrium. On the back wall is the world's largest high-definition screen. It's always on, displaying curious, sometimes *trompe l'oeil* images.

The Walk » Walking south on 17th you'll pass a Lichtenstein sculpture and several hotels. Go right on Sansom for a block of nice little boutiques and then left on 18th or 19th to return to Rittenhouse Square.

New England Trips

CONCOCTED BY A GANG OF HOMESICK (AND UNINSPIRED) BRITS, the name 'New England' has long departed from its literal meaning. Today, the words are synonymous with a memorable medley of sights, smells and sounds: craggy coastlines dotted with lonely lighthouses; lobsters, fresh from the sea, served on weathered picnic tables; the shimmering colors of the autumnal flag flanking a quiet country road; and old, ivy-clad colleges, the hallowed halls of which are filled with hot-blooded scholars.

This collection of trips encompasses the best of New England. Perhaps you'll be moved to pick up a paintbrush, dust off your typewriter, maybe even get a PhD. Somehow, the country's northeast has that effect on folks.

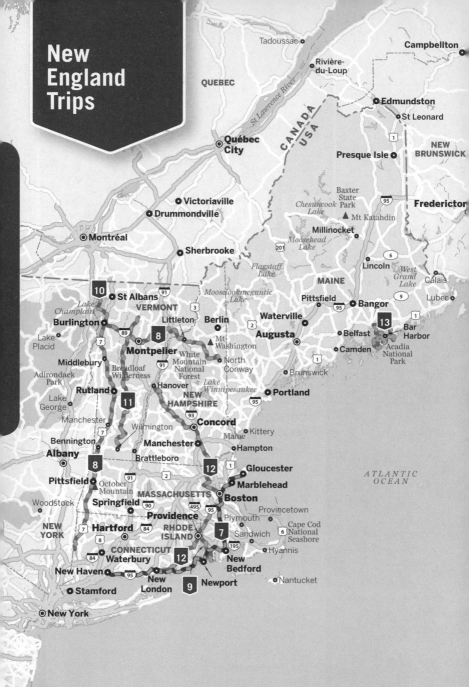

New England Trips

N

| 0 | | | 200 km |
| 0 | | | 100 miles |

DON'T MISS

Stellwagen Bank
This National Marine Sanctuary is a rich feeding ground for humpback whales. See them on Trip **7**

Polo
Enjoy polo in Portsmouth at the Glen Farm country estate on Trip **9**

Ben & Jerry's Factory Tour
Find out how two high-school pals created America's most celebrated ice cream on Trip **11**

Magic Hat Brewery
Take an 'Artifactory' tour at Vermont's most famous microbrewery. Taste your favorite on Trip **10**

Heavenly Views
Lie on the sand and ponder the universe during the Stars over Sand Beach program at Acadia National Park. Enjoy it on Trip **13**

Salem *At Derby Wharf, view the* Friendship *and indulge your inner pirate*

Classic Trip

Coastal New England

7

This drive follows the southern New England coast. A week of whale-watching, maritime museums and sailboats will leave you feeling pleasantly waterlogged.

TRIP HIGHLIGHTS

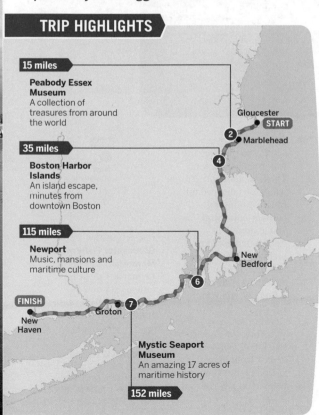

15 miles

Peabody Essex Museum
A collection of treasures from around the world

35 miles

Boston Harbor Islands
An island escape, minutes from downtown Boston

115 miles

Newport
Music, mansions and maritime culture

FINISH
New Haven

Groton

7

6

Gloucester
START

Marblehead

2

4

New Bedford

Mystic Seaport Museum
An amazing 17 acres of maritime history

152 miles

6–8 DAYS
240 MILES / 386KM

GREAT FOR...

BEST TIME TO GO

Sites are open and weather is fine from May to September.

 ESSENTIAL PHOTO

Pose for a photo alongside *The Gloucester Fisherman*.

 BEST TWO DAYS

The first 40 miles (stops one to four) showcase coastal New England, past and present.

MATTHEW IRELAND/GETTY IMAGES ©

Classic Trip

7 Coastal New England

From a pirate's perspective, there was no better base in Colonial America than Newport, given the easy access to trade routes and friendly local merchants. Until 1723, that is, when the new governor ceremoniously hanged 26 sea bandits at Gravelly Point. This classic trip highlights the region's intrinsic connection to the sea, from upstart pirates to upper-crust merchants, from Gloucester fisherfolk to New Bedford whalers, from clipper ships to submarines.

VERMONT

Connecticut River

Greenfield

Deerfield   Millers Falls

Cummington

Williamsburg   Amherst

Leeds

Northampton

Belchertown

Holyoke

Chicopee

Westfield

Southwick   **Springfield**

Granby

Canton

Manchester

Hartford

Glastonbury

Marlborough

Middletown

Meriden

Wallingford

FINISH

9

New Haven   Guilford   Clinton

Long Island Sound

❶ Gloucester

Founded in 1623 by English fisherfolk, Gloucester is among New England's oldest towns. This port on Cape Ann has made its living from fishing for almost 400 years, and inspired works like Rudyard Kipling's *Captains Courageous* and Sebastian Junger's *The Perfect Storm*. Visit the **Marine Heritage Center** (www. gloucestermaritimecenter. org; Harbor Loop; adult/child/ senior/family $8/4/6/18;

⏱10am-6pm daily Jun-Oct) to see the working waterfront in action. There is plenty of hands-on educational fun, including an outdoor aquarium and an excellent exhibit dedicated to Stellwagen Bank, the nearby National Marine Sanctuary. **Capt Bill & Sons Whale Watch** (☎978-283-6995; www. captbillandsons.com; 24 Harbor Loop; adult/senior/ child $48/42/32) boats also depart from here.

Don't leave Gloucester before you pay your

respects at the **Gloucester Fishermen's Memorial**, where Leonarde Craske's famous statue *The Gloucester Fisherman* stands.

🍴 p125

The Drive » Head out of town on Western Ave (MA 127), cruising past *The Gloucester Fisherman* and Stage Fort Park.

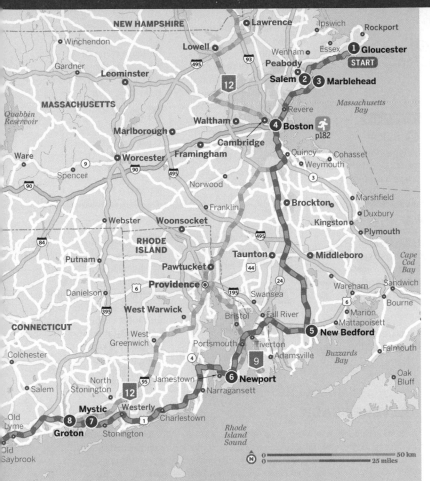

NEW HAMPSHIRE

Winchendon
Gardner
Leominster
Lowell
495
93
Lawrence
Ipswich
Rockport
Wenham
Essex
1 Gloucester
START
Peabody
Salem **2** **3** Marblehead
Massachusetts Bay

12

MASSACHUSETTS

Quabbin Reservoir

Ware
90
Spencer
9
Worcester
Marlborough
Framingham
90
495
Norwood
Revere
Waltham
4 Boston
Cambridge
p182
Quincy
Cohasset
Weymouth
3
Marshfield
Duxbury
Plymouth

Webster
Woonsocket
Franklin
Brockton
495
Kingston
Cape Cod Bay

84
RHODE ISLAND
Putnam
Pawtucket
Taunton
44
Middleboro
Sandwich

Danielson
6
Providence
24
Wareham
6
Bourne

CONNECTICUT
395
West Warwick
West Greenwich
195
Swansea
Bristol
Fall River
Marion
Mattapoisett
5 New Bedford
Buzzards Bay
Falmouth

Colchester
Portsmouth
4
Tiverton
Adamsville
9
Oak Bluff

Salem
North Stonington
12
95
Jamestown
Narragansett
6 Newport

Old Lyme
8 **7**
Mystic
Groton
Westerly
1
Charlestown
Stonington
Rhode Island Sound

Old Saybrook

N
0   50 km
0   25 miles

This winding road follows the coastline south through swanky seaside towns like Manchester-by-the-Sea and Beverly Farms, with occasional glimpses of the bay. After about 14 miles, cross the Essex Bridge and continue south into Salem. For a quicker trip, take MA 128 south to MA 114.

LINK YOUR TRIP

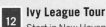

9 Rhode Island: East Bay

Join at Newport, or head north on I-95 and south on RI 77 to start at Little Compton.

12 Ivy League Tour

Start in New Haven and do the Ivy League Tour in reverse.

Classic Trip

TRIP HIGHLIGHT

❷ Salem

Salem's glory dates to the 18th century, when it was a center for clipper-ship trade with the Far East, thanks to the enterprising efforts of the merchant Elias Haskell Derby. His namesake Derby Wharf is now the center of the **Salem Maritime National Historic Site** (www.nps.gov/sama; 193 Derby St; ⏱10am-5pm Sun-Fri, 9am-5pm Sat), which includes the 1871 lighthouse, the tall ship

Friendship and the state custom house.

Many Salem vessels followed Derby's ship *Grand Turk* around the Cape of Good Hope, and soon the owners founded the East India Marine Society to provide warehousing services for their ships' logs and charts. The new company's charter required the establishment of 'a museum in which to house the natural and artificial curiosities' brought back by members' ships. The collection was the basis for what is now the world-class **Peabody Essex Museum** (www.pem.org; Essex St Mall, New Liberty St; adult/child/student/senior

$15/free/11/13; ⏱10am-5pm Tue-Sun). Still today, the museum contains an amazing collection of Asian art, amongst other treasures.

🍴 🛏 p125

The Drive » Take Lafayette St (MA 114) south out of Salem center, driving past the campus of Salem State College. After crossing an inlet, the road bends east and becomes Pleasant St as it enters Marblehead center.

❸ Marblehead

First settled in 1629, Marblehead is a maritime village with winding streets, brightly painted Colonial houses, and 1000 sailing yachts bobbing at moorings in the harbor. This is the Boston area's premier

REVERE BEACH

Cruising through Revere, MA 1A parallels the wide sandy stretch of Revere Beach, which proudly proclaims itself America's first public beach, established in 1896. Scenic but soulless, the condo-fronted beach belies the history of this place, which was a raucous boardwalk and amusement park for most of the 20th century. Famous for roller coasters, dance halls and the Wonderland dog track, Revere Beach attracted hundreds of thousands of sunbathers and fun-seekers during summer months.

The area deteriorated in the 1970s due to crime and pollution. In 1978 a historic blizzard wiped out many of the remaining buildings and businesses and the 'Coney Island of New England' was relegated to the annals of history.

Revere Beach benefitted from a clean-up effort in the 1980s; nowadays, the beach itself is lovely to look at and safe to swim. Unfortunately, dominated by high-end condominium complexes, the area retains nothing of its former charm. Only one vestige of 'old' Revere Beach remains: the world-famous **Kelly's Roast Beef** (www.kellysroastbeef.com; 410 Revere Beach Blvd; sandwiches $6-10; ⏱lunch & dinner), which has been around since 1951, and still serves up the best roast-beef sandwiches and clam chowder in town. There's no indoor seating, so pull up some sand and enjoy the view. Beware of the seagulls: they're crazy for roast beef.

yachting port and one of New England's most prestigious addresses. Clustered around the harbor, Marblehead center is dotted with historic houses, art galleries and waterside parks.

The Drive » Drive south on MA 129, exiting Marblehead and continuing through the seaside town of Swampscott. At the traffic circle, take the first exit onto MA 1A, which continues south through Lynn and Revere. Take the VFW Pkwy (MA 1A) to the Revere Beach Pkwy (MA 16) to the Northeast Expwy (US 1), which goes over the Tobin Bridge and into Boston.

TRIP HIGHLIGHT

④ Boston

Boston's seaside location has influenced every aspect of its history, but it's only in recent years that the waterfront has become an attractive and accessible destination for visitors. Now you can stroll along the **Rose Kennedy Greenway** (www.rosekennedygreenway. org), with the sea on one side and the city on the other. The focal point of the waterfront is the excellent **New England Aquarium** (www.neaq.org; Central Wharf; adult/child/senior $25/18/23; ☺9am-6pm Sun-Thu, 9am-7pm Fri-Sat, 1 hour earlier in winter; **P**), home to seals, penguins, turtles and oodles of fish. Parking is $18.

From Long Wharf, you can catch a ferry

PARKING IN BOSTON

Parking in downtown Boston is prohibitively expensive. For more affordable rates, cross the Fort Point Channel and park in the Seaport District. Park in lots on Northern Ave (near the Institute of Contemporary Art) for a flat rate of $12; the Necco Street Garage (further south, off A St) is only $6.

out to the **Boston Harbor Islands** (www.bostonharborislands.org; ferry adult/child/senior $15/9/11; ☺hourly 9am-6pm May-Sep) for berry picking, beachcombing and sunbathing. Harbor cruises and trolley tours also depart from these docks. For another look at Boston, follow the walking tour, p182.

🍴 🛏 p125

The Drive » Drive south out of Boston on I-93. You'll recognize the urban 'hood of Dorchester by pretty Savin Hill Cove and the landmark Rainbow Swash painted on the gas tank. At exit 4, take MA 24 south toward Brockton, then MA 140 south toward New Bedford. Take I-195 east for 2 miles, exiting onto MA 18 for New Bedford.

⑤ New Bedford

During its heyday as a whaling port (1765–1860), New Bedford commanded some 400 whaling ships – a vast fleet that brought in hundreds of thousands of barrels of whale oil for lighting lamps. Novelist Herman Melville worked on one of these ships for four years, and thus

set his celebrated novel *Moby-Dick* in New Bedford.

The excellent, hands-on **New Bedford Whaling Museum** (www.whalingmuseum.org; 18 Johnny Cake Hill; adult/child/senior & student $14/6/12/9; ☺9am-5pm Jun-Dec, 9am-4pm Tue-Sun Jan-May) celebrates this history. A 66ft skeleton of a blue whale welcomes you at the entrance. Inside, you can tramp the decks of the *Lagoda,* a fully rigged, half-size replica of an actual whaling bark.

The Drive » Take I-195 west for about 10 miles. In Fall River, head south on MA 24, which becomes RI 24 as you cross into Rhode Island. Cross the bridge, with views of Mt Hope Bay to the north and Sakonnet River to the south, then merge onto RI 114, heading south into Newport.

TRIP HIGHLIGHT

⑥ Newport

Blessed with a deepwater harbor, Newport has been a shipbuilding base since 1646. Bowen's and Bannister's Wharf, once working wharves, now typify Newport's transformation from

Classic Trip

WHY THIS IS A CLASSIC TRIP
MARA VORHEES, AUTHOR

Nothing evokes New England's salty air like driving along the old coastal roads. MA 127 winds through some of the state's prettiest seaside towns, giving glimpses of gracious mansions perched at the ocean's edge. Even better, I love cruising along MA 1A with the windows down, feeling the ocean breeze, hearing the seagulls' cries and recalling the glory days of Revere Beach.

Top: Peabody Essex Museum, Salem
Left: Mystic Seaport Lighthouse
Right: Observing marine life at a New England aquarium

a working city-by-the-sea to a resort town. Take a narrated cruise with **Classic Cruises of Newport** (www.cruisenewport.com; Bannister's Wharf; adult $25-30; ☺ mid-May–mid-Oct) on *Rum Runner II,* a Prohibition-era bootlegging vessel, or *Madeleine,* a 72ft schooner. Or ogle the mansions from the Cliff Walk (www.cliffwalk.com).

Jutting out into Naragansett Bay, the gorgeous Fort Adams State Park (www.fortadams.org) is home to America's largest coastal fortification. The park has a beach, and picnic and fishing areas, but the centerpiece is the impressive 1799 fortress. To explore in greater detail join a tour, which takes you deep into its underground tunnels and up onto the ramparts for fabulous views of Newport Harbor and the bay.

In August Fort Adams is the venue for the **Newport Jazz Festival** (www.newportjazzfest.net) and the **Newport Folk Festival** (www.newportfolkfest.net).

✕ p125

The Drive ❯❯ Head west out of Newport on RI 138, swooping over the Newport Bridge onto Conanicut Island and then over the Jamestown Bridge to pick up US 1 for the drive into Mystic. The views of the bay from both bridges are a highlight.

TRIP HIGHLIGHT

❼ Mystic

Many of Mystic's clipper ships launched from George Greenman & Co Shipyard, now the site of the **Mystic Seaport Museum** (www.mysticseaport.org; 75 Greenmanville Ave/CT 27; adult/6-17yr $24/15; ⊘9am-5pm Apr-Oct, 10am-4pm Nov & Mar; 🖶). Today the museum covers 17 acres and includes more than 60 historic buildings, four tall ships and almost 500 smaller vessels. The museum's exhibits include a replica of the 77ft slave ship *Amistad*.

If the call of the sea beckons, the **Sabino** (☎860-572-5351; adult/6-17yr $5.50/4.50), a 1908 steamboat, takes visitors on half-hour excursions up the Mystic River. The boat departs from the museum hourly from 11:30am to 4:30pm.

🛏 ✖ p125

The Drive » The 7-mile drive to Groton along US 1 South is through built-up suburbs and light industrial areas. To hop across the Thames River to New London, head north along North St to pick up I-95 South.

❽ Groton

Groton is home to the US Naval Submarine Base, the first and the largest in the country. It is off-limits to the public, but you can visit the **Historic Ship Nautilus & Submarine Force Museum** (www.ussnautilus.org; 1 Crystal Lake Rd; admission free; ⊘9am-5pm Wed-Sun; Ⓟ), which is home to *Nautilus,* the world's first nuclear-powered submarine and the first sub to transit the North Pole.

Across the river, New London has a similarly illustrious seafaring history, although these days it's built a reputation for itself as a budding creative center. Each summer it hosts **Sailfest** (www.sailfest.org), a three-day festival with free entertainment topped off by the second-largest fireworks display in the Northeast. There's also a **Summer Concert Series**, organized by **Hygienic Art** (www.hygienic.org; 79 Bank St; ⊘11am-3pm Tue-Wed, 11am-6pm Thu-Sat & noon-3pm Sun).

✖ p125

The Drive » It's a 52-mile drive from Groton or New London to New Haven along I-95 South. The initial stages of the drive plough through the suburbs, but after that the interstate runs through old coastal towns such as Old Lyme, Old Saybrook and Guilford.

❾ New Haven

Although most famous for its Ivy League university, Yale, New Haven also played an important role in the burgeoning anti-slavery movement when, in 1839, the trial of mutineering Mendi tribesmen was held in New Haven's District Court.

Following their illegal capture by Spanish slave traders, the tribesmen, led by Joseph Cinqué, seized the schooner *Amistad* and sailed to New Haven seeking refuge. Pending the successful outcome of the trial (for which former president John Quincy Adams came out of retirement to plead their case), the men were held in a jailhouse on the green, where a 14ft-high bronze memorial now stands. It was the first Civil Rights case held in the country.

Stretch your legs with a walking tour of New Haven's art galleries. Or for a unique take on the New Haven shoreline take the 3-mile round trip on the **Shore Line Trolley** (www.shorelinetrolley.com; 17 River St, East Haven; adult/child under 15yr/senior $10/6/8; ⊘10.30am-4.30pm daily Jun-Aug, Sat & Sun May, Sep & Oct; 🖶), the oldest operating suburban trolley in the country, which takes you from East Haven to Short Beach in Branford.

✖ p125

Eating & Sleeping

Gloucester ❶

✗ Two Sisters Coffee Shop Diner $

(27 Washington St; meals $8-10; ⊙ breakfast & lunch; ✍) The fisherfolk go here for breakfast when they come in from their catch. They're early risers, so you may have to wait for a table. Corn beef hash, eggs in a hole and French toast all get rave reviews. Service is a little salty.

Salem ❷

✗ The Old Spot Pub $$

(www.theoldspot.com; 121 Essex St; sandwiches $8-12, mains $15-18; ⊙ lunch Fri-Sun, dinner daily) It's pub food, but so perfectly prepared that it becomes a dining experience. Dim lighting and plush pillows make the place extra comfortable and cozy.

Boston ❹

✗ Barking Crab Seafood $$

(www.barkingcrab.com; 88 Sleeper St; mains $12-30; ⊙ lunch & dinner) Big buckets of crabs, steamers dripping in lemon and butter, paper plates piled high with all things fried... The food is plentiful and affordable, and you eat it at communal picnic tables overlooking the water. Beer flows freely. Service is slack, but the atmosphere is jovial.

🛏 Harborside Inn Boutique Hotel $$

(☎617-723-7500; www.harborsideinnboston. com; 185 State St; r from $169; P ❄ @ 🛜) Ensconced in a former warehouse, this waterfront hostelry strikes the right balance between historic digs and modern conveniences. Nautical-themed guest rooms feature classy, custom-designed teak furniture and plenty of multimedia entertainment options. Add $20 for a city view.

Newport ❻

✗ White Horse Tavern American $$$

(www.whitehorsetavern.us; 26 Marlborough St; mains $14-40; ⊙ 11.30am-9pm) If you'd like to eat at a tavern opened by a 17th-century pirate, then try this gambrel-roofed beauty. Menus for dinner (at which men should wear jackets) might include baked escargot or beef Wellington.

Mystic ❼

🛏 Steamboat Inn Inn $$$

(☎860-536-8300; www.steamboatinnmystic. com; 73 Steamboat Wharf; d incl breakfast $160-295; P 🛜) Located right in the heart of downtown Mystic, the 11 rooms of this romantic, historic inn have wraparound water views and luxurious amenities, including whirlpool tubs, fireplaces and plenty of antiques.

New London ❽

✗ Captain Scott's Lobster Dock Seafood $$

(80 Hamilton St; meals $10-20; ⊙ lunch & dinner May-Oct; 🚻) Captain Scott's is the place to go for seafood in summer. The setting's just picnic tables by the water, but you can feast on succulent (hot or cold) lobster rolls, followed by steamers, fried whole-belly clams, scallops or lobsters.

New Haven ❾

✗ Caseus Fromagerie Bistro Bistro $$

(☎203-624-3373; caseusnewhaven.com; 93 Whitney Ave; meals $10-30; ⊙ 11.30am-2.30pm Mon-Tue & 5.30-9pm Wed-Sat) With a boutique cheese counter piled with locally sourced labels and a concept menu devoted to le grand fromage, Caseus has hit upon a winning combination. After all, what's not to like about a perfectly executed mac'n'cheese?.

Connecticut Break from your tour
with a slice of pumpkin pie

RAY KACHATORIAN/GETTY IMAGES ©

Fall Foliage Tour

8

Touring New England in search of autumn's changing colors has become so popular that it has sprouted its own subculture of 'leaf-peepers.' Immerse yourself in the fall harvest spirit.

TRIP HIGHLIGHTS

212 miles — ⑦ — St Johnsbury

Lake Champlain
Cruise the lake on a
43ft schooner for the
best views

⑧

North
Conway
FINISH

316 miles

Bretton Woods
Zip-line 1000ft
through a golden leaf
canopy

● Manchester

47 miles

Berkshires
Pack a picnic in the
Berkshires' gourmet
shops

④

10 miles

② **Kent**
Sherman ●   Autumn foliage
START   framing the
Housatonic River

**5–7 DAYS
424 MILES / 682KM**

GREAT FOR...

BEST TIME TO GO
August to November
for the harvest and
autumn leaves.

**ESSENTIAL
PHOTO**
Kent Falls set against a
backdrop of autumnal
colors.

**BEST FOR
OUTDOORS**
Zip lining through the
tree canopy in Bretton
Woods.

127

8 Fall Foliage Tour

The brilliance of fall in New England is legendary. Scarlet and sugar maples, ash, birch, beech, dogwood, tulip tree, oak and sassafras all contribute to the carnival of autumn color. But this trip is about much more than just flora and fauna: the harvest spirit makes for family outings to pick-your-own farms, leisurely walks along dappled trails, and tables that groan beneath delicious seasonal produce.

❶ Lake Candlewood

With a surface area of 8.4 sq miles, Candlewood is the largest lake in Connecticut. On the western shore, the **Squantz Pond State Park** (www.ct.gov; 178 Shortwoods Rd, New Fairfield) is popular with leaf-peepers, who come to amble the pretty shoreline.

In Brookfield and Sherman, quiet vineyards with acres of gnarled grapevines line the hillsides.

Visitors can tour the award-winning **DiGrazia Vineyards** (www.digrazia. com; 131 Tower Rd, Brookfield; ⊘11am-5pm daily May-Dec, Sat & Sun Jan-Apr) or opt for something more intimate at **White Silo Farm Winery** (www.whitesilowinery. com; 32 CT 37; tastings $7; ⊘11am-6pm Fri-Sun Apr-Dec), where the focus is on specialty wines made from farm-grown fruit.

For the ultimate bird's-eye view of the foliage, consider a late-afternoon hot-air-balloon ride with **GONE Ballooning** (www.flygoneballooning.com;

88 Sylvan Crest Dr; adult/under 12yr $250/125) **in nearby Southbury.**

✖ p135

The Drive » From Danbury, at the southern tip of the lake, you have a choice of heading north via US 7, taking in Brookfield and New Milford (or trailing the scenic eastern shoreline along Candlewood Lake Rd S); or heading north along CT 37 and CT 39 via New Fairfield, Squantz Pond and Sherman, before reconnecting with US 7 to Kent.

TRIP HIGHLIGHT

❷ Kent

Kent has previously been voted *the* spot in all of New England (yes, even beating Vermont) for fall foliage viewing. Situated prettily in the Litchfield Hills on the banks of the Housatonic River, it is surrounded by dense woodlands. For a

§ **LINK YOUR TRIP**

7 Coastal New England

From North Conway, take NH 16 south to I-95, then head east on MA 128 to Gloucester

12 Ivy League Tour

Follow NH 16 and I-93 northwest into Vermont. Then follow I-91 south all the way to Hanover, NH.

LOCAL KNOWLEDGE
ANNE MCANDREW & DAVE FAIRTY, BACKCOUNTRY OUTFITTERS

Kent is beautiful in the fall. The best hiking trail during the season leads up to Caleb's Peak from Skiff Mountain Rd, hooking up with the Appalachian Trail. At the summit you have the most fantastic views of the Housatonic Valley. If you like, you can camp at any of the shelters on the trail or try Macedonia Brook State Park, which is private and rustic with over 80 miles of hiking trails.

Top: Cornwall Bridge, Housatonic Meadows State Park
Right: Venturing up Mt Equinox, near Manchester

sweeping view of them, hike up Cobble Mountain in **Macedonia Brook State Park** (www.ct.gov; 159 Macedonia Brook Rd), a wooded oasis 2 miles north of town. The steep climb to the rocky ridge affords panoramic views of the foliage against a backdrop of the Taconic and Catskill mountain ranges.

The 2175-mile Georgia-to-Maine **Appalachian National Scenic Trail** (www.appalachiantrail.org) also runs through Kent and up to Salisbury on the Massachusetts border. Unlike much of the trail, the Kent section offers a mostly flat 5-mile river walk alongside the Housatonic, the longest river walk along the entire length of the trail.

The trailhead is accessed on River Rd, off CT 341.

The Drive » The 15-mile drive from Kent to Housatonic Meadows State Park along US 7 is one of the most scenic drives in Connecticut. The single-lane road dips and weaves between thick forests, past Kent Falls State Park with its tumbling waterfall (visible from the road), and through West Cornwall's picturesque covered bridge, which spans the Housatonic River.

❸ Housatonic Meadows State Park

During the spring thaw, the churning waters of the Housatonic challenge kayakers and canoeists. By summer the scenic waterway transforms into a lazy, flat river perfect for fly-fishing. In the **Housatonic Meadows State Park** (☎806-672-6772; US 7; tent sites residents/nonresidents $17/27; ⊙ mid-Apr–mid-Oct), campers vie for a spot on the banks of the river while hikers take to the hills on the Appalachian Trail. **Housatonic River Outfitters** (www.dryflies. com; 24 Kent Rd, Cornwall Bridge) runs guided fishing trips with gourmet picnics.

Popular with artists and photographers, one of the most photographed fall scenes is the **Cornwall Bridge** (West Cornwall), an antique covered bridge that stretches across the broad river, framed by vibrantly colored foliage.

On Labor Day weekend, in the nearby town of Goshen, you can visit the **Goshen Fair** (www.goshenfair.org), one of Connecticut's best old-fashioned fairs, with ox-pulling and wood-cutting contests. Also in Goshen is **Nodine's Smokehouse** (www.nodinesmokehouse.com;

39 North St; ⊙ 9am-5pm Mon-Sat, 10am-4pm Sun), a major supplier to New York gourmet food stores.

The Drive ≫ Continue north along US 7 toward the Massachusetts border and Great Barrington. After a few miles you leave the forested slopes of the park behind you and enter expansive rolling countryside dotted with large red-and-white barns. Look out for hand-painted signs advertising farm produce and consider stopping overnight in Falls Village, which has an excellent B&B (p135).

- - - - - - - - - - - - -

TRIP HIGHLIGHT

❹ Berkshires

Blanketing the westernmost part of Massachusetts, the rounded mountains of the Berkshires turn crimson and gold as early as mid-September. The effective capital of the Berkshires is **Great Barrington**, a formerly industrial town whose streets are now lined with art galleries and upscale restaurants. It's the perfect place to pack your picnic or rest your legs before or after a hike in nearby **Beartown**

State Forest (www.mass. gov/dcr; 69 Blue Hill Rd, Monterey). Crisscrossing some 12,000 acres, hiking trails yield spectacular views of wooded hillsides and pretty Benedict Pond.

Further north, **October Mountain State Forest** (www.mass.gov/dcr; 256 Woodland Rd, Lee) is the state's largest tract of green space (16,127 acres), also interwoven with hiking trails. The name – attributed to Herman Melville – gives a good indication of when this park is at its loveliest, with its multicolored tapestry of hemlocks, birches and oaks.

 p135

The Drive ≫ Drive north on US 7, the spine of the Berkshires, cruising through Great Barrington and Stockbridge. In Lee, the highway merges with scenic US 20, from where you can access October Mountain. Continue 16 miles north through Lenox and Pittsfield to Lanesborough. Turn right on N Main St and follow the signs to the park entrance.

- - - - - - - - - - - - -

TRIP HIGHLIGHT

❺ Mt Greylock State Forest

Massachusetts' highest peak is not so high, at 3491ft, but a climb up the 92ft-high **War Veterans Memorial Tower** rewards you with a panorama stretching up to 100 verdant miles, across the Taconic, Housatonic and Catskill ranges, and

> ✓ **TOP TIP:**
> **NORTHERN BERKSHIRE FALL FOLIAGE PARADE**
>
> If your timing is right, you can stop in North Adams for the **Fall Foliage Parade** (www.fallfoliageparade.com), held in late September or early October. Now in its 57th year, the event follows a changing theme, but it always features music, food and fun – and, of course, foliage.

over five states. Even if the weather seems drab from the foot, driving up to the summit may well lift you above the gray blanket, and the view with a layer of cloud floating between tree line and sky is simply magical.

Mt Greylock State Reservation (www.mass. gov/dcr; park free, summit $2; ☺visitors center 9am-5pm, auto road late May-Oct) has some 45 miles of hiking trails, including a portion of the Appalachian Trail. Frequent trail pull-offs on the road up – including some that lead to waterfalls – make it easy to get at least a little hike in before reaching the top of Mt Greylock.

🍴🛏 p135

The Drive ❯❯ Return to US 7 and continue north through the quintessential college town of Williamstown. Cross the Vermont border and continue north through the historic village of Bennington. Just north of Bennington, turn left on Rte 7A and continue north to Manchester.

- - - - - - - - - -

❻ Manchester

Stylish Manchester is known for its magnificent New England architecture. For fall foliage views, head south of the center to 3828ft-high **Mt Equinox** (☎802-362-1114; www.equinoxmountain. com; car & driver $15, each additional passenger $5;

☺9am-dusk May-Oct), the highest mountain accessible by car in the Taconic Range. Wind up the 5.2 miles – with gasp-inducing scenery at every hairpin turn – seemingly to the top of the world, where the 360-degree panorama unfolds, offering views of the Adirondacks, the lush Battenkill Valley and Montréal's Mt Royal.

If early snow makes Mt Equinox inaccessible, visit 412-acre **Hildene** (☎802-362-1788; www. hildene.org; Rte 7A; museum & grounds adult/child $16/5, grounds only $5/3; ☺9:30am-4:30pm), a Georgian Revival mansion that was once home to the Lincoln family. It's filled with presidential memorabilia and sits nestled at the edge of the Green Mountains, with access to 8 miles of wooded walking trails.

🛏 p135

The Drive ❯❯ Take US 7 north to Burlington. Three miles past Middlebury in New Haven, stop off at Lincoln Peak Vineyard for wine tasting or a picnic lunch on the wraparound porch.

- - - - - - - - - -

TRIP HIGHLIGHT

❼ Lake Champlain

With a surface area of 490 sq miles, straddling New York, Vermont and Quebec, Lake Champlain is the largest freshwater lake in the US after the Great Lakes.

On its northeastern side, **Burlington** is a gorgeous base to enjoy the lake. Explore it by foot on our walking tour. Then scoot down to the wooden promenade, take a swing on the four-person rocking benches and consider a bike ride along the 7.5-mile lakeside bike path.

For the best offshore foliage views we love the *Friend Ship* sailboat at **Whistling Man Schooner Company** (☎802-598-6504; www.whistlingman. com; Boathouse, College St; 2hr cruise adult/child $40/25; ☺May-Oct), a 43ft sloop that accommodates a mere 17 passengers. Next door, **ECHO Lake Aquarium & Science Center** (www.echovermont. org; 1 College St; adult/child $13/10.50; ☺10am-5pm) explores the history and ecosystem of the lake, including a famous snapshot of Champ, Lake Champlain's mythical sea creature.

🍴 p135

The Drive ❯❯ Take I-89 southeast to Montpelier passing Camels Hump State Park and CC Putnam State Forest. At Montpelier, pick up US2 heading east to St Johnsbury, where you can hop on I-91 south to I-93 south. Just after Littleton, take US 302 east to Bretton Woods.

Classic Trip

8 Bretton Woods

Unbuckle your seat belts and step away from the car. You're not just peeping at leaves today, you're swooping past them on zip lines that drop 1000ft at 30mph. The four-season **Bretton Woods Canopy Tour** (☎603-278-4947; www. brettonwoods.com; US 302; per person $110; ☺tours 10am & 2pm) includes a hike through the woods, a stroll over sky bridges and a swoosh down 10 cables to tree platforms.

If this leaves you craving even higher views, cross US 302 and drive 6 miles on Base Rd to the coal-burning, steam-powered **Mount Washington Cog Railway** (☎603-278-5404; www. thecog.com; adult/child/ senior $66/39/59; ☺ 8:30am-4:30pm daily late May-Nov, Sat-Sun Nov-Dec) at the western base of Mt Washington, the highest

DETOUR: KANCAMAGUS SCENIC BYWAY

Start: 9 **North Conway**

From North Conway, the 34.5-mile Kancamagus Scenic Byway, otherwise known as NH 112, passes through the White Mountains from Conway to Lincoln in New Hampshire. You'll drive alongside the Saco River and enjoy sweeping views of the Presidential Range from Kancamagus Pass. Inviting trailheads and pull-offs line the road. From Lincoln, a short drive north on I-93 leads to Franconia Notch State Park, where the foliage in September and October is simply spectacular.

peak in New England. This historic railway has been hauling sightseers to the mountain's 6288ft summit since 1869.

The Drive » Continue driving east on US 302, a route that parallels the Saco River and the Conway Scenic Railroad, traversing Crawford Notch State Park. At the junction of NH 16 and US 302, continue east on US 302 into North Conway.

9 North Conway

Many of the best restaurants, pubs and inns in North Conway come with expansive views of the nearby mountains, making it an ideal place to wrap up a fall foliage road trip. If you're traveling with

kids or you skipped the cog railway ride up Mt Washington, consider an excursion on the antique steam Valley Train with the **Conway Scenic Railroad** (☎603-356-5251; www.conwayscenic.com; 38 Norcross Circle; adult/child 4-12yr/child 1-3yr from $15/11/ free; ☺mid-Jun–mid-Oct); it's a short but sweet round-trip ride through the Mt Washington Valley from North Conway to Conway, 11 miles south. The Moat Mountains and the Saco River will be your scenic backdrop. First-class seats are usually in a restored Pullman observation car.

🛏 p135

Eating & Sleeping

Lake Candlewood ❶

✕ American Pie   Bakery $$

(www.americanpiecompany.com; 29 Sherman Rd/CT 37, Sherman; mains $9-20; ⊙7am-9pm Tue-Sun, to 3pm Mon) A local favorite serving up 20 varieties of homemade pie, including pumpkin and blueberry crumb, alongside burgers, steaks and salads.

Falls Village ❸

🛏 Falls Village Inn   Historic Inn $$$

(☎860-824-0033; www.thefallsvillageinn.com; 33 Railroad St; d/ste $209/299; P 🛜) The heart and soul of one of the smallest villages in Connecticut, this inn originally served the Housatonic Railroad. Now the six rooms are styled by interior decorator Bunny Williams, and the Tap Room is a hangout for Lime Rock's racers.

Berkshires ❹

✕ Castle Street Café   Modern American $$$

(☎413-528-5244; www.castlestreetcafe.com; 10 Castle St; mains $21-29; ⊙dinner Wed-Mon, brunch Sat & Sun; 🛜) The menu reads like a who's who of local farms: loka Valley Farm grass-fed beef, Rawson Brook chevre and Equinox Farm mesclun greens. Prime time to dine is Friday or Saturday, when there's live jazz.

Mt Greylock State Forest ❺

🛏 Bascom Lodge   Lodge $$

(☎413-743-1591; www.bascomlodge.net; 1 Summit Rd, Adams; dm/r $37/125, breakfast & lunch $7-10, dinner $28-32; ⊙breakfast, lunch & dinner Jun-Oct) At the summit of Mt Greylock, this rustic mountain lodge boasts – arguably – the most scenic setting in the state. Come for basic accommodations, straightforward but filling meals and jaw-dropping views.

Manchester ❻

🛏 Equinox   Resort $$$

(☎802-362-4700, 800-362-4747; www.equinoxresort.com; 3567 Main St/Rte 7A; r $280-600, ste $490-1500; @ 🛜 ⊛) Manchester's most famous resort encompasses many worlds: cottages with wood-burning fireplaces, luxury town houses, or antique-filled rooms with canopied beds and oriental rugs. High-end extras abound.

Lake Champlain ❼

✕ Penny Cluse Cafe   Cafe $

(www.pennycluse.com; 169 Cherry St; mains $7-11; ⊙6.45am-3pm Mon-Fri, 8am-3pm Sat & Sun) In the heart of downtown, one of Burlington's most popular breakfast spots whips up pancakes, biscuits and gravy, breakfast burritos, omelettes and tofu scrambles along with sandwiches, fish tacos, salads and the best chile relleno you'll find east of the Mississippi.

North Conway ❾

🛏 Red Elephant Inn   B&B $$

(☎603-356-3548; www.redelephantinn.com; 28 Locust Lane; r $145-260; ⊛ 🛜) Perched on a hill with views of the Moat Mountains, this sweet property offers eight stylish rooms, each with unique attractive decor and amenities. Service is top-notch, as is the delicious, decadent breakfast.

Newport *Stroll Cliff Walk and see how the wealthy vacationed in the 19th century*

Rhode Island: East Bay

9

East Bay is at the heart of Rhode Island's history. Tour the shoreline, and follow the trail from America's humble Colonial roots in Little Compton to the industrial boomtowns of Newport and Providence.

TRIP HIGHLIGHTS

65 miles

6 FINISH

Providence
Explore a 'Mile of History' on Benefit St

Warren

5

38 miles

Bristol
Eight America's Cup yachts were built here

Tiverton

Portsmouth

1 START

3

Newport
Marvel at the mansions of America's capitalist kings

26 miles

Little Compton
Visit the home of Mayflower pilgrims

1 mile

**3–4 DAYS
65 MILES / 105KM**

GREAT FOR...

BEST TIME TO GO

May to October for good weather and farm food.

ESSENTIAL PHOTO

Capture the mansions and sheer cliffs along Cliff Walk.

BEST FOR HISTORY

Find modern America's beginnings in Little Compton.

VISIONS OF AMERICA, LLC/ALAMY ©

137

9 Rhode Island: East Bay

Rhode Island's jagged East Bay tells the American story in microcosm. Start in Little Compton with the grave of Elizabeth Pabodie (1623–1717), the first European settler born in New England. Then meander through historic Tiverton and Bristol, where slave dealers and merchants grew rich. Prosperous as they were, their modest homes barely hold a candle to the mansions, museums and libraries of Newport's capitalist kings and Providence's intelligentsia.

TRIP HIGHLIGHT

1 Little Compton

No doubt tiring of the big-city bustle of 17th-century Portsmouth, early settler Samuel Wilbor crossed the Sakonnet River to Little Compton. His plain family home, **Wilbur House** (www.littlecompton.org; 548 West Main Rd; adult/child $6/3; ☺1-5pm Thu-Sun Apr-Oct, 9am-3pm Tue-Fri Nov-Mar), built in 1690, still stands on a manicured lawn behind a traditional five-bar gate and tells the story of eight generations of Wilburs who lived here.

The rest of Little Compton, from the hand-hewn clapboard houses to the white-steepled **United Congregational Church**, overlooking the **Old Commons Burial Ground**, is one of the oldest and most quaint villages in all of New England. Elizabeth Pabodie, daughter of Mayflower pilgrims Priscilla and John Alden and the first settler born in New England, is buried here. **Gray's Store** (4 Main St), built in 1788 in nearby Adamsville, is the oldest general store in the country.

Lovely, ocean-facing **Goosewing Beach** is the only good public beach. Parking costs $10 at **South Shore Beach** (Little Compton; ☺dawn-dusk),

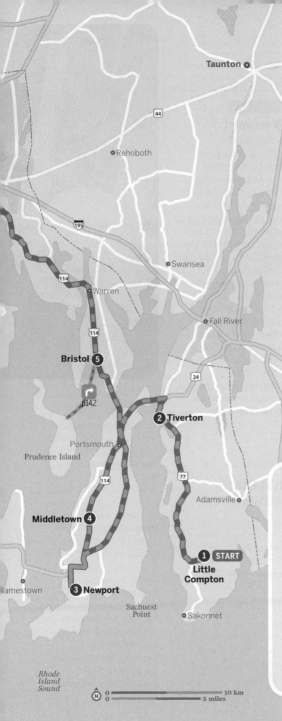

from where you can walk across a small tidal inlet.

📖 p143

The Drive » Head north along RI 77 at a leisurely pace, enjoying the peaceful country scenery of rambling stone walls and clapboard farmhouses. To your left you'll occasionally get glimpses out to the water, which are particularly pretty in the late afternoon as the sun begins to set.

② Tiverton

En route to Tiverton's historic Four Corners, stop in at **Sakonnet Vineyards** (📞1-800-919-4637; www.sakonnetwine.com; 162 West Main Rd; tastings $10; ⏰10am-6pm Mon-Wed, to 8pm Thu-Sun) for daily wine tastings and guided tours. This will set you up nicely for the gourmet treats that await in Tiverton: **Gray's Ice Cream** (graysicecream.com; 16 East Rd; ⏰7am-7pm), where over 40 flavors are made on-site

🔗 LINK YOUR TRIP

2 The Jersey Shore
Drive south on I-95 and take the Garden State Pkwy to Asbury Park.

8 Fall Foliage Tour
Take I-95 south from Providence to CT 9 heading northwest across the state. Take I-84 west to the border. CT 37 and CT 39 lead to Sherman.

daily; artisanal cheeses from the **Milk & Honey Bazaar** (milkandhoneybazaar. com; 3838 Main Rd; ⏰10am-5pm Wed-Sat, noon-5pm Sun); and the gourmet deli bar at **Provender** (www. provenderfinefoods.com; 3883 Main Rd; ⏰9am-5pm mid-Mar–Dec), where you can munch on giant cookies or forage for picnic fare.

Tiverton is an artists' colony so it also offers some of the best shopping in the state, including handwoven Shaker-style rugs from **Amy C Lund** (www. amyclundhandweaver.com; 3964 Main Rd; ⏰10am-5pm Wed-Sat, noon-5pm Sun) and museum-quality art from **Gallery 4** (www. gallery4tiverton.com; 3848 Main Rd; ⏰11am-4:30pm Wed-Sat, noon-4:30pm Sun).

 p143

The Drive >> Head north up Main St, leaving Tiverton and

its green fields behind you, and merge onto the westbound RI 138/RI 24 south, which leads you directly into Newport.

- - - - - - - - - - - -

 TRIP HIGHLIGHT

❸ Newport

Established by religious moderates fleeing persecution from Massachusetts Puritans, the 'new port' flourished to become the fourth richest city in the newly independent colony. Downtown, the Colonial-era architecture is beautifully preserved along with notable landmarks such as Washington Square's **Colony House**, where Rhode Island's declaration of independence was read in May 1776.

Just off the square, the gaslights of the **White Horse Tavern** (☎401-849-3600; www.whitehorsenewport.

BOB ROWAN PROGRESSIVE IMAGE/CORBIS ©

com; 26 Marlborough St), America's oldest tavern, still burn, and on Touro St, America's first synagogue, **Touro Synagogue** (www. tourosynagogue.org; 85 Touro St; tours adult/child $12/free), still stands. Tour the past on guided walks with **Newport History Tours** (www.newporthistorytours.org; tours adult/child $12/5; ⏰10am Thu-Sat May-Sep).

Fascinating as Newport's early history is, it struggles to compete with the town's latter-day success, when wealthy industrialists made Newport their summer vacation spot and built country 'cottages'

💬 LOCAL KNOWLEDGE: POLO IN PORTSMOUTH

Drab though the urban environs of Portsmouth may seem, in-the-know locals rate Portsmouth as a family-friendly destination. Not least because the polo matches hosted at Glen Farm make for a great family day out. Home to the **Newport Polo Club** (www.nptpolo.com; 715 East Main Rd; adult/child $12/free; ⏰gates open 1pm), the 700-acre 'farm' was assembled by New York businessman Henry Taylor, who sought to create a gentleman's country seat in the grand English tradition. In summer, the farm is host to the club's polo matches (check the website for dates), which are a perfect way to enjoy the property and get an authentic taste of Newport high life.

down lantern-lined
Bellevue Ave, modeled
on Italianate palazzos,
French chateaux and
Elizabethan manor
houses, and decorated
them with priceless
furnishings and
artworks. Tour the most
outstanding with the
Preservation Society
(www.newportmansions.org;
424 Bellevue Ave; adult/child
from $14.50/5.50).

✗ 🛏 p143

The Drive ≫ Leave Newport
by way of 10-mile Ocean Dr,
which starts just south of Fort
Adams and curls around the
southern shore, past the grand
mansions, and up Bellevue
Ave before intersecting with

Memorial Blvd. Turn right
here for a straight shot into
Middletown.

- - - - - - - - - -

④ Middletown

Flo's (4 Wave Ave; mains $2.50-
6; ☺ closed Jan-Feb) jaunty
red-and-white clam shack
would be enough reason
to visit Middletown,
which now merges
seamlessly with Newport.
But the best fried clams
in town taste better after
a day on **Second Beach**
(Sachuest Point Rd), the
largest and most beautiful
beach on Aquidneck
Island. Curving around
Sachuest Bay, it is backed
by the 450-acre **Norman**

Bird Sanctuary (www.
normanbirdsanctuary.org; 583
Third Beach Rd; adult/child
$6/3; ☺ 9am-5pm), which
teems with migrating
birds.

The Drive ≫ Leave Aquidneck
Island via East Main Rd, which
takes you north through the
suburbs of Middletown and
Portsmouth. After 6.5 miles,
pick up the RI 114 and cross
the bay via the scenic Mt Hope
suspension bridge. From here it's
a short 3-mile drive into Bristol.

- - - - - - - - - -

TRIP HIGHLIGHT

⑤ Bristol

One-fifth of all slaves
transported to America
were brought in Bristol

DETOUR: PRUDENCE ISLAND

Start: **⑤** Bristol

Idyllic **Prudence Island** (www.prudenceferry.com; adult/
child $6.60/2.90; ⊙6am-6pm Mon-Fri, 8am-6pm Sat &
Sun) sits in the middle of Narragansett Bay, an easy
25-minute ferry ride from Bristol. Originally used
for farming and later as a summer vacation spot
for families from Providence and New York, who
travelled here on the Fall River Line Steamer, the
island now has only 88 inhabitants. There are some
fine Victorian and Beaux Arts houses near Stone
Wharf, a lighthouse and a small store, but otherwise
it's wild and unspoiled. Perfect for mountain biking,
barbecues, fishing and paddling.

ships and by the 18th
century the town was one
of the country's major
commercial ports. The
world-class **Herreshoff
Marine Museum** (www.
herreshoff.org; 1 Burnside St;
adult/child $10/free; ⊙10am-
5pm May-Oct) showcases
some of America's finest
yachts, including eight
that were built for the
America's Cup.

Local resident
Augustus Van Wickle
bought a 72ft Herreshoff
yacht for his wife Bessie
in 1895, but having
nowhere suitable to moor
it, he then had to build
Blithewold Mansion (www.
blithewold.org; 101 Ferry Rd;
adult/child $11/3; ⊙10am-
4pm Tue-Sun mid-Apr–Oct).
The Arts and Crafts
mansion sits in a peerless
position on Narragansett
Bay and is particularly
lovely in spring, when the
daffodils line the shore.
Other local magnates

included slave trader
General George DeWolf
who built **Linden Place**
(☎401-253-0390; www.
lindenplace.org; 500 Hope St;
adult/child $8/5; ⊙10am-4pm
Tue-Sat May-Oct), famous
as a film location for *The
Great Gatsby*.

Bristol's **Colt State
Park** (www.riparks.com;
RI 114; ⊙8:30am-4:30pm)
is Rhode Island's most
scenic park, with its
entire western border
fronting Narragansett
Bay, fringed by 4 miles of
cycling trails and shaded
picnic tables.

🛏 p143

The Drive » From Bristol it's a
straight drive north along RI 114,
through the suburbs of Warren
and Barrington, to Providence.
After 17 miles, merge onto the
I-195 W, which takes you the
remaining 18 miles into the
center of town.

TRIP HIGHLIGHT

⑥ Providence

Providence, the first town
of religious liberal Roger
Williams' new Rhode
Island and Providence
Plantation colony, was
established so that 'no
man should be molested
for his conscience sake.'
Benefit Street's 'Mile
of History' gives a quick
lesson in the city's
architectural legacy with
over 100 Colonial, Federal
and Revival houses.
Amid them you'll find
William Strickland's 1838
Providence Athenaeum
(www.providenceathenaeum.
org; 251 Benefit St; admission
free; ⊙9am-7pm Mon-Thu, to
5pm Fri-Sun), inside which
plaster busts of Greek
gods and philosophers
preside over a collection
that dates to 1753.

Atop the hill sits **Brown
University**, with its Gothic
and Beaux Arts buildings
arranged around the
College Green. Nearby is
John Brown House (www.
rihs.org; 52 Power St; adult/child
$10/6; ⊙tours 1:30pm & 3pm
Tue-Fri, 10:30am-3pm Sat Apr-
Dec), which President John
Quincy Adams thought to
be 'the most magnificent
and elegant mansion...on
this continent.'

End the tour with a nod
toward the bronze statue
of *Independent Man,*
which graces the pearly
white dome of the **Rhode
Island State House**.

✕ 🛏 p143

Eating & Sleeping

Little Compton ❶

🛏 Stone House   Inn $$$

(📞401-635-2222; www.stonehouse1854.com; 122 Sakonnet Point; r $275-400; P 🛜) With its Italianate architecture, granite block and sandstone construction and frilly front porch, fabulous Stone House sits next to the best beaches in town and serves up lovely ocean views.

Tiverton ❷

✕ Evelyn's Drive-In   American $$

(www.evelynsdrivein.com; 2335 Main Rd; mains $5-18; ⏱lunch & dinner Apr-Sep; P 👪) Park on the crushed-shell driveway and eat mildly spiced lobster rolls and burgers on hot-dog buns. The gray clapboard building sits right next to the Nanaquaket Pond.

Newport ❸

✕ Fluke   Seafood $$

(📞401-849-7778; flukewinebar.com; 41 Bowen's Wharf; mains $9-34; ⏱5-11pm Wed-Sat Nov-Apr, daily in summer) Fluke's Scandinavian-inspired dining room, with its blond wood and picture windows, offers an accomplished seafood menu featuring roasted monkfish, seasonal striped sea bass and plump scallops. Upstairs, the bar serves a rock-and-roll cocktail list.

✕ Mooring   Modern American $$

(📞401-846-2260; www.mooringrestaurant. com; Sayers Wharf; mains $6-36; ⏱lunch & dinner; P 👪) You can't get a better view of Narragansett Bay than from the mahogany deck of the Mooring. The grand dining room, with its nautical-themed artwork and marble-topped bar, was once home to the New York Yacht Club.

🛏 Marshall Slocum
Guesthouse   B&B $$

(📞401-841-5120; www.marshallslocuminn.com; 29 Kay St; r $79-275; P ✳🛜) This clapboard

Colonial house, a former parsonage, is situated between Historic Hill and downtown Newport. The period feel is preserved in the interiors, and rooms feature canopy beds, wide wooden floorboards and shuttered windows.

Bristol ❺

🛏 Governor Bradford Inn   Inn $$

(📞401-254-1745; www.mounthopefarm.org; 250 Metacom Ave; r $125-275; P ✳) Administered by the Mount Hope Trust, the Governor Bradford offers four individually styled rooms in a 300-year-old Georgian farmhouse. Once owned by the Haffenreffer family, of beer-brewing fortune, the house sits on 200 acres of pristine farmland.

Providence ❻

✕ Haven Brothers Diner   Diner $

(Washington St; meals $5-10; ⏱5pm-3am) This diner sits on the back of a truck. Legend has it that the business started as a horse-drawn lunch wagon in 1893. Climb up the rickety ladder to get basic diner fare alongside politicians and college kids.

✕ Local 121   Modern American $$$

(www.local121.com; 121 Washington St; mains $16-32; ⏱lunch Tue-Sun, dinner daily) This old-school restaurant, housed in the former Dreyfus hotel, has an unpretentious grandeur. The menu is seasonal, including a local scallop po'boy and duck ham pizza. The tap room is a great place for a casual meal.

🛏 Providence
Biltmore   Historic Hotel $$$

(📞401-421-0700; www.providencebiltmore.com; 11 Dorrance St; r/ste $146/279; P @) Make like an industrialist and check into the granddaddy of Providence's hotels. The Biltmore dates to the 1920s and retains the regal atmosphere in its dark wood details, curving staircases and heavy chandeliers.

South Hero Greet sunrise with postcard-perfect marina views

Lake Champlain Byway

10

Traditional Vermont life meets foodie hub Burlington with sips of Magic Hat beer. Add a spin around islands hugging the Canadian border and your snap-happy self won't be able to stop smiling.

TRIP HIGHLIGHTS

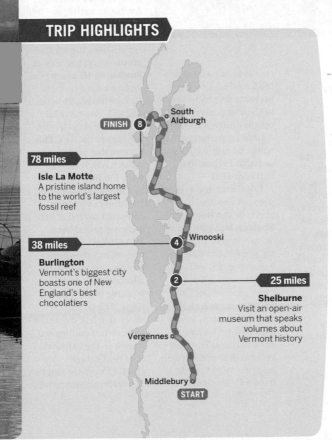

FINISH 8 — South Aldburgh

78 miles

Isle La Motte
A pristine island home to the world's largest fossil reef

4 Winooski

38 miles

Burlington
Vermont's biggest city boasts one of New England's best chocolatiers

2

25 miles

Shelburne
Visit an open-air museum that speaks volumes about Vermont history

Vergennes

Middlebury
START

2–3 DAYS
78 MILES / 125KM

GREAT FOR...

BEST TIME TO GO

June to October for long, summery days and abundant leaf-peeping opportunities.

 ESSENTIAL PHOTO

Grab a shot at water's edge on Isle La Motte.

 BEST FOR FOODIES

Sample the state's most famous beer export and indulge in Burlington's vibrant restaurant scene.

145

Lake Champlain Byway

Vermont's vibrant college towns and the state's most fascinating museum begin this official scenic byway. Then, unfolding like a forgotten ribbon just north of Burlington, you encounter the desolate Champlain Islands, a 27-mile stretch of four largely undeveloped isles – all connected by US 2 and a series of bridges and causeways filled with history and a touch of wine tasting.

❶ Middlebury

In 1800 Middlebury College was founded, and it has been synonymous with the town ever since. Despite Middlebury's history of marble quarrying, most buildings in the town's center are built of brick, wood and schist. **Middlebury College buildings**, however, are made with white marble and gray limestone and the campus is a stunning example of a traditional Vermont college.

The **Middlebury College Museum of Art** (www.middlebury.edu/arts/museum; S Main St, VT 30; admission free; ☺10am-5pm Mon-Fri, noon-5pm Sat & Sun, closed Mon mid-Aug–early Sep & mid-Dec–early Jan) presents fine collections of Cypriot pottery, 19th-century European and American sculpture, and works by luminaries such as Pablo Picasso and Salvador Dalí.

Local and downright peculiar objects sit pretty at the **Henry Sheldon Museum** (www.henrysheldonmuseum.org; 1 Park St; adult/child 6-18yr/senior $5/3/4.50; ☺10am-5pm Tue-Sat year-round, 1-5pm Sun Jun-Oct). Sheldon, a town clerk and storekeeper, avidly collected 19th-century Vermontiana. The 1829 Federal mansion-turned-museum runs the gamut from folk art to bric-a-brac to an upstairs room devoted to curios such as a cigar holder made of chicken claws and Sheldon's own teeth.

✕ ⊨ p151

The Drive » Head north along Rte 7. Three miles past Middlebury, stop off at New Haven's Lincoln Peak Vineyard (www.lincolnpeakvineyard.com) for wine tasting or a picnic lunch on its wraparound porch.

- - - - - - - - - - - - -

TRIP HIGHLIGHT

❷ Shelburne

Feast your eyes on the stunning array of 17th- to 20th-century American artifacts – folk art, textiles, toys, tools, carriages, furniture – spread over the 45-acre grounds and gardens at **Shelburne Museum** (www.shelburnemuseum.org; Rte 7; adult/child $22/11, tickets valid for 2 consecutive days; ☺10am-5pm daily May-Oct, Tue-Sun Nov-Dec; ♿). This remarkable place is set up as a mock village, with 150,000 objects housed in 39 buildings. Highlights include a full-size covered bridge, a classic round barn, an 1871 lighthouse, a one-room schoolhouse, a railway station with a locomotive, and a working blacksmith's forge. The collection's sheer size lets you tailor your visit. Families are drawn to the carousel, the Owl Cottage children's center and the *Ticonderoga* steamship,

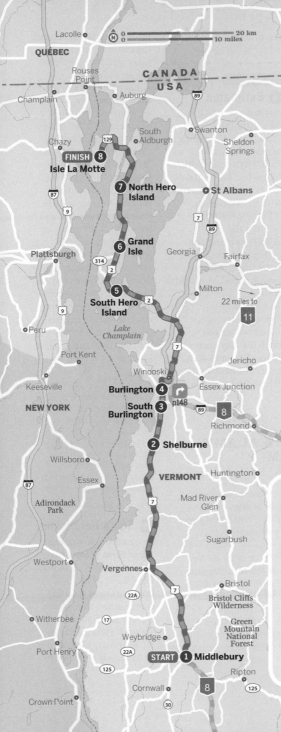

while aficionados of quilts or, say, duck decoys can spend hours investigating their personal passion. Indeed, the buildings themselves are exhibits. Many were moved here from other parts of New England to ensure their preservation.

🛏 p151

The Drive » Continue north on Rte 7 until you reach South Burlington.

- - - - - - - - - - - - - - -

❸ South Burlington

One of the pioneers – and among the most famous – of Vermont's microbreweries is **Magic Hat Brewery** (www.magichat.net; 5 Bartlett Bay Rd; tours free; ⏲10am-6pm Mon-Sat, noon-5pm Sun), which started brewing in 1995. The 'Artifactory' exudes an infectious creative energy, with over 20 varieties flowing from four-dozen taps.

S LINK YOUR TRIP

8 Fall Foliage Tour
Intersect with the Fall Foliage tour in Burlington.

11 Vermont's Spine: Route 100
Drive south on I-89 to hook up with VT 100 at Waterbury.

Half-hour tours (check the website for tour schedule) take you through the history of Vermont breweries and Magic Hat's role, how it makes its beer and keeps environmental impact as low as possible, and its involvement in the community (such as the annual Magic Hat Mardi Gras and its support of the performing arts). Guides happily answer any question you have, such as who writes the sayings on the inside of each bottle cap. You can enjoy free tastes both before and after the tour. Must-trys are the trademark No 9 (pale ale with a hint of apricot); the Orlio organic brews; and Odd Notion, a whimsically changing seasonal creation.

The Drive ⟩⟩ Continue north on Rte 7 to Burlington.

TRIP HIGHLIGHT

④ Burlington

Perched overlooking the glistening Lake Champlain, Vermont's largest city would be a small city in most other states, but Burlington's size is one of its charms. With the University of Vermont (UVM) swelling the city by 13,400 students, and a vibrant cultural and social life, Burlington has a spirited, youthful character. And when it comes to nightlife, this is Vermont's epicenter.

Just before you reach the city center, a chocolate stop is in order. The aroma of rich melted cocoa is intoxicating as you enter the gift shop next to the glass wall that overlooks the small factory at **Lake Champlain Chocolates** (www. lakechamplainchocolates.com; 750 Pine St; tours free; ⏰ tours on the hour 10am-2pm Mon-Fri, shop 9am-6pm Mon-Sat, 11am-5pm Sun). Take the tour to get the history of the chocolatier and ample samples to taste test the gooey goodness. Oh, and this shop is the only one with factory-seconds shelves containing stacks of chocolate at a discount. It tastes the same as the pretty stuff but for cosmetic reasons can't be sold at regular price. The cafe serves coffee drinks and its own luscious ice cream.

 p151

The Drive ⟩⟩ Cast off for the Champlain Islands, cruising 10 miles north of Burlington on I-89 to exit 17, then west on Hwy 2. After Sand Bar State Park – a great picnic and swimming spot – cross the causeway and look for the photo-perfect parking island halfway across.

⑤ South Hero Island

Vermont's first vineyard, **Snow Farm Winery** (www. snowfarm.com; 190 West Shore Rd; ⏰11am-5pm May-Nov) boasts a sweet tasting room tucked away down a dirt road (look for the signs off Hwy 2). Sample its award-winning whites or have a sip of Ice Wine

DETOUR: INTERVALE & ADAM'S BERRY FARM

Start: ④ Burlington

Here, in the midst of Vermont's most urban corridor, you'd scarcely expect to discover pristine farmland. Surprise! Five miles north on Hwy 7, tucked between the urban hubs of Burlington and Winooski, the **Intervale Center** (180 Intervale Rd; www.intervale.org) is a positively bucolic complex of community gardens and farms hugging the fringes of the Winooski River. Descending from Hwy 7, Intervale Rd turns to dirt and passes through a lush tunnel of trees to **Adam's Berry Farm** (📞802-578-9093; http://adamsberryfarm. com; Intervale Rd, Burlington), where pick-your-own strawberry, blueberry and raspberry operations run from late May till the first frost (daily hours vary; call to confirm).

Grand Isle Pear harvest

149

LOCAL KNOWLEDGE: ALLENHOLM ORCHARDS

Just outside the town of South Hero, grab a Creemee (that's Vermont-speak for soft-serve ice cream) at **Allenholm Orchards** (www.allen holm.com; 150 South St; ⊙9am-5pm late May-Christmas Eve; ⓘ), or pick a few apples for the road ahead. This perennially popular orchard sponsors Vermont's largest apple festival (South Hero Applefest) every October.

in the rustic barn (three tastes are free), or drop by on Thursday evening for the free **concert series** (⊙6:30-8:30pm Jun-Sep) on the lawn next to the vines – you can expect anything from jazz to folk to light rock-and-roll.

The Drive » Continue north on Hwy 2.

⑥ Grand Isle

The **Hyde Log Cabin** (228 Hwy 2; adult/child $3/free; ⊙11am-5pm Fri-Sun Jun–mid-Oct), the oldest (1783) log cabin in Vermont and one of the oldest in the US, is worth a short stop to see how settlers lived in the 18th century and to examine traditional household artifacts from Vermont.

The Drive » Continue north on Hwy 2.

⑦ North Hero Island

Boaters for miles around cast anchor at

popular general store **Hero's Welcome** (www. heroswelcome.com; 3537 Hwy 2; ⊙6:30am-6:30pm Mon-Sat, 7am-6pm Sun). The store's amusing wall display of 'World Time Zones' – four clocks showing identical hours for Lake Champlain's North Hero, South Hero, Grand Isle, and Isle La Motte – reflects the prevailing island-centric attitude. Pick up a souvenir, grab a sandwich or coffee and snap some pics on the outdoor terrace overlooking the boat landing.

✕ 🛏 p151

The Drive » From Hwy 2, head west 4 miles on Rte 129 to Isle La Motte.

TRIP HIGHLIGHT

⑧ Isle La Motte

Pristine Isle La Motte is one of the most historic of all the Champlain Islands. Signs along its western shore signal its traditional importance

as a crossroads for Native Americans, and French explorer Samuel de Champlain landed here in 1609.

Meander around the loop road hugging the coast, stopping at **St Anne's Shrine** (www. saintannesshrine.org; 92 St Anne's Rd; ⊙shrine mid-May–mid-Oct, grounds year-round), on the site of Fort St Anne, Vermont's oldest settlement. Though it is welcoming to all, this is a religious place, so be respectful of those who come to pray. The site features a striking granite statue of Samuel de Champlain, and its waterfront has spectacular views and a large picnic area.

Isle La Motte is also home to the 20-acre **Fisk Quarry Preserve** (www. ilmpt.org; West Rd; ⊙dawn-dusk), the world's largest fossil reef, 4 miles south of St Anne's Shrine. Half a million years old, the reef once provided limestone for Radio City Music Hall and Washington's National Gallery. Interpretive trails explain the history of the quarry.

Eating & Sleeping

Middlebury ❶

✗ American Flatbread
Pizza $$

(☎802-388-3300; www.americanflatbread.
com/restaurants/middlebury-vt; 137 Maple St;
flatbreads $14-20; ⊙5-9pm Tue-Sat, to 3pm
Sun) In a cavernous old marble building with a
blazing fire, which keeps things cozy in winter.
The menu is limited to farm-fresh salads, local
microbrews and custom-made flatbreads. Don't
call it pizza or they'll come after you with the
paddle.

🛏 Middlebury Inn
Inn $$

(☎802-388-4961, 800-842-4666; www.
middleburyinn.com; 14 Court House Sq, Rte 7;
r $139-279; 🛜) This inn's fine old main building
(1827) has beautifully restored formal public
rooms and charming guest rooms. The adjacent
Porter Mansion, with Victorian-style rooms, is
full of architectural details. Lower-priced guest
rooms are in the less interesting modern motel
units (basic spaces, no antiques).

Shelburne ❷

🛏 Inn at Shelburne Farms
Inn $$$

(☎802-985-8498; www.shelburnefarms.org/
staydine; 1611 Harbor Rd, Shelburne; r $289-
523, with shared bathroom $169-245, cottage
$289-430, guesthouse $436-926; 🛜) One of
New England's top 10 places to stay, this inn was
once the summer mansion of the wealthy Webb
family. It now welcomes guests with rooms in the
gracious country manor house by the lakefront.

Burlington ❹

✗ August First
Bakery & Cafe
Bakery, Pizzeria $$

(www.augustfirstvt.com; 149 South Champlain
St; meals $9-14; ⊙7:30am-5pm Mon-Fri,
8am-3pm Sat) Most days this bakery-cafe is

a hot spot for a cup of coffee, sandwiches and
its famous breads. Flatbread Friday is a huge
hit – the tables are pushed together and there is
pizza and beer, with unlimited flatbread (pizza
on a flat crust) and salads for $12 ($8 for kids
10 and under). Expect anything from traditional
pepperoni to more exotic gorgonzola and pear
pizzas and everything in between.

✗ Blue Bird Tavern
International $$

(☎802-540-1786; http://bluebirdvermont.
com; 86 Paul St; meals $9-25; ⊙ lunch &
dinner) Nominated for a James Beard award
within its first year of operation, Burlington's
most experimental locavore eatery features a
seasonal menu with small and large plates –
expect anything from hot oysters with seaweed
aioli and maple sugar to mac 'n' cheese with
peas, morel mushrooms and snails. Fries come
with homemade ketchup and mayonnaise. Be
sure to book.

🛏 Sunset House B&B
B&B $$

(☎802-864-3790; www.sunsethousebb.com; 78
Main St; r $120-170; 🛜) This sweet B&B features
four tidy guest rooms. Bathrooms are shared,
and there's a small common kitchen. This is the
only B&B smack in the center of downtown.

North Hero Island ❼

🛏 North Hero House
B&B $$

(☎802-372-4732; Hwy 2; www.northherohouse.
com; r from $140; 🛜) This country inn sits right
across from the water, with quilt-filled rooms,
many with private porch and four-poster bed,
and offers two appealing eating options. The
cozy restaurant serves New American cuisine
(meals $18 to $28; open for dinner) and boasts
water views. The fantastic outdoor Steamship
Pier Bar & Grill (sandwiches $10 to $18; open for
lunch and dinner June to September) feeds you
kababs, burgers and lobster rolls with a fresh
cocktail, smack on the pier, the water glistening
beside you.

COLD HOLLOW CIDER MILL

Legendary Cider Donuts

eal Vermont "Agri"-tainmer

Vermont's Spine: Route 100

11

Yodeling pickles (yes, really), peaceful villages, otherworldly gondola rides and scoops of America's most famous ice cream keep you dazzled and dreamy along Rte 100.

TRIP HIGHLIGHTS

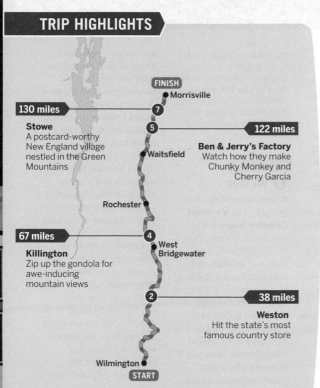

FINISH
● Morrisville

130 miles ⑦

Stowe
A postcard-worthy
New England village
nestled in the Green
Mountains

⑤ ◀ **122 miles**

Ben & Jerry's Factory
Watch how they make
Chunky Monkey and
Cherry Garcia

● Waitsfield

● Rochester

67 miles ④

● West
Bridgewater

Killington
Zip up the gondola for
awe-inducing
mountain views

② ◀ **38 miles**

Weston
Hit the state's most
famous country store

Wilmington ●
START

3–4 DAYS
153 MILES / 246KM

GREAT FOR...

BEST TIME TO GO

May to October for
snow-free roads and
sun-filled days.

ESSENTIAL PHOTO

The 360-degree views
from the K1 Gondola
above Killington.

☑ **BEST FOR FAMILIES**

Poke around the games
at the Weston country
store and take a Ben &
Jerry's Factory tour.

153

11 Vermont's Spine: Route 100

Spanning Vermont from bottom to top, Vermont's revered Rte 100 cuts through the state's most legendary ski resorts, past its best-known and kooky general stores with the verdant Green Mountains always at its side. This drive takes you on a slow meander through the state, though you might speed up in anticipation of the Ben & Jerry's Factory tour looming on the final stretch of road.

1 Wilmington

Chartered in 1751, Wilmington is the winter and summer gateway to Mt Snow, one of New England's best ski resorts and an excellent summertime mountain-biking and golfing spot. There are no main sights per se but the **Historic District** on W Main St contains prime examples of 18th- and 19th-century architecture and is chock full of restaurants and boutiques; the bulk of the village is on the National Register of Historic Places. This is an excellent base to stay overnight and grab a bite before your journey up north.

✗ ⌂ p161

The Drive » Driving north on Rte 100, first you'll pass through ski country (look for Mt Snow on your left) and sleepy hamlets – Jamaica is a prime dose of rural Vermont, with a country store and several antique shops.

TRIP HIGHLIGHT

2 Weston

Picturesque Weston is home to the **Vermont Country Store** (www.vermontcountrystore.com; Rte 100; ◷9am-5:30pm), founded in 1946 and the state's most famous country store. It's a time warp from a simpler era when goods were made to last, and quirky products with appeal had a home. Here you'll discover electronic yodeling plastic pickles, taffeta slips and three kinds of shoe stretchers with customizable bunion and corn knobs – in short, everything you didn't know you needed. Additionally, it carries small toys and games of yesteryear Americana (think wooden pick-up-sticks and vintage tiddlywinks), plus entire sections filled with candy jars and cases of Vermont cheese.

Crowds flock to the renowned summer theater at the **Weston Playhouse** (☏802-824-5288; www.westonplayhouse.org; 703 Main St; tickets $25-50; ◷performances late Jun-early Sep), Vermont's oldest professional theater, just off the gazeboed circular

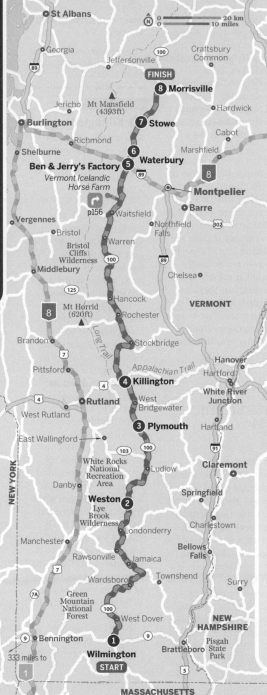

town green. The views upstream to Weston's waterfall and 19th-century mill are the stuff of tourist legend. Recent shows include Arthur Miller's *Death of a Salesman* (starring Christopher Lloyd of *Back to the Future* fame), *Fiddler on the Roof* and child-friendly *You're a Good Man, Charlie Brown.*

The Drive ≫ Continue north on Rte 100. At Plymouth Union, veer off to the right onto Rte 100A for a few miles until you reach Plymouth Center.

❸ Plymouth

Gazing across the high pastures of Plymouth, you feel a bit like Rip Van Winkle – only it's the past you've woken up to. President Calvin Coolidge's boyhood home looks much as it did a century ago, with homes, barns, a church,

LINK YOUR TRIP

8 **Fall Foliage Tour**
Drive west from Rte 100 to pick up the Fall Foliage Tour at Manchester or Lake Champlain.

1 **Finger Lakes Loop**
From Wilmington, drive west across the border into New York, then pick up I-88 to Ithaca.

a one-room schoolhouse and a general store gracefully arrayed among old maples on a bucolic hillside. At Plymouth's heart is the preserved **President Calvin Coolidge State Historic Site** (www.historicvermont. org/coolidge; 3780 Rte 100A; adult/child/family $7.50/2/20; ⏰9:30am-5pm late May–mid-Oct). The village's streets seem sleepy today, but the museum tells a tale of an earlier America filled with elbow grease and perseverance. Tools for blacksmithing, woodworking, butter making and hand-laundering are indicative of the hard work and grit it took to wrest a

living from Vermont's stony pastures. As a boy, Calvin hayed with his grandfather and kept the wood box filled.

Originally co-founded by Coolidge's father, Plymouth's **Plymouth Artisan Cheese** (www. plymouthartisancheese. com; 106 Messer Hill Rd; ⏰9am-5pm) recently resumed production of a traditional farmhouse cheddar known as granular curd cheese. Its distinctively sharp tang and grainy texture are reminiscent of the wheel cheese traditionally found at general stores throughout Vermont. Visitors are invited to browse the photographs and antiques from another era, as well as

observe the cheesemaker at work.

The Drive ≫ Drive back along Rte 100A and turn right to return to Rte 100 N.

- - - - - - - - - - - - -

TRIP HIGHLIGHT

❹ Killington

The largest ski resort in the east, Killington spans seven mountains, highlighted by 4241ft Killington Peak, the second highest in Vermont. It operates the largest snowmaking system in North America and its numerous outdoor activities – from winter skiing and boarding to summer mountain biking and hiking – are all centrally located on the mountain. Killington Resort, the East Coast's answer to Vail, runs the efficient **K1-Express Gondola** (☎800-621-6867; www. killington.com; round-trip $15; ⏰10am-5pm late Jun-early Sep & Oct 1-8, Sat & Sun only early-late Sep), which in winter transports up to 3000 skiers per hour in heated cars along a 2.5-mile cable and is the highest lift in Vermont. In summer and fall it whisks you to impeccable vantage points above the mountains: leaf-peeping atop the cascade rainbow of copper, red and gold in foliage season is truly magical.

Note that, outside the winter peak, establishments restrict

DETOUR: VERMONT ICELANDIC HORSE FARM

Start: ❹ **Killington**

Icelandic horses are one of the oldest, and some say most versatile, breeds in the world. They're also friendly and unbelievably affectionate beasts, and are fairly easy to ride even for novices – they tend to stop and think (rather than panic) if something frightens them. The **Vermont Icelandic Horse Farm** (☎802-496-7141; www.icelandichorses.com; N Basin Rd, Waitsfield; rides 1-3hr $50-100, full day incl lunch $195; ⏰riding tours by appointment), 3 miles west of Rte 100 (the tarmac ends and becomes a dirt road), takes folks on one-to three-hour or full-day jaunts year-round; it also offers two- to five-day inn-to-inn treks (some riding experience required). The farm also runs **Mad River Inn** (www.madriverinn.com; r incl breakfast $125-175), a pleasant inn a short trot away.

their opening times. Be sure to call in advance to confirm hours.

 p161

The Drive >> Continue on Rte 100 N. Roughly 10 miles past Rochester, the road enters a narrow and wild corridor of protected land. A little pullout on the left provides viewing access to pretty Moss Glen Falls. A mile or so later, the small ponds of Granville Gulf comprise one of the state's most accessible moose-watching spots (the best chance of seeing these big critters is at dawn or dusk).

TRIP HIGHLIGHT

❺ Ben & Jerry's Factory

No trip to Vermont would be complete without a visit to the **Ben & Jerry's Factory** (www.benjerry.com; 1281 Waterbury-Stowe Rd/Rte 100, Waterbury; tours $4; ⏰9am-9pm late Jun–mid-Aug, to 7pm mid-Aug–late Oct, 10am-6pm late Oct-late Jun), the biggest production center for America's most famous ice cream. Yeah, the ice-cream making is interesting, but a visit to the factory also explains how school pals Ben and Jerry went from a $5 ice-cream-making correspondence course to a global enterprise and offers a glimpse of the fun in-your-face culture that made these ice-cream pioneers so successful. You're treated to a (very) small free taste at the end, but if

you need a larger dose beeline for the on-site scoop shop.

Quaintly perched on a knoll overlooking the parking lot, the Ben & Jerry's Flavor Graveyard's neat rows of headstones pay silent tribute to flavors that flopped, like Makin' Whoopie Pie and Dastardly Mash. Each memorial is lovingly inscribed with the flavor's brief life span on the grocery store of this earth and a poem in tribute. Rest in Peace Holy Cannoli, 1997–1998! Adieu Miss Jelena's Sweet Potato Pie, 1992–1993!

The Drive >> Continue along Rte 100 for a few miles and you'll start to enter the commercial end of Waterbury – your next stop is on your right.

---

❻ Waterbury

The waft of fresh pressed cider hits you before you reach the door: see how it's made at **Cold Hollow Cider Mill** (www.coldhollow.

com; ⏰8am-7pm Jul-late Oct, to 6pm late Oct-Jun), which features a working cider press to make its cloudy nonalcoholic cider and famous cider doughnuts (guaranteed love at first bite). The cider itself tastes so crisp and fresh you'd swear there was a spigot coming right out of the apple. The gift shop is packed with the most inventive gourmet goodies in town, including corn relish, horseradish jam and piccalilli.

Afterward, walk across the parking lot to the **Grand View Winery** (www.grandviewwinery.com; 4 tastes $2; ⏰11am-5pm) for sips of its award-winning wines. Options vary by season but on our visit we sampled the delicate non-oaky Riesling, strawberry rhubarb fruit wine and, for the first time, dandelion wine. Our verdict? Aromatic and slightly sweet, it's springtime in a glass.

The Drive >> Wipe that ice-cream smile off your face and

LOCAL KNOWLEDGE
WILL WIQUIST,
GREEN MOUNTAIN
CLUB

One of the easiest walking trails in the
area is the Short Trail, right behind
the **Green Mountain Club visitor
center** (www.greenmountainclub.org; 4711
Waterbury-Stowe Rd, Waterbury; ⊙9am-
5pm mid-May–mid-Oct, 10am-5pm Mon-Fri
mid-Oct–mid-May). **It's a fairly flat loop
with picnic areas, and boasts views
of Mt Worcester and Stowe Pinnacle
on the way back. Another option
is the Kirchner Woods Trail** (www.
stowelandtrust.org; Taber Hill Rd), **where
you enjoy fine mountain views while
roaming among hardwoods, maple
trees and a working sugar house.**

Top: Soak up the sun at a resort in Stowe
Left: Hiker takes in Vermont views
Right: Stowe

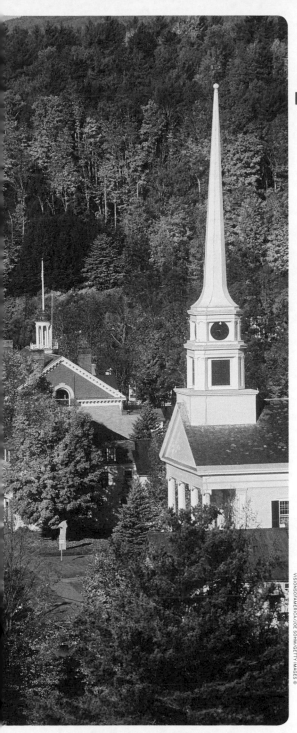
VISIONSOFAMERICA/JOE SOHM/GETTY IMAGES ©

replace it with an ear-to-ear grin as you ascend Rte 100 to the magnificent Vermont ski village of Stowe.

- - - - - - - - - - -

TRIP HIGHLIGHT

❼ Stowe

In a cozy valley where the West Branch River flows into the Little River and mountains rise to the sky in all directions, the quintessential Vermont village of Stowe (founded in 1794) bustles quietly. Nestled in the Green Mountain National Forest, the highest point in Vermont, Mt Mansfield (4393ft), towers in the background, juxtaposed against the town, making this *the* classic Vermont picture-postcard scene. With more than 200 miles of cross-country ski trails, some of the finest mountain biking and downhill skiing in the east, and world-class hiking, this is a natural mecca for adrenaline junkies and active families.

In addition to winter snow sports, **Stowe Mountain Resort** (www. stowe.com; Mountain Rd) opens from spring through to fall with **gondola sky rides** (adult/child $25/17; ⏲10am-4:30pm late Jun–mid-Oct), an alpine slide (adult/child $18/16; ⏲10:30am-4:30pm late Jun–mid-Oct, Sat & Sun only Sep-Oct) and a scenic auto **toll road** (per car $28; ⏲late May–mid-Oct) that

NEW ENGLAND TRIPS **11** VERMONT'S SPINE: ROUTE 100

zigzags to the top of Mt Mansfield.

If *The Sound of Music* is one of your favorite things, the hilltop **Trapp Family Lodge** (www.trappfamily.com; 700 Trapp Hill Rd) boasts sprawling views and oodles of activities, such as hiking, horse-drawn sleigh and carriage rides, lodge tours detailing the family history (often led by a member of the Trapp family), summer concerts on their meadow and frothy goodness at the on-site Trapp Family Brewery.

 p161

The Drive 》 Continue along Rte 100 – you'll pass pretty Christmas-tree farms on either side before reaching your final stop.

THE VERMONT REPUBLIC 1777–91

Vermont held its ground as an independent republic for 14 years (eat your heart out, Texas!) before joining the union. In July 1777, Vermonters drafted the first constitution to outlaw slavery, authorize a public school system and give every man (regardless of property ownership) the right to vote. In recent years, the Second Vermont Republic movement has begun clamoring for secession. Vermont's independent spirit lives on!

❽ Morrisville

When you see the logo bearing a Kokopelli flute-player off to the left, you know you've arrived at **Rock Art Brewery** (www.rockartbrewery.com; 632 Laporte Rd/Rte 100; 4-5 tastes in souvenir glass $4; ⊘9am-6pm Mon-Sat, free tours Fri & Sat 2pm & 4pm). Pop into the friendly tasting room and brewery for samples, including the signature American Red, a malty pale ale that also goes by the nickname 'Super Glide,' because, you know, it glides down oh-so-easily.

Eating & Sleeping

Wilmington ❶

✗ Wahoo's Eatery   American $

(☎802-464-0110; VT 9; burgers, sandwiches &
wraps $5-7.25; ⊙ lunch & dinner May-Oct) This
local institution is a mere roadside snack shack,
less than a mile west of VT 100, but it whips up
quality burgers (made with grass-fed Vermont
beef), hand-cut fries and handmade conch
fritters, plus wraps, sandwiches, hot dogs,
salads and ice cream.

⊨ Old Red Mill Inn & Restaurant   Inn $

(☎802-464-3700; www.oldredmill.com; Rte
100 N; s $55-65, d $65-90; ⊙ closed Apr–mid-
Jun & Nov; 🛜) This converted former sawmill
overlooking the Deerfield River offers simple
rooms (chunky wood furnishings, checkered
bedspreads). Original millworks occupy
common areas and on-site food ($10 to $25)
varies by season: summer picnic fare is served
at Jerry's Deck Bar & Grill; in winter, the rustic
interior dining room takes over with hearty New
England favorites.

Killington ❹

✗ Sunup Bakery   Bakery $

(☎802-425-3865; www.sunupbakery.com; 2250
Killington Rd; dishes $4-8; ⊙ breakfast & lunch)
Fresh muffins and bagels are baked daily along
with yummy breakfast sandwiches, great soy
lattes and an emphasis on friendly (not fast)
service.

⊨ Inn at Long Trail   Inn $$

(☎802-775-7181; www.innatlongtrail.com; 709
US 4; r incl breakfast $79-125, ste $110-150; 🛜)
The first hotel expressly built (in 1938) as a ski
lodge, the rustic decor makes use of tree trunks

(the bar is fashioned from a single log). The
rooms are cozy and suites include fireplaces.

Stowe ❼

✗ Blue Moon Café   International $$$

(☎802-253-7006; www.bluemoonstowe.com;
35 School St; meals $18-31; ⊙ dinner Tue-Sun)
In a converted house with a little sun porch,
this intimate bistro is one of New England's
top restaurants. Mains change monthly, but
the contemporary cuisine usually includes
something like crab cakes, salmon dishes, steak
with chipotle and jicama or dishes utilizing
locally foraged mushrooms.

✗ Depot Street Malt Shoppe   Diner $

(☎802-253-4269; 57 Depot St; dishes $4-10;
⊙11:30am-9pm) Burgers, chocolate sundaes
and old-fashioned malteds reign at this fun,
1950s-themed restaurant. The egg creams hit
the spot in any season.

⊨ Brass Lantern Inn B&B   B&B $$

(☎802-253-2229; www.brasslanterninn.com; 71
Maple St, Rte 100; r incl breakfast $105-245; 🛜)
Just north of the village, this beautiful inn has
spacious, antique-laden rooms with handmade
quilts, some featuring fireplaces and views of
Mt Mansfield.

⊨ Trapp Family Lodge   Lodge $$$

(☎802-253-8511; www.trappfamily.com; 700
Trapp Hill Rd; r from $270; @🛜⛷) This is *the*
spot for taking a twirl and pretending you're
Julie Andrews. The Austrian-style chalet, built
by Maria von Trapp of *The Sound of Music* fame,
houses traditional lodge rooms, or you can rent
one of the modern villas or cozy guesthouses
scattered across the property. Prices are highly
variable; call to enquire.

Dartmouth College *Hallowed halls and tradition await at this campus*

Ivy League Tour

12

This trip celebrates history and education as it rolls between New England's Ivies, where campus tours sneak behind the gates for an up-close look at the USA's greatest universities.

TRIP HIGHLIGHTS

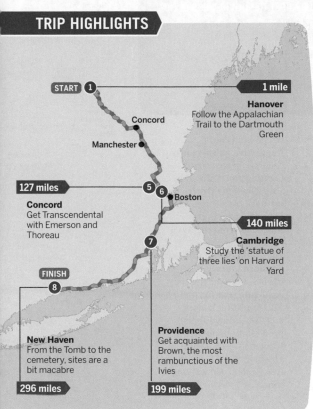

START ① ——————————— **1 mile**

Concord

Manchester ●

Hanover
Follow the Appalachian Trail to the Dartmouth Green

127 miles

⑤ ⑥ ● Boston

Concord
Get Transcendental with Emerson and Thoreau

140 miles

⑦

Cambridge
Study the 'statue of three lies' on Harvard Yard

FINISH
⑧

New Haven
From the Tomb to the cemetery, sites are a bit macabre

296 miles

Providence
Get acquainted with Brown, the most rambunctious of the Ivies

199 miles

**5 DAYS
296 MILES / 476KM**

GREAT FOR...

BEST TIME TO GO
Catch student-filled campuses September to November.

 ESSENTIAL PHOTO

Stand beside the statue of John Harvard, the man who didn't found Harvard.

✓ **BEST HISTORY**

Learn about the USA's oldest university during a Harvard tour.

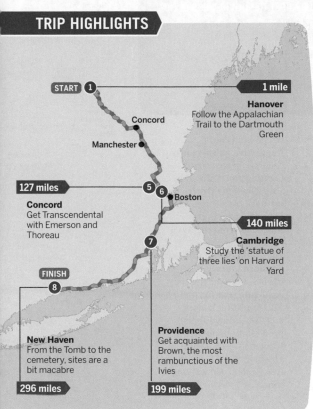

12 Ivy League Tour

What's most surprising about a tour of the Ivy League? The distinct personalities of the different campuses, which are symbiotically fused with their surrounding landscapes. Compare fresh-faced Dartmouth, with its breezy embrace of New Hampshire's outdoors, to enclaved Yale, its Gothic buildings fortressed against the urban wilds of New Haven. But the schools all share one trait – vibrant, diverse and engaged students who dispel any notions that they're out-of-touch elites.

TRIP HIGHLIGHT

❶ Hanover

When the first big snowfall hits **Dartmouth College**, an email blasts across campus, calling everyone to the central Green for a midnight snowball fight. The Green is also the site of elaborate ice sculptures during Dartmouth's **Winter Carnival**, a weeklong celebration that's been held annually for more than 100 years. North of the Green is **Baker Berry Library**, which holds an impressive mural called the *Epic of American Civilization*. Painted by Jose Clemente Orozco, it traces the course of civilization in the Americas from the Aztec era to modern times. At 4pm, stop by the adjacent **Sanborn Library**, where tea is served during the academic year for 10¢. This tradition honors a 19th-century English professor who invited students for chats and afternoon tea. For a free student-led **walking tour** (☎603-646-2875;

www.dartmouth.edu/visit) of the campus, stop by the admissions office on the 2nd floor of McNutt Hall on the west side of the Green. Call or check online to confirm departure times.

The collection at Dartmouth's **Hood Museum of Art** (www. hoodmuseum.dartmouth.edu; 6034 E Wheelock St; admission free; ⏰10am-5pm Tue & Thu-Sat, 10am-9pm Wed, noon-5pm Sun) includes nearly 70,000 items. The collection is particularly strong in American pieces, including Native American art. One highlight is a set of Assyrian reliefs dating to the 9th century BC. From the museum, turn left onto E Wheelock St and walk toward the Hanover Inn. You'll soon cross the **Appalachian Trail**, which runs through downtown. From here, it's 431 miles to Mt Katahdin in Maine.

✖ p171

LINK YOUR TRIP

9 Rhode Island: East Bay

Take a detour from Providence for a drive around the East Bay.

11 Vermont's Spine: Route 100

South of Hanover, take US 4 west to hook up with Rte 100 near Killington.

The Drive » From Hanover, follow NH 120 east to I-89 south. Take exit 117 to NH 4 east, following it to NH 4A. Turn right and follow NH 4A 3.5 miles to the museum.

---

❷ Enfield Shaker Museum

The Enfield Shaker site sits in stark contrast to today's college campuses. In fact, the two couldn't be more different – except for the required communal housing with a bunch of non-relatives. But a trip here is illuminating. Set in a valley overlooking Mascoma Lake, the Enfield Shaker site dates to the late 18th century. At its peak, some 300 members lived in Enfield. Farmers and craftspeople, they built impressive wood and brick buildings and took in converts, orphans and children of the poor – essential for the Shaker future since sex was not allowed in the pacifist, rule-abiding community. By the early 1900s the community had gone into decline and the last family left in 1917.

The **museum** (☎603-632-4346; www. shakermuseum.org; 447 NH 4A; adult/child 10-17 years $12/8; ☻10am-5pm Mon-Sat, noon-5pm Sun) centers on the Great Stone Dwelling, the largest Shaker dwelling house ever built. You can also explore the gardens and grounds.

If you're nice, the guide might let you ring the rooftop bell. Spend the night on the 3rd and 4th floor of the building. **Accommodations** (r $95-135; ☎) feature traditional Shaker furniture, but not phones or TVs, although there is wi-fi.

The Drive » Return to I-89 south. After 54 miles, take I-93 north 3 miles to exit 15E for I-393 east. From there, take exit 1 and follow the signs.

---

❸ Concord

New Hampshire's capital is a trim and tidy city with a wide Main St dominated by the striking **State House**, a granite-hewed 19th-century edifice topped with a glittering dome. New Hampshire schoolteacher Christa McAuliffe, chosen to be America's first teacher-astronaut, is honored at the **McAuliffe-Shepard Discovery Center** (☎603-271-7827; www.starhop.com; 2 Institute Dr; adult/child/senior $10/7/9; ☻10am-5pm Mon-Sat, 11:30am-5pm Sun plus 6:30-9pm Fri; ☗). She died in the *Challenger* explosion on January 28, 1986. The museum also honors New Hampshire native Alan B Shepard, a member of NASA's elite Mercury corps who became America's first astronaut in 1961. Intriguing exhibits chronicle their lives and spotlight aviation,

and earth and space sciences. There's also a planetarium.

The Drive » Return to I-93 south, passing through Manchester before entering Massachusetts. Follow I-495 south toward Lowell.

---

❹ Lowell

In the early 19th century, textile mills in Lowell churned out cloth by the mile, driven by the abundant waterpower of Pawtucket Falls. Today, the historic buildings in the city center – connected by the trolley and canal boats – comprise the Lowell National Historic Park, which gives a fascinating peek at the workings of a 19th-century industrial town. Stop first at the **Market Mills Visitors Center** (www.nps.gov/lowe; 246 Market St, Market Mills; ☻9am-5pm) to pick up a map and check out the general exhibits. Five blocks northeast along the river, the **Boott Cotton Mills Museum** (www.nps.gov/lowe; 115 John St; adult/child/student $6/3/4; ☻9:30am-5pm) has exhibits that chronicle the rise and fall of the industrial revolution in Lowell, including technological changes, labor movements and immigration. The highlight is a working weave room, with 88 power looms. A special exhibit on **Mill Girls &**

Immigrants (40 French St; admission free; ⏱1:30-5pm) examines the lives of working people, while seasonal exhibits are sometimes on display in other historic buildings around town.

The Drive » Take the Lowell Connector to US 3 heading south. In Billerica, exit to Concord Rd. Continue south on Concord Rd (MA 62) through Bedford. This road becomes Monument St and terminates at Monument Sq in Concord center. Walden Pond is about 3 miles south of Monument Sq, along Walden St (MA 126) south of MA 2.

TRIP HIGHLIGHT

⑤ Concord

Tall, white church steeples rise above ancient oaks in Colonial Concord, giving the town a stateliness that belies the American Revolution drama that occurred centuries ago. It is easy to see how so many writers found their inspiration here in the 1800s.

Ralph Waldo Emerson was the paterfamilias of literary Concord and the founder of the Transcendentalist movement (and, incidentally, a graduate of Harvard College). His home of nearly 50 years, the **Ralph Waldo Emerson Memorial House** (www.rwe.org; 28 Cambridge Turnpike; adult/child/senior & student $7/free/5; ⏱10am-4:30pm Thu-Sat, 1-4:30pm Sun mid-Apr–Oct), often hosted

his renowned circle of friends.

One of them was Henry David Thoreau (another Harvard grad), who put Transcendentalist beliefs into practice when he spent two years in a rustic cabin on the shores of **Walden Pond** (www.mass.gov/dcr; 915 Walden St). The glacial pond is now a state park, surrounded by acres of forest. A footpath circles the pond, leading to the site of Thoreau's cabin on the northeast side. Parking is $5.

✕ p171

The Drive » Take MA 2 east to its terminus in Cambridge. Go left on the Alewife Brook Pkwy (MA 16), then right on Massachusetts Ave and into Harvard Sq. Parking spaces are in short supply, but you can usually find one on the street around the Cambridge Common.

TRIP HIGHLIGHT

⑥ Cambridge

Founded in 1636 to educate men for the ministry, Harvard is America's oldest college. The geographic heart of the university – where red-brick buildings and leaf-covered paths exude

academia – is **Harvard Yard**. For maximum visual impact, enter the yard through the wrought-iron Johnston Gate, which is flanked by the two oldest buildings on campus, **Harvard Hall** and **Massachusetts Hall**.

The focal point of the yard is the **John Harvard statue**, by Daniel Chester French. Inscribed 'John Harvard, Founder of Harvard College, 1638,' it is commonly known as the 'statue of three lies': John Harvard was *not* the college's founder but its first benefactor; Harvard was actually founded in 1636; and the man depicted isn't even Mr Harvard himself! This symbol hardly lives up to the university's motto, *Veritas* (truth).

Most Harvard hopefuls rub the statue's shiny foot for good luck; little do they know that campus pranksters regularly use the foot like dogs use a fire hydrant.

So, what's the best thing about Harvard University? The architecture? The history? Arguably, it's the location. Overflowing with coffeehouses and pubs, bookstores and

ALL ABOUT HAAAHHHVAAAHHHD

Want to know more? Get the inside scoop from savvy students on the unofficial **Harvard Tour** (www.harvardtour.com; per person $10).

CHAD EHLERS/ALAMY ©

JOHN NORDELL/GETTY IMAGES ©

LOCAL KNOWLEDGE
EDDIE HORGAN, HARVARD '14; STUDENT MANAGER & GUIDE, THE HAHVAHD TOUR

In the northeast corner of Harvard's campus you'll find the Divinity School. One of our favorite secret spots at the school is the **Harvard Labyrinth**, used for contemplation, meditation and exercise. It's somewhat remote, but easy to find as it sits next to Andover Hall, the main Harvard Divinity School building. The labyrinth takes about 15 minutes to complete.

Top: Connecticut River, near Dartmouth College
Left: Harvard University
Right: Lofty heights at Harvard University

JOHN COLETTI/GETTY IMAGES ©

record stores, street musicians and sidewalk artists, panhandlers and professors, **Harvard Square** exudes energy, creativity and nonconformity – and it's all packed into a handful of streets between the university and the river. Spend an afternoon browsing bookstores, riffling through records and trying on vintage clothing; then camp out in a local cafe.

✗ 🛏 p171

The Drive >> Hop on Memorial Dr and drive east along the Charles River. At Western Ave, cross the river and follow the signs to I-90 heading east ($1.25 toll). Cruise through the tunnel (product of the notorious Big Dig) and merge with I-93 south. Follow I-93 south to I-95 south. Take I-95 to Providence.

TRIP HIGHLIGHT

❼ Providence

College Hill rises east of the Providence River, and atop it sits **Brown University** (www.brown.edu), the rambunctious younger child of an uptight New England household. Big brothers Harvard and Yale carefully manicure their public image, while the little black sheep of the family prides itself on staunch liberalism. Founded in 1764, Brown was the first American college to accept students regardless of religious affiliation, and the first to appoint an African American woman, Ruth Simmons, as president in 2001. Of its small 700-strong faculty, five Brown professors and two alumni have been honored as Nobel laureates.

The campus, consisting of 235 buildings, is divided into the Main Green and Lincoln Field. Enter through the wrought-iron **Van Wickle Gates** on College St. The oldest building on the campus is **University Hall**, a 1770 brick edifice, which was used as a barracks during the Revolutionary War. Free tours of the campus begin from the **Stephen Brown '62 Campus Center** (75 Waterman St). Check the website for times.

✖ p171

The Drive » Take Memorial Blvd out of Providence and merge with I-95 south. The generally pleasant tree-lined interstate will take you around the periphery of Groton, Old Lyme, Guilford and Madison, where you may want to stop for a coffee or snack. Exit at junction 47 for downtown New Haven.

- - - - - - - - - - -

 TRIP HIGHLIGHT

❽ New Haven

Gorgeous, Gothic Yale University is America's third-oldest university. Head to the **Yale University Visitor Center** (www.yale.edu/visitor; cnr Elm & Temple Sts; ⏰9am-4:30pm Mon-Fri, 11am-4pm Sat & Sun) to pick up a free map or take a free one-hour **tour** (⏰10:30am & 2pm Mon-Fri, 1:30pm Sat).

The tour does a good job of fusing historical and academic facts and passes by several standout monuments, including Yale's tallest building, **Harkness Tower**. Guides refrain, however, from mentioning the tombs scattered around the campus. No, these aren't filled with corpses; they're secret hangouts for senior students. The most notorious **Tomb** (64 High St) is the HQ for the Skull & Bones Club, founded in 1832. Its list of members reads like a who's who of high-powered politicos and financiers over the last two centuries.

The original burial ground for alumni, such as Yale's founder, the Reverend James Pierpont (1659–1714), is New Haven's pleasant **Green**, where an estimated 5000 to 10,000 people were buried before the cemetery was moved to **Grove Street Cemetery** (www.grovestreetcemetery.org; 227 Grove St; ⏰9am-4pm). The first chartered cemetery in the country, Grove St's geometric pattern echoes the nine squares of the city, and the elaborate sarcophagi, obelisks and headstones are arranged by family group. Around the turn of the century, Yale medical students would sneak in here at night to dig up bodies for dissection. You can simply join the free guided **tour** (11am Sat May-Nov).

✖ 🛏 p171

Eating & Sleeping

Hanover ❶

✕ Lou's   Diner $

(http://lousrestaurant.net; 30 S Main St; breakfast $7-11, lunch $8-10; ⊙ breakfast & lunch) A Dartmouth institution since 1947, this is Hanover's oldest restaurant and it's always packed with students. From the retro tables or Formica-topped counter, order diner fare that has a bit of panache. The baked goods are highly recommended.

Concord ❺

✕ Country Kitchen   Sandwiches $

(181 Sudbury Ave; sandwiches $5-10; ⊙ breakfast & lunch Mon-Fri) At lunchtime, this little yellow house often has a line out the door, which is testament to its tiny size and amazing sandwiches. The Thanksgiving sandwich, with carved turkey, is the hands-down favorite. No credit cards and no seating, save the picnic table out front.

Cambridge ❻

✕ Cafe Pamplona   Cafe $$

(12 Bow St; mains $8-15; ⊙ 11am-midnight) In a cozy cellar on a backstreet, this no-frills European cafe is the choice among old-time Cantabrigians. In addition to tea and coffee drinks, Pamplona has light snacks, such as gazpacho, sandwiches and biscotti.

⌂ Irving House   Guesthouse $$

(☎ 617-547-4600; www.irvinghouse.com; 24 Irving St; r with shared bath $135-205, with private bath $165-270; P ❋ @ 🛜) The 44 rooms at this property behind Harvard Yard vary, but every bed is covered with a quilt, and big windows let in plenty of light. Museum passes are a nice perk.

Providence ❼

✕ Louis Family Restaurant   Diner $

(www.louisrestaurant.org; 286 Brook St; mains $2-9; ⊙ daily; ⛩) Bleary-eyed students eat strawberry-banana pancakes and drink drip coffee at their favorite greasy spoon. The place is loaded with bad art and faded pictures, and prices are stuck in the 1960s, with spaghetti dinners for $5.

New Haven ❽

✕ Frank Pepe's Pizzeria   Pizzeria $

(www.pepespizzeria.com; 157 Wooster St; pizzas $5-20; ⊙ 4-10pm Mon, Wed & Thu, 11:30am-11pm Fri & Sat, 2:30-10pm Sun) Pepe's serves immaculate pizzas fired in a coal oven in frenetic surroundings, just as it has since 1925 when Frank Pepe got off the boat from Naples. His signature dish is the white-clam pizza, and it's well worth the wait.

⌂ Farnam Guesthouse   B&B $$

(☎ 203-562-7121; www.farnamguesthouse. com; 616 Prospect St; r $149-199; P ❋ 🛜) The Farnams have a long association with Yale as alums, donors and professors, and you can stay in their grand Georgian Colonial mansion in the best neighborhood in town. Expect old-world ambience, with Chippendale sofas, wingback chairs, Victorian antiques and plush oriental carpets.

Cadillac Mountain *Greet the morning with sublime views*

Acadia Byway

13

For adventurers, Mt Desert Island is hard to beat. Mountain hiking. Coastal kayaking. Woodland biking. Bird-watching. When you're done exploring, unwind by stargazing on the beach.

TRIP HIGHLIGHTS

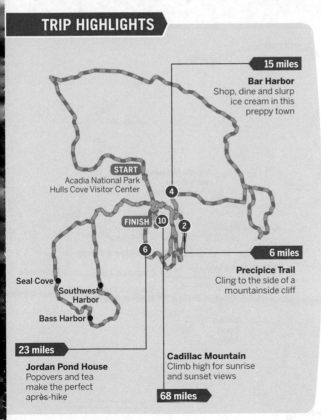

15 miles

Bar Harbor
Shop, dine and slurp ice cream in this preppy town

START
Acadia National Park
Hulls Cove Visitor Center

FINISH

6 miles

Precipice Trail
Cling to the side of a mountainside cliff

Seal Cove
Southwest Harbor
Bass Harbor

23 miles

Jordan Pond House
Popovers and tea make the perfect après-hike

Cadillac Mountain
Climb high for sunrise and sunset views

68 miles

**3 DAYS
68 MILES / 109KM**

GREAT FOR...

BEST TIME TO GO
May through October for good weather and open facilities.

ESSENTIAL PHOTO
Capture that sea-and-sunrise panorama from atop Cadillac Mountain.

BEST FOR OUTDOORS
Hike a 'ladder trail' up a challenging cliff.

13 Acadia Byway

Drivers and hikers alike can thank John D Rockefeller Jr and other wealthy landowners for the aesthetically pleasing bridges, overlooks and stone steps that give Acadia National Park its artistic oomph. Rockefeller in particular, before donating the lands, worked diligently with architects and masons to ensure that the infrastructure — for both carriage roads and motor roads — complemented the surrounding landscape.

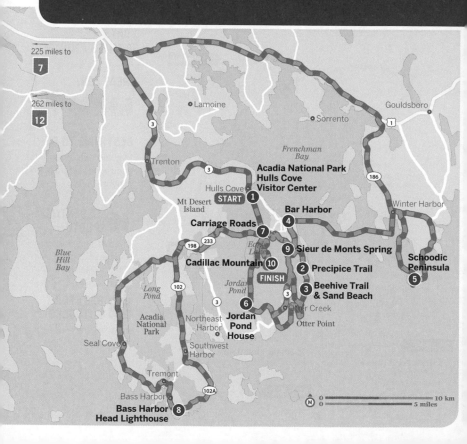

❶ Acadia National Park Hulls Cove Visitor Center

Whoa, whoa, whoa. Before zooming into Bar Harbor on ME 3, stop at the **park visitor center** (☎207-288-3338; www.nps.gov/acad; ⏰8am-4:30pm Apr 15-Oct, extended hours Jul-Sep) to get the lay of the land and pay the admission fee. Inside, head directly to the large diorama, which provides a helpful overview of Mt Desert Island (MDI). As you'll see, Acadia National Park shares the island with several non-park communities, which are tucked here and there beside Acadia's borders.

From the visitor center, the 27-mile Park Loop Rd circumnavigates the northeastern section of the island. The loop is part of the **Acadia All**

LINK YOUR TRIP

7 Coastal New England

For more scenes from Coastal New England, head south on I-95 to Gloucester.

12 Ivy League Tour

Take I-95 south to Augusta, then head west into New Hampshire. Take I-93 north and I-91 south to Hanover.

American Road (http://byways.org), a national scenic byway.

The Drive » From the visitor center, turn right onto the Park Loop Rd, not ME 3, which leads into Bar Harbor. Take in a nice view of Frenchman Bay on your left before passing the spur to ME 233. A short distance ahead, turn left to begin the one-way loop on Park Loop Rd.

TRIP HIGHLIGHT

❷ Precipice Trail

What's the most exciting way to get a bird's-eye view of the park? By climbing up to where the birds are. Two 'ladder trails' cling to the sides of exposed cliffs on the northeastern section of Park Loop Rd, dubbed Ocean Dr. If the season's right, tackle the first of the ladder trails, the 2.2-mile round-trip Precipice Trail, which climbs the side of Champlain Mountain on iron rungs and ladders. (Note that the trail is typically closed March through to the middle of August because it's a nesting area for peregrine falcons. If it is closed, you might catch volunteers and staff monitoring the birds through scopes from the trailhead parking lot.) Skip the trail on rainy days.

The Drive » Drive south on Park Loop Rd. The Beehive Trail starts 100ft north of the Sand Beach parking area.

❸ Beehive Trail & Sand Beach

Another good ladder trail is the Beehive Trail. The 1.6-mile (round-trip) hike includes ladders, rungs, narrow wooden bridges and scrambling – with steep drop-offs. If it's crowded, you can loop back down on a neighboring trail.

Don't let the crowds keep you away from Sand Beach. It's home to one of the few sandy shorelines in the park, and it's a don't-miss spot. But you don't have to visit in the middle of the day to appreciate its charms. Beat the crowds early in the morning, or visit at night, especially for the **Stars over Sand Beach** program. During these one-hour talks, lie on the beach, look up at the sky and listen to rangers share stories and science about the stars. Even if you miss the talk, the eastern coastline along Ocean Dr is worth checking out at night, when you can watch the Milky Way slip right into the ocean.

The Drive » Swoop south past the crashing waves of Thunder Hole and then turn right onto Otter Cliff Rd, which hooks up to ME 3 north into town.

TOP TIP: PARK SHUTTLES

With millions of visitors coming to the park each summer, parking can be a hassle. On arrival, drive the Park Loop Rd straight through for the views and the driving experience. Then leave the driving to others by using the **Island Explorer** (www.exploreacadia.com; ⏱late Jun–early Oct), free with park admission. Shuttles run along eight routes that connect visitors to trails, carriage roads, beaches, campgrounds and in-town destinations. They can even carry mountain bikes.

TRIP HIGHLIGHT

④ Bar Harbor

Tucked on the rugged coast in the shadows of Acadia's mountains, Bar Harbor is a busy gateway town with a J Crew joie de vivre. Restaurants, taverns and boutiques are scattered along Main St, Mt Desert St and Cottage St. Shops sell everything from books to camping gear to handicrafts and art. For a fascinating collection of natural artifacts related to Maine's Native American heritage, visit the **Abbe Museum** (www.abbemuseum.org; 26 Mt Desert St; adult/child $6/2; ⏱10am–5pm daily Jun–Oct, 10am–4pm Thu–Sat Nov–May, closed Jan). The collection holds more than 50,000 objects, such as pottery,

tools, combs and fishing instruments spanning the last 2000 years, including contemporary pieces.

Done browsing? Spend the rest of the afternoon, or early evening, exploring the park by water. Sign up in Bar Harbor for a half-day or sunset kayaking trip. Both **National Park Sea Kayak** (☎800-347-0940; www.acadiakayak.com; 39 Cottage St) and **Coastal Kayaking Tour** (☎207-288-9605; www.acadiafun.com; 48 Cottage St) offer trips along the jagged coast.

✗ ⌷ p181

The Drive » Drive north 16 miles to US 1 north, following it about 17 miles to ME 186 east. ME 186 passes through Winter Harbor and then links to Schoodic Point Loop Rd. It's about an hour's drive one way. Alternatively, hop a Downeast Windjammer ferry (www.downeastwindjammer.com) from the pier beside the Bar Harbor Inn.

⑤ Schoodic Peninsula

The Schoodic Peninsula is the only section of Acadia National Park that's part of the mainland. It's also home to the Schoodic Point Loop Rd, a rugged, woodsy drive with splendid views of Mt Desert Island and Cadillac Mountain. You're more likely to see a moose here than on MDI – what moose wants to cross a bridge?

Much of the drive is one way. There's a picnic area at **Frazer Point** near the park entrance. Further along the loop, turn right for a short ride to **Schoodic Point**, a 440ft-high promontory with ocean views. For historic details about sites along the drive, ask for the Schoodic National Scenic Byway brochure at the Hulls Cove Visitor Center.

The full loop from Winter Harbor is 11.5 miles and covers park, town and state roads. If you're planning to come by ferry, you could rent a bike beforehand at **Bar Harbor Bicycle Shop** (☎207-288-3886; www.barharborbike.com; 141 Cottage St, Bar Harbor; rental per day $24-35; 🚲) – the Schoodic Point Loop Rd's smooth surface and easy hills make it ideal for cycling.

In summer, the Island Explorer Schoodic

ISLAND VISIT PLANNER

Acadia National Park

Admission

Park admission is $20 per vehicle from mid-June to early October, $10 per vehicle late in spring and mid-fall, and $5 for walk-ins and cyclists. Admission is valid for seven days. No admission fee is charged from November to April.

Camping

There are two great rustic **campgrounds** (☎877-444-6777; www.nps.gov/acad, reservations www.recreation.gov; ⛺) on Mt Desert Island, with more than 500 tent sites between them. Both are densely wooded and near the coast. Four miles west of Southwest Harbor, **Seawall** (tent & RV sites $14-20; ☺late May-Sep) has by-reservation and walk-up sites. Five miles south of Bar Harbor on ME 3, **Blackwoods** (tent & RV sites May-Oct $20, Apr & Nov $10; ☺year-round) requires reservations in summer. Both sites have restrooms and pay showers.

Bar Harbor & Mt Desert Island

Before your trip, check lodging availability and connect to hotel, motel and B&B websites via the **Acadia Welcome Center** (☎207-288-5103; www.acadiainfo.com; 1201 Bar Harbor Rd/ME 3, Trenton; ☺8am-6pm Jun-Aug, to 5pm Mon-Fri low season) website, run by the Bar Harbor Chamber of Commerce. Staff can also mail you a copy of the visitor guide. Otherwise, stop by the welcome center itself for lodging brochures, maps and local information. It's located north of the bridge. From here you can call various hotels, motels and B&Bs directly for reservations.

Shuttle runs from Winter Harbor to the peninsula ferry terminal and south along the Schoodic Peninsula. It does not link to Bar Harbor.

The Drive » Return to the Park Loop Rd on MDI. Pass Otter Point then follow the road inland past Wildwood Stable. The Jordan Pond House is 1 mile ahead on the left.

- - - - - - - - - -

TRIP HIGHLIGHT

❻ Jordan Pond House

Share hiking stories with other nature lovers at the lodge-like **Jordan Pond House** (☎207-276-3316; www.jordanpond.com; Park Loop Rd; afternoon tea $9.50, lunch $10-17, dinner $19-27;

☺lunch 11:30am-5:30pm, dinner 6-9pm), where afternoon tea has been a tradition since the late 1800s. Steaming pots of Earl Grey come with hot popovers (hollow rolls made with egg batter and strawberry jam). Eat on the broad lawn overlooking the lake. On clear days the glassy waters of 176-acre Jordan Pond reflect the image of Mt Penobscot like a mirror. Take the 3-mile self-guided nature tour around the pond after finishing your tea.

The Drive » Look up for the rock precariously perched atop South Bubble from the pull-off almost 2 miles north. Continue north to ME 233, following it on

a westerly course to parking at Eagle Lake.

- - - - - - - - - -

TRIP HIGHLIGHT

❼ Carriage Roads

John D Rockefeller Jr, a lover of old-fashioned horse carriages, gifted Acadia with some 45 miles of crisscrossing carriage roads. Made from crushed stone, the roads are free from cars and are popular with cyclists, hikers and equestrians. Several of them fan out from Jordan Pond House, but if the lot is too crowded continue north to the parking area at Eagle Lake on US 233 to link to the carriage road network. If you're

LOCAL KNOWLEDGE
SONJA BERGER,
PARK RANGER

If you're feeling adventurous, and you're not scared of heights, then some of the ladder trails are really fun and really challenging. My favorite is Jordan Cliffs, which is over by the Jordan Pond area. It has an interesting mix of ladders and other kinds of trail-building options that get you up the sheer cliff face and across. Then you've got the popovers and lobster stew at the Jordan Pond House to eat. You can burn off all the calories on the ladder trails.

Top: Bass Harbor Head Lighthouse
Right: Mt Desert Island

planning to explore by bike, the Bicycle Express Shuttle runs to Eagle Lake from the Bar Harbor Village Green from late June through September. Pick up a Carriage Road User's Map at the visitor center.

The Drive » Take ME 233 toward the western part of MDI, connecting to ME 198 west, then drop south on ME 102 toward Southwest Harbor. Pass Echo

Lake Beach and Southwest Harbor, then bear left onto ME 102A for a dramatic rise up and into the park near the seawall.

- - - - - - - - - -

⑧ Bass Harbor Head Lighthouse

There is only one lighthouse on Mt Desert Island, and it sits in the somnolent village of Bass Harbor in the far southwest corner of the park. Built in 1858, the 36ft lighthouse still has a Fresnel lens from 1902. It's in a beautiful location that's a favorite of photographers. The lighthouse is a coast guard residence, so you can't go inside, but you can take photos. You can also stroll to the coast on two easy trails near the property: the **Ship Harbor Trail**, a 1.2-mile loop, and the **Wonderland Trail**, a 1.4-mile round-trip. These trails are spectacular ways to get through the forest and to the coast, which looks different to the coast on Ocean Dr.

The Drive >> For a lollipop loop, return on ME 102A to ME 102 through the village of Bass Harbor. Follow ME 233 back to the Park Loop Rd and the Wild Gardens of Acadia.

9 Sieur de Monts Spring

Nature lovers and history buffs will enjoy a stop at the Sieur de Monts Spring area at the intersection of ME 3 and the Park Loop Rd. Here you'll find a nature center and the summer-only branch of the **Abbe Museum** (adult/child $3/1; ⊙10am-5pm late May-early Oct), which sits in a lush, nature-like setting. Twelve of Acadia's biospheres are displayed in miniature at the **Wild Gardens of Acadia** (admission free), from bog to coniferous woods to meadow. Botany enthusiasts will appreciate the plant labels. There are also some amazing stone-step trails here, appearing out of the talus as if by magic.

The Drive » To avoid driving the full park loop, you can follow ME 3 into Bar Harbor and then hook back onto ME 233 northwest to the exit leading to Cadillac Mountain.

TRIP HIGHLIGHT

10 Cadillac Mountain

Don't leave the park without driving – or hiking – to the 1530ft summit of Cadillac Mountain. For panoramic views of Frenchman Bay, walk the paved 0.5-mile **Cadillac Mountain Summit loop**. The summit is a popular place in the early morning because it's long been touted as the first spot in the US to see the sunrise. The truth? It is, but only between October 7 and March 6. The crown is passed to northern coastal towns the rest of the year because of the tilt of the earth. But, hey, the sunset is always a good bet.

Eating & Sleeping

Bar Harbor ④

✕ 2 Cats   Cafe $

(www.2catsbarharbor.com; 130 Cottage St; mains $6-12; ☺7am-1pm Jan–mid-fall) Cat paws are painted on the tabletops inside this sunny cottage where weekend crowds line up for smoked-trout omelets and homemade muffins. Lunch offers slightly heartier fare. The five-pepper hot sauce is HOT – and sold by the bottle. You might see a cat or two strutting around inside.

✕ Mache Bistro   French $$

(☎207-288-0447; www.machebistro.com; 135 Cottage St; mains $17-24; ☺5:30-9pm Wed-Sat May-Oct) Savor contemporary, French-inflected dishes in a stylish cottage with an interior that looks a bit like a French nightclub. The changing menu highlights local riches – seafood stew with haddock and scallops, and wild blueberry trifles. Open some Mondays and Tuesdays in summer; check the website.

✕ Mt Desert Island Ice Cream   Ice Cream $

(www.mdiic.com; 7 Firefly Lane; scoops $3.75, milkshakes $5; ☺11am-10pm Apr-early fall) A cult hit for edgy flavors such as salted caramel, boozy White Russian and blueberry basil sorbet, this postage-stamp-sized ice-cream counter is a post-dinner must.

✕ Cafe This Way   Cafe $$

(www.cafethisway.com; 14½ Mount Desert St; mains breakfast $6-9, dinner $15-25; ☺7-11:30am Mon-Sat, 8am-1pm Sun, 5:30-9pm nightly; ☑) In a sprawling white cottage, this quirky eatery is the place for breakfast, with plump Maine blueberry pancakes and eggs Benedict with smoked salmon. It also serves eclectic, sophisticated dinners. Sit in the garden.

⌸ Anne's White Columns   Inn $$

(☎207-288-5357; www.anneswhitecolumns.com; 57 Mount Desert St; r incl breakfast $85-175) Once a Christian Scientist church, this B&B's name refers to its dramatic columned entrance. Rooms have a quirky Victorian charm, with plenty of florals and bric-a-brac. Get here in time for the afternoon wine and cheese reception.

⌸ Aurora Inn   Motel $$

(☎207-288-3771; www.aurorainn.com; 51 Holland Ave; r $89-169; ❄☎) This retro motor lodge has 10 clean rooms and a good location within walking distance of downtown. Guests can use the pool and laundry at nearby Quality Inn. Rates drop significantly outside high season (July to early September).

⌸ Bass Cottage   B&B $$$

(☎207-288-1234; www.basscottage.com; 14 The Field; r incl breakfast $185-380; ☺May-Oct; ❄☎) The 10 light-drenched guest rooms here have an elegant summer-cottage chic. Tickle the ivories on the parlor's grand piano or read a novel beneath the Tiffany stained-glass ceiling of the wood-paneled sitting room.

⌸ Holland Inn   B&B $$

(☎207-288-4804; www.hollandinn.com; 35 Holland Ave; r incl breakfast $95-185; ❄☎) In a quiet neighborhood near downtown, this restored 1895 house and adjacent cottage have nine homey, unfrilly rooms. The ambience is so low-key you'll feel like you're staying in a friend's private home.

STRETCH YOUR LEGS
BOSTON

Start/Finish Boston Common

Distance 2.5 miles

Duration Three hours

Everybody knows about the world-class museums and historical sites; but Boston also offers a network of verdant parks, welcoming waterways and delightful shopping streets, making it a wonderful walking city.

Take this walk on Trip

Boston Common

Welcome to the country's oldest public park (with a convenient underground parking facility below – what foresight!). A **bronze plaque** is emblazoned with the words of the treaty between Governor Winthrop and William Blaxton, who sold this land for £30 in 1634. The **Massachusetts State House** (www.sec. state.ma.us; cnr Beacon & Bowdoin Sts; admission free; ☺9am-5pm, tours 10am-3:30pm Mon-Fri) commands a prominent position in the park's northeast corner.

The Walk » Follow the busy Bostonians crisscrossing the common. Exit the park from the western side, cross Charles St, and enter the tranquil Public Garden.

Public Garden

The Public Garden is a 24-acre botanical oasis of Victorian flowerbeds, verdant grass and weeping willows shading a tranquil lagoon. At any time of year, it is an island of loveliness, awash in seasonal blooms, gold-toned leaves or untrammeled snow. Taking a ride on the **Swan Boats** (www.swanboats. com; adult/child/senior $3/1.50/2; ☺10am-4pm mid-Apr–mid-Sep) in the lagoon has been a Boston tradition since 1877. And don't miss the famous statue **Make Way for Ducklings**, based on the beloved children's book by Robert McKloskey.

The Walk » Cross the bridge and exit the garden through the southwestern gate to Arlington St. Stroll west on swanky Newbury St, perfect for window shopping and gallery hopping. Take a left on Clarendon St and continue to Boylston St.

Copley Square

Boston's most exquisite architecture is clustered around this stately Back Bay plaza. The centerpiece is the Romanesque **Trinity Church** (www. trinitychurchboston.org; 206 Clarendon St; adult/child/senior $7/free/5; ☺9am-5pm Mon-Sat, 1-6pm Sun), famed for its stained-glass windows. It's particularly lovely as reflected in the facade of the modern **John Hancock Tower**. This assemblage

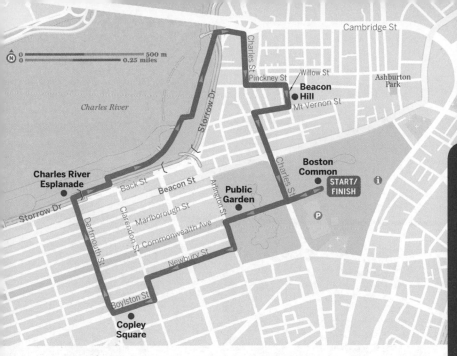

faces off against the elegant neo-Renaissance **Boston Public Library** (BPL; www.bpl.org; 700 Boylston St; admission free; ⊙9am-9pm Mon-Thu, to 5pm Fri & Sat), packed with sculpture, murals and other treasures.

The Walk » Head north on Dartmouth St, crossing the stately, dual-carriageway Commonwealth Ave, the grandest of Back Bay's grand avenues. Continue three more blocks to Back St, from where a pedestrian walkway crosses Storrow Dr to the esplanade.

Charles River Esplanade

The southern bank of the Charles River Basin is an enticing urban escape, with grassy knolls and cooling waterways, all designed by Frederick Law Olmsted. The park is dotted with public art, including an oversized bust of **Arthur Fiedler**, the long-time conductor of the Boston Pops. The **Hatch Memorial Shell** hosts free outdoor concerts and movies, including the famed Fourth of July concert by the Boston Pops.

The Walk » Walk east along the esplanade, enjoying the breezes and views of the Charles River. It's about a half-mile to the Longfellow Bridge, where you can climb the ramp and find yourself at the top of Charles St.

Beacon Hill

With an intriguing history and iconic architecture, Beacon Hill is Boston's most prestigious address. **Charles Street** is an enchanting spot for browsing boutiques and haggling over antiques. To explore further, wander down the residential streets lit with gas lanterns, admire the brick town houses decked with purple windowpanes and blooming flowerboxes, and discover streets such as stately **Louisburg Square** that capture the neighborhood's grandeur.

The Walk » Take your time strolling south along charming Charles St. For a glimpse of Louisburg Sq, walk two blocks east on Pinckney St. Then continue south to Boston Common.

Florida & the South Trips

LIFE IS RICH – MAKE THAT INDULGENT – IN THE SOUTHERN STATES. The food, music, culture, history, all of it is robust, spiced to the hilt, and exhilaratingly full of life.

On these trips, we'll show you the romantic jazz club of your dreams, country calm and city chic. We'll show you sun-kissed beaches and a highway floating above a perfect blue ocean.

Between the Carolinas and the Gulf of Mexico, a different America awaits, warmed by the sultry winds that blow up from the Caribbean. From the mighty Mississippi River to the Florida Keys, from the Blues Highway to Cajun country, from the Smoky Mountains to the art-deco glam of Miami, you'll find that life moves to its own rhythm in the South.

Florida Keys (Trip 14)
JUPITERIMAGES / GETTY IMAGES ©

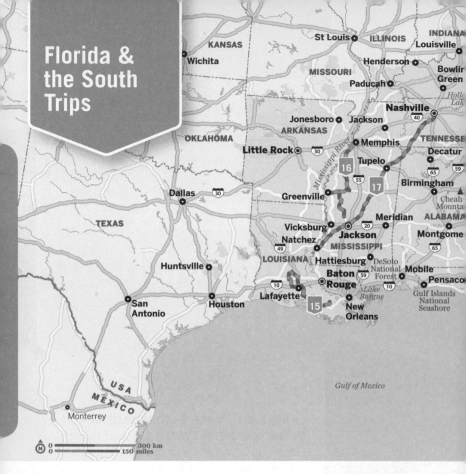

Florida & the South Trips

KANSAS
Wichita

MISSOURI

St Louis
ILLINOIS
Louisville
INDIANA

Henderson
Bowlin Green

Paducah

Holl
Lak

Nashville
40

OKLAHOMA

Jonesboro Jackson
ARKANSAS

Memphis
TENNESSE

Little Rock
30

Tupelo
16
55
17

Decatur
65   59

Birmingham
Cheah
Mounta

Dallas
30

Greenville

Meridian
ALABAMA

TEXAS

Vicksburg
Natchez
49

20
Jackson
MISSISSIPPI

Montgome
65

Huntsville

LOUISIANA Hattiesburg
DeSoto
National
Forest
Mobile
Pensaco

Baton
Rouge
59

San
Antonio

Houston

Lafayette
10

15

Lake
Borgne
10

Gulf Islands
National
Seashore

New
Orleans

USA
MEXICO

Monterrey

Gulf of Mexico

0   300 km
0   150 miles

14 Highway 1 6 Days
Embark on an adventure that runs the length of the Atlantic Coast. (p189)

15 Cajun Country 4 Days
Explore bayous, dance halls, crawfish boils and folk ways in Louisiana's idiosyncratic Acadiana region. (p201)

16 The Blues Highway 3 Days
A soulful ramble to the root of American popular music. (p209)

17 Natchez Trace Parkway 3 Days
The journey south from Nashville stuns with natural beauty and American history. (p221)

Classic Trip

18 Blue Ridge Parkway 5 Days
The beloved byway explores the craggy, misty depths of the Appalachians. (p233)

19 The Great Smokies 4–5 Days
Raft over rapids, scan for wildlife and drive two fantastic nature loops. (p245)

Fort George Island

Peek into old Florida at this Cultural State Park, one of several historical stop-offs in Trip 14

Biltmore Legacy

For less of the formality and more of the family, visit the new 'Vanderbilts at Home and Abroad' exhibit on Trip 18

Museum of the Cherokee Indian

Learn about three Cherokee chiefs who journeyed to England and met with King George III on Trip 19

Clarksdale

The hub of the Delta has the Crossroads, a spectacular juke joint and comfortable digs from which to explore the blues. Visit it on Trip 16

Natchez

This laid-back river town is an antebellum time capsule, and a charming respite for a few days of strolling and contemplation. See it on Trip 16

Ocean Drive Miami Beach (Trip 14)

Miami Beach Art deco treasures
as far as the eye can see

Classic Trip

Highway 1

14

Glittering Miami provides a spectacular grand finale to this epic coastal road trip featuring miles and miles of beaches interspersed with fascinating historical sights.

TRIP HIGHLIGHTS

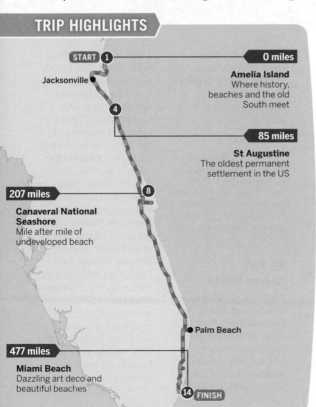

START **1** ──────────── **0 miles**

Jacksonville ●

4

Amelia Island
Where history, beaches and the old South meet

85 miles

St Augustine
The oldest permanent settlement in the US

207 miles ──── **8**

Canaveral National Seashore
Mile after mile of undeveloped beach

● Palm Beach

477 miles

Miami Beach
Dazzling art deco and beautiful beaches

14 **FINISH**

6 DAYS
475 MILES / 764KM

GREAT FOR...

BEST TIME TO GO

November to April, when it's warm but not too hot.

ESSENTIAL PHOTO

Rows of colorful art-deco hotels along Ocean Ave at Miami Beach.

BEST FOR HISTORY

St Augustine, the oldest permanent settlement in the US.

Classic Trip

14 Highway 1

Drive the length of Florida all the way down the coast and you'll get a sampling of everything we love about the Sunshine State. You'll find the oldest permanent settlement in the United States, family-friendly attractions, the Latin flavor of Miami and – oh, yeah – miles and miles of beaches traveling right along beside you, inviting you to stop as often as you want.

TRIP HIGHLIGHT

① Amelia Island

Start your drive just 13 miles south of the Georgia border in Amelia Island, a glorious barrier island with the moss-draped charm of the Deep South. Vacationers have been flocking here since the 1890s, when Henry Flagler's railroad converted the area into a playground for the rich. The legacy of that golden era remains visible today in Amelia's central town of **Fernandina Beach**, with 50 blocks of historic buildings, Victorian B&Bs, and restaurants housed in converted fishing cottages. The best introduction to the town is a half-hour horse-drawn carriage tour with the **Old Towne Carriage Co** (☎904-277-1555; www.ameliacarriagetours.com; ½ hr adult/child $15/7).

✕ 🛏 p198

The Drive » Meander down Hwy 1A for about half an hour, passing both Big and Little Talbot Island State Parks. After you enter Fort George Island, take the right fork in the road to get to the Ribault Club.

② Fort George Island

History runs deep at **Fort George Island Cultural State Park** (12157 Heckscher Dr; ☺8am-sunset, visitor center 9am-5pm Wed-Sun). Enormous shell middens date the island's habitation by Native Americans to over 5000 years ago. In 1736 British General James Oglethorpe built a fort in the area, though it's long since vanished and its exact location is uncertain. In the 1920s flappers flocked to the ritzy **Ribault Club** (www.nps.gov/timu; ☺9am-5pm) for Gatsby-esque bashes with lawn bowling and yachting. Today it houses the island's visitor center, which can provide you with a CD tour of the area. Perhaps most fascinating, and certainly most sobering, is **Kingsley Plantation**, (11676 Palmetto Ave; admission free; ☺9am-5pm), Florida's oldest plantation house built in 1798. Because of its remote location, it's not a grand southern mansion, but

it does provide a fairly unflinching look at slavery through exhibits and the remains of 23 slave cabins.

The Drive » Follow Hwy 105 inland 15 miles to I-95, then shoot straight south into downtown Jacksonville.

- - - - - - - - - - -

❸ Jacksonville

With its high-rises, freeways and chain hotels, Jacksonville is a bit of a departure from our coastal theme, but it offers lots of dining options, and its restored historic districts are worth a wander. Check out the **Five Points** and **San Marco** neighborhoods; both are charming, walkable areas lined with bistros, boutiques and bars.

It's also a good chance to work in a little culture at the **Cummer Museum of Art** (www.cummer.org; 829 Riverside Ave; adult/

🔗 LINK YOUR TRIP

15 Cajun Country

Follow I-10 west, then head south from Baton Rouge to Thibodaux to start your Cajun Country trip.

18 Blue Ridge Parkway

Take the I-95 north along the coast and head inland on I-26 through Columbia. From there take Hwy 321 all the way to Boone.

Classic Trip

student $10/6; ⊙10am-9pm Tue, to 4pm Wed-Sat, noon-4pm Sun), which has a genuinely excellent collection of American and European paintings, Asian decorative art and antiquities; or the **Jacksonville Museum of Modern Art** (www .mocajacksonville.org; 333 N Laura St; adult/child $8/5; ⊙11am-5pm Tue-Sat, to 9pm Thu, noon-5pm Sun), which houses contemporary paintings, sculptures, prints, photography and film.

✕ p198

The Drive ≫ Take US 1 southwest for an hour straight into St Augustine, where it becomes Ponce de Leon Blvd.

TRIP HIGHLIGHT

❹ St Augustine

Founded by the Spanish in 1565, St Augustine is the oldest permanent settlement in the US. Tourists flock here

to stroll the ancient streets, and horse-drawn carriages clip-clop past townsfolk dressed in period costume. It's definitely tourist-centric, with tons of museums, tours and attractions vying for your attention. Start with the **Spanish Quarter Museum** (33 St George St; adult/child $13/7; ⊙9am-6pm), a re-creation of 18th-century St Augustine complete with craftspeople demonstrating trades such as blacksmithing and leather working.

While you're here, don't miss the **Lightner Museum** (☎904-824-2874; www.lightnermuseum.org; 75 King St; adult/child $10/5; ⊙9am-5pm) located in the former Hotel Alcazar. We love the endless displays of everything from Gilded Age furnishings to collections of marbles and cigar-box labels.

Stop by the **Visitor Information Center** (☎904-825-1000; www .ci.st-augustine.fl.us; 10 Castillo Dr; ⊙8:30am-5:30pm) to find out about your other options, including

ghost tours, the Pirate and Treasure Museum, Castillo de San Marcos National Monument, and the Fountain of Youth, a goofy tourist attraction disguised as an archeological park that is purportedly the very spot where Ponce de Leon landed.

✕ ⌂ p198

The Drive ≫ Take the Bridge of Lions toward the beach then follow Hwy 1A south for 13 miles to Fort Matanzas. To catch the 35-person ferry, go through the visitor center and out to the pier. The ride lasts about five minutes and launches hourly from 9:30am to 4:30pm, weather permitting.

----

❺ Fort Matanzas National Monument

By now you've seen firsthand that the Florida coast isn't all about fun in the sun; it also has a rich history that goes back hundreds of years. History buffs will enjoy a visit to this tiny Spanish **fort** (www.nps.gov/foma; 8635 Hwy A1A; admission free; ⊙9am-5:30pm) built in 1742. Its purpose? To guard **Matanzas Inlet** – a waterway leading straight up to St Augustine – from British invasion.

On the lovely (and free!) boat ride over, park rangers narrate the fort's history and explain the gruesome origins of the name. ('Matanzas' means 'slaughters' in

✓ **TOP TIP: THE ROAD LESS TAKEN**

Despite its National Scenic Byway designation, oceanfront Hwy A1A often lacks ocean views, with wind-blocking vegetation growing on both sides of the road. Unless you're just moseying up or down the coast, Hwy 1 or I-95 are often better choices for driving long distances.

Spanish; let's just say things went badly for a couple hundred French Huguenot soldiers back in 1565.)

The Drive » Hopping over to I-95 will only shave a little bit off the hour-long trip; you might as well enjoy putting along Hwy 1A to Daytona Beach, 40 miles south.

6 Daytona Beach

With typical Floridian hype, Daytona Beach bills itself as 'The World's Most Famous Beach.' But its fame is less about quality than the size of the parties this expansive beach has witnessed during spring break, SpeedWeeks and motorcycle events when half-a-million bikers roar into town. One Daytona title no one disputes is 'Birthplace of NASCAR,' which started here in 1947. Its origins go back as far as 1902 to drag races held on the beach's hard-packed sands.

NASCAR is the main event here. Catch a race at the **Daytona International Speedway** (☎800-748-7467; www .daytonaintlspeedway.com; 1801 W International Speedway Blvd; tickets from $20, tours adult $16-23, child 6-12yr $10-17). When there's no race, you can wander the massive stands for free or take a tram tour of the track and pit area. Race-car fanatics can indulge in the **Richard Petty Driving Experience**

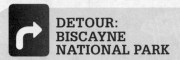

DETOUR: BISCAYNE NATIONAL PARK

Start: 14 **Miami Beach**

About an hour's drive south of Miami Beach, **Biscayne National Park** (☎305-230-7275, 305-230-1100; www.biscayneunderwater.com; 9700 SW 328th St) is a protected marine sanctuary harboring amazing tropical coral reef systems, most within sight of Miami's skyline. It's only accessible by water: you can take a glass-bottomed-boat tour, snorkel or scuba dive, or rent a canoe or kayak to lose yourself in this 300-sq-mile system of islands, underwater shipwrecks and mangrove forests.

(☎800-237-3889; www .drivepetty.com) and feel the thrill of riding shotgun or even taking the wheel themselves.

✕ ⌂ p198

The Drive » Take South Atlantic Ave 10 miles south along the coast to get to Ponce Inlet.

7 Ponce Inlet

What's a beach road trip without a good lighthouse? About 10 miles south of Daytona Beach is the **Ponce Inlet Lighthouse & Museum** (www.ponceinlet.org; 4931 S Peninsula Dr; adult/child $5/1.50; ◷10am-6pm winter, to 9pm summer). Stop by for a photo op with the handsome red-brick tower built in 1887, then climb the 203 steps to the top for great views of the surrounding beaches. A handful of historical buildings comprise

the museum portion of your tour, including the lightkeeper's house and the **Lens House**, where there's a collection of Fresnel Lenses.

The Drive » Backtrack up Atlantic, then cut over to US 1/FL-5 and head south 20 minutes. Preplanning pays here, because your route depends on where you're heading. One road goes 6 miles south from New Smyrna Beach, and another 6 miles north from the wildlife refuge. Both dead-end, leaving 16 miles of beach between them.

TRIP HIGHLIGHT

8 Canaveral National Seashore

These 24 miles of pristine, windswept beaches comprise the longest stretch of undeveloped beach on Florida's east coast. On the north end is family-friendly **Apollo Beach**, which shines in a class of its own with gentle surf

WHY THIS IS A CLASSIC TRIP
MARIELLA KRAUSE, AUTHOR

Who doesn't love cruising down the coast? This trip is a natural for shoreline, seafood and sunshine – but it doesn't rely solely on beach culture. It's a remarkably well-rounded drive that culminates in the world-class city of Miami, with diversions along the way that include worthwhile art exhibits, peaceful nature preserves and some of the United States' oldest historical sites.

Top: Daytona International Speedway
Left: Ponce Inlet Lighthouse
Right: Kennedy Space Center

DENNIS K JOHNSON / GETTY IMAGES ©

and miles of solitude. On the south end, **Playalinda Beach** is surfer central.

Just west of (and including) the beach, the 140,000-acre **Merritt Island National Wildlife Refuge** (www.fws.gov/merrittisland; I-95 exit 80; ☉ park dawn-dusk, visitor center 8am-4:30pm Mon-Fri, 9am-5pm Sat & Sun, closed Sun Apr-Oct) is an unspoiled oasis for birds and wildlife. It's one of the country's best **birding** spots, especially from October to May (early morning and after 4pm), and more endangered and threatened species of wildlife inhabit the swamps, marshes and hardwood hammocks here than at any other site in the continental United States.

Stop by the visitor center for more information; an easy quarter-mile boardwalk will whet your appetite for everything the refuge has to offer. Other highlights include the **Manatee Observation Deck**, the 7-mile **Black Point Wildlife Drive**, and a variety of **hiking trails**.

The Drive » Although Kennedy Space Center is just south of the Merritt Island Refuge, you have to go back into Titusville, travel south 5 miles on US 1/Hwy 5, then take the Nasa Causeway back over to get there.

❾ Space Coast

The Space Coast's main claim to fame (other than being the setting for the iconic 1960s TV series *I Dream of Jeannie*) is being the real-life home to the Kennedy Space Center and its massive visitor complex. Once a working space-flight facility, Kennedy Space Center is shifting from a living museum to a historical one since the end of NASA's space shuttle program in 2011.

🍴 p199

The Drive » Hop back onto the freeway (I-95) for the 2½-hour drive south to Palm Beach.

❿ Palm Beach

History and nature give way to money and culture as you reach the southern part of the coast, and Palm Beach looks every inch the playground for the rich and famous that it is. But fear not: the rest of us can stroll along the beach – kept pleasantly seaweed-free by the town – ogle the massive gated compounds on A1A or window-shop in uber-ritzy Worth Ave, all for free.

The best reason to stop here is **Flagler Museum** (www.flaglermuseum.us; 1 Whitehall Way; adult/child $18/10; ⊙10am-5pm Tue-Sat, noon-5pm Sun), housed in the spectacular, Beaux-art-styled Whitehall Mansion built by Henry Flagler in 1902. You won't get many details about the railroad mogul himself, but you will get a peek into his opulent lifestyle, including his own personal train car.

The Drive » When you're ready to be back among the commoners, head back inland. West Palm Beach is just a causeway away.

⓫ West Palm Beach

While Palm Beach has the money, West Palm Beach has the largest art museum in Florida, the **Norton Museum of Art** (☎561-832-5196; www.norton.org; 1451 S Olive Ave; adult/child $12/5; ⊙10am-5pm Tue-Sat, to 9pm Thu, 11am-5pm Sun). The Nessel Wing features a colorful crowd-pleaser: a ceiling made from nearly 700 pieces of handblown glass by Dale Chihuly. Across the street, the **Ann Norton Sculpture Garden** (www.ansg.org; 253 Barcelona Rd; adult/child under 5yr $7/free; ⊙10am-4pm Wed-Sun) is a real West Palm gem.

Come evening, if you're not sure what you're in the mood for, head to **CityPlace** (www.cityplace.com; 700 S Rosemary Ave; ⊙10am-10pm Mon-Sat, noon-6pm Sun), a massive outdoor shopping and entertainment center. Here you'll find a slew of stores, about a dozen restaurants, a 20-screen movie theater and the Harriet Himmel Theater; not to mention free concerts in the outdoor plaza.

🍴 🛏 p199

The Drive » Fort Lauderdale is a straight shot down I-95, 45 miles south of Palm Beach. Taking Hwy 1A will add more than half an hour to your trip.

⓬ Fort Lauderdale

Fort Lauderdale Beach isn't the spring-break destination it once was, although you can still find outposts of beach-bummin' bars and motels in between the swanky boutique hotels and multimillion-dollar yachts. Few visitors venture far inland except maybe to dine and shop along Las Olas Blvd;

3, 2, 1...BLASTOFF!

Along the Space Coast, even phone calls get a countdown, thanks to the local area code: 321. It's no coincidence; in 1999 residents led by Robert Osband petitioned to get the digits in honor of the rocket launches that took place at Cape Canaveral.

most spend the bulk of their time on the coast, frolicking at water's edge. The **promenade** – a wide, brick, palm-tree-dotted pathway swooping along the beach – is a magnet for runners, in-line skaters, walkers and cyclists. The white-sand beach, meanwhile, is one of the nation's cleanest and best.

The best way to see Fort Lauderdale is from the water. Hop onboard the **Carrie B** (☎954-642-1601, 888-238-9805; www .carriebcruises.com; tours adult/child $23/13) for a 1½-hour riverboat tour that lets you get a glimpse of the ginormous mansions along the Intracoastal and New River. Or, for the best unofficial tour of the city, hop on the **Water Taxi** (www.watertaxi .com; all-day pass adult/child $20/13), whose drivers offer lively narration of the passing scenery.

✖ 🛏 p199

The Drive ≫ Things are heating up. Miami is just half an hour south of Fort Lauderdale down I-95.

- - - - - - - - - - - -

⑬ Miami

Miami moves to a different rhythm from anywhere else in the USA, with pastel-hued,

subtropical beauty and Latin sexiness at every turn. Just west of downtown on Calle Ocho (8th St), you'll find **Little Havana**, the most prominent community of Cuban Americans in the US. One of the best times to come is the last Friday of the month during **Viernes Culturales** (www .viernesculturales.org), a street fair showcasing Latino artists and musicians. Or catch the vibe at **Máximo Gómez Park** (SW 8th St, at SW 15th Ave; ☺9am-6pm), where old-timers gather to play dominoes to the strains of Latin music.

Wynwood and the **Design District** are Miami's official arts neighborhoods; don't miss the amazing collection of murals at **Wynwood Walls** (www .thewynwoodwalls.com; NW 2nd Ave, btwn 25th & 26th St; ☺11am-11pm Mon-Sat, noon-6pm Sun), surrounded by blocks and blocks of even more murals that form a sort of drive-though art gallery.

✖ 🛏 p199

The Drive ≫ We've saved the best for last. Cross over the Julia Tuttle Causeway or the MacArthur Causeway to find yourself in art-deco-laden Miami Beach.

TRIP HIGHLIGHT

⑭ Miami Beach

Miami Beach dazzles at every turn. It has some of the best beaches in the country, with white sand and warm, blue-green water, and it's world-famous for its people-watching. Then there's the deco. Miami Beach has the largest concentration of deco anywhere in the world, with approximately 1200 buildings lining the streets around Ocean Dr and Collins Ave. Arrange a tour at the Art Deco Welcome Center (p256) or pick up a walking-tour map in the gift shop.

Running alongside the beach, **Ocean Avenue** is lined with cafes that spill out onto the sidewalk; stroll along until you find one that suits your cravings. Another highly strollable area is **Lincoln Road Mall**, a pedestrian promenade lined with stores, restaurants and bars.

Get a taste of everything Miami Beach has to offer with our walking tour (p256).

✖ 🛏 p199

Classic Trip

Eating & Sleeping

Amelia Island ❶

✖ Café Karibo & Karibrew   Fusion, Pub $$

(☎904-277-5269; www.cafekaribo.com; 27 N 3rd St; mains $7-22; ⏱11am-9pm Tue-Sat, 11am-8pm Sun, 11am-3pm Mon) With a large and eclectic menu and two separate spaces to choose from – a courtyard cafe or adjacent brewpub – you're bound to find something that's just right.

🛏 Elizabeth Pointe Lodge   B&B $$$

(☎904-277-4851; www.elizabethpointelodge. com; 98 S Fletcher Ave; r $225-335, ste $385-470; ❄🛜) Out at the beach, this Nantucket-style inn looks like a glorious old sea captain's house, with wraparound porches, gracious service and beautifully appointed rooms.

Jacksonville ❸

✖ Aix   Mediterranean $$$

(☎904-398-1949; www.bistrox.com; 1440 San Marco Blvd; mains $10-28; ⏱11am-10pm Mon-Thu, to 11pm Fri, 5-11pm Sat, 5-9pm Sun) Dine with the fashionable food mavens on fusion-y Mediterranean dishes that burst with global flavors. Reservations recommended.

✖ Clark's Fish Camp   Southern $$

(☎904-268-3474; www.clarksfishcamp.com; 12903 Hood Landing Rd; mains $13-22; ⏱4:30-9:30pm Mon-Thu, 4:30-10pm Fri, 11:30am-10pm Sat, 11:30am-9:30pm Sun) Sample Florida's Southern 'Cracker' cuisine of gator, snake, catfish and frog's legs in this unforgettable swamp shack far south of downtown Jacksonville.

St Augustine ❹

✖ Floridian   New American $$

(☎904-829-0655; www.thefloridianstaug.com; 39 Cordova St; mains $12-20; ⏱11am-3pm Wed-Mon, 5-9pm Mon-Thu, 5-10pm Fri & Sat) Though it oozes with locavore earnestness, this farm-to-table restaurant is so fabulous you won't mind. Dine on whimsical neo-Southern creations in a cool eclectic space.

✖ Spanish Bakery   Bakery $

(www.thespanishbakery.com; 42½ St George St; mains $3.50-5.50; ⏱9:30am-3pm) This diminutive stucco bakeshop serves empanadas, sausage rolls and other conquistador-era favorites. Don't hesitate; it sells out quick.

🛏 Casa Monica   Historical Hotel $$$

(☎904-827-1888; www.casamonica.com; 95 Cordova St; r $179-379; P❄🛜🏊) Built in 1888, this is *the* luxe hotel in town, with turrets, richly appointed rooms and fountains adding to the Spanish-Moorish castle atmosphere.

Daytona Beach ❻

✖ Dancing Avocado Kitchen   Mexican $

(110 S Beach St; mains $6-10; ⏱8am-4pm Tue-Sat; 🌱) Fresh, healthful, yummy Mexican dishes dominate the menu at this vegetarian-oriented cafe, but the signature dancing avocado melt is tops.

🛏 Tropical Manor   Resort $$

(☎386-252-4920; www.tropicalmanor.com; 2237 S Atlantic Ave; r $80-315; P❄🛜🏊) This beachfront property is vintage Florida, with motel rooms, efficiencies and cottages all blanketed in a frenzy of murals and bright pastels.

Space Coast ❾

✕ Coconuts on the Beach — Seafood $$

(☎321-784-1422; www.coconutsonthebeach. com; 2 Minutemen Causeway; mains $8-18; ⏰11am-10pm) Coconuts isn't just a name; it's a favored ingredient. The oceanfront 'party deck' hosts regular live music, so head indoors if you're seeking a family atmosphere.

West Palm Beach ⓫

✕ Rhythm Cafe — Fusion $$

(☎561-833-3406; www.rhythmcafe.cc; 3800 S Dixie Hwy; mains $17-30; ⏰5:30-10pm Tue-Sat, to 9pm Sun) There's no lack of flair at this colorful, upbeat bistro located in a converted drugstore. The menu bops happily from goat-cheese pie to tuna tartar to pomegranate-infused catch of the day.

⌂ Hotel Biba — Motel $

(☎561-832-0094; www.hotelbiba.com; 320 Belvedere Rd; r $69-129; ❈🛜📶) The retro-funky exterior looks like a cute 1950s motel, but the rooms have a modern boutique style that would be right at home in Miami's SoBe.

Fort Lauderdale ⓬

✕ Gran Forno — Italian $

(www.gran-forno.com; 1235 E Las Olas Blvd; mains $6-12; ⏰7am-6pm Tue-Sun) This delightfully old-school Milanese-style bakery and cafe serves warm crusty pastries, bubbling pizzas, and fat golden loaves of ciabatta.

✕ Le Tub — Burgers, American $$

(www.theletub.com; 1100 N Ocean Dr; mains $9-20; ⏰11am-1am Mon-Fri, noon-2am Sat & Sun; 🚸) Decorated exclusively with flotsam collected along Hollywood Beach, this quirky burger joint is routinely named 'Best in America.' Expect a wait, both for seating and cooking time. It's worth it.

⌂ Riverside Hotel — Hotel $$

(☎954-467-0671; www.riversidehotel.com; 620 E Las Olas Blvd; r $129-224; P❈🛜📶🍴) Fabulously located on Las Olas, with three room types: more modern rooms in the newer tower, restored rooms in the original property and the more old fashioned 'classic' rooms.

Miami ⓭

✕ Michy's — Fusion $$$

(☎305-759-2001; http://michysmiami.com; 6927 Biscayne Blvd; meals $29-38; ⏰6-10:30pm Tue-Thu, to 11pm Fri & Sat, to 10pm Sun; 🍴) Organic, locally sourced ingredients and a stylish, fantastical decor are what you'll find at Michelle 'Michy' Bernstein's place – one of the brightest stars in Miami's culinary constellation.

⌂ Biltmore Hotel — Historical Hotel $$$

(☎855-311-6903; www.biltmorehotel.com; 1200 Anastasia Ave; r from $209; P❈🛜📶🍴) This 1926 hotel is a National Historic Landmark and an icon of luxury. Standard rooms are small, but public spaces are palatial; its fabulous pool is the largest hotel pool in the country.

Miami Beach ⓮

✕ 11th St Diner — Diner $

(www.eleventhstreetdiner.com; 1065 Washington Ave; mains $9-18; ⏰24hr except Tue midnight-7am Wed) This deco diner housed inside a gleaming Pullman train car sees round-the-clock activity and is especially popular with people staggering home from clubs.

✕ Joe's Stone Crab Restaurant — American $$$

(☎305-673-0365; www.joesstonecrab.com; 11 Washington Ave; mains $11-60; ⏰11:30am-2pm Wed-Sun Oct-Jun, 6-10pm Wed-Sun year-round) Opened as a 1913 lunch counter, this swanky seafood and chophouse is tops. (Tip: hit the cheaper take-out window for a beach picnic.)

⌂ Clay Hotel — Hotel $

(☎800-379-2529, 305-534-2988; www.clay hotel.com; 1438 Washington Ave; r $88-190; ❈@🛜) Located in a 100-year-old Spanish-style villa – legend has it that Al Capone once slept here – the Clay has clean and comfortable rooms and is located right on Espanola Way.

⌂ Pelican Hotel — Boutique Hotel $$$

(☎305-673-3373; www.pelicanhotel.com; 826 Ocean Dr; r $165-425, ste $295-555; ❈🛜) The name and deco facade don't hint at anything unusual, but the decorators went wild inside with great themes such as 'Best Whorehouse,' 'Executive Zebra' and 'Me Tarzan, You Vain.'

Breaux Bridge *Steamy swampland and outstanding Cajun cuisi*

Cajun Country

15

Enter a maze of bayous, lakes, swamps and prairies where the crawfish boils, and all-night jam sessions and dance parties don't end.

TRIP HIGHLIGHTS

160 miles

Chicot State Park
Wander between bayous and cypress stands

3
Mamou

105 miles

Breaux Bridge
Dine on decadent Cajun fare

2

6
FINISH

New Iberia

Morgan City

Thibodaux
START

230 miles

Lafayette
Split time between live music and Cajun cuisine

4 DAYS
370 MILES / 595KM

GREAT FOR...

BEST TIME TO GO

March to June for festivals in Acadiana, plus warm weather and lots of parties.

 ESSENTIAL PHOTO

Cajun concerts rocking Fred's Lounge every Saturday morning.

 BEST FOR CULTURE

The unique folkways of Acadiana permeating south Louisiana.

201

15 | Cajun Country

Cross into south Louisiana, and you venture into a land that's intensely, immediately unique. You will drive past dinosaur-laced wetlands where standing water is uphill from the floodplain, through villages where French is still the language of celebration (and, sometimes, the home) and towns that love to fiddle, dance, two-step and, most of all, eat well. *Bievenue Louisianne, cher*: this is Cajun Country, a waterlogged, toe-tapping nation unto itself.

❶ Thibodaux

Thibodaux (tib-ah-doe), huddled against the banks of Bayou Lafourcge, is the traditional gateway to Cajun country for those traveling from New Orleans. Thanks to a city center lined with historical homes, it's a fair bit more attractive than nearby Houma, which is often also cited as a major Cajun country destination but is in reality more of a charmless oil town. The main attraction in Thibodaux is the **Wetlands Acadian Cultural Center** (✆985-448-1375; www.nps.gov/jela; 314 St Mary St; admission free; ⊙9am-8pm Mon, to 6pm Tue-Thu, to 5pm Fri & Sat, closed Sun Jun-Aug, plus Christmas & Mardi Gras; 👫🎫), part of the **Jean Laffitte National Park** system. NPS rangers lead boat tours from here into the bayou during spring and fall; you can either chug to the **ED White Plantation** (⊙10am-noon; admission $5) on Wednesday or the **Madewood Plantation** (⊙10am-2:30pm; admission $28.25) on Saturday, where you're given a house tour and lunch. The Center also hosts an excellent on-site museum, and helpful staff provide free walking tours of Thibodaux town (2pm Monday, Tuesday and Thursday). If you're lucky, you'll land here on a Monday evening, when Cajun musicians jam out (5:30pm to 7pm).

🍴 p207

The Drive » Get on Hwy 90 and drive to Breaux Bridge. It's about two hours nonstop, but don't be afraid to occasionally peel off and check out some side roads.

(Map labels)

Bun
(3042)
Chicot State Park ❸ — 10
Ville Pla
Mamou ❹ — 10
167
Oberlin — 13
Opelousa
Eunice ❺
367
13
Crowley° — Rayne
10
Gueydan — Kaplan
Intracoastal Waterway
Grand Lake
White Lake
Gulf of Mexico

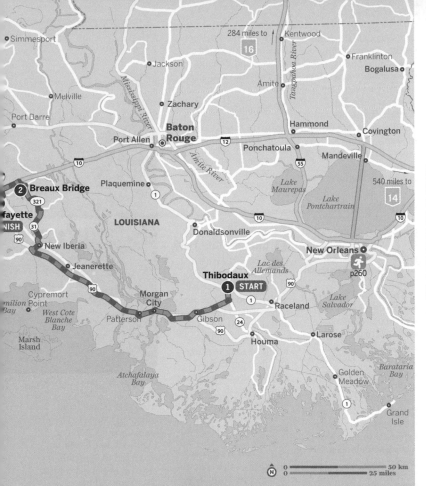

Simmesport

Jackson

284 miles to 16 Kentwood

Franklinton

Bogalusa

Melville

Amite

Zachary

Port Darre

Baton Rouge

Port Allen

Hammond

Covington

Ponchatoula

Mandeville

12

Breaux Bridge

321

Plaquemine

540 miles to 14

fayette

31

NISH

90

LOUISIANA

Donaldsonville

New Iberia

Jeanerette

Cypremort
milion Point
Bay

West Cote
Blanche
Bay

Patterson

Morgan
City

Gibson

24

Thibodaux

1 START

Raceland

Lake
Salvador

Larose

New Orleans

p260

Marsh
Island

Atchafalaya
Bay

Houma

Golden
Meadow

Baratatia
Bay

Grand
Isle

Lac des
Allemands

Lake
Maurepas

Lake
Pontchartrain

N
0   50 km
0   25 miles

TRIP HIGHLIGHT

❷ Breaux Bridge

Little Breaux Bridge
boasts a pretty
'downtown' of smallish
side streets, Cajun
hospitality and a silly
amount of good food.
Your main objective is
to eat at the ridiculously

LINK YOUR TRIP

14 Highway 1
From Thibodaux
make your way to Baton
Rouge then head east on
the I-12 and I-10 all the
way to the start of your
Florida coast cruise.

16 The Blues Highway
From Thibodaux head
north to Baton Rouge
then east on I-12. At
Hammond, head north
on the I-55 to Memphis.

delicious Café des Amis (p207), where sinfully good Cajun fare is often served alongside local live music. The shows are scheduled for Wednesday nights and Sunday mornings (zydeco brunch!), but performers have a habit of dropping in unexpectedly. Otherwise there's not a lot to do in Breaux Bridge but stroll around the handsome town center and, if you're here during the first weekend in May, check out the **Breaux Bridge Crawfish Festival** (www.bbcrawfest.com).

Three miles south of Breaux Bridge is **Lake Martin** (Lake Martin Rd), a bird sanctuary that hosts thousands of great and cattle egrets, blue heron and more than a few gators. A small walkway extends over the algae-carpeted black water and loops through a pretty cypress swamp, while birds huddle in nearby trees.

Stop by Henderson, 8 miles northeast of Breaux Bridge. On Sunday afternoons, **Angelle's Whiskey River** (📞337-228-8567; 1006 Earlene Dr; cover varies; ⊘call for opening hours) rocks to zydeco and Cajun tunes. It's a small house, and it gets packed. Locals dance on tables, on the bar and in the water. Nearby **Pat's** (📞337-228-7512; www.patsfishermanswharf.com; 1008 Henderson Levee Rd; mains $12-24; ⊘11am-10pm, to 10:30pm Fri-

Sun; 🅿 🚻) serves decent seafood of the fried variety, and dancing of the two-step and Cajun genre.

✂️ 🛏️ p207

The Drive ›› From Breaux Bridge you can take Hwy 49 north for about 24 miles, then US 167 north to Ville Platte, then LA-3042 to Chicot State Park, a total trip time of about 80 minutes.

TRIP HIGHLIGHT

❸ Chicot State Park

Cajun country isn't just a cultural space – it's a physical landscape as well, a land of shadowy, moss-draped pine forest and slow-water bayous and lakes. Sometimes it can be tough seeing all this from the roadways, as roads have understandably been built away from floodable bottomlands. **Chicot State Park** (📞888-677-2442, 337-363-2403; www.crt.state.la.us/parks/ichicot.aspx; 3469 Chicot Park Rd; per person $1; 🅿 🚻 🛶) is a wonderful place to access the natural beauty of Cajun Country. An excellent interpretive center is fun for kids and informative for adults, and deserves enormous accolades for its open, airy design. Miles of trails extend into the nearby forests, cypress swamps and wetlands. If you can, stay for early evening; the sunsets over the Spanish moss–draped

trees that fringe Lake Chicot are superb. There are campsites ($16 per night October to March, $20 April to September), six- and 15-person cabins ($85/120) and boat rentals (per hour/day $5/20) all available.

The Drive ›› Head back toward Ville Platte, then turn onto LA-10 west. After 7 miles turn south onto LA-13; it's about 4 miles more to Mamou.

❹ Mamou

Deep in the hart of Cajun Country, Mamou is a typical south Louisiana small town six days of the week, worth a peek

Lafayette La Chapelle des Attakapas, Vermilionville

and a short stop before rolling to Eunice. But on Saturday mornings, Mamou's hometown hangout, little **Fred's Lounge** (420 6th St; ⏰8am-1:30pm Sat), becomes the apotheosis of a Cajun dancehall.

OK, to be fair: Fred's is more of a dance shack than hall. It's a little bar and it gets more than a little crowded from 8:30am to 2pm-ish, when owner 'Tante' (auntie) Sue and her staff host a Francophone-friendly music morning, with bands, beer, cigarettes and dancing (seriously, it gets smoky in here. Fair warning). Sue herself will often take to the stage to dispense wisdom and song in Cajun French, all while taking pulls off a bottle of brown liquor she keeps in a pistol holster.

The Drive ≫ Eunice is only 11 miles south of Mamou; just keep heading straight on LA-13.

----

❺ Eunice

Eunice lies in the heart of the Cajun prairie, its associated folkways, and music. Musician Mark Savoy builds accordions at his **Savoy Music Center** (☎337-457-9563; www.savoymusiccenter.com; Hwy 190; ⏰9am-5pm Tue-Fri, 9am-noon Sat), where you can also pluck some CDs and catch a Saturday morning jam session. Saturday night means the Rendez-Vous Cajuns are playing the **Liberty Theater** (☎337-457-7389; 200 Park Ave; admission $5), which is just two blocks from the **Cajun Music Hall of Fame & Museum** (☎337-457-6534; www.cajunfrenchmusic.org; 230 S CC Duson Dr; admission free; ⏰9am-5pm Tue-Sat) – a small affair, to be sure, but charming in its way. The NPS-run **Prairie Acadian Cultural Center** (☎337-457-8499; www.nps.gov/jela; 250 West Park Ave;

CAJUNS, CREOLES AND...CREOLES

A lot of tourists in Louisiana use the terms 'Cajun' and 'Creole' interchangeably, but the two cultures are different and distinct. 'Creole' refers to descendants of the original European settlers of Louisiana, a blended mix of mainly French and Spanish ancestry. The Creoles tend to have urban connections to New Orleans and considered their own culture refined and civilized. Many (but not all) were descended from aristocrats, merchants and skilled tradesmen.

The Cajuns can trace their lineage to the Acadians, colonists from rural France who settled Nova Scotia. After the British conquered Canada, the proud Acadians refused to kneel to the new crown, and were exiled in the mid-18th century – an act known as the *Grand Dérangement*. Many exiles settled in south Louisiana; they knew the area was French, but the Acadians ('Cajun' is an English bastardization of the word) were often treated as country bumpkins by the Creoles. The Acadians-cum-Cajuns settled in the bayous and prairies, and to this day self-conceptualize as a more rural, frontier-stye culture.

Adding confusion to all of the above is the practice, standard in many post-colonial French societies, of referring to mixed-race individuals as 'creoles.' This happens in Louisiana, but there is a cultural difference between Franco-Spanish Creoles and mixed-race creoles, even as these two communities very likely share actual blood ancestry.

admission free; ⊘8am-5pm Tue-Fri, to 6pm Sat) is another worthy stop, and often hosts music nights and educational lectures.

The Drive » Head east on US 190 (Laurel Ave) and turn right onto LA-367. Follow LA-367 for around 19 miles (it becomes LA-98 for a bit), then merge onto I-10 eastbound. Follow I-10 for around 14 miles, then take exit 101 onto LA-182/N University Ave; follow into downtown Lafayette.

TRIP HIGHLIGHT

❻ Lafayette

Lafayette, capital of Cajun Country and fourth-largest city in Louisiana, has a wonderful concentration of good eats and culture for a city of its size (around 120,000). On most nights you can catch fantastic zydeco, country, blues, funk, swamp rock and even punk blasting out of the excellent **Blue Moon Saloon** (www .bluemoonpresents.com; 215 E Convent St; cover $5-8); the crowd here is young, hip and often tattooed, but they'll get down to a fiddle as easily as drum-and-bass. During the last weekend in April Lafayette hosts **Festival International de Louisiane** (www.festival international.com), the largest Francophone musical event in the Western Hemisphere.

Vermilionville (☎337-233-4077; www.vermilionville .org; 300 Fisher Rd; adult/ student $8/6; ⊘10am-4pm Tue-Sun; 🚹), a restored/ re-created 19th-century Cajun village, wends its way along the bayou near the airport. Costumed docents explain Cajun, Creole and Native American history, local bands perform on Sundays, and boat tours of the bayou are offered.

The not-as-polished **Acadian Village** (☎337 981 2364; www.acadianvillage.org; 200 Greenleaf Dr; adult/student $7/4; ⊘10am-4pm) offers a similar experience, minus the boat tours.

Next to Vermilionville, the NPS runs the **Acadian Cultural Center** (www .nps.gov/jela; 501 Fisher Rd; ⊘8am-5pm), containing exhibits on Cajun life; it's a little dry compared to the above, but still worth a visit.

✕ 🛏 p207

Eating & Sleeping

Thibodaux ❶

✕ Fremin's   Cajun $$

(☏985-449-0333; 402 West Third St; mains
$11-23; ⏱11am-2pm Tue-Fri, 5-9pm Tue-Thu,
to 10pm Fri & Sat) Fremin's is one of the great
granddaddies of high-end, classic Cajun cuisine.
The menu doesn't change much, and while there
are some items that could use an update, overall
this is a solid menu. Case in point: soft-shell
crab served over pasta with a meltingly good
mushroom brandy sauce.

Breaux Bridge ❷

✕ Café des Amis   Cajun $$$

(www.cafedesamis.com; 140 E Bridge St; mains
$17-26; ⏱11am-2pm Tue, to 9pm Wed & Thu,
7:30am-9:30pm Fri & Sat, 8am-2pm Sun) What's
better than the Creole and Cajun menu at this
joint? Not much really, but there's a strong case
to be made for the surreal folk art on the walls
and the live zydeco breakfast that goes off every
Saturday morning.

⌫ Bayou Cabins   Cabin $

(☏337-332-6158; www.bayoucabins.com; 100 W
Mills Ave; cabins $60-125) Each of the 14 cabins
on the Bayou Teche is completely individual.
Cabin 1 has 1949 newspapers as wallpaper
(aka insulation), and cabin 7 has fine Victorian
antiques and a claw-foot tub. Your full, hot
breakfast is served at 9am and the on-site store
sells homemade cracklings and boudin.

Lafayette ❻

✕ Artmosphere   American $

(☏337-233-3331; 902 Johnston St; mains
under $10; ⏱11am-2am Mon-Sat, to midnight

Sun) Your place if you're jonesing for vegan/
vegetarian food, or even just a hookah, plus
a lovely selection of beer on offer. Live music
every night and a crowd that largely consists of
the student and artist set.

✕ Dwyer's   Diner $

(☏337-235-9364; 323 Jefferson St; mains $5-12;
⏱7am-3pm; 🚶) This family-owned joint is
especially fun on Wednesday mornings when
local Cajuns shoot the breeze in their old-school
French dialect.

✕ French Press   Breakfast $$$

(www.thefrenchpresslafayette.com; 214 E
Vermillion; breakfast $6-$10.50, dinner mains
$29-38; ⏱7am-2pm Tue-Thu, 7am-2pm & 5:30-
9pm Fri, 9am-2pm & 5:30-9pm Sat, 9am-2pm
Sun; 🛜) This French-Cajun hybrid is the best
culinary thing going in Lafayette. Breakfasts
are mind blowing, with a sinful Cajun benedict
(boudin instead of ham), cheddar grits (that
will kill you dead) and organic granola (offset
the grits). Dinner is wonderful as well; that rack
of lamb with the truffle gratin is a special bit of
gastronomic dreaminess.

⌫ Blue Moon
Guest House   Guesthouse $

(☏877-766-2583, 337-234-2422; www.blue
moonguesthouse.com; 215 E Convent St; dm
$18, r $73-94; 🅿❄@🛜) There's a backyard
nightclub and hostel environs (dorms and
some private rooms) in this tidy old Lafayette
home. Does it get loud? Hell yes, but the music
is great.

⌫ La Maison de Belle B&B   B&B $$

(☏337-235-2520; 608 Girard Park Dr; r
$110-150) Overnight where John Kennedy
Toole dreamed up *Confederacy of Dunces*. The
grounds and adjacent park are lovely.

Clarksdale The ideal base for a
Mississippi blues tour

The Blues Highway

16

Listen to living blues legends howl their sad enlightenment and pay homage to the music that saturated northern Mississippi for a century, and bloomed rock'n'roll.

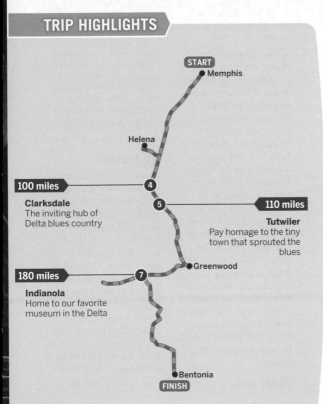

TRIP HIGHLIGHTS

START
● Memphis

● Helena

100 miles
④

⑤

110 miles
Tutwiler
Pay homage to the tiny town that sprouted the blues

Clarksdale
The inviting hub of Delta blues country

180 miles
⑦

● Greenwood

Indianola
Home to our favorite museum in the Delta

● Bentonia
FINISH

3 DAYS
350 MILES / 563KM

GREAT FOR...

BEST TIME TO GO
May and June for blues festivals in the Delta.

ESSENTIAL PHOTO

Red's smoky, burgundy glow when a bluesman is wailing on stage.

BEST FOR MUSIC

The music and soul of the Mississippi Delta – a cultural immersion with an epic soundtrack.

209

16 The Blues Highway

In the plains, along Hwy 61, American music took root. It arrived from Africa in the souls of slaves, morphed into field songs, and wormed into the brain of a sharecropping troubadour waiting for a train. In Clarksdale, at the Crossroads, legend has it that Robert Johnson made a deal with the devil and became America's first guitar hero. But to fully grasp its influence, start in Memphis.

❶ Memphis

The Mississippi Delta and Memphis have always been inextricably linked. Memphis was a beacon for the Delta bluesmen, with its relative freedoms, African American–owned businesses and the bright lights and foot-stamping crowds of Beale St, which is still rocking.

Rum Boogie Cafe (📞912-528-0150; www.rumboogie.com; 182 Beale St) is a Cajun-themed blues bar with a terrific house band. The original **BB King's** (📞901-524-5464; www.bbkingclubs.com; 143 Beale St; ⏲noon-1am, kitchen open until 11pm) is a living monument to the Missisippi genius who made good here.

And it was in Memphis where WC Handy was first credited with putting the blues to paper when he wrote 'Beale Street Blues' in 1916. You can visit the house where he lived. The Mississippi Delta legacy bubbles up at Sun Studio, where you can tour the label that launched Elvis, whose interpretation of the blues birthed rock'n'roll. And it's running through the veins of the wonderful Stax Museum of American Soul Music. Those connections are explained perfectly at the Memphis Rock 'n' Soul Museum.

✕ ⍾ p218

The Drive ≫ US 61 begins in Memphis, where it is a wide avenue snaking through the city's rough seam. Eventually urbanity gives way to flat farmland, and the highway goes rural as you enter Mississippi

❷ Tunica

A gathering of casinos rests near the riverbanks in Tunica, Hwy 61's most prosperous and least authentic town. Nevertheless, it is the gateway to the blues and home to their juke-joint mock-up of a **Tunica Visitors Center** (📞662-363-3800; www.tunicatravel.com; 13625 US 61; ⏲9am-6pm), where a cool interactive digital guide comes packed with information on famed blues artists and the

Mississippi Blues Trail itself. It's a good place to get inspired about what you are about to experience, and perhaps do some plotting and planning. Unless you play cards, however, Tunica is not otherwise noteworthy.

The Drive » Continue on the arrow-straight road for 19 miles, then veer west on US 49 and over the Mississippi River into Helena, Arkansas.

③ Helena

Helena, Arkansas, a depressed mill town 32 miles north and across the Mississippi River from Clarksdale, was once the home of blues legend Sonny Boy Williamson. He was a

LINK YOUR TRIP

15 Cajun Country

From Bentonia take Hwy 49 to Jackson and then south on I-55 until Hammond. From there head west to Baton Rouge and then south to Thibodaux and Cajun Country.

17 Natchez Trace Parkway

From Memphis head east on I-40 to Nashville where the Natchez Trace trail begins.

regular on *King Biscuit Time*, America's original blues radio show. It still broadcasts out of the **Delta Cultural Center** (📞870-338-4350; www .deltaculturalcenter.com; 141 Cherry St; admission free; 🕐9am-5pm Tue-Sat), a worthwhile blues museum. Down the street you'll find the Delta's best record store, **Bubba's Blues Corner** (📞870-995-1326; 105 Cherry St; admission free; 🕐9am-5pm Tue-Sat; 🚻). Delightfully disorganized, it's supposedly a regular stop on Robert Plant's personal blues pilgrimages. Bubba himself is warm and friendly and a wealth of knowledge. If the shop isn't open when you fall by, give him a ring, and he'll happily open up. Helena hosts two festivals of note.

The **King Biscuit Blues Festival** (www .kingbiscuitfestival.com; tickets $45; 🕐Oct) is held over three days each October. In 2013, the headliners were Greg Allman and Robert Cray. It also hosts a **Live On The Levee** (www.kingbiscuitfestival.com/ live-on-the-levee; adult/child $30/free) concert series, with regular concerts in the spring and summer. Rockabilly fans will want to land here in May, for the annual **Arkansas Delta Rockabilly Festival** (www.deltarockabillyfest.com; tickets $30; 🕐May).

The Drive 》 US 49 converges with the US 61 in Mississippi, and from there it's 30 miles south until you reach the Crossroads. Peeking out above the trees on the northeast corner of US 61 and US 49, where the roads diverge once again, is the landmark weathervane of three interlocking blue guitars. You have arrived in the Delta's beating heart.

DAVID LYONS / ALAMY ©

KING BISCUIT TIME

Sonny Boy Williamson was the host of *King Biscuit Time* when BB King was a young buck. King recalls listening to the lunch-hour program, and dreaming of possibilities. When he moved to Memphis as a teenager and began playing Beale St gigs, Williamson invited King to play on his radio show, and a star was born. Williamson remained an important mentor for King as his career took off. The radio show, which begins weekdays at 12:15pm, is still running, and has been hosted by Sunshine Sonny Payne since 1951.

TRIP HIGHLIGHT

❹ Clarksdale

Clarksdale is the Delta's most useful base – with more comfortable hotel rooms and modern, tasteful kitchens here than the rest of the Delta combined. It's also within a couple of hours of all the blues sights. If you want to know who's playing where, come see Roger Stolle at **Cat Head** (📞662-624-5992; www.cathead.biz; 252 Delta Ave; 🕐10am-5pm Mon-Sat; 🚻). He also sells a good range of blues souvenirs, and is the main engine

Memphis Rum Boogie Cafe

behind the annual **Juke Joint Festival** (www.jukejointfestival.com; tickets $15). Wednesday through Saturday live music sweeps through Clarksdale like a summer storm. Morgan Freeman's **Ground Zero Blues Club** (www.groundzerobluesclub.com; 0 Blues Alley; ⊙11am-2pm Mon & Tue, to 11pm Wed & Thu, to 1am Fri & Sat) has the most professional bandstand and sound system, but it will never compare to **Red's** (☎662-627-3166; 395 Sunflower Ave; cover $10; ⊙live music 9pm Fri & Sat), a funky, red-lit, juke joint run with in-your-face charm by Red himself. He'll fire up his enormous grill outside on special occasions. The **Delta Blues Museum** (www.deltabluesmuseum.org; 1 Blues Alley; adult/senior & student $7/5; ⊙9am-5pm Mon-Sat), set in the city's old train depot, has a fine collection of blues memorabilia, including Muddy Waters' reconstructed Mississippi cabin. The creative, multimedia exhibits also honor BB King, John Lee Hooker, Big Mama Thornton and WC Handy.

✗ 🛏 p218

The Drive » From Clarksdale, take US 49 south from the Crossroads to the tiny town of Tutwiler.

- - - - - - - - - - -

TRIP HIGHLIGHT

⑤ Tutwiler

Sleepy Tutwiler is where WC Handy heard that ragged guitar man in 1903. Handy, known as the 'father of the blues,' was inspired to (literally) write the original blues song, in 12 bars with a three-chord progression and AAB verse pattern, in 1912, though he wasn't widely recognized as an originator until 'Beale Street Blues' became a hit

213

THE BLUES HIGHWAY
ADAM SKOLNICK, AUTHOR

The story of America is one of arrival from elsewhere, suffering at the mercy of nature – or an oppressor or time – and it's also a story of rebirth. The blues is America's soundtrack. Beautiful and wild, it thrums up in those darkest hours and explodes like catharsis. It's a painkiller, a purification. In the moment, it feels like liberation. It's a sound that revolutionized America. And it happened here.

Top: Instrument display, Delta Blues Museum; © Delta Blues Museum
Left: Tunica Visitors Center
Right: James 'Chicken' Dooris, Ground Zero Blues Club

in 1916. That way-back divine encounter, which birthed blues and jazz, is honored along the **Tutwiler Tracks** (off Hwy 49; ), where the train station used to be. The mural also reveals the directions to **Sonny Boy Williamson's Grave** (off Hwy 49;). He's buried amid a broken-down jumble of gravestones. Williamson's headstone is set back in the trees. Rusted harmonicas, candles and half-empty whiskey bottles have been left here out of respect.

The Drive » Continue on the other Blues Highway, US 49 south through more farmland, across the Yazoo River, and into the rather charming and tony town of Greenwood.

❻ Greenwood

Greenwood is the Delta's most prosperous town that doesn't involve slot machines. The financial backbone here is the Viking Range corporation which builds its magnificent ranges in town and whose wares you can buy in upmarket showrooms. There is also a fantastic cafe and a fine hotel – the best in the Delta – within these city limits. And each May, the town gets behind the local music scene, with its annual **River to the Rails** (662-453-7625; www.rivertotherails. org; 325 Main St) festival. Along with two days of live blues, there is a barbecue and an art competition. As far as history goes, Greenwood happens to be the hometown of Byron de la Beckwith, the presumed murderer of Medgar Evers.

 p219

The Drive » From Greenwood, take US 82 east, over the Yazoo River, through leafy horse country, and through an ugly commercial bloom of big chain stores and kitchens, into Indianola.

7 Indianola

You have reached the home town of arguably the Delta's biggest star. When BB King was still a child, Indianola was home to **Club Ebony** (☎662-887-3086; www .clubebony.biz; 404 Hannah St; no cover; ☺noon-late daily, live music 6-10pm Sun), a

fixture on the so-called 'chitlin circuit.' Ebony gave BB his first steady work, and hosted legends including Howlin' Wolf, Muddy Waters, Count Basie and James Brown. The corner of Church and 2nd is where BB used to strum his beloved guitar, Lucille, for passers-by. Nearby, the **BB King Museum & Delta Interpretive Center** (☎662-887-9539; www.bbkingmuseum.org; 400 Second St; adult/child 5-12yr/under 5yr $12/$5/ free; ☺10am-5pm Tue-Sat, noon-5pm Sun & Mon) is set in a complex around the old Indianola cotton gin. The experience starts with a 12-minute film covering his life's work. Afterward you are free to roam halls packed with interactive exhibits, tracing King's

history and his musical influences – African, gospel and country. Other interactive exhibits demonstrate his influence on the next generation of artists, including Jimmie Hendrix and the Allman Brothers. Oh, and his 12 Grammy awards are here too. King returns to Indianola for a free annual show as part of his annual **BB King Homecoming Festival** (www.bbkingmuseum. org; Fletcher Park; advance purchase/day of $12/18).

The Drive » From Indianola, go west through the fast-food jumble along US 82 into Leland.

8 Leland

Leland is a small, down-on-its-luck town, but one with a terrific museum. **Highway 61 Blues Museum** (☎662-686-7646; www.highway61blues.com; 400 N Broad St; admission $7; ☺10am-5pm Mon-Sat; ♿) offers details on local folks including Ruby Edwards and David 'Honeyboy' Edwards. It also puts on a lauded blues festival each October, held in Warfield Point Park, right on the Mississippi River.

Local luminary Jim Henson, the creator of the Muppets, is also from Leland, and his life and work are celebrated at the **Jim Henson Exhibit** (☎662-686-7383; www .birthplaceofthefrog.com; 415

BB KING'S BLUES

BB King grew up in the cotton fields on the outskirts of Indianola, a leafy middle-class town, and it didn't take long before he learned what it meant to have the blues. His parents divorced when he was four. His mother died when he was nine. His grandmother passed away when he was 14. All alone, he was forced to leave Indianola – the only town he ever knew – to live with his father. He quickly became homesick, and made his way back. As a young man he was convinced he would become a cotton farmer. There weren't many other possibilities to consider. Or so he thought. When he went to Memphis for the first time in the 1940s, his world opened. From there he drifted into West Memphis, Arkansas, where he met Sonny Boy Williamson, who put the young upstart on the radio for the first time, launching his career.

S Deer Creek Dr; donations encouraged; ⏰10am-4pm Mon-Sat) on the bank of Deer Creek.

The Drive » Head west on US 82 for 25 miles until it ends near the river.

- - - - - - - - - - - - - -

❾ Greenville

The Mississippi River town of Greenville was a fixture on the riverboat route and has long been a gambling resort area. For years it supported blues and jazz musicians who played the resorts, and some – including BB King – make appearances to this day. Although it's scruffy around the edges, Greenville can be pleasant along the river. But the real reason to visit is to try the steaks, tamales and chili at **Doe's Eat Place** (📞662-334-3315; 502 Nelson St; ⏰5-9pm Mon-Sat), a classic hole-in-the-wall joint you may never forget.

The Drive » Return to Indianola then drive south on US 49W to humble Bentonia.

- - - - - - - - - - - - - -

❿ Bentonia

Bentonia, once a thriving farming community, now has fewer than 100 people and the downtown is gutted, but it's still home to one of Mississippi's most historical jukes. The Holmes family opened the **Blue Front** (📞662-755-2278; downtown Bentonia; ⏰hours vary, call ahead) during the Jim Crow

DETOUR: PO MONKEYS

Start: ❹ **Clarksdale**

Take US 61 south from Clarksdale for about 27 miles and head west on Dillon Rd through farmland. Po Monkeys, in Merigold, Mississippi, is one of the Delta's most beloved juke joints. It only has live music about once a month, but there's sweet trouble to be found here on Mondays when naked Shack Dancers prowl, and on Thursdays when college kids dance to DJ sets till the wee hours. Being a night-time venue, you'll be doubling back to Clarksdale after partying here.

period, when African Americans weren't even allowed to sip Coca-Cola. They sold house-stilled corn liquor (to blacks and whites) during Prohibition and welcomed all the Delta blues artists of the day: Sonny Boy, Percy Smith and Jack Owens among them. The joint still opens in the evenings, but live blues only blooms during Bentonia's annual **festival** (www.facebook.com/BentoniaBluesFestival; Downtown Bentonia; tickets $10; ⏰mid-Jun) when the town comes back to life, if ever so briefly.

FAVORITE BLUES FESTS

To make the most of your music-loving dollar, hit the Delta during one of its many blues festivals. Rooms can be scarce. Book well in advance.

» **Juke Joint Festival** (www.jukejointfestival.com; tickets $15) Clarksdale, mid-April

» **King Biscuit Blues Festival** (www.kingbiscuitfestival.com; tickets $45) Helena, October

» **BB King Homecoming** (www.bbkingmuseum.org; Fletcher Park; tickets $18) Indianola, early June

» **Highway 61 Blues Festival** (www.highway61blues.com; Warfield Point Park) Leland, early June

» **Bentonia Blues Festival** (www.facebook.com/BentoniaBluesFestival; Downtown Bentonia; tickets $10) Bentonia, mid-June

» **Sunflower River Blues & Gospel Festival** (www.sunflowerfest.org) Clarksdale, August

Eating & Sleeping

Memphis ❶

✕ Arcade
Diner $

(www.arcaderestaurant.com; 540 S Main St; mains $8-10; ⏰7am-3pm, plus dinner Fri) Elvis used to eat at this ultra-retro diner, Memphis' oldest. Crowds still pack in for sublime sweet-potato pancakes and greasy-spoon cheeseburgers. It's walking distance from downtown and Beale St.

✕ Charlie Vergos' Rendezvous
Barbecue $$

(☎901-523-2746; www.hogsfly.com; 52 S 2nd St; mains $10-20; ⏰4:30-10:30pm Tue-Thu, 11am-11pm Fri, from 11:30am Sat) Tucked in an alleyway off Union Ave, this subterranean institution sells an astonishing 5 tons of its exquisite dry-rubbed ribs weekly. The ribs don't come with any sauce, but the pork shoulder does, so try a combo and you'll have plenty of sauce to enjoy. The beef brisket is also tremendous. With a superb, no-nonsense waitstaff, and walls plastered with historical memorabilia, eating here is an event. Expect a wait.

✕ Gus's World Famous Fried Chicken
Chicken $

(☎901-527-4877; www.facebook.com/pages/Guss-World-Famous-Fried-Chicken-Memphis-TN/103867756323858; 310 S Front St; mains $6-9; ⏰11am-9pm Sun-Thu, to 10pm Fri & Sat) Fried-chicken connoisseurs across the globe twitch in their sleep at night, dreaming about the gossamer-light fried chicken at this downtown concrete bunker with the fun, neon-lit interior and vintage juke box. On busy nights, waits can top an hour. So worth it.

🛏 Heartbreak Hotel
Hotel $$

(☎877-777-0606, 901-332-1000; www.elvis.com/epheartbreakhotel; 3677 Elvis Presley Blvd; d from $120; P✻@🔊🖳) At the end of Lonely St (seriously) across from Graceland, this basic hotel is tarted up with all things Elvis. Ramp up the already palpable kitsch with one of the themed suites, such as the red-velvet monstrosity that is the Burnin' Love room.

🛏 Madison Hotel
Boutique $$$

(☎901-333-1200; www.madisonhotelmemphis.com; 79 Madison Ave; r from $264; P✻@🔊🖳) If you're looking for a sleek treat, check in to this swanky, boutique sleep. The rooftop garden is one of the best places in town to watch a sunset, and rooms have nice touches, including high ceilings, Italian linens and whirlpool tubs.

Clarksdale ❹

✕ Abe's
BBQ $

(☎662-624-9947; 616 State St; sandwiches $4-6, plates $6-14; ⏰10am-9pm Mon-Thu, 10am-10pm Fri & Sat, 11am-2pm Sun; 🖳) In business at the crossroads since 1924, the slow-burning, chili-smothered tamales and melt-off-the-bone ribs are dynamite, and it does brisket and pulled pork sandwiches and plates too.

✕ Delta Donuts
Donuts $

(☎662-627-9094; 610 N State St, Clarksdale; doughnuts $2; ⏰6am-11am; 🖳) Forget calories, and enjoy one of these delectably warm doughnuts stuffed with chocolate and vanilla cream.

✕ Oxbow
Deli $

(115 3rd St; ⏰10am-6pm Mon-Fri, to 5pm Sat) Self-caterers will want to stop by this fresh gourmet market and art gallery with some produce and a selection of specialty deli meats, cheeses, artisan breads, and an array of house-made salads including a tasty-looking quinoa salad and citrus ginger slaw.

✘ Rust   Southern $$

(www.rustclarksdale.com; 218 Delta Ave; mains $12-36; ⊘6-9pm Tue-Thu, to 10pm Fri & Sat) Upscale comfort food done with some degree of aplomb. The crawfish cakes (seasonal) are nice and the grilled asparagus with balsamic reduction is a winner. The burger is decent too. Overall, it's good, not great, unless you count the atmospherics. Think: wood floors, intimate booths and cozy corners. It's definitely a nice spot for a dinner out before a blues show.

✘ Yazoo Pass   Cafe $$

(www.yazoopass.com; 207 Yazoo Ave; lunch mains $6-10, dinner mains $13-26; ⊘7am-9pm Mon-Sat; 🛜) A contemporary new space in town with exposed brick walls, polished concrete fl oors, rattan furnishings and leather booths where you can enjoy fresh scones and croissants in the mornings, a salad bar, sandwiches and soups at lunch, and pan seared ahi, fi let mignon, burgers and pastas at dinner.

🛏 Lofts at the Five & Dime   Lofts $$

(☎888-510-9604; www.fiveanddimelofts. com; 211 Yazoo St; lofts $150-175) Set in a 1954 building are six plush, loft-style apartments with molded concrete counters in the full kitchen, massive flat screens in living room and bedroom, exposed rafters, terrazzo showers and free sodas and water throughout your stay. Units sleep up to four people comfortably.

🛏 Shack Up Inn   Inn $

(☎662-624-8329; www.shackupinn.com; Hwy 49; d $75-165; P ❄ 🛜) Guests stay in refurbished sharecropper cabins or the creatively renovated cotton gin. The whole place reeks of down-home dirty blues and Deep South character – possibly the coolest place you'll ever stay.

Greenwood ❻

✘ Delta Bistro   Southern Fusion $$

(☎662-455-9575; www.deltabistro.com; 117 Main St; mains $9-24; ⊘11am-9pm Mon-Sat) A tasty upmarket cafe serving southern treats such as fried catfish and barbecue shrimp po' boys and crab bisque, as well as fine departures including tender elk brisket, and a seared duck breast served with pork belly and grilled baby asparagus. This is the best kitchen in the Delta.

🛏 Alluvian   Boutique Hotel $$$

(☎662-453-2114; www.thealluvian.com; 318 Howard St; r $200-215; P ❄ @ 🛜) A stunning four-star boutique hotel done up by the Viking corporation, with a gushing fountain in the courtyard and spacious rooms and suites with all the trimmings: soaker tubs, high ceilings, granite wash basins and checkerboard parlor floors in the bath. Some rooms have courtyard views. Others overlook the antiquated downtown. Book ahead, especially on weekdays. This is a business hotel, after all.

Natchez Trace Parkway *Stirring history and natural beauty*

Natchez Trace Parkway

17

With emerald mounds, opulent mansions and layers of history, the Natchez Trace Parkway winds 444 gorgeously wooded miles from Nashville all the way to southern Mississippi.

TRIP HIGHLIGHTS

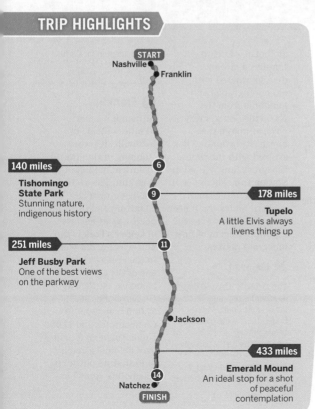

START
Nashville
Franklin

140 miles

6

Tishomingo State Park
Stunning nature, indigenous history

9

178 miles

Tupelo
A little Elvis always livens things up

251 miles

11

Jeff Busby Park
One of the best views on the parkway

Jackson

433 miles

Emerald Mound
An ideal stop for a shot of peaceful contemplation

14

Natchez

FINISH

3 DAYS
444 MILES / 714KM

GREAT FOR...

BEST TIME TO GO
September to November and April to June to dodge the sweltering heat.

ESSENTIAL PHOTO
Emerald Mound for magical sunset views.

BEST FOR HISTORY
The whole route for glimpses of indigenous ways, echoes of a pioneering past, and the birthplace of Elvis.

221

17 Natchez Trace Parkway

America grew from infancy to childhood then adolescence in the late 18th and 19th centuries. That's when settlers explored and expanded, traded and clashed with Native Americans, and eventually confronted their own shadows during the Civil War. Evidence of this drama can be found along the Natchez Trace, but before you begin, hit the honky-tonks and enjoy a little night music.

❶ Nashville

Although this leafy, sprawling southern city – with its thriving economy and hospitable locals – has no scarcity of charms, it really is all about the music. Boot-stomping honky-tonks lure aspiring stars from across the country in the hopes of ascending into royalty, of the type on display at the Country Music Hall of Fame. Don't miss Bluebird Cafe: tucked into a suburban strip mall, this singer-songwriter haven was made famous in the recent television series *Nashville*. No chitchat or you will get bounced. Enjoy a less-controlled musical environment at Tootsie's Orchid Lounge, a glorious dive smothered with old photographs and handbills from the Nashville Sound glory days, although the music (still country) has evolved with the times. Bluegrass fans will adore Station Inn, where you'll sit at one of the small cocktail tables, swill beer (only), and marvel at the lightning fingers of fine bluegrass players.

🍴 🛏 p230

The Drive » The next day head south, and you will traverse the Double-Arch Bridge, 155ft above the valley, before settling in for a pleasant country drive on the parkway. You'll notice dense woods encroaching and arching elegantly over the baby-bottom-smooth highway for the next 444 miles.

❷ Franklin

Although it's just 10 miles outside of Nashville, it's worth stopping in the tiny historical hamlet of Franklin. The Victorian-era downtown is charming and the nearby artsy enclave of **Leiper's Fork** is fun and eclectic. But you're in the area to check out one of the Civil War's bloodiest battlefields. On November 30, 1864, 37,000 men (20,000 Confederates and 17,000 Union soldiers) fought over a 2-mile stretch of Franklin's outskirts. Nashville's sprawl has

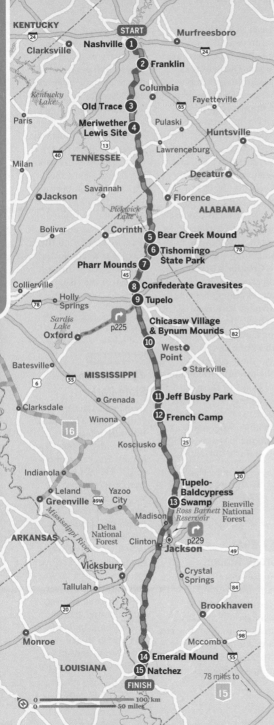

turned much of that battlefield into suburbs, but the **Carter House** (☎615-791-1861; www.carter-house.org; 1140 Columbia Ave; adult/senior/child $8/7/4; ⏱9am-5pm Mon-Sat, 1-5pm Sun; 👨👪) property is a preserved 8-acre chunk of the Battle of Franklin. The house is still riddled with 1000-plus bullet holes.

The Drive » The parkway carves a path through dense woodland as you swerve past another historical district at Leiper's Fork before coming to the first of several Old Trace turnouts.

- - - - - - - - - - - - - -

❸ Old Trace

At Mile 403.7 (don't mind the 'backward' mile markers, we think a north–south route works best) you'll find the first of several sections of the Old Trace. In the early 19th

LINK YOUR TRIP

15 Cajun Country

Head south on Hwy 61 from Natchez to Cajun Country's launching point in Thibodaux.

16 The Blues Highway

At Tupelo head northwest on I-78 to Memphis to link up with the Blues Highway.

century, Kaintucks (boatmen from Ohio and Pennsylvania) floated coal, livestock and agricultural goods down the Ohio and Mississippi Rivers aboard flat-bottom boats. Often their boats were emptied in Natchez, where they disembarked and began the long walk home up the Old Trace to Nashville, where they could access established roads further north. This walking path intersected Choctaw and Chicasaw country, which meant it was hazardous. In fact, indigenous travellers were the first to beat this earth. You can walk a 2000ft section of that original trail at this turnout.

The Drive » There's beaucoup beauty on a 20-mile stretch of road, as the parkway flows past Jackson Falls and the Baker Bluff overlook, which offers views over the Duck River.

- - - - - - - - - - - - - - - -

❹ Meriwether Lewis Site

At Mile 385.9, you'll come to the Meriwether Lewis Site, where the famed explorer and first governor of the Louisiana territory died of mysterious gunshot wounds at nearby Grinders Inn. His fateful journey began in September, 1809. His plan was to travel to Washington, DC to defend his spending of government funds. Think of it as an early-days subpoena before a Congressional committee. At Fort Pickering, a remote wilderness outpost near modern-day Memphis, he met up with a Chicasaw agent named James Neely. Neely was to escort the Lewis party safely through Chicasaw land. They traveled north, through the bush, and along the Old Trace to **Grinder's Stand**, and checked in to the inn run by the pioneering Grinder Family. Mrs Grinder made up a room for Lewis and fed him, and after he retired, two shots rang out. The legendary explorer was shot in the head and chest and died at 35. Lewis' good friend, Thomas Jefferson, was convinced it was suicide. His family disagreed.

The Drive » Continue on and you will cross into Alabama at Mile 341.8, and Mississippi at Mile 308.

- - - - - - - - - - - - - - - -

❺ Bear Creek Mound

Just across the Alabama state line and in Mississippi, at Mile 308.8, you'll find Bear Creek Mound, an ancient indigenous ceremonial site. There are seven groups of mounds found along the parkway, all of them in Mississippi. They vary in shape from Mayan-like pyramids to domes to small rises, and were used for worship or to bury the dead. Some were also seen as power spots for local chiefs who sometimes lived on top of them. That was arguably the case at Bear Creek, which was built between 1100 and 1300 AD. Archaeologists who did the 1965 excavation work here are convinced that there was a temple and/or a chief's dwelling on the top of the rise.

The Drive » The highway bisects Tishomingo State Park at Mile 304.5.

- - - - - - - - - - - - - - - -

TRIP HIGHLIGHT

❻ Tishomingo State Park

Named for the Chicasaw Indian Chief Tishomingo, this park offers the opportunity to take it slow. You can **camp** (☎662-438-6914; www.mississippistateparks.reserveamerica.com; Mile 304.5, Natchez Trace Parkway, Tishomingo; campsite $16; 🚻🐾) among the evocative, moss-covered sandstone cliffs and rock formations, fern gullies and waterfalls of Bear Creek canyon. Hiking trails abound, canoes are available for rent if you wish to paddle Bear Creek, and spring wildflowers bloom once the weather warms. It's a special oasis, and one that was utilized by the Chicasaw and their Paleo Indian antecedents. There is proof of their civilization in the park dating back to 7000 BC.

The Drive >> Just under 20 miles of more wooded beauty leads from Tishimongo State Park to the next in a series of Native American mounds at Mile 286.7

---

7 Pharr Mounds

The Pharr Mounds is a 2000-year-old, 90-acre complex of eight indigenous burial sites. Four of them were excavated in 1966 and found to have fireplaces and low platforms where the dead were cremated. Ceremonial artifacts were also found, along with copper vessels, which raised some eyebrows. Copper is not indigenous to Mississippi, and its presence here indicated an extensive trade network with other nations and peoples.

The Drive >> About 17 miles on, at Mile 269.4, you'll come across a turnout that links up to another section of the Old Trace and offers a bit more recent history.

---

8 Confederate Gravesites

Just north of Tupelo, on a small rise overlooking the Old Trace, lies a row

DETOUR: OXFORD

Start: 9 Tupelo

If you plan on driving the entire Natchez Trace from Nashville to Natchez, you should make the 50-mile detour along Hwy 6 to Oxford, Mississippi, a town rich in culture and history. This is Faulkner country, and Oxford is a thriving university town with terrific restaurants and bars. Don't miss the catfish dinner at Taylor Grocery, 15 minutes south of Oxford.

of 13 graves of unknown Confederate soldiers. What led to their fate has been lost in time, but theories range from their having died during the Confederate retreat from Corinth, Mississippi, following the legendary **Battle of Shiloh**. Others believe they were wounded in the nearby **Battle of Brices Cross Roads**, and buried by their brothers, here. Today they rest as reminders of the ultimate cost of war in any time and place.

The Drive >> Less than 10 miles later you will loop into the comparatively large hamlet of Tupelo, at Mile 266, where you can gather road supplies for the southward push.

TRIP HIGHLIGHT

9 Tupelo

Here, the **Natchez Trace Parkway Visitors Center** (800-305-7417; www.nps. gov/natr; Mile 286.7, Natchez Trace Parkway; 8am-5pm, closed Christmas;) is a fantastic resource

with well-done natural and American history displays, and detailed parkway maps. You should pick the brains of local rangers behind the counter, who may know a secret or two. Of course, music buffs will know that Tupelo is world famous for its favorite son. Elvis Presley's Birthplace is a pilgrimage site for those who kneel before the king. The original structure has a new roof and furniture, but no matter the decor, it was within these humble walls that Elvis was born on January 8, 1935, where he learned to play the guitar and began to dream big. His family's church, where Elvis first was bit by the music bug, has been transported and restored here, as well.

The Drive >> Just barely out of Tupelo, at Mile 261.8, is Chicasaw Village. The Bynum Mounds are another nearly 30 miles south. You'll see the

NATCHEZ TRACE PARKWAY
ADAM SKOLNICK, AUTHOR

When you combine natural beauty with deep history, and add to that a smooth road (that makes for terrific cycling) and hiking trails and streams, you have 444 miles of enriching, vacation reverie at your disposal. Versatile enough to suit existential soloists, active retirees or even young families, it takes hard work to have a bad time on the Trace.

Above: Emerald Mound
Right: Confederate gravesites

turnoff just after leaving the Tombigbee National Forest.

---

⑩ Chicasaw Village & Bynum Mounds

South from Tupelo, the Trace winds past the Chickasaw Village Site, where displays document how the Chickasaw lived and traveled during the fur-trade heyday of the early 19th century. It was

1541 when Hernan De Soto entered Mississippi under the Spanish flag. They fought a bitter battle, and though De Soto survived, the Chickasaw held strong. By the 1600s the English had engaged the Chickasaw in what became a lucrative fur trade. Meanwhile, the French held sway just west in the massive Louisiana territory. As an ally to England, the Chickasaw found themselves up against not only the French, but their Choctaw allies. That was the state of affairs when this now leveled village and fort compound was built in the 18th century. Further down the road is the site of six 2100-year-old Bynum Mounds. Five of them were excavated just after WWII, and copper tools and cremated remains were found. Two of the mounds have been restored for public viewing.

The Drive » Between Miles 211 and 205 this gold and green riverine parkway turns post-apocalyptic thanks to an April 2011 tornado that decimated the forest, with hundreds of trees snapped like so many toothpicks. This profound and astonishing dead zone is a sight to behold. Jeff Busby Park can be found at Mile 193.1.

⓫ Jeff Busby Park

Don't miss this hilltop park with picnic tables and a fabulous overlook taking in low-lying, forested hills that extend for miles, all the way to the horizon. Exhibits at the top include facts and figures about local flora and fauna, as well as a primer on indigenous tools. **Little Mountain Trail**, a half-mile loop that takes 30 minutes to complete, descends from the parking lot into a shady hollow. Another half-mile spur trail branches from that loop to the campground below.

The Drive » Thirteen miles down the road, at Mile 180, the forest clears and an agrarian plateau emerges, jade and perfect, as if this land has been cultivated for centuries.

⓬ French Camp

At this site of a former French pioneer settlement, you can tour a cute antebellum two-story home, built by Revolutionary War veteran Colonel James Drane. An end table is set for tea, aged leather journals are arranged on the desk and Drane's original US flag is in an upstairs bedroom along with an antique loom. Even more noteworthy is the ornate stagecoach of Greenwood LeFlore, which carried the last chief of the Choctaw nation east of the Mississippi on his two trips to Washington to negotiate with President Andrew Jackson, a route that demanded the navigation of a hazardous piece of the Old Trace known as the Devil's Backbone. For more recent French camp history you can peruse the **French Camp Museum**. Set

in a vintage log cabin, there is a number of historical photos on the porch, as well as framed newspaper articles and maps in the museum itself.

🛏 p231

The Drive » As you head south, the forest clears for snapshots of horses in the prairie, before the trees encroach again and again.

⓭ Tupelo-Baldcypress Swamp

At Mile 122, you can examine some of these trees up close as you tour the stunning Tupelo-Baldcypress Swamp. The 20-minute trail snakes through an abandoned channel and continues on a boardwalk over the milky green swamp shaded by water tupelo and bald cypresses. Look for turtles on the rocks and gators in the murk.

The Drive » The swamp empties into the Ross R Barnett Reservoir, which you'll see to the east as you speed toward and through the state capital of Jackson. The next intriguing sight is just 10.3 miles from Natchez, accessible by graded road that leads west from the parkway.

⓮ Emerald Mound

Emerald Mound is by far the best of the indigenous mound sites. Using stone tools, pre-Columbian

LOCAL KNOWLEDGE: KAYAKING THE OLD RIVER

According to Keith Benoist, a photographer, landscaper and co-founder of the **Phatwater Challenge** marathon kayak race, the Mississippi has more navigable river miles than any other state in the union. Natchez-born Benoist trains for his 42-mile race by paddling 10 miles of the Old River, an abandoned section of the Mississippi fringed with cypress and teeming with gators. If you're lucky enough to meet him at Under the Hill, he may just take you with him.

ancestors to the Natchez people graded this 8-acre mountain into a flat-topped pyramid. It is now the second-largest mound in America. There are shady, creekside picnic spots here, and you can and should climb to the top where you'll find a vast lawn along with a diagram of what the temple may have looked like. It would have been perched on the secondary and highest of the mounds. A perfect diversion on an easy spring afternoon just before the sun smolders, when birdsong rings from the trees and co-mingles with the call of a distant train.

The Drive » As you approach Natchez, the mossy arms of southern oaks spread over the roadway, and the air gets just a touch warmer and more moist. You can almost smell the river from here.

- - - - - - - - - - - - -

15 Natchez

When the woods part, revealing historical antebellum mansions, you have reached Natchez, Mississippi. In the 1840s, Natchez had more millionaires per capita

DETOUR: JACKSON

Start: 13 Tupelo-Baldcypress Swamp

Twenty-two miles south of the swamp, and just a bit further along the interstate, is Mississippi's capital. With its fine downtown museums, and artsy-funky **Fondren District** – home to Mississippi's best kitchen – Jackson offers a blast of 'now' if you need a pick-me-up. The city's two best sites are the Mississippi Museum of Art, which promotes home-grown artists and offers rotating exhibitions, and the Eudora Welty House. This is where the literary giant, and Pulitzer Prize winner, crafted every last one of her books. And do not leave town without enjoying lunch or dinner at Walker's Drive-In.

than any city in the world (because the plantation owners didn't pay their staff). Yes, old cotton money built these homes with slave labor, but they are graced all the same with an opulent, *Gone With the Wind* charm. 'Pilgrimage season' is in the spring and fall, when the mansions open for tours, though some are open year-round. The brick-red **Auburn Mansion** (☎601-446-6631; www .natchezpilgrimage.com; Duncan Park; ☺11am-3pm Tue-Sat, last tour 2:30pm; ♿) is famous for its freestanding spiral staircase. Built in 1812, the architecture here

influenced countless mansions throughout the South.

Natchez has dirt under its fingernails too. When Mark Twain came through town (and he did on numerous occasions), he crashed in a room above the local watering hole. **Under the Hill Saloon** (☎601-446-8023; www.underthehillsaloon. com; 25 Silver St; ☺9am-late), across the street from the mighty Mississippi River, remains the best bar in town, with terrific (and free) live music on weekends.

✗ ⊫ p231

Eating & Sleeping

Nashville ❶

✗ City House   New Southern $$$

(📞615-736-5838; www.cityhousenashville.
com; 1222 4th Ave N; mains $15-24; ⏱5-10pm
Mon, Wed-Sat, to 9pm Sun) This signless brick
building in Nashville's gentrifying Germantown
hides one of the city's best restaurants.
The food, cooked in an open kitchen in the
warehouselike space, is a crackling bang-up
of Italy-meets–New South. They do tangy kale
salads, a tasty chickpea and octopus dish
flavored with fennel, onion, lemon and garlic,
and pastas feature twists such as rigatoni
rabbit, or gnocchi in cauliflower ragu. They cure
their own sausage and salamis, and take pride
in their cocktail and wine list. Save room for
dessert. Sunday supper features a stripped-
down menu.

✗ Monell's   Southern $$

(📞615-248-4747; www.monellstn.com; 1235 6th
Ave N; all-you-can-eat $13-19; ⏱10:30am-2pm
Mon, 10:30am-2pm & 5-8:30pm Tue-Fri, 8:30am-
3pm & 5-8:30pm Sat, 8:30am-4pm Sun) In an old
brick house just north of the District, Monell's is
beloved for down-home Southern food served
family-style. This is not just a meal, it's an
experience. Especially at breakfast when platter
after platter of sausage, bacon, bone in ham,
skillet-fried chicken, hominy, corn pudding,
baked apples and potatoes are served along
with baskets of biscuits and bowls of sugary
cinnamon rolls.

✗ Prince's Hot Chicken   Fried Chicken $

(www.facebook.com/pages/Princes-Hot-
Chicken/166097846802728; 123 Ewing Dr;
quarter/half/whole chicken $5/9/18, cash only;
⏱noon-10pm Tue-Thu, noon-4am Fri, 2pm-
4am Sat; Ⓟ) Cayenne-rubbed 'hot chicken,'

fried to succulent perfection and served on a
piece of white bread with a side of pickles, is
Nashville's unique contribution to the culinary
universe. Tiny, faded Prince's, in a gritty,
northside strip mall, is a local legend that's
gotten shout-outs everywhere from the *New
York Times* to *Bon Appétit*. In mild, medium,
hot and death-defying extra hot, its chicken
will burn a hole in your stomach and you'll be
begging for more.

🛏 Hutton Hotel   Hotel $$$

(📞615-340-9333; www.huttonhotel.com; 1808
West End Ave; r from $289; Ⓟ❄@📶) Our
favorite Nashville boutique hotel riffs on mid-
century Modern design with bamboo-paneled
walls and grown-up beanbags in the lobby. Rust-
and chocolate-colored rooms are sizable and
well appointed with marble rain showers, glass
wash basins, king beds, ample desk space, fat
flat screens, high-end carpet and linens, and top
level service.

🛏 Indigo Nashville Downtown   Hotel $$

(📞877-846-3446; www.ichotelsgroup.com;
301 Union St; r from $139; Ⓟ❄📶) Most of
downtown's midrange hotels are corporate
behemoths catering to conventioneers. Not
so the Indigo, with its mod high-ceiling lobby,
space-age violet-and-lime color schemes, and
arty floor-to-ceiling photomurals of Nashville
landmarks. Parking is $20.

🛏 Union Station Hotel   Hotel $$$

(📞615-726-1001; www.unionstationhotel
nashville.com; 1001 Broadway; r from $359;
Ⓟ❄📶) Set in the old grey stone, church-like
edifice that was once the Nashville train station.
The lobby is especially glorious with an arched,
stained-glass ceiling, and roaring fireplace.
Rooms are elegant, modern and Marriott
approved.

French Camp 🕛

🛏 French Camp B&B   B&B $

(📞662-547-6835; www.frenchcamp.org; Mile 180.7, Natchez Trace Pkwy; r $85; 🐾) Stay the night in a log cabin built on a former French pioneer site that was further developed by a Revolutionary War hero.

Natchez 🕕

🍴 Cotton Alley   Cafe $$

(www.cottonalleycafe.com; 208 Main St; mains $10-15; ⏰11am-10pm Mon-Sat) This cute whitewashed dining room is chock-a-block with knickknacks and artistic touches and the menu borrows from local tastes. Think grilled chicken sandwich on Texas toast and jambalaya pasta, but it does a nice chicken Ceasar and a tasty grilled salmon salad too.

🍴 Magnolia Grill   Southern Fusion $$

(📞601-446-7670; www.magnoliagrill.com; 49 Silver St; mains $13-20; ⏰11am-9pm, to 10pm Fri & Sat; 🐾) Down by the riverside, this attractive wooden storefront grill with exposed rafters and outdoor patio is a good place for a pork tenderloin po'boy, or a fried crawfish spinach salad.

🛏 Historic Oak Hill Inn   Inn $$

(📞601-446-2500; www.historicoakhill.com; 409 S Rankin St; r incl breakfast from $125; 🅿 ❄ 🛜) Staying at classic Natchez B&B, Historic Oak Hill Inn, you'll get a taste of antebellum aristocratic living, from period furniture to china. A high-strung staff makes for an immaculate experience.

🛏 Mark Twain Guesthouse   Guesthouse $

(📞601-446-8023; www.underthehillssaloon. com; 33 Silver St; r without bath $65-85; ❄ 🛜) Riverboat captain Samuel Clemens used to drink till late at the saloon and pass out in one of three upstairs bedrooms (room 1 has the best view) with shared baths. Can be noisy until after 2am.

Blue Ridge Parkway *Wildlife, waterfalls and winsome towns*

Classic Trip

Blue Ridge Parkway

18

This drive on America's favorite byway curves through the leafy Appalachians, where it swoops up the East Coast's highest peak and stops by the nation's largest mansion.

TRIP HIGHLIGHTS

5 DAYS
210 MILES / 338KM

GREAT FOR...

BEST TIME TO GO
May to October for leafy trees and open attractions.

ESSENTIAL PHOTO
The mile-high suspension bridge at Grandfather Mountain.

BEST FOR FAMILIES
The route has steam-train rides, gem mining, easy hiking and old-fashioned candy.

21 miles

Grandfather Mountain
Cross a mile-high suspension bridge for a parkway panorama

START
Valle Crucis

35 miles

Linville Falls
A family-friendly hike leads to views of a 90ft waterfall

Waterrock Knob Visitor Center
FINISH

Downtown Asheville
Enjoy indie shops and microbreweries

101 miles

Biltmore Estate
Peer at gargoyles, dumbwaiters and a bowling alley

109 miles

233

18 Blue Ridge Parkway

The Blue Ridge Parkway stretches 469 miles, from Shenandoah National Park in Virginia to Great Smoky Mountains National Park in North Carolina. In the Tar Heel State, the road carves a sinuous path through a rugged landscape of craggy peaks, crashing waterfalls, thick forests and charming mountain towns. Three things you'll see? White-tail deer, local microbrews and signs for Grandfather Mountain. And one piece of advice: at breakfast, never say no to a biscuit.

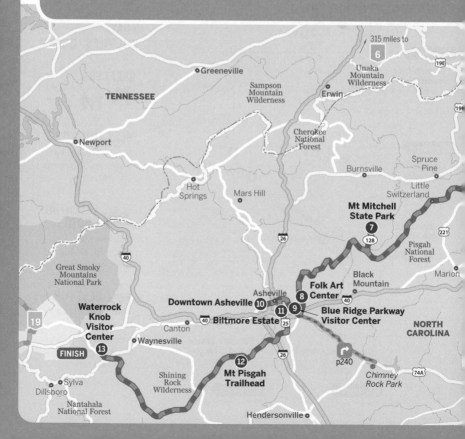

❶ Valle Crucis

How do you start a road trip through the mountains? With a good night's sleep and all the right gear. You'll find both in Valle Crucis, a bucolic village west of Boone. After slumbering beneath sumptuous linens at the Mast Farm Inn (p242), a 200-year-old farmhouse, ease into the day sipping coffee from a rocking chair on the inn's front porch.

Down the road is the **Original Mast General Store** (📞828-963-6511; www.mastgeneralstore.com; Hwy 194, Valle Crucis; ☉7am-6:30pm Mon-Sat, noon-6pm Sun; 🏠) and its **Annex** (Hwy 194; ☉10am-6pm Mon-Sat, noon-6pm Sun). The first of several Mast general stores across the region, the original sells many of the same products that it did when it opened in 1883. Today you'll find bacon and hard candy as well as hiking shoes and French Country hand towels. The Annex building sells outdoor apparel and hiking gear.

🍴 p242

The Drive >> Drive south on Hwy 194, also known as Broadstone Rd, through 3 miles of rural splendor. At Hwy 105 turn left.

---

❷ Boone

If you're traveling with kids or wannabe prospectors, stop at **Foggy Mountain Gem Mine** (📞828-963-4367; www.foggymountaingems.com; 4416 Hwy 105 S; buckets $17-120; ☉10am-6pm; 🏠) to pan for semi-precious stones, which are sold by the bucketload. There are several gem-mining spots near the parkway, but Foggy Mountain, a smaller company, is operated by graduate gemologists who may take their craft a bit more seriously. After sifting your rocks in a miner's flume line, the gemologists will cut and mount your favorite finds in any number of settings.

In downtown Boone, home of Appalachian State, you'll find shopping and dining on **King Street**. Keep an eye out for the bronze statue of local bluegrass legend Doc Watson. He's strumming a Gallagher guitar like nobody's business at the corner of King and Depot Sts.

🍴 p242

The Drive >> From King St, turn onto Hwy 321 just past the Daniel Boone Inn restaurant. Drive 4 miles then turn right at the theme park.

 LINK YOUR TRIP

6 Skyline Drive
Head north from Asheville on I-26 till you reach I-81. Follow that northeast for 300 miles to Strasburg where you'll take I-66 east to Front Royal.

19 The Great Smokies
From Waterrock Knob Visitor Center, head north until you reach Hwy 19. Follow this west through Cherokee to the start of the Great Smokies at Nantahala Outdoor Center.

Classic Trip

❸ Blowing Rock

The parkway runs just above the village of Blowing Rock, which sits at an elevation of 4000ft. On a cloudy morning, drive south on Hwy 321 to the top of the mountain to check out the cloud-capped views of surrounding peaks. The eastern continental divide runs through the bar at the Green Park Inn (p242), a white-clapboard grand hotel that opened in 1891. They say author Margaret Mitchell worked on *Gone with the Wind* while staying here.

A rite of passage for every North Carolina child is the **Tweetsie Railroad** (☑877-893-3874; www.tweetsie.com; 300 Tweetsie Railroad Ln; adult/ child $37/23; ☺9am-6pm daily Jun-Aug, 9am-6pm Fri-Sun mid-Apr–May, 9am-6pm Sat & Oct; 👶), a theme park where Appalachian culture meets the Wild West. The highlight? A 1917 coal-fired steam locomotive that chugs past marauding Indians and heroic cowboys. Midway rides, fudge shops and family-friendly shows round out the fun.

✕ 🛏 p242

The Drive ›› The entrance to the Blue Ridge Parkway is in Blowing Rock, 2.3 miles south of the Tweetsie Railroad. Once on the parkway, drive south 2 miles.

❹ Moses H Cone Memorial Park

Hikers and equestrians share 25 miles of carriage roads on the former estate (Mile 294) of Moses H Cone, a wealthy philanthropist and conservationist who made his fortune in denim. His mansion and grounds were given to the national park service in the 1950s. His Colonial Revival mansion, completed in 1901, now houses the **Parkway Craft Center** (☑828-295-7938; www.craftguild.org; Mile 294, Blue Ridge Parkway; ☺9am-5pm mid-Mar–Nov). The shop sells high-end crafts made by members of the Southern Highland Craft Guild. Free tours of the 2nd floor of the mansion, Flat Top Manor, are offered on Saturdays and Sundays June through mid-October at 10am, 11am, 2pm and 3pm. Tours do fill up. To reserve a spot call ☑828-295-3782 on the Friday before your visit.

The Drive ›› Head south on the parkway, passing split rail fences, stone walls, streams and meadows. Just south of Mile 304 the parkway curves across the Linn Cove Viaduct, the last section of the parkway to be completed, in 1987, because of the terrain's fragility. Exit onto US 221 at Mile 305 and drive 1 mile south.

TRIP HIGHLIGHT

❺ Grandfather Mountain

Don't let a fear of heights keep you from driving up to the famed swinging bridge near the peaks of **Grandfather Mountain** (☑828-733-4337; www.grandfather.com; Mile 305, Blue Ridge Pkwy; adult/child 4-12yr $18/8; ☺8am-7pm Jun-Aug). Yes, the 228ft-long bridge is 1 mile above sea level and yes, you can hear its steel girders 'sing' on gusty days, but the ground is just 80ft below the span. Nothing to sneeze at, for sure, but it's not the Grand Canyon, and the views of nearby mountains are superb. The small **Nature Museum** spotlights local flora and fauna as well as regional explorer Daniel Boone. Behind the museum, black bears, deer and otters roam a small animal habitat. Grandfather Mountain is a Unesco Biosphere Reserve.

Park attractions have been privately managed by the Morton family since the 1950s. The North Carolina State Park System purchased the mountain's backcountry lands in 2008, and **Grandfather Mountain State Park** (www.ncparks.gov) was established the following year. State park trails can be accessed from the parkway for free, or from parking lots inside the attraction with paid admission. The strenuous but varied **Grandfather Trail** runs 2.4 miles from the suspension bridge parking lot along the mountain's crest, ending atop Calloway Peak; the trail includes cables and ladders.

The Drive » Follow the parkway south and turn left just south of Mile 316 to reach Linville Falls.

TRIP HIGHLIGHT

❻ Linville Falls

Have time for just one hike? Then hop out of your car for the moderate 1.6-mile round-trip **Erwin's View Trail** at popular Linville Falls. Here, the Linville River sweeps over two separate falls before crashing 2000ft through a rocky gorge. The trail crosses the river then follows it downstream. At 0.5 miles, a spur trail leads to a view of the Upper Falls. The 90ft Lower Falls are visible from the Chimney View and Gorge View overlooks just ahead. At the latter you'll also see the imposing Linville Gorge. Ponder the scope of it all at the trail's last stop, the Erwin's View Overlook.

The Drive » Drive south on the parkway and turn right, south of Mile 355, onto NC 128. Follow NC 128 into the park.

❼ Mt Mitchell State Park

A trip to **Mt Mitchell** (☎828-675-4611; www .ncparks.gov; 2388 State Hwy 128; admission free; ⏰8am-9pm May-Aug, closes earlier rest of the year) might lead to a fight. Will you drive to the top of the highest mountain east of the Mississippi, or will you hike there? Make your decision at the **park office** (⏰8am-5pm Apr-Oct, closed weekends Nov-Mar), which sits beside a 2-mile trail to the 6684ft summit.

At the top you'll see the grave of the mountain's namesake, Dr Elisha Mitchell. A dedicated professor from the University of

BLUE RIDGE PARKWAY TRIP PLANNER

Construction of the parkway began in 1935, during the Great Depression, after the government harnessed the strength of thousands of out-of-work young men in the Civilian Conservation Corps. The parkway wasn't fully linked together until 1987, when the Lynn Cove viaduct opened.

Travel Tips

» The maximum speed limit is 45 mph.

» Long stretches of the road close in winter and may not reopen until March. Many visitor centers and campgrounds are closed until May. Check the park service website (www.nps.gov/blri) for the latest information about road closures and the opening dates for facilities.

» The North Carolina section of the parkway begins at Mile 216.9, between the Blue Ridge Mountain Center in Virginia and Cumberland Knob in North Carolina.

» There are 26 tunnels on the parkway in North Carolina (and just one in Virginia). Watch for signs to turn on your headlights.

» For more trip planning tools, check the websites for the **Blue Ridge Parkway Association** (www.blueridgeparkway.org) and the **Blue Ridge National Heritage Area** (www.blueridgeheritage.com).

Classic Trip

ANDRE JENNY / ALAMY ©

LOCAL VOICE
JENNIFER PHARR
DAVIS, OWNER,
BLUE RIDGE HIKING
CO; AUTHOR OF
CALLED AGAIN, ABOUT HER
46-DAY TRAVERSE OF THE
APPALACHIAN TRAIL

Past Mt Pisgah you come to a
lookout along the parkway for
Graveyard Fields. It's a beautiful
area with several different hiking
trails to choose from. There's a
great waterfall right there that's
very close to the parkway. It's called
Lower Falls, or Second Falls. There's
also an Upper Falls, which is not as
spectacular, but it's a nice walk up.

Top: Bass Lake, Moses H Cone Memorial Park
Left: Horseriding, Moses H Cone Memorial Park
Right: Chimney Rock, Chimney Rock Park

North Carolina, he died after a fall while trying to verify the height of the mountain in 1857. A circular ramp beside the grave leads to panoramic views of the surrounding Black Mountains and beyond.

The Drive » Return to the parkway and drive south to Mile 382. During the last two weeks of June look for blooming rhododendrons.

❽ Folk Art Center

As you enter the lobby at the **Folk Art Center** (📞828-298-7928; www .craftguild.org; Mile 382; ⏰9am-6pm Apr-Dec, to 5pm Jan-Mar), look up. A row of handcrafted Appalachian chairs hangs from the walls above. They're an impressive calling card for the gallery here, which is dedicated to southern craftsmanship. The chairs are part of the Southern Highland Craft Guild's permanent collection, which holds more than 2400 traditional and modern crafts. Items from the collection – pottery, baskets, quilts, woodcarvings – are displayed on the 2nd floor. The Allanstand Craft Shop on the 1st floor sells a range of fine traditional crafts.

The Drive » Turn right onto the parkway and drive south. After crossing the Swannanoa River and I-40, continue to Mile 384.

Classic Trip

❾ Blue Ridge Parkway Visitor Center

Sit back and let the scenery come to you at this helpful **visitor center** (☎828-298-5330; www.nps.gov/blri; Mile 384; ⏱9am-5pm), where the beauty and wonder of the drive is captured in a big-screen film, *Blue Ridge Parkway – America's Favorite Journey*. A park service representative can provide details about trails along the parkway at the front desk. For a list of regional sites and activities, slide the digital monitor across the interactive I-Wall map at the back of the main hall. The adjacent regional information desk has brochures and coupons for Asheville area attractions.

The Drive » Drive north, backtracking over the interstate and river, and exit at Tunnel Rd, which is US 70. Drive west to US 240 and follow it to the exits for downtown Asheville.

TRIP HIGHLIGHT

❿ Downtown Asheville

Hippies. Hipsters. Hikers. And a few high-falutin' preppies. This 4H Club gives Asheville its funky charm. Just look around. Intellectual lefties gather at **Malaprops Bookstore and Café** (www.malaprops.com; 55 Haywood St), where the shelves stretch from Banned Books to Southern Cooking. And the hipsters? They're nibbling silky truffles at **Chocolate Fetish** (www.chocolatefetish.com; 36 Haywood St) or sipping homegrown ale at microbreweries such as the convivial – and hoppy – **Wicked Weed** (www.wickedweedbrewing.com; 91 Biltmore Ave). At the engaging **Thomas Wolfe Memorial** (www.wolfememorial.com; 52 N Market St; museum free, house tour $5; ⏱9am-5pm Tue-Sat), the city celebrates its most famous angsty son, Thomas Wolfe, who penned the Asheville-inspired novel *Look Homeward, Angel*.

Hikers can shop for new boots at impressive **Tops for Shoes** (www.topsforshoes.com; 27 N Lexington Ave) and outdoor gear at **Mast General Store** (www.mastgeneralstore.com; 15 Biltmore Ave). The preppies? They're working at downtown banks and law firms – and checking out the same places as everybody else.

The finishing touch? A sidewalk busker fiddling a lonesome mountain tune. It'll put a spring in your step while maybe just breaking your heart.

The Drive » Follow Asheland Ave (which becomes McDowell St) south. After crossing Swannanoa River, the entry to Biltmore Estate is on the right.

TRIP HIGHLIGHT

⓫ Biltmore Estate

The destination that put Asheville on the map is the 175,000-sq-ft **Biltmore Estate** (☎800-543-2961; www.biltmore.com; 1 Approach Rd; adult/child under 16yr $59/30;

DETOUR: CHIMNEY ROCK PARK

Start: ❿ Downtown Asheville

The US flag flaps in the breeze atop this popular park's namesake 315ft granite monolith. The top can be reached by elevator or by stairs – lots and lots of stairs. Once on top, look east for amazing views of **Lake Lure**. Another draw is the hike around the cliffs to 404ft **Hickory Nut Falls**. Scenes from *The Last of the Mohicans* were filmed at the **park** (www.chimneyrockpark.com; Hwy 64/74A; adult/child $15/7; ⏱8:30am-5:30pm late Mar-Oct, hours vary rest of the year). There's a small exhibit about the movie inside the Sky Lounge. From Asheville, follow US 74A east for 20 scenic, but very curvy, miles.

⊙house 9am-4:30pm, restaurants & shops vary). The French Chateau–style mega-mansion, built by shipping and railroad heir George Vanderbilt II, was completed in 1895 after six years of work by hundreds of artists, craftsmen and educated professionals. The Vanderbilt-Cecil family still owns the estate. The entrance fee is steep, so arrive early to get your money's worth, and note that tours of the house are self-guided. The $10 audio tour is worth purchasing for the extra details. For an additional $17 you can take a general guided tour or join a specialized behind-the-scenes guided tour focusing on the architecture, the family or the servants. Children ages 10 to 16 are free June through August with an adult paid admission.

In addition to the mansion there are gardens, trails, lakes, restaurants, an inn and a winery, with complimentary wine tasting. At the estate's Antler Hill Village, don't miss the new **Vanderbilts at Home & Abroad** exhibit in the Biltmore Legacy building. With a focus on family history and stories, the exhibit includes a family tree – look for Anderson Cooper's name – and a samurai sword owned by George Vanderbilt.

BLUEGRASS & MOUNTAIN MUSIC

For locally grown fiddle-and-banjo music, head deep into the hills of the High Country. Regional shows and music jams are listed on the Blue Ridge Music Trails (www.blueridgemusic.org) and the Blue Ridge National Heritage Area (www.blueridgeheritage. com) websites. Here are three to get you started, from north to south:

» **Mountain Home Music Concert Series** (www .mountainhomemusic.com) Spring through fall, enjoy shows by Appalachian musicians in Boone on scheduled Saturday nights.

» **Old Fort Mountain Music Jam** (www .mcdowellnc.org) Tap your toes Friday nights from 7pm to 10pm in downtown Old Fort, east of Asheville.

» **Historic Orchard at Altapass** (www .altapassorchard.org) On weekends May through October, settle in for an afternoon of music at Little Switzerland, at Mile 328.

The Drive ⟫ After exiting the grounds, turn right onto US 25 and continue to the parkway, not quite 3.5 miles, and drive south.

- - - - - - - - - - - -

⑫ Mt Pisgah Trailhead

For a short hike to a panoramic view, pull into the parking lot beside the Mt Pisgah Trailhead just beyond Mile 407. From here, a 1.6-mile trail (one way) leads to the mountain's 5721ft summit, which is topped by a lofty TV tower. The trail is steep and rocky in its final stretch, but you'll be rewarded with views of the **French Broad River Valley** and **Cold Mountain**, the latter made famous by Charles Frazier's novel of the same name. One mile

south are a campground, a general store, a restaurant and an inn.

The Drive ⟫ The drive south passes the Graveyard Fields Overlook, which has short trails to scenic waterfalls. The 6047ft Richland-Balsam Overlook at Mile 431.4 is the highest point on the parkway. From here, continue south another 20 miles.

- - - - - - - - - - - -

⑬ Waterrock Knob Visitor Center

This trip ends at the Waterrock Knob Visitor Center (Mile 451.2), which sits at an elevation of nearly 6000ft. With a four-state view, this scenic spot is a great place to see where you've been and to assess what's ahead. Helpful signage attaches names to the mountains on the distant horizons.

Classic Trip

Eating & Sleeping

Valle Crucis ❶

🛏 **Mast Farm Inn & Simplicity Restaurant**　　　B&B $$$

(📞828-963-5857; www.themastfarminn.com; 2543 Broadstone Rd; r incl breakfast $209-249, cabins $349-419, restaurant mains $22-34, prix fixe $48-53; P ✳ 🛜) The farmhouse and adjacent cabins define rustic chic, with hardwood floors and claw-foot tubs. The upscale mountain cuisine at Simplicity is worth a trip in itself. Each guest receives a personalized menu for dinner – 'Slow Chicken NASCAR style but mighty low on points and Ashe County cheese trucked over by Junior Johnson.' Enjoy!

Boone ❷

🍴 **Dan'l Boone Inn**　　　Southern $$

(📞828-264-8657; www.danlbooneinn.com; 130 Hardin St; breakfast adult $10, child $5-7, dinner adult $17, child $6-10; ⏱11:30am-9pm Mon-Fri, 8am-9pm Sat & Sun Jun-Oct, hours vary rest of the year; 👶) Quantity is the name of the game at this restaurant, and the family-style meals are a Boone (sorry) for hungry hikers. Open since 1959. Cash or check only.

🍴 **Hob Nob Farm Cafe**　　　Cafe $$

(www.hobnobfarmcafe.com; 506 West King St; breakfast & lunch $3-12, dinner $8-15; ⏱10am-10pm Wed-Sun; 🍴) Inside a wildly painted cottage, mountain town hippie types gobble up avocado-tempeh melts, Thai curry bowls and sloppy burgers made from local beef. Brunch is served until 5pm.

Blowing Rock ❸

🍴 **Six Pence Pub**　　　Pub $$

(www.sixpencepub.com; 1121 Main St; mains $9-18; ⏱restaurant 11:30am-10:30pm Sun-Thu, to midnight Fri & Sat, bar to 2am nightly) The bartenders keep a sharp but friendly eye on things at this lively British pub where the shepherd's pie comes neat, not messy.

🛏 **Cliff Dwellers Inn**　　　Motel $$

(📞828-295-3098; www.cliffdwellers.com; 116 Lakeview Terrace; r $99-129, apt $179; P ✳ 🛜 🏊) From its perch above town, this well-named motel lures guests with good service, reasonable prices, stylish rooms and balconies with sweeping views.

🛏 **Green Park Inn**　　　Hotel $$

(📞828-414-9230; www.greenparkinn.com; 9239 Valley Blvd; r incl breakfast $149-189; P ✳ 🛜 🏊) Under new management, this historical gabled inn serves up history, refreshed Victorian style and made-to-order breakfasts. Pets are $25 per night. The GPS address is 5995 Lenoir Turnpike.

Asheville

🍴 **12 Bones**　　　Barbecue $

(www.12bones.com; 5 Riverside Dr; dishes $4-20; ⏱11am-4pm Mon-Fri) Soooooiieee, 12 Bones is good. The slow-cooked meats are smoky tender, and the sides, from the jalapeno cheese grits to the buttery green beans, will have you kissing your mama and blessing the day you were born. Order at the counter, grab a picnic table, die happy. Lunch only, closed weekends.

🍴 **Admiral**　　　Modern American $$

(📞828-252-2541; www.theadmirainc.com; 400 Haywood Rd; small plates $10-14, large plates $22-30; ⏱5-10pm) This concrete bunker, which sits beside a car junkyard, looks divey on the outside. But inside? That's where the magic happens. This low-key West Asheville spot is one of the state's finest New American restaurants, serving wildly creative dishes – flat iron steak with soy-sauce mashed potatoes and Vietnamese slaw – that taste divine.

✕ Sunny Point Cafe   Cafe $

(www.sunnypointcafe.com; 626 Haywood
Rd; breakfast & lunch $8-12, dinner $8-17;
⊙8:30am-2:30pm Sun & Mon, 8:30am-9pm
Tue-Sat) In the morning, solos, couples and
ladies-who-breakfast fill this bright West
Asheville spot that's loved for its hearty,
homemade fare. The huevos rancheros, with
feta cheese and chorizo sausage, is deservedly
popular. The cafe embraces the organic and
fresh, and even has its own garden. The biscuits
are divine.

✕ Tupelo Honey   New Southern $$

(📞828-255-4863; www.tupelohoneycafe.com;
12 College St; breakfast $7-15, lunch & dinner
$10-28; ⊙9am-10pm) This long-time favorite is
known for New Southern fare, such as shrimp
and grits with goat cheese. Tupelo-born Elvis
would have surely loved the nutty fried chicken
with milk gravy and smashed sweet potatoes.
Breakfasts are superb, but no matter the meal,
say yes to the biscuit. And add a drop of honey.

🛏 Aloft Asheville   Hotel $$$

(📞828-232-2838; www.aloftasheville.com; 51
Biltmore Ave; r from $242; ⓟ❄@🛜🏊🐾) At
first glance this new downtown hotel looks like
the 7th ring of hipster – giant chalkboard in the
lobby, groovy young staff, a neon lounge with
bright retro chairs. The only thing missing is a
wool-cap-wearing bearded guy drinking a hoppy
microbrew – oh, wait, over there. We jest. Once
settled, you'll find the staff knowledgeable, the
rooms large with lots of counter space, and the
atmosphere convivial. Aloft is also close to the
downtown action. Parking is $5 per day; pets
are free.

🛏 Campfire Lodgings   Campground $$

(📞828-658-8012; www.campfirelodgings.com;
116 Appalachian Village Rd; tent/RV sites $38/45,
yurts from $115, cabins $160; ⓟ❄) All yurts
should have flat-screen TVs, don't you think?
Sleep like the world's most stylish Mongolian
nomad in one of these furnished multiroom
tents, on the side of a hill with stunning valley
views. Cabins and tent sites are also available.

🛏 Grove Park
Inn Resort & Spa   Resort $$$

(📞828-252-2711; www.groveparkinn.com; 290
Macon Ave; r from $269; ⓟ❄@🛜🏊🐾)
This titanic arts-and-crafts-style lodge,
which celebrated its centennial in 2013, has
hale-and-hearty decor that conjures an era of
adventure. But don't worry modern mavens, the
well-appointed rooms come with 21st-century
amenities. Look for inspirational quotes
scattered across the property. Fees include a
$25 daily resort fee and a $5 self-parking fee.
The pet fee is $130 per reservation.

🛏 Sweet Peas   Hostel $

(📞828-285-8488; www.sweetpeashostel.
com; 23 Rankin Ave; dm/pod/r $28/35/60;
ⓟ❄@🛜) This spick-and-span hostel gleams
with IKEA-like style. Picture shipshape steel
bunk beds and blond-wood sleeping 'pods'.
Noise can filter up from the bar below, but the
hostel's style, sociability and downtown location
make it a winner.

The Great Smokies *Hike, camp,
mountain bike and stargaze*

The Great Smokies

19

Alas, Hobbiton and Narnia don't exist. But the Smokies are a wonderland of their own: home to technicolor greenery, strutting wildlife, whispering waterfalls and the irrepressible Dollywood.

TRIP HIGHLIGHTS

85 miles

Cades Cove
Wild animals, old cabins and, well, Sunday drivers

FINISH
● Sevierville

● Dollywood

Pigeon ●
Forge

115 miles

Roaring Fork Motor Road
Follow an old wagon road past hardwoods and waterfalls

Gatlinburg ● ⑫

⑩

50 miles

Clingmans Dome
The last half-mile is a doozy on the hike to the summit

⑥

③

Bryson ●
City

Museum of The Cherokee Indian
Stories of triumph and tragedy are movingly told

START

25 miles

4–5 DAYS
160 MILES / 257KM

GREAT FOR...

BEST TIME TO GO

September to October for fall color; April to June for greenery and waterfalls.

 ESSENTIAL PHOTO

The tree-covered slopes snapped from the Newfound Gap Overlook.

 BEST FOR OUTDOORS

Cycling the Cades Cove loop on an official 'no-car' morning.

245

DENNIE CODY / GETTY IMAGES ©

19 The Great Smokies

While the beauty of the Great Smokies can be seen from your car, the exhilarating, crash-bang, breathe-it-in wonder of the place can't be fully appreciated until you leave your vehicle. Hold tight as you bounce over Nantahala rapids. Give a nod to foraging black bears as you cycle Cades Cove. And press your nose against windows in downtown Gatlinburg, where ogling short stacks is the best way to choose the right pancake place.

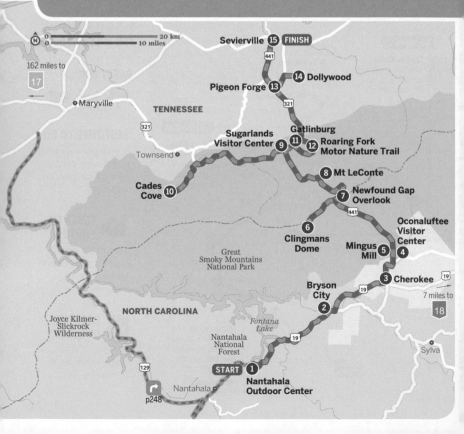

❶ Nantahala Outdoor Center

Splash, bang, wheeeeee... There's no easing into this trip, which starts in the mountain-fed rivers and rugged valleys of western North Carolina, a region famed for its fantastic kayaking and white-water rafting.

The **Nantahala Outdoor Center** (NOC; ☎828-488-2176, 888-905-7238; www.noc.com; 13077 Hwy 19/74; kayak/canoe rental per day $30/50, guided trips $30-189) launches trips on the class II and III rapids of the Nantahala River from its sprawling outpost near Bryson City. Ride a group raft or a two-person ducky through the wide, brown river gorge. The company also offers white-water trips on six other Appalachian rivers.

LINK YOUR TRIP

17 Natchez Trace Parkway

Head northwest on Hwy 321/Rte 73 from Maryville until you reach I-40. Take this west until you hit on musical Nashville.

18 Blue Ridge Parkway

Continue east on Hwy 19 from Cherokee to link up with Blue Ridge Parkway.

Experienced paddlers can brave the 9-mile trip down the roiling class IV-V Cheoah ($169 to $189), launching from nearby Robbinsville.

At the Adventure Center, which is part of the NOC campus, sign up to zipline or to climb an alpine tower. Also on-site are an outdoor store, a year-round restaurant and lodging, which includes campsites, cabins, a hostel and an inn. The Appalachian Trail crosses the property, and the Great Smoky Mountain Railroad stops here.

The Drive » Follow US 19 north about 12.5 miles on a twisty, wooded path that winds past rafting companies and oh-so-many signs for boiled peanuts. Take exit 67 into downtown Bryson City.

❷ Bryson City

This friendly mountain town is a great base camp for exploring the North Carolina side of the Smokies. The marquee attraction is the historic **Great Smoky Mountains Railroad** (☎800-872-4681; www.gsmr.com; 226 Everett St; Nantahala Gorge trip adult/child 2-12yr from $55/31; ⏰Mar-Dec), which departs from downtown and plows through the dramatic Nantahala Gorge and across the Fontana Trestle. The former Murphy Branch Line, built in the late 1800s, brought unheard-of luxuries such as books,

factory-spun cloth and oil lamps into town. Trips on the red-and-yellow trains include a Great Pumpkin–themed trip in the fall and the Christmas-time Polar Express, which stops at the North Pole to pick up Santa.

✗ 🛏 p254

The Drive » Continue 10 miles north on US 19.

TRIP HIGHLIGHT

❸ Cherokee

The Cherokee people have lived in this area since the last ice age, though many died on the Trail of Tears. The descendents of those who escaped or returned are known as the Eastern Band of the Cherokee. Make time for the **Museum of the Cherokee Indian** (☎828-497-3481; www.cherokeemuseum.org; 589 Tsali Blvd/Hwy 441, at Drama Rd; adult/child 6-12yr $10/6; ⏰9am-5pm daily, until 7pm Mon-Sat Jun-Aug). The earth-colored halls trace the history of the tribe, with artifacts such as pots, deerskins, woven skirts and an animated exhibit on Cherokee myths. The tribe's modern story is particularly compelling, with a detailed look at the tragedy and injustice of the **Trail of Tears**. This mass exodus occurred in the 1830s, when President Andrew Jackson ordered more than 16,000 Native Americans be removed from their southeastern homelands and resettled in what's now Oklahoma. The museum also spotlights a fascinating moment in Colonial-era history: the 1760s journey of three Cherokees to England, where they met with King George III.

The Drive >> Drive 3 miles north on US 441, passing the Blue Ridge Parkway.

④ Oconaluftee Visitor Center

If they're offering samples of regional preserves at the **Oconaluftee Visitor Center** (☎865-436-1200; www.nps.gov/grsm; Hwy 441; admission free; ⊙8am-7pm Jun-Aug, closing hours vary rest of the year), say yes. But pull out your money because you'll want to take a jar home. Here you'll also find interactive exhibits about the park's history and ecosystems. Helpful guides ($1) about specific attractions are also available. For this trip, the *Day Hikes* pamphlet and the guides to **Cades Cove** and the **Roaring Fork Motor Nature Trail** are helpful supplements.

Behind the visitor center, the pet-friendly **Oconaluftee River Trail** follows the river for 1.5 miles to the boundary of the Cherokee reservation. Pick up a free backcountry camping permit if you plan to go off-trail. The adjacent **Mountain Farm Museum** (☎423-436-1200; www.nps.gov/grsm; ⊙9am-5pm mid-Mar–mid-Nov & Thanksgiving weekend) is a 19th-century farmstead assembled from buildings from various locations around the park. The worn, wooden structures, including a barn, a blacksmith shop and a smokehouse, give a glimpse into the hardscrabble existence of Appalachian settlers.

The Drive >> Drive half a mile north on US 441. The parking lot is on the left.

⑤ Mingus Mill

Interested in old buildings and 1800s commerce? Then take the short walk to **Mingus Mill** (self-guided tours free; ⊙9am-5pm mid-Mar–mid-Nov). This 1886 gristmill was the largest in the Smokies. If the miller is here, he can explain how the mill grinds corn into cornmeal. Outside, the 200ft-long wooden millrace directs water to the building. There's no water wheel here because the mill used a cast-iron turbine.

The Drive >> Return to US 441 and turn left, continuing toward Gatlinburg. Turn left and drive 7 miles on Clingmans Dome Rd.

DETOUR: THE TAIL OF THE DRAGON

Start: ❶ **Nantahala Outdoor Center**

A dragon lurks in the rugged foothills of the southwestern Smokies. This particular monster is an infamous drive that twists through Deals Gap beside the national park. According to legend, the 11-mile route, known as the Tail of the Dragon, has 318 curves. From the Nantahala Outdoor Center, drive south on US 19/74 to US 129. Follow US 129 north. The dragon starts at the North Carolina and Tennessee state line. Godspeed and drive slowly. And may you tame the dragon like a Targaryen.

TRIP HIGHLIGHT

⑥ Clingmans Dome

At 6643ft, Clingmans Dome is the third-highest mountain east of the Mississippi. You can drive almost all the way to the top, but the final climb to the summit's Jetsons-like observation tower requires a half-mile walk on a paved trail. It's a very steep ascent, but there are resting spots along the way. The trail crosses the 2174-mile

NATIONAL PARK TRIP PLANNER

Established in 1934, **Great Smoky Mountains National Park** (☎865-436-1200; www.nps.gov/grsm) attracts more than nine million travelers per year, making it the most-visited national park in America.

Newfoundland Gap Rd/US 441 is the only thoroughfare crossing the entire 521,000-acre park, traversing 33 miles of deep oak and pine forest, and wildflower meadows. The park sits in two states, North Carolina and Tennessee. The Oconaluftee Visitor Center welcomes visitors arriving on US 441 in North Carolina; Sugarlands Visitor Center is the Tennessee counterpart.

Orientation & Fees

Great Smoky charges no admission fee, nor will it ever; this proviso was written into the park's original charter as a stipulation for a $5 million Rockefeller family grant. Stop by a visitor center to pick up a park map and the free *Smokies Guide* newspaper. The park is open all year although some facilities are only open seasonally, and roads may close due to bad weather. Leashed pets are allowed in campgrounds and on roadsides, but not on trails, with the exception of the Gatlinburg and Oconaluftee River trails.

Camping

The park currently operates seven developed campgrounds. None have showers or hook-ups. **Reservations** (☎877-444-6777; www.recreation.gov) are required at Cataloochee Campground, and they may be made at Elkmont, Smokemont, Cosby and Cades Cove. Big Creek and Deep Creek are first-come, first-served.

Traffic

If you're visiting on a summer weekend, particularly on the Tennessee side, accept that there is going to be a lot traffic. Take a break by following trails into the wilderness.

Appalachian Trail, which reaches its highest point on the Dome.

From the tower, on a clear day, enjoy a 360-degree view that sweeps in five states. Spruce- and pine-covered mountaintops sprawl for miles. The **visitor contact station** (☺10am-6pm Apr-Oct, 9:30am-5pm Nov) beside the parking lot has a bookstore and shop.

The weather here is cooler than at lower elevations, and rain can arrive quickly. Consider wearing layers and bringing a rain poncho.

And in case you're wondering, a dome is a rounded mountain.

The Drive » Follow Clingmans Dome Rd back to US 441. Cross US 441 and pull into the overlook parking area.

⑦ Newfound Gap Overlook

There's a lot going at the intersection of US 441 and Clingmans Dome Rd. Here, the **Rockefeller Monument** pays tribute to a $5 million donation from the Rockefeller Foundation that

helped to complete land purchases needed to create the park. President Franklin D Roosevelt formally dedicated Great Smoky Mountains National Park in this spot in 1940. The overlook sits at the border of North Carolina and Tennessee, within the 5046ft Newfound Gap. Enjoy expansive mountain views from the parking area or hop on the **Appalachian Trail** for a stroll.

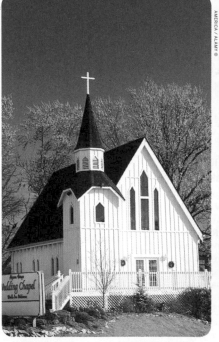

THE GREAT SMOKIES
AMY C BALFOUR, AUTHOR

As a kid, I loved reading adventure novels set in imaginary kingdoms, those otherworldly places filled with misty mountains, abandoned fortresses and a giant or two. The Great Smokies feel like one of those kingdoms, especially in spring when the forest is a luminous green, the animals are waking up and the trails meander into drifting fog.

Top: Cascades, Great Smoky Mountains National Park
Left: Wedding Chapel, Pigeon Forge
Right: Great Smoky Mountains National Park

The Drive » From here, follow US 441 north into Tennessee for about 5 miles to the parking lot.

8 Mt LeConte

Climbing 6593ft Mt LeConte is probably the park's most popular challenge, sure to give serious hamstring burn. The **Alum Cave Trail**, one of five routes to the peak, starts from the Alum Cave parking area on the main road. Follow a creek, pass under a stone arch and wind your way steadily upward. It's a 5.5-mile hike to LeConte Lodge, where you can join the **Rainbow Falls Trail** to the summit.

✕ ⊨ p254

The Drive » Continue on Newfound Gap Rd. Turn left into the parking lot at Little River Rd.

9 Sugarlands Visitor Center

At the juncture of Little River and Newfound Gap Rds is the **Sugarlands Visitor Center** (☎865-436-1291; www.nps.gov/grsm; ⊙8am-7pm Jun-Aug, closing hours vary rest of year), the park headquarters and main Tennessee entrance. Step inside for exhibits about plant and animal life (there's a stuffed wild boar only a mama boar could love), and a bookstore. Several ranger-led talks and tours meet at Sugarlands.

TIM FITZHARRIS / GETTY IMAGES ©

MALCOLM MACGREGOR / GETTY IMAGES ©

The Drive » Turn onto Little River Rd for a gorgeous 25-mile drive beside lively flowing waterways. The road passes Elkmont Campground then becomes Laurel Creek Rd. Watch for cars stopping suddenly as drivers pull over to look at wildlife.

TRIP HIGHLIGHT

🔟 Cades Cove

This secluded valley contains the remnants of a 19th-century settlement. It's accessed by an 11-mile, one-way loop road that has numerous pull-offs. From these, you can poke around old churches and farmhouses or hike trails through postcard-perfect meadows filled with deer, wild turkeys and the occasional bear. For good wildlife viewing, come in the late afternoon when the animals romp with abandon.

The narrow loop road has a speed limit of 10mph and can get crowded (and maddeningly slow) in high season. For a more tranquil experience, ride your bike, or walk, on a Wednesday or Saturday morning from early May through late September when cars are banned from the road between 7am and 10am. Rent a bike at the Cades Cove Campground Store ($4 to $6 per hour). Also recommended is the 5-mile round-trip hike to **Abrams Falls**. Trailhead parking is after the Elijah Oliver Place.

Stop by the **Cades Cove Visitor Center** (📞877-444-6777; 🕙9am-7pm Apr-Aug, closes earlier rest of year) for ranger talks.

🛏 p254

The Drive » Return to the Sugarlands Vistor Center then turn left onto US 441, which is called Parkway between Gatlinburg and Sevierville. Drive 2 miles to Gatlinburg.

⓫ Gatlinburg

Driving out of the park on the Tennessee side is disconcerting. All at once you pop out of the tranquil green tunnel of trees and into a blinking, shrieking welter of cars, motels, pancake houses, mini-golf courses and Ripley's Believe It or Not Museums. Welcome to Gatlinburg. It's Heidi meets Hillbilly in this vaguely Bavarian-themed tourist wonderland, catering to Smokies visitors since the 1930s. Most of the tourist attractions are within the compact, hilly little downtown.

The **Gatlinburg Sky Lift** (📞865-436-4307; www. gatlinburgskylift.com; 765 Parkway, Parkway light 7; adult/ child $14/10.50; 🕙9am-11pm Jun-Aug, varies rest of year), a repurposed ski-resort chairlift, whisks you high over the Smokies. You'll fill up your camera's memory card with panoramic snapshots.

🍴 🛏 p254

From Parkway in downtown Gatlinburg, turn right onto Historic Nature Trail/Airport Rd at the Gatlinburg Convention Center. Follow it into the national park, continuing to the marked entrance for the one-way Roaring Fork Motor Nature Trail.

WATERFALLS OF THE SMOKIES

The Smokies are full of waterfalls, from icy trickles to roaring cascades. Here are a few of the best:

» **Grotto Falls** You can walk behind these 25ft-high falls, off Trillium Gap Trail.

» **Laurel Falls** This popular 80ft fall is located down an easy 2.6-mile paved trail.

» **Mingo Falls** At 120ft, this is one of the highest waterfalls in the Appalachians.

» **Rainbow Falls** On sunny days, the mist here produces a rainbow.

12 Roaring Fork Motor Nature Trail

Built on the foundations of a 150-year-old wagon road, the 6-mile Roaring Fork loop twists through strikingly lush forest. Sights include burbling cascades, abundant hardwoods, mossy boulders and old cabins once inhabited by farming families. The isolated community of Roaring Fork was settled in the mid-1800s, along a powerful mountain stream. The families that lived here were forced to move when the park was established about 100 years later.

For a waterfall hike, try the 2.6-mile round-trip walk to **Grotto Falls** from the Trillium Gap Trailhead. Further down the road, check out the Ephraim Bales cabin, once home to 11 people.

The Roaring Fork Auto Tour Guide, for sale for $1 in the Oconaluftee and Sugarlands visitor centers, provides details about plant life and buildings along the drive. No buses, trailer or RVs are permitted on the motor road.

The Drive » At the end of Roaring Fork Rd turn left onto E Parkway. Less than 1 mile ahead, turn right at US 321S/ US 441. Drive 7 miles to Pigeon Forge.

13 Pigeon Forge

The town of Pigeon Forge is an ode to that big-haired, big-busted angel of East Tennessee, Dolly Parton – who's known to be a pretty cool chick.

Born in a one-room shack in the nearby hamlet of Locust Ridge, Parton started performing on Knoxville radio at the age of 11 and moved to Nashville at 18 with all her worldly belongings in a cardboard suitcase. She's made millions singing about her Smoky Mountain roots and continues to be a huge presence in her hometown, donating money to local causes and riding a glittery float in the annual Dolly Parade.

Wacky museums and OTT dinner shows line Parkway, the main drag.

Are you an Elvis fan? Step into the low-key **Elvis Museum** (☎865-428-2001; www.elvismuseums.com; 2638 Parkway; adult/child $17/7.50; ☺10am-6pm Sun-Fri, 10am-8pm Sat), which is chock-full of clothing, jewelry and cars (including a 1967 Honeymoon Cadillac) given away by the generous singer. Tickets are steep, but you can save $5 by pre-purchasing online.

The Drive » Turn right onto Parkway and drive 2 miles southeast. Then turn left onto Dollywood Ln/Veterans Blvd and follow signs to Dollywood, about 2½ miles away.

14 Dollywood

Dolly Parton's theme park **Dollywood** (☎865-428-9488; www.dollywood.com; 2700 Dollywood Parks Blvd; adult/child $57/45; ☺Apr-Dec) is an enormous love letter to mountain culture. Families pour in to ride the country-themed thrill rides and see demonstrations of traditional Appalachian crafts. You can also tour the bald-eagle sanctuary or worship at the altar of Dolly in the Chasing Rainbows life-story museum. The adjacent Dollywood's Splash Country takes these themes and adds water.

The Drive » Return to Parkway and follow it north 4½ miles into downtown Sevierville. Turn left onto Bruce St and drive one block to Court Ave.

15 Sevierville

On the front lawn of the downtown **courthouse** (125 Court Ave) you might see a few happy folks getting their pictures taken in front of the statue of a young Dolly Parton. Wearing a ponytail, her guitar held loose, it captures something kind of nice. You know where's she's from, where her music is going to take her, and how it all ties in to this tough, but always beautiful, mountain country.

Eating & Sleeping

FLORIDA & THE SOUTH TRIPS **19** THE GREAT SMOKIES

Bryson City ❷

✖ Cork & Bean — Cafe $$

(☎828-488-1934; www.brysoncitycorkandbean.com; 16 Everett St; breakfast $6-12, lunch $7-9, dinner $7-25; ☺8am-9pm) Big windows frame the Cork & Bean, a chic restaurant and coffee house in downtown Bryson City. With an emphasis on locally grown and organic fare, you'll feel less guilty digging into the eatery's crepes and sandwiches after your local hike. Look for eggs benedict, huevos rancheros and Belgian waffles on the weekend brunch menu. The adjacent coffee house is a welcoming, cozy place to surf the net.

🛏 Fryemont Inn — Inn $$

(☎828-488-2159; www.fryemontinn.com; 245 Fryemont St; lodge/ste/cabins from $110/$180/245, nonguest breakfast $6-9, dinner $20-29; ☺restaurant 6-8pm Sun-Tue, 6-9pm Fri & Sat mid-Apr–late Nov; ⓟ☏☒) The view of Bryson City and the Smokies from the porch of the lofty Fryemont Inn is hard to beat. This family-owned mountain lodge, which opened in 1923, feels like summer camp with its bark-covered main building and a common area flanked by a stone fireplace. No TVs or air-con in the lodge rooms. Wi-fi is available in the lobby. The room rate includes breakfast and dinner at the on-site restaurant, which is open to the public. Dinner entrees include trout, steak and lamb.

Mt LeConte ❽

🛏 LeConte Lodge — Cabins $$

(☎865-429-5704; www.lecontelodge.com; cabins per person adult/child 4-12yr $126/85) These rough-hewn log cabins near the summit of Mt LeConte are the park's only non-camping accommodation. There's no electricity, no real showers, and you have to hike at least 5.5 miles

to get here. But you'll be amply rewarded by glowing purple sunrises from the eastern-facing cliffs at Myrtle Point. As for meals, there's beef and gravy with mashed potatoes for dinner, scrambled eggs and Canadian bacon for breakfast.

Elkmont Campground

🛏 Elkmont Campground — Campground $

(☎865-436-1271; www.information nps.gov/grsm; Little River Rd; sites $17-23; ☺early Mar-Nov; ♿) The park's largest campground is on Little River Rd, 5 miles west of Sugarlands Visitor Center. Little River and Jakes Creek run through this wooded site and and the sound of rippling water adds tranquility. There are 200 tent and RV campsites and 20 walk-in sites. All are reservable beginning May 15. Like other campgrounds in the park, there are no showers, or electrical or water hook-ups. There are restrooms.

Cades Cove ❿

🛏 Cades Cove Campground — Campground $

(☎865-448-2472; information www.nps.gov/grsm; sites $20) This woodsy campground with 159 sites is a great place to sleep if you want to get a jump on visiting Cades Cove. There's a camp store, drinking water and bathrooms, but no showers. There are 29 tent-only sites.

Gatlinburg ⓫

✖ Pancake Pantry — Breakfast, American $

(☎865-436-4724; www.pancakepantry.com; 628 Parkway; breakfast $7-11, lunch $8-10; ☺7am-4pm Jun-Oct, to 3pm Nov-May; ♿) This welcoming place is the granddaddy of

254

Gatlinburg's many pancake houses. Chow down on a wide variety of pancakes, from wild blueberry to Sugar & Spice, as well as cheese-swollen omelets and whipped-cream-smothered waffles. The building looks like an overgrown Smurf house. Breakfast offered all day.

✖ Smoky Mountain Brewery   Pub $$

(www.smoky-mtn-brewery.com; 1004 Parkway; mains $9-23; ⊙11:30am-1am) For filling pub grub and decent microbrews, head to this busy brewery with lots of TVs and walls covered with dollar bills. Can't make up your mind from the menu? Go with the pizza.

✖ Wild Boar Saloon & Howard's Steakhouse   Steaks $$

(⏺865-436-3600; www.wildboarsaloon.com; 976 Parkway; mains $9-30; ⊙10am-10pm Sun-Thu, until 1:30am Fri & Sat) Since 1947 this dark creekside saloon has been serving burgers, ribs and a tasty pulled pork shoulder drenched in homemade sauce. But it's known for its steaks and for being the oldest joint in town.

🛏 Bearskin Lodge   Lodge $$

(⏺877-795-7546; www.thebearskinlodge.com; 840 River Rd; r from $110) This shingled riverside lodge is blessed with timber accents and a bit more panache than other Gatlinburg comers. All rooms have flat-screens and fireplaces, as well as private balconies jutting over the river. And it's excellent value.

🛏 Hampton Inn   Hotel $$

(⏺865-436-4878; www.hamptoninn3.hilton. com; 967 Parkway; r $139-179, ste $219; P @ 🛜 🐕) Yep, it's part of a chain, but the hotel sits in the thick-of-the-action on Parkway. Decor is modern, and furnishings include an easy chair and ottoman. Rooms with king beds have a fireplace. Ahhh.

STRETCH YOUR LEGS
MIAMI BEACH

Start/Finish: Ocean Drive

Distance: 3 miles

Duration: 3 hours

Greater Miami sprawls, but compact Miami Beach packs in the sights, making it perfect for an afternoon of exploring on foot. Get a taste of its famous art-deco district, as well as its luscious, white-sand beaches.

Take this walk on Trip

14

Ocean Drive

Ocean Drive is the classic Miami strip, where neon-accented art-deco buildings line the way for an endless parade of cars, in-line skaters and pedestrians. Stop at the **Art Deco Welcome Center** (📞305-672-2014; www.mdpl.org; 1001 Ocean Dr, South Beach; ⊙9:30am-5pm, to 7pm Thu) if you really want to immerse yourself in the world of decorative finials and cantilevered eyebrows.

The Walk ≫ Head north. To fully appreciate the architecture, stick to the park side of the street. At 13th St, note the Carlyle Hotel, where *The Birdcage* was filmed. Cross Lummus Park to get to the beach.

Lummus Park & South Beach

Take off your shoes and dig your toes into some of the most luscious sand you've ever felt, and stare out at (or run straight toward) the teal-green water that's shallow and warm enough to splash around in for hours. Run up and down if you must – cartwheels in the sand would not be inappropriate – but be sure to notice the six floridly colored lifeguard stands that stretch along this strip.

The Walk ≫ Walk (or wade) up the beach and find the path that takes you to Lincoln Rd just past the Loews Hotel. (If you get to the Sagamore you've gone too far.) Walk two blocks along Lincoln until you reach Washington Ave.

Lincoln Road Mall

Calling Lincoln Rd a mall is technically accurate, but misses the point. Yes, you can shop, and there are sidewalk cafes galore. But this outdoor pedestrian promenade between Alton Rd and Washington Ave is really about seeing and being seen; there are times when it feels less like a road and more like a runway.

The Walk ≫ Head south down busy Collins Ave, another thoroughfare that's lined with deco treasures. At 13th St, hop over one block to Washington Ave.

Miami Beach Post Office

Ahhh, Miami Beach – even its municipal buildings are treasured works of art. A fine example of Streamline Moderne, the **Miami Beach Post Office** (1300 Washington Ave) was built in 1937 as pa rt of the Works Progress Administration. Duck inside to mail some postcards and check out the striking ceiling mural of a stylized night sky.

The Walk » Just two blocks down – and they're not very interesting blocks, so we're tempted to send you back over to Collins – is a vintage dining experience.

11th St Diner

Many art-deco buildings evoke modes of transportation, such as planes, trains or ships. Well, the shiny little 11th St Diner does more than evoke: it's actually housed in a classic Pullman train car. Pull over for refreshments; the inside is as cute as the outside.

The Walk » Now that you're refreshed, head just a few doors down; your next stop is in the same block.

Wolfsonian-FIU

A fascinating museum that's part of Florida International University, the **Wolfsonian-FIU** (www.wolfsonian .org; 1001 Washington Ave; adult/child 6-12yr $//5; ☻noon-6pm Thu-Tue, to 9pm Fri) showcases artifacts from the height of the Industrial Revolution from the late 19th to mid-20th century. The exhibits span transportation, urbanism, industrial design, advertising and political propaganda, and give some intriguing insight as to what was going on in the world while all that deco was being built.

The Walk » It's just two short blocks along 10th St to get back to Ocean Dr. Between 7th and 8th is a fetching strip of buildings including the Colony Hotel, which you'll recognize instantly if you've ever watched anything set in Miami Beach.

STRETCH
YOUR LEGS
SAVANNAH

Start/Finish: Sentient Bean, Forsyth Park

Distance: 3.3 miles

Duration: 3 hours

Savannah is a living museum of Southern architecture and antebellum charm. Gorgeous and full of Old South charisma, its historical heart is freckled with pleasant squares shaded by spreading oaks dripping with Spanish moss. This town was made for walking.

Sentient Bean

Savannah is a coffee-loving town, and there's no better place to start your morning than **Sentient Bean** (www .sentientbean.com; 13 E Park Ave; ⊙7am-10pm; 🛜), a fabulous bohemian cafe with terrific coffee, gourmet scones, a hipster clientele and baristas with attitude (the good kind). Plus, it's just across the street from Forsyth Park.

The Walk » Step across the street and stroll through Savannah's most central, and most beautiful, park.

Forsyth Park

Gushing with fountains, draped with mossy oaks, unfurled with vast lawns and basketball and tennis courts, this is one dynamite city park. The Visitor Center has a number of brochures and maps that delve into local architecture and history and is worth stopping by. You also might consider staying the night at the hip and swanky Mansion on Forsyth Park.

The Walk » From the north end of the park continue straight to elegant Monterey Sq, your first of many such rectangular oases of charm.

Mercer-Williams House

The location of an infamous homicide, the **Mercer-Williams House** (www .mercerhouse.com; 429 Bull St; adult/child $12.50/8) was bought and restored by eccentric art dealer Jim Williams in 1969. Inside you'll find the room in which Danny Hansford was murdered in 1981. That story is at the heart of *Midnight in the Garden of Good and Evil*, the book and subsequent film that put Savannah on the map.

The Walk » From Monterey Sq, take Bull St north for four blocks, past a row of historical homes to E Charlton St on Madison Sq.

Shop SCAD

Creative impulses charge through Savannah's veins, thanks in large part to the Savannah College of Art & Design (SCAD). SCAD students are legion, its

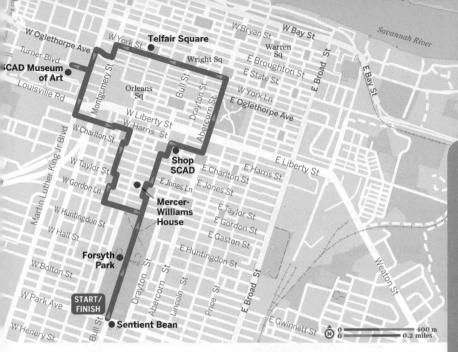

graduates often settling in town to paint or open flower shops, textile depots or design businesses. All the wares – throw pillows, art books, jewelry and T-shirts – on sale at **ShopSCAD** (www.shopscadonline. com; 340 Bull St; ⊙9am-5:30pm Mon-Wed, to 8pm Thu & Fri, 10am-8pm Sat, noon-5pm Sun) were imagined by SCAD students, alumni or faculty.

The Walk » Make a right on Harris St and meander through Laffayette Sq (one of our favorites) then make a left on Abercorn St and another on York St.

Telfair Square

Two of Savannah's most popular museums are set around this leafy residential plaza. The **Telfair Academy of Arts & Sciences** (www.telfair.org; 121 Barnard St; adult/child $12/5; ⊙noon-5pm Mon, 10am-5pm Tue-Sat, 1-5pm Sun) is filled with 19th-century American art and silver, and a smattering of European pieces. Nearby, **Jepson Center for the Arts** (JCA; www.telfair.org; 207 W York St; adult/child $12/5; ⊙10am-5pm Mon, Wed, Fri & Sat, 10am-8pm Thu, noon-5pm Sun; ♿) has 20th- and 21st-century art.

The Walk » Take York St west to Montgomery, head south to Oglethorpe and west again. Cross Martin Luther King Jr Blvd, one of town's major streets, and walk two long blocks to Turner Blvd.

SCAD Museum of Art

More than the sum of its parts, the **SCAD Museum of Art** (www.scadmoa .org; 601 Turner Blvd; adult/child under 14yr $10/free; ⊙10am-5pm Tue, Wed & Fri, to 8pm Thu, noon-5pm Sat & Sun) is a new brick, steel, concrete and glass longhouse carved with groovy sitting areas inside and out, and filled with fun rotating exhibitions – including an installation of video screens strobing various karaoke interpretations of Madonna's *Lucky Star*. It has intriguing mixed-media pieces and an inviting cafe.

The Walk » Your 1¼ mile walk back to the start follows MLK to Harris St. Make a left to Barnard, and head south, through Pulaski and Chatham Sqs. Make a left on Gaston to enter Forsyth Park.

STRETCH YOUR LEGS
NEW ORLEANS

Start/Finish: New Orleans African American Museum

Distance: 2.6 miles

Duration: 3 hours

Few destinations have as many sensational ways to kill time as the Crescent City. Its history runs deep, the colonial architecture is exquisite, and there's mouthwatering Cajun and Creole food, historical dive bars, a gorgeous countryside, and lashings of great free live music.

New Orleans African American Museum

We'll start in the Treme (pronounced truh-may), one of the country's oldest African American neighborhoods, at the **New Orleans African American Museum** (www.thenoaam.org; 1418 Governor Nicholls St; adult/student/child $7/5/3; ⊙11am-4pm Wed-Sat), a window into the African American experience in Louisiana, which stands out from the rest of the country due to the French-colonial connection.

The Walk ≫ Go southeast along Governor Nicholls St and turn right onto Henriette Delille St.

Backstreet Cultural Museum

New Orleans is often described as both the least American city in America and the northernmost city in the Caribbean. This is due to a unique colonial history that preserved the bonds between black New Orleanians and Africa and the greater black diaspora. Learn about this deep culture at the **Backstreet Cultural Museum** (www.backstreetmuseum .org; 1116 St Claude Ave; admission $8; ⊙10am-5pm Tue-Sat), a small but fascinating peek into the street-level music, ritual and communities that underlie the singular New Orleans experience.

The Walk ≫ Return to Governor Nicholls St and continue southeast. Once you cross busy Rampart St, you've entered the French Quarter. Turn right onto Royal St, a pretty lane with cute art galleries, antique shops and wonderful architecture.

Historic New Orleans Collection

The **Historic New Orleans Collection** (www.hnoc.org; 533 Royal St; admission free, tours $5; ⊙9:30am-4:30pm Tue-Sat, 10:30am-4:30pm Sun) is an interesting museum, spread over several exquisitely restored buildings and packed with well-curated exhibits. Rotating exhibitions are inevitably fascinating. Separate home, architecture/courtyard and history tours run at 10am, 11am, 2pm and 3pm, the home tour being the most interesting.

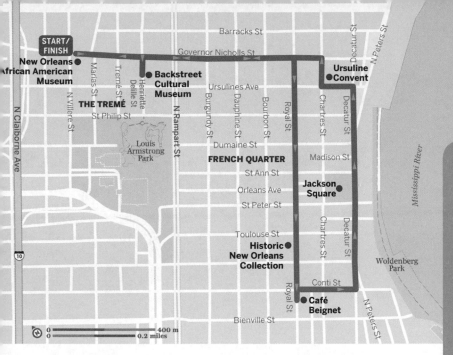

The Walk » Continue in a southerly direction on Royal St; at the 400 block, you'll pass the marbled magnificence of the Louisiana State Supreme Court. It's only about 500ft to the next stop.

Café Beignet

You've likely heard about the beignets (fried, sugar-covered doughnuts) at Café du Monde. They're good, but the place is horribly crowded. Instead, head to **Café Beignet** (📞504 524 5530; 334B Royal St; meals $6-8; 🕑7am-5pm) on Royal St. Watch pedestrians stroll by, drink your espresso in peace and try a beignet; they're delicious.

The Walk » Turn around and turn right on Conti St, follow it for two blocks, then turn left on Decatur St. To your right, over the levee, is the Mississippi River. Walk north four blocks to get to Jackson Sq.

Jackson Square

Stroll over to Jackson Square, the city green of New Orleans. Lovers' lanes and trimmed hedges surround a monument to Andrew Jackson, the hero of the Battle of New Orleans and the seventh president of the USA. But the real star is the magnificent, French-style St Louis Cathedral, flanked by the Cabildo and Presbytere. The former houses a Louisiana state history museum; the latter an exhibition on Mardi Gras.

The Walk » Continue north on Decatur St for three blocks, then turn left onto Ursulines Ave. After one block, turn right onto Chartres St.

Ursuline Convent

In 1727, 12 Ursuline nuns arrived in New Orleans to care for the French garrison's 'miserable little hospital' and educate the colony's young girls. Between 1745 and 1752 the French army built the **Ursuline Convent** (1112 Chartres St; adult/child $5/3; 🕑 tours 10am-4pm Mon-Sat), now the only remaining French building in the quarter. A self-guided tour takes in various rotating exhibits and the beautiful St Mary's chapel.

The Walk » Walk up Chartres St and turn left on Govenor Nicholls St. From here it's a half-mile back to the African American Museum and your starting point.

Great Lakes Trips

DON'T BE FOOLED BY ALL THE CORN.
The Midwest is more than a flat, endless field.
Intrepid road-trippers will find that out as soon
as they set wheels on red-cliffed, forest-cloaked
Hwy 61 in northern Minnesota; on the dune-
backed, lighthouse-dotted thoroughfares of
western Michigan; or on the River Road rising
and twisting along the Big Muddy.

The Great Lakes themselves are huge, like
inland seas. Dairy farms and orchards blanket
the region, meaning fresh pie and ice cream
await trip-takers. Big cities such as Chicago
and Minneapolis rise up and provide awesome
doses of culture and entertainment.

And when the Midwest does flatten out? There's
always a goofball roadside attraction to revive
imaginations.

Lake Michigan A stretch of beach on Michigan's Gold Coast (Trip 21)

Great Lakes Trips

N

0   200 km
0   100 miles

Thunder Bay

Lake Superior

Boundary Waters Canoe Area Wilderness

Isle Royale National Park

CANADA
USA

Grand Portage

Bemidji
Chippewa National Forest
Grand Rapids
Superior National Forest
Tofte

23

Leech Lake Indian Reservation

MINNESOTA

Apostle Islands

Hancock

Marquette

Duluth
Superior
Ashland
Ironwood

MICHIGAN

Ottawa National Forest

Hiawatha National Forest

Mackinaw City

22

Fond du Lac Indian Reservation

Mille Lacs Lakes

Chequamegon National Forest

Lake Chippewa

Lac du Flambeau Indian Reservation

Escanaba

Petoskey

Boyne City

35

Saint Croix National Scenic Riverway

Nicolet National Forest

Menominee

St Cloud

94

WISCONSIN

Eau Claire
Wausau

Menominee Indian Reservation

Green Bay

Traverse City

Sleeping Bear Dunes National Lakeshore

Minneapolis

Appleton

Manistee

Cadillac

35

Mankato

Rochester
Winona
La Crosse

Oshkosh
Lake Winnebago
Fond Du Lac

Manitowoc

Manistee National Forest

Isabe Indi Reservati

21

Albert Lea

90

Mason City

Prairie Du Chien

Madison

Janesville

Sheboygan

Port Washington

Lake Michigan

Milwaukee

Muskegon

Grand Rapids

Lansing

Fort Dodge

IOWA

Kenosha

Holland

Waterloo

Dubuque

Freeport
Rockford

Benton Harbor

Kalamazoo

Marsh

Jewell

Cedar Rapids

New Buffalo

South Bend

80

Iowa City

Chicago

Gary

Three Oaks

Des Moines

Davenport

Wilmington

Fort Wayne

35

Galesburg

Kankakee

Fort Madison
Burlington

Peoria

20

Bloomington

55

INDIANA

Lafayette

Muncie

MISSOURI

22

Quincy

Champaign

Danville

Indianapolis

Richmond

Chillicothe

Hannibal

Urbana

Springfield

Decatur

Terre Haute

Columbus

Moberly

ILLINOIS

Columbia

Litchfield

St Louis

Mississippi River

Des Moines River

Cedar River

Rock River

Illinois River

Split Rock Lighthouse (Trip 23)

Classic Trip

20 Route 66 14 Days
America's 'Mother Road' offers a time-warped journey from Chicago to LA. (p267)

21 Michigan's Gold Coast 4 Days
A spin along Lake Michigan's shore features beaches, wineries and island-hopping. (p281)

22 Along the Great River Road 6–7 Days
Trace the Mississippi River through bluff-strewn scenery and retro small towns. (p291)

23 Highway 61 2–3 Days
The Minnesota byway hugs Lake Superior's rugged edge, passing waterfalls and moose. (p301)

 DON'T MISS

Pie
The region's prolific orchards result in flaky, scrumptious desserts at hot spots such as Crane's Pie Pantry and Betty's Pies. Try them out on Trips 21 23

Hemingway Haunts
Literary buffs can find the places Papa wrote about and the bars where he tossed back drinks. Retrace the writer's steps on Trip 21

Harbor View Cafe
It's in the middle of nowhere, but foodies have been trekking to check out the riverside cafe's chalkboard menu for 30-plus years. Make a visit on Trip 22

Judge CR Magney State Park
You've never seen a waterfall like Devil's Kettle, where half the flow disappears down a hole. See it for yourself on Trip 23

Cozy Dog Drive In
Not only is the eatery crammed with Route 66 relics, it's the mythic birthplace of the corn dog. Make the stop on Trip 20

Route 66 Experience the classic US road trip cruising the 'Main Street of America'

Classic Trip

Route 66 **20**

America's 'Mother Road' offers a time-warped journey from Chicago to LA past neon-lit diners, drive-in movie theaters and roadside attractions that beg for a photo.

TRIP HIGHLIGHTS

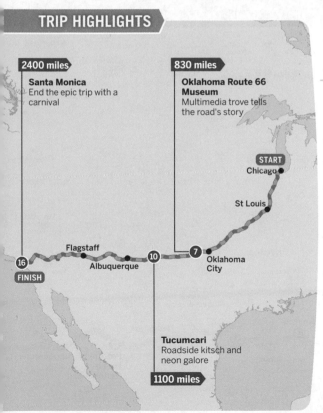

2400 miles
Santa Monica
End the epic trip with a carnival

830 miles
Oklahoma Route 66 Museum
Multimedia trove tells the road's story

START
Chicago

St Louis

Flagstaff

Albuquerque

10

7

Oklahoma City

16
FINISH

Tucumcari
Roadside kitsch and neon galore

1100 miles

14 DAYS
2400 MILES /
3862KM

GREAT FOR...

BEST TIME TO GO
May–Sep

 ESSENTIAL PHOTO

The Gemini Giant, a fiberglass spaceman, in Wilmington, IL.

 BEST 2 DAYS
California's stretch of road offers tumbleweed landscapes, tipi motels and malted milkshakes.

20 Route 66

It's a lonely road – a ghost road really – that appears for a stretch then disappears, gobbled up by the interstate. You know you've found it again when a 20ft lumberjack holding a hot dog rises up from the side, or a sign points you to the 'World's Largest Covered Wagon,' driven by giant Abe Lincoln. And that's just Illinois – the first of eight states on the nostalgic, kitschy, slowpoke drive west.

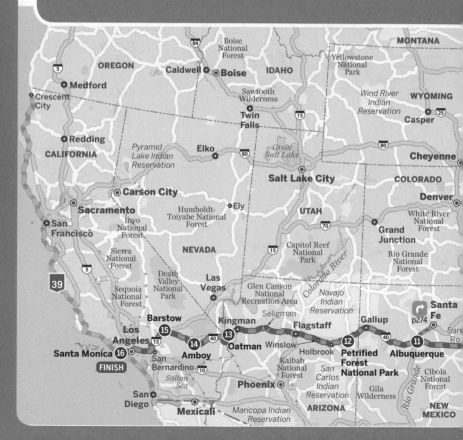

❶ Chicago

Route 66 kicks off in downtown Chicago on Adams St just west of Michigan Ave. Before you snap the obligatory photo with the 'Route 66 Begin' sign (on the south side of Adams, FYI), spend some time exploring the Windy City. Wander through the **Art Institute** (☏312-443-3600; www.artic.edu; 111 S Michigan Ave; adult/child $23/free; ⏰10:30am-5pm, to 8pm Thu; ♿) – literally steps from the Mother Road's launching point – and browse Edward Hopper's *Nighthawks* (a diner scene) and Grant Wood's *American Gothic* (a farmer portrait) to set the scene for what you'll see en route. Nearby **Millennium Park** (☏312-742-1168; www.millenniumpark.org; 201 E Randolph St; ⏰6am-11pm; ♿; Ⓜ Brown, Orange, Green, Purple, Pink Line to Randolph) is just plain cool, with mod public artworks and concerts at lunchtime

LINK YOUR TRIP

22 Along the Great River Road

The epic roadway (actually a series of roads) traces the meanderings of the Mississippi River. Pick it up in St Louis.

39 Pacific Coast Highways

This route along the edge of the continent cruises along an equally iconic numbered route: Hwy 1. When you finish Route 66, follow Hwy 1 north or south.

GREAT LAKES TRIPS **20** ROUTE 66

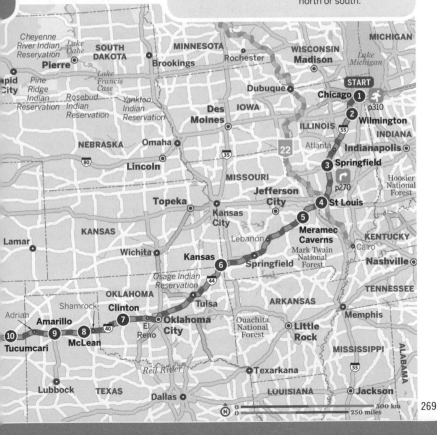

269

and most evenings June through August. Our Chicago walking tour (p310) has more suggestions.

🍴 p278

The Drive ≫ Stay on Adams St for 1.5 miles until you come to Ogden Ave. Go left, and continue through the suburbs of Cicero and Berwyn. At Harlem Ave, turn left (south) and stay on it briefly until you jump onto Joliet Rd. Soon Joliet Rd joins southbound I-55 (at exit 277), and you're funneled onto the interstate.

- - - - - - - - - - - -

2 Gemini Giant

Our first stop rises from the cornfields 60 miles south of Chicago. Leave I-55 at exit 241, and follow Hwy 44 south a short distance to Hwy 53, which rolls into the town of Wilmington. Here the Gemini Giant – a 28ft

fiberglass spaceman – stands guard outside the **Launching Pad Drive-In** (810 E Baltimore St). The restaurant is now shuttered, but the humongous green rocket-holding statue remains a quintessential photo op.

The Drive ≫ Get back on I-55. Take exit 154 for Funks Grove, a 19th-century maple-sirup farm (yes, that's sirup with an 'i'). Get on Old Route 66 (a frontage road that parallels the interstate here), and in 10 miles you'll reach Atlanta and its pie-filled cafe (p278). Springfield is 50 miles southwest.

- - - - - - - - - - - -

3 Springfield

Illinois is the Land of Lincoln, according to local license plates, and the best place to get your Honest Abe fix is Springfield, the state capital. Fans of the 16th president get weak-kneed at the holy trio of sights: **Lincoln's Tomb** (www.lincolntomb. org; 1441 Monument Ave;

🕓9am-5pm, closed Sun & Mon Sep-May), the **Lincoln Presidential Library & Museum** (☎217-558-8444; www.presidentlincoln.org; 212 N 6th St; adult/child \$12/6; 🕓9am-5pm; 🛗) and the **Lincoln Home** (☎217-492-4150; www.nps.gov/liho; 426 S 7th St; 🕓8:30am-5pm), all in or near downtown. Oh, and Springfield's Route 66 claim to fame? It's the birthplace of the corn dog (a cornmeal-battered, fried hot dog on a stick).

🍴 p278

The Drive ≫ Return to I-55, which supersedes Route 66 here as in most of the state. The **Route 66 Association of Illinois** (www.il66assoc.org) tells you where to veer off for restored gas stations, vintage cafes and giant Lincoln statues. Near Edwardsville get on I-270, on which you'll swoop over the Mississippi River and enter Missouri.

- - - - - - - - - - - -

4 St Louis

Just over the border is St Louis, a can-do city that has launched westbound travelers for centuries. To ogle the city's most iconic attraction, exit I-270 onto Riverview Dr and point your car south toward the 630ft-tall **Gateway Arch** (www.gatewayarch.com; tram ride adult/child \$10/5; 🕓8am-10pm Jun-Aug, 9am-6pm Sep-May), a graceful reminder of the city's role in westward expansion. For up-close views of the stainless-steel span and the Jefferson National

**DETOUR:
OLD CHAIN OF
ROCKS BRIDGE**

Start: 3 Springfield

Before driving into Missouri, detour off I-270 at exit 3. Follow Hwy 3 (aka Lewis and Clark Blvd) south, turn right at the first stoplight and drive west to the 1929 **Old Chain of Rocks Bridge** (Old Chain of Rocks Rd; 🕓9am-dusk). Open only to pedestrians and cyclists these days, the mile-long span over the Mississippi River has a 22-degree angled bend (the cause of many a crash, hence the ban on cars). Hide your valuables and lock your car if you leave it to go exploring.

Expansion Memorial surrounding it, turn left onto Washington Ave from Tucker Blvd (12th St). To explore the city in greater detail, see our St Louis walking tour (p358).

✕ p278

The Drive >> From here, I-44 closely tracks – and often covers – chunks of original Mother Road. Take the interstate southwest to Stanton, then follow the signs to Meramac Caverns.

⑤ Meramec Caverns

Kitschy billboards have been touting **Meramec Caverns** (www.americascave. com; Exit 230 off I-44; adult/child $20/10; ⊙8:30am-7:30pm summer, reduced hours rest of year) for miles. The family-mobbed attraction and campground has lured road-trippers with its offbeat ads since 1933. From gold panning to riverboat rides, you'll find a day's worth of distractions, but don't miss the historically and geologically engaging cave tour. Note to kitsch seekers: the restaurant and gift store are actually inside the mouth of the cave.

The Drive >> Continue on I-44. Lebanon (p278) makes a good pit stop. Ditch the interstate west of Springfield, taking Hwy 96 to Civil War–era Carthage with its historic town square and 66 Drive-In Theatre. From Joplin, follow Hwy 66 to Old Route 66 then hold tight: Kansas is on the horizon.

⑥ Kansas

The tornado-prone state holds a mere 13 miles of Mother Road (less than 1% of the total) but there's still a lot to see. First you'll pass through mine-scarred **Galena**, where a rusty old tow truck inspired animators from Pixar to create the character Mater in *Cars*. A few miles later, stop at the red-brick **Eisler Brothers Old Riverton Store** (☑620-848-3330; www.eislerbros.com; 7109 SE Hwy 66; ⊙7:30am-8pm Mon-Sat, noon-7pm Sun) and stock up on batteries, turkey sandwiches and Route 66 memorabilia. The 1925 property looks much like it did when built – note the pressed-tin ceiling and the outhouse – and it's on the National Register of Historic Places. Cross Hwy 400 and continue to the **1923 Marsh Rainbow Arch Bridge**, from where it's 3 miles south to **Baxter Springs**, site of a Civil War massacre and numerous bank robberies.

The Drive >> Enter Oklahoma. From Afton, Route 66 parallels I-44 (now a tollway) through Vinita, home to a famed fried-chicken cafe (p278). Tulsa to Oklahoma City offers one of the longest continuous stretches of Mother Road (110 miles). From here it joins Business I-40 for 20 miles to El Reno and its distinctive burgers (p278), and then parallels I-40 to Clinton.

TRIP HIGHLIGHT

⑦ Oklahoma Route 66 Museum

Flags from all eight Mother Road states fly high beside the memorabilia-filled **Oklahoma Route 66 Museum** (☑580-323-7866; www.route66.org; 2229 W Gary Blvd, Clinton, OK; adult/child $4/1; ⊙9am-5pm Mon-Sat, 1-5pm Sun, with variations, closed Sun & Mon Dec & Jan; ⊞) in Clinton. This fun-loving treasure trove, run by the Oklahoma Historical Society, isn't your typical mishmash of photos, clippings and knickknacks (though there is an artifact-filled Cabinet of Curios). Instead, it uses music and videos to dramatize six decades of Route 66 history. Last exhibit? A faux-but-fun drive-in theater.

The Drive >> Continue west 70 miles to the Texas border. From here old Route 66 runs immediately south of I-40 through barely changed towns such as Shamrock, with its restored 1930s buildings like the Tower Station and U-Drop Inn, and miniscule McLean.

⑧ Devil's Rope Museum

The sprawling grasslands of Texas and other western cattle states were once open range, where steers and cowboys could wander where they darn well

Classic Trip

LOCAL KNOWLEDGE
SARA BENSON,
AUTHOR

As you follow the
National Old Trails Rd,
look for the installation of recycled
glass-bottle trees (over 200 of
them) by folk artist Elmer Long.
Then motor across the Mojave River
into dusty downtown Victorville,
with its Hollywood-Western
atmosphere. Near Cajon Pass, I
always pull over at the Summit Inn
truck stop for an ostrich burger and
date milkshake.

Top: Roy's Motel & Cafe, Amboy
Left: Petrified Forest National Park
Right: Gemini Giant, Wilmington

GEMINI GIANT

66

pleased. That all changed in the 1880s when the devil's rope – more commonly known as barbed wire – began dividing up the land into private parcels. This **museum** (www. barbwiremuseum.com; 100 Kingsley St, McLean; ☺9am-5pm Mon-Fri, 10am-4pm Sat Mar-Nov) in the battered town of McLean has vast barbed-wire displays and a small but homey and idiosyncratic room devoted to Route 66. The detailed map of the road in Texas is a must.

The Drive » I-40 west of McLean glides over low-rolling hills. The landscape flattens at Groom, home of the tilting water tower and a 19-story cross at exit 112. Take exit 96 for Conway to snap a photo of the forlorn VW Beetle Ranch, aka the Bug Ranch, on the south side of I-40. For the Big Texan, take exit 74.

----

❾ Amarillo

This cowboy town holds a plethora of Route 66 sites: the Big Texan Steak Ranch (p278) (you've seen the billboards), the historic livestock auction and the San Jacinto District, which still has original Route 66 businesses.

As for the Big Texan, this hokey but classic attraction opened on Route 66 in 1960. It moved to its current location when I-40 opened in 1971 and has never looked back. The attention-grabbing gimmick here is the 'free

273

Classic Trip

72oz steak' offer – you have to eat this enormous portion of cow plus a multitude of sides in under one hour, or you pay for the entire meal ($72). Contestants sit at a raised table to 'entertain' the other diners. Less than 20% pass the challenge.

 p278

The Drive » Continue west on I-40. To see the Cadillac Ranch, an art installation of spray-painted cars, take exit 60 then backtrack on the southern frontage road from the Love's gas station. From there, follow I-40 west through Adrian and the Midpoint Cafe (p278) to the New Mexico border. Tucumcari is 40 miles west.

TRIP HIGHLIGHT

⑩ Tucumcari

A ranching and farming town sandwiched between the mesas and the plains, Tucumcari is home to one of the best preserved sections of Route 66 in the country. It's a great place to drive through at night, when dozens of neon signs – relics of the town's Route 66 heyday – cast a crazy rainbow-colored glow. Tucumcari's Route 66 motoring legacy and other regional highlights are recorded on 35 murals in downtown and the surrounding area. Pick up a map for the murals at the **chamber of commerce** (404 W Route 66; ☺8:30am-5pm Mon-Fri).

The engaging **Mesalands Dinosaur Museum** (www.mesalands. edu/community/dinosaur-museum; 222 E Laughlin St; adult/child $6.50/4; ☺10am-6pm Tue-Sat Mar-Aug, noon-5pm Tue-Sat Sep-Feb; 🚼) showcases real dinosaur bones and has hands-on exhibits for kids. Casts of dinosaur bones are done in bronze (not the usual plaster of Paris), which shows fine detail.

🍴 🛏 p279

The Drive » West on I-40, dry and windy plains spread into the distance, the horizon interrupted by flat-topped mesas. To stretch your legs, take exit 273 from Route 66/I-40 to downtown Santa Rosa and the Route 66 Auto Museum, which has upwards of 35 cars from the 1920s through the 1960s, all in beautiful condition.

---

⑪ Albuquerque

After 1936, Route 66 was realigned from its original path, which linked north through Santa Fe, to a direct line west into Albuquerque. Today, the city's Central Ave follows the post-1937 route. It passes through Nob Hill, the university, downtown and Old Town.

The patioed Kelly's Brewery (p279), in today's trendy Nob Hill, was an art moderne gas station on the route, commissioned in 1939. West of I-25, look for the spectacular tile-and-wood artistry of the **KiMo Theatre** (www.cabq.gov/kimo; 423 Central Ave NW, downtown), across from the old Indian trading post. This 1927 icon of pueblo deco architecture blends Native American culture with art deco design. It also screens classic movies. For prehistoric designs, take exit 154, just west of downtown, and drive north 3 miles to **Petroglyph National**

DETOUR: SANTA FE

Start: ⑪ Albuquerque

New Mexico's capital city is an oasis of art and culture lifted 7000ft above sea level, against the backdrop of the Sangre de Christo Mountains. It was on Route 66 until 1938, when a realignment left it by the wayside. It's well worth the detour to see the Georgia O'Keeffe Museum and to fork into uber-hot green chili dishes in the superb restaurants. See our Sante Fe walking tour (p482) for more to-dos. Route 66 follows the Old Pecos Trail (NM466) into town.

SINDRE ELLINGSEN / ALAMY ©

Wigwam Motel, Holbrook Spend the night in a tipi

275

Classic Trip

more than 20,000 rock etchings.

 p279

The Drive » Route 66 dips from I-40 into Gallup, becoming the main drag past beautifully renovated buildings, including the 1926 Spanish Colonial El Morro Theater. Cool murals also adorn many buildings. From Gallup, it's 21 miles to Arizona. In Arizona, take exit 311 to enter Petrified Forest National Park.

⑫ Petrified Forest National Park

The 'trees' of the **Petrified Forest** (📞928-524-6228; www.nps.gov/pefo; vehicle/walk-in, bicycle & motorcycle $10/5; ⏰7am-8pm Jun & Jul, shorter hr Aug-May) are fragmented, fossilized 225-million-year-old logs; in essence, wood that has turned to stone, scattered over a vast area of semidesert grassland. Many are huge – up to 6ft in diameter.

The scenic drive has about 15 pullouts with interpretive signs and some short trails. Two trails near the southern entrance provide the best access for close-ups of the petrified logs: the 0.6-mile Long Logs Trail, which has the largest concentration, and the 0.4-mile Giant Logs Trail, which is entered through the Rainbow Forest Museum and sports the park's largest log.

North of the I-40, enjoy sweeping views of the Painted Desert, where nature presents a hauntingly beautiful palette, especially at sunset.

The park, which straddles the I-40, has an entrance at exit 311 in the north and another off Hwy 180 in the south. A 28-mile paved scenic road links the two. To avoid backtracking, westbound travelers should start in the north, eastbound travelers in the south.

The Drive » Take I-40 west 25 miles to Holbrook, a former Wild West town now home to

the photo-ready Wigwam Motel. Motor on through lonesome Winslow, which has an elegant hotel (p279), and college-y Flagstaff. At Seligman grab a burger (p279) before the Mother Road arcs northwest away from I-40 through scrub-covered desert, then rejoins the interstate at quiet Kingman. From here you corkscrew through the Black Mountains and Sitgreaves Pass to Oatman.

- - - - - - - - - - -

⑬ Oatman

Since the veins of ore ran dry in 1942, crusty Oatman has reinvented itself as a movie set and Wild West tourist trap, complete with staged gun fights (daily at 1:30pm and 3:30pm) and gift stores named Fast Fanny's Place and the Classy Ass.

Speaking of asses, there are plenty of them (the four-legged kind, that is) roaming the streets. Stupid and endearing, they're descendents from pack animals left by the early miners. These burros may beg for food, but do not feed them carrots. Instead, buy healthier hay cubes for $1 per bag at nearby stores.

Squeezed among the shops is the 1902 Oatman Hotel, a surprisingly modest shack (no longer renting rooms) where Clark Gable and Carole Lombard spent their wedding night in 1939. On July 4 the town holds a sidewalk egg-frying contest. Now that's hot!

TOP TIP: NAVIGATING ROUTE 66

Because Route 66 is no longer an official road, it doesn't appear on most maps. We've provided high-level directions, but you'll fare best using one of these additional resources: free turn-by-turn directions at www.historic66.com, or maps from the National Historic Route 66 Federation (www.national66.org).

The Drive » From here, Route 66 twists down to Golden Shores and I-40. Soon you'll enter California at Needles. About 40 miles later, the road dips south and joins with the National Old Trails Rd. This is some of the coolest stretch of road, with huge skies and vintage signs rusting in the sun.

- - - - - - - - - - - -

⑭ Amboy

Potholed and crumbling in a romantic way, the USA's original transnational highway was established in 1912, more than a decade before Route 66 first ran through here. The rutted highway races through tiny towns, sparsely scattered across the Mojave. Only a few landmarks interrupt the horizon, including **Roy's Motel & Cafe** (www.rt66roys.com; National Old Trails Hwy; ⊙vary), a landmark Route 66 watering hole. If you'll believe the lore, Roy once cooked his famous Route 66 double cheeseburger on the hood of a '63 Mercury. Although the motel is abandoned, the gas station and cafe are occasionally open. It's east of **Amboy Crater** (☏760-326-7000; www. blm.gov/ca; 1 mile west of Amboy; ⊙sunrise-sunset), an almost perfectly symmetrical volcanic cinder cone. You can hike to the top, but it's best to avoid the midday sun – the 1.5-mile hike doesn't have a stitch of shade.

The Drive » Stay on the National Old Trails Rd to Ludlow. Turn right onto Crucero Rd and pass under I-40, then take the north frontage road west and turn left at Lavic Rd. Keep heading west on the National Old Trails Rd through windswept Daggett. Join I-40 at Nebo Rd. Drive for about 15 minutes before taking the exit for Barstow Road.

- - - - - - - - - - - -

⑮ Barstow

Exit the interstate onto Main St, which runs through Barstow, a railroad settlement and historic crossroads, where murals adorn empty buildings downtown. Follow 1st St north across the Mojave River over a trestle bridge to the 1911 Harvey House, nicknamed 'Casa del Desierto,' designed by Western architect Mary Colter. Next to a small railroad museum is the **Route 66 'Mother Road' Museum** (☏760-255-1890; www.route66museum.org; 681 N 1st St; ⊙10am-4pm Fri-Sun), displaying black-and-white historical photographs and odds and ends of everyday life in the early 20th century. Back in the day, it was also a Harvey House.

✗ p279

The Drive » Rejoin the National Old Trails Rd. At Victorville take I-15 out of town, heading south to San Bernardino, home to an iconic Route 66 motor court. From there follow Foothill Blvd/Route 66 west through retro-suburban Pasadena and check out the diner. Finally, for your Hollywood ending, take Arroyo Seco Pkwy to LA, where Sunset Blvd connects to Santa Monica Blvd.

- - - - - - - - - - - -

TRIP HIGHLIGHT

⑯ Santa Monica

This is the end of the line: Route 66 reaches its finish, over 2400 miles from its starting point in Chicago, on an ocean bluff in **Palisades Park**, where a Will Rogers Hwy memorial plaque marks the official end of the Mother Road. Celebrate on **Santa Monica Pier** (☏310-458-8900; www. santamonicapier.org; 🚻), where you can ride a 1920s carousel featured in *The Sting*, gently touch tide-pool critters at the **Santa Monica Pier Aquarium** (☏310-393-6149; www.healthebay. org; 1600 Ocean Front Walk; adult/child $5/free; ⊙2-5pm Tue-Fri, 12:30-5pm Sat & Sun; 🚻), and soak up a sunset atop the solar-powered Ferris wheel at **Pacific Park** (☏310-260-8744; www. pacpark.com; ⊙11am-9pm Sun-Thu, to midnight Fri & Sat Jun-Aug, shorter hours Sep-May; 🚻). Year-round carnival rides include the West Coast's only oceanfront steel roller coaster – a thrilling ride to end this classic trip.

🛏 p279

Classic Trip

Eating & Sleeping

Chicago ①

✖ Lou Mitchell's   Breakfast $

(www.loumitchellsrestaurant.com; 565 W Jackson Blvd; mains $6-11; ⏰5:30am-3pm Mon-Sat, 7am-3pm Sun; 🚻; Ⓜ Blue Line to Clinton) Lou's old-school waitresses deliver omelets that hang off the plate and thick-cut French toast while calling you 'honey' and filling your coffee cup. Free donut holes and Milk Duds sweeten the deal. It's located near Route 66's starting point.

Atlanta

✖ The Palms Grill Cafe   Cafe $

(☎217-648-2233; www.thepalmsgrillcafe.com; 110 SW Arch St; pie slices $3; ⏰5am-8pm) Thick slabs of gooseberry, sour cream raisin and other retro pies tempt from the glass case. Then walk across the street to snap a photo with Tall Paul, a sky-high statue of Paul Bunyan clutching a hot dog.

Springfield ③

✖ Cozy Dog Drive In   American $

(www.cozydogdrivein.com; 2935 S 6th St; mains $2-4.50; ⏰8am-8pm Mon-Sat) It's a Route 66 legend – the reputed birthplace of the corn dog! – with memorabilia and souvenirs in addition to the deeply fried main course on a stick.

St Louis ④

✖ Ted Drewes Frozen Custard   Ice Cream $

(☎314-481-2652; www.teddrewes.com; 6726 Chippewa St; mains under $5; ⏰11am-11pm Feb-Dec; 🚻) Get in line at this icicle-trimmed shack to order a 'concrete' – a super-creamy ice-cream-like treat so thick they hand it to you upside down.

Lebanon

🛏 Munger Moss Motel   Motel $

(☎417-532-3111; www.mungermoss.com; 1336 E Rte 66; r from $50; ❄🌐🛏) The 1940s motel has a monster of a neon sign and Mother Road–loving owners. Munger and Moss? Surnames of the original owner's first two husbands.

Vinita

✖ Clanton's   American $

(www.clantonscafe.com; 319 E Illinois Ave; mains $4-10; ⏰6am-8pm Mon-Fri, to 2pm Sat & Sun) Clanton's dates back to 1927 and is the place for chicken fried steak and calf fries (don't ask).

El Reno

✖ Sid's   Burgers

(300 S Choctaw Ave; ⏰11am-7pm) El Reno is the birthplace of the fried onion burger, a local specialty in which ground beef is combined with raw onions and then cooked and caramelized on the grill. Sid's makes a mean one.

Amarillo ⑧

✖ Big Texan Steak Ranch   Steakhouse $$

(www.bigtexan.com; 7701 I-40 E, exit 74; mains $10-40; ⏰7am-10:30pm; 🚻) Consume the 72oz steak, plus all the fixin's, in an hour and it's free; otherwise you pay $72.

Adrian

✖ Midpoint Cafe   Cafe $

(☎806-538-6379; cnr Business 40 & CR 22; mains $3-7; ⏰8am-4pm Mar-Dec) Vibrant vinyl chairs and 1950s-esque knickknacks form the backdrop of this burger joint and gift shop. It marks the halfway point between LA and Chicago, and serves some darn good 'ugly crust' pie.

Tucumcari 🔟

✖ Kix on 66 — Diner $

(www.kixon66.com; 1102 E Tucumcari Blvd; mains $5-10; ⏱6am-2pm; 🛜) A classic diner with a hint of style, Kix serves American and Southwest specialties right beside the Mother Road.

🛏 Blue Swallow Motel — Historic Motel $

(📞575-461-9849; www.blueswallowmotel.com; 815 E Tucumcari Blvd; r from $65; ❄🛜🍽) Spend the night in this beautifully restored motel and feel time slide in reverse. The place has a great lobby, friendly owners and vintage, uniquely decorated rooms.

Albuquerque 1️⃣1️⃣

✖ Frontier — New Mexican $

(www.frontierrestaurant.com; 2400 Central Ave SE; mains $3-11; ⏱5am-1am; 🅿🚼) Get in line for enormous cinnamon rolls and some of the best huevos rancheros in town. The food, people-watching and Western art are all outstanding.

✖ Kelly's Brewery — Brewery

(www.kellysbrewpub.com; 3222 Central Ave SE; ⏱8am-10:30pm Sun-Thu, to midnight Fri & Sat) Come to this former Route 66 service station for patio dining, lots of local microbrews and 20-somethings hanging out.

Winslow

🛏 La Posada — Historic Hotel $$

(📞928-289-4366; www.laposada.org; 303 E 2nd St; r $119-169; ❄🛜🍽) The Mary Colter–designed 1930s *hacienda* features elaborate tile work, glass-and-tin chandeliers, Navajo rugs and other details that accent its rustic Western-style elegance. The period-styled rooms are named for illustrious former guests.

Seligman

✖ Snow Cap Drive-In — Burgers $

(📞928-422-3291; 301 E Rte 66; dishes $3-6; ⏱10am-6pm mid-Mar–Nov) It's a Route

66 institution. The crazy decor is only the beginning. Beware the fake mustard bottle...

Barstow 1️⃣5️⃣

✖ Idle Spurs Steakhouse — Steakhouse $$

(📞760-256-8888; www.idlespurssteakhouse.com; 690 Hwy 58; mains $13-27; ⏱11am-9pm Mon-Fri, from 4pm Sat & Sun) This Old West steakhouse and fully stocked saloon (it's even got microbrews) will slake your desert thirst. There's a tree growing inside the dining room.

San Bernardino

🛏 Wigwam Motel — Motel $

(📞909-875-3005; www.wigwammotel.com; 2728 W Foothill Blvd, Rialto; r $65-80; 🍽) This vintage motor court lets travelers sleep in concrete tepees, which have been Route 66 icons since 1949.

Pasadena

✖ Fair Oaks Pharmacy — Diner $

(📞626-799-1414; www.fairoakspharmacy.net; 1526 Mission St; mains $4-8; ⏱9am-9pm Mon-Fri, to 10pm Sat, 10am-7pm Sun; 🚼) Road weary? Stop by this early 20th-century soda fountain for egg creams, hand-dipped malts and gooey-good chili cheeseburgers.

🛏 Saga Motor Hotel — Motel $

(📞626-795-0431, 800-793 7242; www.thesagamotorhotel.com; 1633 E Colorado Blvd; r incl breakfast $79-99; 🅿❄@🛜) Take a dip in the heated outdoor swimming pool surrounded by Astroturf, and pretend it's the 1950s. The vintage property still hands out quaint metal room keys to its guests, living up to its motto 'timeless appeal with modern luxuries.'

Santa Monica 1️⃣6️⃣

🛏 Sea Shore Motel — Motel $$

(📞310-392-2787; www.seashoremotel.com; 2637 Main St; r from $110; 🅿❄🛜) Say 'So long!' to your retro Route 66 road trip at this time-warped motel. Although the noisy, no-frills rooms have seen better days, they're so close to the beach that you can inhale the sea-salted breezes.

Sleeping Bear Dunes *Climb 200ft of sand for stunning lake vistas*

Michigan's Gold Coast

21

They don't call it the Gold Coast for nothing. Michigan's western shoreline features endless stretches of beach, dunes, wineries, orchards and B&B-filled towns that boom in summer.

TRIP HIGHLIGHTS

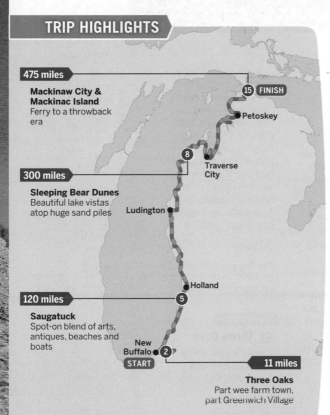

475 miles

Mackinaw City & Mackinac Island
Ferry to a throwback era

15 FINISH

● Petoskey

8

● Traverse City

300 miles

Sleeping Bear Dunes
Beautiful lake vistas atop huge sand piles

Ludington ●

120 miles

Saugatuck
Spot-on blend of arts, antiques, beaches and boats

● Holland

5

New Buffalo ●
2
START

11 miles

Three Oaks
Part wee farm town, part Greenwich Village

**4 DAYS
475 MILES / 765KM**

GREAT FOR...

BEST TIME TO GO

July through October for pleasant weather and orchard harvests.

 ESSENTIAL PHOTO

Atop the Dune Climb at Sleeping Bear Dunes.

✓ BEST FOR FOODIES

Traverse City has artisan food shops selling local wines, ciders and produce.

21 Michigan's Gold Coast

While Michigan's shore has been a holiday hot spot for over a century, it still surprises: the Caribbean-azure water, the West Coast surfing vibe, the French-style cider house that pops up by the road. Ernest Hemingway used to spend summers in the northern reaches, and he never forgot it. Even after traveling the world, he once wrote that the best sky is in 'Northern Michigan in the fall'.

1 New Buffalo

Hit the waves first in New Buffalo. While it looks like a typical resort town, it's also the Midwest's surfing hub. You heard right. You can surf Lake Michigan, and the VW-bus-driving dudes at **Third Coast Surf Shop** (☎269-932-4575; www.thirdcoastsurfshop.com; 110-C N Whittaker St; ☺10am-6pm mid-May–late Sep) will show you how. They rent wetsuits and boards (per day $20 to $35). For novices they offer 1½-hour lessons ($55 to $75) from the public beach right out the front door. Reserve in advance.

Not a surfer? Not a problem. Lounge on the wide, sandy beach (lifeguards patrol in summer); watch boats glide in and out of the busy marina; lick an ice cream cone or three; and peruse the festive shops and the town's popular **farmers market** (cnr Red Arrow Hwy & Lakeshore Rd; ☺9am-3pm Sat & Sun).

 p289

The Drive » Follow Hwy 12 as it curves inland for 6 miles to the wee town of Three Oaks.

TRIP HIGHLIGHT

2 Three Oaks

Three Oaks is where Green Acres meets Greenwich Village in

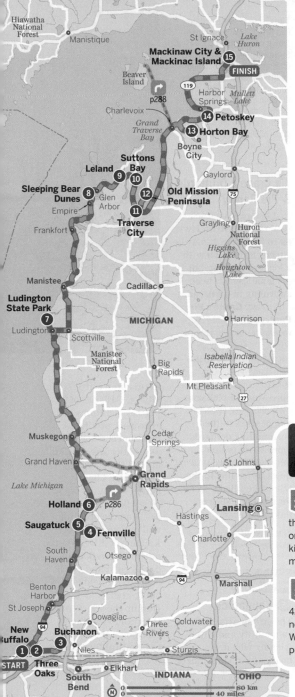

a funky farm-and-arts blend. Rent bikes at **Dewey Cannon Trading Company** (☎269-756-3361; www.applecidercentury.com; 3 Dewey Cannon Ave; bike per day $20; ⏱9am-5pm) and cycle lightly used rural roads past orchards and vineyards. In the evening, catch a provocative play or art-house flick at Three Oaks' theaters.

Or just swing by for an hour or two to putter around the antique stores and concrete lawn ornament shops. The whole town spans about five blocks. Be sure to stop in at **Drier's Meat Market** (www.driers.com; 14 S Elm St; ⏱9am-5pm Mon-Sat, 11am-5pm Sun), a butcher shop that has been around since Civil War days. It's filled with antique grinders and cleavers, as well as the famous smoked meats.

 LINK YOUR TRIP

20 **Route 66**
The time-warped thoroughfare is America's original road trip, and it kicks off in Chicago, 70 miles west of New Buffalo.

23 **Highway 61**
Ready to drive? It's 420 miles across the wild northwoods of Michigan and Wisconsin to your starting point in Duluth.

The Drive » Head north on Elm St, which becomes Three Oaks Rd. After about 5 miles you'll zig left onto Sawyer Rd, then right onto the Red Arrow Hwy. About 1 mile later, turn right on Browntown Rd. When it ends at Hills Rd turn left, and then right on Mt Tabor Rd.

❸ Buchanon

By now you've noticed all the wineries around. A dozen or so cluster between New Buffalo and Saugatuck. Connoisseurs often regard **Tabor Hill Winery** (☑800-283-3363; www.taborhill.com; 185 Mt Tabor Rd; tours free, tastings $6; ☺tours noon-4:30pm, tastings from 10am Mon-Sat, from noon Sun) as the region's best. The vintner provides tours and lets you belly up in the tasting room for swigs of its blood-red cabernet franc and crisp sparkling wines. There's also a restaurant overlooking the vineyard.

A mile north (take Hills Rd), **Round Barn Winery** (www.roundbarnwinery.com; 10983 Hills Rd; tastings $8; ☺11am-6pm Mon-Sat, from noon Sun) goes beyond vino with its grapes. It also uses the fruit to make DiVine Vodka, a smoother elixir than the kind made with grains or potatoes. Try it in the tasting room. During the week, you're welcome to picnic on the grounds; there's a cafe for weekend snacking.

The Drive » Return to the Red Arrow Hwy. Head north until it intersects with I-94 and Business I-94. Follow the latter through downtown St Joseph. Soon it converges with shore-hugging Hwy 63, which meets the Blue Star Hwy. This scenic thoroughfare moseys north to South Haven, a fine ice-cream stop (p289), and onward to Saugatuck.

❹ Crane's Orchards & Pie Pantry

Just before Saugatuck, turn right (east) on Hwy 89 to Fennville. It may be a teeny farm town with a lone traffic light, but pie fanatics have been swarming in for decades. The draw: **Crane's Pie Pantry** (☑269-561-2297; www.cranespiepantry.com; 6054 124th Ave; pie slices $4; ☺9am-8pm Mon-Sat, from 11am Sun May-Oct, reduced hours Nov-Apr). Sure, you can pick your own cherries, apples and peaches in the surrounding orchards (open 10am to 6pm), but those in need of a quick fix beeline to the tchotchke-filled bakery for a bulging slice of flaky goodness.

The Drive » Return to the Blue Star Hwy. Drive north for 4 miles to Saugatuck.

TRIP HIGHLIGHT

❺ Saugatuck

The strong arts community and gay-friendly vibe draw boatloads of vacationers

CRAIG STERKEN PHOTOGRAPHY / GETTY IMAGES ©

to this pretty little village. Galleries of pottery, paintings and glasswork proliferate downtown along Water and Butler streets. Climb aboard the clackety **Saugatuck Chain Ferry** (Mary St; one way $1; ☺9am-9pm late May-early Sep), and the operator will pull you across the Kalamazoo River. On the other side, walk to the dock's right and you'll come to Mt Baldhead, a 200ft-high sand dune. Huff up the stairs to see the grand view, then race down the north side to beautiful **Oval Beach** (Oval Beach Rd; ☺9am-10pm).

Big Sable Point Lighthouse Volunteer as a lighthouse keeper in Ludington State Park

Can't get enough sand? **Saugatuck Dune Rides** (☎269-857-2253; www. saugatuckduneride.com; 6495 Blue Star Hwy; adult/child $18/10; ⏱10am-7:30pm Mon-Sat, from 11:30am Sun, closed late Oct-late Apr) provides a half-hour of good, cheesy fun zipping over nearby mounds.

✕ ⏢ p289

The Drive ≫ The Blue Star Hwy (aka County Rd A-2) makes its slowpoke, two-lane way northeast through farmland. It becomes Washington Ave, then Michigan Ave, then River Ave before reaching downtown Holland 12 miles later.

6 Holland

You don't have to cross the ocean for tulips, windmills and clogs. Holland, Michigan, has the whole kitschy package. **Veldheer Tulip Farm** (www.veldheer.com; 12755 Quincy St; ⏱9am-5pm) is a popular place to immerse in all things Dutch. A wooden-shoe factory and traditional blue-and-white pottery workshop are also on site. While it veers from the Dutch theme, be sure to stop by the **New Holland Brewing Company Pub** (www.

newhollandbrew.com; 66 E 8th St; ⏱11am-midnight, to 10pm Sun). The microbrewery is known for its robust beers such as Dragon's Milk stout (10% alcohol) and its housemade rums. The pub is the place to sample them.

The Drive ≫ From Holland to Grand Haven, Lake Shore Ave is the back-road alternative to Hwy 31. Pick it up from Ottawa Beach Rd just before entering Holland State Park, and you're golden for 22 miles. After Grand Haven, filter back onto Hwy 31 for 75 miles to Ludington. Take exit 166 for the park.

❼ Ludington State Park

It's time to stretch the legs at **Ludington State Park** (☏231-843-8671; tent & RV sites $16-29, cabins $45), beyond the city limits on Hwy 116. If you don't have one already, buy a vehicle permit (per day/year $9/31) at the entrance booth, valid at all Michigan parks. Once inside, people simply pull over on the roadside and make a break for the beautiful stretches of beach. There's also a top-notch trail system and the renovated **Big Sable Point Lighthouse** to hike to (or live in, as the volunteer lighthouse

keeper). Tours of the 112ft fog-buster cost $3.

The Drive » Get back on Hwy 31 and head to Manistee. Three miles beyond, hop on Hwy 22 which clasps the coast for the next 115 miles. Inland lakes, clapboard towns and historic lighthouses flash by en route to the Sleeping Bear Dunes.

TRIP HIGHLIGHT

❽ Sleeping Bear Dunes National Lakeshore

Stop at the park's **visitor center** (☏231-326-5134; www.nps.gov/slbe; 9922 Front St; ⏰8:30am-6pm Jun-Aug, to 4pm Sep-May) in Empire for information, trail maps and vehicle entry permits (week/annual $10/20). Then steer north for 2 miles to Hwy 109

DETOUR: GRAND RAPIDS

Start: ❻ Holland

The second-largest city in Michigan, Grand Rapids, once known for office-furniture manufacturing, has become a mecca for beer tourism. Twenty craft breweries operate in the area. **Grand Rapids Convention and Visitors Bureau** (www.experiencegr. com) has maps and self-guided tour information online.

If you've only got time for one brewery, make it rock-and-roll **Founders Brewing Company** (www. foundersbrewing.com; 235 Grandville Ave SW; ⏰11am-2am Mon-Sat, noon-midnight Sun). The ruby-tinged Dirty Bastard Ale is good swillin'. Want to try one more? Head to **Brewery Vivant** (www.breweryvivant.com; 925 Cherry St SE; ⏰from 3pm Mon-Fri, from 11am Sat, from noon Sun), which specializes in Belgian-style beers. It's set in an old chapel with stained glass, a vaulted ceiling and farmhouse-style communal tables.

The city lies 29 miles inland from Holland via I-196.

and the **Pierce Stocking Scenic Drive**. The 7-mile, one-lane, picnic-grove-studded loop is one way to absorb the stunning lake vistas. Another is the **Dune Climb**, which entails trudging up a 200ft-high sand pile. It's likewise on Hwy 109. There's also the **Sleeping Bear Heritage Trail** (www. sleepingbeartrail.org), which paves 5 miles from the town of Glen Arbor to the Dune Climb; it's a view-a-licious jaunt, which is why walkers and cyclists are all over it.

The Drive » Hwy 109 ends in bustling Glen Arbor, a good choice for lodging (p289). Rejoin Hwy 22 for 18 miles as it continues through the national lakeshore to Leland.

❾ Leland

Little Leland is cute as a button. Grab a bite at a waterfront restaurant downtown, and poke around atmospheric Fishtown with its weather-beaten fishing-shanties-cum-shops. **Ferries** (round-trip adult/child $35/20, 1½hr) depart from here for the forest-cloaked Manitou Islands; day trips are doable in July and August. Check with **Manitou Island Transit** (☏231-256-9061; www. manitoutransit.com), which also runs a sunset cruise (per adult/child $20/13) along the lighthouse-dotted shoreline four days per week.

 p289

The Drive » Take Hwy 22 north for 4 miles. Zig right on N Eagle Hwy, then left on E Kolarik Rd. A mile onward, take the first right you come to, which is Setterbo Rd. You'll spy the cider house 3.5 miles later.

⑩ Suttons Bay

On the outskirts of Suttons Bay, **Tandem Ciders** (www.tandemciders. com; 2055 Setterbo Rd; ⊙noon-6pm Mon-Sat, to 5pm Sun) pours delicious hard ciders in its cozy tasting room on the family farm. Pull up a stool at the bar and sip elixirs such as Cidre Royale (tart and high-powered) and Honey Pie (sweetened by a local beekeeper's wares). Draught ciders are free to taste; their bottled counterparts cost $1 per tasting. In town, **Grand Traverse Bike Tours** (☎231-421-6815; www. grandtraversebiketours.com; 118 N Saint Mary's St; ⊙10am-5:30pm Mon-Fri, to 4pm Sat & Sun) offers guided rides (6.5-hour tour is $89) to local wineries, as well as self-guided tours (per person $59) for which staff provide route planning and van pickup of your wine purchases.

The Drive » Hwy 22 rides down the Leelanau Peninsula and eventually rolls into Traverse City.

⑪ Traverse City

Traverse City is the region's 'big' city, with an unabashed love for cherries. It's a happening place with kiteboarding and sailing, music and movie festivals, and brewpubs and chic restaurants.

Front St is the main drag to wander and for window shopping. Be sure to pop in to **Cherry Republic** (www.cherryrepublic. com; 154 E Front St; ⊙9am-10pm). It's touristy but a hoot to see all the products: cherry ketchup, cherry-dusted tortillas, cherry butter, cherry wine – you get the point. Most of it tastes better than you think. And the shop is *very* generous with samples (hence the crowds).

✕ p289

The Drive » Take Front St (aka Hwy 31) heading east out of town. When you get to Garfield Ave, turn left. It soon becomes Hwy 37, sallying through the grape- and cherry-planted Old Mission Peninsula.

⑫ Old Mission Peninsula

Taste-tripping through the peninsula's wineries is a popular pastime. With eight vineyards in 19 miles, you won't go thirsty. **Chateau Grand Traverse** (www.cgtwines.com; ⊙10am-7pm Mon-Sat, to 6pm Sun) and **Chateau Chantal** (www.chateauchantal.com; ⊙11am-8pm Mon-Sat, to 6pm Sun) pour crowd-pleasing Chardonnay and Pinot Noir. **Peninsula Cellars** (www.peninsulacellars.com; ⊙10am-6pm), in an old schoolhouse, makes fine whites and is often less crowded. Whatever bottle you buy, take it out to Lighthouse Park beach at the peninsula's tip and enjoy it with the waves chilling your toes.

🛏 p289

The Drive » Retrace your path back to Hwy 31 and head north. In roughly 50 miles, north of yacht-riddled Charlevoix, look for Boyne City Rd. It skirts Lake Charlevoix and eventually arrives at the Horton Bay General Store.

⑬ Horton Bay General Store

Ernest Hemingway fans will recognize the **Horton Bay General Store** (☎231-582-7827; www.hortonbaygeneralstore. com; 05115 Boyne City Rd; ⊙8am-2pm mid-May–mid-Oct), with its 'high false front', from his short story *Up in Michigan*. Hemingway idled away some youthful summers telling fish stories on the big porch. His family had a cottage on nearby Walloon Lake. Next door to the general store, the erratically open **Red Fox Inn Bookstore** (05156 Boyne City Rd; ⊙late May–early Sep) holds the mother lode of Hemingway books and souvenirs. The proprietor is a font of local lore.

The Drive » Head east on Boyne City Rd. Take the second left onto Sumner Rd, and then left again on Camp Daggett Rd. The latter meets Hwy 31 in 6 miles, which carries you to Petoskey.

DETOUR: BEAVER ISLAND

Start: ⑬ Horton Bay

For an alternative to Mackinac Island, sail to quieter **Beaver Island** (www.beaverisland.org), an Irish-influenced enclave, home to 600 people, that offers hiking, fishing, kayaking and snorkeling to shipwrecked schooners. The **ferry** (☎231-448-2500; www.bibco.com) departs from downtown Charlevoix. The two-hour journey costs $29/90 one-way per person/car.

⑭ Petoskey

Petoskey is yet another resort town with a yacht-filled marina and compact downtown dotted with gourmet restaurants and gift boutiques. It also has a couple of Hemingway sights. The **Little Traverse History Museum** (☎231-347-2620; www.petoskeymuseum.org; 100 Depot Ct; admission $3; ☺10am-4pm Mon-Fri, from 1pm Sat late May–mid-Oct) has a collection dedicated to the author, including rare first-edition books that Hemingway autographed for a friend when he visited in 1947. Afterward, toss back a drink at **City Park Grill** (☎231-347-0101; www.cityparkgrill.com; 432 E Lake St; ☺11:30am-midnight), where Hemingway was

a regular. Just north of town you can hunt for famed Petoskey stones (honeycomb-patterned fragments of ancient coral) at **Petoskey State Park** (☎231-347-2311; 2475 Hwy 119; tent & RV sites $27-29).

The Drive ≫ Time for a choice on this final stretch: take the 'fast' way to Mackinaw City via Hwy 31, or dawdle on narrow Hwy 119. The latter dips and curves through thick forests and along bluffs as part of the Tunnel of Trees scenic route.

TRIP HIGHLIGHT

⑮ Mackinaw City & Mackinac Island

Touristy Mackinaw City serves mainly as the jump-off point to Mackinac Island, but it does have an intriguing sight: **Colonial Michilimackinac**

(☎231-436-5564; www.mackinacparks.com; adult/child $11/6.50; ☺9:30am-7pm Jun-Aug, to 5pm May & Sep–mid-Oct), a National Historic Landmark that features a reconstructed stockade first built in 1715 by the French; the visitor center is beneath the enormous Mackinac Bridge.

Mackinac Island floats a few miles offshore and is the big draw up here. Cars are banned, and all travel on the 3.8-sq-mile isle is by horse-drawn carriage or bicycle. It's a charming, old-time place, speckled with fudge shops, Victorian cottages and 18th-century forts. The ferry ride over takes 15 to 30 minutes, so it's easy to do as a day trip. Better yet, spend the night.

Three ferry companies, **Arnold Line** (☎800-542-8528; www.arnoldline.com); **Shepler's** (☎800-828-6157; www.sheplersferry.com); and **Star Line** (☎800-638-9892; www.mackinacferry.com) make frequent trips and charge the same rates: round-trip adult/child $25/13. They have parking lots where you can leave your car.

✗ ⍽ p289

Eating & Sleeping

New Buffalo ❶

✖ Redamak's
Burgers $

(www.redamaks.com; 616 E Buffalo St; burgers $5-10; ⊘ noon-10:30pm Mar-Oct) **This burgers-and-beer roadhouse dates from the 1940s; the spicy curly fries reign supreme. Cash only.**

South Haven

✖ Sherman's Dairy Bar
Ice Cream $

(☎269-637-8251; www.shermanicecream.com; 1601 Phoenix Rd; cones from $3; ⊘ 11am-11pm Mon-Sat, noon-11pm Sun, closed Nov-Feb; 🖐) Beloved Sherman's scoops massive cones in 50 flavors (try the Mackinac Island fudge). It can't get any fresher, since it's made in the onsite factory. Lines can be lengthy.

Saugatuck ❺

✖ Wicks Park Bar & Grill
American $$

(☎269-857-2888; www.wickspark.com; 449 Water St; mains $11-25; ⊘ 11:30am-9pm) Located by the chain ferry, Wicks gets props for its lake perch and live music.

🛏 Pines Motorlodge
Motel $$

(☎269-857-5211; www.thepinesmotorlodge. com; 56 Blue Star Hwy; r incl breakfast $139-199; 🖥) Retro tiki lamps, pinewood furniture and communal lawn chairs create a fun, social ambiance amid the fir trees.

Glen Arbor

🛏 Glen Arbor B&B
B&B $$

(☎231-334-6789; www.glenarborbnb.com; 6548 Western Ave; r $131-196; ⊘ closed mid-Nov–Apr) The owners have renovated this century-old farmhouse into a sunny, French country inn with six themed rooms.

Leland ❾

✖ Cove
Seafood $$$

(☎231-256-9834; www.thecoveleland.com; 111 River St,; mains $20-29; ⊘ 11am-10pm, closed Nov-Apr) The Cove's specialty is whitefish that it prepares four ways (baked with almonds, stuffed with crab, encrusted with garlic, and foil-baked with peppers).

Traverse City ⓫

✖ North Peak Brewing Company
Brewery $$

(☎231-941-7325; www.northpeak.net; 400 W Front St; mains $10-20; ⊘ 11am-11pm Mon-Thu, to midnight Fri & Sat, noon-10pm Sun) Munch pizzas, mussels and pretzel-crusted walleye with the housemade suds. A five-beer sampler costs $6. North Peak also makes root beer.

Old Mission Peninsula ⓬

🛏 Grey Hare Inn
B&B $$$

(☎231-947-2214; www.greyhareinn.com; Carroll St; r $185-285; ❄🖥) It's an intimate, three-room B&B on a working vineyard, with French–style decor and bay views. Many of the peninsula's other vineyards also double as B&Bs.

Mackinac Island ⓯

✖ Horn's Bar
Burgers, Mexican $$

(☎906-847-6154; www.hornsbar.com; Main St; mains $10-19; ⊘ 11am-2am) Horn's saloon serves American burgers and south-of-the-border fare, and there's live entertainment nightly.

🛏 Cloghaun B&B
B&B $$

(☎906-847-3885; www.cloghaun.com; Market St; r incl breakfast $112-197; ⊘ mid-May–late Oct; 🖥) The garden-encircled Victorian home offers 11 rooms, some with shared bath. It's an easy walk from the boat docks.

Dubuque *The river road unfurls through Iowa farmland*

Along the Great River Road

22

This epic roadway edges the Mississippi River. In its northern half, it passes pine forests and eagles' nests, 18th-century forts and the World's Largest Six-Pack.

TRIP HIGHLIGHTS

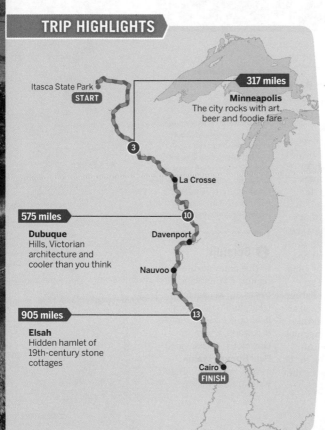

Itasca State Park
START

317 miles

Minneapolis
The city rocks with art, beer and foodie fare

3

La Crosse

10

575 miles

Dubuque
Hills, Victorian architecture and cooler than you think

Davenport

Nauvoo

905 miles

Elsah
Hidden hamlet of 19th-century stone cottages

13

Cairo
FINISH

**6–7 DAYS
1075 MILES /
1730KM**

GREAT FOR...

BEST TIME TO GO

June through September for snow-free weather.

ESSENTIAL PHOTO

Paul Bunyan and his blue ox Babe in Bemidji.

BEST FOR TWO DAYS

The road between stops four and 10 offers bluff-strewn scenery, historic towns and foodie pit stops.

Along the Great River Road

It happens time and again. The road curves around a bluff and Old Man River appears, wider than you remember, a swift-moving expanse dotted with woodsy islands and behemoth barges. An eagle swoops overhead, diving to the water and rising with a floppy fish. Every once in a while you reach a city, say Minneapolis or Dubuque, but mostly the road unfurls through forgotten towns where it becomes Main Street.

❶ Itasca State Park

Begin where the river begins, in Minnesota's **Itasca State Park** (📞218-266-2100; www.dnr. state.mn.us/itasca; off Hwy 71 N; per vehicle $5; 🚻🐕). A carved pole denotes the headwaters of 'the Mighty Mississippi' – a good thing, because it's puny enough to mistake for a creek. Wade in the knee-deep flow and hop over a couple of stepping stones, then boast you walked across the Father of Waters. The park also offers canoeing, hiking, biking and camping, plus a lodge and hostel, all operated according to the principles of 'Minnesota

nice' (the state's proverbial hospitality).

🛏 p299

The Drive » Drive northeast, zigzagging on various county roads. Take County Rd 2 to 40 to 9, through Becida. Turn left onto 169th Ave, which becomes County Rd 7 and rolls into Bemidji (an overall trip of 30 miles). For free maps that help navigation, see www.mnmississippiriver.com.

❷ Bemidji

In this piney northwoods region of Minnesota, the towns are known for lakes, lumberjacks and fishing. A classic example is Bemidji, where an enormous, mustachioed **Paul Bunyan statue** awaits. Standing 18ft and weighing 2.5 tons, he

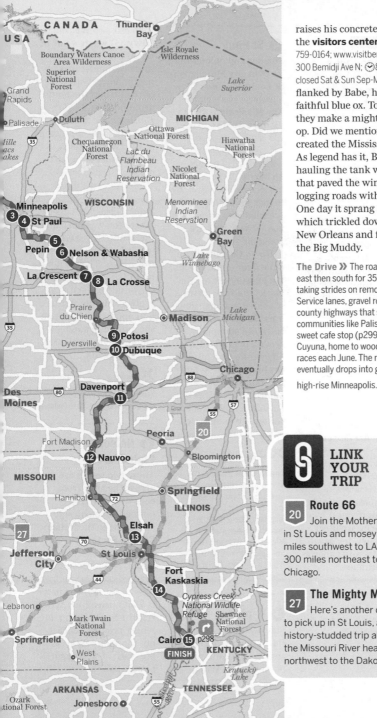

raises his concrete head by the **visitors center** (☎218-759-0164; www.visitbemidji.com; 300 Bemidji Ave N; ☉8am-5pm, closed Sat & Sun Sep-May), flanked by Babe, his faithful blue ox. Together they make a mighty photo op. Did we mention they created the Mississippi? As legend has it, Babe was hauling the tank wagon that paved the winter logging roads with ice. One day it sprang a leak, which trickled down to New Orleans and formed the Big Muddy.

The Drive » The road drifts east then south for 350 miles, taking strides on remote Forest Service lanes, gravel roads and county highways that skirt wee communities like Palisade, a sweet cafe stop (p299), and Cuyuna, home to wood-tick races each June. The road eventually drops into glassy, high-rise Minneapolis.

LINK YOUR TRIP

20 Route 66

Join the Mother Road in St Louis and mosey 2100 miles southwest to LA or 300 miles northeast to Chicago.

27 The Mighty Mo

Here's another one to pick up in St Louis, a history-studded trip along the Missouri River heading northwest to the Dakotas.

TRIP HIGHLIGHT

❸ Minneapolis

The Riverfront District at downtown's northern edge makes a fine pause with its parks, museums, bars and polka clubs. At the foot of Portland Ave is the car-free **Stone Arch Bridge** over the Mississippi, from which you can view the cascading St Anthony Falls. A few blocks east is the cobalt-blue **Guthrie Theater** (📞612-377-2224; www.guthrietheater.org; 818 2nd St S). Make your way up to its 'Endless Bridge', a cantilevered walkway overlooking the river. You don't need a theater ticket – it's intended as a public space.

A stone's throw downstream, 50,000 students hit the books (and live-music venues) at the University of Minnesota. The uni's **Weisman Art Museum** (📞612-625-9494; www.weisman.umn.edu; 333 E River Rd; ⏱10am-5pm Tue-Fri, to 8pm Wed, 11am-5pm Sat & Sun) occupies a swooping, silver waterfront structure by architect Frank Gehry. It's worth a peek for its airy galleries of American art.

✗ p299

The Drive ≫ Take I-94 E to exit 241B for downtown St Paul. It's about a 10-mile drive.

❹ St Paul

Smaller and quieter than its twin city Minneapolis, St Paul has more of a historic character. The **Mississippi River Visitors Center** (📞651-293-0200; www.nps.gov/miss; ⏱9:30am-5pm Sun-Thu, to 9pm Fri & Sat) occupies an alcove in the science museum's lobby. Stop by to pick up trail maps and see what sort of ranger-guided activities are going on.

Up on Cathedral Hill, named for – that's right – the hulking church that marks the spot, a string of Gilded Age mansions lines **Summit Ave**. This is the old stomping ground of author F Scott Fitzgerald, who lived in the brownstone at 599 Summit Ave when he published *This Side of Paradise*. A block south, Grand Ave holds a slew of foodie cafes and shops.

✗ 🛏 p299

The Drive ≫ 25 miles beyond St Paul, near Hastings, the River Road splits into eastern and western sections as the Mississippi becomes the border between states. It's the Minnesota–Wisconsin line at this juncture, and our trip starts flip-flopping between the two to cover the best sights.

❺ Pepin

Stay on the Minnesota side (Hwy 61) of the river to shoe and pottery purveyor Red Wing, then cross to Wisconsin (Hwy 35) where some of the Mississippi Valley's prettiest landscapes begin. A great stretch of road edges the bluffs around Pepin. *Little House on the Prairie* fans can make a pit stop at the **Laura Ingalls Wilder Museum** (www.lauraingallspepin.com; 306 Third St; suggested donation adult/child $2/1; ⏱10am-5pm mid-May–mid-Oct). This is where she was born and the abode that starred in *Little House in the Big Woods*. There's not a lot in the museum (and the building itself is a replica), but die-hards will appreciate being on the authentic patch of land once owned by Ma and Pa Ingalls.

✗ p299

The Drive ≫ Continue 8 miles southeast on Hwy 35 to Nelson.

❻ Nelson & Wabasha

These two towns are across the river from each other. Nelson is on the Wisconsin side and home to the **Nelson Cheese Factory** (www.nelsoncheese.com; S237 N Main St; ice cream scoops from $1.50; ⏱9am-6pm Sun-Thu, to 7pm Fri & Sat; 🌞). The name is a bit misleading: the refurbished building no longer produces cheese, but the shop carries a big stash of Wisconsin hunks, and the cozy wine

Itasca State Park Camp, hike and canoe where the mighty Mississippi begins

ROAD RESOURCES

Turn-by-turn directions for the Great River Road are complex, spanning an incredible number of highways and byways. We've provided some road information here, but for nitty-gritty instructions you'll need additional resources. **Minnesota** (www.mnmississippiriver.com), **Wisconsin** (www.wigreatriverroad.org), **Illinois** (www.greatriverroad-illinois.org) and **Iowa** (www.iowagreatriverroad.com) each maintain their own River Road website. Or check the **National Scenic Byways** (www.byways.org/explore/byways/2279/directions.html) for designated sections. The one constant, wherever you are: the green paddle-wheel sign that marks the way.

bar serves 'em on tasting plates. The queues, though, are for the ice cream (emphasis on cream, which is used in abundance in the mega-rich treat).

Across the water in Wabasha, Minnesota, is the **National Eagle Center** (☎651-565-4989; www.nationaleaglecenter.org; 50 Pembroke Ave; adult/child $8/5; ◷10am-5pm). Large populations of bald eagles flock to the area each winter, where they nest in waterside trees and catch themselves fat silvery fish. The center has the lowdown. It also introduces you to Donald, Harriet and the other rehabilitated birds who live on-site.

✖ p299

The Drive » From Wabasha, stay on Hwy 61 as it opens into a gorgeous drive for nearly 60 miles past sandbars, marshes and untamed green hills en route to La Crescent, Minnesota.

❼ La Crescent

It's no wonder it's nicknamed 'the Apple Capital'. Orchards sprout from the land and roadside stands sell the tart wares, particularly bountiful from August through October. Strawberries, sweet corn and pumpkins fill baskets during other seasons. Hardy **Bauer's Market** (☎507-895-4583; www.bauersmarketplace.com; 221 N 2nd St; ◷8am-8pm Mon-Fri, to 6pm Sat & Sun) is open year-round selling local produce as well as garden supplies and giftware – say, a fish-toting gnome or giant mushroom – many painted by a local artist.

The Drive » Cross the Mississippi again via Hwy 61 to La Crescent's twin city La Crosse, Wisconsin.

❽ La Crosse

The road (which becomes 3rd St S on the Wisconsin side) swings by the **World's Largest Six-Pack**. The 'cans' are actually storage tanks for City Brewery, formerly G Heileman Brewing, maker of Old Style lager. As the sign in front says: they hold enough to fill 7.3 million cans, or enough to provide one lucky person with a six-pack a day for 3351 years. Yowza.

The historic center of **La Crosse** (www.explorelacrosse.com) nestles several restaurants and pubs downtown around Main St. **Grandad Bluff** offers grand views of the river. It's east of town along Main St (which becomes Bliss Rd); follow Bliss Rd up the hill and then turn right on Grandad Bluff Rd.

The Drive » Return to Hwy 35, which clasps the river for 24 miles to the Iowa border, then 35 miles more to the old fur-trading post of Prairie du Chien. Continue to Bloomington, then turn right on Hwy 133 for 40 rural, rolling miles to Potosi.

❾ Potosi

The River Road becomes Main St as it moseys into town. The **Potosi Brewing Company** (☎608-763-4002; www.potosibrewery.com; 209 S Main St; ◷10:30am-9pm) is your one-stop shop for food, drink, memorabilia and historical information. The thick-stone building began brewing beer in 1852. Imbibe indoors amid neon-lit beer signs or outdoors in the pretty beer garden. Supplement with a burger and the famous beer cheese soup.

The building also holds the **National Brewery Museum** (admission $5), stuffed with old beer bottles, cans, coasters and advertising signs, and a **transportation museum** (admission free) that shows early beer-hauling equipment. And there's one more item of interest inside: the **Great River Road interpretation center**, which offers maps, history and internet kiosks.

The Drive » Go east on Hwy 133 to Hwy 35/61; turn right. Follow it for 8 miles to the junction with Hwy 151. The three roads merge into one for 10 miles. Veer off for Dubuque at the 9th St–11th St exit.

TRIP HIGHLIGHT

⑩ Dubuque

Dubuque has some surprises up its sleeve. Nineteenth-century Victorian homes line its narrow and lively streets between the Mississippi River and seven steep limestone hills. The **4th Street Elevator** (www. dbq.com/fenplco; cnr 4th St & Fenelon; adult/child round-trip $3/1.50; ☺8am–10pm Apr–Nov), built in 1882, climbs a steep hill for huge

views. Ring the bell to begin the ride.

At the hands-on **National Mississippi River Museum & Aquarium** (www. rivermuseum.com; 350 E 3rd St; adult/child $15/10; ☺9am–6pm summer, 10am–5pm rest of year), at the Port of Dubuque, enjoy a big-screen soar over the river, pilot a simulated barge, or touch river-dwelling creatures in a wet lab. An American alligator lurks in the Mississippi Bayou aquarium, one of six creature-filled habitats.

🛏 p299

The Drive » Take Hwy 52 south for 45 miles toward Sabula, then follow Hwy 67 to Davenport for 55 miles.

⑪ Davenport

Davenport is arguably the coolest of the 'Quad Cities' (www. visitquadcities.com), a foursome that also includes Bettendorf in Iowa and Moline and Rock Island in Illinois. Downtown, the glass-walled **Figge Art Museum** (📞563-326-7804; www.figgeart.org; 225 W 2nd St; adult/child $7/4; ☺10am–5pm Tue, Wed, Fri & Sat, to 9pm Thu, noon–5pm Sun; ♿) sparkles above the River Road. The museum's Midwest Regionalist Collection includes the only self-portrait by *American Gothic* painter Grant Wood; you can also stroll through the world-class

Haitian and Mexican Colonial collections.

The Drive » A leisurely network of roads continues south in Iowa, with Hwy 61 rolling into Fort Madison. Cross the Mississippi on the Fort Madison Toll Bridge ($2), a double-decker swing-span accommodating trains and cars on separate levels. On the Illinois side, take Hwy 96 into striking Nauvoo.

⑫ Nauvoo

Little Nauvoo (www. seenauvoo.com) has long been a pilgrimage site for Mormons. Joseph Smith, the religion's founder, brought his flock here in 1839 after they were kicked out of Missouri. Nauvoo (Hebrew for 'beautiful place') grew quickly. Almost 12,000 Mormons took up residence, rivaling Chicago's population. By 1846 they were gone. Tension rose, Smith was killed, and Brigham Young led the group west to Utah. Today the tiny town is a historic district loaded with impressive structures, such as the homes of Smith and Young. The centerpiece is the gleaming white temple, built in 2002 on the site of the Mormons' burned-down original sanctuary.

The Drive » Follow Hwy 96 south to I-72, taking it west across the Mississippi to Hannibal, Missouri (p354), hometown of writer Mark Twain. Back in Illinois, take Hwy 96 to Hwy 100. The road becomes incredibly scenic

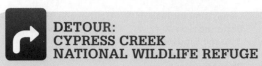

DETOUR: CYPRESS CREEK NATIONAL WILDLIFE REFUGE

Start: 15 Cairo

You certainly don't expect to find southern-style swampland, complete with moss-draped cypress trees and croaking bullfrogs in Illinois. But it's here, at **Cypress Creek National Wildlife Refuge** (📞618-634-2231; www.fws.gov/midwest/cypresscreek). For River Road–trippers who aren't going onward to Louisiana, this is an opportunity to see the eerie swamp ecosystem in action. From Cairo drive north 25 miles on Hwy 37 to Cypress, and stop in at the **Cache River Wetlands Center** (📞618-657-2064; 8885 Hwy 37; 🕙9am-4pm Wed-Sun). Staff can sort you out with hiking, biking and canoeing information.

around Grafton. As you slip under wind-hewn bluffs, watch for the turnoff to Elsah.

TRIP HIGHLIGHT

13 Elsah

You can't help but slow down in itty-bitty Elsah (www.elsah.org), a hidden hamlet of 19th-century stone cottages, wood-buggy shops and farmhouses. Most of the town sits on two parallel streets. Around the bend lies Principia College, a small liberal arts school and one of the few for Christian Scientists. Outdoors enthusiasts can zip line and cycle bluff-side trails.

🛏 p299

The Drive » Take Hwy 100 to Alton. After that, the River Road gets lost around St Louis (see our walking tour (p358) if you plan to make it a stop). A good place to pick up the trail again is Ellis Grove, Illinois, 75 miles south via I-255, Hwy 159 and Hwy 3.

----

14 Fort Kaskaskia

A few miles south of Ellis Grove, **Fort Kaskaskia** (4372 Park Rd; 🕙9am-5pm Wed-Sun) sits on a bluff beside the river. The French built it around 1759 to defend against British attacks. All that remains today are lonely earthworks around the perimeter, a cemetery from the late 1800s, and a view-tastic overlook. It's a great spot for a picnic, with tables and grills. If you're into French colonial architecture, take the footpath down to ogle the **Pierre Menard Home**, built in 1802 for the gent who eventually became Illinois' first lieutenant governor. Trivia tip: the town of Kaskaskia was Illinois' first capital,

though its tenure barely lasted a year.

The Drive » About 6 miles down Hwy 3 you'll roll through Chester. It's the hometown of EC Segar, creator of the cartoon character Popeye – hence the statues of the spinach-eating sailor and pals Wimpy, Olive Oyl and Swee'Pea throughout town. Continue south on Hwy 3 for 85 miles until it ends at Cairo.

----

15 Cairo

It's the end of the line for the Great River Road's northern half. The town – pronounced *kay*-ro – has seen better days, but the surrounding area's swampy parklands are nifty. For those continuing on the thoroughfare, this is roughly the half-way point. The next 1000 miles meander past blues joints and barbecue shacks, steamboats and plantations, en route to New Orleans.

Eating & Sleeping

Itasca State Park ❶

🛏 Douglas Lodge   Lodge $$

(☎866-857-2757; r $95-140; 🛜) The venerable Douglas Lodge, run by the park, offers rustic charm in its rooms; some share a bathroom. The Douglas also has cabins and a good restaurant.

Palisade

✕ Palisade Cafe   American $

(210 Main St; mains $5-11; ⊙ 7am-7pm Mon-Sat, to 2pm Sun) This woodsy little joint in the middle of nowhere is a welcome respite, whipping up stuffed hash browns (as in stuffed with gooey cheese) and killer pies.

Minneapolis ❸

✕ Butcher & the Boar   American $$$

(☎612-238-8887; www.butcherandtheboar. com; 1121 Hennepin Ave; mains $25-32; ⊙5pm-midnight; 🛜) The coppery, candlelit room is carnivore nirvana. Get your carving knife ready for wild boar ham with country butter, chicken-fried veal sausage and more house-crafted meats. The 30 taps flow with regional brews, backed up by a lengthy bourbon list. Reservations are essential.

St Paul ❹

✕ Mickey's Dining Car   Diner $

(www.mickeysdiningcar.com; 36 W 7th St; mains $4-9; ⊙24hr) The art-deco-styled, vintage diner is the kind of place where the friendly waitress calls you 'honey' and satisfied regulars line the bar with their coffee cups and newspapers. The food has timeless appeal, too: burgers, malts and apple pie.

🛏 Covington Inn   B&B $$

(☎651-292-1411; www.covingtoninn.com; 100 Harriet Island Rd; r incl breakfast $150-235; 🅿🌂) This four-room, Harriet Island B&B is on a tugboat floating in the Mississippi River; watch the river traffic glide by while sipping your morning coffee.

Pepin ❺

✕ Harbor View Cafe   American $$$

(www.harborviewpepin.com; 314 First St; mains $19-26; ⊙11am-2:30pm Mon & Thu-Sun, closed mid-Nov–mid-Mar) The book-stuffed Harbor View is a Slow Food stalwart. Staff write the changing menu on a chalkboard twice daily – once for lunch, once for dinner. Cross your fingers the list shows the four-cheese stuffed mushrooms, caper-sauced halibut, and lemon cake with ginger. Deck chairs line the sidewalk outside, each with a water view. Cash only.

Nelson ❻

✕ Stone Barn   Pizzeria $$

(☎715-673-4478; www.nelsonstonebarn.com; S685 Country Rd KK; pizzas $11-19; ⊙5-9pm Fri-Sun mid-May–late Sep) Browse the antique store or amble through the herb garden while waiting for your wafer-thin-crusted pizza to emerge from the wood-fired oven. All tables are set outdoors, surrounded by hilly farmland.

Dubuque ❿

🛏 Hotel Julien   Historic Hotel $$

(☎563-556-4200; www.hoteljuliendubuque. com; 200 Main St; r $110-250; 🌂🛜) The eight-story hotel was built in 1914 and was once a refuge for Al Capone. A lavish renovation has turned it upscale and it's a real antidote to chains.

Elsah ⓭

🛏 Maple Leaf Cottage Inn   B&B $$

(☎618-374-1684; www.mapleleafcottages.com; 12 Selma St; r $90-110; 🛜) Iron-rail beds, claw-foot tubs and other antique accoutrements throw the Maple Leaf back in time. Cash or check only.

Split Rock Lighthouse Picture-perfect clifftop views of Lake Superior

Highway 61

23

Waterfalls, moose and Bob Dylan vestiges roll by on Minnesota's Hwy 61. The road grips Lake Superior's shore, tucked between red-tinged cliffs and towering firs from Duluth to Canada's edge.

TRIP HIGHLIGHTS

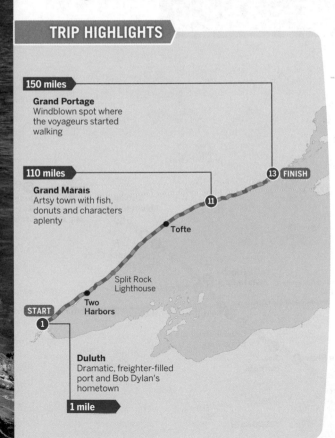

150 miles

Grand Portage
Windblown spot where the voyageurs started walking

110 miles

Grand Marais
Artsy town with fish, donuts and characters aplenty

13 FINISH

11

Tofte

Split Rock Lighthouse

START
1

Two Harbors

Duluth
Dramatic, freighter-filled port and Bob Dylan's hometown

1 mile

2–3 DAYS
150 MILES / 241KM

GREAT FOR...

BEST TIME TO GO
July to mid-October for pleasant weather and fall colors.

ESSENTIAL PHOTO

Split Rock Lighthouse on its perfect clifftop.

BEST FOR WILDLIFE

Drive the Gunflint Trail and watch for moose.

301

23 Highway 61

Mention Hwy 61 and many folks hum Bob Dylan. But this North Shore road is not about murder, poverty or any other mean-street mumblings from his 1965 album *Highway 61 Revisited*. Instead it's a journey dominated by water, where ore-toting freighters ply the ports, little fishing fleets haul in the day's catch, and wave-bashed cliffs offer Superior views if you're willing to trek.

TRIP HIGHLIGHT

❶ Duluth

Dramatically spliced into a cliff that tumbles down to Lake Superior, Duluth is one of the busiest ports in the nation. Canal Park downtown is a good spot to see the action. Start at the **Aerial Lift Bridge**, Duluth's landmark that raises its mighty arm to let horn-bellowing ships into port. About 1000 freighters a year glide through. The screens outside the **Maritime Visitors Center** (☏218-

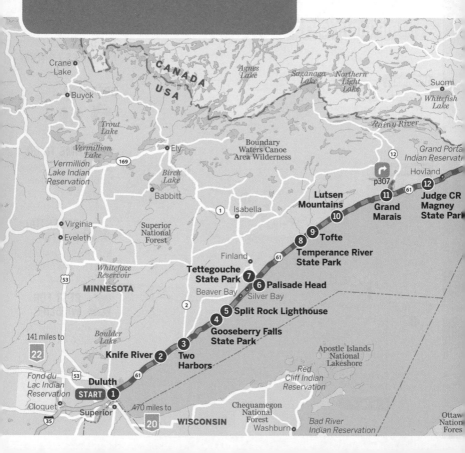

720-5260; www.lsmma.com; 600 Lake Ave S; ⊘10am-9pm Jun-Aug, reduced hours Sep-May) announce when the big boats come and go; inside holds first-rate exhibitions on Great Lakes shipping and shipwrecks.

Duluth is also the birthplace of Bob Dylan, though the town is pretty laid-back about its famous son. You're on your own to find **Dylan's childhood home** (519 N 3rd Ave E), up a hill a few blocks northeast of downtown. Dylan lived on the top floor until age six, when his family moved inland to Hibbing. It's a private residence (and unmarked), so all you can do is check it out from the street.

✗ 🛏 p309

The Drive ⟫ Take London Rd, aka Hwy 61, heading northeast out of town. Follow the signs for the North Shore Scenic Dr (also called Scenic 61 or Old Hwy 61). There's a Hwy 61 expressway that also covers the next 20 miles, but steer clear and dawdle on the original, curvy, two-lane route instead.

- - - - - - - - - - - - - - - -

❷ Knife River

Unspoiled shoreline and fisherfolk casting at river mouths are your companions along the way until you reach **Russ Kendall's Smoke House** (☎218-834-5995; 149 Scenic Dr; salmon per pound $17; ⊘9:30am-5:30pm) in Knife River. A groovy neon sign beckons you in. Four generations of Kendall folk have cooked up the locally plucked trout and line-caught Alaskan salmon. Buy a brown-sugar-cured slab, staff will wrap it in newspaper, and you'll be set for picnics for miles to come.

The Drive ⟫ Continue northeast on Hwy 61. The Knife River fish may well be demolished by Two Harbors, a couple of miles up the road.

- - - - - - - - - - - - - - - -

❸ Two Harbors

Minnesota's only operating **lighthouse** (www.lakecountyhistoricalsociety.org; admission $3; ⊘10am-6pm Mon-Sat, to 4pm Sun) rises up over Agate Bay. The 1892 fog-buster sticks to a rhythm – 0.4-second flash, 4.6 seconds of darkness, 0.4-second flash, 14.6 seconds of darkness. That's how it goes all day, every day; check it out. You can also watch iron-ore freighters maneuvering around the docks that jut into Agate Bay, and there's an old tugboat you can tour (per person $3). Oh, the other harbor that gives the town its name? Burlington Bay, around the point to the north.

Thunder Bay
Kakabeka Falls
Grand Portage
❸ FINISH
p308
Isle Royale National Park
Lake Superior
Ontonagon Indian Reservation
Ontonagon
MICHIGAN

0 — 40 km
0 — 20 miles

🔗 LINK YOUR TRIP

20 **Route 66**
It's a haul to Chicago – 470 miles – but the payoff is a slowpoke ride on America's Main Street.

22 **Along the Great River Road**
Pick up the Mississippi River–edged route in Grand Rapids, about 83 miles east via Hwy 2.

Hiking buffs should stop in the **Superior Hiking Trail Headquarters** (www.shta. org; 731 7th Ave; ⊘9am-5pm Mon-Fri, 10am-4pm Sat, noon-4pm Sun). The awesome 290-mile footpath follows the lake-hugging ridgeline between Duluth and the Canadian border. Trailheads with parking lots pop up every 5 to 10 miles, making it ideal for day hikes. Overnight hikers will find 81 backcountry campsites and several lodges along the way. The headquarters has maps and information.

✕ 🛏 p309

The Drive 》 Motor onward on Hwy 61, past the hamlet of Castle Danger (named for a boat that ran aground nearby) to Gooseberry Falls State Park, a 13-mile drive.

AMERICA / ALAMY ©

❹ Gooseberry Falls State Park

The five cascades, scenic gorge and easy trails draw carloads of visitors to **Gooseberry Falls State Park** (☏218-834-3855; www. dnr.state.mn.us; 3206 Hwy 61; per vehicle/campsites $5/$20; ⊘8am-10pm; 🚻). Several cool stone and log buildings, built by Civilian Conservation Corps in the 1930s, dot the premises and hold exhibits and concessions.

The **Lower and Middle Falls** offer the quickest access via a 0.6-mile paved walkway. Hardier types can trek the 2-mile **Gooseberry River Loop**, which is part of the Superior Hiking Trail. To embark, leave your car at the visitor center lot (at milepost 38.9). Follow the trail to the Upper Falls, then continue upstream on the Fifth Falls Trail. Cross the bridge at Fifth Falls, then return on the river's other side to where you started. Voila! It's one of the simplest Superior trail jaunts you'll find.

The Drive 》 Yep, it's back to Hwy 61 heading northeast, this time for 6 miles.

❺ Split Rock Lighthouse

Split Rock Lighthouse State Park (☏218-226-6377; www.dnr.state.mn.us; 3755 Split Rock Lighthouse

Gooseberry Falls State Park Follow the Superior Hiking Trail to the Upper Falls

Rd; per vehicle/campsites/ lighthouse $5/12/8; ⊙10am-6pm) is the most visited spot on the entire North Shore. The shiner itself is a state historic site with a separate admission fee. Guided tours are available (they depart hourly), or you can explore on your own. If you don't mind stairs, say 170 or so each way, tramp down the cliff to

the beach for incredible views of the lighthouse and surrounding shore.

The lighthouse was built after a whopping storm in November 1905 battered 29 ships in the area. Modern navigation equipment rendered it obsolete by 1969. No matter. It remains one of the most picture-perfect structures you'll come across.

The Drive » Onward on Hwy 61 for 10 miles. Not long after cruising by taconite-crazed Silver Bay, watch for the sign to Palisade Head.

– – – – – – – – – –

6 Palisade Head

Palisade Head is an old lava flow that morphed into some awesomely sheer, rust-red cliffs. A narrow road winds around to the top, where

HIGHWAY 61'S OTHER INCARNATION

Hwy 61 is also used to reference the fabled Blues Highway that tracks the Mississippi River en route to New Orleans (see our Blues Highway trip (p209). That road is actually US 61, and it starts near St Paul, Minnesota. Our Hwy 61 is the state scenic road that starts in Duluth.

there's a small parking lot. The view that unfurls is tremendous. On a clear day you can see Wisconsin's Apostle Islands. Rock climbers love the Head, and you'll probably see a lot of them hanging around.

The Drive » Return to Hwy 61. Palisade Head is actually part of Tettegouche State Park, though it's not contiguous. The park's main span begins 2 miles up-road.

⑦ Tettegouche State Park

Like most of the parks dotting the North Shore, **Tettegouche State Park** (📞218-226-6365; www.dnr. state.mn.us/tettegouche; 5702 Hwy 61; per vehicle/ campsites $5/20; ⊙9am-8pm) offers fishing, camping, paddling and hiking trails to waterfalls and little lakes, plus skiing and snowshoe trails in winter.

There are two unique to-dos, both accessed near the park entrance (milepost 58.5). Leave your car in the parking lot by the new visitors center, then hit the trail to **Shovel Point**. It's a

1.5-mile round-trip jaunt over lots of steps and boardwalks. It pays off with sublime views of the rugged landscape from the point's tip. Watch the lake's awesome power as waves smash below. And keep an eye out for peregrine falcons that nest in the area. Tettegouche's other cool feature is the idyllic **swimming hole** at the Baptism River's mouth. Walk along the picnic area by the visitors center and you'll run into it.

The Drive » Hwy 61 rolls by more birch trees, parks and cloud-flecked skies for the next 22 miles. Not far past Taconite Harbor (now used to load and unload coal for the adjacent power plant), you'll come to Temperance River.

⑧ Temperance River State Park

Get ready for another gorgeous, falls-filled landscape. The eponymous waterway at **Temperance River State Park** (www. dnr.state.mn.us; 7620 Hwy 61; per vehicle/ campsites $5/20; ⊙9am-8pm) belies its moderate name and roars

through a narrow, twisting gorge. The scene is easy to get to, with highway-side parking. Then hike over footbridges and around rock pools to see the action.

The Drive » It's a quick 2 miles up Hwy 61 to Tofte.

⑨ Tofte

The teeny town of Tofte is worth a stop to browse the **North Shore Commercial Fishing Museum** (www. commercialfishingmuseum. org; 7136 Hwy 61; adult/child $3/1; ⊙9am-3pm Sun-Thu, to 5pm Fri & Sat). The twin-gabled red building holds fishing nets, a fishing boat and other tools of the trade, as well as intriguing photos, most of them from the original Norwegian families who settled and fished here in the late 1800s.

Nearby **Sawtooth Outfitters** (📞218-663-7643; www.sawtoothoutfitters.com; 7216 Hwy 61; ⊙7am-7pm late May-early Sep, reduced hours rest of the year) offers guided kayaking tours (half-/full-day tours $50/100) for all levels of paddling. They have trips on the Temperance River and out on Lake Superior, as well as easier jaunts on wildlife-rich inland lakes. Sawtooth also rents mountain bikes (per day from $22) to pedal over the many trails in the area, including the popular Gitchi Gami

State Bike Trail (www.
ggta.org).

The Drive » Get back on
Hwy 61 and head 7 piney miles
northeast.

⑩ Lutsen Mountains

Lutsen (📞218-406-1320;
www.lutsen.com; 10am-5pm)
is a ski resort – the
biggest alpine ski area in
the Midwest, in fact. So
it bustles in winter when
skiers and snowboarders
pile in for the 92 runs on
four mountains.

In summer, visitors
come for the **aerial
tramway** (round-trip adult/
child $12/8) to the top
of Moose Mountain.
The red gondola cars
glide at treetop level
into the valley and over
the Poplar River before
reaching the mountain
top 1000ft later. Gape at
the view from the chalet
and hike the paths. The
Superior Hiking Trail
cuts through and you can
take it plus a spur for the
4.5-mile trek back down
the mountain.

Kids go crazy for the
alpine slide (per person
$8) on Eagle Mountain;
it's accessed by chairlift.
The resort also arranges
family-friendly canoe
trips in voyageur-style
vessels (per person $15;
at 8:30am and 10:30am)
on the Poplar River.

The Drive » Back to Hwy
61, past maple- and birch-rich
Cascade River State Park
(particularly pretty in fall), for
20 miles to Grand Marais.

TRIP HIGHLIGHT

⑪ Grand Marais

Artsy little Grand Marais
makes an excellent base to
explore the region. Stroll
the waterfront, watch the
small fishing fleet head
out, and take advantage
of the characterful local
eateries. Do-it-yourself
enthusiasts can learn to
build boats, tie flies or
brew beer at the **North
House Folk School** (📞218-
387-9762; www.northhouse.
org; 500 Hwy 61). The course
list, which strives to
preserve local traditions,
is phenomenal – as is
the school's two-hour
sailing trip aboard the
Vikingesque schooner
Hjordis (per person $35
to 45).

 p309

The Drive » Beyond Grand
Marais Hwy 61 widens, you
see fewer people, and the lake
reveals itself more. After 14
miles, you'll arrive at Magney
State Park.

⑫ Judge CR Magney State Park

The namesake of the
park (www.dnr.state.mn.us;
4051 Hwy 61; per vehicle/
campsites $5/20; ☉9am-
8pm) was a former mayor
of Duluth and Minnesota
Supreme Court justice
who helped preserve the
area. His own patch of
land is a beauty. Hiking
to **Devil's Kettle**, the
famous falls where
the Brule River splits
around a huge rock, is
a must. Half of the flow

DETOUR: GUNFLINT TRAIL

Start: ⑪ **Grand Marais**

The **Gunflint Trail** (www.gunflint-trail.com), aka Hwy
12, slices inland from Grand Marais and ends near
Saganaga Lake. The paved, 57-mile-long byway dips
into the **Boundary Waters Canoe Area Wilderness**
(www.fs.usda.gov/attmain/superior/specialplaces), the
legendarily remote paddlers' paradise. For Boundary
permits and information, visit the **Gunflint Ranger
Station** (📞218-387-1750; ☉8am-4:30pm May-Sep), a
stone's throw southwest of Grand Marais on Hwy 61.

Even if you're not canoeing, the road has excellent
hiking, picnicking and moose-viewing. Look for the
big antlered guys and gals around dawn or dusk in
wet, swampy areas.

It takes 1½ hours to drive the Gunflint Trail one way,
but you'll want longer for hiking, zip-lining and moose
stops. There aren't any towns along the route, but
several lodges tuck in woods where you can grab a
meal or snack.

DETOUR: ISLE ROYALE NATIONAL PARK

Start: ⓭ Grand Portage

Isle Royale National Park (www.nps.gov/isro; fee per day $4; ☉mid-May–Oct) is technically part of Michigan, but it's easily accessed from Grand Portage by daily **ferries** (☎218-475-0024; www.isleroyaleboats.com; day trip adult/child $58/32) between May and October. The unspoiled, 210-sq-mile island is totally free of vehicles and roads, and gets fewer visitors in a year than Yellowstone National Park gets in a day – which means the packs of wolves and moose creeping through the forest are all yours.

The ferry ride takes 90 minutes. Day trips leave Grand Portage in the morning, spend four hours on the island, then return by 3pm.

Wilderness buffs will want to linger. Around 165 miles of hiking trails lace the island and connect dozens of campgrounds along Lake Superior and inland waterways. It's a full-on wilderness adventure for which you'll need a tent, camping stove, sleeping bag, food and water filter. Or you can bunk at the island's lone accommodation, the **Rock Harbor Lodge** (☎906-337-4993; www.isleroyaleresort.com; r & cottages $237-271; ☉late May-early Sep).

drops 50ft in a typically gorgeous North Shore gush, but the other half disappears down a huge hole and flows underground. Where it goes is a mystery – scientists have never been able to determine the water's outlet. It's a moderately breath-sapping 1.1-mile walk each way.

Across the road from the park is **Naniboujou Lodge**. Built in the 1920s, the property was once a private club for Babe Ruth and his contemporaries, who smoked cigars in the Great Hall, and warmed by the 20ft-high stone fireplace. The pièce de résistance is the hall's massive domed ceiling painted with mind-blowing, psychedelic-colored Cree Indian designs. The hall is now the lodge's dining room, and you're welcome to walk in for a peek (or meal).

🛏 p309

The Drive » The final 26-mile stretch of highway passes through the Grand Portage Indian Reservation and, finally, Grand Portage National Monument.

- - - - - - - - - -

TRIP HIGHLIGHT

⓭ Grand Portage

Grand Portage National Monument (☎218-475-0123; www.nps.gov/grpo; ☉9am-5pm mid-May–mid-Oct) is where the early voyageurs had to carry their canoes (hence the name) around the Pigeon River rapids. This was the center of a fur-trading empire, and the reconstructed 1788 trading post and Ojibwe village show how the community lived in the harsh environment. Learn how the original inhabitants prepared wild rice and pressed beaver pelts as you wander through the Great Hall and other buildings with costumed interpreters. A big powwow takes place the second weekend in August.

The half-mile paved path that goes to Mount Rose rewards with killer views. Or walk the 17-mile round-trip Grand Portage Trail that traces the early fur men's route.

Grand Portage is impressively lonely and windblown – fitting for the end of the road. Because with that, Hwy 61 stops cold at the Canadian border.

Eating & Sleeping

Duluth ①

✖ Duluth Grill   American $$

(www.duluthgrill.com; 118 S 27th Ave W; mains $8-16; ⊘7am-9pm; ⚡🐾) The garden in the parking lot is the tip-off that the Duluth Grill is a sustainable, hippy-vibed place. The dineresque menu is huge, ranging from eggy breakfast skillets to curried-polenta stew to bison burgers. It's a couple of miles southwest of Canal Park.

✖ Pizza Luce   Pizzeria $$

(☎218-727-7400; www.pizzaluce.com; 11 E Superior St; mains $10-20; ⊘8am-1:30am Sun-Thu, to 2:30am Fri & Sat; ⚡) Downtown on Superior St, Pizza Luce cooks locally sourced breakfasts and gourmet pizzas. It's plugged into the local music scene and hosts bands, too.

🛏 Fitger's Inn   Hotel $$

(☎218-722-8826; www.fitgers.com; 600 E Superior St; r incl breakfast $149-239; @🛜) Fitger's carved its 62 large rooms, each with slightly varied decor, from an old brewery. The pricier rooms have great water views. There's still a brewhouse inside, and it makes fantastic suds.

Two Harbors ③

✖ Betty's Pies   American $

(www.bettyspies.com; 1633 Hwy 61; sandwiches $5-9; ⊘7am-9pm, reduced Oct-May) Racks of pie are Betty's claim to fame. Consider the five-layer chocolate tinful, stacked with dark chocolate, cinnamon meringue, regular whipped cream and chocolate whipped cream. It's 2 miles north of town.

🛏 Lighthouse B&B   B&B $$

(☎888-832-5606; www.lighthousebb.org; r incl breakfast $135-155) You can't beat this real-deal lighthouse for nautical ambiance and lake views. Three rooms share a bathroom; there's a fourth, en suite room in a separate building.

Grand Marais ⑪

✖ Dockside Fish Market   Deli $

(www.docksidefishmarket.com; 418 Hwy 61; mains $7-11) The boat heads out in the morning and by noon the freshly caught herring has been fried into fish-and-chips at the deli counter. Seven tables scatter on the outdoor deck, and another seven are indoors. Before leaving, check the freezer case for briny-tanged Superior Gold Caviar (aka herring roe), a local delicacy.

✖ Sven and Ole's   American $

(☎218-387-1713; www.svenandoles.com; 9 Wisconsin St; sandwiches $6-9; ⊘11am-8pm, to 9pm Thu-Sat) It's a classic for sandwiches and pizzas, plus beer at the attached pub. Go ahead: ask about the lutefisk pizza.

✖ World's Best Donuts   Bakery $

(☎218-387-1345; www.worldsbestdonutsmn. com; 10 E Wisconsin St; donuts $1-2; ⊘4:30am-4:30pm Mon-Sat, to 2pm Sun, closed mid-Oct–mid-May) Mmm, doughnuts. Staff nobly arrive at 3am each morning to fry and glaze. Try the elephant-ear-like skizzle.

🛏 Harbor Inn   Hotel $$

(☎218-387-1191; www.harborinnhotel.com; 207 Wisconsin St; r $115-135; 🛜) The rooms may look plain Jane, but they're comfy and well located in town.

Judge CR Magney State Park ⑫

🛏 Naniboujou Lodge   Lodge $$

(☎218-387-2688; www.naniboujou.com; 20 Naniboujou Trail; r $95-115; ⊘late May-late Oct) Rooms at the historic property vary in decor, but each offers an away-from-it-all experience.

STRETCH YOUR LEGS
CHICAGO

Start/Finish: Millennium Park

Distance: 2 miles

Duration: 3 hours

The Windy City will blow you away with its blend of high culture and earthy pleasures. This walk swoops through the action-packed downtown Loop, highlighting Chicago's revered art and architecture.

Take this walk on Trip

Millennium Park

Where to start amid the mod designs of Millennium Park (🖉312-742-1168; www.millenniumpark.org; 201 E Randolph St; 🕙6am-11pm; 🚹; MBrown, Orange, Green, Purple, Pink Line to Randolph)? Pritzker Pavilion, Frank Gehry's rippling silver band shell? *Crown Fountain*, Jaume Plensa's splashy waterwork, where images of locals spout gargoyle-style? Or 'the Bean' (officially *Cloud Gate*), Anish Kapoor's 110-ton, silver-drop sculpture? That's the one. Join the visitors swarming it to see the skyline reflections.

The Walk 》 Walk across Monroe St to the Art Institute's Modern Wing entrance. You can also take the silvery pedestrian bridge that rises from Millennium Park and arches over the street. It deposits you at the institute's free, third-floor sculpture garden.

Art Institute of Chicago

The Art Institute (🖉312-443-3600; www.artic.edu; 111 S Michigan Ave; adult/child $23/free; 🕙10:30am-5pm, to 8pm Thu; 🚹) is the second-largest art museum in the country. The collection of impressionist and post-impressionist paintings is second only to those in France, and the number of surrealist works is tremendous. Download the free app for DIY tours. It offers 50 jaunts, everything from highlights to a 'birthday-suit tour' of naked works.

The Walk 》 Walk south on Michigan Ave to Jackson Blvd; turn right. Pass under the rumbling El train. Four business-y blocks later you'll pass the 1930 art deco Board of Trade (look for *Ceres*, the goddess of agriculture, on top). Turn right on LaSalle St.

Rookery

The 1888 **Rookery** (www.gowright.org/rookery; 209 S LaSalle St; 🕙9:30am-5:30pm Mon-Fri; MBrown, Orange, Purple, Pink Line to Quincy) looks fortresslike from the outside, but the inside is light and airy thanks to Frank Lloyd Wright, who overhauled the atrium. You can walk in and look around for free. The Frank

Lloyd Wright Preservation Trust has a groovy shop in the lobby and offers lunchtime tours ($5 to $10) at noon on weekdays.

The Walk ⟩⟩ Continue on LaSalle St, the heart of Chicago's financial district, to Washington St. Turn right and behold what rises up when you get to Daley Plaza.

The Picasso

Pablo Picasso's abstract sculpture is the granddaddy of Chicago's public art. Baboon, dog, woman? Picasso couldn't decide either, which is why it's officially titled *Untitled* (50 W Washington St; Ⓜ Blue Line to Washington).

The Walk ⟩⟩ Stay on Washington St, passing the Hotel Burnham (at 1 W Washington). The building is an 1890s landmark that set the bar for modern skyscraper design. A block and a half later you'll reach Toni's place.

Toni Patisserie & Cafe

Parisian-style **Toni Patisserie & Cafe** (www.tonipatisserie.com; 65 E Washington St ; Ⓧ8am-8pm Mon-Sat, to 5pm Sun; Ⓜ Brown,

Orange, Green, Purple, Pink Line to Randolph or Madison) provides a refuge from the Loop hullabaloo. Order a coffee to sip at the close-set tables while you try to resist the eclairs, macarons and tiered cakes tempting you from the glass case.

The Walk ⟩⟩ Walk a half block down Washington St and cross the street.

Chicago Cultural Center

There's always something cool and free going on at the **Cultural Center** (☎312-744-6630; www.chicagoculturalcenter. org; 78 E Washington St; Ⓧ8am-7pm Mon-Thu, to 6pm Fri, 9am-6pm Sat, 10am-6pm Sun; Ⓜ Brown, Orange, Green, Purple, Pink Line to Randolph): art exhibitions, foreign films, lunchtime jazz and classical concerts. The grand building also contains the world's largest Tiffany stained-glass dome, Chicago's main visitor center and StoryCorps' recording studio (where folks tell their tale and have it preserved in the Library of Congress). Depart from the Cultural Center's Randolph St exit, and you're back where you started.

Great Plains Trips

THE STATES OF THE GREAT PLAINS ARE MORE THAN HAPPY TO TRANSITION you between east and west. But if you slow down for just a moment, they'll open the door, invite you in and share with you some of the country's finest history, scenery and yarns of adventure. You'll hear the stories of outlaws, pioneers and the likes of Geronimo, Crazy Horse and the Five Civilized Tribes, as well as the original duo of explorers, Lewis and Clark.

All this, and we haven't mentioned Gateway Arch, Mt Rushmore or Scotts Bluff. One required stop? The prairie. Scratchy blue stems, unabashed birdsong, the smell of cut grass – by tickling the senses, it reinvigorates the soul. Pull over, get out of the car, breathe deep. We think you'll see what we mean.

Kansas Checkerboard farmland (Trip 27)

Great Plains Trips

Bison Badlands National Park (Trip 26)

24 **Oklahoma's Tribal Trails 4–5 days**
Learn the heart-breaking stories of Oklahoma's Native Americans. (p317)

25 **On the Pioneer Trails 5–7 days**
Follow the trails and tales of early travelers as you explore Nebraska. (p327)

Classic Trip
26 **Black Hills Loop 2–3 days**
Icons, beauty and fun combine for the perfect driving loop. (p337)

27 **The Mighty Mo 7 days**
America's longest river first lured Lewis and Clark, now it's your turn. (p349)

DON'T MISS

Washita Battlefield National Historic Site

This Native American camp was raided at dawn in 1868. A National Park Service facility tells the tragic story; visit the site on Trip `24`

Homestead National Monument

The Homestead Act of 1862 opened up much of the American West to settlers. Among the earliest were the Freeman's, whose story is recalled on Trip `25`

Iron Mountain Road

A real-life roller coaster, this road passes through the unparalleled beauty of Custer State Park on Trip `26`

Lewis & Clark Historical Trail Visitors Center

On the Missouri riverfront in Omaha, this center lets you plan your own journey of discovery on Trip `27`

Knife River Indian Villages Site

The centuries barely seem to have touched this remote site. Revel in the desolation on Trip `27`

Anadarko *A hub for many Plains tribes*

Oklahoma's Tribal Trails

24

Oklahoma's flag is the only state flag that honors Native Americans. What's the history behind the tribal heritage? This trip uncovers the answers from Tahlequah to Washita.

TRIP HIGHLIGHTS

453 miles

Washita Battlefield National Historic Site
A harrowing and heartbreaking sight of battle and slaughter

188 miles

Oklahoma City
All the state's drama in one bustling city

Tulsa

START
1

10 **FINISH**

6

Muskogee

Anadarko

8

Fort Sill
An 1870s fort used for battles against Apaches and Cherokees

283 miles

Tahlequah
Learn about the iconic Cherokee nation

1 mile

4–5 DAYS
453 MILES / 729KM

GREAT FOR...

BEST TIME TO GO
Enjoy this trip April to October, when the weather can be lovely.

 ESSENTIAL PHOTO

Dawn at Washita Battlefield National Historic Site.

 BEST FOR HISTORY

The unmissable Cherokee Heritage Center with its moving displays in Tahlequah.

24 Oklahoma's Tribal Trails

There's no soft-pedaling the Trail of Tears, the forced removal and march of five Indian tribes from the southeastern US to what was then called the Indian Territory in present-day eastern Oklahoma. The tales of death, deception and duplicity are sobering. You can visit sites connected to these tragedies (and others) across Oklahoma. In addition you can learn about the vital role of Native Americans in the state today.

TRIP HIGHLIGHT

❶ Tahlequah

Subtle, forested hills interspersed with lakes and iconic red dirt cover Oklahoma's northeast corner, aka Green Country (www.greencountryok.com), which includes Tahlequah, the Cherokee capital since 1839.

Of the tragedies visited on Indian tribes, perhaps none is more tragic than the relocation of the Cherokees. The history and horror

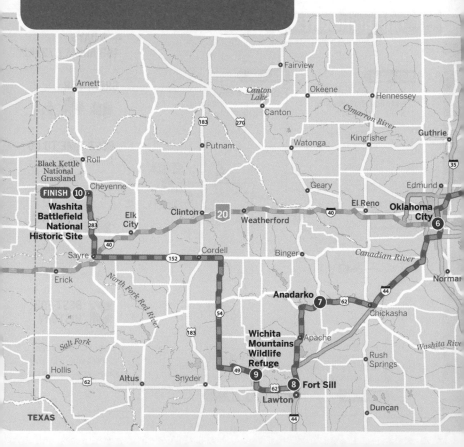

behind the forced march is movingly traced at the six-gallery **Cherokee Heritage Center** (www.cherokeeheritage.org; 21192 Keeler Rd; adult/child $8.50/5; ⏰9am-5pm Jun-Aug, short hours rest of year) outside of town. Interactive displays describe key events, including court battles and stockade imprisonment, that preceded the forced removal then focus on the army-commanded marches between 1838 and 1839. Disease, starvation and the cold killed scores on the 800-mile journey.

Outside, at the **Ancient Village**, visitors can learn what life was like in a Cherokee community before the arrival of Europeans. The one-hour guided tour includes pottery-making and blowgun demonstrations.

The Drive » The Cherokee Heritage Center is on the

LINK YOUR TRIP

20 Route 66
In one of the richest states for Route 66 sites, the Native American heritage of Oklahoma makes an excellent add-on as the two routes weave in and out across the state.

25 On the Pioneer Trails
See yet more ways people spread out across the US. The drive north to Nebraska features classic Great Plains open vistas. Take I-29 430 miles north to Omaha.

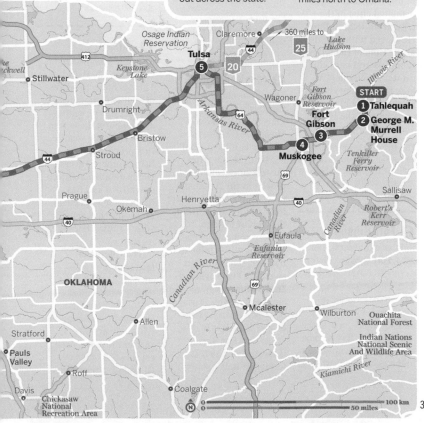

southwest side of Tahlequah. From here it is a short drive (1 mile) south on South Keeler Dr to your next stop.

- - - - - - - - - - -

❷ George M Murrell House

A large estate from the mid-19th century, this historic **house** (19479 E Murrell Home Rd, Park Hill; donation requested; ☺9am-5pm Tue-Sat) belies some of the images of the Cherokees as downtrodden. Murrell, who was of European descent, was married to Minerva Ross, a member of a prominent Cherokee family (her father was principal chief of the tribe from 1828 to 1866). He moved with his family at the time of the forced removals and built this estate, which offers a look at the more genteel aspects of life in the early days of the Indian Territory.

The Drive ❯❯ The third stop on the tour is an easy 18 miles southwest along US 62. Enjoy the gently rolling countryside and iconic red Oklahoma earth.

- - - - - - - - - - -

❸ Fort Gibson

Built as a frontier fort in 1824, **Fort Gibson** (907 N Garrison Rd, Fort Sill; adult/child $3/1; ☺10am-5pm Tue-Sun Jun-Aug, Thu-Sun rest of year) came to play an integral – and notorious – role in the Trail of Tears. It was home to the removal commission in the 1830s and is where

surviving Creek and Seminole Indians were brought after the forced march. From here they were dispatched around the Indian Territory. You can get a good sense of military life 180 years ago at the restored grounds and buildings. Fort Gibson is a National Historic Landmark managed by the Oklahoma Historical Society.

Washington Irving wrote his landmark *A Tour of the Prairies* in 1835 based on trips he took with Fort Gibson troops in 1832 and 1833 looking for local bands of Native Americans.

The Drive ❯❯ Continue on US 62 southwest 9 miles to Muskogee.

- - - - - - - - - - -

❹ Muskogee

The namesake of Merle Haggard's 1969 hit 'Okie from Muskogee?', Muskogee ('where even squares can have a ball') is a bit different from the rest of Oklahoma. It is deep in the Arkansas River valley and there are hints of humid air from the Gulf of Mexico.

Here you can learn more about the relocated tribes at the small but engaging **Five Civilized Tribes Museum** (www. fivetribes.org; Honor Heights Dr, Agency Hill; adult/student $4/2; ☺10am-5pm Mon-Fri, to 2pm Sat). The museum is located in a 1875 former Indian Agency

office that was used as a meeting place for the leaders of the five tribes. The museum dedicates one wall to each tribe; displays cover an eclectic array of topics from Choctaw code talkers in WWI to variations in lacrosse sticks. The gift shop sells pottery, painting and jewelry made by members of the five tribes.

The Drive ❯❯ Skip the tolls and monotony of the Muskogee Turnpike and opt instead for US 64, which wanders through classic small towns such as Haskell that give a timeless sense of rural Oklahoma. The 60-mile drive to Tulsa will take about 90 minutes.

- - - - - - - - - - -

❺ Tulsa

Self-billed as the 'Oil Capital of the World,' Tulsa is home to scores of energy companies drilling for oil, selling it or supplying those who do. The steady wealth this provides once helped create Tulsa's richly detailed art-deco downtown and has funded some excellent museums that give the state's Indian heritage its due.

The **Gilcrease Museum** (www.gilcrease. org; 1400 Gilcrease Museum Rd; adult/child $8/free; ☺10am-5pm Tue-Sun) is a superb museum with a great story: it sits on the manicured estate of Thomas Gilcrease, a part-Native

BENJAMIN G. RANDLE / GETTY IMAGES ©

Rural Oklahoma

American who grew up on Creek tribal lands. He later was eligible for a tribal allotment which contained a little surprise – oil! Over his life, Gilcrease built up one of the world's great collections of art and artifacts relating to the cultures of the American West. The museum is northwest of downtown, off Hwy 64.

South of town is another oil magnate's property, a converted Italianate villa also ringed by fabulous foliage. It houses some fine Native American works at the **Philbrook**

Museum of Art (www. philbrook.org; 2727 S Rockford Rd, east of Peoria Ave; adult/ child $9/free; 🕙10am-5pm Tue-Sun, to 8pm Thu).

 p325

The Drive ≫ Link Oklahoma's two largest cities via the quick route of I-44, otherwise known as the Turner Turnpike. In return for the tolls you'll minimize your time between the big-name attractions as you zip along slightly more than 100 miles.

➏ Oklahoma City

At the impressive **Oklahoma History Center** (www.okhistorycenter. org; 2401 N Laird Ave; adult/

child $7/4; 🕙10am-5pm Mon-Sat), you can explore the heritage of the 39 tribes headquartered in the state. Artifacts include an 1890 cradleboard, a Kiowa pictorial calendar and an original letter from Thomas Jefferson that Lewis and Clark gave to the Otoe tribe. In it, Jefferson invites the tribe to the nation's capital. Be sure to look up before you leave – there's a Pawnee star chart on the ceiling.

The contributions of Indians to Oklahoma's life past and present are highlighted in engaging and interactive exhibits at the **Gaylord-Pickens Museum** (www.oklahomaheritage.com; 1400 Classen Dr; ⊘9am-5pm Tue-Fri, from 10am Sat).

Stay tuned for the much-anticipated opening of the **American Indian Cultural Center & Museum** (www.theamericanindiancenter.org; junction I-40 & I-35). This landmark center with its arresting design is meant to be one of the premier Native American institutions in the world. Its construction has slowed due to state budget cuts and at the time of writing was not open to the public.

Meanwhile, you can experience the frontier in a manner familiar to anyone who has seen an old Western movie at the **National Cowboy & Western Heritage Museum** (www.nationalcowboymuseum.org; 1700 NE 63rd St; adult/child $12.50/6; ⊘10am-5pm).

 p325

The Drive » A 40-mile drive southwest on I-44 (the Baily Turnpike toll road) leads to Chickasha at exit 83. Head 20 miles west on US 62 through Native American lands to Anadarko.

---

⑦ Anadarko

Eight tribal lands are located in this area, and students from 46 different tribes are enrolled in Anadarko schools. The town regularly hosts powwows and Native American events.

To mix a little shopping with your learning, visit the **Southern Plains Indian Museum** (📞405-247-6221; www.doi.gov/iacb/museums/museum_s_plains.html; 715 E Central Blvd, Anadarko, OK; ⊘9am-5pm Tue-Sat; 🚻). It houses a small but diverse collection of Plains Indian clothing, weaponry and musical instruments. There's also a small collection of Native American dolls. The gift shop sells museum-quality crafts including jewelry, dolls and beadwork items

(barrettes, purses and moccasins). About 85% of the store's customers are Native American.

Just east is the **National Hall of Fame for Famous American Indians** (📞405-247-5555; 851 E Central Blvd, Hwy 62, east of Anadarko; ⊘site 24hr, visitors center 9am-5pm Mon-Sat, 1-5pm Sun). A short outdoor walk leads past the bronze busts of well-known Native Americans including Pocahontas, Geronimo and Sitting Bull. The nearby visitors center has a good selection of books on Oklahoma Indians.

The Drive » US 62 continues to figure prominently in this tour as you drive 35 miles south to Fort Sill. The historic portion is just west of US 62 on the edge of this very active military base.

TRIP HIGHLIGHT

⑧ Fort Sill

Oklahoma isn't just home to eastern tribes. Numerous western and Plains tribes, including the Apache, Comanche, Kiowa and Wichita, were also forced here as the US expanded west. The US Army built Fort Sill in 1869 in Kiowa and Comanche territory to prevent raids into settlements in Texas and Kansas. By the 1880s and 1890s its role had changed, and the fort was serving as a protective sanctuary for many tribes.

THE CHOCTAWS AND OKLAHOMA'S IDENTITY

The Choctaws were skilled farmers living in brick and stone homes in Mississippi and Alabama in the early 1800s. They were relocated to Oklahoma in the 1830s – after 16 broken treaties with the US. Oklahoma's name derives from the Choctaw words for 'red man', and the state flag is derived in part from a flag carried by Choctaw soldiers fighting for the Confederacy during the Civil War.

TRAIL OF TEARS ACROSS THE US

From Alabama to Oklahoma, across nine states, the National Park Service administers the **Trail of Tears National Historic Trail** (www.nps.gov/trte), which features and highlights important sites from the tragedy. Among the highlights:

» **Alabama** – Fort Payne Cabin Site. Dates to 1838 when federal troops arrived to force the Cherokee to Oklahoma.

» **Georgia** – Rockdale Plantation. An 18th-century plantation building once owned by a slave-owning Cherokee man.

» **Tennessee** – Brainerd Mission Cemetery. The remains of a mission for the Cherokees near Chattanooga. Most of the missionaries accompanied the tribe's removal to Oklahoma.

» **Kentucky** – Trail of Tears Commemorative Park. Used as a cemetery for chiefs who died during the removals.

» **Illinois** – Trail of Tears State Forest. A bleak forest where hundreds of Native Americans died during the horrible winter of 1838–39.

» **Missouri** – Trail of Tears State Park. Another natural area that commemorates the horrible events of the removals.

The **Fort Sill National Historic Landmark Museum** (☎580-442-5123; sill-www.army.mil; 437 Quanah Rd, Fort Sill; �) 8:30am-5pm Tue-Sat; 👍), which fills several original stone buildings, explores the history of the fort. Another highlight is the 1872 **Post Guardhouse**, the center of law enforcement for the Indian Territory. Step inside to see where Apache leader **Geronimo** was detained on three separate occasions. Geronimo and other Apache warriors were brought here in 1894 as prisoners of war. Geronimo's grave, marked by an eagle-topped stone pyramid, is on fort grounds a few miles from the guardhouse.

Today, Fort Sill is home to the US Army Field Artillery School.

The Drive » Leave booming artillery in your wake as you roll west on Hwy 62 to state Hwy 115 north. Black-eyed susans, scrubby trees and barbed-wire fences line the two-lane byway as it unfurls from tiny Cache toward the hill-dappled Wichita Mountains Wildlife Refuge.

- - - - - - - - - - - - - -

❾ Wichita Mountains Wildlife Refuge

Southwest Oklahoma opens into expansive prairie fields all the way to Texas. Beautiful mountains provide texture.

The 59,202-acre **Wichita Mountains Wildlife Refuge** (☎580-429-3222; http://wichitamountains.fws.gov; 32 Refuge Headquarters, Indiahoma, OK; primitive sites $6, single units $8-16; ☉ visitors center 8am-6pm summer, to 4:30pm winter; 👍🎣) protects bison, elk, longhorn cattle and a super-active prairie-dog town. Wildlife is abundant; observant drivers might even see a spindly, palm-sized tarantula tiptoeing across the road. At the visitors center, informative displays highlight the refuge's flora and fauna. A massive glass window yields inspiring views of prairie grasslands. For a short-but-scenic hike, try the creek-hugging **Kite Trail** to the waterfalls and rocks at the Forty Foot Hole. It starts at the Lost Lake Picnic Area.

FIVE CIVILISED TRIBES

Two of eastern Oklahoma's earliest known tribes, the Osage and the Quapaw, ceded millions of acres to the US government in the 1820s. The US then gave the land to five east-coast tribes: the Cherokee, Chickasaw, Choctaw, Creek and Seminoles. Because these five tribes had implemented formal governmental and agricultural practices in their communities, they were collectively called the Five Civilized Tribes.

The Five Civilized Tribes were forced to move to the Oklahoma area, known then as the Indian Territory, after settlers in the southern states decided they wanted the tribes' fertile farmlands for themselves. Between 1830 and 1850, the five tribes were forcibly relocated; their routes are collectively known as the Trail of Tears.

How many people died in this forced march is unknown, however records suggest deaths were in the tens of thousands. Often overlooked are the thousands of African Americans who were held as slaves by the Native Americans. Scores died during the removals.

As for their new homes in the Indian Territory, the US government said it would belong to the five tribes 'for as long as the stars shine and the rivers may flow'. The reality? More like 70 years. In the mid-1800s the country was quickly expanding west, and white settlers wanted the land. Through legislative maneuvering, certain Indian-owned lands were deemed 'unassigned', opening them up for settlement. The Oklahoma Land Rush began on April 22, 1889, when 50,000 would-be settlers made a mad dash for their own 160-acre allotment.

The Drive » Hwy 49 west of the refuge continues the natural beauty of the mountains. After 15 miles turn north on Hwy 54, which runs through tribal lands. Look for schools, tiny towns and small farms on the 38.5 miles. When you reach Hwy 152, just north of the evocatively named village of Cloud Chief, turn west for 44 miles to US 283. Go north through cattle country for 24 miles to Cheyenne and follow the signs to the Washita site.

✖ p325

- - - - - - - - - - - - - -

TRIP HIGHLIGHT

⑩ Washita Battlefield National Historic Site

At the **Washita Battlefield National**

Historic Site (www.nps.gov/ waba; Hwy 47A, 2 miles west of Cheyenne; ☾ site dawn-dusk, visitor center 9am-5pm, talks & tours 10am-2pm Sat & Sun Jun-Aug) George Custer's troops launched a dawn attack on November 27, 1868 on the peaceful village of Chief Black Kettle. It was a slaughter of men, women, children and domestic animals, an act some would say led to karmic revenge on Custer eight years later. Among those who died was the peace-promoting chief, Black Kettle. Even today, you may encounter current members of the US military studying what exactly transpired here that cold, pre-winter morning.

Self-guiding **trails** at the site traverse the site of the killings, which is remarkably unchanged. A new visitor center 0.7 miles away contains a good **museum**. Seasonal tours and talks are very worthwhile. A small garden shows how traditional plants were grown for medicine, spiritual rituals and food.

Eating & Sleeping

Tulsa 5

X Ike's Chili House
Diner $

(5941 E Admiral Pl; mains under $7; ⊙10am-7pm Mon-Fri, to 3pm Sat) Ike's has been serving chili for over 100 years and its classic version is much-loved. You can get it straight or over Fritos, a hot dog, beans or spaghetti. Top with red peppers, onions, jalapenos, saltines and cheddar cheese for classic joy.

X Tavern
American $$

(www.taverntulsa.com; 201 N Main St; mains $10-30; ⊙11am-late) This beautiful pub anchors the Brady Arts District and serves excellent fare. The hamburgers are legendary or you can opt for steaks, salads or seasonal specials. The bartenders are true mixologists.

⊨ Desert Hills Motel
Motel $

(☎918-834-3311; www.deserthillstulsa.com; 5220 E 11th St; r from $40; ❄ 🛜) The glowing neon cactus out front beckons you to this lovingly restored 1950s motor court with 50 rooms (with fridges and microwaves). It's 5 miles east of downtown, on historic Route 66.

⊨ Hotel Ambassador
Hotel $$$

(☎918-587-8200; www.hotelambassador-tulsa.com; 1324 S Main St; r from $200-300; P ❄ @ 🛜) Look in the hallway for the photos of this 1929 nine-story hotel before its opulent renovation. Public spaces are suitably grand; the 55 rooms have a contemporary feel that helps the somewhat close quarters seem a tad larger.

Oklahoma City 6

X Tucker's Onion Burgers
Burgers $

(www.tuckersonionburgers.com; 324 NW 23rd St; mains from $4; ⊙11am-9pm) A new kind of burger joint with and old-time Route 66 vibe,

Tucker's has high-quality food (locally sourced) that includes iconic OK onion burgers, fresh-cut fries, and shakes. They even have a green ethos and a fine patio.

X Cattlemen's Steakhouse
Steakhouse $$

(www.cattlemensrestaurant.com; 1309 S Agnew Ave; mains $5-25; ⊙6am-10pm Sun-Thu, to midnight Fri & Sat) OKC's most storied restaurant, this Stockyards City institution has been feeding cowpokes and city slickers slabs of beef and lamb's fries (that's a polite way of saying gonads) since 1910.

⊨ Carlyle Motel
Motel $

(☎405-946-3355; 3600 NW 39th St; r from $40) Little has changed (other than the sheets) since the 1950s at this simple 15-room place, which is popular with Route 66 buffs.

⊨ Colcord Hotel
Boutique Hotel $$

(☎405-601-4300; www.colcordhotel.com; 15 N Robinson Ave; r $150-200; P ❄ @ 🛜) OKC's first skyscraper, built in 1910, is now a 12-story luxurious hotel. Many original flourishes, such as the marble-clad lobby, survive, while the 108 rooms have a stylish, contemporary touch. It's walking distance to Bricktown.

Wichita Mountains Wildlife Refuge 9

X Meers Store & Restaurant
Burgers

(☎580-429-8051; www.meersstore.com; Hwy 115, north of refuge; mains $4-11; ⊙10:30am-8:30pm Sun, Mon, Wed & Thu, to 9pm Fri & Sat; 👶) Meers Store & Restaurant is a ramshackle burger-and-beer joint hunkered at the end of a twisty, country-road junction north of the refuge. Its smashed-flat, 7in Meers burger – made from the beef of the restaurant's own longhorns – is a 'must-eat' in the region.

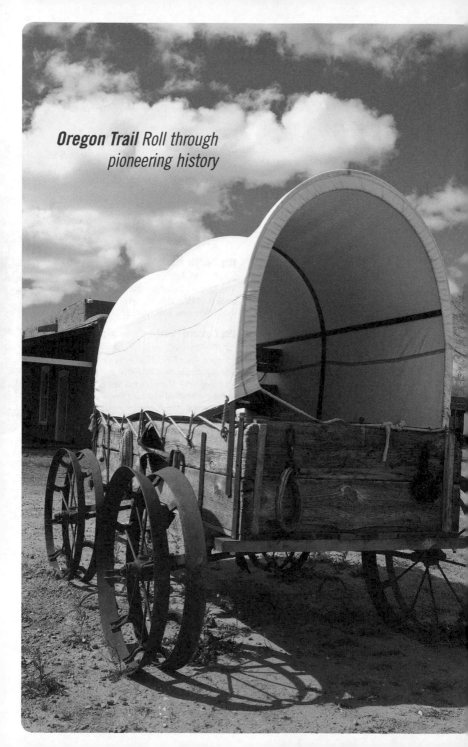

Oregon Trail *Roll through
pioneering history*

On the Pioneer Trails

25

Follow in the wagon tracks of thousands of pioneers who crossed Nebraska on iconic treks including the Oregon Trail. Visit windswept settlements of those who stayed behind.

TRIP HIGHLIGHTS

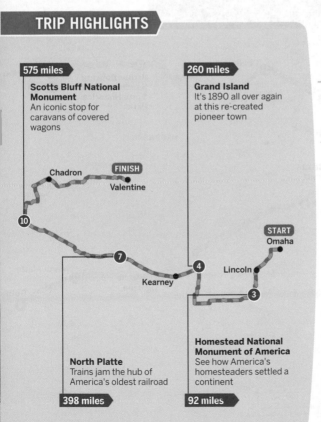

575 miles

Scotts Bluff National Monument
An iconic stop for caravans of covered wagons

260 miles

Grand Island
It's 1890 all over again at this re-created pioneer town

Chadron **FINISH**
Valentine

10

7

4 Lincoln

START
Omaha

Kearney

3

North Platte
Trains jam the hub of America's oldest railroad

398 miles

Homestead National Monument of America
See how America's homesteaders settled a continent

92 miles

5–7 DAYS
802 MILES / 1291KM

GREAT FOR...

BEST TIME TO GO
May to September when everything is open and the wildflowers are in bloom.

 ESSENTIAL PHOTO
The postcard-worthy buttes of Scotts Bluff.

 BEST FOR EXPLORING
Explore off-the-beaten-paths in a land many blithely whiz through.

327

25 On the Pioneer Trails

Balmy days driving through lush green valleys and barren buttes; nights hanging outside a small-town ice-cream stand recalling the day's adventures to the background sound of crickets. These are just some of the charms of exploring the backroads of Nebraska, which, like the ubiquitous state plant, corn, when left on the fire, pops with attractions. Eschew I-80 and be a modern-day pioneer.

1 Omaha

Omaha's location on the Missouri River and proximity to the Platte made it an important stop on the Oregon, California and Mormon trails. Many heading west paused here before plunging into Nebraska and you should do the same. Learn tales from these pioneer trails at the beautiful **Durham Museum** (☎402-444-5071; www.durhammuseum.org; 801 S 10th St; adult/child $9/6; ⊙10am-8pm Tue, to 5pm Wed-Sat, 1-5pm Sun), housed in

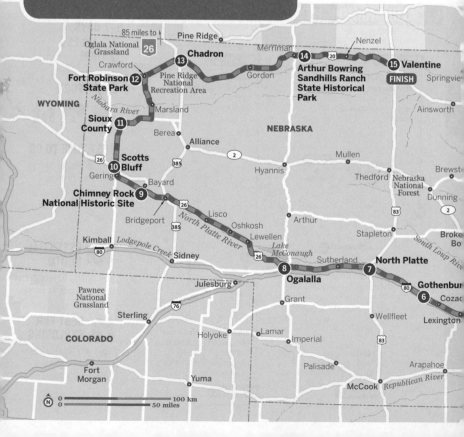

the once-bustling Union Station.

 p335

Scoot along US 6, with its old drive-ins still peddling soft-serve cones and other pleasures, for the 57 miles to Lincoln.

----

❷ Lincoln

Home to the historic **Haymarket District** and the huge downtown campus of the University of Nebraska, the capital city is a good place to get the big picture of the state's story. You can almost hear the wagon wheels creaking and the sound of sod busting at the **Museum of Nebraska History** (www.nebraskahistory.org; 131 Centennial Mall N; admission by donation; ⏰9am-4:30pm Mon-Fri, 1-4:30pm Sat & Sun).

 p335

The Drive » Drive 35 miles south of Lincoln on Hwy 77, until you're 4 miles west of Beatrice.

LINK YOUR TRIP

26 Black Hills Loop
It's a cornucopia of icons, colorful history and natural beauty on this trip. Take US-20 and then US-18 west through the Pine Ridge Reservation and then go north on scenic US-385.

27 The Mighty Mo
Follow in the tracks of famous explorers Lewis and Clark along America's longest river, which includes an iconic stretch in Nebraska. You can join the trip right in Omaha.

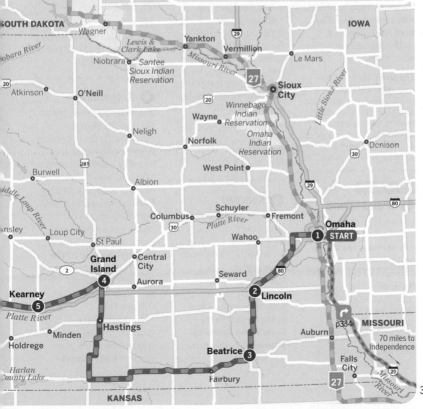

❸ Homestead National Monument of America

The **Homestead National Monument** (www.nps.gov/home; Hwy 4; ☻heritage center 9am-5pm) just north of Beatrice is on the site of the very first homestead granted under the landmark *Homestead Act of 1862,* which opened much of the US to settlers who received land for free if they made it productive. The pioneering Freeman family is buried here and you can see their reconstructed log house and hike the site. The heritage center is a striking building with good displays.

The Drive 》 An even 100 miles west on US 136 takes you through near ghost towns, where the solitary gas stations serve as town centers and quaint brick downtowns slowly crumble. Head north at Red Bluff and drive for 68 miles on US 281.

❹ Grand Island

For a wide-ranging introduction to pioneer life, spend a few hours at the 200-acre **Stuhr Museum of the Prairie Pioneer** (www.stuhrmuseum.org; I-80 exit 312, 3133 W Hwy 34; adult/child $8/6; ☻9am-5pm Mon-Sat, noon-5pm Sun) in Grand Island, Nebraska. In summer,

period reenactors go about their business in an 1890s railroad town, answering questions about their jobs and home life. Also on view is an 1860s log-cabin settlement, a one-room schoolhouse and a Pawnee earth lodge.

On the 2nd floor of the museum's Stuhr Building, a covered wagon overflows with furniture and clothes – an inspiring symbol of the pioneers' can-do optimism. A few steps away, a display of black-and-white photos of a primitive sod house and a prairie funeral depict the darker, harsher realities lurking behind the romance of the pioneer dream. Interesting fact? In 1880, 20% of Nebraska's population was foreign born, with most settlers emigrating from Germany, Sweden and Ireland.

The Drive 》 The leaves of cottonwoods shimmer in the sunlight on this lonely yet lush 42 miles of US 30.

❺ Kearney

A shimmering brown arch sweeps across four lanes of I-80 like an imposing medieval drawbridge. This horizon-breaking distraction – it depicts a setting Nebraska sun – is the **Great Platte River Road Archway Monument** (www.archway.org; adult/child $12/5; ☻9am-

6pm summer, reduced hours rest of year). A little bit hokey, a little bit history, it's a relentlessly cheery ode to the West that puts a high-tech, glossy spin on the pioneer journey and western travel, sweeping in everything from stampeding buffalo to the gold-seeking '49ers. The mini-adventure begins with a dramatic escalator ride up to the enclosed, two-story bridge.

Kearney's compact, cute and walkable downtown, near US 30 and the busy Union Pacific (UP) mainline, has good cafes and bars.

✕ ⊨ p335

The Drive 》 Count the corn silos and see if they outnumber the passing trains along the next 60 miles of US 30.

❻ Gothenburg

The Pony Express (1860–61) was the FedEx of its day, using a fleet of young riders and swift horses to carry letters between Missouri and California in an astounding 10 days. Each horseman rode full-bore for almost six hours – changing horses every 10 miles – before passing the mail to the next rider. Their route through Nebraska generally followed the Oregon Trail.

In Gothenburg, step inside what some researchers think is an original **Pony Express**

Station (www.ci.gothenburg. ne.us; 1500 Lake Ave, Gothenburg, NE; ☺8am-8pm Jun-Aug, shorter hours rest of year; ♿), one of just a few still in existence. The engaging array of artifacts includes a mochila, the rider's mail-holding saddlebag. Afterwards, wander a few of the streets downtown lined with beautiful old Victorian houses. Buy one for a song and stay awhile.

The Drive » A never-ending procession of UP trains zip along the world's busiest freight line for the next 36 miles of US 30.

TRIP HIGHLIGHT

❼ North Platte

North Platte, a rail-fan mecca, is home to the **Buffalo Bill Ranch State Historical Park** (www. outdoornebraska.ne.gov; 2921 Scouts Rest Ranch Rd; house adult/child $2/1, vehicle permit $5; ☺9am-5pm daily summer, to 4pm Mon-Fri mid-Mar–May & Sep–mid-Oct), 2 miles north of US 30. Once the home of Bill Cody – an iconic figure of the American West and the father of rodeo and the famed Wild West Show – it has a fun museum that reflects his colorful life.

Enjoy sweeping views of UP's **Bailey Yard**, the world's largest railroad yard, from the **Golden Spike Tower** (www. goldenspiketower.com; 1249 N Homestead Rd; adult/child $7/5; ☺9am-7pm Mon-Sat, from 1pm Sun summer, to 5pm

TOP TIP: AVOID I-80

America's top transcontinental highway, I-80 zips across Nebraska for 455 miles. But while it speeds travelers on their way, it does the state no favors with its endless succession of exits populated with gaudy generic chains and nary a hint of the highlights and pleasures that lie beyond the interchanges.

But for the entire length of I-80, you have fine alternatives in fascinating two-lane roads just to the north. Take US 6 out of Omaha to Lincoln, US 34 on the Grand Island and then the best stretch of all, historic US 30 all the way to Wyoming.

You'll hug the lush Platte River valley for much of this route and bounce through the hearts of a succession of picturesque small towns such as Gothenburg. Fast trains on the busy parallel Union Pacific (UP) main line pace your progress. Think of it as a grad-school version of Route 66.

rest of year), an eight-story observation tower with indoor and outdoor decks.

The Drive » Set the cruise control on 'chill' as you drive a straight line 52 miles due west on US 30.

❽ Ogallala

Set your clocks to mountain time just west of Sutherland. Ogallala was once known as the 'Gomorrah of the Cattle Trail'. It now has all the salacious charm of a motel's nightstand bible.

The Oregon and California trails turn north near here, following the Platte River toward Wyoming and the wild blue yonder.

The Drive » Cornfields give way to untamed prairie grasses and desolate bluffs on two-lane

US 26, known as Nebraska's Western Trails Historic & Scenic Byway. Look right soon after leaving Ogallala to glimpse sparkling Lake McConaughy through the low hills. Otherwise, cattle herds, passing trains with coal from Wyoming and tumbleweed towns are the biggest distractions for the next 101 miles.

❾ Chimney Rock National Historic Site

Heading west, centuries-old bluff formations rise up from the horizon, their striking presence a visual link connecting modern-day travelers (and Oregon Trail gamers) with their pioneer forebears. One of these links is Chimney Rock, located inside the **Chimney Rock National Historic Site**

(📞308-586-2581; www.nps. gov/chro; Chimney Rock Rd, Bayard, NE; adult/child with parent $3/free; 🕐9am-5pm; ♿). It's visible 12 miles after Bridgeport off Hwy 92. Chimney Rock's fragile 120ft spire was an inspiring landmark for pioneers, and it was mentioned in hundreds of journals. It also marked the end of the first leg of the journey and the beginning of the tough – but final – push to the coast.

The Drive ⟫ Stay on Hwy 92 for 21 miles west after Chimney Rock. As you enter Gering, just south of the city of Scottsbluff, continue straight onto M St which leads to Old Oregon Trail Rd. It follows the actual route of the trail and leads straight to Scotts Bluff National Monument after just 3 miles.

TRIP HIGHLIGHT

❿ Scotts Bluff National Monument

Spend a few minutes in the visitors center of this picturesque **monument** (www.nps.gov/scbl; Gering, NE; per car $5; 🕐visitor center 9am-5pm; ♿) run by the National Park Service – there's a nice collection of Western art in the William Henry Jackson Gallery – then hit the trail. You can hike the 1.6-mile **Saddle Rock Trail** (one way) or drive the same distance up to the South Overlook for bird's-eye views of Mitchell Pass.

Before you leave, spend a few moments hiking the trail through Mitchell Pass itself. The covered wagons on display here look unnervingly frail as you peer through the bluff-flanked gateway, a narrow channel that spills onto the Rocky Mountain–bumping plains. For pioneers, reaching this pass was a significant milestone; it marked the completion of 600 miles of Great Plains trekking.

🍴 p335

The Drive ⟫ From Scottsbluff, we leave the Great Platte River Rd and head north to a historic military fort and a lonely trading post, important bastions that paved the way for long-term settlers. Along the way, revel in Nebraska's prairie, which is aptly described as a 'sea of grass'. This analogy proves true on the 52-mile drive north on Hwy 71.

⓫ Sioux County

Prairie grasses bend and bob as strong winds sweep over 360 degrees of low-rolling hills, punctuated by the occasional wooden windmill or lonely cell-phone tower as you drive through Sioux County, named for the Plains tribe that hunted and traveled throughout Nebraska.

Enjoy the drive, this is roll-down-your-window-and-breathe-in-America country.

The Drive ⟫ Like bristles on the visage of a trail-weary pioneer, trees begin appearing amid the rolling grasslands as you head north for 27 miles on Hwy 2.

GO WEST!

An estimated 400,000 people trekked west across America between 1840 and 1860, lured by tales of gold, promises of religious freedom and visions of fertile farmland. They were also inspired by the expansionist credo of President James Polk and the rallying cry of New York editor John O'Sullivan, who urged Americans in 1845 to 'overspread the continent allotted by Providence for the free development of our yearly multiplying millions'.

These starry-eyed pioneers became the foot soldiers of 'manifest destiny', eager to pursue their own dreams while furthering America's expansionist goals. The movement's success depended on the safe, reliable passage of these foot soldiers through the Great Plains and beyond. The California, Oregon and Mormon pioneer trails served this purpose well, successfully channeling the travelers and their 'prairie schooners' on defined routes across the country.

North Platte Buffalo Bill Ranch State Historical Park

⑫ Fort Robinson State Park

Sioux warrior Crazy Horse was fatally stabbed on the grounds of Fort Robinson, now **Fort Robinson State Park** (www.outdoornebraska. ne.gov; Hwy 20; per vehicle $5; ☉ sunrise-sunset), on September 5, 1877, at the age of 35. The fort – in operation between 1874 and 1948 – was the area's most important military post during the Indian Wars.

In summer, visitors descend on the 22,000-acre park for stagecoach rides, steak cookouts, trout fishing and hiking. There are two museums on the grounds, the Fort Robinson Museum and the Trailside Museum, as well as the reconstructed Guardhouse where Crazy Horse spent his final hours.

The Drive » If you prefer your historic digs in an urban setting, drive 20 miles east to Chadron.

⑬ Chadron

Chadron's **Museum of the Fur Trade** (www.furtrade. org; off US 20; adult/child $5/ free; ☉ 8am-5pm May-Oct) is a well-curated tribute to the mountain men

DETOUR: INDEPENDENCE, MO

Start: ❶ Omaha

Long associated with colorful US president Harry S Truman, Independence, Missouri, was also a popular jumping-off point for pioneers preparing to follow the Oregon and California trails. For an enjoyable history of these two trails and others, spend an hour or two at the city's **National Trails Museum** (www.frontiertrailsmuseum.org). Exhibits include a wall-sized map of the major trail routes, a mock general store and diary entries from the pioneers.

Independence is near Kansas City, 200 miles south of Omaha off I-29.

and trappers who paved the way for the pioneers. For a small museum, it holds a fascinating array of artifacts: from 1820s mountain-man leggings and hand-forged animal traps to blankets, pelts and liquor bottles. Kit Carson's shotgun is displayed beside the world's largest collection of Native American trade guns.

In back, there's a reproduction of the Bordeaux Trading Post; it was in operation here from 1837 to 1876. The harsh reality of life on the plains is evident the moment you step inside the squat, unnervingly cramped building. Though it's not the original structure, the reproduction is so precisely done it's listed on the National Register of Historic Places.

The Drive ›› Continue east to the Sandhills for 77 miles on US 20, known as the Bridges to Buttes Byway. The little towns along here are just hanging on amid the buttes, canyons and rolling hills of the often-dramatic landscape.

- - - - - - - - - - - - -

❶❹ Arthur Bowring Sandhills Ranch State Historical Park

The hardscrabble lives of Nebraskan ranchers is faithfully recalled at this preserved 1920s ranch near the South Dakota border. Owned by the Bowring clan, it includes an early sod house which easily makes clear that *any* farm house was a major step up.

Still, you'll find comforts here as Eva Bowring, who lived here for much of her long life, collected crystal, china and some antique furniture that must have old-house-owners drooling. Her story is an interesting one: in 1954 she took a break from chasing cows to ride

herd in the US Senate where she served for a brief period after another Senator died.

The Drive ›› Keep the camera ready for moody shots of lonely windmills amid the sandy bluffs on the 60 miles west on US 20 to Valentine.

- - - - - - - - - - - - -

❶❺ Valentine

What better way to immerse yourself in a timeless Nebraska from before the pioneer days than floating down a scenic river – especially on a steamy summer day.

Valentine sits on the edge of the Sandhills and is a great base for canoeing, kayaking and inner-tubing the winding canyons of the federally protected **Niobrara National Scenic River** (www.nps.gov/niob). The river crosses the **Fort Niobrara National Wildlife Refuge** (www.fws.gov/fortniobrara; Hwy 12; ⊙ visitor center 8am-4:30pm daily Jun-Aug, Mon-Fri Sep-May). Driving tours take you past bison, elk and more.

Floating down the river draws scores of people through the summer. Sheer limestone bluffs, lush forests and spring-fed waterfalls along the banks shatter any 'flat Nebraska' stereotypes. Most float tours are based in Valentine (www.visitvalentine.com).

🛏 p335

Eating & Sleeping

Omaha 1

Ted & Wally's Ice Cream Ice Cream $

(www.tedandwallys.com; 1120 Jackson St; ice cream from $3; ⌚11am-10pm) Ultra-creamy ice cream in myriad flavors made fresh daily.

Bronco's Burgers $

(4540 Leavenworth St; mains $4-7; ⌚7am-11pm) Classic local burger joint with a great neon sign and a few tables scattered inside and out. Everything, including the burgers, is ultrafresh.

Upstream Brewing Company American $$

(☎402-344-0200; 514 S 11th St; mains $10-30; ⌚11am-1am) In a big old firehouse, the beer here is also big on flavor. The Caesar salads have enough garlic to propel you over the Missouri to Iowa. Steaks are thick and up to local standards. There are sidewalk tables, a rooftop deck and a huge bar.

Magnolia Hotel Historic Hotel $$

(☎402-341-2500; www.magnoliahotelomaha.com; 1615 Howard St; r $130-200; ❄@📶🐾) Not far from Old Market, the Magnolia is a boutique hotel housed in a restored 1923 Italianate high-rise. The 145 rooms have a vibrant, modern style. Rates include a full buffet breakfast and bedtime milk and cookies.

Lincoln 2

Indigo Bridge Cafe $

(701 P St; mains under $5; ⌚8am-10pm; 📶) This fine cafe in a fantastic bookstore serves coffees and snacks through the day. At lunch (Monday, Wednesday and Friday), enjoy hearty organic soup and bread and pay what you can afford.

Yia Yia's Pizza Pizzeria $$

(1423 O St; mains $8-15; ⌚11am-1pm Mon-Sat, 11am-9pm Sun) Many a hangover has been chased away by the cheesy, gooey goodness here at this Lincoln legend. The pizzas are cracker-thin; the regional beer list thick. Sit at a sidewalk table or inside amid the gregarious college crowd.

Rogers House B&B $$

(☎402-476-6961; www.rogershouseinn.com; 2145 B St; r $90-170; ❄📶) Close to downtown, the 11 rooms here are spread out over two 100-year-old houses. Refreshingly, the decor eschews the froufrou silliness of many B&Bs.

Kearney 5

Thunderhead Brewing Co American

(www.thunderheadbrewing.com; 18 E 21st St; mains $5-10; ⌚noon-1am) The place for good IPAs and pizza.

Midtown Western Inn Motel $

(☎308-237-3153; www.midtownwesterninn.com; 1401 2nd Ave; r $50-80; ❄📶🏊) A good indie choice near downtown, this vintage motel has huge, clean rooms.

Scottsbluff 10

Emporium Coffeehouse & Café American $$

(www.emporiumdining.com; 1818 1st Ave; mains $7-30; ⌚7am-10pm, to 3pm Sun, to 5pm Mon) This umbrella-fronted vintage house in downtown Scottsbluff is a regional gem. Great meals from breakfasts to late-night sandwiches are served. The wine and spirits list has more than 100 selections.

Valentine 15

Trade Winds Motel Motel $

(☎402-376-1600; www.tradewindslodge.com; 1009 E US 20/83; r $50-100; ❄📶🏊) The classic red-brick Trade Winds Motel has 32 comfy and clean rooms with fridges and microwaves. It's a great indie choice.

Mt Rushmore *Meet the giants of American history*

Classic Trip

Black Hills Loop

26

Shaggy bison lumber across the plains. Giant monuments praise great men. Windswept prairies unfurl below towering mountains. This drive embraces the region's heritage in all its messy glory.

TRIP HIGHLIGHTS

1 mile

Rapid City
A surprising city with great food and drink

Spearfish

Lead **10**

192 miles

Deadwood
Relive the Wild West in this gold rush town

1 START/FINISH

Hill City

3

4

Jewel Cave
National Monument

Wind Cave
National Park

**Mt Rushmore
National Memorial**
The familiar icon is stunning in person

24 miles

**Peter Norbeck
Scenic Byway**
A roller-coaster ride through beautiful scenery

27 miles

**2 – 3 DAYS
265 MILES / 426KM**

GREAT FOR...

BEST TIME TO GO
May to September, when all sights are open.

**ESSENTIAL
PHOTO**

Any angle that puts a new angle on the four mugs at Mt Rushmore.

**BEST FOR
OUTDOORS**

Where the buffalo roam is just the start of critter-filled days amid beautiful scenery.

26 Black Hills Loop

In the early 1800s, 60 million buffalo roamed the plains. Rampant overhunting decimated their ranks and by 1889 fewer than 1000 remained. Today, their numbers have climbed to 250,000; several Black Hills parks manage healthy herds. On this tour you'll see the iconic buffalo and other legendary sights, including the Badlands, Mt Rushmore, the Crazy Horse Memorial, sprawling parks and the town made famous for having no law at all: Deadwood.

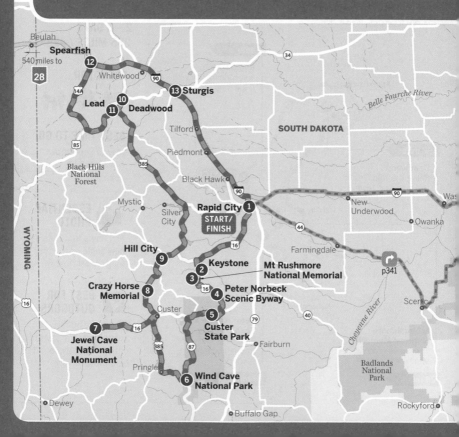

❶ Rapid City

A worthy capital to the region, 'Rapid' has an intriguing, lively and walkable downtown. Well-preserved brick buildings, filled with quality shops and places to dine, make it a good urban base and hub for your looping tour. Get a walking-tour brochure of Rapid's historic buildings and public art from the visitor center. Check out the watery fun on **Main St Square**.

280 miles to

27

Wall

14

Cottonwood

90

Buffalo Gap
National
Grassland

dlands
ational
Park

240

44   *White River*

Cedar
Pass

44

*Pine Ridge Indian
Reservation*

Cheyenne River

While strolling, don't miss the **Statues of Presidents** (www.cityofpresidents.com; 631 Main St; ⊘info center noon-9pm Mon-Sat Jun-Sep) on downtown street corners. From a shifty-eyed Nixon in repose to a triumphant Harry Truman, lifelike statues dot corners throughout the center. Collect all 42.

Learn about how dramatic natural underground events over the eons have produced some stellar rocks. See these plus dinosaur bones and some stellar fossils at the **Museum of Geology** (www.museum.sdsmt.edu; 501 E St Joseph St, O'Harra Bldg; ⊘9am-5pm Mon-Fri, to 6pm Sat, noon-5pm Sun summer, 9am-4pm Mon-Fri, 10am-4pm Sat rest of year), located at the South Dakota School of Mines & Technology.

✕ ⬦ p346

The Drive ❯❯ Choose from the commercial charms on Hwys 16 and 16A on the 21-mile drive to Keystone.

❷ Keystone

One indisputable fact about the Black Hills? It will always, always, always take longer than you think to reach a key attraction. Trust us. Slow-moving Winnebagos, serpentine byways and kitschy roadside distractions will deaden your pace. And the distractions start early on Hwy 16 where family-friendly and delightfully hokey tourist attractions vie for dollars on the way to Mt Rushmore, including the animal-happy **Bear Country USA** (www.bearcountryusa.com; Hwy 16; adult/child $16/10; ⊘8am-6pm summer, reduced hours rest of year, closed winter; ⊞) and **Reptile Gardens** (www.reptilegardens.com; Hwy 16; adult/child $16/11; ⊘8am-6pm summer, reduced hours rest of year, closed winter; ⊞).

Kitsch reigns supreme in Keystone, a gaudy town bursting with rah-rah patriotism, Old West spirit and too many fudgeries. The fuss is

---

🔗 LINK YOUR TRIP

27 The Mighty Mo
Join the route in Pierre, SD, a 170-mile trip east of Rapid City via I-29 plus scenic legs on US 14 and Hwy 34.

28 Grand Teton to Yellowstone
More great American parks are west through Montana.

directly attributable to its proximity to Mt Rushmore 2 miles west.

 p346

The Drive » It's a mere 3-mile jaunt uphill to Mt Rushmore. Keep yours eyes peeled for the first glimpse of a prez.

- - - - - - - - - -

TRIP HIGHLIGHT

❸ Mt Rushmore National Memorial

Glimpses of Washington's nose from the roads leading to this hugely popular monument never cease to surprise and are but harbingers of the full impact of this mountainside sculpture once you're up close (and past the less impressive parking area and entrance walk). George Washington, Thomas Jefferson, Abraham Lincoln and Theodore Roosevelt each iconically stare into the distance in 60ft-tall granite glory.

It's hugely popular, but you can easily escape the crowds and fully appreciate **Mt Rushmore** (www.nps.gov/moru; off Hwy 244; parking $11; ⊙8am-10pm summer, 8am-5pm rest of year) while marveling at the artistry of sculptor Gutzon Borglum and the immense labor of the workers who created the

memorial between 1927 and 1941.

The **Presidential Trail** loop passes right below the monument for some fine nostril views and gives you access to the worthwhile Sculptor's Studio. Start clockwise and you're right under Washington's nose in under five minutes. The **nature trail** to the right as you face the entrance connects the viewing and parking areas, passing through a pine forest and avoiding the crowds and commercialism.

The official Park Service information centers have excellent bookstores with proceeds going to the park. Avoid the schlocky Xanterra gift shop and the disappointing Carvers Cafe, which looked much better in the scene where Cary Grant gets plugged in *North by Northwest*. The main **museum** is far from comprehensive but the fascinating **Sculptor's Studio** conveys the drama of how the monument came to be.

The Drive » Backtrack slightly from Mt Rushmore and head southwest for the 16 miles of thrills on the Iron Mountain Rd.

- - - - - - - - - -

TRIP HIGHLIGHT

❹ Peter Norbeck Scenic Byway

Driving the 66-mile Peter Norbeck Scenic Byway is like flirting with a brand-new crush:

always exhilarating, occasionally challenging and sometimes you get a few butterflies. Named for the South Dakota Senator who pushed for its creation in 1919, the oval-shaped byway is broken into four roads linking the most memorable destinations in the Black Hills (drivers of large RVs should call Custer State Park for tunnel measurements).

Iron Mountain Rd (Hwy 16A) is the real star, beloved for its pigtailing loops, Mt Rushmore–framing tunnels and one gorgeous glide through sun-dappled pines. It's a 16-mile roller coaster of wooden bridges, virtual loop-the-loops, narrow tunnels and stunning vistas. Expect lots of drivers going even slower than you are.

The 14-mile **Needles Hwy** (Hwy 87) swoops below granite spires, careens past rocky overlooks and slings though a super-narrow tunnel.

The Drive » Once past the Iron Mountain Rd, other Peter Norbeck Scenic Byway options aside, it is only 3 miles along Hwy 16 west to the Custer State Park visitor center.

- - - - - - - - - -

❺ Custer State Park

The only reason 111-sq-mile **Custer State Park** (www.custerstatepark.info; 7-day pass per car $15) isn't a national park is that

DETOUR:
BADLANDS NATIONAL PARK & MORE

Start: ❶ Rapid City

More than 600 buffalo, also known as North American bison, roam **Badlands National Park** (☎605-433-5361; www.nps.gov/badl; Hwy 240; 7-day pass per person/carload $7/15; ⊗Ben Reifel Visitor Center 7am-7pm summer, 8am-5pm spring & fall, 9am-4pm winter; ⚿). The name originated with French trappers and the Lakota Sioux, who described the park's jagged spires and crumbling buttes as 'bad lands'. Today, this crumbling former floodplain is visually compelling, its corrugated hillsides enlivened by a palette of reds and pinks.

You can see the eroding rocks up close on the **Notch Trail**, a 1.5-mile (round-trip) leg stretcher that twists through a canyon, scampers up a wooden ladder then curves along a crumbly ridgeline to an expansive view of grasslands and more serrated walls. At the **Ben Reifel Visitor Center** just down the road, a visually stunning film captures the park's natural diversity with jaw-dropping close-ups of the plants and animals that thrive in the mixed-grass prairie.

From Rapid City, head about 50 miles east on I-90, where **Badlands Loop Rd** (Hwy 240) links with I-90 at exits 131 and 110. The loop stretches west from the visitors center into the park's north unit, curving along a narrow ridge of buttes known as the Badlands Wall. It can be driven in an hour, but stopping at the numerous overlooks can easily fill a morning. Exit 110 off I-90 also serves Wall, home to the eponymous **Wall Drug** (www.walldrug.com; 510 Main St; ⊗6:30am-6pm, extended hours in summer; ⚿), one of the world's great – and unmissable – tourist traps.

To avoid I-90 back to Rapid City, pick up Hwy 44. Jagged bluffs give way to rolling prairie on this made-for-convertibles byway that swings through the **Buffalo Gap National Grassland** (www.fs.fed.us/grasslands; 798 Main St, Wall; ⊗8am-4:30pm Mon-Fri) on its way west.

the state grabbed it first. It boasts one of the largest free-roaming bison herds in the world (about 1500), the famous 'begging burros' (donkeys seeking handouts) and more than 200 bird species. Other wildlife include elk, pronghorns, mountain goats, bighorn sheep, coyotes, prairie dogs, mountain lions and bobcats. Meandering over awesome stone bridges and across sublime alpine meadows, the 18-mile **Wildlife Loop Road** allows plenty of spotting.

The **Peter Norbeck Visitor Center** (☎605-255-4464; www.custerstatepark.info; US 16A; ⊗8am-8pm summer, 9am-5pm rest of year), situated on the eastern side of the park, contains good exhibits and offers gold-panning demonstrations and guided nature walks. The nearby **Black Hills Playhouse** (www.blackhillsplayhouse.com; adult/child $32/15; ⊗schedule varies Jun–mid-Aug) hosts summer theater.

Hiking through the pine-covered hills and prairie grassland is a great way to see wildlife and rock formations. **Trails** through Sylvan Lake Shore, Sunday Gulch, Cathedral Spires and French Creek Natural Area are all highly recommended.

The park is named for the notorious George A Custer, who led a scientific expedition into the Black Hills in 1874. The expedition's discovery of gold drew so many new settlers that an 1868 treaty granting the Sioux a 60-million-acre reservation in the area was eventually broken. Crazy Horse and

Classic Trip

DANITA DELIMONT / GETTY IMAGES ©

WHY THIS IS A CLASSIC TRIP
RYAN VER BERKMOES, AUTHOR

From the moment you catch a glimpse of George Washington's nose poking out between a couple of pine trees, you are in for one surprise after another in South Dakota's beautiful Black Hills. There are thrills: the drive through the twists and turns of the Iron Mountain Road are like a Disney ride; and there's the wild and woolly: the Deadwood cemetery's graves of notorious characters including Calamity Jane.

Top: Badlands National Park
Left: Cowboy hats for sale
Right: Prairie dog

the Lakotas retaliated, killing Custer and 265 of his men at Montana's Battle of the Little Big Horn in 1876.

🛏 p346

The Drive ›› Near the western edge of Custer State Park, head due south on Hwy 87 for 19 miles from US 16. It's beautiful ride through a long swath of wilderness and park.

- - - - - - - - - - -

⑥ Wind Cave National Park

This park, protecting 44 sq miles of grassland and forest, sits just south of Custer State Park. The central feature is, of course, the cave, which contains 132 miles of mapped passages. The cave's foremost feature is its 'boxwork' calcite formations (95% of all that are known exist here), which look like honeycomb and date back 60 to 100 million years. The strong gusts of wind that are felt at the entrance, but not inside, give the cave its name. For an introduction to the cave's history and geology, wander the exhibits at the **visitor center** (www.nps.gov/wica; ⊙9am-6pm summer, reduced hours rest of year) prior to one of the ranger-led cave **tours** (☎reservations 605-745-4600; adult $7-23, child $3.50-4.50) (most are one to 1½ hours; the four-hour Wild Cave Tour offers an orgy of spelunking).

Classic Trip

Not all of the park's treasures are underground. Wind Cave's above-ground acres abound with bison and prairie dogs.

The Drive ≫ Scenic drives continue as you go from one big hole in the ground to another. Jewel Cave is 38 miles northwest on US 385 and US 16.

➐ Jewel Cave National Monument

Another of the Black Hills' many fascinating caves is Jewel Cave, 13 miles west of Custer on US 16, so named because calcite crystals line nearly all of its walls. Currently 168 miles have been surveyed, making it the third-longest known cave in the world, but it is presumed to be the longest. **Tours** (adult $4-27, child free-$4) range in length and difficulty and are offered on a first-come basis. Make arrangements at the **visitor center** (www.nps.gov/jeca; ⊙8am-5:30pm summer, to 4:30pm rest of year).

The Drive ≫ Retrace your route for 13 miles until US 385 joins US 16 and then go north for 5 miles.

➑ Crazy Horse Memorial

The world's largest monument, the **Crazy Horse Memorial** (www.crazyhorsememorial.org; US 385; per person/car $10/27; ⊙8am-dusk summer, to 5pm rest of year), is a 563ft-tall work-in-progress. When finished it will depict the Sioux leader astride his horse, pointing to the horizon saying, 'My lands are where my dead lie buried.'

Never photographed or persuaded to sign a meaningless treaty, Crazy Horse was chosen for a monument that Lakota Sioux elders hoped would balance the presidential focus of Mt Rushmore. In 1948 a Boston-born sculptor, the indefatigable Korczak Ziolkowski, started blasting granite. His family have continued the work since his death in 1982. (It should be noted that many Native Americans oppose the monument as desecration of sacred land.)

No one is predicting when the sculpture will be complete (the face was dedicated in 1998). A rather thrilling laser-light show tells the tales of the monument on summer evenings.

The visitor center complex includes a Native American museum, a cultural center, cafes and Ziolkowski's studio.

The Drive ≫ It's a short 10-mile drive north on US 16/385 to the refreshments of Hill City.

➒ Hill City

One of the most appealing towns up in the hills, **Hill City** (www.hillcitysd.com) is less frenzied than places such as Keystone. Its main drag has cafes and galleries.

The **1880 Train** (www.1880train.com; 222 Railroad Ave; adult/child round-trip $28/12; ⊙early May–mid-Oct) is a classic steam train running through rugged country to and from Keystone. An interesting little train museum is next door.

✕ 🛏 p346

The Drive ≫ Lakes, rivers, meadows and a few low-key tourist traps enliven the 42 miles on US 385 to Deadwood through the heart of the Black Hills.

TRIP HIGHLIGHT

➓ Deadwood

'No law at all in Deadwood, is that true?' So began the iconic HBO TV series. Today things have changed, although the 80 gambling halls, big and small, would no doubt put a sly grin on the faces of the hard characters who founded the town.

Deadwood's atmospheric streets are lined with gold-rush-era buildings lavishly restored with gambling dollars. Its storied past is easy to find at its museums and cemeteries. There's eternal devotion

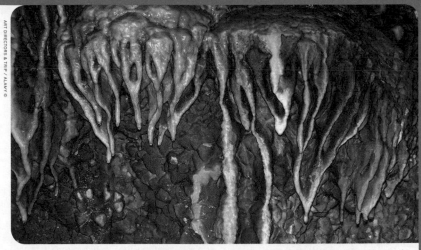

ART DIRECTORS & TRIP / ALAMY ©

Jewel Cave National Monument

to Wild Bill Hickok, who was shot in the back of the head here in 1876 while gambling.

Actors reenact famous **shootouts** (⊘2pm, 4pm & 6pm Jun-Aug) on Main St during summer. **Hickok's murder** (657 Main St; ⊘1pm, 3pm, 5pm & 7pm Jun–mid-Sep) is acted out in Saloon No 10. A trial of the killer takes place in the **Masonic Temple** (cnr Main & Pine Sts).

✗ ⊨ p347

The Drive » Lead is just 4 miles uphill from Deadwood, through land scarred by generations hunting for gold.

- - - - - - - - - - -

⑪ Lead

Lead (pronounced *leed*) has an unrestored charm and still bears plenty of scars from the mining era. Gape at the 1250ft-deep **Homestake gold mine** (☎605-584-3110;

www.homestaketour.com; 160 W Main St; viewing area free, tours adult/child $7.50/6.50; ⊘tours 9am-4pm May-Sep) to see what open-pit mining can do to a mountain. Nearby are the same mine's shafts, which plunge more than 1.5 miles below the surface and are now being used for physics research.

⊨ p347

The Drive » Climb out of steep canyons for 11 miles on US 14A until you plunge back down into Spearfish Canyon.

- - - - - - - - - - -

⑫ Spearfish

Spearfish Canyon Scenic Byway (www.byways.org; US 14A) is a waterfall-lined, curvaceous 20-mile road that cleaves from the heart of the hills into Spearfish. There's a sight worth stopping for around every bend; pause for longer than a minute

and you'll hear beavers hard at work.

⊨ p347

The Drive » It's a quick 22 miles east on I-90 to Sturgis. That solitary headlight in the rearview mirror is a hog hoping to blow past. From Sturgis back to Rapid City is only 36 miles.

- - - - - - - - - - -

⑬ Sturgis

Fast food, Christian iconography and billboards for glitzy biker bars featuring dolled-up models unlikely to ever be found on the back of a hog are just some of the cacophony of images of this tacky small town on I-90 (exits 30 and 32). Things get even louder for the annual **Sturgis Motorcycle Rally** (www. sturgismotorcyclerally.com; ⊘early Aug), when around 500,000 riders, fans and curious onlookers take over the town.

Eating & Sleeping

Rapid City ❶

✕ Murphy's Pub & Grill   American $$

(www.murphyspubandgrill.com; 510 9th St;
mains $6-20; ⏲ food 11am-10pm, bar to 1am)
Pub fare with creative flair makes this bustling
downtown bar an excellent dining choice,
especially for salads, burgers and pasta.
Specials feature seasonal and local ingredients.
The vast terrace is matched by the big interior.

✕ Tally's   American $$

(530 6th St; mains $6-20; ⏲7am-9pm Mon-Thu,
to 10pm Fri & Sat) Carter or Reagan? Both
statues are out front and you can ponder your
preference while you savor the upscale diner
fare at this stylish cafe and bar. Breakfasts are
as good as ever; more creative regional fare is
on offer at night.

✕ Independent Ale House   Pub

(www.independentalehouse.com; 625 St
Joseph St; ⏲3pm-late) Enjoy a fabulous (and
changing) line-up of the best microbrews from
the region in this vintage-style bar. There are
chairs on the sidewalk and a short snack menu
that features individual-sized pizzas.

🛏 Town House Motel   Motel $$

(☎605-342-8143; www.blackhillsmotels.
com; 210 St Joseph St; r $60-110; ❄🛜🏊) A
classic yet clean 40-room motel within walking
distance of all the downtown joys. The exterior
corridors in the two-story blocks of rooms
overlook the parking area and pool.

🛏 Hotel Alex Johnson   Hotel $$

(☎605-342-1210; www.alexjohnson.com; 523
6th St; r $60-200; ❄@🛜) The design of
this 1927 classic magically blends Germanic
Tudor architecture and traditional Lakota Sioux
symbols – note the lobby's painted ceiling and
the chandelier made of war lances. The 127
rooms are modern and slightly posh but the real

appeal here is that it hasn't been turned into a
boutique hotel. Its timeless qualities include a
portrait of guest Al Capone near the front desk.
The rooftop bar is a delight.

🛏 Adoba Eco Hotel   Hotel $$

(☎605-348-8300; www.adobahotelrapidcity.
com; 445 Mt Rushmore Rd; r $80-200;
❄@🛜🏊) A former high-rise Radisson has
been reborn as a high-concept downtown hotel
with green accents. Furniture is made from
recycled materials yet there's no skimping
on comfort. The marble floor in the lobby is a
stunner.

Keystone ❷

✕ Teddy's Deli   Deli $

(236 Winter St; mains from $5; ⏲9am-9pm
summer, shorter hours rest of year) Best
sandwiches in the region, far better than what
you'll get at nearby Mt Rushmore. And if you're
in the mood for dessert, Keystone doesn't lack
for fudge.

Custer State Park ❺

🛏 Custer State Park Resorts   Resort

(☎888-875-0001; www.custerresorts.com) The
park has four impressive resorts with a mix of
lodge rooms and cabins starting at $95 and going
much higher. Book well ahead. The Blue Bell
Lodge includes a one-room rustic cabin that's a
hit with nature-lovers with an inner grizzly.

Hill City ❾

✕ Desperados   American $$

(301 Main St; mains $9-20; ⏲11:30am-9pm)
Dine amid frontier charm in rustic surrounds on
the town's main drag. Have the burger. Service
is quick and casual.

🛏 Lantern Inn   Motel $$

(📞605-574-2582; www.lanterninn.com; 580 E Main St; r $70-130; ❄🛜🏊) Lantern Inn is an 18-room motel-style place spread over two stories fronting attractive grounds. Think of Jefferson's huge granite nose while you're enjoying a blissful end-of-day float in the pool.

🛏 Alpine Inn   Historic Hotel $$

(📞605-574-2749; www.alpineinnhillcity.com; 133 Main St; r $80-160) Right in the center of the city, the Alpine Inn dates to 1886 and has comfy rooms in bright red. You can't get more central, and the historic train is a short walk away. Rock yourself silly on the porch. It also serves filling German fare.

Deadwood ⑩

🍴 Midnight Star   Steak $$

(📞605-578-1555; 677 Main St; mains $15-40; ⏰food 8am-10pm) Owned by actor Kevin Costner, this attractive boozer and casino displays costumes and photos from Costner's movies. The restaurant serves pricey steaks.

🍴 Saloon No 10   Bar $$

(www.saloon10.com; 657 Main St; mains $10-25; ⏰food noon-10pm, bar 8am-2am) Dark paneled walls and sawdust on the floor are features of this storied bar. The original, where Hickok literally lost big time, stood across the street, but the building burned to the ground and the owners brought the bar over here. There's a rooftop and decent Italian-accented food.

🛏 Bullock Hotel   Historic Hotel $$

(📞605-578-1745; www.historicbullock.com; 633 Main St; r $75-160; ❄🛜) Fans of the TV show will recall the conflicted but upstanding sheriff Seth Bullock. This hotel was opened by the real Bullock in 1895. The 28 rooms are modern and comfortable while retaining the period charm of the building.

🛏 Deadwood Dick's   Hotel $$

(📞605-578-3224; www.deadwooddicks.com; 51 Sherman St; r $60-160; ❄🛜) These home-style and idiosyncratic rooms feature furniture from the owner's ground-floor antique shop and range in size from small doubles to large suites with kitchens. The characterful bar on the ground floor abuts the shop.

Lead ⑪

🛏 Main Street Manor Hostel   Hostel $

(📞605-717-2044; www.mainstreetmanorhostel. com; 515 W Main St; per person/d $25/50; ⏰closed Dec & Jan; ❄🛜) This hostel in a house is a gem in its own right. Guests get use of the kitchen, garden and laundry at this very friendly place. You can stretch the legs on hilly climbs in all directions.

Spearfish ⑫

🛏 Spearfish Canyon Lodge   Lodge $$

(📞605-584-3435; www.spfcanyon.com; US 14A; r $90-220; ❄🛜🏊) For a rural retreat, this lodge is a mere 13 miles south of Spearfish near trails and streams. The massive lobby fireplace adds charm and the 54 modern piney rooms are cozy.

Bison *The Missouri and its tributaries support plentiful wildlife*

The Mighty Mo

27

Follow the course of North America's longest river as it runs past great cities, evocative wilderness and sites embedded in US history.

1388 miles

Williston
The Missouri meets the
Yellowstone in a mighty
river confluence

13 FINISH

12 **Bismark**

1219 miles

Stanton
Visit the village site
where Lewis and Clark
met Sacagawea

Pierre

Sioux City

Omaha

309 miles

Kansas City
Jazz, barbecue and
great neighborhoods
make KC hard to leave

4

START
1

1 mile

St Louis
The landmark arch
recalls Lewis and Clark
and their adventure west

**7 DAYS
1388 MILES /
2234KM**

GREAT FOR...

BEST TIME TO GO
May to September,
when all the sights are
open.

 ESSENTIAL PHOTO
Any shot that shows
the Missouri River's
impressive girth.

 BEST FOR HISTORY
Much of America's 19th-
century sense of self
was formed by events
along the river.

27 | The Mighty Mo

In 1804–05, Lewis and Clark followed the Missouri River during the first stages of their legendary journey west. With their Corps of Discovery, they canoed up the river, meeting Native Americans – some friendly, others hostile – and discovering vast expanses of land, untouched for eons and teeming with wildlife. Exploring the river today, you can make your very own discoveries.

TRIP HIGHLIGHT

❶ St Louis

Slide into St Louis and revel in the unique vibe of the largest city in the Great Plains. Beer, bowling and baseball are some of the top attractions, but history and culture, much of it linked to its unique position as the 'Gateway to the West', give it texture.

Fur-trapper Pierre Laclede knew prime real estate when he saw it, putting down stakes at the junction of the Mississippi and Missouri Rivers in 1764. The hustle picked up considerably when prospectors discovered gold in California in 1848 and St Louis became the jump-off point first for get-rich-quick dreamers and later for waves of settlers.

As a symbol for the city, the **Gateway Arch** (www.gatewayarch.com; tram ride adult/child $10/5; ⏰8am-10pm Jun-Aug, 9am-6pm Sep-May) has soared above any expectations its backers could have had in 1965 when it opened. The centerpiece of this National Park Service property, the silvery, shimmering 630ft-high arch is the Great Plains' own Eiffel Tower. A tram ride takes you to the tight confines at the top.

The arch is part of the **Jefferson National Expansion Memorial** which honors the vision of the namesake president who sponsored the Lewis and Clark expedition. It began here on May 14, 1804 and followed the Missouri River, much as you'll do on this tour.

 p357

The Drive » To use a cliché, from the arch, Go West (about 24 miles on busy I-70).

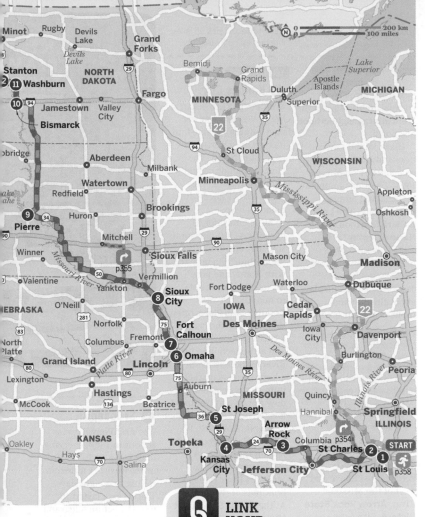

---

② St Charles

This Missouri River town, founded in 1769 has a cobblestoned Main St. Within the well-preserved downtown you can visit the **first state capitol** (200 S Main St; admission free, tours adult/child $4/2.50; ◷10am-4pm Mon-Sat, noon-4pm Sun, closed Mon Nov-Mar). **Ask at**

🔗 LINK YOUR TRIP

26 Black Hills Loop

A plethora of sites await in South Dakota's Black Hills. Start the route in Rapid City, a 170-mile trip east of Pierre along scenic legs on Hwy 34 and US 14 plus I-29.

22 Along the Great River Road

Link up with the more famous – yet shorter – Mississippi River north of St Louis to see America's two greatest rivers.

the **visitor center** (☎800-366-2427; www.historicstcharles.com; 230 S Main St; ☺8am-5pm Mon-Fri, 10am-5pm Sat, noon-5pm Sun) about tours, which pass some rare French colonial architecture in the **Frenchtown neighborhood** just north.

Clark joined Lewis here and they began their epic journey on May 21, 1804. Their encampment is reenacted annually on that date. The **Lewis & Clark Boathouse and Nature Center** (www.lewisandclarkcenter.org; 1050 Riverside Dr; adult/child $5/2; ☺10am-5pm Mon-Sat, noon-5pm Sun) has displays about the duo and replicas of their boats.

The Drive >> Skip the elusive charms of I-70 and instead stay close to the river, taking first Hwy 94 and then cutting north via Columbia (which has good cafes downtown) on US 63. From here take Hwy 740, Hwy 240, US 40 and Hwy 41 in that order for a total journey of 190 miles.

- - - - - - - - - - - -

❸ Arrow Rock

Perched just above and west of the Missouri River, **Arrow Rock State Historic Site** (www.mostateparks.com/park/arrow-rock-state-historic-site; ☺visitor center 10am-4pm daily Mar-Nov, Fri-Sun Dec-Feb) is a small preserved town that feels little changed since the 1830s when it was on the main stagecoach route west.

The Drive >> Hwy 41 followed by US 65 and US 24 take you through rolling Missouri

countryside and, after 95 miles, into the heart of Kansas City.

- - - - - - - - - - - -

TRIP HIGHLIGHT

❹ Kansas City

Kansas City (KC) began life in 1821 as a trading post, but really came into its own once westward expansion began. The Oregon, California and Santa Fe trails all met steamboats loaded with pioneers here.

KC is famed for its barbecues (100-plus joints smoke it up), fountains (more than 200; on par with Rome) and jazz.

Neighborhoods not to miss include the **Country Club Plaza**, often shortened to 'the Plaza', a 1920s shopping district and an attraction in itself; **River Market**, home to a large farmers market, immediately north of downtown; and **Westport**, located on Westport Rd, just west of Main St, it's filled with locally owned restaurants and bars.

The unpredictable Missouri River claimed hundreds of riverboats. At the **Arabia Steamboat Museum** (www.1856.com; 400 Grand Blvd; adult/child $16/6; ☺10am-5:30pm Mon-Sat, noon-5:30pm Sun, last tour 90min before closing) you can see 200 tons of salvaged 'treasure' from an 1856 victim.

✖ ⊨ p357

The Drive >> Quickly escape KC's endless suburbs by darting north 55 miles on I-29.

- - - - - - - - - - - -

❺ St Joseph

The first Pony Express set out in 1860, carrying mail from 'St Jo' 2000 miles west to California, taking just eight days. The service lasted 18 months before telegraph lines made it redundant. The **Pony Express National Museum** (www.ponyexpress.org; 914 Penn St; adult/child $6/3; ☺9am-5pm Mon-Sat, 11am-5pm Sun) tells the story of the dangerous Express and its riders.

St Jo, just east of the Missouri River, was home to outlaw Jesse James. He was killed at what

Omaha Old Market district

is now the **Jesse James Home Museum** (www.ponyexpressjessejames.com; cnr 12th & Penn Sts; adult/child $4/2; ⏰9am-4pm Mon-Sat, 1-4pm Sun Apr-Oct, Sat & Sun only Nov-Mar). The bullet hole is still in the wall.

Housed in the former 'State Lunatic Asylum No 2', the **Glore Psychiatric Museum** (www.stjosephmuseum.org; 3406 Frederick Ave; adult/child $5/3; ⏰10am-5pm Mon-Sat, 1-5pm Sun) gives a frightening and fascinating look at lobotomies, the 'bath of surprise' and other discredited treatments.

The Drive ›› Cross west to Nebraska on US 36 and then head north on US 75. While on this 157-mile-long leg, look for views of the Missouri from old river towns like Nebraska City.

- - - - - - - - - - - -

⑥ Omaha

Home to the brick-and-cobblestoned **Old Market** neighborhood downtown, a lively music scene and several quality museums, Omaha can turn a few hours into a few days.

Omaha's location on the Missouri River and proximity to the Platte made it an important stop on the Oregon, California and Mormon Trails. Later, the first transcontinental railroad to California stretched west from here. Its history is recounted at the **Union Pacific Railroad Museum** (www.uprr.com; 200 Pearl St, Council Bluffs, IA; ⏰10am-4pm Tue-Sat) in nearby Council Bluffs.

The downtown **riverfront** (8th St & Riverfront Dr) has been massively spiffed up. Among the highlights: the architecturally stunning **Bob Kerry Pedestrian Bridge**, which soars over to Iowa; the **Heartland of America Park**, with fountains and lush botanical gardens; and **Lewis & Clark Landing**,

DETOUR: HANNIBAL

Start: ❷ St Charles

When the air is sultry in this old river town, you almost expect to hear the whistle of a paddle steamer on that *other* river, the Mississippi. Mark Twain's boyhood home, 100 miles northwest of St Louis, has some authentically vintage areas and plenty of sites where you can get a sense of the muse and his creations, Tom Sawyer and Huck Finn.

The **Mark Twain Boyhood Home & Museum** (www.marktwainmuseum.org; 415 N Main St; adult/child $11/6; ☺9am-5pm) presents eight buildings, including two homes Twain lived in and that of Laura Hawkins, the real-life inspiration for Becky Thatcher. Afterward, float down the Mississippi on the **Mark Twain Riverboat** (www.marktwainriverboat.com; Center St; 1hr sightseeing cruise adult/child $16/11; ☺Apr-Nov, schedule varies). **National Tom Sawyer Days** (www.hannibaljaycees.org; ☺around Jul 4 weekend) feature frog-jumping and fence-painting contests and much more.

From St Charles, Hannibal is 95 miles northwest through low, rolling hills via US 61.

centuries. A looping driving route shows you what the land crossed by the Missouri once looked like before farms and development changed things forever.

The Drive › Farm towns hoping to be remembered by time dot the 84 miles of US 75 north from Fort Calhoun. The road's general route gently bends with the overall course of the Missouri River to the east.

---

❽ Sioux City

On high bluff, the modest city of Sioux City, Iowa, has grand views looking west over the Missouri River. There's a good **overlook** at the corner of W Fourth and Burton Sts.

On August 20, 1804, Sergeant Charles Floyd became the only person to die on the Lewis and Clark expedition team, probably from appendicitis. You can learn much more about this and other aspects of the journey at the beautiful **Lewis & Clark Interpretive Center** (www.siouxcitylcic.com; 900 Larsen Park Rd; ☺9am-5pm Tue-Fri, to 8pm Thu, noon-5pm Sat & Sun), which is right on the river.

The Drive › Enjoy the smallest of rural two-laners to reach the first capitol of the Dakota states. Angle out of Sioux City on Hwy 12, then cross over to South Dakota at Westfield and pick up the alternately sinuous and angular Hwy 50, which closely follows the river. The final 64 miles of this 306-mile-long leg are on Hwy 34.

---

where the explorers did just that in 1804. It's home to the **Lewis & Clark Historical Trail Visitors Center** (www.nps.gov/lecl; 601 Riverfront Dr; ☺9am-5pm summer, Mon-Fri only rest of the year) where you can get information and advice for following in their footsteps.

 p357

The Drive › Just beyond the outer reaches of ever-growing Omaha, Fort Calhoun is 16 miles north on US 75.

---

❼ Fort Calhoun

Just north of Omaha, the small town of Fort Calhoun has two sights

which take you back to days long gone on the Missouri. **Fort Atkinson State Historical Park** (www.outdoornebraska.ne.gov; Madison St; adult/child $2/1; ☺8am-5pm) preserves the first US military fort built west of the Missouri River. It was built in 1820 on a recommendation of Lewis and Clark, who besides being explorers, were keen military officers.

Just east of town, **Boyer Chute National Wildlife Refuge** (www.fws.gov/refuge/boyer_chute; CR 34; ☺dawn-dusk) has marshes and other open areas on the river that are little changed in

⑨ Pierre

Pierre (pronounced 'peer'), SD, is just too small (population 14,100) and ordinary to feel like a seat of power. Small-town Victorian homes overlook the imposing 1910 **State Capitol** (500 E Capitol Ave; ⊙8am-7pm Mon-Fri, to 5pm Sat & Sun) with its black copper dome.

Hard by the Missouri River, it lies along the Native American Scenic Byway and lonely, stark US 14. Imagine this area when it was rich with bison, beavers, elk and much more.

Exhibits at the **South Dakota Cultural Heritage Center** (www.history.sd.gov; 900 Governor's Dr; adult/child $4/free; ⊙9am-6:30pm Mon-Sat, 1-4:30pm Sun summer, to 4:30pm rest of year) include a bloody Ghost Dance shirt from the Battle of Wounded Knee.

At a bend on the river, **Framboise Island** has several hiking trails and plentiful wildlife. It's across from where the Lewis and Clark expedition spent four days in late September, 1804. The expedition was nearly derailed when they inadvertently offended members of the local Brule tribe.

The Drive » Dams cause the Missouri to look like a lake for much of the 208 miles you'll drive north along US 83 to the other Dakota capitol.

⑩ Bismarck

Compared with the sylvan charms of Pierre, the stark 1930s **State Capitol** (☎701-328-2480; N 7th St; ⊙8am-4pm Mon-Fri, tours hourly except noon, plus 9am-4pm Sat & 1-4pm Sun summer) in Bismarck, ND, is often referred to as the 'skyscraper of the prairie' and looks like a Stalinist school of dentistry.

Behind the Sacagawea (a Native American woman whose friendship proved invaluable to Lewis and Clark) statue, the huge **North Dakota Heritage Center** (www.history.nd.gov; Capitol Hill; ⊙8am-5pm Mon-Fri, 10am-5pm Sat & Sun) has details on everything from Norwegian bachelor farmers to the scores of nuclear bombs perched on missiles in silos across the state.

Fort Abraham Lincoln State Park (www.parkrec.nd.gov; per vehicle $5, plus adult/child to tour historical sites $6/4; ⊙park 9am-5pm, tours May-Sep), 7 miles south of nearby Mandan on SR 1806, is well worth the detour. Its **On-A-Slant Indian Village** has five re-created Mandan earth lodges, while the fort, with several replica buildings, was Custer's last stop before the Battle of Little Bighorn.

The Drive » Maybe pancakes are popular around here because that's how flat much of the land is. See for yourself on this 40-mile drive north on US 83.

⑪ Washburn

There are several worthwhile attractions near the spot where

DETOUR: MITCHELL

Start: ⑧ Sioux City

Why not honor the starch you'll see growing in profusion in vibrant green fields all along the Missouri? Every year, half a million people pull off I-90 (exit 332) to see the Taj Mahal of agriculture, the all-time-ultimate roadside attraction, the **Corn Palace** (www.cornpalace.org; 604 N Main St; ⊙8am-9pm summer, reduced hours rest of year). Close to 300,000 ears of corn are used each year to create a tableaux of murals on the outside of the building. Ponder the scenes and you may find a kernel of truth or just say 'aw shucks'. Mitchell is 150 miles northwest of Sioux City via I-29 and I-90. Rejoin the drive at Pierre, 150 miles northwest via I-90 and US 83.

Lewis and Clark wintered with the Mandan in 1804–05. They offer an evocative look at the lives of the Native Americans and the explorers amid lands that even today seem little changed.

Learn about the duo's expedition and the Native Americans who helped them at the **North Dakota Lewis & Clark Interpretive Center** (www.fortmandan.com; junction US 83 & ND Hwy 200A; adult/child $7.50/5; 9am-5pm daily year-round, from noon Sun winter).

Fort Mandan (CR 17), a replica of the fort built by Lewis and Clark, is 2.5 miles west (10 miles downstream from the flooded original site). It sits on a lonely stretch of the Missouri River marked by a monument to Seaman, the expedition's dog.

The Drive ≫ Head 22 miles west of Washburn through verdant rolling prairie on Hwy 200 to just north of the small town of Stanton.

TRIP HIGHLIGHT

⑫ Stanton, ND

At **Knife River Indian Villages National Historical Site** you can still see the mounds left by three earthen villages of the Hidastas, who lived on the Knife River, a narrow tributary of the Missouri, for more than 900 years. The National Park Service has re-created one of the earthen lodges. A stroll through the mostly wide-open and wild site leads to the village where Lewis and Clark met Sacagawea.

The Drive ≫ More dams cause the Missouri to balloon out into a tangle of waters that look like a couple of lizards doing a mating dance. Hwy 200 takes you for most of the 169 miles of your final leg.

TRIP HIGHLIGHT

⑬ Williston

Twenty-two miles southwest of Williston along SR 1804, **Fort Buford** (www.history.

nd.gov; adult/child $5/2.50; 10am-6pm mid-May–mid-Sep) is the bleak army outpost where Sitting Bull surrendered. The adjacent **Missouri-Yellowstone Confluence Interpretive Center** (9am-7pm mid-May–mid-Sep, 9am-4pm Wed-Sat, 1-5pm Sun rest of year) includes the fort's visitor center and has good views of where the Yellowstone River joins the Missouri, greatly increasing the latter's flow.

About 2 miles west, on the Montana–North Dakota border, the more evocative **Fort Union Trading Post** (www.nps.gov/fous; SR 1804; 8am-6:30pm summer, 9am-5:30pm rest of year) is a reconstruction of the American Fur Company post built in 1828.

Over the border in Montana, the Missouri frays out into myriad tributaries. Lewis and Clark had numerous portages as they continued their epic journey west.

Eating & Sleeping

St Louis ❶

✕ Crown Candy Kitchen   Cafe $
(1401 St Louis Ave; mains $5-10; ⊙10:30am-9pm Mon-Sat, to 5pm Sun) An authentic family-run soda fountain that's been making families smile since 1913. Malts come with spoons; try their famous BLT.

✕ Bridge Tap House & Wine Bar   Bar
(www.thebridgestl.com; 1004 Locust St; ⊙11am-1am) Slip onto a sofa or rest your elbows on a table at this romantic bar where you can savor fine wines, the best local beers and a variety of exquisite little bites from a seasonal menu.

✕ Eleven Eleven
Mississippi   Modern American $$
(☎314-241-9999; www.1111-m.com; 1111 Mississippi Ave; mains $9-22; ⊙11am-10pm Mon-Thu, to midnight Fri & Sat; ✎) This popular bistro and wine bar fills an old shoe factory. Dinner mains draw on regional specialties with an Italian accent.

⨿ Moonrise Hotel   Boutique Hotel $$
(☎314-721-1111; www.moonrisehotel.com; 6177 Delmar Blvd; r $120-280; P❄@🛜🐾) The stylish eight-story Moonrise has a high profile amid the high energy of the Loop neighborhood. The 125 rooms sport a lunar motif.

Kansas City ❹

✕ Arthur Bryant's   Barbecue $$
(www.arthurbryantsbbq.com; 1727 Brooklyn Ave; mains $8-15; ⊙10am-9:30pm Mon-Thu, to 10pm Fri & Sat, 11am-8pm Sun) Not far from the Jazz District, this famous institution serves up piles of superb BBQ in a somewhat slick setting.

✕ Oklahoma Joe's   Barbecue $$
(www.oklahomajoesbbq.com; 3002 W 47th Ave; mains $6-15; ⊙11am-8:30pm Mon-Thu, to

9:30pm Fri & Sat) The best reason to cross the state border, this legendary BBQ joint is housed in a brightly lit old gas station.

✕ Rieger Hotel
Grill & Exchange   American $$$
(☎816-471-2177; www.theriegerkc.com; 1924 Main St; mains $20-30; ⊙11am-2pm Mon-Fri, 5-10pm Mon-Sat) One of KC's most innovative restaurants is in what was once a humdrum 1915 vintage hotel.

⨿ Q Hotel   Hotel $$
(☎816-931-0001; www.theqhotel.com; 560 Westport Rd; r $110-140; P❄@🛜🐾) This environmentally conscious indie hotel is centrally located in Westport. All 123 rooms have a bright color scheme that seems as fresh as spring.

Omaha ❻

✕ Upstream
Brewing Company   American $$
(☎402-344-0200; 514 S 11th St; mains $10-30; ⊙11am-1am) In a big Old Market firehouse, the beer and food here is also big on flavor. There are sidewalk tables, a rooftop deck and a huge bar.

✕ Spencer's   Steakhouse $$$
(☎402-280-8888; www.spencersforsteaksand chops.com; 102 S 10th St; mains $25-55; ⊙5-10pm) Omaha's famous for steaks and this lavish restaurant is the current reigning champ for seared meat. You can enjoy excellent casual fare in the bar for a fraction of the price.

⨿ Magnolia Hotel   Historic Hotel $$
(☎402-341-2500; www.magnoliahotelomaha. com; 1615 Howard St; r $130-200; ❄@🛜🐾) Not far from Old Market, the Magnolia is a boutique hotel housed in a restored 1923 Italianate high-rise.

STRETCH YOUR LEGS
ST LOUIS

Start/Finish: Forest Park Visitor and Education Center

Distance: 4 miles

Duration: 3 hours

The Gateway Arch downtown is an obvious drawcard, but for real walking pleasure, join the masses in leafy, museum- and attraction-filled Forest Park. The Central West End neighborhood to the east adds to the fun.

Take this walk on Trips

Forest Park

New York City may have Central Park, but St Louis has the bigger (by 528 acres) **Forest Park** (www.stlouis.missouri.org/citygov/parks/forestpark; ⊗6am-10pm). The superb, 1371-acre spread was the setting of the 1904 World's Fair. It's a beautiful escape and is dotted with attractions.

The **Visitor and Education Center** (www.forestparkforever.org; 5595 Grand Dr; ⊗8:30am-7pm Mon-Fri, 9am-4pm Sat & Sun) is in an old streetcar pavilion and has a cafe. Park your car here and start your walk, which runs roughly counterclockwise.

The Walk » Walk northwest through the well-tended grounds some 300m.

Missouri History Museum

The **Missouri History Museum** (www.mohistory.org; 5700 Lindell Blvd; ⊗10am-5pm, to 8pm Tue) presents the story of St Louis, starring such worthies as a World's Fair and aviator Charles Lindbergh (look for the sales receipt for his first plane – he bought it at a variety store!).

The Walk » Walk south past the tennis courts to the lake's small marina.

Post-Dispatch Lake

Still showing signs of its central position during the World's Fair, this large lake isn't just for ogling: rent a boat from the **Boathouse** (www.boathouseforestpark.com; 6101 Government Dr; boat rental per hr $15; ⊗10am-approx 1hr before sunset) and explore the placid waters.

The Walk » Walk directly southwest to the art museum, or alternatively take the longer and prettier sinuous path along the northside of the lakes, then drop down south past the Grand Basin and across the grassy expanse of Art Hill.

St Louis Art Museum

A grand beaux-arts palace originally built for the World's Fair, it now houses the storied **St Louis Art Museum** (www.slam.org; 1 Fine Arts Dr; ⊗10am-5pm Tue-Sun, to 9pm Fri), which has collections spanning time and styles. A stunning new wing opened in 2013.

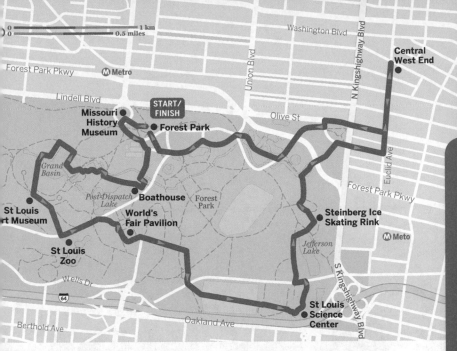

The Walk >> A short verdant stroll south and you are at the north entrance to the zoo.

St Louis Zoo

A world-class facility, the vast **St Louis Zoo** (www.stlzoo.org; 1 Government Dr; fee for some exhibits; ⏰8am-5pm daily, to 7pm Fri-Sun Jun-Aug; 👶) includes a fascinating River's Edge area with African critters.

The Walk >> Walk straight east through the tree-shaded grounds, watching for the planetarium in the distance. You might pause at the beautiful 1909 **World's Fair Pavilion**, a grand open-air shelter built with proceeds from the 1904 fair.

St Louis Science Center

Live demonstrations, dinosaurs, a planetarium and an IMAX theater are just some of the highlights of the **St Louis Science Center** (www.slsc.org; 5050 Oakland Ave; ⏰9:30am-5:30pm Mon-Sat, from 11am Sun Jun-Aug, to 4:30pm rest of year; 👶), much of which is reached via a dramatic glass walkway over I-64. The park entrance is anchored by the planetarium here.

The Walk >> Follow the wide main pedestrian path past Jefferson Lake.

Steinberg Ice-Skating Rink

If it's too cold to rent a boat, it's probably just right to go ice-skating with lots of other happy skaters at the **Steinberg Ice Skating Rink** (www. steinbergskatingrink.com; off N Kingshighway Blvd; admission $6, skates rental $4; ⏰10am-9pm Sun-Thu, to midnight Fri & Sat mid-Nov–Feb).

The Walk >> Leave the park, crossing S Kingshighway Blvd.

Central West End

This posh center for cafes and shopping is anchored by Euclid St. **Duff's** (www. duffsrestaurant.com; 392 N Euclid Ave; mains $8-20; ⏰11:30am-10pm Sun-Thu, to 11pm Fri, 10am-11pm Sat) has an eclectic menu of sandwiches, salads and more ambitious fare. Score a sidewalk table outside under the trees. **Left Bank Books** (www.left-bank. com; 399 N Euclid Ave; ⏰10am-10pm Mon-Sat, 11am-6pm Sun) is a great indie bookstore.

The Walk >> Return to the car park via some of the nicest gardens in Forest Park. Follow the paths along the waterways linking Round and Deer Lakes.

Rocky Mountains Trips

RIDE BELOW THESE ROWS OF SNOWCAPPED PEAKS and alongside clear-running rivers and rugged canyons: the Rockies emanate vitality. Certainly everything about this place – from the bears to the beers – feels larger than life.

With an emphasis on farm-fresh food and an urban edge to those monolith mountains, you could say the Wild West has transformed into more of a frame of mind. But the thrills – such as meandering through valleys, skiing the champagne powder of Aspen or Vail, or watching Yellowstone wolves on the hunt – still remain.

Tap the adrenaline and hold on, or retreat into the deep peace of this pine-scented nirvana.

Grand Teton National Park Reflection of Teton's craggy peaks (Trip 28)
JOHN WOODWORTH / GETTY IMAGES ©

Rocky Mountains Trips

N 0   400 km
      0   200 miles

Saskatoon

Regina

SASKATCHEWAN

Medicine Hat

Cranbrook

Lethbridge

Estevan

ALBERTA

CANADA

USA

IDAHO

Glacier National Park

29

Whitefish

Shelby

Havre

Fort Peck Indian Reservation

Williston

Lake Sakakawea

Kalispell

Rocky Mountains

15

NORTH DAKOTA

Coeur d'Alene

Bob Marshall Wilderness

Great Falls

Lewistown

Fort Peck Lake

Glendive

Dickinso

Missoula

Missouri River

94

Lewiston

Helena

MONTANA

Yellowstone River

Miles City

Standing Ro
Ind
Reservat

Anaconda

Butte

Billings

Cheyer
River Ind
Reservat

Continental Divide

90

Bozeman

Livingston

Crow Indian Reservation

Sheridan

IDAHO

Dillon

15

Buffalo

Rapid City

Sawtooth National Recreation Area

28

Yellowstone National Park

Big Horn Mountains

Gillette

SOUTH DAKOT.

84

Grand Teton National Park

89

WYOMING

Thermopolis

Boise

Idaho Falls

Jackson

Wind River Range

Riverton

Casper

Mountain Home

Pocatello

Lander

Douglas

NEBRASK.

Twin Falls

15

Kemmerer

Rawlins

25

Laramie

Cheyenne

Brigham City

Evanston

Green River

Rock Springs

Rocky Mountains

Fort Collins

Ogden

Great Salt Lake

Greeley

Elko

80

Craig

Rocky Mountain National Park

Boulder

Denver

Salt Lake City

Provo

Glenwood Springs

Vail

Burlingto

UTAH

Grand Junction

Aspen

24

Conifer

Ely

70

Fairplay

30

Colorado Sprin

Montrose

Florence

87

Pueblo

Lama

Telluride

550

Monte Vista

COLORADO

Cedar City

Glen Canyon National Recreation Area

Colorado River

Mesa Verde National Park

31

Durango

Alamosa

Trinidad

NEVADA

15

Taos

Las Vegas

Grand Canyon National Park

Farmington

Navajo Indian Reservation

Continental Divide

NEW MEXICO

Hualapai Indian Reservation

ARIZONA

Hopi Indian Reservation

Santa Fe

Kingman

Gallup

Colorado Skiing in the Rockies (Trip 30)

Classic Trip

28 **Grand Teton to Yellowstone**
7 days
With outstanding wildlife, gushing geysers and alpine scenery, this trip is the consummate parks experience. (p365)

29 **Going-to-the-Sun Road 3 days**
Glacier National Park's backbone has steep switchbacks, waterfalls and glistening glacier views. (p377)

30 **Top of the Rockies 4–5 days**
Wild West ghost towns, soaring ski resorts and alpine bliss. (p385)

31 **San Juan Skyway &**
Million Dollar Highway 6–8 days
Motor from mysterious cliff dwellings to lost mining villages and Colorado chic. (p395)

 DON'T MISS

Balcony House
Often sold out, the most adventurous Mesa Verde cliff dwelling features steep ladder climbs and narrow passageways to crawl through. Take the climb on Trip **31**

Wolf Watching
Get up early to see wolf packs roaming Lamar Valley. Joining a biologist-led course is a good place to start. See what you can spot on Trip **28**

Maroon Bells
Once you've seen these chiseled peaks, you'll forget all about Aspen's glamorous airs – this is a hard place not to love. See for yourself on Trip **30**

Lake McDonald
Immerse yourself in these immense blue waters ringed by Glacier National Park by renting a rowboat from Glacier Park Boat Co on Trip **29**

James Ranch
Dig in to farm-fresh burgers at this roadside farmstand near Durango on Trip **31**

Grand Prismatic Spring Watch out for
spurting geysers and bubbling mud pots

Classic Trip

Grand Teton to Yellowstone

28

Iconic Yellowstone and Grand Teton may be our closest connections to wild America. Take a hike under the sublime Teton spires and witness spurting geysers, herds of bison and howling wolves.

TRIP HIGHLIGHTS

FINISH
Mammoth

10 ━━ **190 miles**

Lamar Valley
Spy on grizzlies, wolves and antelope in action

Canyon

100 miles

Grand Prismatic Spring
Rainbow thermals, geysers and bubbling mud

6

Yellowstone Lake

Old Faithful

3 ━━ **27 miles**

String & Leigh Lakes
Stroll and swim the Tetons' backyard

1 mile

Jackson
Cowboy grit meets high-alpine adventure

1

START

7 DAYS
250 MILES / 402 KM

GREAT FOR...

BEST TIME TO GO
Jun–Sep

 ESSENTIAL PHOTO

Oxbow Bend, Grand Teton National Park. Moose and elk frequent this Snake River haven with the booming backdrop of Mt Moran.

 BEST FOR WILDLIFE

A North American wildlife safari at dawn in the valleys of Yellowstone.

365

28 Grand Teton to Yellowstone

A life-list must, Yellowstone is nature's *tour de force*. On view are herds of bison, lumbering grizzlies and packs of wolves. Yellowstone's unique supervolcano features half the world's geysers, the country's largest high-altitude lake and a mass of blue-ribbon rivers and waterfalls. To the south, Grand Teton National Park complements with craggy peaks, peaceful waterways and sublime alpine terrain prime for exploration.

TRIP HIGHLIGHT

❶ Jackson

Just south of Grand Teton National Park's southern entrance, Jackson is much more than a park gateway. A chic destination on its own, this ski town is also a summer stunner, with plentiful outdoor activities, galleries and a shopping scene that reaches beyond trinketry, with cool boutiques and tailored outdoor gear. Don't skip the **National Museum of Wildlife Art** (☏307-733-5771; www.wildlifeart.org; 2820 Rungius Rd; adult/child $12/6; ⊙9am-5pm), where major works by Remington and Bierstadt offer perspectives on nature that will make your skin prickle. Across the street, elk herds, bison and bighorn sheep congregate in winter at the **National Elk Refuge** (☏307-733-9212; www.fws.gov/nationalelkrefuge; Hwy 89; horse-drawn sleigh ride adult/child $18/14; ⊙8am-5pm Sep-May, 8am-7pm Jun-Aug, horse-drawn sleigh ride 10am-4pm mid-Dec–Mar), though it's mostly a feast for birders in summer. Finally, take advantage of a foodie scene that's among the best in the West, with renowned chefs and an emphasis on local, farm-raised food.

✕ 🛏 p374

The Drive » From Jackson take Rte 22 to the Moose-Wilson Road (Rte 390), so narrow it's closed to trucks and trailers. Drive slowly; grizzly sightings are not uncommon along this back road. A booth on the roadway marks the **Granite Canyon Entrance** (⊙7-day permit per vehicle $25) to Grand Teton National Park. Pay your entry fee here. Turn into the Laurance S Rockefeller Preserve on your right, 16 miles from Jackson.

❷ Laurance S Rockefeller Preserve

In contrast to conventional visitor centers, the **Laurance S Rockefeller Preserve Center** (☏307-739-3654; Moose-Wilson Rd; ⊙8am-6pm Jun-Aug, 9am-5pm rest of year) aims to provide a meditative experience that turns out not unlike a spiritual guide to the park. Sparely furnished and LEED certified, it sets the scene for your foray

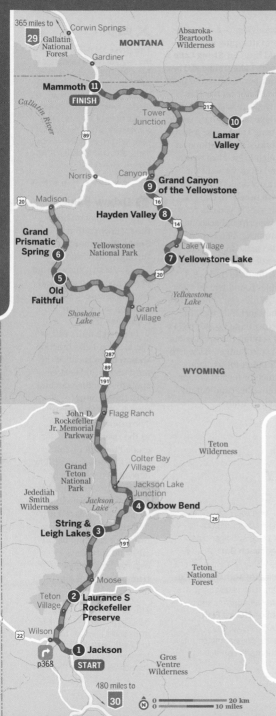

into nature, with great quotes from naturalists etched into the walls and a gorgeous conservation library with oversized titles best enjoyed from the leather armchairs.

From here, you might take an easy stroll to **Phelps Lake**. The 7-mile loop takes about 3.5 hours. If you just have two hours, and your swimsuit, make your goal Jump Rock. A 24ft drop into clear cobalt water, it's a favorite of swimmers and picnickers, located about an hour in on the trail.

The Drive » The road ends in 4 miles at Teton Park Rd. Go left for the Moose entrance booth or go right for the Craig Thomas Visitors Center or Dornan's. Teton Park Rd runs parallel to a newly constructed cycling path that starts in Jackson (ending at Jenny Lake).

LINK YOUR TRIP

29 Going-to-the-Sun Road

From Mammoth, take 89 north through Paradise Valley, join I-90 at Bozeman and take 93N at Missoula, a seven-hour trip to glaciers and grandeur.

30 Top of the Rockies

From Jackson take 191 south to I-80 east, join up with I-25 south to Denver, an eight-hour trip to Colorado high country.

Drive slowly, as wildlife are often on the road. Take advantage of the numerous scenic overlooks on the left side of the road. Turn left for Leigh and String Lake trailheads; continue on the same one-way loop for the scenic drive to Jenny Lake.

TRIP HIGHLIGHT

3 String & Leigh Lakes

In **Grand Teton National Park** (📞307-739-3399; www. nps.gov/grte; Teton Park Rd, Grand Teton National Park; admission $25) the drive-by views are so dramatic it's hard to keep your eyes on the road.

The adventure starts in Moose, where you can rent a canoe at **Dornan's** (📞307-733-2522; www.dornans.com;

Moose Village) – ask staff for help strapping it down – and head for **String Lake & Leigh Lake** trailhead. Have your permits in hand from the visitor center. This adventure is good for the whole family. First, paddle String Lake, make a short portage and continue on Leigh Lake. Float, swim and enjoy views of the craggy peaks from your own beach. To make a night of it, you can reserve a waterfront backcountry campsite. These shores also make for a great, gentle hike, apt for all ages. String Lake trail is 3.3 miles round-trip on foot.

While you're here, take the short loop road to Jenny Lake Lodge (p374). If staying the night is out of your budget, it's worth stopping for a casual lunch or formal dinner – a romantic, candlelit, five-course affair.

DETOUR: WILSON, WY

Start: ❶ Jackson

Big barns and the open range make this outpost 13 miles from Jackson feel more like Marlboro country – even though the median home price averages a cool $3 million. Don't miss the **Stagecoach Bar** (📞307-733-4407; http://stagecoachbar.net; 5755 W Hwy 22, Wilson), where fun bands have ranch hands mingling with rhinestone cowgirls, hippies and hikers. Thursday is disco night and on Sundays the popular house country band croons until 10pm. Local institution **Nora's Fish Creek Inn** (📞307-733-8288; 5600 W Hwy 22, Wilson; mains $7-35; ⏱6am-2pm, 5-9:30pm) dishes up heaping country breakfasts, fresh trout and homemade cobbler.

🍴 🛏 p374

The Drive » Take a left out of the Jenny or String Lake areas to Teton Park Rd. Heading north the landscape turns from sagebrush to pine forest, climbing near densely forested Signal Mt Road. Partial views of Jackson Lake come on the left. At the Jackson Lake Junction go right to Oxbow Bend, almost immediately after the turn on your right.

- - - - - - - - - - - -

4 Oxbow Bend

Families enjoy rafting the mellow section of **Snake River** that runs through the park, with views of sharp snowbound peaks and the occasional wading moose. Contact a Jackson outfitter to book a half-day trip.

Located 2 miles east of the Jackson Lake Junction, **Oxbow Bend** is one of the most scenic and desired spots for wildlife-watching, with the stunning backdrop of Mt Moran. The oxbow was created as the river's faster water eroded the outer bank while the slower inner flow deposited the sediment.

These wet lowlands have prime wildlife-watching, so bring binoculars. Early morning and dusk are prime for spotting moose, elk, sandhill cranes, ospreys, bald eagles, trumpeter swans and other birds.

The Drive » From Oxbow Bend, go right on 287/89. The road parallels Jackson Lake to the left. The last chance for camping with services on Jackson Lake is Lizard Creek.

After entering Yellowstone National Park, the straight road reaches the Continental Divide (7988ft) and descends. At Yellowstone Lake, take the left-hand fork over Craig Pass (8262ft) to Old Faithful.

5 Old Faithful

Heading north of the Tetons, the road climbs and pine forest stretch along the horizon. America's first national park, **Yellowstone National Park** (☎307-344-2263; www.nps.gov/yell; Grand Loop Rd, Mammoth, Yellowstone National Park; admission $25; ⊙ north entrance year-round, south entrance May-Oct) **covers an astounding 3472 sq miles** – that's more than three times the size of Rhode Island. Entering through the South Gate, show your valid Grand Teton admission ticket so you don't pay twice, and go west on the loop road to the **Old Faithful Visitor Center** (☎307-344-2107; www.nps.gov/yell/planyourvisit/backcountryhiking.htm; Grand Loop Rd, Yellowstone National Park; campsites $12; ⊙8:30am-4pm Jun-Aug) for information.

Spouting some 8000 gallons of water some 180ft high, **Old Faithful** erupts about every 90 minutes. Check for eruption time estimates at the visitor center. Almost hourly throughout the day, ranger-led geology talks

TOP TIP: BEAT THE CROWDS

To avoid Yellowstone crowds, think strategically. Visit in May, September or October, and do like the wildlife do by being most active at dawn and dusk. Pack your own picnic lunches and eat lodge dinners after 9pm. Pitch your tent in the the wild (permit required) – only 1% of visitors stay overnight in Yellowstone's backcountry.

help explain the strange subterranean plumbing that causes geysers.

If you just missed an eruption, fill the wait with a 1.1-mile walk to **Observation Hill**, for an overview of the entire basin. Loop back via Solitary Geyser, its sudden bursts come every 4 to 8 minutes, before rejoining the boardwalk.

Another prime viewing spot is the porch of historic **Old Faithful Inn**. Even if you're not staying over, it's worth a dinner splurge.

✕ 🛏 p375

The Drive » From Old Faithful it's only 16 miles to Madison Junction, but these are action-packed. If driving out and back (to loop back to Yellowstone Lake), you might consider taking all the easterly right-hand turnouts first, and following with the west-side turnouts the following day after camping at Madison, while driving south.

TRIP HIGHLIGHT

6 Grand Prismatic Spring

Exploring **Geyser Country** can take the better part of a day.

If you rent or have a bicycle, you can enjoy many attractions via designated paths. Unlike the wildlife, these spurting geysers, multihued springs and bubbling mud pots are guaranteed to show up for the picture.

Leaving Madison Campground, backtrack south 2 miles and take Firehole Canyon Dr on your right. Pass the rhyolite cliffs and rapids to **Firehole Falls** and swimming area for a morning dip.

Five miles south, a pullout offers fine views of the smoking geysers and pools of **Midway Geyser Basin** to the right, and Firehole Lake Basin to the left, with bison making it a classic Yellowstone vista.

One mile on, take a right for **Fountain Paint Pot**, a huge pool of plopping goop. Next up is Midway Geyser Basin. Its main attraction is the breathtaking rainbow-hued **Grand Prismatic Spring**. Walk the boardwalk to appreciate

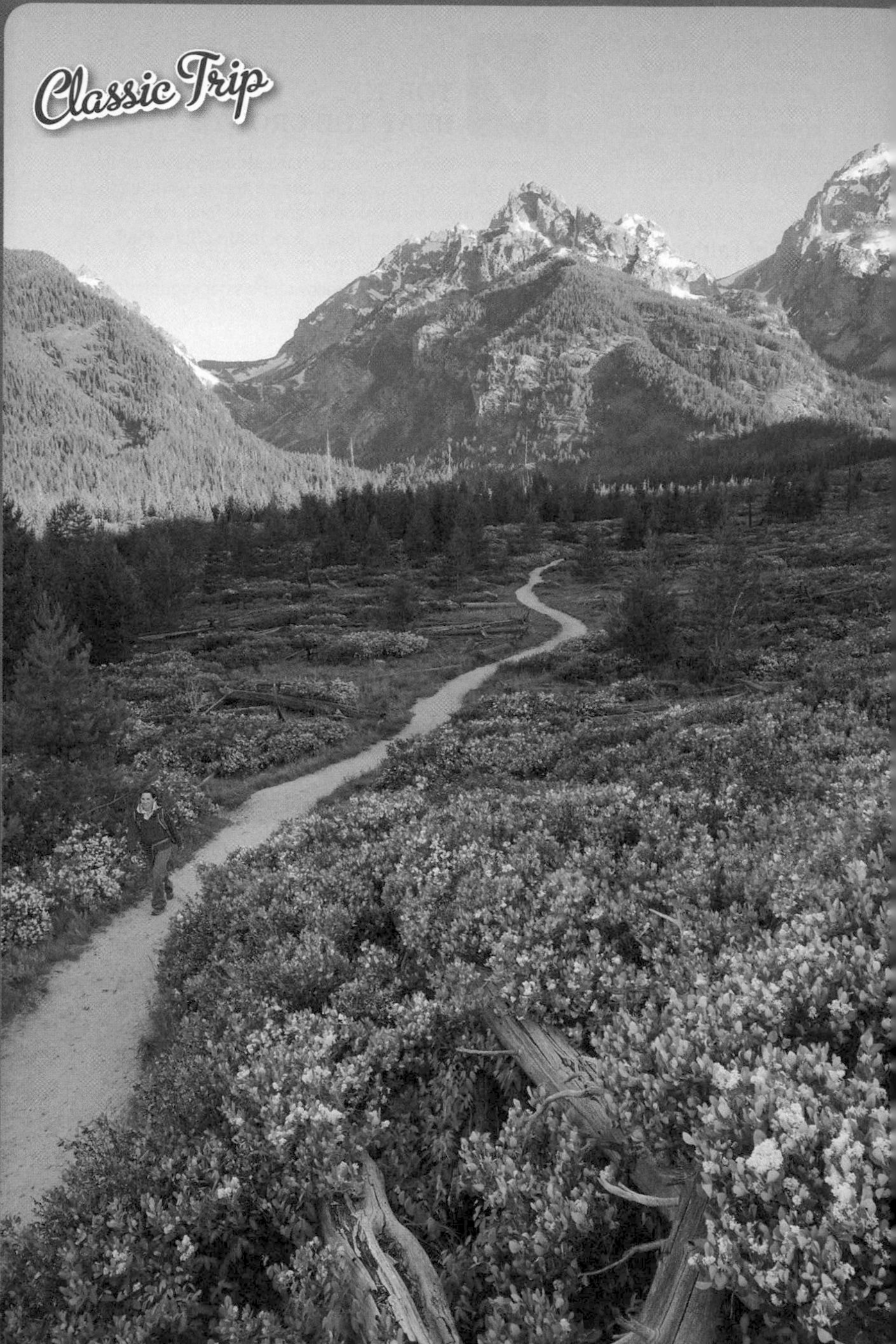
Classic Trip

its 370ft expanse. It drains into **Excelsior Pool**, a teal blown-out geyser that last erupted in 1985; the boiling water later fuels the Firehole River.

The Drive » From Grand Prismatic Spring, drive south toward Old Faithful. The road climbs to Craig Pass (8262ft) before descending to West Thumb, an information station on Yellowstone Lake. Go left on the shoreline road to Lake Village.

❼ Yellowstone Lake

Imbibe the shimmering expanse of **Yellowstone Lake** (7733ft), one of the world's largest alpine lakes. Grand Loop Road hugs much of the western shore. Stop to picnic at **Sand Point**, where it's worth taking a short walk to the lagoon and black sand beach, looking beyond to the rugged Absaroka Range.

Continue north and have a look at the 1891 **Lake Yellowstone Hotel**, the park's oldest building. This buttercup yellow southern mansion has a sprawling sunroom perfect for classical concerts and cocktail hour – you may want to return at the day's end.

At the crossroads further north, take a right for **Fishing Bridge**, the springtime haunt of grizzlies scooping up fish (the lake and river have the country's highest cutthroat trout population). Don't miss the 5pm ranger talk here if your hour coincides.

A bit east, **Pelican Valley** is famed for its meadows and sagebrush, popular with moose and grizzlies. A number of great trails depart from this area. Try Storm Point, a 2.3-mile, 90-minute walk through diverse wildlife habitats.

✖ ⊨ p375

The Drive » Drive along Yellowstone Lake to Lake Village, turning right for Fishing Bridge. Bear jams are frequent here. Drive slowly, as it gets congested with both human and animal traffic, and stop only at turnouts. A few miles on, Storm Point trail is on your right. Retrace your steps to Fishing Bridge and head north toward Hayden Valley.

❽ Hayden Valley

Flowing from Yellowstone Lake, the **Yellowstone River** is broad and shallow as it meanders gently through the grasslands of Hayden Valley, the park's

LOCAL KNOWLEDGE
NATHAN VARLEY, WILDLIFE BIOLOGIST & GUIDE

If you want to get away from the crowds, in the central part of Yellowstone, upper Broad Creek trail and Mist Creek both have campsites which stay empty every night. It's spectacular because you have a lot of wildlife, it's very scenic and there are also thermal areas and pots of boiling mud.

Left: Grand Teton National Park
Right: Moose among the autumn foliage in Grand Teton

Classic Trip

largest valley and one of its premier wildlife-watching spots.

A former lake bed, the valley's fine silt and clay keeps shrubs and grasses thriving, attracting bison by the herd. There's also coyotes, springtime grizzlies, and elk that turn out in great numbers for the fall rut.

Rangers lead **wildlife-watching trips** at 7am several times weekly to pullouts 1 mile north of Sulphur Cauldron and 1.5 miles north of Trout Creek.

Also check out the mud pots and sulphur pits at **Mud Volcano**, a thermal area 6 miles north of Fishing Bridge Junction. Earthquakes in 1979 generated enough heat and gases in the mud pots to cook nearby lodgepole pines. Follow the 2.3-mile loop boardwalk to see the sights.

The Drive » The road runs parallel to the Yellowstone River to the east. It's another spot famous for bear jams (though the offender is usually bison). These buff creatures blissfully meander onto the road, so keep your distance. After the open valley changes to densely forested terrain, keep watch for the right-hand South Rim Dr with views of Yellowstone's Grand Canyon.

❾ Grand Canyon of the Yellowstone

Here the Yellowstone River takes a dive over the Upper Falls (109ft) and Lower Falls (308ft) before raging through the thousand-foot Grand Canyon of the Yellowstone.

Heading north on Grand Loop Rd, take the right-hand turn to South Rim Dr. A steep 500ft descent, **Uncle Tom's Trail** offers the best view of both falls. Hop in the car again to continue to **Artist Point**. Canyon walls shaded salmon pink, chalk white, ochre and pale green make this a masterpiece. A short 1-mile trail continues here to Point Sublime, worth following just to bask in the landscape.

Returning to the Grand Loop, go north and turn right on North Rim Dr, a 2.5-mile one-way with overlooks. **Lookout Point** offers the best views of the Lower Falls. Hike the steep 500ft trail for closer action. This is where landscape artist Thomas Moran sketched for his famous canyon painting, supposedly weeping over his comparatively poor palette.

The Drive » Complete the South Rim Dr and return to the Grand Loop. Heading north, the second right is the one-way North Rim Dr, which loops you to the crossroads of Canyon Village. Head right here for

Dunraven Pass. This section is narrow and curvy with huge drops. It descends to Tower-Roosevelt, where you can head right (east) for Lamar Valley.

TRIP HIGHLIGHT

❿ Lamar Valley

Take the winding road to **Tower-Roosevelt** (⊙late May–mid-Oct), stopping at **Washburn Hot Springs Overlook** for views of the Yellowstone Caldera. On clear days you can even see the Teton range. The road climbs Dunraven Pass (8859ft), surrounded by fir and whitebark pines.

Stop at **Antelope Creek turnouts**, with great wildlife-watching in prime grizzly habitat. It's worth hunkering down at these high vantage points with a spotting scope.

If Yellowstone was a reality show, Lamar Valley would be the set of predator-prey sparring. Wolves, bears, foxes and their prey are all commonly spotted here, although visitors are relatively few. Stop at roadside turnouts between Pebble and Slough Creek campgrounds for prime wolf-spotting.

Along this road, Buffalo Ranch hosts **Yellowstone Institute** (www.yellowstoneassociation. org) courses, with biologist-led wildlife-watching. The wolf-

YELLOWSTONE SAFARI

The Lamar Valley is dubbed the 'Serengeti of North America' for its large herds of bison, elk and the occasional grizzly or coyote. It's the best place to spot wolves, particularly in spring. Wolf-watchers should ask staff at the visitor center for the wolf-observation sheet, which differentiates the various packs and individual members.

The central Hayden Valley is the other main wildlife-watching area, where spotters crowd the pullouts around dusk. It's a good place to view large predators such as wolves and grizzlies, especially in spring when thawing winter carcasses offer almost guaranteed sightings. Coyotes, elk and bison are all common. The tree line is a good place to scan for wildlife. The more you know about animals' habitats and habits, the more likely you are to catch a glimpse of them.

In general, spring and fall are the best times to view wildlife, but each season has its own highlight. Wapati calves and baby bison are adorable in late spring, while bugling elk come out in the fall rut. In summer, observe at dawn or dusk, as most animals withdraw to forests to avoid midday heat.

It's worth having good binoculars or even renting a spotting scope. A high-end telephoto lens can also help obsere wildlife at a safe distance.

watching course is particularly fascinating.

The Drive » To continue to Mammoth, turn around at Pebble Creek campground and return to Tower-Roosevelt. From here it's 18 miles to Mammoth Hot Springs, with a visitor center and full services. A short section of the road around the Mammoth Hot Springs terraces is steep with hairpin turns. The Upper Terraces are on the right coming from Tower, reached via a one-way loop not suitable for trailers and RVs.

- - - - - - - - - - - - -

🕘 Mammoth Hot Springs

Go west to Mammoth Hot Springs. At over 115,000 years old, it's North America's oldest known, and most volatile, continuously active thermal area. Here the mountain is actually turning itself inside-out, depositing dissolved subterranean limestone that builds up in white sculpted layers bordering the surreal.

Take the one-way loop around the **Upper Terraces** for views, but it's best to park at the **Lower Terraces** to walk the hour's worth of boardwalks, so you can end on a descent.

End your trip with a dip in the **Boiling River**, a hot-spring swimming hole, reached via an easy half-mile footpath from a parking lot on the eastern side of the road 2.3 miles north of Mammoth. The hot springs here tumble over travertine rocks into the cool Gardner River, creating a waterfall and warm swimming hole. Though usually crowded, soaking here is still a treat.

Leave the park via the north entrance at the Montana state line.

✗ 🛏 p375

Classic Trip

Eating & Sleeping

Jackson ❶

✖ Snake
River Grill
Modern American **$$$**

(📞307-733-0557; 84 E Broadway; mains $21-52; 🕐from 5:30pm) With a roaring stone fireplace, extensive wine list and snappy linens, this grill creates notable American *haute cuisine*. Start with tempura string beans with spicy sriracha dipping sauce. The crispy pork falls off the bone and grilled elk chops show earthy goodness. One dessert easily satisfies two.

✖ Pearl Street Meat Co
Deli **$**

(260 W Pearl Ave; sandwiches $9; 🕐8am-7pm Mon-Sat, 11am-7pm Sun) Jackson's answer to Dean & Deluca is this busy deli stocked with artisan cheeses, gourmet products and natural local meats. Takeout sandwiches are perfect for park picnics.

✖ Coco Love
Dessert **$**

(📞307-733-3253; 55 N Glenwood Dr; desserts $5-8; 🕐9am-8pm) Master dessert-chef Oscar Ortega shows off his French training with a pastry case of exquisite *objet d'art* desserts and handmade chocolates that make you quiver in delight. Do it.

🛏 Alpine House
B&B **$$$**

(📞307-739-1570; www.alpinehouse.com; 285 N Glenwood St; d incl breakfast $250, cottage $450; 📶) Two former Olympic skiers have infused this downtown home with sunny Scandinavian style. They offer great personalized service and there's a cozy library specializing in mountaineering books. Plus plush robes, down comforters, a shared Finnish sauna and an outdoor Jacuzzi.

🛏 Buckrail Lodge
Motel **$$**

(📞307-733-2079; www.buckraillodge.com; 110 E Karnes Ave; r from $93; ❄🛜) With spacious and charming log-cabin-style rooms, this steal is centrally located, with ample grounds and an outdoor Jacuzzi.

String & Leigh Lakes ❸

✖ Jenny Lake Lodge
Dining Room
Modern American **$$$**

(📞307-543-3352; breakfast $24, lunch mains $12-15, prix-fixe dinner $85; 🕐7am-9pm) A real splurge, but totally worth it, this may be the only five-course wilderness meal of your life. For breakfast, crab-cake eggs benedict is prepared to perfection. Trout with polenta and crispy spinach satisfies hungry hikers. Dress up in the evening, when reservations are a must.

🛏 Jenny Lake Lodge
Lodge **$$$**

(📞307-733-4647; www.gtlc.com; Jenny Lake; cabins incl half-board $655; 🕐Jun-Sep) Worn timbers, down comforters and colorful quilts cozy up this elegant park lodging. Perks include breakfast, a five-course dinner, complimentary bicycles and horseback riding. Log cabins sport a deck but there are no TVs or radios (phones are available on request).

🛏 Climbers' Ranch
Cabin **$**

(📞307-733-7271; www.americanalpineclub. org; Teton Park Rd; dm $25; 🕐Jun-Sep) A hiker's paradise, these rustic log cabins have a spectacular in-park location. The basics are covered: a well-kept bathhouse, climbing wall and a sheltered cook station. Just bring your own sleeping bag and pad.

🛏 Lizard
Creek Campground
Campground **$**

(📞800-672-6012; sites $21; 🕐June-early Sep) In a forested peninsula along Jackson Lake's north shore, about 8 miles north of Colter Bay Junction, these secluded sites (60 in total) rarely fill up.

Old Faithful ⑤

✖ Old Faithful
Inn Dining Room   American $$$

(☎307-545-4999; dinner mains $13-29;
⏱6:30-10:30am, 11:30am-2:30pm, 5-10pm; 🔧)
The buffets here will maximize your time spent
geyser-gazing but the à la carte options are
more innovative, with elk sliders, bison ravioli
and a sizzling pork osso buco. There are gluten-
free options. Reserve dinner 24 hours ahead.

🛏 Old Faithful Inn   Hotel $$

(☎866-439-7375; www.yellowstone
nationalparklodges.com; old house d with
shared/private bath from $103/140, standard
from $164; ⏱early May-early Oct) Next to the
signature geyser, this national historic landmark
features an immense timber lobby with huge
stone fireplaces and sky-high knotted-pine
ceilings. Prices vary, and many of the most
interesting historic rooms share baths. Public
areas offer plenty of allure.

🛏 Madison
Campground   Campground $

(☎307-344-7311; www.yellowstone
nationalparklodges.com; site $21; ⏱early
May-late Oct) The closest campground to Old
Faithful, with 250 sites in open forest. Though
it's large, sites are well-spaced. Bison and elk
are known to frequent the meadows to the west.
There are nightly ranger talks.

Yellowstone Lake ⑦

✖ Lake Yellowstone
Hotel Dining Room   American $$$

(☎307-344-7311; mains $13-33; ⏱6:30-10am,
11:30am-2:30pm, 5-10pm; 🔧) Keep one outfit
unwrinkled to dine in style at the dining room
of the Lake Yellowstone Hotel – the best in
the park. Lunch options include Montana
lamb sliders, lovely salads and bison burgers.

There are local and gluten-free options.
Dinner consists of heavier fare. Reservations
recommended.

🛏 Lake Yellowstone Hotel   Hotel $$

(☎866-439-7375; www.yellowstone
nationalparklodges.com; cabins $130, r $149-
299; ⏱mid-May–Sep) Oozing 1920s Western
ambiance, this romantic, historic hotel is a
class act. It has Yellowstone's most divine
lounge, with big lakeview picture windows and
a live string quartet playing. Rooms are well
appointed, cabins more rustic.

Mammoth Hot Springs ⑪

✖ Old West Cookout   BBQ $$$

(Roosevelt Country; ☎866-439-7375; dinner &
wagon ride adult/child $57/46; ⏱5pm, Jun to
early Sep; 🚌) From the Roosevelt Lodge, guests
travel by wagon or ride horses to a cookout with
steak, beans and the kind of cowboy coffee you
have to filter through your teeth. Kids love it.
Reserve way ahead.

🛏 Roosevelt Lodge Cabins   Cabin $

(☎866-439-7375; www.yellowstone
nationalparklodges.com; cabins $69-115; 🐾)
For families or groups, the Roughrider cabins
are among the park's greatest bargains, as the
price remains the same despite the number of
occupants. While they feature a log-burning
stove, baths are separate and shared. Frontier
cabins are a step up; book them well in advance.

🛏 Norris Campground   Campground $

(http://www.nps.gov/yell; site $20; ⏱mid-
May–late Sep) Overlooking the Gibbon River,
this is one of the park's nicest campsites,
with riverside options (on the popular Loop A)
adjacent to meadows with plenty of fishing and
wildlife-watching opportunities. At night there is
a ranger-led campfire program. No reservations
required.

Highline Trail Traverse Glacier National
Park on one of America's best hikes

Going-to-the-Sun Road

29

From grandeur to grizzlies, Glacier National Park is the soul of the great American wilderness. Hugging cliffs with hairpin turns, the Going-to-the-Sun Road is your passageway across the park.

FENG WEI PHOTOGRAPHY / GETTY IMAGES ©

TRIP HIGHLIGHTS

1 mile

Whitefish
Cowboy charm just south of Canada

50 miles

Garden Wall
Stunning steep slopes, cascading streams and wildflower meadows

5

7

FINISH
St Mary

St Mary Lake

Lake McDonald

Apgar

West Glacier

1 **START**

Logan Pass
Gaze onto the grandeur in four cardinal directions

57 miles

3 DAYS
76 MILES / 122KM

GREAT FOR...

BEST TIME TO GO
Jul–Sep

ESSENTIAL PHOTO

Oberlin Bend for arresting views of Garden Wall.

BEST FOR WILDLIFE

Spy on elk herds and roaming coyotes at Two Dog Flats.

29

Going-to-the-Sun Road

Few national parks are as magnificent and pristine as Glacier, the only spot in the lower 48 where grizzly bears roam in the wilderness that's both accessible and authentically wild. It's renowned for its historic 'parkitecture' lodges, intact pre-Columbian ecosystem and the spectacular Going-to-the-Sun Road. This 53-mile mountain route is a National Historic Landmark, with excellent hiking trails served by a free shuttle.

TRIP HIGHLIGHT

❶ Whitefish

A gateway to Glacier National Park, this charismatic and caffeinated New West ski town would merit a long-distance trip itself. One square mile of rustic Western chic, its strong suits are both the great outdoors and downtown's welcoming shops and restaurants.

Summer at **Whitefish Mountain Resort** (📞406-862-2900; www.bigmtn.com) has intrepid

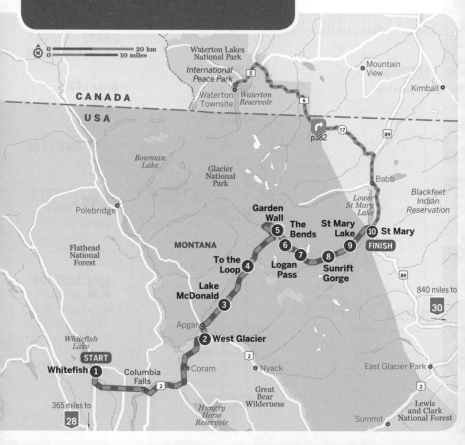

explorers touring the treetops via suspended canopy, mountain biking white-knuckle trails and finishing with beers at the Summit House. But our pick is to hike its Big Mountain in mid-August to gather a basket of succulent huckleberries! Extra points if you find the teensy (and tasty) whortleberries near the top. If you're too tuckered to descend on foot, ride the gondola down.

There is rail service to West and East Glacier from the **railroad depot** (☑406-862-2268; 500 Depot St; ⏰6am-1:30pm, 4:30pm-midnight). Once in the park, hook up with the hop-on-hop-off shuttle service to explore Going-to-the-Sun Road.

LINK YOUR TRIP

28 Grand Teton to Yellowstone

For Yellowstone's spectacular wildlife, MT take US89 N to Bozeman for I-90W. At Missoula take Rte 35 to 82 for Whitefish. It's a 6½ hour, 410-mile trip.

30 Top of the Rockies

From St Mary take US-89 S and work your way to I-90 E and I-25 S to Denver; the fine Colorado high country is a 13-hour, 931-mile trip.

🍴 📖 p383

The Drive » From Whitefish head south on Hwy 93 and go left on MT 40 East, which becomes Hwy 2. West Glacier is an easy 26-mile trip.

② West Glacier

The busiest entrance to the park, West Glacier is just an entryway. Services, including a visitor center and backcountry permit office, are found in the nearby hub of Apgar where the cross-park shuttles also start. If you have time, check out the original schoolhouse which dates from 1915. Nearby, the tiny 1929 **Discovery Cabin** acts as an activity center for children.

Though a motel, **Village Inn** (☑406-888-5632; www.glacierparkinc.com; Apgar Village; r $146-263; ⏰late May-late Sep) is a top choice for lodging in Apgar Village. It's both comfy and rustic, a gadget-free zone where you can feast on lake views just beyond the balcony.

The **Going-to-the-Sun Road** (⏰mid-Jun–late Sep) is undergoing road rehabilitation until 2017. That means the summer opening date may be later than the usual mid-June, so check online before traveling.

🍴 p383

The Drive » Pick up the paved Going-to-the-Sun Road to your left and head north to Apgar Village, with restaurants and services. The campground is slightly further on. At lower

elevations, the speed limit is 40mph. Note that vehicles over 8ft wide and 21ft long are not permitted.

③ Lake McDonald

The lush, verdant valley of Lake McDonald boasts some of the park's oldest temperate rainforest. Paddling your rowboat over the glassy surface of the largest lake in the park may be the best way to experience serenity on a super scale. Rent a boat from **Glacier Park Boat Co** (☑406-257-2426; www.glacierparkboats.com; St Mary Lake cruise adult/child $25/12) at the lodge dock. On the opposite shore, burned areas are evidence of the 2003 Robert Fire.

Shrug off the crowds and sleep under the fragrant pines at **Sprague Creek**, our favorite lakeside campground. There's only tent camping allowed and with just 25 sites, you can really enjoy the serenity of these shores.

Reaching the eastern end of the shore, rustic **Lake McDonald Lodge** was first built in 1895, though it was replaced with Swiss-style architecture in 1913. Enter via the back door which faces the lake.

📖 p383

The Drive » Rimmed by pines, this flat section skirts shimmering Lake McDonald's eastern shore, serving up views of Stanton Mountain beyond the northern shore. Both Sprague Creek and Lake McDonald Lodge are to the left.

TAKE A FREE RIDE

Fewer cars on the road means less fossil-fuel emissions, so help the park combat global warming by taking the park's **free shuttle** (⊘9am-3:45pm Apgar Village, Jul & Aug) across Going-to-the-Sun Road rather than driving. For RV travelers it may be obligatory due to large vehicle restrictions. The shuttle runs between Apgar Transit Center and St Mary, making 16 shuttle stops. Departing every 30 minutes from the west side, shuttles allow you to get on or off at these key points of interest. Some express shuttles go directly to Logan Pass. No tickets are necessary. Bring a day pack and water with you. To go totally green, plan your trip to the park via Amtrak's Empire Builder train from Minneapolis, Chicago, Seattle or Portland.

4 To the Loop

The road runs parallel to blue-green McDonald Creek and **McDonald Falls** – beautiful cascades gushing through cut rock. Photos are best from the observation platform that juts into the river.

Though often crowded, it's worth appreciating the old-growth cedars and hemlocks of **Avalanche Creek**. Beyond the campground and picnic area, Trail of the Cedars loops 1 mile. Keep going for a pleasant hike that leads to snow-fed Avalanche Lake, a 4-mile round-trip through spruce and fir to a cirque.

The 1926 **West Tunnel** took years to drill. An interior sidewalk borders the view of Heaven's Peak through observation windows.

It may be hard to believe that a sharp hairpin turn is the defining feature of the whole road, but **The Loop** was an elegant engineering solution to one *very* vertical climb. Instead of making the proposed 15 switchbacks, The Loop follows McDonald Creek with just one hairpin, also taking in full dramatic views of the Garden Wall. As the Highline Trail endpoint, the parking lot gets busy in high season.

The Drive » The road ascends parallel to McDonald Creek before angling sharply to the Garden Wall, which forms the 9000ft spine of the Continental Divide. In early summer, there may be standing water on the road from the Weeping Wall; westbound passengers will be treated to a soaking.

TRIP HIGHLIGHT

5 Garden Wall

Powerful glaciers carved this dramatic arête running parallel to Going-to-the-Sun Road millions of years ago. The steep western slopes of Garden Wall feature lush wildflower meadows traversed by the Highline Trail.

Located 610ft below the Garden Wall, the glistening **Weeping Wall** creates seasonal waterfalls that formed when drilling during road construction unleashed a series of mountain springs. Water falls over the lip of a 30ft man-made cliff and frequently gives westbound car passengers a good soaking in early summer. By early August the torrent reverts to its more gentle namesake: weeping.

For a more natural waterfall, look across the valley to the distant **Bird Woman Falls**, a spectacular 500ft spray emerging from a hanging valley between Mt Oberlin and Mt Cannon.

Throughout this section there is ample evidence of why Going-to-the-Sun Road is renowned as a marvel of civil engineering. Highlights include the bridge that Haystack Falls flows through and the 1932 Triple Arches, with a small turnout.

The Drive » Continue the ascent to Logan Pass. In alpine sections the speed limit is 25mph. This is the picture-perfect section of the road (you might recognize it from the tourist brochures!). Be sure to pull over and snap your own postcard shot.

6 The Bends

Just beyond the Weeping Wall, **Big Bend** features magnificent views of Mt Oberlin, Heaven's Peak and Cannon Mountain amid blooming beargrass and fireweed. It's midway between The Loop and Logan Pass. It's a good spot for a break. Bighorn sheep blend well into the cliffs – grab your binoculars to find them.

Just west of Logan Pass, **Oberlin Bend** sits below the cascading waterfalls of Mt Oberlin. Take the short boardwalk for breathtaking views of hanging valleys and Going-to-the-Sun Road itself. On a clear day, views extend all the way to Canada. It may also be the best spot to see the park's signature mountain goats hanging out on steep rock ledges.

The Drive » This section between The Loop and Logan Pass has views onto the Garden Wall. Stop at designated pullouts for both Big Bend and Oberlin Bend. Wildlife may get close here – try to keep a respectful distance.

TRIP HIGHLIGHT

7 Logan Pass

The highest point of Going-to-the-Sun Road, panoramic Logan Pass (6646ft) also marks the Continental Divide. Stop at **Logan Pass Visitor Center** (☏406-888-7800; Going-to-the-Sun Rd, Logan Pass; admission free; ☺Jun– mid-Oct) with interesting natural-history displays and a browse-worthy bookstore. Take the 1.5-mile boardwalk trail behind it to the wildflower meadows of **Hidden Lake Overlook**.

Across the way, the **Highline Trail** is lauded as one of America's best hikes and a huge highlight for trekkers. Cutting like a scar across the famous Garden Wall, this rugged 18.5-mile path traces mountain-goat terrain along the Continental Divide with huge vistas of glaciated valleys and jagged peaks. Though it isn't difficult (there's minimal elevation change), the trail is quite exposed. For a shorter sample, stop at Granite Park, 7.6-miles, one way.

Most hikers arrive to the Highline via private vehicles and return by shuttle. You can avoid the long shuttle lines by leaving your car at the finish of the hike (The Loop or Granite Park) and taking shuttle transportation to the start.

The Drive » Descend Going-to-the-Sun Road toward East Glacier, taking special care at the Siyeh Bend switchbacks. The Jackson Glacier overlook comes up on the right. From here the road makes a relatively straight descent to St Mary Lake.

8 Sunrift Gorge

Pull out near Gunsight Pass Trailhead for telescopic views of **Jackson Glacier**. It's a short walk to the overlook. The park's fifth-largest glacier, it's also the only one you will see from this road, viewed at a 5-mile distance. As it has melted over the years, it has actually split into two glaciers called Jackson and Bigfoot. In 1850 the park had 150 glaciers – today there are a scant 26.

Just off the road and adjacent to a shuttle stop to your left, Sunrift Gorge is a narrow canyon that's 80ft deep and 800ft long. It was carved over millennia by the gushing glacial meltwaters of Baring Creek. Its shady, moist microclimate supports different vegetation and wildlife, like the water ouzels that navigate rapid currents.

Constructed in 1093, the picturesque **Baring Bridge** is considered the most beautiful man-made feature on the road. It was once a main transit point when horses were used to travel the park. Follow the short quarter-mile wooded trail here to Baring Falls.

The Drive » The road skirts north of St Mary Lake for the remainder of the drive.

9 St Mary Lake

Located on the park's drier eastern side, where the mountains melt imperceptibly into the Great Plains, St Mary

DETOUR:
INTERNATIONAL PEACE PARK

Start: ⑩ St Mary Visitor Center

Hello, Canada! This three-day detour takes Hwy 17 northeast from St Mary Visitor Center to Canada's Hwy 6 and Hwy 5 to Waterton Lakes National Park, Glacier's sister park in Alberta, Canada (bring your passport). Together these two stunners compose the Waterton-Glacier International Peace Park, declared a World Heritage Site in 1995. Once there, ditch your latte habit and enjoy high tea at the venerable old **Prince of Wales Hotel** (☎403-859-2231; www.princeofwaleswaterton.com; Prince of Wales Rd; r from $239; ☺mid-May–Sep; [P][📶]), perched on a hill with stunning views. The hotel is only open June through August.

Another way to take in the majestic landscape without regard to borders is to participate in the free International Peace Park Hike. Every Saturday in summer, rangers bring a group of hikers from Waterton on a gentle 8.5-mile hike alongside twinkling Upper Waterton Lake in Canada to Goat Haunt in Glacier National Park in the US. A boat (adult US$12) returns hikers to Waterton. The program is wildly popular; reserve a spot at the Waterton Visitor Center.

Lake fills a deep, glacier-carved valley famous for its astounding views and ferocious winds. Known to the Blackfeet as the Walled-in Lake, its long shoreline features numerous trailheads and viewpoints.

Windy and spectacular, **Sun Point** is a rocky promontory overlooking the lake. Take in views of the magnificent Going-to-the-Sun Mountain (9642ft) to the north. You will also see Wild Goose Island, a tiny stub in the middle of St Mary Lake. The former site of some of the park's earliest and most luxurious chalets that no longer stand, Sun Point is now a good picnic spot. Lace up your boots if you want to take the trails linking to Baring Falls and St Mary Falls.

Large pullout **Golden Staircase** abuts limestone cliffs. The 500ft retaining wall was built in the 1930s. Across the lake there's evidence of the 2006 Red Eagle Fire.

✗ 🛏 p383

The Drive » Continue heading east. Services at Rising Sun are found on your right, 18 miles before reaching St Mary Campground. The visitor center is slightly beyond it at the eastern park entrance. There are more services and gas stations in the town of St Mary.

- - - - - - - - - - - - - - -

⑩ St Mary
Visitor Center

Handy shuttle stop **Rising Sun** has a lovely backdrop and many hotels and services (including showers for campers). A 1½ hour lake cruise is combined with a 3-mile hike to St Mary Falls with Glacier Park Boat Co.

An amazing biological diversity is found where the prairies and mountains meet at **Two Dog Flats**. These shortgrass prairies, wildflower meadows and forest are home to coyotes, badgers, deer, songbirds and predators. Prolific in winter, elk hang around for fall and spring, best seen in the morning or evening.

The eastern gateway to Glacier National Park, the St Mary Visitor Center is classic 1950s parkitecture, restored and featuring classic lines that imitate mountain silhouettes. In addition to offering information, rangers present evening programs here throughout the summer. Backpackers can obtain backcountry permits here too.

✗ 🛏 p383

Eating & Sleeping

Whitefish ❶

✗ Buffalo Café   Cafe $

(www.buffalocafewhitefish.com; 514 3rd St E; breakfast $7-10) Locals love the plates piled high with food and old-fashioned milkshakes. Breakfast features mountains of hash browns and hearty *huevos rancheros*. Lunch offers burgers and grilled sandwiches.

The Great Northern Brewing Co   Brewpub

(☎406-863-1000; www.greatnorthernbrewing. com; 2 Central Avenue; ⏰tours 1pm & 3pm Mon-Thu) This place is a real classic, brewing some of Montana's best beers including Huckleberry Wheat. With no kitchen, they stock take-out menus from Whitefish restaurants and offer recommendations. Take the tour.

⌸ Downtowner Inn   Motel $$

(☎406-862-2535; www.downtownermotel. cc; 224 Spokane Ave; d $123; ❄🐾) Featuring a gym, Jacuzzi and morning bagel bar, this friendly motel is more than a roadside stop. There's lots of information on local activities, and helpful staff.

⌸ Garden Wall   B&B $$

(☎406-862-3440; www.gardenwallinn.com; 504 Spokane Ave; r incl breakfast $155-215, ste $275; 🐾) An efficiently run B&B with art-deco rooms, living-room log fires on chilly days and gourmet breakfasts. But first a wake-up coffee tray is delivered to your room. The suite sleeps up to four.

West Glacier ❷

✗ West Glacier Restaurant   American $

(☎406-888-5359; 200 Going-to-the-Sun Rd; mains $6-18; ⏰7am-10pm mid-May–Oct; 👶) Virtually unchanged for the last 50 years. Order something with huckleberry, the same Montana fruit the grizzly bears like.

Lake McDonald ❸

⌸ Lake McDonald Lodge   Lodge $$

(☎406-888-5431; www.lakemcdonaldlodge. com; Going-to-the-Sun Rd, Lake McDonald Valley; r $79-191; ⏰Jun-Sep) Built in 1913, this old hunting lodge is adorned with stuffed-animal trophies and exudes relaxation. The 100 rooms are lodge-, chalet- or motel-style. There are nightly park-ranger talks and lake cruises, as well as a restaurant and pizzeria.

⌸ Sperry Chalet   Chalet $$

(☎888-345-2649; www.sperrychalet.com; Lake McDonald Valley; s/d incl full board $135/332; ⏰Jul 7-Sep 8) A hike-in-only Swiss-style chalet with phenomenal views. The 7-mile trail starts opposite Lake McDonald Lodge. This impressive stone structure was constructed a century ago by Great Northern Railway in the heart of the high country. It has modern outdoor composting toilets and cold-water-only showers. Mules can be hired to carry gear.

⌸ Apgar Campground   Campground $

(☎406-888-7800; Apgar; campsite $20; ⏰early May-Oct, Dec-late Mar) A large wooded campground with a cycle path and lake access, very convenient to Apgar Village and its restaurants.

St Mary Visitor Center ❿

✗ Park Café and Grocery   Cafe

(☎406-732-4482; www.parkcafe.us; St Mary; mains $6-12; ⏰May-Sep) This family-run cafe is known for excellent homemade pies. Numerous selections from fruit to cream are fresh-baked each morning.

⌸ St Mary Campground   Campground $

(☎406-888-5632; St Mary; campsite $23; ⏰late May-late Sept, Dec-late Mar) Cottonwoods and aspens flank these shady campsites, though there are parts of the campground (around B loop) that are less protected.

Aspen *Climb high in this alpine gem of a town*

Top of the Rockies

30

Ride the Great Divide as you climb past snow-dusted peaks, glitzy resorts, abandoned ghost towns and big-sky wilderness.

TRIP HIGHLIGHTS

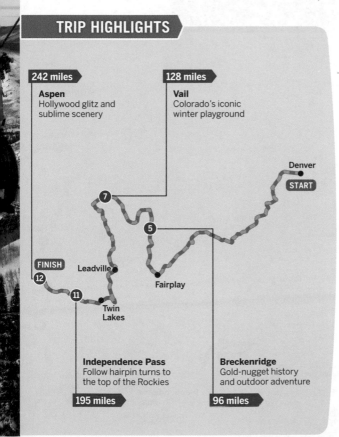

242 miles

Aspen
Hollywood glitz and sublime scenery

128 miles

Vail
Colorado's iconic winter playground

Denver

START

7

5

FINISH

Leadville

12

Fairplay

11

Twin Lakes

Independence Pass
Follow hairpin turns to the top of the Rockies

195 miles

Breckenridge
Gold-nugget history and outdoor adventure

96 miles

4–5 DAYS
242 MILES / 389KM

GREAT FOR...

BEST TIME TO GO
June to October, for the sky-high drive over Independence Pass.

 ESSENTIAL PHOTO

Maroon Bells, Colorado's most iconic peaks.

 BEST TWO DAYS

Head from Breckenridge to Aspen to hit the highlights; Vail is optional.

30

Top of the Rockies

This high-altitude adventure follows Colorado's backroads from one spectacular mountain pass to the next. Along the way you'll get a glimpse of countless jagged peaks (including the two tallest in the state, Mt Elbert and Mt Massive), rich veins of Wild West history and alpine gems such as Breckenridge, Vail and Aspen, each of which has its own distinct style. Come here to hike, bike, ski or spot wildlife – for lovers of the great outdoors, this here's paradise.

❶ Denver

While Denver has its moments – see our walking tour for tips on exploring the city – it won't be long before you feel the urge to head up into those gorgeous snowcapped peaks west of town. But while everyone else will be leaving via the interstate, this trip will introduce you to the Rockies' prettiest backdoor secret: Hwy 285.

The Drive ❯❯ Kenosha Pass is 65 miles southwest of downtown Denver, on Hwy 285.

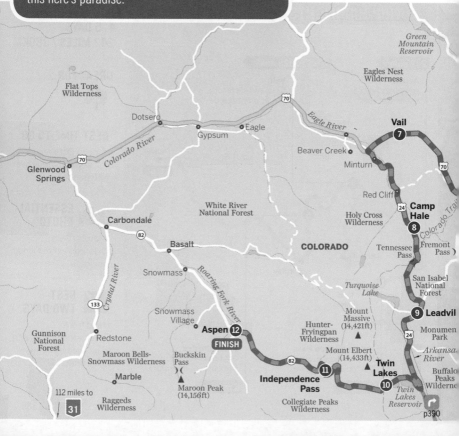

② Kenosha Pass

The climb out of Denver is pretty enough, but it's not until you reach Kenosha Pass (10,000ft) that you really start to feel that Rocky Mountain magic. Although there's a scenic overlook at the pass, the best views, ironically, are not at the overlook at all, but after you round the bend on the way down. Suddenly, you'll find yourself looking out over the distant peaks of the Mosquito range, rising mightily above the high-altitude prairie

of the South Park basin. Inspired? You're not the first. Walt Whitman wrote about this same view on a trip West in 1879.

The Drive » Fairplay is 21 miles southwest of Kenosha

Pass on Hwy 285. When you reach town, turn north onto Hwy 9 to access Main St. Much of the highway between here and Denver follows an old stagecoach road – originally an 18-hour-long journey, broken up over two days.

LINK YOUR TRIP

31 San Juan Skyway & the Million Dollar Highway

Follow backroads 250 miles south to the peaks and pueblos of Telluride and Mesa Verde.

36 High Road & Low Road to Taos

Take Hwy 285 south to magical New Mexico and Santa Fe (300 miles), passing Salida and the Great Sand Dunes.

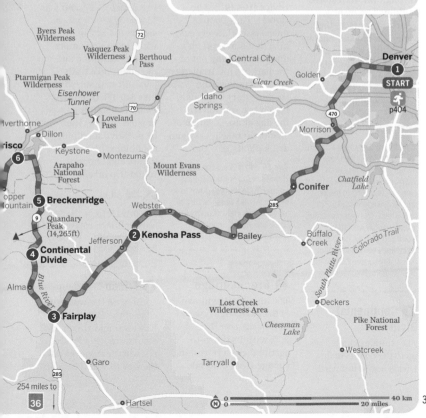

❸ Fairplay

Tiny Fairplay was originally a mining settlement and supply town for Leadville (pack burros used to clop back and forth over 13,000ft-Mosquito Pass to the west), and you can stop here to visit **South Park City** (www.southparkcity. org; 100 4th St; adult/child 6-12yr $10/4; ⏰9am-7pm, mid-May–mid-Oct, shorter hours May & Oct; ♿), a re-created 19th-century Colorado boomtown. Get a taste of life back in the good-old, bad-old days of the gold rush through the 40 restored buildings on display, which range from the general store and saloon to a dentist's office and morgue. And yes, *South Park* fans, Fairplay does bear more than a passing resemblance to the hometown of Kyle, Cartman and the boys.

The Drive ›› Hoosier Pass and the Continental Divide are 11 miles north of Fairplay on Hwy 9. The pass is hemmed in by Mt Lincoln (14,286ft) to the west and Mt Silverheels (13,822ft) to the east. The latter is named after a dancer who stayed behind to care for the ill during a smallpox epidemic in Alma, eventually succumbing to the disease herself.

❹ Continental Divide

The stunning climb up to the Continental Divide begins just north of Fairplay. A mere 5.5-mile drive will bring you to Alma, the highest incorporated town in the United States, at an elevation of 10,578ft. It's surrounded by four '14ers' (mountains over 14,000ft), thousand-year-old bristlecone pines and scores of old mining claims. If you want to explore, follow the unpaved Buckskin Rd (County Rd 8) 6 miles west toward Kite Lake – 4WD and high clearance is recommended for the last mile.

Otherwise, keep climbing up Hwy 9 and you'll soon reach Hoosier Pass and the Continental Divide (11,539ft). The Hoosier Pass Loop (3 miles) is a relatively easy hike that starts off on a dirt road leading out of the parking lot. It allows you to get above the treeline quickly, though remember you started the day at an elevation of 5280ft, so take it easy and drink plenty of water.

The Drive ›› Breckenridge is 11 miles north of Hoosier Pass on Hwy 9. On the way down from the pass, you'll pass the turnoff for Quandary Peak (County Rd 850), which is 7.5 miles from Breckenridge.

TRIP HIGHLIGHT

❺ Breckenridge

The historic downtown of **Breckenridge** (www. breckenridge.com; lift ticket $115) with its down-to-earth vibe is a refreshing change from Colorado's glitzier resorts. Its gold-nugget history survives in the numerous heritage buildings scattered around town, but make no mistake, it's the endless outdoor activities that draw the crowds. Regardless of whether it's snow or shine, the BreckConnect Gondola (free) up to the base of Peak 8 is where the fun begins. In winter, skiers can catch the T-bar up to the Imperial Express Superchair, which, at 12,840ft, is the highest chairlift in the US. In summer, kids will rock the **Fun Park** (☏800-789-7669; www.breckenridge.com; Peak 8; day pass 3-7yr/8yr & up $34/68; ⏰9:30am-5:30pm mid-Jun–mid-Sep; ♿), while teens and adults can hit the hiking and mountain-bike trails (chairlift without/with bike $10/17). **Quandary Peak** (14,265ft) is a popular 14er to climb, but be prepared for alpine conditions; it's a 6-mile (figure eight hours) round-trip hike.

🍴 🛏 p393

The Drive ›› Follow Hwy 9 north for 10 miles until you reach the turnoff (on your left) for Frisco's Main St.

❻ Frisco

Located on the western edge of the Dillon Reservoir and ringed by mountains, tiny Frisco is a worthy stopover on the way to Vail. The main

Aspen Alpine adventure playground

DETOUR: SALIDA
Start ⑩ Twin Lakes

If you're on the road from November to May, chances are Independence Pass will be closed. If this is the case, don't fret – simply follow Hwy 24 and the Arkansas River south for 50 miles until you reach the town of Salida. Home to one of the largest historic downtown areas in the state, funky Salida is Colorado's white-water-rafting hub and a great base from which to explore the Collegiate Peaks, whether you're on foot, bike or skis. A favorite with Coloradans, Salida is less well known than the big ski towns and has a much more local, small-town feel. Alternatively, if you simply can't miss Aspen, retrace your steps from Twin Lakes back to I-70, head west to Glenwood Springs, then follow Hwy 82 east up the Roaring Fork Valley until you reach town. It's roughly 150 miles or three hours of driving.

attraction is the **Historic Park & Museum** (www.townoffrisco.com; cnr 2nd Ave & Main St; ☉10am-4pm Tue-Sat, 10am-2pm Sun; 👪) which has a collection of restored log cabins and the town jail and chapel. Frisco is also a great place to get on two wheels and exercise your lungs – Summit County's paved bike lanes (www.summitbiking.org) extend around the reservoir all the way from Vail to Keystone to Breck. Get the scoop on local trails and rent a bike at **Team Managers** (☎970-668-3321; www.team-managers.com; 1121 Dillon Dam Rd; bike rental 4hr/full day $17/27, ski rental from $10; ☉8:30am-6pm).

The Drive » From Frisco, take I-70 west 27 miles to exit 176 and follow signs to either Vail Village

(the main town) or Lionshead further west. Either way, look for the public parking garages ($25 per day in winter, free in summer) – they're the only places to park, unless you're spending the night.

- - - - - - - - - - - -

TRIP HIGHLIGHT

❼ Vail
Vail Mountain Resort
(www.vail.com; lift ticket winter/summer $119/26) is Eagle County's legendary winter playground. This is where the movie stars and tycoons ski, and it's not unusual to see Texans in 10-gallon hats and women in mink coats zipping down the slopes. Whether you're here for the powdery back bowls or it's your first time on a snowboard, the largest ski resort in the US rarely disappoints – so long as you're prepared for the

price tag. There's plenty of action in summer too. For mountain-bike rental see **Bike Valet** (☎970-476-5385; www.bikevalet.net; 520 E Lionshead Circle; bike rental per day from $30; ☉10am-5pm; 👪) and **Bearcat Stables** (☎970-926-1578; www.bearcatstables.com; 2701 Squaw Creek Rd, Edwards; 1/2/4hr ride $60/90/160; ☉by reservation; 👪) for horseback riding. Book ahead if you plan on teeing off at the **Vail Golf Club** (☎888-709-3939; www.vailrec.com; 1778 Vail Valley Dr; 9-/18-holes $55/90 May-Oct). Check out the **Holy Cross Ranger Office** (☎970-827-5715; www.fs.usda.gov/whiteriver; 24747 Hwy 24; ☉9am-4pm Mon-Fri) for hiking and camping info. Families stay occupied at **Adventure Ridge** (☎970-754-8245; lift ticket adult/child $26/5, activity prices vary; ☉10am-6pm, to 9pm Thu-Sat, mid-Jun–Sep; 👪), which features a plethora of activities 10,000ft up at the top of Eagle Bahn Gondola (access is from Lionshead). It's slated to expand into the much larger **Epic Discovery** (www.epicdiscovery.com) in 2015, with everything from a ropes course and zip lines to an adrenaline-pumping 'forest coaster'.

 p393

The Drive » From Vail, take I-70 west for 4.5 miles to exit 171, and then turn onto Hwy 24 east. After you pass through the town of Minturn, the road begins to wind up along a cliff face, with impressive views of Notch Mountain (13,237ft) and the Holy Cross Wilderness on your right. After 17 miles you'll reach the turnoff for Camp Hale – now no more than a grassy meadow.

--- --- --- --- --- --- ---

8 Camp Hale

Established in 1942, Camp Hale was created specifically for the purpose of training the 10th Mountain Division, the US Army's only battalion on skis. At its height during WWII, there were over 1000 buildings and some 14,000 soldiers housed in the meadow here.

After the war Camp Hale was decommissioned, only to be brought back to life again in 1958, this time by the CIA. Over the next six years, CIA agents trained Tibetan freedom fighters in guerrilla warfare, with the goal of driving the communist Chinese out of Tibet.

In 1965 Camp Hale was officially dismantled, and the land returned to the US Forest Service. Many vets from the 10th Mountain Division returned to Colorado to become involved in the burgeoning ski industry, including Pete Seibert, who co-founded Vail Resort in 1962.

 p393

The Drive ⟫ Hwy 24 is known as the 'Top of the Rockies Scenic Byway'. On the way down from Tennessee Pass you'll be treated to a panorama of Colorado's two highest peaks

– Mt Massive and Mt Elbert – stretching away to the south. All told, it's 16 miles from Camp Hale to Leadville.

--- --- --- --- --- --- ---

9 Leadville

Originally known as Cloud City, Leadville was once Colorado's second-largest municipality. It was silver, not gold, that made the fortunes of many here; the best place to learn about the town's mineral-rich history is at the surprisingly interesting **Mining Hall of Fame** (www.mininghalloffame.org; 120 W 9th St; adult/child 6-12yr $7/3; ⏱9am-5pm Jun-Oct, 11am-6pm Nov-May; ♿), which can be combined with a visit to the **Matchless Mine** (E 7th Rd; adult/child 6-12yr $7/3, combo ticket with Mining Hall of Fame $10/5; ⏱9am-5pm Jun-Sep) exterior in summer. The historic downtown makes for a pleasant stroll; check out landmarks such as the **Healy House Museum** (www.historycolorado.org; 912 Harrison Ave; adult/child 6-12yr $6/4.50; ⏱10am-4:30pm mid-May–Sep) and the **Tabor Opera House** (www.taboroperahouse.

net; 308 Harrison Ave; adult/child $5/2.50; ⏱10am-5pm Mon-Sat Jun-Aug), where the likes of Houdini and Oscar Wilde once appeared.

 p393

The Drive ⟫ From Leadville, take Hwy 24 south for 14 miles, following the not-yet-mighty Arkansas River until you reach the turnoff for Hwy 82. Follow Hwy 82 west for 6.5 miles until you reach Twin Lakes. The turnoff for the Mt Elbert trailhead is actually just south of Leadville on Rte 300. The turnoff for the Interlaken trailhead is 0.6 miles after you turn onto Hwy 82, after Lost Canyon Rd.

--- --- --- --- --- --- ---

10 Twin Lakes

A short drive from Leadville is Twin Lakes, the two largest glacial lakes in the state and an excellent spot to spend a night. A few cabins are all that's left of Dayton, the original town, but the scenery is fabulous and there are plenty of opportunities to get out and hike or fish. On the south shore of the main lake is Interlaken, the vestiges of what was once Colorado's largest resort,

✓ **TOP TIP:
ALTITUDE**

Much of this drive is above 9000ft: don't underestimate the altitude. Essential gear includes sunglasses, sunscreen, hat, Ibuprofen, windbreaker and fleece. Staying hydrated is crucial.

built in 1889. You can get here along the Colorado and Continental Divide trails; it's about 5 miles round-trip with little elevation gain.

If you're up for something more challenging, Colorado's tallest peak, Mt Elbert (14,433ft), is also a possibility. This is a 9-mile round-trip hike with nearly 5000ft of elevation gain, so figure on spending the entire day.

📖 p393

The Drive ⟫ It's 17 miles from Twin Lakes to the top of Independence Pass along Hwy 82. The ghost town of Independence is roughly 3 miles west of the summit.

- - - - - - - - - -

TRIP HIGHLIGHT

⓫ Independence Pass

Looming at 12,095ft, Independence Pass (open June-October) is one of the more high-profile passes along the Continental Divide. The views along the narrow ribbon of road range from pretty to stunning to downright cinematic, and by the time you glimpse swatches of glacier just below the

knife edge of peaks, you'll be living in your own IMAX film. A paved nature trail leaves the parking area at the top of the pass – you're above the treeline here, so dress warmly. On your way down into Aspen, don't miss the ghost town of **Independence** (www.aspenhistorysociety. com; suggested donation $3; ⏱10am-6pm mid-Jun–Aug). Operated and preserved by the Aspen Historical Society, it has the remains of the old livery, general store and a few cabins.

The Drive ⟫ Aspen is 20 miles west of Independence Pass on Hwy 82. Although in theory you can find metered street parking, it's simplest to park in the public garage ($15 per day) next to the Aspen Visitor Center on Rio Grande Pl.

- - - - - - - - - -

TRIP HIGHLIGHT

⓬ Aspen

A cocktail of cowboy grit, Hollywood glam, Ivy League brains and fresh powder, Aspen is a town unlike any place else in the American West. And whatever the season, you'll find plenty here to keep you occupied. The **Aspen Skiing**

Company (☎800-525-6200; www.aspensnowmass. com) runs the area's four resorts – Aspen, Snowmass, Buttermilk and the Highlands – while the historic red-brick downtown has some of Colorado's best restaurants, a great **art museum** (☎970-925-8050; www.aspenartmuseum. org; cnr East Hyman Ave & Spring St; ⏱10am-6pm Tue-Sat, to 7pm Thu, noon-6pm Sun), plenty of galleries and boutiques, and the noteworthy **Aspen Center for Environmental Studies** (ACES; ☎970-925-5756; www.aspennature.org; Hallam Lake, 100 Puppy Smith St; ⏱9am-5pm Mon-Fri; 🅿️ ♿). Whether you go on a tour with ACES or venture out on your own, the backcountry here is simply spectacular: hikers and bikers have a range of trails to choose from, including several in the iconic Maroon Bells Wilderness Area. Go to the **Aspen Ranger Office** (☎970-925-3445; www. fs.usda.gov/whiteriver; 806 W Hallam St; ⏱8am-4:30pm Mon-Fri) for maps and hiking tips.

🍴 📖 p393

Eating & Sleeping

Breckenridge ⑤

✕ Hearthstone Modern American $$$

(✆970-453-1148; http://hearthstonerestaurant.biz; 130 S Ridge St; mains $26-44; ⏲4pm-late; 🅿) One of Breck's favorites, this restored 1886 Victorian serves up creative mountain fare such as blackberry elk and almond-crusted Colorado bass. There are great deals on small plates during happy hour (4pm to 6pm). Reserve.

🛏 Abbet Placer Inn B&B $$

(✆970-453-6489; www.abbettplacer.com; 205 S French St; r summer $99-179, winter $119-229; 🅿❄@🖥) This violet house has five large rooms decked out with wood furnishings, iPod docks and fluffy robes. The top floor has massive views of the peaks.

Vail ⑦

✕ bōl Modern American $$

(✆970-476-5300; www.bolvail.com; 141 E Meadow Dr; mains $14-28; ⏲5pm-1am, from 2pm winter; 🖥🅿🚹) Half hip eatery, half space-age bowling alley, bōl is hands down the funkiest hangout in Vail. You can go bowling in the back, but it's the surprisingly eclectic menu that's the real appeal. Book ahead.

🛏 The Sebastian Hotel $$$

(✆800-354-6908; www.thesebastianvail.com; 16 Vail Rd; r summer/winter from $230/500; 🅿❄🖥🏊🐶) Deluxe and modern, this sophisticated hotel showcases tasteful contemporary art and an impressive list of amenities. Room rates dip to reasonable in the summer.

Camp Hale ⑧

✕ Tennessee Pass Cookhouse Modern American $$$

(✆719-486-8114; www.tennesseepass.com; Tennessee Pass; lunch from $14, 4-course dinner $80; ⏲lunch Sat & Sun, dinner daily Dec–mid-Apr, dinner only Thu-Sun late Jun-Sep; 🅿) If you've never had a gourmet dinner in a yurt before, this is your chance. Diners get to hike, snowshoe or cross-country ski 1 mile in to the yurt, where an elegant four-course meal awaits. They also have sleep yurts ($225 per six-person yurt). Reservations only.

Leadville ⑨

✕ Tennessee Pass Cafe Cafe $$

(222 Harrison Ave; sandwiches $8.75-12.75, mains $9.25-15.75; ⏲7am-9pm; 🅿🚹) This artsy cafe has the best menu in town, with specials ranging from veggie enchiladas and buffalo burgers to Thai-style stir-fries.

Twin Lakes ⑩

🛏 Twin Lakes Lodge Hotel $$

(✆719-486-7965; www.thetwinlakesinn.com; 6435 Hwy 82; r $100-160, cabin from $250; 🖥) Over 130 years old, this green-shuttered inn was reopened in 2013. Not all rooms have private baths, but you can't beat the lakeside location. The downstairs restaurant (dinner $15 to $27) is recommended.

Aspen ⑫

✕ Justice Snow's Gastro Pub $$

(✆970-429-8192; www.justicesnows.com; 328 E Hyman Ave; mains $10-22; ⏲11am-2am; 🖥🅿) Located in the historic Wheeler Opera House, Justice Snow's is a retro-fitted old saloon that marries antique wooden furnishings with a deft modern touch. The affordable, locally sourced menu ($10 gourmet burger! in Aspen!) keeps the locals coming back.

🛏 Hotel Aspen Hotel $$$

(✆970-925-3441; www.hotelaspen.com; 110 W Main St; r summer/winter from $135/300; 🅿❄🖥🏊🐶) The hip Hotel Aspen offers one of the best deals in town, with a casual vibe, four hot tubs and affordable luxury. If you opt for the fireplace suite, you'll also have access to your own private solarium.

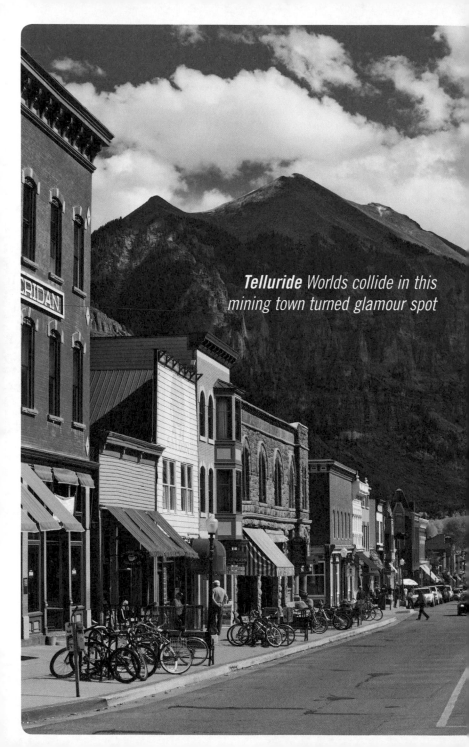

Telluride *Worlds collide in this mining town turned glamour spot*

San Juan Skyway & Million Dollar Highway

31

Encompassing the vertiginous Million Dollar Highway, the San Juan Skyway loops southern Colorado, traveling magnificent passes to alluring Old West towns.

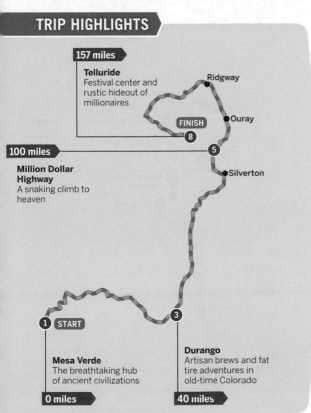

157 miles

Telluride
Festival center and rustic hideout of millionaires

Ridgway

FINISH
8

Ouray

100 miles

Million Dollar Highway
A snaking climb to heaven

5

Silverton

1 **START**

3

Mesa Verde
The breathtaking hub of ancient civilizations

0 miles

Durango
Artisan brews and fat tire adventures in old-time Colorado

40 miles

**6–8 DAYS
157 MILES / 253KM**

GREAT FOR...

BEST TIME TO GO
Visit from June to October for clear roads and summer fun.

 ESSENTIAL PHOTO
Snap Mesa Verde's dramatic cliff dwellings.

☑ **BEST FOR FOODIES**
The farm-to-table options in Mancos and Durango.

395

31 San Juan Skyway & Million Dollar Highway

This is the west at its most rugged: a landscape of twisting mountain passes and ancient ruins, with burly peaks and gusty high desert plateaus, a land of unbroken spirit. Beyond the thrills of outdoor adventure and the rough charm of old plank saloons, there remains the lingering mystery of the region's earliest inhabitants whose awe-inspiring cliff dwellings make up Mesa Verde National Park.

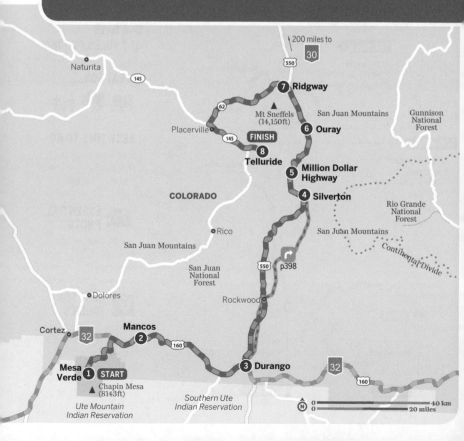

① Mesa Verde

More than 700 years after Ancestral Puebloans left, the mystery behind their last known home remains. Amateur anthropologists love it; the incredible cultural heritage makes it unique among American national parks. Ancestral Puebloan sites are scattered throughout the canyons and mesas, perched on a high plateau south of Mancos, though many remain off-limits to visitors.

If you only have a few hours, stop at **Mesa Verde Visitor & Research Center** (☎800-305-6053, 970-529-5034; www.nps.gov/meve; North

LINK YOUR TRIP

30 Top of the Rockies

Head north from Ridgway on 550 to Grand Junction. Turn right to join I-70 towards Glenwood Springs, then take 82 to Aspen.

32 Four Corners Cruise

Join the super-sized Four Corners drive on the U-160 at Durango.

Rim Rd; ⊙8am-7pm daily Jun-early Sep, 8am-5pm early Sep–mid-Oct, closed mid-Oct–May; 🚗) and drive around **Chapin Mesa** where you can take the short walk to the easily accessible Spruce Tree House, the park's best-preserved cliff dwelling.

If you have a day or more, buy tickets in advance for popular ranger-led tours of Cliff Palace and Balcony House. These active visits involve climbing rung ladders and scooting through ancient passages. The heat in summer is brutal – go early if you want to hike or cool off at the informative **Chapin Mesa Museum** (☎970-529-4475; www.nps.gov/meve; Chapin Mesa Rd; admission included with park entry; ⊙8am-6:30pm Apr–mid-Oct, 8am-5pm mid-Oct–Apr; P 🚗) near Spruce Tree House.

The Drive 》 Entering Mesa Verde, go immediately left for the visitor center. Return to the main access road. It takes 45 minutes to reach the main attractions on Wetherill Mesa and the road is steep and narrow in places. Leaving the park, head east on US-160 for Mancos, exit right for Main St and follow to the intersection with Grand Ave.

② Mancos

Blink and you'll miss this hamlet embracing the offbeat, earthy and slightly strange (witness

the puppets dangling through the roof of the local coffee shop).

With a vibrant arts community and love for locavore food, Mancos is the perfect rest stop. You will find most points of interest in a three-block radius. These include a distillery, custom hat shop, galleries and good cooking. During the last Friday of each month, the Arts Walk fires up what locals deem 'downtown.'

The area's oddest accommodations is **Jersey Jim Lookout Tower** (☎970-533-7060; r $40; ⊙mid-May–mid-Oct), a watch tower standing 55ft high with panoramic views. This sought-after lodging is 14 miles north of Mancos at 9800ft. It comes with an Osborne Fire Finder and topographic map.

The Drive 》 Drive east on US-160. Reaching Durango turn left onto Camino del Rio and right onto W 11th St in half a mile. Main Ave is your second right.

③ Durango

A regional darling, Durango's style straddles its ragtime past and a cool, cutting-edge future where townie bikes, caffeine and farmers markets rule. Outdoor enthusiasts get ready to be smitten. The **Animas River** floats right through town; float it or fly-fish it, while hundreds of mountain-bike rides range from scenic dirt roads to steep single track. When you've gotten your kicks, you can join the summer crowds strolling **Main Avenue**, stopping at book stores, boutiques and breweries.

Leave town heading north on the **San Juan Skyway** (US 550), which passes farms and stables as it starts the scenic climb toward Silverton. Bring your hunger to the family-run **James Ranch** (Animas River Valley; mains $6-13; ⊙11am-7pm Mon-Sat) just 10 miles out of Durango. The outstanding farmstand grill features the farm's own organic grass-fed beef, cheese and fresh produce market. Steak sandwiches and

focaccia cheese melts with caramelized onions simply rock. Kids dig the goats. Thursday features Burgers & Bands from July to October (adult/child $20/10). A two-hour farm tour ($18) is held on Mondays and Fridays at 9:30am and Tuesdays at 4pm.

✕ 🛏 p403

The Drive ≫ Take Main Ave heading north. Leaving Durango it becomes US 550, also part of the San Juan Skyway. James Ranch is 10 miles in on the right side. A band of 14,000ft peaks becomes visible to the right and frequent pullouts offer scenic views. Before Silverton the road climbs both Coal Banks Pass (10,640ft) and Molas Pass (10,910).

- - - - - - - - - - - - - - -

❹ Silverton

Ringed by snowy peaks and proudly steeped in tawdry mining-town lore,

Silverton would seem more at home in Alaska than the lower 48. At 9318ft the air is thin, but that discourages no one from hitting the bar stool.

Explore it all and don't shy away from the mere 500 locals – they're happy to see a fresh face. It's a two-street town, but only respectable **Greene Street**, now home to restaurants and trinket shops, is paved. One block over, notorious **Blair Street** was a silver-rush hub of brothels and boozing establishments, banished to the back street where real ladies didn't stroll.

Stop at the **Silverton Museum** (🕿970-387-5838; www.silvertonhistoricsociety. org; 1557 Greene St; adult/child $5/free; ⊙10am-4pm Jun-Oct; P 👪), housed in the old San Juan County Jail, to see the original cells. It tells the Silverton story from terrible mining accidents to 'saloons, alcohol, prostitution, gambling, robbery...there were many opportunities to die violently.'

Most visitors use Silverton as a hub for jeep tours – sketchy mining roads climbing in all directions offer unreal views. In winter, **Silverton Mountain** (🕿970-387-5706; www. silvertonmountain.com; State Hwy 110; daily lift ticket $49, all-day guide & lift ticket $99) offers experts some

---

DETOUR: NARROW GAUGE RAILROAD

Start: ❸ Durango

Climb aboard the steam driven **Durango & Silverton Narrow Gauge Railroad** (🕿970-247-2733, toll-free 877-872-4607; www.durangotrain.com; 479 Main Ave; adult/child return from $85/51; ⊙departure at 8am, 8:45am & 9:30am; 👪) for the train ride of the summer. The train, running between Durango and Silverton, has been in continuous operation for 123 years, and the scenic 45-mile journey north to Silverton, a National Historic Landmark, takes 3½ hours one way. Most locals recommend taking it one way and returning from Silverton via bus, it's faster. It's most glorious in late September and early October when the Aspens turn golden.

serious powder skiing on ungroomed terrain.

 p403

The Drive » Leaving Silverton head north on US 550, the Million Dollar Highway. It starts with a gentle climb but becomes steeper. Hairpin turns slow traffic at Molas Pass to 25mph. The most hair-raising sections follow, with 15mph speed limits in places. The road lacks guardrails and drops are huge, so stay attentive. Pullouts provide relief between mile markers 91 and 93.

- - - - - - - - - - - - - -

TRIP HIGHLIGHT

❺ Million Dollar Highway

The origin of the name of this 24-mile stretch between Silverton and Ouray is disputed – some say it took a million dollars a mile to build it in the 1920s; others purport the roadbed contains valuable ore.

Among America's most memorable drives, this breathtaking stretch passes old mine head frames and larger-than-life alpine scenery. Though paved, its blind corners, tunnels and narrow turns would put the Roadrunner on edge. It's often closed in winter, when it's said to have more avalanches than the entire state of Colorado. Snowfall usually starts in October.

Leaving Silverton, the road ascends Mineral Creek Valley, passing the Longfellow mine ruins 1 mile before **Red Mountain Pass** (11,018ft), with sheer drops and hairpin turns slowing traffic to 25mph.

Descending toward Ouray, visit **Bear Creek Falls**, a large turnout with a daring viewing platform over the crashing several-hundred-foot falls. A difficult 8-mile trail here switchbacks to even greater views – not for vertigo sufferers.

Stop at the **lookout** over Ouray at mile marker 92. Turn right for the lovely **Amphitheater Campground** (📞877-444-6777; http://www.recreation.gov; US Hwy 550; tent sites $16; 🕐Jun-Aug).

LOCAL KNOWLEDGE: COLORADO'S HAUTE ROUTE

An exceptional way to enjoy hundreds of miles of single track in summer or virgin powder slopes in winter, **San Juan Hut System** (📞970-626-3033; www.sanjuanhuts.com; per person $30) continues the European tradition of hut-to-hut adventures with five backcountry mountain huts. Bring just your food, flashlight and sleeping bag – amenities include padded bunks, propane stoves, wood stoves for heating and firewood.

Mountain-biking routes go from Durango or Telluride to Moab, winding through high alpine and desert regions. Or pick one hut as your base. There's terrain for all levels, though skiers should have knowledge of snow and avalanche conditions or go with a guide. The website has helpful tips and information on rental skis, bikes and (optional) guides based in Ridgway or Ouray.

The Drive » The Million Dollar Highway makes a steep descent into Ouray and becomes Main St.

- - - - - - - - - - - - - -

❻ Ouray

A well-preserved mining village snug beneath imposing peaks, Ouray breeds enchantment. It's named after the legendary Ute chief who kept the peace between the white settlers and the crush of miners invading the San Juan Mountains in the early 1870s, by relinquishing the Ute tribal lands.

The area is rife with hot springs. One cool cave spring, now located underneath the **Wiesbaden Hotel** (📞970-325-4347; www.wiesbadenhotsprings.com; 625

SAN JUAN SKYWAY & MILLION DOLLAR HIGHWAY
CAROLYN MCCARTHY, AUTHOR

This trip is Colorado at its most breathtaking, with winding country roads and spunky mining towns backed by the chiseled San Juan mountains. Want to feel the Wild West? Try making small talk with the barkeeps and hotel hosts in Ouray, Silverton and Telluride. In these parts, every 19th-century saloon or historic hotel has a ghost story to share. Check out the bullet holes in Telluride's New Sheridan bar.

Above: Durango & Silverton Narrow Gauge Railroad
Left: Spruce Tree House, Mesa Verde
Right: Hiking near Telluride

5th St; r $132-347; ⊖🛜🖵),
was favored by Chief
Ouray. Now you can soak
there by the hour.

The annual Ouray
Ice Festival draws elite
climbers for a four-day
competition. But the
town also lends thrills
to hikers and 4WD fans.
If you're skittish about
driving yourself, **San
Juan Scenic Jeep Tours**
(📞970-325-0089; http://
sanjuanjeeptours.com; 206
7th Ave; adult/child half-day
$59/30; 🚹) takes open-
air Jeeps into the high
country, offering special
wildflower or ghost-town
trips.

It's worth hiking up
to **Box Canyon Falls** (off
Box Canyon Rd; adult/child
$4/2; ⊗8am-8pm Jun-Aug;
🅿🚹) from the west
end of 3rd Avenue. A
suspension bridge leads
you into the belly of
this 285ft waterfall. The
surrounding area is rich
in birdlife – look for the
protected black swift,
which nests in the rock
face.

🛏 p403

The Drive » Leave Ouray
heading north via Main St,
which becomes US 550 N. It's a
flat 10-mile drive to Ridgway's
only traffic light. Turn left onto
Sherman St. The center of
town is spread over the next
half-mile.

❼ Ridgway

Wide open meadows backed by snowcovered San Juans and the stellar Mt Sneffels, Ridgway is an inviting blip of a burg. The backdrop of John Wayne's 1969 cowboy classic *True Grit*, today it sports a sort of neo-Western charm.

Sunny rock pools at **Orvis Hot Springs** (📞970-626-5324; www.orvishotsprings.com; 1585 County Rd 3; per hr/day $10/14) make this clothing-optional hot spring hard to resist. Though it gets its fair share of exhibitionists, a variety of soaking areas (100°F to 114°F) mean you can probably scout out the perfect quiet spot. Less appealing are the private indoor pools lacking fresh air. It's 9 miles north of Ouray, outside Ridgway.

The Drive » Leaving town heading west, Sherman St becomes CO 62. Take this easy drive 23 miles. At the crossroads go left onto CO 145 S for Telluride. Approaching town there's a traffic circle, take the second exit onto W Colorado Ave. The center of Telluride is in half a mile.

TELLURIDE FESTIVALS

For information see www.visittelluride.com/festivals-events.

Mountainfilm (late May) A four-day screening of high-caliber outdoor adventure and environmental films.

Telluride Bluegrass Festival (late Jun) Thousands enjoy a weekend of top-notch rollicking alfresco bluegrass going well into the night.

Telluride Film Festival (early Sep) National and international films are premiered throughout town, and the event attracts big-name stars.

TRIP HIGHLIGHT

❽ Telluride

Surrounded on three sides by mastodon peaks, exclusive Telluride was once a rough mining town. Today it's dirtbag-meets-diva – where glitterati mix with ski bums, and renowned music and film festivals create a frolicking summer atmosphere.

The very renovated center still has palpable old-time charm. Stop into the plush **New Sheridan Bar** (📞970-728-3911; www.newsheridan.com; 231 W Colorado Ave; ⏰5pm-2am) to find out the story of those old bullet holes in the wall and the plucky survival of the bar itself, even as the adjoining hotel sold off chandeliers to pay the heating bills during waning mining fortunes.

Touring downtown, check out the **free box** where you can swap unwanted items, the tradition is a point of civic pride. Then take a free 15-minute **gondola** (⏰7am-midnight; 🚲) ride up to the Telluride Mountain Village, where you can rent a mountain bike, dine or just bask in the panoramas.

If you are planning on attending a festival, book your tickets and lodging months in advance.

🍴 🛏 p403

Eating & Sleeping

Durango ❸

🍴 East by Southwest   Fusion, Sushi $$$
(📞970-247-5533; http://eastbysouthwest.com;
160 E College Dr; sushi $4-13, mains $12-24;
🕐11:30am-3pm & 5-10pm Mon-Sat, 5-10pm
Sun; 🖋️🚼) Locals rave about this hip enclave
serving pan-Asian and creative sushi in a
congenial low-key setting. The food rocks, but
don't skip the sake cocktails.

🍴 Ska Brewing Company   Brewpub $$
(📞970-247-5792; www.skabrewing.com; 225
Girard St; mains $7-13; 🕐11am-3am Mon-Wed,
11am-3pm & 5-8pm Thu, 11am-8pm Fri) Ska
ranks among Colorado's finest brews. This
tasting-room bar was once just a production
facility, today it gets packed with locals after
work. Its on-site restaurant, the Container,
serves delicious brick-oven pizzas, heaping
sandwiches with local beef and cheese, and
fresh salads.

🛏️ Rochester House   Hotel $$
(📞970-385-1920, toll-free 800-664-1920; www.
rochesterhotel.com; 721 E 2nd Ave; d $169-229;
😊❄️📶) Influenced by old Westerns, with
movie posters and marquee lights, this adorable
hotel splices the new West with old Hollywood.
Rooms are spacious and breakfast is served in
an old train car. There's a free summer concert
series in the courtyard, Wednesdays at 4:30pm.

Silverton ❹

🍴 Montanya Distillers   Pub $$
(www.montanyadistillers.com; 1309 Greene St;
mains $6-13; 🕐noon-10pm) Dangerous
bartenders at this mod bar on Greene St can
talk you into anything while crafting exotic
cocktails with homemade syrups, berries and
its very own award-winning rum. It has a fun
atmosphere, especially on the rooftop deck in
summer. Order a fruit and cheese plate or the
famous house spinach and artichoke dip.

Ouray ❻

🛏️ Box Canyon
Lodge & Hot Springs   Lodge $$
(📞970-325-4981, 800-327-5080; www.
boxcanyonouray.com; 45 3rd Ave; r $110-165, apt
$278-319; 📶) Not every hotel offers geothermal
heated rooms, and these are spacious and
accommodating. The real treat here is four
wooden spring-fed hot tubs, perfect for a
romantic stargazing soak. Book well ahead.

Telluride ❽

🍴 La Cocina de Luz   Mexican, Organic $$
(www.lacocinatelluride.com; 123 E Colorado Ave;
mains $9-19; 🕐9am-9pm; 🖋️) Lovingly serving
organic and Mexican, it's no wonder that the
lunch line runs deep at this healthy *taquería*.
Perks are a salsa and chip bar, handmade
tortillas and margaritas with organic lime
and agave nectar. With vegan, gluten-free
options too.

🍴 New Sheridan
Chop House   Modern American $$$
(📞970-728-4531; www.newsheridan.com; 231
W Colorado Ave; mains from $19; 🕐5pm-2am)
For an intimate dinner on embroidered velvet
benches. Start with a cheese plate, from there
the menu gets Western, for example pasta with
wild mushroom and sage. Carnivores should try
the elk shortloin in a hard cider reduction. For a
treat, end with a flourless dark chocolate cake in
fresh caramel sauce. Service is superb.

🛏️ Telluride Town
Park Campground   Campground $
(📞970-728-2173; 500 E Colorado Ave; campsite
vehicle/walk-in $23/15; 🕐mid-May–mid-Oct;
📶) Right in the center of town, this lovely
spot has 20 sites with great views, some river
beaches and bathhouse access. It fills up
quickly in the high season.

STRETCH YOUR LEGS
DENVER

Start/Finish: Highlands

Distance: 4 miles

Duration: 4 hours

The Mile High City has some of the best walking paths in the nation, world-class art museums, brewpubs aplenty, urban white-water parks, Rocky Mountain–chic boutiques and eateries, and a new urban scene that is transforming this classic Western city.

Take this walk on Trip

Highlands

One of Denver's top up-and-coming neighborhoods, Highlands sits conveniently next to I-70, offering a bird's-eye vantage of the city, B-Share bicycles (if you prefer to bike this route), and free two-hour parking. In the hipper-than-thou Lower Highlands neighborhood check out some cool boutiques, raucous brewpubs and great lunchtime restaurants, such as **Linger** (☎303-993-3120; www.lingerdenver.com; 2030 W 30th Ave; mains $8-14; ⏰11:30am-2:30pm, 4pm-2am Tue-Sat, 10am-2:30pm Sun), before heading into the city.

The Walk » Trundle over to the 16th St pedestrian bridge that will take you over I-70, past John McEnroe's pile of public art known as National Velvet, and across another pedestrian bridge to Commons Park.

Commons Park

Affording views of the city and a bit of fresh air, spacious and hilly Commons Park has bike paths, benches, river access, and plenty of people-watching. A lyrical curving stairway to nowhere known as Common Ground by artist Barbara Grygutis is an undeniable centerpiece. The stairway is just east of the pedestrian bridge over the Platte River.

The Walk » Cruise straight through the park to the massive and hard-to-miss Millennium Bridge.

Millennium Bridge

A defining piece of city infrastructure, the Millennium Bridge is the world's first cable-stayed bridge using a post-tensioned structural construction (yowsa!). If the technical jargon goes over your head, you'll be impressed enough by just looking up – the sweeping forms of the cables and white mast are a dramatic sight against Denver's consistently blue sky.

The Walk » Stop on the bridge to take in the views of Coors Field and Union Station, before plunging down into the chaos of Lower Downtown (LoDo).

16th Street Mall

The 16th Street Pedestrian Mall is an unavoidable tourist trap, with plenty of T-shirt shops, plus a few good restaurants and bars and some decent public art on display. The funkier LoDo, around Larimer Sq, is the best place to have a drink or browse the boutiques.

The Walk » Cruise south on 16th St to the end of the pedestrian mall. From there, it's a quick scurry across Colfax Ave to Civic Center Park. To save time, hop on the free bus that runs the entirety of the mall.

Civic Center Park

In the shadow of the State Capitol's golden dome, Civic Center Park hosts lounging drifters, politicos yammering into Bluetooth headsets and some of the most iconic public sculptures in the city, including the 1920 Bronco Buster, whose model was arrested for murder before the statue was finished. If you have time, head over to the State Capitol for a free tour, plus a photo op on the 13th step that sits exactly a mile above sea level.

The Walk » Continue south past the whimsical Yearling statue (how did that horse get onto that chair?), more public art and the postmodern Denver Library, before you hit the iconic Denver Art Museum.

Denver Art Museum

If you are only going to visit one museum in Denver, this is it. The DAM puts on special avant-garde multimedia exhibits. The Western American Art section of the permanent collection is justifiably famous. The landmark $110-million Frederic C Hamilton wing, designed by Daniel Libeskind, is simply awesome. If you run out of time, grab a B-Cycle here to pedal back to Highlands along the Cherry Creek Bike Path.

The Walk » Go past the Convention Center's Big Blue Bear, continuing west down Champa St past the Denver Performing Arts Complex and its signature Dancers statue. From there, take the Cherry Creek Bike Path all the way to Confluence Park and Highlands.

Southwest Trips

MOTHER NATURE HAD SOME FUN IN THE SOUTHWEST. Red rock canyons crack across ancient plateaus. Hoodoos cluster like conspirators on remote slopes. Whisper-light sand dunes shimmer on distant horizons. Wildflowers, saguaros and ponderosa pines lure you in for a closer look.

Our trips across the Southwest swoop from scrubby deserts to the majestic Grand Canyon, from sandstone buttresses sculpted by desert winds to the shimmering lights of Las Vegas. En route, dramatic landscapes and movie locations unfold on all sides – this is the road trip as it was meant to be driven! Fill your tank, don your Ray-Bans and set off in search of the Southwest!

Las Vegas (Trip 32)

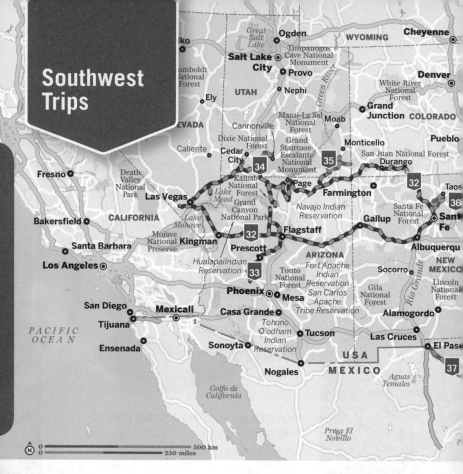

Southwest Trips

Classic Trip
32 Four Corners Cruise 10 Days
Loop past the Southwest's biggest and boldest parks and sights. (p411)

Classic Trip
33 Fantastic Canyon Voyage 4–5 Days
Cowboy up in Wickenburg, enjoy views in Jerome, then applaud the Grand Canyon. (p423)

34 Zion & Bryce National Parks 6 Days
Red-rock grandeur in two stunning national parks. (p435)

35 Monument Valley & Trail of the Ancients 5 Days
Ancient and modern-day indigenous tribal cultures on display. (p445)

36 High & Low Roads to Taos 2–4 Days
Take the mountains up and the canyons down, looping between iconic destinations. (p453)

DON'T MISS

Horseshoe Bend

If you're a sucker for a gobsmacking view, stroll to this cliff-side perch to look at the Colorado River – 1100ft below, on Trip 32

Santuario de Chimayó

This 1816 adobe church is home to miracle healings and is the site of the largest Catholic pilgrimage in the US. Find it on Trip 36

Beer Drinking

Grab an ice-cold Shiner Bock and join the locals at Gruene Hall or on the Terlingua Porch, in Trips 37 38

Canyoneering

Rock-climb up then rappel down through narrow slot canyons on Trip 34

Airport Mesa

It's an easy scramble to a sweeping 360-degree view of Sedona's monolithic red rocks on Trip 33

37 Big Bend Scenic Loop 5–7 Days
Minimalist art, mystery lights and star parties lead the way to Big Bend. (p463)

38 Hill Country 2–5 Days
This drive strings together some of Texas' most welcoming towns. (p471)

Horseshoe Bend *A sheer drop – both beautiful and terrifying*

Classic Trip

Four Corners Cruise

32

This road trip is super-sized, covering the grandest views and biggest wows in the Southwest – from Vegas to Zion to the Grand Canyon and beyond. The timid should stay at a home.

TRIP HIGHLIGHTS

195 miles

Zion National Park
Hike Walter's Wiggles to reach Angels Landing

425 miles

Horseshoe Bend
A serpentine twist in the Colorado River – far below

St George
Las Vegas
START/ FINISH
Kingman
Williams
Santa Fe
Albuquerque

1355 miles

Grand Canyon South Rim
The Rim Trail rolls past views and history

525 miles

Monument Valley
Look for the Three Sisters on the 17-mile drive

**10 DAYS
1850 MILES /
2980KM**

GREAT FOR...

BEST TIME TO GO
Spring and fall for lighter crowds and pleasant temperatures.

ESSENTIAL PHOTO
The glory of the Grand Canyon from Mather Point on the South Rim.

BEST FOR OUTDOORS
Angels Rest Trail in Zion National Park.

411

Classic Trip

32 Four Corners Cruise

From a distance, the rugged buttes of Monument Valley look like the remains of a prehistoric fortress, red-gold ramparts protecting ancient secrets. But their sun-reflected beauty lures you in. Up close, the rocks are mesmerizing, an alluring mix of the familiar and elusive. Yes, they're recognizable from multitudes of Westerns, but the big screen doesn't capture the changing patterns of light, the imposing height or the strangeness of the angles. It's a captivating spell — one cast by breathtaking vistas across the Southwest.

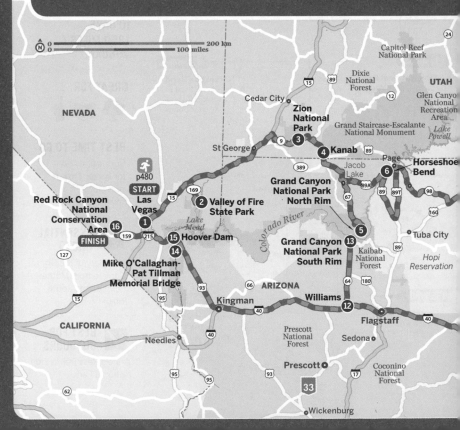

❶ Las Vegas

The giant pink stiletto in the lobby of Vegas' **Cosmopolitan** (www. cosmopolitanlasvegas. com; 3708 Las Vegas Blvd S; ⊙24hr) is an eye-catcher. Designed by Roark Gourley, the 9ft-tall shoe was supposed to be a piece of art on display. But its protective ropes were soon pushed aside by party girls who stepped inside the shoe to pose for photos. In response, the Cosmopolitan removed the ropes. After 16 months, the stiletto

was sent out for repairs because of all the love, proving that what the crowd wants is what the crowd gets in Vegas.

Take in more of the city's excess with a morning walk past the

icons of the Strip (see p480), then spend the afternoon downtown at the new **Mob Museum** (www.themobmuseum. org; 300 Stewart Ave; adult/ child $20/14; ⊙10am-7pm Sun-Thu, to 8pm Fri & Sat), a

LINK YOUR TRIP

33 Fantastic Canyon Voyage

For red rocks and mining history swing south from Flagstaff on I-17 to Hwy 89A.

36 High & Low Roads to Taos

Art, scenery and history are highlights on these two drives that link Santa Fe and Taos.

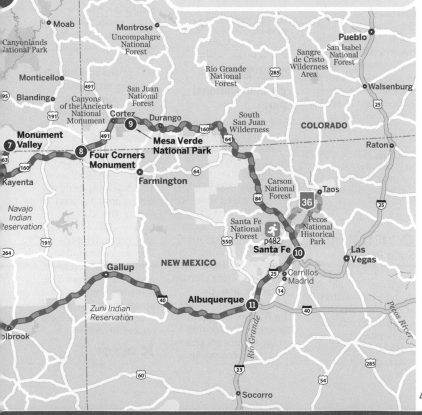

Classic Trip

three-story collection of exhibits examining the development of organized crime in America and the mob's connection to Las Vegas. One block south, you can zip line over **Fremont St** from Slotzilla's 11th-story launchpad (www.vegasexperience.com) then end the night with an illuminated stroll at the **Neon Museum** (☎702-387-6366; www.neonmuseum.org; 770 Las Vegas Blvd N; day tour adult/child $18/12, night tour $25/22; ☺9-10am & 7:30-9pm Jun-Aug, extended daytime hours beginning at 10am rest of the year). A money-saving combo ticket for the Mob Museum and the Neon Museum is now available for $30 per person.

✕ 🛏 p421

The Drive » Follow I-15 north for 37 miles then take exit 7. From here, Hwy 169/Valley of Fire Hwy travels 15 miles to the park.

❷ Valley of Fire State Park

Before the sandstone bacchanal of Utah, swing through this masterwork of desert scenery. It's an easy detour, with Hwy 169 running through the **park** (☎702-397-2088; www.parks.nv.gov/parks/valley-offire-state-park; per vehicle $10; ☺visitor center 8:30am-4:30pm) and passing close to the psychedelically shaped red rock outcroppings. From the visitor center, take the winding scenic side road out to **White Domes**, an 11-mile round-trip. En route you'll pass **Rainbow Vista**, followed by the turnoff to **Fire Canyon** and **Silica Dome** (where Captain Kirk perished in *Star Trek: Generations*).

Spring and fall are the best times to visit; summer temperatures typically exceed 100°F (more than 37°C).

The Drive » Return to I-15 north, cruising through Arizona and into Utah. Leave the highway at exit 16 and follow Hwy 9 east for 32 miles.

TRIP HIGHLIGHT

❸ Zion National Park

The climb up Angels Landing in **Zion National Park** (www.nps.gov/zion; Hwy 9; 7-day per vehicle $25; ☺24hr, Zion Canyon visitor center 8am -7:30pm Jun-Aug, closes earlier rest of year) may be the best day hike in North America. From Grotto Trailhead, the 5.4-mile round-trip crosses the Virgin River, hugs a towering cliffside, squeezes through a narrow canyon, snakes up Walters Wiggles, then traverses a razor-thin ridge where steel chains and the encouraging words of strangers are your only safety net. Your reward after the final scramble to the 5790ft summit? A bird's-eye view of Zion Canyon. The hike reflects what's best about the park: beauty, adventure and the shared community of people who love the outdoors.

The Drive » Take Hwy 9 east, driving almost 25 miles to Hwy 89. Follow Hwy 89 south to outdoorsy Kanab.

❹ Kanab

Sitting between Zion, Grand Staircase-Escalante and the Grand Canyon North Rim, Kanab is a good spot for a base camp. Hundreds of Western movies were filmed here, and John Wayne and other gun-slingin' celebs really put the town on the map. Today, animal lovers know that the town is home to the **Best Friends Animal Sanctuary** (☎435-644-2001; www.bestfriends.org; Angel Canyon, Hwy 89; admission free; ☺9:30am-5:30pm; 🐾), the country's largest no-kill animal shelter. Tours of the facility – home to dogs, cats, pigs and birds – are free, but call ahead to confirm times and to make a reservation. The sanctuary's welcome center (open 8am to 5pm) is between mile markers 69 and 70 on Hwy 89.

✕ 🛏 p421

The Drive » Continue into Arizona – now on Hwy 89A – and climb the Kaibab Plateau. Turn right onto Hwy 67 at Jacob Lake and drive 44 miles to Grand Canyon Lodge.

- - - - - - - - - - - - - -

❺ Grand Canyon National Park North Rim

While driving through the ponderosa forest that opens onto rolling meadows in Kaibab National Forest, keep an eye out for mule deer as you approach the entrance to the **park** (per vehicle $25; ☺ closed winter). Stop by the **North Rim Visitor Center** (☎928-638-7864; www.nps.gov/grca; ☺8am-6pm mid-May–mid-Oct, 9am-4pm Oct 16-31), beside Grand Canyon Lodge, for information and to join ranger-led nature walks and night-time programs. Enjoy a cocktail from the **Roughrider Saloon** on the lodge terrace while soaking up the view.

For an easy but scenic half-day hike, follow the 4-mile **Cape Final Trail** (round-trip) through ponderosa pines to great canyon views. The difficult 14-mile **North Kaibab Trail** is the only maintained rim-to-river trail and connects with trails to the South Rim near Phantom Ranch. The trailhead is 2 miles north of Grand Canyon Lodge.

TOP TIP: NO BOTTLED WATER

As a conservation measure, Grand Canyon National Park no longer sells bottled water. Instead, fill your thermos at water filling stations along the rim or at Canyon View Marketplace. Water bottles had constituted 20% of the waste generated in the park.

For inner-canyon hiking, walk 0.75 miles down to Coconino Overlook or 2 miles to the Supai Tunnel.

The Drive » At press time, the highway department had closed Hwy 89 between Bitter Springs and Page because a landslide had buckled the road. It should be closed until 2015. Hwy 89T is the temporary route. Turn right onto Hwy 89A heading east at Jacob Lake. Follow Hwy 89A down the Kaibab Plateau, past Lees Ferry and the closed section of Hwy 89, to Hwy 89T. Turn left onto Hwy 89T and take it north to Page.

- - - - - - - - - - - - - -

TRIP HIGHLIGHT

❻ Horseshoe Bend

The clifftop view at Horseshoe Bend will sear itself onto your memory. One thousand feet below, the Colorado River carves a perfect U through towering sandstone. It's simultaneously beautiful and terrifying. There are no railings – it's just you, a sheer drop and dozens of people you don't know. Free-range toddlers are not a good idea. From the parking lot it's a 0.75-mile one-way hike to the rim. There's a steep hill

along the way, and the trail is unshaded, but it's worth it. The trailhead is on Hwy 89 south of Page, south of mile marker 541.

The Drive » From the parking lot, turn left onto Hwy 89 and drive north a short distance to Hwy 98. Turn right onto Hwy 98 and follow it southeast to Hwy 160. Turn left and drive 32 miles, passing the entrance to Navajo National Monument. In Kayenta, turn left onto Hwy 163 north for almost 24 miles to Monument Valley, which sits beside the Arizona and Utah border.

- - - - - - - - - - - - - -

TRIP HIGHLIGHT

❼ Monument Valley

'May I walk in beauty' is the final line of a famous Navajo prayer. Beauty comes in many forms on the Navajo's sprawling reservation, but makes its most famous appearance at Monument Valley, a majestic cluster of buttes and spires. For up-close views of the formations, drive into the Monument Valley **Navajo Tribal Park** (☎435-727-5874; www.navajonationparks. org/htm/monumentvalley.htm; adult/child $5/free; ☺ drive 6am-8:30pm May-Sep, 8am-4:30pm Oct-Apr; visitor center

LOCAL VOICE
ROBIN TELLIS, NORTH RIM SUPERVISORY RANGER FOR INTERPRETATION

A really good day hike is Cape Final. It's a beautiful hike and the viewpoints at the end are incredible. It starts out in the ponderosa forest, and it's a really good example of a healthy ponderosa forest. It has big trees and is wide open. It's a great hike.

Above: Grand Canyon National Park
Opposite: Plaque at the Four Corners Monument

6am-8pm May-Sep, 8am-5pm Oct-Apr) and follow the unpaved 17-mile scenic loop that passes some of the most dramatic formations such as the East and West Mitten Buttes and the Three Sisters. For a guided tour (1½/2½ hours $75/95) into areas off-limits to private vehicles, stop by one of the kiosks in the

parking lot beside the View hotel.

🛏 p421

The Drive » Follow Hwy 163 back to Kayenta. Turn left and follow Hwy 160 east about 72 miles to tiny Tee Noc Pos. Take a sharp left to stay on Hwy 160 and drive 6 miles to the monument.

⑧ Four Corners Monument

It's seriously remote, but you can't skip the **Four Corners Monument** (📞928-871-6647; www. navajonationparks.org; admission $3; ⏱8am-7pm May-Sep, 8am-5pm Oct-Apr) in a road trips guide about the Southwest! Once you arrive, don't be shy: put a foot into Arizona and

plant the other in New Mexico. Slap a hand in Utah and place the other in Colorado. Smile for the camera. It makes a good photo, even if it's not 100% accurate – an April 2009 news story had government surveyors admitting that the marker is almost 2000ft east of where it should be, but it remains a legally recognized border point.

417

Classic Trip

Half the fun is watching the acrobatics performed on the marker.

The Drive » Return to Hwy 160 and turn left. It's a 50-mile drive across New Mexico and into Colorado.

- - - - - - - - - - - - - -

9 Mesa Verde National Park

Ancestral Puebloan sites are found throughout the canyons and mesas of **Mesa Verde** (970-529-4465; www.nps.gov/meve; 7-day pass car/motorcycle $15/8 Jun-Aug, low season $10/5; **P** **⊞**), perched on a high plateau south of Cortez and Mancos. According to the park, the Ancestral Pueobloans didn't 'disappear' 700 years ago, they simply migrated south, becoming the ancestors of today's Native Americans. If you only have time for a short visit, check out the **Chapin Mesa Museum** (p397) and walk through the **Spruce Tree House**, where you can climb down a wooden ladder into a kiva.

Mesa Verde rewards travelers who set aside a day or more to take the ranger-led tours of **Cliff Palace** and **Balcony House**, explore **Wetherill Mesa** (the quieter side

of the canyon), visit the museum or participate in one of the campfire programs at **Morefield Campground** (970-529-4465; www.visitmesaverde.com; North Rim Rd; ☺May-early Oct; 🐾). The park also offers plenty of hiking, skiing, snowshoeing and mountain-biking options. Camp out or stay in luxury at the lodge.

The Drive » Hop onto US 160, following it 35 miles east to Durango and then another 60 miles to join US 84 S. In New Mexico, US 84 S passes through Abiquiú, home of artist Georgia O'Keeffe from 1949 until 1986. Continue toward Santa Fe, exiting onto N Guadalupe St to head toward the Plaza.

- - - - - - - - - - - - - -

10 Santa Fe

This 400-year-old city is pretty darn inviting. You've got the juxtaposition of art and landscape, with cow skulls hanging from sky-blue walls and slender crosses topping century-old missions. And then there's the comfortable mingling of Native American, Hispanic and Anglo cultures, with ancient pueblos, 300-year-old haciendas and stylish modern buildings standing in easy proximity.

The beauty of the region was captured by New Mexico's most famous artist, Georgia O'Keeffe. Possessing the world's largest collection of her work,

the **Georgia O'Keeffe Museum** (505-946-1000; www.okeeffemuseum.org; 217 Johnson St; adult/child $12/free; ☺10am-5pm, to 7pm Fri) showcases the thick brushwork and luminous colors that don't always come through on the ubiquitous posters; take your time to relish them firsthand. The museum is housed in a former Spanish Baptist church with adobe walls that has been renovated to form 10 skylit galleries.

The city is anchored by the Plaza, which was the end of the Santa Fe Trail between 1822 and 1880. For more sights, see Stretch Your Legs, p482.

✕ 🛏 p421

The Drive » The historic route to Albuquerque is the Turquoise Trail, which follows Hwy 14 south for 50 miles through Cerrillos and Madrid. If you're in a hurry, take I-25 south.

- - - - - - - - - - - - - -

11 Albuquerque

Most of Albuquerque's top sites are concentrated in Old Town, which is a straight shot west on Central Ave from Nob Hill and the University of New Mexico (UNM).

The most extravagant route to the top of 10,378ft Sandia Crest is via the **Sandia Peak Tramway** (www.sandiapeak.com; Tramway Blvd; vehicles $1, adult/youth 13-20yr/child $20/17/12; ☺9am-8pm Wed-Mon, from 5pm Tue Sep-May, 9am-9pm Jun-Aug). The 2.7-

mile tram ride starts in the desert realm of cholla cactus and soars to the pine-topped summit. For exercise, take the beautiful 8-mile (one-way) **La Luz Trail** back down, connecting with the 2-mile Tramway Trail to return to your car. The La Luz Trail passes a small waterfall, pine forests and spectacular views. It gets hot, so start early. Take Tramway Blvd east from I-25 to get to the tramway.

 p421

The Drive » From Albuquerque to Williams, AZ, I-40 overlaps or parallels Route 66. It's 355 miles to Williams.

⑫ Williams

Train buffs, Route 66 enthusiasts and Grand Canyon–bound vacationers all cross paths in Williams, a small town with all the charm and authenticity of 'Main Street America.' If you only have time for a day visit to the park, the **Grand Canyon Railway** (☎800-843-8724, 928-635-4253; www.thetrain. com; Railway Depot, 233 N Grand Canyon Blvd; round-trip adult/child from $75/45; ♿) is a fun and hassle-free way to get there and back. After a **Wild West show** beside the tracks, the train departs for its two-hour ride to the South Rim, where you can explore by foot or shuttle. Late May

through early November passengers can ride in an open-air **Pullman** (adult/child $59/29).

On Route 66 the divey **Sultana Bar** (☎928-635-2021; 301 W Rte 66; ⊙10am-2am, from noon in winter), which once housed a speakeasy, recently had its 100th birthday.

TRIP HIGHLIGHT

⑬ Grand Canyon National Park South Rim

A walk along the **Rim Trail** in **Grand Canyon Village** brings stunning views of the **Grand Canyon** (www.nps.gov/grca; per vehicle $25, per person arriving on foot, bicycle or motorcycle $12, admission good for 7 days; ⊙ visitor centre 8am-5pm) as well as historic buildings, Native American crafts and geologic displays.

Starting from the plaza at **Bright Angel**

Trailhead, walk east on the Rim Trail to **Kolb Studio**, which holds a small bookstore and an art gallery.

Next door is **Lookout Studio**, designed by noted architect Mary Colter to look like the stone dwellings of the Southwest's Puebloans. There's a small shop, and the popular **Condor Talks** are given here.

Step into the **El Tovar** hotel to see its replica Remington bronzes, stained glass, stuffed mounts and exposed beams, or to admire the canyon views from its porches. Despite renovations, this rambling 1905 wooden lodge hasn't lost any of its genteel historic patina.

Next door, the **Hopi House** has offered high-quality Native American jewelry and crafts since 1904. Just east, the **Trail**

PHOTO FINISH: KOLB STUDIO

Before digital photography, brothers Ellsworth and Emery Kolb were shooting souvenir photos of mule-riding Grand Canyon visitors as they began their descent down the Bright Angel Trail. The brothers would sell finished prints to the tourists returning to the rim at the end of the day. But in the early 1900s there was no running water on the South Rim – so how did they process their prints?

After snapping photos from their studio window that overlooked a bend in the trail, one of the brothers would run 4.6 miles down to the waters of Indian Garden with the negatives, print the photos in their lab there and then run, or perhaps hike briskly, back up the Bright Angel to meet visitors with their prints.

Classic Trip

of Time interpretative display traces the history of the canyon's formation. End at the big-windowed **Yavapai Museum** and its superb geology exhibit.

🛏 p421

The Drive ≫ Return to I-40 west. Drive 116 miles then take exit 48 for US 93 north. Take US 93 north for 72 miles, crossing into Nevada. In Nevada take exit 2 for Hwy 172 to the dam.

- - - - - - - - - - - -

🔟 Mike O'Callaghan-Pat Tillman Memorial Bridge

This graceful span, dedicated in 2010, was named for Mike O'Callaghan, governor of Nevada from 1971 to 1979, and for NFL star Pat Tillman, a safety for the Arizona Cardinals who enlisted as a US Army Ranger after September 11. Tillman was killed by friendly fire during a battle in Afghanistan in 2004.

Open to pedestrians along a walkway separated from traffic on Hwy 93, the bridge sits 890ft above the Colorado River. It's the second-highest bridge in the US, and provides a bird's-eye view of Hoover Dam and Lake Mead behind it.

The Drive ≫ Turn right onto the access road and drive a short distance down to the dam.

- - - - - - - - - - - -

🔟 Hoover Dam

A statue of bronze winged figures stands atop **Hoover Dam** (☎866-730-9097, 702-494-2517; www.usbr.gov/lc/hooverdam; Hwy 93; visitor center $8, incl powerplant tour adult/child $11/9, all-inclusive tour $30; ⊙9am-6pm, last ticket sold 5:15pm), memorializing those who built the massive 726ft concrete structure, one of the world's tallest dams. This New Deal public works project, completed ahead of schedule and under budget in 1936, was the Colorado River's first major dam. Thousands of men and their families, eager for work during the Depression, came to Black Canyon and worked in excruciating conditions – dangling hundreds of feet above the canyon in 120°F (about 50°C) desert heat. Hundreds lost their lives.

Today, guided tours begin at the visitor center, where a video screening features original footage of the construction. After the movie take an elevator ride 50 stories below to view the dam's massive power generators, each of which alone could power a city of 100,000 people. Parking costs $7.

The Drive ≫ Return to US 93, following it north as it joins I-515. Take exit 61 for I-215 north. After 11 miles I-215 becomes Clark County 215. Follow it just over 13 miles to Charleston Blvd/Hwy 159 at exit 26 and follow it west.

- - - - - - - - - - - -

🔟 Red Rock Canyon National Conservation Area

The awesome natural forces in this **national conservation area** (☎702-515-5350; www.redrockcanyonlv.org; day-use per car/bicycle $7/3; ⊙scenic loop 6am-8pm Apr-Sep, earlier Oct-Mar, visitor center 8am-4:30pm) can't be exaggerated. Created about 65 million years ago, the canyon is more like a valley, with a steep, rugged red rock escarpment rising 3000ft on its western edge, evidence of tectonic-plate collisions.

The 13-mile, one-way scenic drive passes some of the canyon's most striking features, where you can access hiking trails and rock-climbing routes. The 2.5-mile round-trip hike to **Calico Tanks** climbs through the sandstone and ends atop rocks offering a grand view of the desert and mountains, with Vegas thrown in for sizzle.

National park passes are accepted for admission.

Eating & Sleeping

Las Vegas ❶

✖ Gordon Ramsay Steak
Steakhouse $$$

(☏877-346-4642; www.parislasvegas.com;
3655 Las Vegas Blvd S, Paris; mains $32-63;
⏱4:30-10:30pm, bar to midnight Fri & Sat)
Ribboned in red and domed by a jaunty Union
Jack, Gordon Ramsay's new steakhouse is one
of the top seats in town.

✖ Lotus of Siam
Thai $$

(☏702-735-3033; www.saipinchutima.com;
953 E Sahara Ave; mains $9-30; ⏱11:30am-
2:30pm Mon-Fri, buffet to 2pm, 5:30-10pm daily)
According to *Gourmet* magazine, this is the top
Thai restaurant in the US. One bite of the simple
pad thai – or any of the exotic northern Thai
dishes – will have you nodding in agreement.

🛏 Vdara
Hotel $$

(☏702-590-2767; www.vdara.com; 2600
W Harmon Ave; r $159-196; P 🛜 ☲) Cool
sophistication and warm hospitality merge
seamlessly at new-on-the scene Vdara, a no-
gaming, all-suites hotel in City Center.

Kanab ❹

✖ Rocking V Cafe
American $$

(www.rockingvcafe.com; 97 W Center St; lunch
$9-14, dinner $15-29; ⏱11:30am-10pm; 🌿)
Fresh ingredients star in dishes like hand-cut
buffalo tenderloin and chargrilled zucchini with
curried quinoa. Local artwork decorating the
1892 brick storefront is as creative as the food.
Off-season hours vary.

🛏 Quail Park Lodge
Motel $$

(☏435-215-1447; www.quailparklodge.com;
125 N 300 W; r $115-159; ❄ @ 🛜 ☲ 🐾) A
colorful retro style pervades all 13 rooms at
this refurbished 1963 motel. Mod cons include
microwaves and minifridges.

Monument Valley ❼

🛏 View Hotel
Hotel $$$

(☏435-727-5555; www.monumentvalleyview.
com; Hwy 163; r $209-265, ste $299-329;
❄ @ 🛜) Southwestern-themed rooms are nice
but nothing compared to their balconies, which
have straight-on views of the famous red rock
formation. Wi-fi available in the lobby only.

Santa Fe ❿

✖ Horseman's Haven
New Mexican $

(4354 Cerrillos Rd; mains $8-12; ⏱8am-8pm
Mon-Sat, 8:30am-2pm Sun; 🚶) The hottest
green chili in town! (The timid should order it on
the side.) Service is friendly and fast, and the
enormous 3D burrito might fill you for the day.

🛏 El Rey Inn
Hotel $$

(☏505-982-1931; www.elreyinnsantafe.com;
1862 Cerrillos Rd; r incl breakfast $105-165, ste
from $150; P ❄ @ 🛜 ☲) A classic courtyard
hotel with super rooms, a great pool and hot
tub, and a kids' playground scattered around 5
acres of greenery. Most rooms have air-con.

Albuquerque ⓫

✖ Flying Star Café
American $

(www.flyingstarcafe.com; 3416 Central Ave SE;
mains $6-12; ⏱6am-11pm Sun-Thu, to midnight
Fri-Sat; 🛜 🌿 🚶) With seven constantly packed
locations, this is the place to go for creative
diner food made with regional ingredients,
including homemade soups, main dishes from
sandwiches to stir-fry, and yummy desserts.

Grand Canyon ⓭

🛏 El Tovar
Lodge $$$

(www.grandcanyonlodges.com; d $178-273, ste
$335-426; ⏱year-round; ❄ 🛜) Standard rooms
are on the small side, so those in need of elbow
room should go for the deluxe rooms. Both offer
casual luxury and high standards of comfort.

Jerome *'The Wickedest Town in the West' in its mining heyday*

Classic Trip

Fantastic Canyon Voyage

33

Old West meets New West on this scenic route to the Grand Canyon, climbing from cowboy country to mining towns, stylish wineries and red rocks, with a grand finale at the Big Ditch.

TRIP HIGHLIGHTS

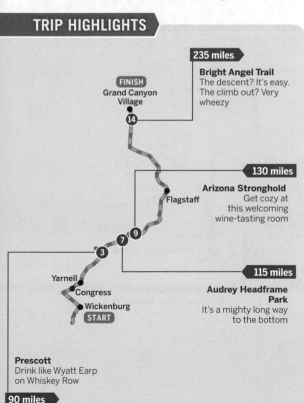

235 miles

FINISH
Grand Canyon Village

14

Bright Angel Trail
The descent? It's easy. The climb out? Very wheezy

130 miles

Flagstaff

Arizona Stronghold
Get cozy at this welcoming wine-tasting room

7 **9**

3

115 miles

Yarnell
Congress
Wickenburg
START

Audrey Headframe Park
It's a mighty long way to the bottom

Prescott
Drink like Wyatt Earp on Whiskey Row

90 miles

4–5 DAYS
285 MILES / 459KM

GREAT FOR...

BEST TIME TO GO
Visit in fall and spring, to beat the heat and summer crowds.

ESSENTIAL PHOTO
The Grand Canyon from Mather Point.

☑ BEST FOR HISTORY & CULTURE
Push through the swinging doors of history in Wickenburg, Prescott and Jerome.

Classic Trip

33 Fantastic Canyon Voyage

This road trip wins Best All Round. It's pretty, it's wild and it embraces Arizona's rough-and-tumble history. Scenic trails wind past sandstone buttes, ponderosa pines and canyon views. Wild West adventures include horseback rides, saloon crawls and taking a stand atop a 1910ft mine shaft. But the route's not stuck in the past. A burgeoning wine scene and a new ale trail add 21st-century sparkle.

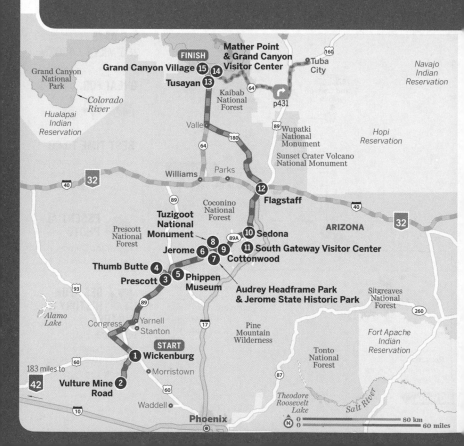

❶ Wickenburg

With its saddle shops and Old West storefronts, Wickenburg looks like it fell out of the sky – directly from the 1890s. At the newly expanded **Desert Caballeros Western Museum** (☎928-684-2272; www.westernmuseum.org; 21 N Frontier St; adult/child/senior $9/free/7; ◷10am-5pm Mon-Sat, noon-4pm Sun, closed Mon Jun-Aug), the artwork celebrates the West. The *Spirit of the Cowboy* collection examines the raw materials behind the cowboy myth, showcasing rifles, ropes and saddles. The *Cowgirl Up!* exhibit and sale in March and April is a fun and impressive tribute to an eclectic array of Western women artists.

LINK YOUR TRIP

32 Four Corners Cruise

Trade natural wonders for Sin City wows by driving west on I-40 to Hwy 93 north.

42 Palm Springs & Joshua Tree Oases

From Wickenburg, take Hwy 60 west to I-10 for lush desert getaways and outdoor fun.

Scattered across downtown are statues of the town's founders and colorful characters. One of the latter was George Sayers, a 'bibulous reprobate' who was chained to the **Jail Tree** on Tegner St in the late 1800s. Press the button to hear his tale then walk next door to the beloved **Chaparral** (45 N Tegner St; 1 scoop $3.50; ◷11am-7pm Tue-Sat, noon-5pm Sun & Mon) for a scoop of homemade ice cream.

Wickenburg is pleasant anytime but summer, when temperatures can top 110°F (43°C).

The Drive » Head west on Hwy 60, turn left onto Vulture Mine Rd. It's 12 miles to the mine. Saguaros and cattle guards mark the lonely drive.

---

❷ Vulture Mine Road

At the remote and dusty **Vulture Mine** (www.vultureminetours.com; 36610 N 355th St, off Vulture Mine Rd; donation $10; ◷tour 8:30am-10:30am Sat early May–mid-Oct, 10am-noon rest of year), Austrian immigrant Henry Wickenburg staked his claim and made his fortune. The site holds the main shaft, where $30 million worth of gold was mined, the blacksmith shop and other decrepit old buildings, and the Hanging Tree. Under new ownership, you can

visit by guided tour on Saturday mornings.

On the way back into town, consider spending the night at rustically posh **Rancho de Los Caballeros** (☎928-684-5484; www.ranchodeloscaballeros.com; 1551 S Vulture Mine Rd; r incl 3 meals $485-660; ◷Oct–mid-May; ❄❂), where guests can sign up for a trail ride (half-day ride $50 to $60).

The Drive » From downtown Wickenburg, pick up Hwy 93 north and drive 5 miles to 89N. Continuing north, the route leaves the Sonoran Desert and tackles the Weaver Mountains, climbing 2500ft in 4 miles. On top, tiny Yarnell was the site of a devastating forest fire in June 2013, when 19 members of the Granite Mountain Hotshots were killed while battling the blaze.

---

❸ Prescott

Fire raged through Whiskey Row in downtown Prescott ('press-kit') on July 14, 1900. Quick-thinking locals saved the town's most prized possession: the 24ft-long Brunswick Bar that anchored the Palace Saloon. After lugging the solid oak bar onto Courthouse Plaza, they grabbed their drinks and continued the party. Prescott's cooperative spirit lives on, infusing the city with a welcoming vibe.

The columned County Courthouse, situated in

SOUTHWEST TRIPS **33** FANTASTIC CANYON VOYAGE

an elm-shaded plaza, anchors the **Historic Downtown**. Just west is Whiskey Row, where 40 drinking establishments once supplied suds to rough-hewn cowboys, miners and wastrels. The fire in 1900 destroyed 25 saloons, five hotels and the red-light district, but several early buildings remain. Stroll through the **Palace Saloon**, rebuilt in 1901, which displays photographs and artifacts (including the still-in-use Brunswick Bar). Wyatt Earp and Doc Holliday drank here back in the day.

To learn more about Prescott, which was Arizona's first territorial capital, visit the engaging **Sharlot Hall Museum** (☎928-445-3122; www.sharlot.org; 415 W Gurley St; adult/child $7/3; ◷10am-5pm Mon-Sat, noon-4pm Sun May-Sep,

10am-4pm Mon-Sat, noon-4pm Sun Oct-Apr), named for its 1928 founder, pioneer woman Sharlot Hall. The city is also home to the **World's Oldest Rodeo** (www.worldsoldestrodeo.com), which dates to 1888 and is held the week before July 4th.

✕ 🛏 p433

The Drive ≫ From the County Courthouse downtown, drive west on Gurley St, which turns into Thumb Butte Rd, for 3.5 miles.

❹ Thumb Butte

Prescott sits in the middle of the Prescott National Forest, a 1.2 million-acre playground well stocked with mountains, lakes and ponderosa pines. The **Prescott National Forest Office** (☎928-443-8000; www.fs.fed.us/r3/prescott; 344 S Cortez St; ◷8am-4:30pm Mon-Fri) has information about local hikes, drives, picnic areas and campgrounds. A $5 day-use fee is required – and payable – at many area trailheads.

Intra-agency passes, including the America the Beautiful pass, cover this fee.

For a short hike, head to the hard-to-miss Thumb Butte. The 1.75-mile **Thumb Butte Trail #33** (◷7am-7pm) is a moderate workout and offers nice views of the town and mountains. Leashed dogs are OK.

The Drive ≫ Follow Hwy 89N out of Prescott, passing the Granite Dells rock formations on the 7-mile drive. Granite Dells Rd leads to a trail through the granite boulders on the **Mile High Trail System** (http://cityofprescott.net/services/parks/trails).

❺ Phippen Museum

Strutting its stuff like a rodeo champ, the recently expanded **Phippen Museum** (☎928-778-1385; www.phippenartmuseum.org; 4701 Hwy 89N; adult/child $7/free; ◷10am-4pm Tue-Sat, 1-4pm Sun) ropes in visitors with an entertaining mix of special exhibits spotlighting cowboy and Western art. Named for the late George Phippen, a local self-taught artist who helped put Western art on the map, it's worth a stop to see what's brewing. As you'll discover, Western art is broader than oil paintings of weather-beaten faces under broad hat brims – although you might see some of that too.

◗ LOCAL KNOWLEDGE: THE GREEN FROG

Perhaps this box should be called Local Pranksters. You'll see what we mean as you leave the village of Congress, which sits at the junction of Hwy 71 and Hwy 89N. Look left for the **big green frog**; this painted rock was created in 1928 and has been maintained by locals ever since.

The Drive » Just north, leave Hwy 89 for Hwy 89A. This serpentine road brooks no distraction as it approaches hillside Jerome, tucked in the Mingus Mountains. If you dare, glance east for stunning glimpses of the Verde Valley.

- - - - - - - - - - - -

6 Jerome

As the road snakes down steep Cleopatra Hill, it can be hard to tell whether the buildings are winning or losing their battle with gravity. Just look for the **Sliding Jail** – it's waaaay down there at the bottom of town.

Shabbily chic, this resurrected ghost town was known as the 'Wickedest Town in the West' during its late-1800s copper-mining heyday. In those days it teemed with brothels, saloons and opium dens. When the mines petered out in 1953, Jerome's population plummeted. Then came the '60s, when scores of hippies snapped up crumbling buildings for pennies, more or less restored them and injected the town with a groovy *joie de vivre*.

Join the party with a stroll past the galleries, indie shops, old buildings and wine-tasting rooms that are scattered up and down the hillside. Local artists sell their work at the **Jerome Artists Cooperative Gallery**

(☎928-639-4276; www.jeromeartistscoop.com; 502 N Main St; ☉10am-6pm) while burly but friendly-enough bikers gather at the **Spirit Room Bar** (☎928-634-8809; www.spiritroom.com; 166 Main St; ☉10:30am-1am).

✕ 🛏 p433

The Drive » Follow Main St/Hwy 89A out of downtown then turn left onto Douglas Rd.

- - - - - - - - - - - -

TRIP HIGHLIGHT

7 Audrey Headframe Park & Jerome State Historic Park

Holy moly! Wow! That's no joke! I'm not stepping on that! Yep, the glass platform covering the mining shaft at **Audrey Headframe Park** (55 Douglas Rd; admission free; ☉8am-5pm) isn't your everyday roadside attraction. It's death staring you in the face. If the cover shattered, the drop is 1910ft – which is 650ft longer than the Empire State Building!

Sufficiently disturbed? Chill out next door at the excellent **Jerome State Historic Park** (☎928-634-5381; www.azstateparks.com; adult/child $5/2; ☉8:30am-5pm), which explores the town's mining past. The museum is inside the 1916 mansion of eccentric mining mogul Jimmy 'Rawhide' Douglas. The folksy video is worth watching

before you explore the museum.

The Drive » Hwy 89A drops to tiny Clarkdale. At the traffic circle, take the second exit onto the Clarkdale Pkwy and into town. Follow Main St east to S Broadway then turn left onto Tuzigoot Rd.

- - - - - - - - - - - -

8 Tuzigoot National Monument

Squatting atop a ridge, **Tuzigoot National Monument** (☎928-634-5564; www.nps.gov/tuzi; adult/child $5/free, combination ticket with Montezuma Castle National Monument $8/free; ☉8am-5pm), a Sinaguan pueblo like nearby Montezuma, is believed to have been inhabited from AD 1000 to 1400. At its peak as many as 225 people lived in its 110 rooms. Stop by the revamped visitor center to examine tools, pottery and arrowheads then climb a short, steep trail (not suitable for wheelchairs) for memorable views of the Verde River Valley.

The Drive » Return to S Broadway and follow it south just over 1.5 miles into Old Town Cottonwood.

- - - - - - - - - - - -

TRIP HIGHLIGHT

9 Cottonwood

Cottonwood has kicked up its cool quotient, particularly in its pedestrian-friendly Old Town District. On this low-key strip

Classic Trip

RICHARD CUMMINS/ROBERT HARDING WORLD IMAGERY/CORBIS ©

WHY THIS IS A CLASSIC TRIP
AMY BALFOUR, AUTHOR

You know you're on a good road trip when you see a horde of motorcyclists roaring up in your rearview mirror. That happens all the time on Hwy 89/89A. I love it. The red rock and Verde Valley views are superb, plus the route ends at the best show in the Southwest: the Grand Canyon. Along the way, every stop is loaded with possibilities for adventure.

Top: Desert View Watchtower
Left: Welcome sign, Cottonwood
Right: Jerome

JOHN ELK/GETTY IMAGES ©

there are loads of good restaurants and several interesting indie stores. The inviting **Arizona Stronghold** (www.azstronghold.com; 1023 N Main St; tastings $9; ⊘noon-7pm Sun-Thu, to 9pm Fri & Sat) tasting room has welcoming staff, comfy couches, and live music on Friday nights. Enjoy a few more wine samples across the street at the chocolate-and-wine pairing **Pillsbury Wine Company** (www.pillsburywine.com; 1012 N Main St; ⊘11am-6pm Sun-Thu, 11am-8pm Fri). For wet-and-wild wine tasting in Cottonwood, join a Water to Wine kayak tour ($97.25) with **Sedona Adventure Tours** (📞928-204-6440; www.sedonaadventuretours.com; 2020 Contractors Rd; 🚹) on the Verde River to Alcantara Vineyards.

The Drive » Follow Main St south to reconnect with Hwy 89A N. Follow it into Sedona. At the roundabout at the junction of Hwy 89A and Hwy 179, called the Y, continue into Uptown Sedona. The visitor center sits at the junction of Hwy 89A and Forest Rd.

---

⑩ Sedona

The stunning red rocks here have an intensely spiritual pull for many visitors. Some New Age believers even think that the sandstone formations hold vortices that exude high-octane spiritual energy. See for

WITOLD SKRYPCZAK/GETTY IMAGES ©

Classic Trip

yourself atop **Airport Mesa**, the vortex closest to downtown. Here, a short scramble leads to a lofty view of the surrounding sandstone monoliths, which blaze a psychedelic red and orange at sunset. To get to the viewpoint, drive up Airport Rd for 0.5 miles and look for a small parking area on the left.

Another pretty site is the **Chapel of the Holy Cross** (☎928-282-4069; www.chapeloftheholycross. com; 780 Chapel Rd; ⊙9am-5pm Mon-Sat, 10am-5pm Sun), a church tucked between spectacular red-rock columns 3 miles south of town. This modern, non-denominational chapel was built by Marguerite Brunwig Staude in the tradition of Frank Lloyd Wright.

The Drive ❯❯ Follow Hwy 179 south past Bell Rock, passing the Village of Oak Creek.

⑪ South Gateway Visitor Center

Outdoor adventurers love the super-scenic hiking and biking trails in and around Sedona. The US Forest Service provides the helpful and free *Recreation Guide to Your National Forest*, which has brief descriptions of popular trails and a map pinpointing routes and trailheads. Pick one up at the **USFS South Gateway Visitor Center** (☎928-203-2900; www. redrockcountry.org; 8375

DAVID C TOMLINSON / GETTY IMAGES ©

Sedona Red rocks at sunset

Hwy 179; ⊘8am-5pm) just south of the village of Oak Creek. Staff can guide you to trails suited to your interests.

The Drive » Hwy 89A rolls north through the riparian greenery of scenic Oak Creek Canyon, where red cliffs flank the drive. North of the canyon pick-up I-17 north. Sedona is 30 miles from Flagstaff.

⑫ Flagstaff

From its pedestrian-friendly historic downtown to its high-altitude pursuits like skiing and hiking, Flagstaff's charms are countless. Humphrey's Peak, the highest point in Arizona, provides an inspiring backdrop. Start at the **visitor center** (📞800-842-7293; www. flagstaffarizona.org; 1 E Rte 66; ⊘8am-5pm Mon-Sat, 9am-4pm Sun), which has free brochures for walking tours, including a guide to Flagstaff's haunted places.

The interesting **Lowell Observatory** (📞928-233-3212; www.lowell.edu; 1400 W Mars Hill Rd; adult/child $12/5; ⊘9am-10pm Jun-Aug, shorter hours Sep-May), built in 1894, sits on a hill just outside downtown. It witnessed the first sighting of Pluto in 1920. During the day, take a guided tour. At night, weather permitting, try stargazing.

Flagstaff's microbreweries are the stars on the one-mile

DETOUR: DESERT VIEW DRIVE

Start: ⑭ Mather Point & Grand Canyon Visitor Center

This scenic road meanders 25 miles to the East Entrance on Hwy 64, passing some of the park's finest viewpoints, picnic areas and historic sites. **Grand View Point** marks the trailhead where miner Peter Berry opened his Grand View Hotel in 1897. Views are indeed spectacular. Another stunning view awaits at **Moran Point**, named for Thomas Moran, a landscape painter whose work aided in designating the Grand Canyon as a national monument in 1908. Further along is **Tusayan Ruin & Museum**, where you can walk around the remains of an excavated Puebloan village dating to 1185. At the end of the road is the **Watchtower**, designed by Mary Colter and inspired by ancient Puebloan watchtowers. The terrace gives panoramic views of the canyon and river. The circular staircase inside leads past Hopi murals to 360-degree views on the top floor.

Flagstaff Ale Trail (www. flagstaffaletrail.com). Or hop on the **Alpine Pedaler** (📞928-213-9233; www. alpinepedaler.com; per person $25), a 15-passenger 'party on wheels' that stops at bars and breweries.

✕ 🛏 p433

The Drive » The next morning – and mornings are best for the 90-mile trip – take Hwy 180 west and enjoy the views of the San Francisco Peaks through the treetops. When you reach Hwy 64 at the town of Valle, turn right and drive north on the big flat of the Coconino Plateau.

⑬ Tusayan

This little town sits 1 mile south of the

Grand Canyon's South Entrance, along Hwy 64. It's basically a half-mile strip of hotels and restaurants. Stop at the **National Geographic Visitor Center & IMAX** (📞928-638-2468; www. explorethecanyon.com; 450 Hwy 64; adult/child $13/10; ⊘8am-10pm Mar-Oct, 10:30am-6:30pm Nov-Feb) to pre-pay the $25 per-vehicle park fee and save yourself what could be a long wait at the entrance. Currently screening in the IMAX theater is the terrific 34-minute film *Grand Canyon – The Hidden Secrets*. With exhilarating river-running scenes and

Classic Trip

virtual-reality drops off canyon rims, the film plunges you into the history and geology of the canyon through the eyes of ancient Native Americans, John Wesley Powell and a soaring eagle.

In summer, you can leave your car here and catch the Tusayan shuttle into the park.

The Drive » Follow Hwy 64 1 mile north to the park entrance. Admission to the national park is $25 per vehicle or $12 for someone entering by foot, bicycle or motorcycle, and is good for 7 days.

TRIP HIGHLIGHT

🍴 Mather Point & Grand Canyon Visitor Center

Park at the visitor center but don't go inside. Not yet. Walk, or run, directly to **Mather Point**, the first overlook after the South Entrance. It's usually packed elbow-to-elbow with a global array of tourists, all taking photos, but even with the crowds there's a sense of communal wonder that keeps the scene polite. You'll see – the sheer immensity of the canyon

just grabs you, then pulls you in for a look at the gorgeous details – rugged plateaus, crumbly spires and colorful ridges.

Three hundred yards behind Mather Point is the main **visitor center** (www.nps.gov/grca; ☉8am-5pm), with a theater and a bookstore. On the plaza, bulletin boards and kiosks display information about ranger programs, the weather, tours and hikes. Inside is a ranger-staffed information desk and a lecture hall, where rangers offer daily talks on a variety of subjects. The theater screens a 20-minute movie, *Grand Canyon: A Journey of Wonder*, on the hour and half-hour.

From here, explore the park via park shuttle, rent a **bike** (☎928-638-3055; www.bikegrandcanyon. com; 10 S Entrance Rd, Grand Canyon Visitor Center; full-day adult/child $40/30; ☉8am-6pm May-Oct, 10am-4pm Mar, Apr, Oct & Nov), or your own four wheels. In summer, parking can be a challenge in Grand Canyon Village.

The Drive » The Village Loop Rd leads into Grand Canyon Village. Pass El Tovar, Kachina and Thunderbird lodges and Bright Angel Lodge. The Bright Angel Trailhead is just west of Bright Angel Lodge.

🍴 Grand Canyon Village

In 2013 the park opened a new plaza and parking area beside the Bright Angel Trailhead. The **Bright Angel** is the most popular of the corridor trails, and its steep and scenic 8-mile descent to the Colorado River has four logical turn-around points: Mile-and-a-half Resthouse, Three Mile Resthouse, Indian Garden and Plateau Point. Summer heat can be crippling and the climb is steep. Day hikers should turn around at one of the two resthouses (a 3- to 6-mile round-trip).

If you're more interested in history and geography than strenuous hiking, follow the easy **Rim Trail** east from here (see p419). Heading west, the Rim Trail passes every overlook on the way to **Hermits Rest**, offering spectacular views. The Hermits Rest shuttle runs parallel to the trail, so hike until you're tired then hop on the shuttle to continue or return. But be sure to hop off for the sunset, which is best at Hopi Point (which draws crowds) or Pima Point.

🛏 p433

Eating & Sleeping

Prescott ③

✗ Iron Springs Cafe   Cafe $$
(☎928-443-8848; www.ironspringscafe.com;
1501 Iron Springs Rd; mains brunch $10-13, lunch
$10-15, dinner $10-21; ⊘8am-8pm Wed-Sat,
9am-2pm Sun) Savory Cajun and Southwestern
specialties, often spicy, are highlights at this
cafe inside a former train station.

✗ Lone Spur Cafe   Cafe $
(☎928-445-8202; www.thelonespur.com; 106 W
Gurley St; breakfast & lunch $8-17, dinner $14-24;
⊘8am-2pm daily, 4:30-8pm Fri) Portions are
huge, and the sausage gravy will knock your hat
off. Decor includes stuffed mounts, cowboy gear
and an antler chandelier.

🛏 Motor Lodge   Bungalow $$
(☎928-717-0157; www.themotorlodge.com;
503 S Montezuma St; r $99-119, ste $149, apt
$159; ❄🛜) Rooms in the 12 snazzy bungalows
at this welcoming place come with whimsical
prints and stylish but comfy bedding.

Jerome ⑥

✗ Grapes   American $$
(☎928-639-8477; www.grapesjerome.com;
111 Main St; lunch & dinner $9-17; ⊘11am-9pm)
Everything on the menu has a wine pairing
suggestion. Top-drawer pizza, pasta and steak
in a classy but lively environment.

🛏 Jerome Grand Hotel   Hotel $$
(☎928-634-8200; www.jeromegrandhotel.
com; 200 Hill St; r $120-205, ste $270-460;
❄🛜) Built in 1926 as a hospital for the mining
community, this sturdy fortress plays up its
unusual history with relics of the past, from
incinerator chutes to patient call lights. For
$20 hotel guests can join the evening ghost
tour. Enjoy fine dining and and a dazzling

valley panorama at the attached **Asylum
Restaurant** (lunch $10 to $16, dinner $20
to $32).

Flagstaff ⑫

✗ Beaver Street Brewery   Brewpub $$
(www.beaverstreetbrewery.com; 11 S Beaver
St; lunch $8-13, dinner $10-20; ⊘11am-11pm
Sun-Thu, to midnight Fri & Sat; 👶) This place
packs in families, river guides, ski bums and
businesspeople. The menu is typical brewpub
fare, with delicious pizzas, burgers and salads,
and there's usually five handmade beers on tap.

🛏 Hotel Monte Vista   Hotel $$
(☎928-779-6971; www.hotelmontevista.com;
100 N San Francisco St; d $65-110, ste $120-140;
🛜) In downtown Flagstaff. Ask for a quiet room
if you think the live music at the downstairs bar
will irritate. Wi-fi and ghosts are free.

Grand Canyon Village ⑮

🛏 Bright Angel Lodge   Lodge $$
(www.grandcanyonlodges.com; r with/without
private bath $94/83, suites $185-362, cabins
$120-340; ⊘year-round; ❄@🛜) The cabins
are most coveted, but lodge rooms (some with
shared shower) are cozy and immaculate. The
Bright Angel Bar is perfect for those who
want to unwind with a burger and a beer without
cleaning up too much.

🛏 El Tovar   Lodge $$$
(www.grandcanyonlodges.com; d $178-273, ste
$335-426; ⊘year-round; ❄🛜) The rugged
yet elegant (it's possible!) El Tovar remains a
grande dame of national park lodges. Standard
rooms can be small, so go for deluxe if you
need elbow room. At the stone-and-oak **dining
room** enjoy a steak beside the best views in
the state.

Bryce Canyon National Park
Sandcastle-like spires

Zion & Bryce National Parks

34

From canyon floor to cliff-top perches, the red-rock country in southwestern Utah will delight your eyes and challenge your muscles.

TRIP HIGHLIGHTS

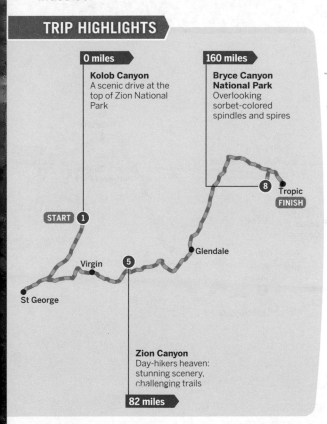

0 miles

Kolob Canyon
A scenic drive at the top of Zion National Park

160 miles

Bryce Canyon National Park
Overlooking sorbet-colored spindles and spires

START 1

8 Tropic
FINISH

Virgin   5

● Glendale

St George

Zion Canyon
Day-hikers heaven: stunning scenery, challenging trails

82 miles

6 DAYS
178 MILES / 286KM

GREAT FOR...

BEST TIME TO GO
In April and September you'll likely have warm weather both at low and high elevations.

 ESSENTIAL PHOTO
The amphitheater's color at sunrise on Fairyland Point.

 BEST FOR HIKING
Zion Canyon has easy river walks to strenuous, canyon-climbing hikes.

Zion & Bryce National Parks

Standing in the umber earth atop Observation Point (6507ft), Zion Canyon spreads before you. The sinuous green river belt snakes through towering crimson cliffs, and hikers below on Angels Landing resemble ants. If you climbed the 4-mile trail up 2148ft from the canyon floor – bravo! But insiders know that the views look just as sweet if you hiked the backcountry East Mesa trail and descended to the point.

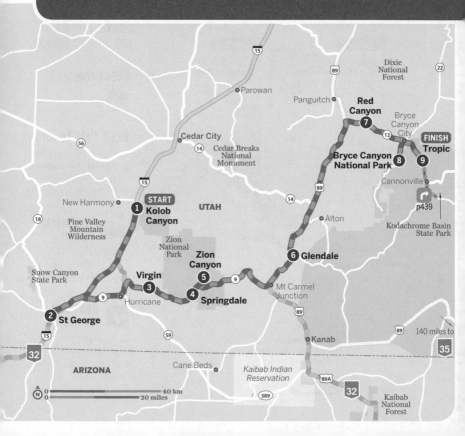

TRIP HIGHLIGHT

1 Kolob Canyon

Start your visit at the **Kolob Canyons Visitor Center** (☎435-586-0895; www.nps.gov/zion; Kolob Canyons Rd, Zion National Park; 7-day vehicle pass $25; ⏲park 24hr, center 8am-6pm Jun-Sep, to 4:30pm Oct-May), gateway to the less-visited, higher elevation section of Zion National Park off I-15. Even in peak season you'll see relatively few cars on the scenic 5-mile **Kolob Canyon Rd**, a high-plateau route where striking canyon and rangeland views alternate. The road terminates at **Kolob Canyon Overlook** (6200ft); from there the **Timber Creek Trail** (1-mile round-trip) follows a 100ft ascent to a small peak with great views of the Pine Valley Mountains beyond. In early summer the trail area is covered with wildflowers. Note that the upper section of the road may be closed due to snow from November through May.

The best longer hike in this section of the park is the **Taylor Creek Trail** (5-mile round-trip), which passes pioneer ruins and crisscrosses a creek, with little elevation change.

The Drive » Distant rock formations zoom by as you cruise along at 70-plus mph on I-15. St George is 41 miles south.

LINK YOUR TRIP

32 Four Corners Cruise

Twist east from Zion on Hwy 9 then follow Hwys 89 and 89A south to the Grand Canyon North Rim.

35 Monument Valley & Trail of the Ancients

For majestic monoliths, take Hwy 9 then Hwy 89 southeast to Page then follow Hwys 98 and 160 east to Hwy 163 north.

2 St George

A spacious Mormon town with an eye-catching temple and a few pioneer buildings, St George sits about equidistant between the two halves of Zion. The **Chamber of Commerce** (☎435-628-1658; www.stgeorgechamber.com; 97 E St George Blvd; ⏲9am-5pm Mon-Fri) can provide information on the historic downtown. Otherwise, use this time to stock up on food and fuel in this trip's only real city (population 75,561). Eleven miles north of town, **Snow Canyon State Park** (☎435-628-2255; http://stateparks.utah.gov; 1002 Snow Canyon Dr, Ivins; per vehicle $6; ⏲day use 6am-10pm; 👪) is a 7400-acre sampler of southwest Utah's famous land features. Easy trails that are perfect for kids lead to tiny slot canyons, cinder cones, lava tubes and fields of undulating slickrock.

p443

The Drive » Off the interstate, Hwy 9 leads you into canyon country. You'll pass the town of Hurricane before sweeping curves give way to tighter turns (and slower traffic). Virgin is 27 miles east of St George.

3 Virgin

The tiny-tot town of Virgin, named after the river (what else?), has an odd claim to fame – in 2000 the city council passed a largely symbolic law requiring every resident (about 600 of them) to own a gun. You can't miss the **Virgin Trading Post** (☎435-635-3455; 1000 W Hwy 9; village $2; ⏲9am-7pm), which sells homemade fudge, ice cream and every Western knickknack known to man. Stop and have your picture taken in the 'Virgin Jail' or 'Wild Ass Saloon' in the replica Old West village here. It's pure, kitschy fun.

The Drive » Springdale is 14 miles further along Hwy 9 (55 minutes from St George).

➍ Springdale

Stunning orangish-red mountains, including the **Watchman** (6555ft), form the backdrop for a perfect little park town. Here eclectic cafes and eateries are big on locally sourced ingredients. Galleries and artisan shops line the long main drag, interspersed with indie motels, lodges and a few B&Bs. Make this your base for three nights exploring Zion Canyon and surrounds. Outfitters **Zion Rock & Mountain Guides** (☏435-772-3303; www.

zionrockguides.com; 1458 Zion Park Blvd; ⊙8am-8pm Mar-Oct, hours vary Nov-Feb) and **Zion Adventure Company** (☏435-772-1001; www.zionadventures.com; 36 Lion Blvd; ⊙8am-8pm Mar-Oct, 9am-noon & 4-7pm Nov-Feb) lead canyoneering, climbing and 4WD trips outside the park; the latter has inner-tube rentals for summer float trips. They both outfit for backcountry hikes through the Narrows.

Three times daily **Zion Canyon Giant Screen Theatre** (www.zioncanyontheatre.com; 145 Zion Park Blvd; adult/child $8/6) shows the 40-minute *Zion Canyon:*

Treasure of the Gods. The film's light on substance but long on beauty.

 p443

The Drive » The entrance to the Zion Canyon section of Zion National Park is only 2 miles east of Springdale. Note that here you're at about 3900ft, the lowest (and hottest) part of your trip.

TRIP HIGHLIGHT

➎ Zion Canyon

More than 100 miles of trails cut through the surprisingly well-watered, deciduous tree-covered Virgin River canyon section of Zion National Park. Map out your routes at the **Zion Canyon Visitor Center** (☏435-772-3256; www.nps.gov/zion; Hwy 9, Zion National Park; 7-day vehicle pass $25; ⊙8am-7:30pm late May-early Sep, to 5pm late Sep-early May). Your first activity should be the 6-mile **Scenic Drive**, which pierces the heart of the park. From April through October using the free shuttle is mandatory, but you can hop off and on at any of the scenic stops and trailheads along the way.

The paved, mile-long one-way **Riverside Walk** at the end of the road is an easy stroll. When the trail ends, you can continue hiking along

---

LOCAL KNOWLEDGE: EAST MESA TRAIL

It feels deliciously like cheating to wander through open stands of tall ponderosa pines and then descend to Observation Point instead of hiking more than 2100ft uphill from the Zion Canyon floor. On **East Mesa Trail** (6.4 miles round-trip, moderate difficulty) you can do just that, because your vehicle does all the climbing. North Fork Rd is about 2.5 miles beyond the park's east entrance; follow it 5 miles north up Hwy 9 from there. Getting to the trailhead in some seasons requires 4WD; enquire about conditions and maps at the Zion Canyon Visitor Center. Nearby **Zion Ponderosa Ranch Resort** (☏800-293-5444, 435-648-2700; www.zionponderosa.com; N Fork Rd, off Hwy 9; cabins $70-160, tent sites $10, RV sites with hookups $49; @🛜🏊), which also has accommodation and activities, can provide hiker shuttles. Note that at 6500ft, these roads and the trail may be closed due to snow November through May.

in the Virgin River for 5 miles. Alternatively, a half-mile one-way trail leads up to the lower of the **Emerald Pools** where water tumbles from above a steep overhang stained by desert varnish.

The strenuous, 5.4-mile round-trip **Angels Landing Trail** (four hours, 1400ft elevation gain) is a vertigo-inducer with narrow ridges and 2000ft sheer drop-offs. Succeed and the exhilaration is unsurpassed. Canyon views are even more phenomenal from the top of the even higher **Observation Point** (8 miles round-trip; 2148ft elevation change).

For the 16-mile one-way trip down through the **Narrows**, the spectacular slot canyons of the Virgin River, you need to plan ahead. An outfitter, shuttle and gear (see Springdale) plus a backcountry permit from the park are required; make advance reservations via the park website.

🛏 p443

The Drive » Driving east, Hwy 9 undulates over bridges and up 3.5 miles of tight switchbacks before reaching the impressive gallery-dotted Zion–Mt Carmel Tunnel. From there until the east park entrance, the canyon walls are made of etched, light-colored slickrock, including Checkerboard Mesa. Glendale

DETOUR: KODACHROME BASIN STATE PARK

Start: 9 Tropic

Dozens of red, pink and white sandstone chimneys punctuate **Kodachrome Basin State Park** (📞435-679-8562; www.stateparks.utah.gov; off Cottonwood Canyon Rd; day-use per vehicle $6; 🕐day use 6am-10pm), named for its photogenic landscape by the National Geographic Society in 1948. The moderately easy, 3-mile round-trip **Panorama Trail** provides an overview of the otherworldly formations. Be sure to take the side trails to **Indian Cave**, where you can check out the handprints on the wall (cowboys' or Indians'?), and **Secret Passage**, a short spur through a narrow slot canyon. **Red Canyon Trail Rides** (📞800-892-7923; www.redcanyontrailrides.com; Kodachrome Basin State Park; 1-hr ride $40; 🕐Mar-Nov) offers horseback riding in Kodachrome.

The park lies 26 miles southeast of Bryce Canyon National Park, off Cottonwood Canyon Rd, south of Cannonville.

lies 32 miles (50 minutes) northwest of Zion Canyon.

- - - - - - - - - - - - -

6 Glendale

Several little towns line Hwy 89 north of the Hwy 9 junction. As you drive, look for little rock shops, art galleries and home-style cafes. Glendale is a small Mormon settlement founded in 1871. **Buffalo Bistro** (📞435-648-2778; www.buffalobistro.net; 305 N Main St; burgers & mains $8-24; 🕐4-9:30pm Thu-Sun mid-Mar–mid-Oct) conjures a laid-back Western spirit with a breezy porch, sizzling grill and eclectic

menu that includes wild boar ribs and elk burgers. Reservations recommended.

🛏 p443

The Drive » Hwy 89 is a fairly straight shot through pastoral lands; turn off from there onto Scenic Byway 12 where the red rock meets the road. Red Canyon is 41 miles northeast of Glendale.

- - - - - - - - - - - - -

7 Red Canyon

Impossibly red monoliths rise up roadside as you reach **Red Canyon** (📞435-676-2676; www.fs.usda.gov/recarea/dixie; Scenic Byway 12, Dixie National Forest; admission free; 🕐park 24hr,

LOCAL VOICE
LYMAN HAFEN,
DIRECTOR, ZION
NATURAL HISTORY
ASSOCIATION

My favorite time of year in Zion is the first full week of November when 24 amazing artists come to paint in the Zion National Park Plein Air Art Invitational. Cool but bearable weather, fall colors, fewer visitors, interaction with artists, and a major art exhibition and sale, open a new perspective on the magic of Zion.

Above: Bridge across the Virgin River, Zion National Park
Left: Rock tower, Kodachrome Basin State Park
Right: The Narrows, Zion National Park

visitor center 9am-6pm Jun-Aug, 10am-4pm May & Sep). These parklands provide super-easy access to eerie, intensely colored formations. Check out the excellent geologic displays and pick up maps at the visitor center, where several moderate hiking trails begin. The 0.7-mile one-way **Arches Trail** passes 15 arches as it winds through a canyon. Legend has it that outlaw Butch Cassidy once rode in the area; a tough 8.9-mile hiking route, **Cassidy Trail**, bears his name.

The Drive » Stop to take the requisite photo before you drive through two blasted-rock arches to continue on. Bryce Canyon National Park is only 9 miles down the road.

- - - - - - - - - - - -

TRIP HIGHLIGHT

❽ Bryce Canyon National Park

The pastel-colored, sandcastle-like spires and hoodoos of **Bryce Canyon National Park** (📞435-834-5322; www.stateparks.utah.gov; Hwy 63; 7-day vehicle pass $25; ⏰24hr, visitor center 8am-8pm May-Sep, to 4:30pm Oct-Apr) look like something straight out of Dr Seuss' imagination. The 'canyon' is actually an amphitheater of formations eroded from the cliffs. **Rim Road Scenic Drive** (18 miles one way), roughly follows the canyon rim past the visitor center (8000ft), the lodge, incredible overlooks and trailheads, ending at **Rainbow Point** (9115ft). From early May through early October, an optional free shuttle bus (8am until at least 5:30pm) departs from a staging area just north of the park.

The easiest walk would be to follow the **Rim Trail** that outlines Bryce Amphitheater from Fairyland Point to Bryce Point (up to 5.5 miles one way). Several sections are paved and wheelchair accessible, the most level being the half mile between Sunrise and Sunset Points.

A number of moderate trails descend below the rim to the maze of fragrant juniper and undulating high-mountain desert. The **Navajo Loop** drops 521ft from Sunset Point. To avoid a super-steep ascent, follow the **Queen's Garden Trail** on the desert floor and hike up 320ft to Sunrise Point. From there take the shuttle, or follow the Rim Trail back to your car (2.9-mile round-trip).

Note that the high altitude means cooler temperatures – 80°F (27°C) average in July – here than at scorching Zion National Park.

🛏 p443

The Drive » Only 11 miles east of Bryce Canyon, the town of Tropic is 2000ft lower in elevation – so expect it to be 10 degrees warmer there.

- - - - - - - - - - -

❾ Tropic

A farming community at heart, Tropic does offer a few services for park goers. There's a grocery store, a couple of restaurants and several motels. Basing yourself here for two nights is definitely less expensive than staying in the park. Note that the town is entirely seasonal; many businesses shut their doors tight from October through March.

🛏 p443

Eating & Sleeping

St George ②

✕ Painted Pony Modern American $$$

(📞435-634-1700; www.painted-pony.com; 2 W St George Blvd, Ancestor Sq; sandwiches $9-12, dinner mains $24-35; ⏰11am-10pm) Expect gourmet comfort food such as meatloaf with a port wine reduction and rosemary mashed potatoes.

🛏 Seven Wives Inn B&B $$

(📞800-600-3737, 435-628-3737; www.sevenwivesinn.com; 217 N 100 West; r & ste incl breakfast $99-185; 🌢@🛜🌢) Individually furnished guest rooms occupy two 1800s homes at this charming inn with a small pool.

Springdale ④

✕ Bit & Spur Restaurant & Saloon Southwestern $$

(www.bitandspur.com; 1212 Zion Park Blvd; mains $16-28; ⏰5-10pm daily Mar-Oct, 5-10pm Thu-Sat Nov-Feb) Sweet-potato tamales and chili-rubbed rib-eyes are two of the classics at this Western-inspired eatery. Full bar.

🛏 Canyon Ranch Motel Motel $$

(📞866-946-6276, 435-772-3357; www.canyonranchmotel.com; 668 Zion Park Blvd; r $99-119, apt $120-140; 🌢🛜🌢) At this 1930s motor-court motel the cottages that surround a shaded lawn with redwood swings give the place a cool, retro vibe but interiors are thoroughly updated.

🛏 Red Rock Inn B&B $$

(📞435-772-3139; www.redrockinn.com; 998 Zion Park Blvd; cottages incl breakfast $127-132; 🌢🛜) Five romantic country-contemporary cottages spill down a small desert hillside. Enjoy the full hot breakfast on your private patio.

Zion Canyon ⑤

🛏 Zion Lodge Lodge $$

(📞435-772-7700, 888-297-2757; www.zionlodge.com; Zion Canyon Scenic Dr; r $185,

cabins $195, ste $225; 🌢@🛜) Though not as grand as some park lodges, the wooden cabins and motels here are refined rustic. Here in the middle of Zion Canyon you're surrounded by stunning red-rock cliffs on all sides.

Glendale ⑥

🛏 Historic Smith Hotel B&B $

(📞800-528-3558, 435-648-2156; http://historicsmithhotel.com; 295 N Main St; r incl breakfast $79-89; 🌢) The seven-room Historic Smith Hotel is more comfortable than a favorite old sweater. Don't let the small rooms turn you off. The proprietors are great and the big breakfast table is a perfect place to meet other intrepid travelers.

Bryce Canyon National Park ⑧

🛏 Bryce Canyon Lodge Lodge $$

(📞877-386-4383, 435-834-8700; www.brycecanyonforever.com; Hwy 63; r & cabins $175-200; ⏰Apr-Oct; @) The 1920s Bryce park lodge exudes mountain charm with a large stone fireplace and exposed timbers. Rooms are in two-story wooden satellite buildings or in cabins.

🛏 Ruby's Inn Motel $$

(📞866-866-6616, 435-834-5341; www.rubysinn.com; 1000 S Hwy 63; r $135-180; 🌢@🛜🌢) More like a town than a resort complex. Choose from several motel-hotel lodging options, then take a helicopter ride, watch a rodeo, shop for groceries and Western art, fill up with gas, dine at one of several restaurants and post a letter about it all.

Tropic ⑨

🛏 Bryce Country Cabins Cabins $$

(📞888-679-8643, 435-679-8643; www.brycecountrycabins.com; 320 N Main St; cabins $99-139; ⏰Feb-Oct; 🌢🛜) Knotty-pine walls and log beds add charm to roomy one- and two-bedroom cabins on the edge of town.

Moki Dugway Hairpin turns and hair-raising heights

Monument Valley & Trail of the Ancients

35

Extreme desert isolation has preserved rocky natural wonders and numerous Ancestral Puebloan sites in far southeastern Utah and into Arizona.

TRIP HIGHLIGHTS

210 miles

Moki Dugway
Hairpin turns, 1100ft descent: one helluva road

●Blanding

8

FINISH
Goosenecks State Park

START
1

Monument Valley
Monolithic buttes and mesas defining the desert Southwest

0 miles

2

Hovenweep National Monument

46 miles

Bluff
A comfortable outpost in a remote and rugged landscape

---

5 DAYS
262 MILES / 422KM

GREAT FOR...

BEST TIME TO GO
October through April to avoid searing heat.

 ESSENTIAL PHOTO
Monument Valley's monolithic buttes at sunrise or sunset.

 BEST FOR ANCIENT SITES

Hire a guide in either Bluff or Monument Valley to get you off the beaten track and see rock art and ruins.

Monument Valley & Trail of the Ancients

Capturing the sheer scale of Monument Valley in a photo poses a big challenge. The best perspective shots have clouds or the moon in the background or something such as cactus or juniper trees in the foreground. To make the many shades of deepest red stand out, avoid the harsh noon sun and either use a polarizing filter or adjust your white balance accordingly.

TRIP HIGHLIGHT

❶ **Monument Valley**

Don't worry if you feel like you've seen this place before. Monument Valley's monolithic chocolate-red buttes and colossal, colorful mesas have starred in countless films, TV shows and commercials. The most famous formations are visible from the 17-mile, rough-dirt **scenic drive** looping through **Monument Valley Navajo Tribal Park** (📞435-727-5874; www.navajonationparks.

Monument Valley & Trail of the Ancients map

- 0 / 20 km
- 0 / 10 miles
- Manti-La Sal National Forest
- 191
- COLORADO
- 95 Natural Bridges National Monument ❼ 275
- Mule Canyon Ruins ❻
- Butler Wash Ruins ❺
- ❹ Blanding
- 95
- 262
- 20 miles to 31
- Grand Gulch
- Cedar Mesa
- UTAH
- Comb Ridge
- ❸ Hovenweep National Monument
- 261
- Valley of the Gods ❾
- 191
- San Juan River
- Moki Dugway ❽
- Bluff ❷
- 162
- San Juan River
- FINISH
- Goosenecks State Park ❿
- Mexican Hat
- 163
- Navajo Indian Reservation
- 191
- Monument Valley ❶ START
- 163
- Monument Valley Navajo Tribal Park
- 32
- ARIZONA
- 32
- 160

org/htm/monumentvalley.htm; adult/child $5/free; ⊙drive 6am-8:30pm May-Sep, 8am-4:30pm Oct-Apr, visitor center 6am-8pm May-Sep, 8am-5pm Oct-Apr), down a four-mile spur road south of **Goulding's Lodge** (📞435-727-3231; www.gouldings.com; Hwy 163; r $180), which has a small museum and offers tours. The park and scenery straddle the Utah–Arizona line.

The only way to get into the backcountry to see rock art, natural arches and coves is by taking a Navajo-led tour by foot, horseback or vehicle. Easygoing guides have booths in the parking lot at the visitor center. Tours are peppered with details about Dine culture, life

LINK YOUR TRIP

31 San Juan Skyway & Million Dollar Highway

Swap Utah's ancient wonders for Colorado cliff dwellings via Hwy 162 southeast and Hwy 160E.

32 Four Corners Cruise

With the Mittens Buttes in the rearview mirror, pick up US 163 south to Hwy 160 East.

on the reservation and movie trivia.

✕ 🛏 p451

The Drive ≫ The monument's mesas diminish in your rearview mirror as you head north, crossing the San Juan River and continuing along its valley the 45 total miles to Bluff, Utah.

TRIP HIGHLIGHT

❷ Bluff

Tiny tot Bluff (population 258) isn't much, but a few good motels and a handful of restaurants – surrounded by stunning red rock – make it a cool base for exploring. We've set up the trip for two nights in Monument Valley, two here in Bluff and one in Mexican Hat or back in the Valley. But distances are short enough that you could spend every night in Bluff and take daily forays.

Descendants of the town's pioneers re-created a log cabin settlement called **Bluff Fort** (www.hirf.org/bluff.asp; 5 E Hwy 191; admission free; ⊙9am-6pm Mon-Sat). Three miles west of town on public lands, the accessible **Sand Island petroglyphs** (www.blm.gov; Sand Island Rd, off Hwy 163; admission free; ⊙24hr) were created between 800 and 2500 years ago.

A few outfitters in town lead backcountry excursions that access rock art and ruins.
Far Out Expeditions (📞435-672-2294; www.

faroutexpeditions.com; half-day from $125) offers single and multiday hikes.
Wild Rivers Expeditions (📞800-422-7654; www.riversandruins.com; 101 Main St; day trip adult/child $175/133), a history- and geology-minded outfit, rafts along the San Juan. And **Buckhorn Llama** (📞435-672-2466; www.llamapack.com; per day $400) leads five- and six-day, llama-supported treks.

✕ 🛏 p451

The Drive ≫ The best route to Hovenweep is the paved Hwy 262 (past Hatch Trading Post, turn off on to Hwy 191 and follow the signs). From Bluff to the main entrance is a slow, 42-mile drive total (1¼ hours).

----

❸ Hovenweep National Monument

Meaning 'deserted valley' in the Ute language, the archeological sites of **Hovenweep National Monument** (📞ext 10 970-562-4282; www.nps.gov/hove; Hwy 262; park 7-day per vehicle $6, tent & RV sites $10; ⊙park dusk-dawn, visitor center 8am-6pm Jun-Sep, 9am-5pm Oct-May) exist in splendid isolation. Most of the eight towers and unit houses you'll see in the **Square Towers Group**, accessed near the visitor center, were built from 1230 to 1275 AD. Imagine stacking each clay-formed block to create such tall structures on tiny ledges. You could easily spend a half day or more hiking around the gorge's ruins. Other sites, which lie across the border in Colorado, require long hikes.

The Drive ≫ Bluff is the only base in the area, so you'll have to drive both to Hovenweep and back in one day. Moving on to Blanding, 28 miles north of Bluff, Hwy 191 is a rural road unimpeded by too many twists or turns.

GIORGIO FOCHESATO/GETTY IMAGES ©

④ Blanding

A special museum elevates small, agriculturally oriented Blanding a little above its totally drab name. The **Edge of the Cedars State Park Museum** (www.stateparks.utah.gov; 660 W 400 N; adult/child $5/3; ⊙9am-5pm Mon-Sat) is where you can learn more about the area's ancients, with its trove of archeological treasures that have been gathered from across southeastern Utah. Outside, climb down the rickety ladder into a dark, earthy-smelling ceremonial kiva (an Ancestral Puebloan ceremonial structure) c AD 1100. Can you feel a power to the place? (Just ignore the encroaching subdivision noise.)
Blue Mountain Artisans (www.facebook.com/pages/Blue-Mountain-Artisans; 215 E Center St; ⊙11am-6pm Wed-Sat) sells professional photographs of area archeological and geological sites, plus local jewelry.

🍴 p451

The Drive ≫ Heading west on Hwy 95, the scenery gets up close and personal. Butler Wash is only 14 miles along on free public lands; look for the signs.

⑤ Butler Wash Ruins

No need of hike days into the backcountry here: it's only a half-mile tramp to views of the freely accessible **Butler Wash Ruins**, a 20-room cliff dwelling on public lands. Scramble over the slickrock boulders (follow the cairns) to see the sacred kivas, habitation and storage rooms associated with the Ancestral Puebloan (or Anasazi) Kayenta group of northern Arizona c 1300 AD.

Monument Valley

The Drive » Continue west on Hwy 95, after the road veers north, look for a sign announcing more ruins – about 25 miles along.

- - - - - - - - - -

⑥ Mule Canyon Ruins

Though not particularly well preserved or evocative, the base of the tower, kiva and 12-room **Mule Canyon Ruins** sit almost roadside. Pottery found here links the population (c 1000 to 1150 AD) to the Mesa Verde group in southern Colorado.

The Drive » Continue along through the cliffs and canyons of Hwy 95 until you branch off on to the even smaller Hwy 275. The monument is 26 miles west of Mule Canyon.

- - - - - - - - - -

⑦ Natural Bridges National Monument

The views at **Natural Bridges** (www.nps.gov/nabr; Hwy 275; park 7-day per vehicle $6, tent & RV sites $10; ⊙24hr, visitor center 8am-6pm May-Sep, 9am-5pm Oct-Apr) are of a white sandstone canyon (it's not red!). All three impressive and easily

TAKE ONLY PICTURES

Sadly enough, many invaluable archeological sites in the area have been vandalized by thieves. Even casual visitors do irreparable damage by climbing on old dwelling walls or picking up 'just one' little pot shard. The old maxim 'take only pictures' bears repeating. Do not touch, move or remove any artifacts; it's against the law. The best way to explore ancient backcountry sites is with a well-informed, responsible guide.

accessible bridges are visible from a nine-mile winding **Scenic Drive** loop with overlooks. The oldest is also the closest: take a half-mile hike to the beautifully delicate **Owachomo Bridge**, spanning 180ft at only 9ft thick. Note that trails to Kachina and Siapu bridges are not long, but they require navigating super-steep sections or ladders. Near the end of the drive, don't skip the 0.3-mile trail to the **Horsecollar Ruin** cliff dwelling overlook.

The Drive >> Ochre-yellow to reddish-orange sandstone canyons surround you as you wend your way south on Rte 261. To your right is **Cedar Mesa-Grand Gulch primitive area**, a seriously challenging wilderness environment. To drive the 36 miles to Moki Dugway will take at least an hour.

TRIP HIGHLIGHT

8 Moki Dugway

Along a roughly paved, hairpin-turn-filled section of road, **Moki Dugway** descends 1100ft in just three miles. Miners 'dug out' the extreme switchbacks in the 1950s to transport uranium ore. Note that the road is far from wide by today's standards, but there are places to pull out. You can't always see what's around the next bend, but you can see down the sheer dropoffs. Those afraid of heights (or in trailers over 24ft long), steer clear.

The Drive >> At the bottom of the dugway, prepare yourself for another wild ride. The turnoff for Valley of the Gods is less than five miles ahead on your left.

9 Valley of the Gods

Think of the gravel road through the freely accessible **Valley of the Gods** as a do-it-yourself roller coaster, with sharp, steep hills and quick turns around some amazing scenery. Locals call it 'mini-Monument Valley'. Download the public lands office pamphlet from www. blm.gov to identify the strangely shaped sandstone monoliths and pinnacles (Seven Sailors, Lady on a Tub, Rooster Butte...). Allow an hour-plus for the 17 miles between highways 261 and 163. Do not attempt it without 4WD if it's rained recently.

The Drive >> Once you emerge from the valley, follow Hwy 163 back west and take the little jog up Hwy 261 to the Goosenecks State Park spur, a total of 8 miles away.

10 Goosenecks State Park Overlook

Following the 4-mile spur to **Goosenecks State Park** (http://stateparks.utah. gov; Rte 261; admission free; ☺24hr) brings you to a mesmerizing view. From 1000ft above you can see how the San Juan River's path carved tight turns through sediment, leaving gooseneck-shaped spits of land untouched. The dusty park itself doesn't have much to speak of besides pit toilets and picnic tables.

Eating & Sleeping

Monument Valley ❶

✕ Stagecoach Dining Room $$

(mains $8-27; ⊙6:30am-9:30pm Central Time, shorter hours in winter) Goulding's restaurant is a replica of a film set built for John Ford's 1949 Western *She Wore a Yellow Ribbon*. Tuck into the steaks or Navajo tacos piled high with chili and cheese.

🛏 Goulding's Lodge   Motel $$

(☎435-727-3231; www.gouldings.com; r $205-242, cabins $92, tent sites $26, RV sites $5; ❄🛜🏊🐾) This historical hotel a few miles west of Monument Valley has modern rooms, most with some view of the megaliths in the distance. Each has a DVD player so you can rent one of the many movies shot here.

🛏 View Hotel   Hotel $$$

(☎435-727-5555; www.monumentvalleyview.com; Hwy 163; r $209-265, ste $299-329; ❄@🛜) Probably the most aptly named hotel in Arizona. Rooms that end in numbers higher than 15 (for example 216) have unobstructed panoramas of Monument Valley below. Wi-fi available in the lobby only; restaurant on site.

Bluff ❷

✕ San Juan River Kitchen   New Mexican $$

(www.sanjuanriverkitchen.com; 75 E Main St; mains $14-20; ⊙5:30-10pm Tue-Sat) The inventive, regionally sourced Mexican-American dishes here use organic ingredients whenever possible. Don't skip the homemade chipotle chocolate ice cream.

✕ Twin Rocks Cafe & Trading Post   Native American $$

(913 E Navajo Twins Dr; mains $6-18; ⊙7am-9pm) A full diner-style menu is available, but we recommend trying fry bread (deep-fried dough) as part of a breakfast sandwich or wrapped up as a Navajo taco.

🛏 Desert Rose Inn   Motel $$

(☎888-475-7673, 435-672-2303; www.desertroseinn.com; Hwy 191; r $105-119, cabins $139-179; ❄@🛜) Wood porches wrap completely around a dramatic, two-story log building at the edge of town. Quilts on pine beds add to the comfort of extra-large rooms and cabins.

🛏 Recapture Lodge   Motel $

(☎435-672-2281; www.recapturelodge.com; Hwy 191; r incl breakfast $70-90; ❄@🛜🏊) A locally owned, rustic motel with super-knowledgeable staff who can help out with trek planning. There's plenty of shade around the small pool and on the property's 3½ miles of walking trails.

Blanding ❹

✕ Fattboyz Grillin   American $$

(www.facebook.com/pages/Fattboyz-Grillin; 164 N Hwy 191; mains $7-18; ⊙noon-9pm Mon-Sat) Good barbecued ribs, sandwiches and burgers. A Brian Kirby burger has it all: beef patty, barbecued pork, cheese *and* chili.

Mexican Hat

✕ Old River Grille   Diner $$

(http://sanjuaninn.net; Hwy 163; mains $7-15; ⊙7am-9pm) Southwestern home cooking here includes some Navajo Nation dishes.

🛏 San Juan Inn   Motel $

(☎800-447-2022, 435-683-2220; www.sanjuaninn.net; Hwy 163; r $85-100; ❄) The cliffside motel perches high above the San Juan River. Rooms are pretty basic, but are the nicest in town. Trading post on site.

Taos Pueblo
*Visit in July for
the summer
pow-wow*

High & Low Roads to Taos

36

Santa Fe, Taos, the Rio Grande, the Sangre de Cristos. And all the adobe villages, art galleries, Spanish-colonial churches and burrito stands in between make this loop a classic.

TRIP HIGHLIGHTS

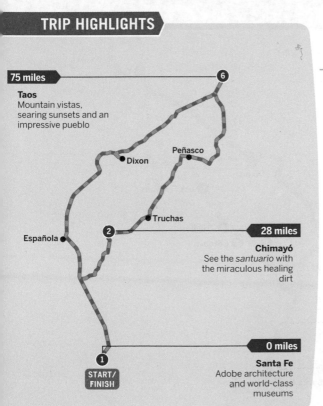

75 miles — **6**

Taos
Mountain vistas, searing sunsets and an impressive pueblo

Peñasco

● Dixon

● Truchas

Española ● **2**

28 miles

Chimayó
See the *santuario* with the miraculous healing dirt

0 miles

Santa Fe
Adobe architecture and world-class museums

1
START/ FINISH

2–4 DAYS
150 MILES / 241KM

- - - - - - - - - - - - - -

GREAT FOR...
📖 🍷

- - - - - - - - - - - - - -

BEST TIME TO GO
June to March.

- - - - - - - - - - - - - -

📷 **ESSENTIAL PHOTO**

Get the gorge and mountains at once, from Hwy 68 near Taos.

- - - - - - - - - - - - - -

☑ **BEST FOR CULTURE**

The 'miracle church' – and the chili – in Chimayó.

453

36 High & Low Roads to Taos

Starting in hip, historic Santa Fe, you'll rise from scrub-and-sandstone desert into ponderosa forests, snaking between the villages at the base of the 13,000ft Sangre de Cristos, until you reach the Taos plateau. After checking out this little place that's lured artists, writers and hippies for the past century, head back south through the ruggedly sculpted Rio Grande gorge, with the river coursing alongside you.

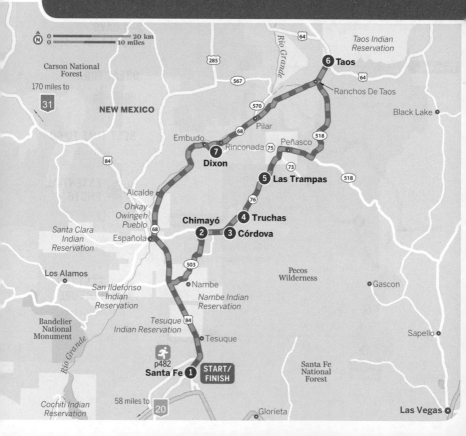

❶ Santa Fe

Walking among the historic adobe neighborhoods, and even around the tourist-filled plaza, there's no denying that 400-year-old Santa Fe has a timeless, earthy soul. Known as 'the city different,' it seamlessly blends historical and contemporary styles and casts a spell that's hard to resist: it's the second-oldest city in the US, the oldest state capital, and throws the oldest annual party (Fiesta) while boasting the second-largest art market in the nation, plus gourmet restaurants, world-class museums, opera, spas and more. At 7000ft above sea level, Santa Fe is also the

LOCAL KNOWLEDGE: NATURE CALLS

Want to see the scenery without a pane of glass in front of your face? Off the High Road, take a stroll on the **Santa Barbara Trail**, which follows a trout-filled creek through mixed forest into the Pecos Wilderness; it's pretty flat and easygoing. To reach the trailhead, take Hwy 73 from Peñasco and follow the signs.

Off the Low Road, turn onto Hwy 570 at Pilar and check out the **Orilla Verde Recreation Area** (day-use $3, tent/RV sites $7/15), where you can hang out or camp along the Rio Grande (or tube on it or fish in it). Hike up to the rim on Old 570, a dirt road blocked by a landslide, with expansive vistas of the Taos Plateau and the Sangre de Cristos.

Some of the best views in the state are from the top of **Lake Peak** (12,409ft), which can be reached on a day hike starting at the Santa Fe Ski Basin.

From Taos Ski Valley, you can day hike to the top of **Wheeler Peak** (13,161ft), New Mexico's highest summit (the views are pretty good up there, too). For trail maps and more information, go to the **Travel Bug** (www.mapsofnewmexico.com; 839 Paseo de Peralta; ⏰7:30am-5:30pm Mon-Sat, 11am-4pm Sun; 📶) bookshop in Santa Fe or the Taos **visitor center** (📞575-758-3873; Paseo del Pueblo Sur, Paseo del Cañon; ⏰9am-5pm; 📶).

LINK YOUR TRIP

31 San Juan Skyway & Million Dollar Highway

The landscape becomes the art after leaving Española on US 84 north to US 160 east to Mesa Verde.

20 Route 66

From Santa Fe drive south on I-25 to Albuquerque for green chili specialties on Route 66.

highest US state capital, and a fantastic base for hiking, mountain biking, backpacking and skiing. The plaza area has the highest concentration of sights but it's also worth a trip to Museum Hill for the fantastical **Museum of International Folk Art** (www.internationalfolkart.org; 706 Camino Lejo; NM resident/nonresident/child $6/9/free, free 5-8pm Fri summer; ⏰10am-5pm, closed Mon Sep-May) and the excellent (and free) **Wheelwright Museum of the American**

Indian (www.wheelwright.org; 704 Camino Lejo; ⏰10am-5pm Mon-Sat, 1-5pm Sun), among others.

✕ 🛏 p461

The Drive » For this 27-mile leg, take Hwy 84/285 north, then exit right onto Hwy 503 towards Nambé. Turn left onto Juan Medina Rd, toward the Santauario de Chimayó.

❷ Chimayó

Tucked into this little village is the so-called 'Lourdes of America,' **El**

Santuario de Chimayó

(www.elsantuariodechimayo. us; ⊙9am-5pm Oct-Apr, to 6pm May-Sep), one of the most important cultural sites in New Mexico. In 1816, this two-towered adobe chapel was built over a spot of earth said to have miraculous healing properties. Even today, the faithful come to rub the *tierra bendita* – holy

dirt – from a small pit inside the church on whatever hurts; some mix it with water and drink it. The walls of the dirt room are covered with crutches, left behind by those healed by the dirt. During Holy Week, about 30,000 pilgrims walk to Chimayó from Santa Fe, Albuquerque and beyond in the largest Catholic pilgrimage in the US. The artwork in the *santuario* is worth a trip on its own.

Chimayó also has a centuries-old tradition of producing some of the finest weavings in the area and has a handful of family-run galleries. Irvin Trujillo, a seventh-generation weaver, whose carpets are in collections at the Smithsonian in Washington, DC and the Museum of Fine Arts in Santa Fe, works out of his gallery **Centinela Traditional Arts** (www. chimayoweavers.com; NM 76; ⊙9am-6pm Mon-Sat, 10am-5pm Sun). Naturally dyed blankets, vests and pillows are sold, and you can watch the artists weaving on handlooms.

✗ p461

The Drive » Follow Hwy 76 north for a few miles, and take the right-side turn off to Córdova.

WINTER THRILLS

One of the biggest winter draws to this part of New Mexico is the skiing and snowboarding, and **Taos Ski Valley** (www.skitaos.org; half-/full-day lift ticket $64/77) is the premier place to hit the slopes. There's just something about the snow, challenging terrain and laid-back atmosphere that makes this mountain a wintery heaven-on-earth – that is, if heaven has a 3275ft vertical drop.

Offering some of the most difficult terrain in the USA, it's a fantastic place to zip down steep tree glades into untouched powder bowls. Seasoned skiers luck out, with more than half of the 70-plus trails at the Taos Ski Valley ranked expert; but there's also an award-winning ski school, so complete beginners thrive here, too. The valley has a peak elevation of 11,819ft and gets an average of more than 300in of all-natural powder annually – but some seasons are much better than others. The resort also has a skier-cross obstacle course at its popular terrain park.

That said, **Ski Santa Fe** (☎505-982-4429, snow report 505-983-9155; www.skisantafe.com; lift ticket adult/child $66/46; ⊙9am-4pm late Nov-Apr) is no slouch. Less than 30 minutes from the Santa Fe plaza, it boasts the same fluffy powder (though usually a little less of it), with an even higher base elevation (10,350ft) and higher chairlift service (12,075ft). Briefly admire the awesome desert and mountain vistas, then fly down powder glade shoots, steep bump runs or long groomers. The resort caters to families and expert skiers alike with its varied terrain. The quality and length of the ski season can vary wildly from year to year depending on how much snow the mountain gets, and when it falls (you can almost always count on a good storm in late March).

❸ Córdova

Down in the Rio Quemado Valley, this little town is best known for its unpainted, austere *santos* (saint) carvings created by local masters like George Lopez, Jose Delores Lopez, and Sabinita Lopez Ortiz – all members of the same artistic family. Stop and see their work at the **Sabinita Lopez Ortiz shop** (☎505-351-4572; County Rd 9; ⊘variable) – one of a few galleries in town.

The Drive » Hop back on Hwy 76 north, and climb higher into the Sangre de Cristo Mountains, about 4 miles.

- - - - - - - - - - - -

❹ Truchas

Rural New Mexico at its most sincere is showcased in Truchas, originally settled by the Spaniards in the 18th century. Robert Redford's *The Milagro Beanfield War* was filmed here (but don't bother with the movie – the book it's based on, by John Nichols, is waaaay better). Narrow roads, many unpaved, wend between century-old adobes. Fields of grass and alfalfa spread toward the sheer walls and plunging ridges that define the western flank of the Truchas Peaks. Between the run-down homes are some wonderful art galleries, which double as workshops for local weavers, painters, sculptors and other artists. The best place to get an overview of who's painting/sculpting/carving/weaving what, is the **High Road Marketplace** (www.highroadnewmexico.com; 1642 Hwy 76; ⊘10am-5pm, to 4pm winter), a cooperative art gallery with a huge variety of work by area artists.

The Drive » Continue north on Hwy 76 for around 8 miles, transecting the little valleys of Ojo Sarco and Cañada de los Alamos.

HIGH/LOW ROAD FESTIVALS

Try to catch – or avoid, if you hate crowds – some of the highlights from around the year on the High and Low Roads. Check websites for exact dates each year:

» **Easter** (Chimayó) – March/April

» **Taos Solar Music Festival** (www.solarmusicfest.com) – June

» **Taos Pueblo Pow-Wow** (www.taospueblopowwow.com; adult/child $10/free) – July

» **International Folk Art Market** (www.folkartmarket.org; Santa Fe) – July

» **Spanish Market** (www.spanishcolonial.org; Santa Fe) – July

» **Indian Market** (www.swaia.org; Santa Fe) – August

» **Santa Fe Fiesta** (www.santafefiesta.org) – September

» **High Road Art Tour** (www.highroadnewmexico.com; Hwy 76 to Peñasco) – September

» **Dixon Studio Tour** (www.dixonarts.org) – November

» **Christmas on Canyon Rd** (Santa Fe) – December

- - - - - - - - - - - -

❺ Las Trampas

Completed in 1780 and constantly defended against Apache raids, the **Church of San José de Gracia** (Hwy 76; ⊘9am-5pm Fri & Sat) is considered one of the finest surviving 18th-century churches in the USA and is a National Historic Landmark. Original paintings and carvings remain in excellent condition, and self-flagellation bloodstains from Los Hermanos Penitentes (a 19th-century religious order with a strong following in the northern

HIGH & LOW ROADS TO TAOS
MICHAEL BENANAV, AUTHOR

In this one loop, you delve into the enchanted essence of New Mexico: its oldest settlement, its most sacred sight, its highest peaks, its biggest river, its best food. From top art galleries and museums to rural villages where horse pastures and orchards are laced together by *acequias* (irrigation ditches), this is the state as you most imagined it might be. And more.

Above: Church at Taos Pueblo
Left: Wood crafts by Gloria Lopez Cordova at the Santa Fe Spanish Market
Right: Chili ristras and dried flowers

mountains of New Mexico) are still visible. On your way out of town, look right to see the amazing irrigation aqueduct, carved from tree trunks!

The Drive » Continue north on Hwy 76, through lovely Chamisal. At the T, turn right onto Hwy 75 and stay on it through Peñasco and Vadito. At Hwy 518, turn left towards Taos. At the end of the road, turn right on Paseo del Pueblo Sur/Hwy 68 and take it on into Taos – around 32 miles in total.

TRIP HIGHLIGHT

⑥ Taos

Taos is a place undeniably dominated by the power of its landscape: 12,300ft often-snowcapped peaks rise behind town, a sage-speckled plateau unrolls to the west before plunging 800ft straight down into the Rio Grande Gorge. The sky can be a searing sapphire blue or an ominous parade of rumbling thunderheads. And then there are the sunsets...

The pueblo here is one of the oldest continuously inhabited communities in the United States and it roots the town in a long history with a rich cultural legacy – including conquistadors, Catholicism, and cowboys. Taos remains a relaxed and eccentric place, with classic mud-brick buildings, quirky cafes and excellent restaurants. It's both rural and worldly, and a little bit otherworldly.

The best thing to do is walk around the plaza area soaking in the aura of the place. But you also won't want to miss **Taos Pueblo** (☏505-758-1028; www.taospueblo.com; Taos Pueblo Rd; adult/child $10/free, photography or video permit $6; ◷8am-4:30pm). Built around 1450 and continuously inhabited ever since, it's the largest existing multistoried pueblo structure in the USA and one of the best surviving examples of traditional adobe construction. Also well worth a visit is the **Millicent Rogers Museum** (www.millicentrogers.org; 1504 Millicent Rogers Rd; adult/child $10/2; ◷10am-5pm, closed Mon Nov-Mar), filled with pottery, jewelry, baskets and textiles from the private collection of a model and oil heiress who moved to Taos in 1947 and acquired one of the best collections of Indian and Spanish colonial art in the USA.

✗ 🛏 p461

The Drive » On this 26-mile leg, cruise the Low Road back to Santa Fe by taking Hwy 68 South. Just before the road drops downhill, there's a large pullout with huge views, so hop out and see what you're leaving behind. Then head down into the Rio Grande gorge. Go left on Hwy 75 to Dixon.

- - - - - - - - - - - - -

❼ Dixon

This small agricultural and artistic community is spread along the gorgeous Rio Embudo valley. It's famous for its apples but plenty of other crops are grown here too, including some of the grapes used by two award-winning local wineries, **Vivac** (www.vivacwinery.com; ◷10am-6pm Mon-Sat, from noon Sun) and **La Chiripada** (www.lachiripada.com; NM 75; ◷11am-6pm Mon-Sat, from noon Sun), both of which have tasting rooms. In summer and fall, there's a farmers market on Wednesday afternoons, with food fresh from the fields. Our favorite art gallery is actually on Hwy 68, in Rinconada, just north of Hwy 75; **Rift Gallery** (www.saxstonecarving.com; Hwy 68; ◷10am-5pm Wed-Sun) features masterful ceramics and stonework. On the first weekend in November, local artists open their homes and studios to the public in New Mexico's oldest studio tour. In summer, ask at the local food co-op and some kind soul might point you to the waterfalls, up a nearby dirt road.

✗ p461

The Drive » Back on Hwy 68, head south along the river, through Embudo and out of the gorge. Continue through Española, where you'll meet Hwy 84/285, and can take it back to Santa Fe. Both these towns are great lunch stops (p461). This leg is around 47 miles.

Eating & Sleeping

Santa Fe ❶

✗ Harry's
Roadhouse — American, New Mexican $

(☎505-989-4629; www.harrysroadhouse-santafe.com; 96 Old Las Vegas Hwy; mains breakfast $5-8, lunch $7-11, dinner $9-16; ⏰7am-10pm; 🚸) This longtime favorite on the southern edge of town feels like a rambling cottage. And, seriously, *everything* is good here. Especially dessert! The mood is casual and there's a full bar.

🛏 El Paradero — B&B $$

(☎505-988-1177; www.elparadero.com; 220 W Manhattan Ave; r $110-200; P ❄ @ 📶) Just a few blocks from the Plaza, this 200-year-old adobe B&B is one of Santa Fe's oldest inns. Each room is unique and loaded with character; our favorite is No 6.

Chimayó ❷

✗ Rancho de Chimayo — New Mexican $$

(☎505-984-2100; www.ranchodechimayo.com; County Rd 98; mains $8-18; ⏰8:30-10:30am Sat & Sun, 11:30am-9pm daily, closed Mon Nov-Apr) Classic New Mexican home cooking and the perfect margarita in atmospheric Southwestern ambiance.

Taos ❻

✗ El Gamal — Middle Eastern $

(www.elgamaltaos.com; 12 Doña Luz St; mains $7-12; ⏰9am-5pm Sun-Wed, to 9pm Thu-Sat; 📶 🍴 🚸) We're not sure the falafel at this vegetarian Middle Eastern place quite achieves its goal to 'promote peace...through evolving people's consciousness and taste buds,' but it just might. There's a kids' playroom in the back, plus a pool table and free wi-fi.

✗ Michael's Kitchen — New Mexican $$

(www.michaelskitchen.com; 304C Paseo del Pueblo Norte; mains $7-16; ⏰7am-2:30pm

Mon-Thu, to 8pm Fri-Sun; 🚸) Locals and tourists converge on this old favorite because the menu is long, the food's reliably good, and it's an easy place for kids. Plus, it serves the best damn breakfast in town. The fresh pastries fly out the door.

🛏 Historic Taos Inn — Historic Hotel $$

(☎575-758-2233; www.taosinn.com; 125 Paseo del Pueblo Norte; r $75-275; P ❄ 📶) With a cozy lobby, a top-notch restaurant, a sunken fireplace, a prime location, and lots of live local music at its famed Adobe Bar, the Taos Inn is more than the sum of its parts. The older rooms, some from the 19th century, are the nicest.

Dixon ❼

✗ Zuly's Cafe — Cafe $

(www.zulyscafe.org; 234 Hwy 75; mains $5-11; ⏰7:30am-3pm Tue-Thu, 7:30am-8pm Fri, 9am-8pm Sat) Scarf down a burrito, enchilada or buffalo burger at this excellent local cafe that surprises with some of the best green and red chili anywhere in the state. Seriously.

Embudo

✗ Sugar's BBQ — BBQ $

(1799 Hwy 68; mains $5-12; ⏰11am-6pm Thu-Sun) This bustling roadside stand serves up juicy burgers and succulent barbeque. Brisket burritos = mmmmmm.

Española

✗ El Parasol — New Mexican $

(☎www.elparasol.com; 603 Santa Cruz Rd; mains $2-5; ⏰7am-9pm) As local as it gets. Line up outside of this tiny trailer for the greasy-good chicken-guacamole tacos (order at least two) or the *carne adovada* (pork in red chile) burrito. Eat at a shaded picnic table.

McDonald Observatory A celestial show in clear, dark skies

Big Bend Scenic Loop

37

Although it's known for wide open spaces, west Texas is packed with surprising experiences that makes this a supremely well-rounded drive.

TRIP HIGHLIGHTS

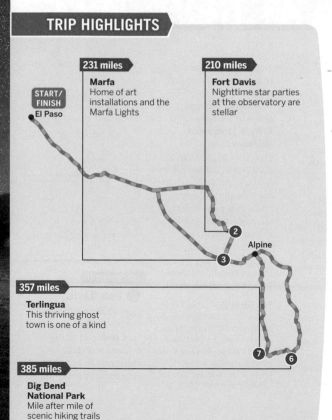

231 miles

Marfa
Home of art installations and the Marfa Lights

210 miles

Fort Davis
Nighttime star parties at the observatory are stellar

START/FINISH
El Paso

Alpine

357 miles

Terlingua
This thriving ghost town is one of a kind

385 miles

Big Bend National Park
Mile after mile of scenic hiking trails

5–7 DAYS
255 MILES / 410KM

GREAT FOR...

BEST TIME TO GO

Best between February and April – before the heat sets in.

ESSENTIAL PHOTO

Prada Marfa, a quirky roadside art installation.

BEST FOR OUTDOORS

McDonald Observatory's nighttime star parties.

37 Big Bend Scenic Loop

Getting to visit Big Bend National Park and experience the endless vistas straight out of an old Western are reason enough to make this trip. But you'll also get to have plenty of fun along the way, exploring the quirky small towns that are prime road-trip material. West Texas offers an unforgettable set of experiences, including minimalist art installations, nighttime astronomy parties and thriving ghost towns.

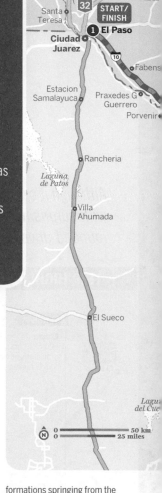

1 El Paso

Start your trip in El Paso, a border city that's wedged tightly into a remote corner of west Texas. Before you get out of town, take advantage of the great Mexican food you can find all over the city – it's right across the river from Mexico – and take time to enjoy some of El Paso's many free museums. Downtown, the **El Paso Museum of Art** (915-532-1707; www.elpasoartmuseum.org; 1 Arts Festival Plaza; special exhibits charge admission; ⊘9am-5pm Tue-Sat, to 9pm Thu, noon-5pm Sun) has a terrific Southwestern collection, and the engaging modern pieces round out the display nicely.

Another one you shouldn't miss is the **El Paso Holocaust Museum** (www.elpasoholocaustmuseum.org; 715 N Oregon St; ⊘9am-4pm Tue-Fri, 1-5pm Sat & Sun). It may seem a little out of place in a predominately Hispanic town, but it hosts amazingly thoughtful and moving exhibits that are imaginatively presented for maximum impact.

The Drive » Head east on I-10 for two hours, then turn onto TX-118 towards Fort Davis. The area is part of both the Chihuahuan Desert and the Davis Mountains, giving it a unique setting where the endless horizons are suddenly interrupted by rock formations springing from the earth.

TRIP HIGHLIGHT

2 Fort Davis

Here's why you'll want to plan on being in Fort Davis on either a Tuesday, Friday or Saturday: to go to an evening star party at

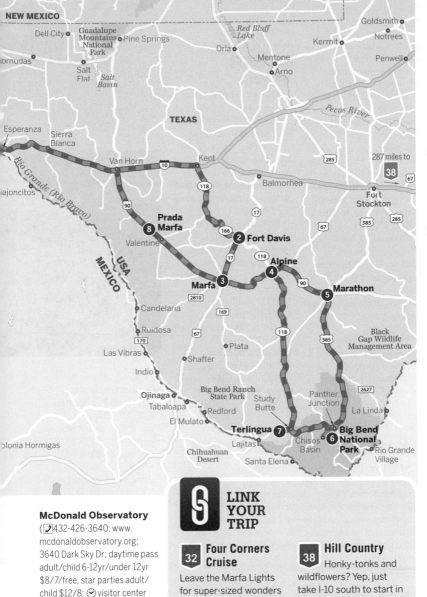

McDonald Observatory

(📞432-426-3640; www.
mcdonaldobservatory.org;
3640 Dark Sky Dr; daytime pass
adult/child 6-12yr/under 12yr
$8/7/free, star parties adult/
child $12/8; ⏱ visitor center
10am-5:30pm; ♿). The
observatory has some of
the clearest and darkest
skies in North America,
not to mention some
of the most powerful

LINK YOUR TRIP

32 Four Corners Cruise

Leave the Marfa Lights
for super-sized wonders
in the Southwest via I-10
west to I-25 north.

38 Hill Country

Honky-tonks and
wildflowers? Yep, just
take I-10 south to start in
San Antonio.

telescopes – a perfect combination for gazing at stars, planets and assorted celestial bodies with astronomers on hand to explain it all.

Other than that, nature lovers will enjoy **Davis Mountains State Park** (☎432-426-3337; http://www.tpwd.state.tx.us; Hwy 118; adult/child under 12yr $6/free), and history buffs can immerse themselves at the 1854 **Fort Davis National Historic Site** (☎432 426-3224; www.nps.gov/foda; Hwy 17; adult/child $3/free; ☉8am-5pm), a well-preserved frontier military post that's impressively situated at the foot of Sleeping Lion Mountain.

🛏 p469

The Drive » Marfa is just 20 minutes south on TX-17, a two-lane country road where tumbleweeds bounce slowly by and congregate around the barbed-wire fences.

- - - - - - - - - -

TRIP HIGHLIGHT

❸ Marfa

Marfa got its first taste of fame when Rock Hudson, Elizabeth Taylor and James Dean came to town to film the 1956 film *Giant*, and has served as a film location for movies like *There Will Be Blood* and *No Country for Old Men*.

But these days, this tiny town with one stoplight draws visitors from around the world for an entirely different reason: its art scene. Donald Judd single-handedly put Marfa on the art-world map in the 1980s when he used a bunch of abandoned military buildings to create one of the world's largest permanent installations

WITOLD SKRYPCZAK/GETTY IMAGES ©

of minimalist art at the **Chinati Foundation** (☎432-729-4362; www.chinati.org; 1 Calvary Row; adult/student $25/10; ☉by guided tour only 10am & 2pm Wed-Sun).

You'll find a variety of art galleries sprinkled around town exploring everything from photography to sculpture to modern art. **Ballroom Marfa** (☎432-729-3600; www.ballroommarfa.org; 108 E San Antonio; ☉10am-6pm Wed-Sat, to 3pm Sun) is a great gallery to catch the vibe.

🍴 🛏 p469

MARFA LIGHTS VIEWING AREA

The Marfa Lights that flicker beneath the Chinati Mountains have captured the imagination of many a traveler over the decades, with accounts of mysterious lights that appear and disappear on the horizon that go all the way back to the 1800s. Numerous studies have been conducted to explain the phenomenon, but the only thing scientists all agree on is that they have no idea what causes the apparition.

Catch the show at the Marfa Lights Viewing Area, on the right side of the road between Marfa and Alpine. From the platform, look south and find the red blinking light (that one's real). Just to the right is where you will (or won't) see the Marfa Lights doing their ghostly thing.

Terlingua Historic cemetery

The Drive » Alpine is about half an hour east of Marfa on Hwy 90/67.

- - - - - - - - - - - -

④ Alpine

The biggest little town in the area, Alpine is the county seat, a college town (Sul Ross University is here) and the best place to stock up on whatever you need before you head down into the Chihuahuan Desert.

Stop by the **Museum of the Big Bend** (☎432-837-8143; www.sulross.edu/museum; 400 N Harrison St; donations accepted; ◷9am-5pm Tue-Sat, 1-5pm

Sun) to brush up on the history of the Big Bend region. But don't expect it to be dry and dusty. A renovation in 2006 added spiffy new exhibits, and reading is kept to a minimum. Most impressive? The enormous wing bone of the Texas pterosaur found in Big Bend – the largest flying creature ever found, with an estimated wing span of more than 50ft – along with the intimidatingly large re-creation of the whole bird that's big enough to snatch up a fully grown human and carry him off for dinner.

✕ ⌸ p469

The Drive » Keep heading east – half an hour later you'll reach the seriously tiny town of Marathon (pronounced mar-a-thun). The views aren't much during this stretch of the drive, but Big Bend will make up for all that.

- - - - - - - - - - - -

⑤ Marathon

This tiny railroad town has two claims to fame: it's the closest town to Big Bend's north entrance, providing a last chance to fill up your car and your stomach. And it's got the **Gage Hotel** (☎432-386-4205; www.gagehotel.com; 102 NW 1st

St/Hwy 90), a true Texas treasure that's worth a peek if not an overnight stay.

The Drive » Heading south on US 385, it's 40 miles to the northern edge of Big Bend, and 40 more to get to the Chisos Basin, the heart of the park. The flat road affords miles and miles of views for most of the drive.

TRIP HIGHLIGHT

⑥ Big Bend National Park

Talk about big. At 1252 sq miles, this national park is almost as big as the state of Rhode Island. Some people duck in for an afternoon, hike a quick trail and head back out, but we recommend staying at least two nights to hit the highlights.

With over 200 miles of trails to explore, it's no wonder hiking is one of the most popular activities, with many of the best hikes leaving from the Chisos Basin. Hit the short, paved **Window View Trail** at sunset, then hike the 4.4-mile **Window Trail** the next morning before it gets too hot. Spend the afternoon hiking the shady 4.8-mile **Lost Mine Trail**, or take a scenic drive to see the eerily abandoned **Sam Nail Ranch** or the scenic **Santa Elena Canyon**.

Another great morning hike is the **Grapevine**

Hills Trail, where a much-photographed formation of three acrobatic boulders form an inverted-triangle 'window.'

The visitor centers have tons of information and great maps. Pick up the *Hiker's Guide to Trails of Big Bend National Park* ($1.95 at park visitor centers) to learn about all your options.

🛏 p469

The Drive » From the west park entrance, turn left after 3 miles then follow the signs for Terlingua Ghost Town, just past Terlingua proper. It's about a 45-minute drive from the middle of the park.

TRIP HIGHLIGHT

⑦ Terlingua

Quirky Terlingua is a unique combination: it's both a ghost town and a social hub. When the local cinnabar mines closed down in the 1940s, the town dried up and blew away like a tumbleweed, leaving buildings that fell into ruins.

But the area has slowly repopulated, businesses have been built on top of the ruins, and locals gather here for two daily rituals: in the late afternoon, everyone drinks beer on the porch of **Terlingua Trading Company** (☎432-371-2234; www.historic-terlingua.com;

100 Ivey Rd; ⏰10am-9pm). And after the sun goes down, the party moves next door to Starlight Theater (p469), where there's live music every night.

Come early enough to check out the fascinating **stone ruins** (from the road – they're private property) and the old **cemetery**, which you're welcome to explore.

🍴 p469

The Drive » Head north to Alpine, then cut west on US 90. It's a little over five hours back to El Paso, but there's one last stop on your way out that you can't miss.

⑧ Prada Marfa

So you're driving along a two-lane highway out in the middle of nowhere, when suddenly a small building appears in the distance like a mirage. You glance over and see...a Prada store? Known as the 'Prada Marfa' (although it's really closer to Valentine) this art installation set against the backdrop of dusty west Texas is a tongue-in-cheek commentary on consumerism. You can't go in, but you're encouraged to window shop or snap a photo.

The Drive » Take US 90 back to the I-10 and head west to El Paso.

Eating & Sleeping

Fort Davis ②

🛏 Indian Lodge   Inn $$
(📞lodge 432-426-3254, reservations 512-
389-8982; Hwy 118; d $95-125, ste $135-150;
❄️🛜🏊) In Davis Mountains State Park, the
surprisingly spacious and comfortable guest
rooms in this historic, Spanish-style adobe
lodge are a steal.

Marfa ③

🍴 Cochineal   American $$$
(📞432-729-3300; 107 W San Antonio St;
breakfast $4-10, small plates $5-15, dinner
$24-28; 🕐9am-1pm Sat & Sun, 6-10pm Thu-
Tue) This is where foodies get their fix, with a
menu that changes regularly due to a focus
on local, organic ingredients. Reservations
recommended.

🍴 Future Shark   American $
(📞432-729-4278; www.foodsharkmarfa.com;
120 N Highland Ave; mains $7-13; 🕐11am-7pm
Mon-Fri) Hooray! The Food Shark truck finally
has a brick-and-mortar restaurant serving up
similarly awesome fare as the popular truck, but
cafeteria style.

🛏 El Cosmico   Campground $$
(📞432-729-1950; www.elcosmico.com; 802 S
Highland Ave; tent camping per person $12, safari
tents $65, teepees $80, trailers $110-180; 🛜)
Sleep in an Airstream, a teepee or a safari tent
at one of the funkiest choices in all of Texas.
The cool lounge and hammock grove make
particularly pleasant common areas.

Alpine ④

🍴 Reata   Steakhouse $$
(📞432-837-9232; www.reata.net; 203 N 5th
St; lunch $9-14, dinner $10-25; 🕐11:30am-2pm
& 5-10pm Mon-Sat, 11:30am-2pm Sun) In the

dining room, Reata turns on the upscale ranch-
style charm. Step back into the lively bar or
shady patio and it's a completely different vibe
where you can nibble your way around the menu
and enjoy a margarita.

🛏 Holland Hotel   Historic Hotel $$
(📞800-535-8040, 432-837-3844; www.
thehollandhoteltexas.com; 209 W Holland Ave;
d $99-120, ste $120-220; ⊖❄️🛜🏊) Built in
1928 and beautifully renovated in 2009, the
Holland is a Spanish Colonial building furnished
in an understated, hacienda-style decor that
retains all of its 1930s charm.

Big Bend National Park ⑥

🛏 Chisos Mountain Lodge
& Dining Room   Lodge $$
(📞432-477-2291; http://chisosmountainslodge.
com; lodge & motel r $123-127, cottages $150;
🕐restaurant 7-10am, 11am-4pm & 5-8pm)
Decent accommodations and dining service
within the park. You can do better outside
Big Bend, but it's nice not to have to drive 45
minutes to rest up after your hike.

Terlingua ⑦

🍴 Espresso…Y Poco Mas   Cafe $
(📞432-371-3044; 100 Milagro Rd; food $2.50-
6.50; 🕐8am-2pm, to 1pm summer; 🛜) We love
this friendly little walk-up counter at La Posada
Milagro where you can find pastries, breakfast
burritos, lunches and what might just be the
best iced coffee in all of west Texas.

🍴 Starlight Theater   American $$
(📞432-371-2326; www.thestarlighttheatre.com;
631 Ivey St; mains $9-25; 🕐5pm-midnight) This
former movie theater had fallen into roofless
disrepair (thus the 'starlight' name) before
being converted into a restaurant with nightly
live music that makes it the center of Terlingua's
nightlife.

Wildflowers *Fields of bluebonnets show Texas' soft side*

Hill Country

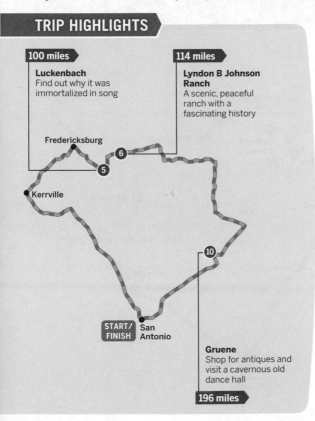

38

Take a drive through the countryside where gently rolling hills are blanketed with wildflowers, friendly folks enjoy an easy way of life, and there's plenty to do along the way.

TRIP HIGHLIGHTS

100 miles

Luckenbach
Find out why it was immortalized in song

114 miles

Lyndon B Johnson Ranch
A scenic, peaceful ranch with a fascinating history

Fredericksburg

6

5

Kerrville

10

START/FINISH · San Antonio

Gruene
Shop for antiques and visit a cavernous old dance hall

196 miles

2–5 DAYS
229 MILES / 368KM

GREAT FOR...

BEST TIME TO GO
In March and April for wildflower season.

 ESSENTIAL PHOTO

Bluebonnets – pose your kids or yourself in a field full of wildflowers.

 BEST FOR CULTURE

Two-stepping at Texas' oldest dance hall in Gruene.

471

38 Hill Country

In March and early April when wildflowers are blooming, this is one of the prettiest drives in all of Texas – perfect for a day trip or a lazy, meandering vacation. Along this route, you can rummage through antique stores, listen to live music, dig in to a plate of barbecue, and learn about the president who called this area home.

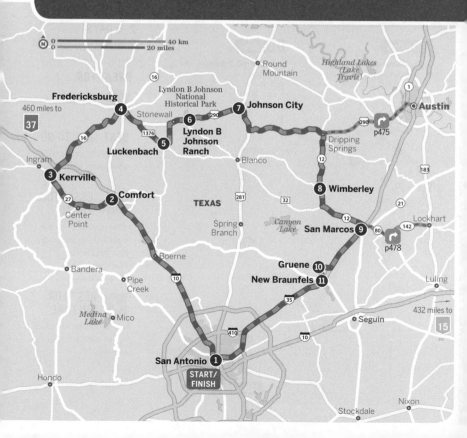

❶ San Antonio

While sprawling San Antonio isn't part of the Hill Country, it's a great launching point for your trip. Don't miss the lovely, European-style River Walk, a paved canal that winds its way through downtown and is lined with colorful cafes, hotel gardens and stone footbridges. For the best overview, hop on a Rio San Antonio **river cruise** (📞800-417-4139; www.riosanantonio.com; adult/child under 5yr $8.25/2; ⏰9am-9pm), a 40-minute ride that loops through downtown.

Pay your respects at the **Alamo** (📞210-225-1391; www.thealamo.org; 300 Alamo Plaza; ⏰9am-5:30pm Mon-Sat, from 10am Sun), where revolutionaries fought for Texas' independence from Mexico.

LINK YOUR TRIP

15 **Cajun Country**
For po'boys and crawfish, take I-10 east to Lafayette then head south on US 90 with a left to Thibodaux.

37 **Big Bend Scenic Loop**
West Texas? Breathtaking, quirky, and big. Head northwest on I-10 to El Paso.

The Drive ❯❯ Head northwest on I-10 to get to Comfort, less than an hour from downtown San Antonio. When the wildflowers are blooming, detour north on Waring-Welfare Rd then back on TX-27.

❷ Comfort

Remarkably under the tourist radar, Comfort is a 19th-century German settlement and perhaps the most idyllic of the Hill Country bunch, with rough-hewn limestone homes from the late 1800s and a beautifully restored historic center in the area around High and 8th Sts.

Shopping for antiques is the number-one activity, but you'll also find a few good restaurants, a winery and, as the town's name suggests, an easy way of life. Start at the **Comfort Antique Mall** (📞830-995-4678; 734 High St; ⏰10am-5pm Sun-Fri, to 6pm Sat) where you can pick up a map of antique stores, or go to the **Comfort Chamber of Commerce** (www.comfort-texas.com) website for options.

🍴 p479

The Drive ❯❯ The interstate is a straight shot, but we prefer the back road of TX-27 west to Kerrville that takes you through serene farmland.

❸ Kerrville

The Hill Country can feel a bit fussy at times, but not Kerrville. What it lacks in historic charm, it makes up for in size, offering plenty of services for travelers, as well as easy access to kayaking, canoeing and swimming on the Guadalupe River. The best place to hop in the water is **Kerrville-Schreiner Park** (2385 Bandera Hwy; day-use adult/child/senior $4/1/2; ⏰8am-10pm).

While you're in town, check out one of the world's best collections of cowboy art at the **Museum of Western Art** (📞830-896-2553; www.museumofwesternart.com; 1550 Bandera Hwy; adult/student/under 8yr $7/5/free; ⏰10am-4pm Tue-Sat). The building itself is beautiful, with hand-made mesquite parquet floors and unique vaulted domes overhead, and it's chock-full of paintings and sculptures depicting scenes from the Old West.

🍴 🛏 p479

The Drive ❯❯ Take TX-16 northeast of town for half an hour to get to Fredericksburg.

❹ Fredericksburg

The unofficial capital of the Hill Country, Fredericksburg is a 19th-century German settlement that specializes in 'quaint.' The town packs a lot of charm into a relatively small amount of space, with a boggling array of welcoming inns and B&Bs and a main street lined with historic buildings housing German restaurants, *biergartens*, antique stores and shops.

Many of the shops are typical tourist-town offerings, but there are enough interesting stores to make it fun to wander. Plus, the town is a great base for checking out the surrounding peach orchards and vineyards. Just a few miles east of town, **Wildseed Farms** (www.wildseedfarms.com; 100 Legacy Dr; ⊙9:30am-6:30pm) has cultivated fields of wildflowers and sells seed packets along with just about every wildflower-related gift you can imagine.

✕ ⊨ p479

The Drive ≫ Five miles southeast of town on US 290, turn right on Ranch Rd 1376 and follow it 4.5 miles into Luckenbach. There are only a handful of buildings, so don't worry that the actual town is somewhere else.

- - - - - - - - - -

TRIP HIGHLIGHT

❺ Luckenbach

You won't find a more laid-back place than Luckenbach, where the main activity is sitting at a picnic table under an old oak tree with a cold bottle of Shiner Bock and listening to guitar pickers, who are often accompanied by roosters. Come prepared to relax, get to know some folks, and bask in the small-town atmosphere.

Start at the old trading post established back in 1849 – now the **Luckenbach General Store** (⊙10am-9pm

Mon-Sat, noon-9pm Sun), which also serves as the local post office, saloon and community center. Out back you'll find the picking circle, and there's often live music on the weekends in the old dance hall; go online to check out the town's **music schedule** (www.luckenbachtexas.com).

The Drive ≫ Take Luckenbach Rd back north to US 290. The LBJ Ranch is just 7 miles down and the entrance is right off the highway.

- - - - - - - - - -

TRIP HIGHLIGHT

❻ Lyndon B Johnson Ranch

You don't have to be a history buff to appreciate the family home of the 36th president of the United States. Now the **Lyndon Johnson National Historic Park** (www.nps.gov/lyjo; Hwy 290; park admission and driving tour free, house tour $3; ⊙9am-5:30pm, house tours 10am-4:30pm), this beautiful piece of Texas land is where Lyndon Johnson was born, lived and died.

The park includes the Johnson birthplace, the one-room schoolhouse where he briefly attended school and a neighboring farm that now serves as a living history museum. The centerpiece of the park is the ranch house where LBJ and Lady Bird lived and where he spent so much time during

---

SCENIC DRIVE: WILDFLOWER TRAILS

You know spring has arrived in Texas when you see cars pulling up roadside and families climbing out to take the requisite picture of their kids surrounded by bluebonnets – Texas' state flower. From March to April in Hill Country, Indian paintbrushes, winecups and bluebonnets are at their peak.

Check the **Wildflower Hotline** (☎800-452-9292) to find out what's blooming where. Taking Rte 16 and FM 1323, north from Fredericksburg and east to Willow City, is usually a good route.

his presidency that it became known as the 'Texas White House.'

You can also see the airfield that he and other foreign dignitaries flew into, the private jet he used as president, and the Johnson family cemetery, where LBJ and Lady Bird are both buried under sprawling oak trees.

Stop by the visitor center to get your free park permit, a map and a free CD audio tour.

The Drive >> LBJ's childhood home is just 15 minutes east on US 290.

❼ Johnson City

You might assume Johnson City was named after President Johnson, but the bragging rights go to James Polk Johnson, a town settler back in the late 1800s. The fact that James Johnson's grandson went on to become president of the United States was just pure luck.

Here you'll find **Lyndon Johnson's Boyhood Home** (100 E Ladybird Lane; ⊙tours half hourly 9am-11:30 & 1-4:30pm), which Johnson himself had restored for personal posterity. Park rangers from the **visitor center** (Ladybird Ln & Ave G; ⊙8:45am-5pm) – where you can also find local information and exhibits on the president and First Lady – offer

DETOUR: AUSTIN

Start: ❼ Johnson City

Since this trip is all about winding your way through the Hill Country, we didn't list Austin as a stop. After all, it warrants its own whole trip, which we hope your central Texas itinerary already includes.

However, we'd be remiss if we didn't mention that, when you get to Dripping Springs, you're only half an hour from the Texas state capital..

free guided tours every half hour that meet on the front porch. On the surface, it's just an old Texas house, but it's fascinating when you think about the boy who grew up here.

The Drive >> Follow US 290 south toward Blanco then east toward Dripping Springs. At Dripping Springs, turn right on Ranch Rd 12 towards Wimberley.

❽ Wimberley

A popular weekend spot for Austinites, this artists' community gets absolutely bonkers during summer weekends – especially on the first Saturday of each month from April to December, when local art galleries, shops and craftspeople set up booths for **Wimberley Market Days**, a bustling collection of live music, food and more than 400 vendors at Lion's Field on RR 2325.

For excellent scenic views of the surrounding limestone hills near

Wimberley, take a drive on FM 32, also known as the Devil's Backbone. From Wimberley, head south on RR 12 to FM 32, then turn right toward Canyon Lake. The road gets steeper, then winds out onto a craggy ridge – the 'backbone' – with a 360-degree vista.

Afterwards, cool off at Wimberley's famous **Blue Hole** (📱512-847-9127; www.friendsofbluehole.org; 100 Blue Hole Lane, off CR 173; adult/child/under 4yr $8/4/ free; ⊙10am-6pm Mon-Fri, to 8pm Sat, 11am-6pm Sun), one of the Hill Country's best swimming holes. It's a privately owned spot in the calm, shady and crystal-clear waters of Cypress Creek.

🍴 p479

The Drive >> Keep going south on Ranch Rd 12; San Marcos is about 15 minutes southeast through some more (mostly) undeveloped countryside.

HILL COUNTRY
MARIELLA KRAUSE, AUTHOR

Easily accessed from both San Antonio and Austin (my home town), the Hill Country is a popular getaway for both its natural beauty and easygoing nature. You can drive this entire loop in under five hours, but what's the rush? There are so many great little towns and interesting things to do, you'll be glad you decided to linger.

Above: Luckenbach General Store
Left: Lyndon Johnson National Historic Park
Right: Oak tree in Hill Country

NKBIMAGES/GETTY IMAGES ©

⑨ San Marcos

Around central Texas, 'San Marcos' is practically synonymous with 'outlet malls,' and bargain shoppers can make a full day of it at two side-by-side shopping meccas. It's not exactly in keeping with the spirit of the Hill Country, but it's a popular enough activity we had to point it out.

The fashion-oriented **San Marcos Premium Outlets** (☏512-396-2200; www.premiumoutlets.com; 3939 S IH-35, exit 200; ⊙10am-9pm Mon-Sat, to 7pm Sun) is enormous – and enormously popular – with 140 brand-name outlets. Across the street, **Tanger Outlets** (☏512-396-7446; www.tangeroutlet.com/sanmarcos; 4015 S IH-35; ⊙9am-9pm Mon-Sat, 10am-7pm Sun) has more modest offerings with brands that aren't that expensive to start with, but it's still fun to hunt.

The Drive » Shoot 12 miles down I-35 to the turnoff for Canyon Lake. Gruene is just a couple miles off the highway.

TRIP HIGHLIGHT

⑩ Gruene

Get a true taste of Texas at **Gruene Hall** (www.gruenehall.com; 1280 Gruene Rd; ⊙11am-midnight Mon-Fri, 10am-1am Sat, 10am-9pm Sun), a dance hall where folks have been

477

congregating since 1878, making it Texas' oldest. It opens early, so you can stop by anytime to toss back a longneck, two-step on the well-worn wooden dance floor, or play horseshoes out in the yard. There's only a cover on weekend nights and when big acts are playing, so at least stroll through and soak up the vibe.

The town is loaded with antique stores and shops selling housewares, gifts and souvenirs, and **Old Gruene Market Days** are held the third weekend of the month, February through November.

 p479

The Drive » You don't even have to get back on the interstate; New Braunfels is just 3 miles south.

----

⑪ New Braunfels

The historic town of New Braunfels was the first German settlement in Texas. In summer, visitors flock here to float down the Guadalupe River in an

DETOUR: LOCKHART

Start: ⑨ San Marcos

People travel from all over the state to dig into brisket, sausage and ribs in Lockhart, officially designated in 1999 as the Barbecue Capital of Texas. Lucky for you, you only have to detour 18 miles to experience the smoky goodness. You can eat very well for under $10 at:

Black's Barbecue (215 N Main St; sandwiches $4-6, brisket per pound $11; ⊙10am-8pm Sun-Thu, to 8:30pm Fri & Sat) A longtime Lockhart favorite since 1932, with sausage so good Lyndon Johnson had them cater a party at the nation's capital.

Kreuz Market (☎512-398-2361; 619 N Colorado St; brisket per pound $11.90, sides extra; ⊙10:30am-8pm Mon-Sat) Serving Lockhart since 1900, the barn-like Kreuz Market uses a dry rub, which means you shouldn't insult them by asking for barbecue sauce; they don't serve it, and the meat doesn't need it.

Smitty's Market (208 S Commerce St; lunch plates $6, brisket per pound $11.90; ⊙7am-6pm Mon-Fri, 7am-6:30pm Sat, 9am-3pm Sun) The blackened pit room and homely dining room are all original (knives used to be chained to the tables). Ask them to trim off the fat on the brisket if you're particular about that.

inner tube – a Texas summer tradition. There are lots of outfitters in town, like **Rockin' R River Rides** (☎830-629-9999; www.rockinr.com; 1405 Gruene Rd; tubes $17). Its rental prices include shuttle service, and for an additional fee it can also hook you up with an ice chest and a tube to float your ice chest on.

 p479

The Drive » From New Braunfels it's 32 miles on the I-35 back to San Antonio.

Eating & Sleeping

Comfort ②

🛏 Hotel Faust
B&B $$

(✆830-995-3030; www.hotelfaust.com; 717 High St; d $110-160, 2-bedroom cottage $175-195; 😊 ❄) For some true historic charm, spend the night in one of the beautifully restored rooms in this late-1800s hotel. Better yet, stay in the 1820s log cabin that was moved to its present location from Kentucky.

Kerrville ③

✕ Grape Juice
American $$

(✆830-792-9463; www.grapejuiceonline. com; 623 Water St; mains $10-15; ⊙11am-11pm Tue-Sat) Calling it a 'wine bar' would be ignoring our favorite thing about this place: the purely awesome macaroni and cheese made with smoked Gouda.

🛏 Inn of the Hills Resort & Conference Center
Motel $

(✆830-895-5000, 800-292-5690; www. innofthehills.com; 1001 Junction Hwy; d $77-104; 😊 ❄ 🛜 🛏) The lovely renovated rooms that open onto the pool are done in soothing earth tones with boutique-hotel flair, but the best feature of all is the beautiful Olympic-style pool that's surrounded by shade trees.

Fredericksburg ④

✕ Pink Pig
American $$

(✆830-990-8800; www.pinkpigtexas.com; 6266 E US Hwy 290; lunch $9-12, dinner $18-28; ⊙11am-2:30pm Tue & Wed, 11am-2:30pm & 5:30-9pm Thu-Sat, from 10am Sun) Pick up baked goods or a boxed lunch from the bakery counter, or enjoy a meal inside the historic log building. And save room for dessert: the Pink Pig was opened by Rebecca Rather, AKA The Pastry Queen.

🛏 Gastehaus Schmidt
Accommodation Services

(✆830-997-5612, 866-427-8374; www. fbglodging.com; 231 W Main St) Nearly 300 B&Bs do business around here; this reservation service helps sort them out.

Wimberley ⑧

✕ Leaning Pear
American $

(✆512-847-7327; www.leaningpear.com; 111 River Rd; mains $7-9; ⊙11am-3pm Sun, Mon, Wed & Thu, to 8pm Fri & Sat) This cafe exudes Hill Country charm like a cool glass of iced tea, serving salads and sandwiches in a restored stone house outside of downtown.

Gruene ⑩

✕ Gristmill Restaurant
American $$

(www.gristmillrestaurant.com; 1287 Gruene Rd; mains $7-20; ⊙11am-9pm Sun-Thu, to 10pm Fri & Sat) Located within the brick remnants of a long-gone gristmill, the Gristmill has character to spare. Indoor seating affords a rustic ambiance, and outdoor tables get a view of the river.

🛏 Gruene Mansion Inn
Inn $$$

(✆830-629-2641; www.gruenemansioninn. com; 1275 Gruene Rd; d $195-250) Choose from rooms in the mansion, former carriage house or old barns. All are richly decorated in a style the owners call 'rustic Victorian elegance,' featuring lots of wood, floral prints and pressed-tin ceiling tiles.

New Braunfels ⑪

✕ Naegelin's Bakery
Bakery $

(✆830-625-5722; www.naegelins.com; 129 S Seguin Ave; ⊙6:30am-5:30pm Mon-Fri, to 5pm Sat) More than just a great place to pick up German strudels and Czech *kolaches*, Naegelin's is also the oldest bakery in Texas, opened in 1868.

STRETCH YOUR LEGS
LAS VEGAS

Start/Finish: Bellagio

Distance: 1.8 miles/2.9km

Duration: Four hours

This loop takes in the most dazzling sites on the Strip: the canals of Venice, the graceful Eiffel Tower, the world's tallest Ferris wheel and a three-story chandelier. And remember, objects on the Strip are further away than they appear.

Take this walk on Trip

Bellagio

For floral inspiration, pause in the lobby at the ever-stylish **Bellagio** (www. bellagio.com; 3600 Las Vegas Blvd S) to admire the room's showpiece: a Dale Chihuly sculpture composed of 2000 hand-blown glass flowers in vibrant colors. Just beyond the lobby, the **Bellagio Conservatory & Botanical Gardens** (admission free; ☺24hr) dazzles passers-by with gorgeously ostentatious floral designs that change seasonally. If you're hankering for fine art, see what's on display at the **Bellagio Gallery of Fine Art** (adult/student/child $16/11/free; ☺10am-8pm), which hosts blockbuster traveling exhibits.

The Walk » Walk north on S Las Vegas Blvd and cross E Flamingo Rd. Caesar's Palace will be just ahead on your left.

Caesar's Palace

It's easy to get lost inside this labyrinth-like Greco-Roman **fantasyland** (www.caesarspalace.com; 3570 Las Vegas Blvd S) where maps are few (and not oriented to the outside). The interior is captivating, however, with marble reproductions of classical statuary, including a 4-ton Brahma shrine near the front entrance. Towering fountains, goddess-costumed cocktail waitresses and the swanky haute couture of the Forum Shops up the glitz factor. For lunch, consider the fantastic **Bacchanal Buffet** (www.caesarspalace.com; 3570 Las Vegas Blvd S), a gastronomic celebration of global proportions.

The Walk » Continue north on Las Vegas Blvd S, passing the Mirage. At night, its faux-Polynesian volcano erupts. Just north, take the walkway over Las Vegas Blvd S.

Venetian

The spectacular **Venetian** (www.venetian. com; 3355 Las Vegas Blvd S; gondola ride adult/ private $19/76) is a facsimile of a doge's palace, inspired by the splendor of Italy's most romantic city. It features roaming mimes and minstrels in period costume, hand-painted ceiling frescoes and full-scale reproductions of the Italian port's famous landmarks. Flowing canals, vibrant piazzas and stone walkways attempt to capture the spirit of La Serenissima Repubblica, reputedly the home of the world's first casino. Take a **gondola ride** or stroll through the atmospheric **Grand Canal Shoppes**.

The Walk » It's a 0.7-mile trek to Paris, but sights along the way should keep it interesting, particularly the $55 million LINQ shopping and entertainment district set to open in December 2013. It will be home to the 550ft-tall High Roller, billed as the world's tallest Ferris wheel.

Paris-Las Vegas

Evoking the gaiety of the City of Light, **Paris-Las Vegas** (www.parislv.com; 3655 Las Vegas Blvd S) strives to capture the essence of the grand dame by recreating her landmarks. Fine likenesses of the Opera, the Arc de Triomphe, the Champs-Élysées, the soaring Eiffel Tower and even the Seine frame the property. The signature attraction is the **Eiffel Tower Experience** (☎702-946-7000; adult/child from $11.50/7.50; ☺9:30am-12:30am Mon-Fri, to 1am Sat & Sun, weather permitting). Ascend in a glass elevator to the observation deck for panoramic views of the Strip, notably the Bellagio's dancing fountains.

The Walk » Walk a short distance south on Las Vegas Blvd S. Cross Las Vegas Blvd S on Paris Dr.

Cosmopolitan

The twinkling three-story chandelier inside this sleek addition to the Strip isn't purely decorative. Nope, it's a step-inside, sip a swanky cocktail and survey your domain kind of place, worthy of your wildest fairy tale. A bit much? Not really. Like the rest of Vegas, the **Cosmopolitan** (www.cosmopolitanlasvegas.com; 3708 Las Vegas Blvd S; ☺24hr) is just having fun.

The Walk » From here, walk north on Las Vegas Blvd S to catch the dazzling choreographed dancing fountain show at Bellagio.

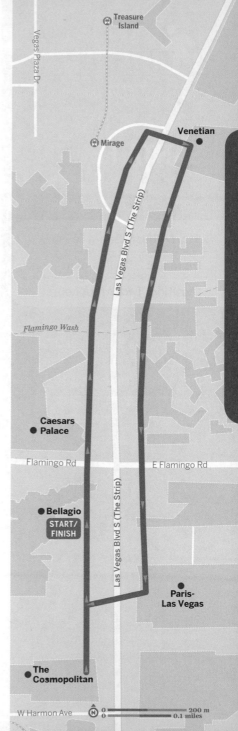

STRETCH YOUR LEGS
SANTA FE

Start/Finish: Santa Fe Plaza

Distance: 2.5 miles/4km

Duration: Two to four hours

The only way to see the best of Santa Fe is on foot, strolling through it's old adobe soul and into its renowned museums, churches, art galleries and historic buildings.

Take this walk on Trips

New Mexico Museum of Art

At the plaza's northwest corner, the **Museum of Art** (www.nmartmuseum. org; 107 W Palace Ave; ☺10am-5pm, closed Mon Sep-May) features collections of the Taos Society of Artists, Santa Fe Society of Artists and other legendary collectives – it's a who's who of the geniuses who put this dusty town on par with Paris and New York.

The Walk » Cross Lincoln Ave.

Palace of the Governors

Built in 1610, the **Palace of the Governors** (☎505-476-5100; www. palaceofthegovernors.org; 105 W Palace Ave; adult/child $9/free; ☺10am-5pm, closed Mon Oct-May) is one of the oldest public buildings in the USA. It displays a handful of historic relics, but most of its holdings are now shown in an adjacent exhibition space called the **New Mexico History Museum** (113 Lincoln Ave), a glossy, 96,000-sq-ft expansion that opened in 2009.

The Walk » Browse the selection of Native American pottery and jewelry, talking to the artisans about their work. Then cross Palace Ave.

Shiprock

In a 2nd-floor loft at the northeast corner of the Plaza, **Shiprock** (www. shiprocktrading.com; 53 Old Santa Fe Trail, Plaza) has an extraordinary collection of Navajo rugs. Run by a fifth-generation Indian country trader, the vintage pieces are the real deal.

The Walk » Walk one block south, then turn left on E San Francisco St. If you're hungry, make a pit stop across the plaza at the casual Plaza Cafe.

St Francis Cathedral

Jean Baptiste Lamy was sent to Santa Fe by the pope with orders to tame the Wild Western outpost town through culture and religion. Convinced that the town needed a focal point for religious life, he began construction of **St Francis Cathedral** (www.cbsfa.org; 131 Cathedral Pl; ☺8:30am-5pm) in 1869. Inside

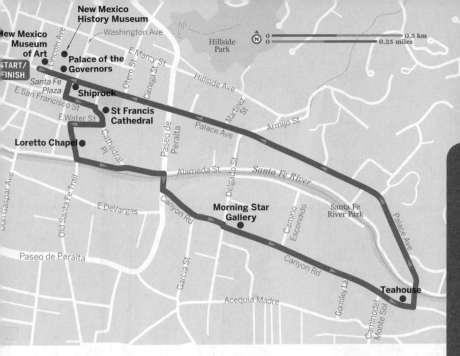

is a small chapel that houses the oldest Madonna statue in North America.

The Walk » Just south of the cathedral, turn right on Water St, to the corner with Old Santa Fe Trail.

Loretto Chapel

Modeled on Sainte Chapelle in Paris, **Loretto Chapel** (www.lorettochapel.com; 207 Old Santa Fe Trail; admission $3; ⊙9am-5pm Mon-Sat, 10:30am-5pm Sun) was built between 1873 and 1878 for the Sisters of Loretto, the first nuns to come to New Mexico. Today it's a museum popular for **St Joseph's Miraculous Staircase** – which seems to defy the laws of physics by standing with no visible support.

The Walk » Walk south and turn left on E Alameda St. Turn right on Paseo de Peralta, then left onto Canyon Rd – the legendary heart of Santa Fe's gallery scene.

Morning Star Gallery

Of all the Canyon Rd shops dealing in Indian antiquities, **Morning Star** (www.morningstargallery.com; 513 Canyon Rd; ⊙9am-5pm Mon-Sat) remains the best: weaving, jewelry, beadwork, *kachina* (Hopi spirit) dolls and even a few original ledger drawings are just some of the stars at this stunning gallery, which specializes in pre-WWII Plains Indian ephemera. Some artifacts here are finer than those in most museums and sell for hundreds of thousands of dollars.

The Walk » Meander on down Canyon Rd, stopping into whichever galleries catch your eye.

Teahouse

Prepare for a dilemma – at the **Teahouse** (www.teahousesantafe.com; 821 Canyon Rd; mains $8-17; ⊙9am-7pm; 🛜), you'll be confronted with the list of 150 types of tea. There's coffee, too, and a great food menu, from baked polenta with poached eggs to wild mushroom porcini panini to grilled salmon salad. Oh, and freshly baked desserts. It's a perfect last stop on Canyon Rd.

The Walk » Turn left on Palace Ave and walk it back to the plaza.

California
Trips

Only California gives great American road trips a Hollywood ending. Ever since the early days of Spanish conquistadors and gold-rush pioneers, the eternal quest for fortune and fame has inevitably led to California's golden shores. But even gold will seem overrated once you've seen the platinum glint of the Pacific, and no movie star will ever be as big as California's mighty old-growth redwoods or giant sequoia trees.

Hang tight around curves that hug the coastline on legendary Hwy 1, stringing together sandy beaches, surf and seafood shacks; follow country lanes to famous Napa and Sonoma Valley vineyards. Honestly, there's no such thing as a wrong turn here.

In California, dreaming comes with the territory.

Yosemite National Park (Trip 40)

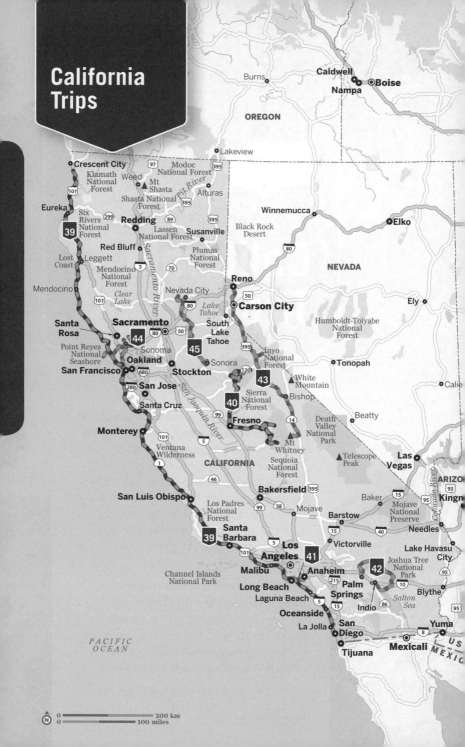

California
Trips

DON'T MISS

Kings Canyon Scenic Byway

Wind down into the USA's deepest river canyon carved by glaciers to Road's End in Cedar Grove, on Trip **40**

Point Arena

Ascend 145 corkscrew steps inside the tallest lighthouse in California that you can still climb to the top of, on Trip **39**

Alabama Hills

Where famous Western movies and TV shows were filmed outside of Lone Pine, just below Mt Whitney, on Trip **43**

Seal Beach

Slow way down for this old-fashioned beach town, squeezed between LA and the OC, where you can learn to surf by the weather-beaten wooden pier, on Trip **41**

Marin Headlands

Gawk at million-dollar views of San Francisco and the Pacific while exploring abandoned military bunkers tucked into hillsides, on Trip **44**

Big Sur coast *Precipitous cliffs dominate the seascape*

Classic Trip

Pacific Coast Highways

39

Our top pick for classic California dreamin' snakes along the Pacific coast for 1000 miles. Uncover beaches, seafood shacks and piers for catching sunsets over boundless ocean horizons.

TRIP HIGHLIGHTS

950 miles

Redwood National & State Parks
See the world's tallest trees

FINISH
14
Eureka

600 miles

San Francisco
By Golden Gate Park, cross the famous bridge

Mendocino

10

375 miles

Around Hearst Castle
Tour a hilltop mansion, then gape at elephant seals

Monterey

7

240 miles

Santa Barbara
Bountiful beaches and nearby wine country

5

Los Angeles

San Diego **START**

7–10 DAYS
1000 MILES/ 1610KM

GREAT FOR...

BEST TIME TO GO
Year-round, but July to October for the sunniest skies.

ESSENTIAL PHOTO
Golden Gate Bridge on San Francisco Bay.

BEST TWO DAYS
Santa Barbara north to Monterey via Big Sur.

Classic Trip

39 Pacific Coast Highways

Make your escape from California's tangled, traffic-jammed freeways and cruise in the slow lane. Once you get rolling, it'll be almost painful to leave the ocean behind for too long. Officially, only the short, sun-loving stretch of Hwy 1 through Orange and Los Angeles Counties can legally call itself the Pacific Coast Highway (PCH). But never mind that technicality, because equally bewitching ribbons of Hwy 1 and Hwy 101 await all along this route.

Crescent City
Mt Sha (14,18
FINISH
14 **Redwood National & State Parks**
Arcata
13 **Eureka**
Fortuna
Redding
Red Bluff
Mendocino & Fort Bragg
Leggett
12
Willits
Around Point Arena
11
Clearlak
Santa Rosa
44
Bodega Bay
Point Reyes National Seashore p496
San Francisco 10
p564
Santa Cruz
Monterey
PACIFIC OCEAN

① San Diego

Begin at the bottom of the state map, where the pretty peninsula beach town of **Coronado** is connected to the San Diego mainland by the white-sand beaches of the **Silver Strand**. If you've seen Marilyn Monroe cavort in *Some Like It Hot*, you'll recognize the **Hotel Del Coronado**, which has hosted US presidents, celebrities and royalty, including Edward VIII who gave up his throne to marry a Coronado divorcée. Wander the turreted palace's labyrinthine corridors, then quaff tropical cocktails at ocean-view Babcock & Story Bar.

Be thrilled by driving over the 2.1-mile-long **Coronado Bay Bridge**. Detour inland to **Balboa Park** (☎619-239-0512; www.balboapark.org). Head west, then south to Point Loma's **Cabrillo National Monument** (www.nps.gov/cabr; per car $5; ⊙9am-5pm, last entry 4:30pm; 🚻) for captivating

0 ——— 100 km
0 ——— 50 miles

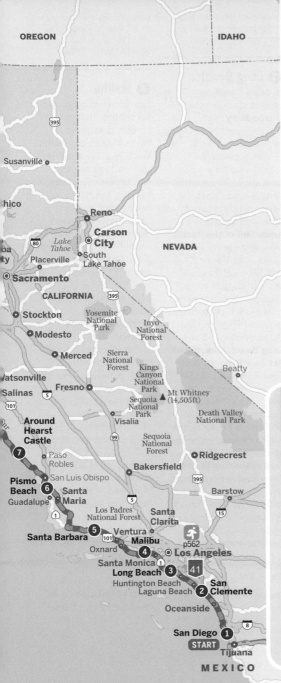

OREGON

IDAHO

Susanville

Reno

Carson City

NEVADA

Lake Tahoe

South Lake Tahoe

Placerville

Sacramento

CALIFORNIA

Stockton

Modesto

Yosemite National Park

Inyo National Forest

Merced

Sierra National Forest

Beatty

Fresno

Kings Canyon National Park

Salinas

Mt Whitney (14,505ft)

Sequoia National Park

Death Valley National Park

Visalia

Around Hearst Castle

Sequoia National Forest

Ridgecrest

Paso Robles

Bakersfield

San Luis Obispo

Pismo Beach

Santa Maria

Barstow

Guadalupe

Los Padres National Forest

Santa Clarita

Santa Barbara

Ventura

Malibu

Oxnard

p562

Los Angeles

Santa Monica

Long Beach

Huntington Beach

Laguna Beach

San Clemente

Oceanside

San Diego

START

Tijuana

MEXICO

bay panoramas from the 19th-century lighthouse and a monument to the West Coast's first Spanish explorers. Rolling north of **Mission Beach**, where an old-fashioned amusement park is dwarfed by SeaWorld, suddenly you're in hoity-toity **La Jolla**, beyond which lie North County's beach towns.

 p500

The Drive » It's a 50-mile trip from La Jolla north along coastal roads then the I-5 into Orange County (aka the 'OC'), passing Camp Pendleton Marine Corps Base and buxom-shaped San Onofre Nuclear Generating Station. Exit at San Clemente and follow Avenida del Mar downhill to the beach.

CALIFORNIA TRIPS **39** PACIFIC COAST HIGHWAYS

LINK YOUR TRIP

41 Disneyland & Orange County Beaches

Soak up the SoCal sunshine in glam beach towns along PCH, then take the kids to Anaheim's world-famous theme parks.

44 San Francisco, Marin & Napa Loop

Linger in Northern California's cultural capital and follow rural roads along the coast and into wine country.

Classic Trip

➋ San Clemente

Life behind the conservative 'Orange Curtain' is far different than in most other laid-back, liberal California beach counties. Apart from glamorous beaches where famous TV shows and movies have been filmed, you can still uncover the beach culture of yesteryear here in off-the-beaten-path spots like San Clemente. Home to living surfing legends, top-notch surfboard companies and *Surfer* magazine, this may be the last place in the OC where you can authentically live the surf lifestyle. Ride your own board or swim at the city's main beach beside San Clemente Pier. A fast detour inland, the community's **Surfing Heritage Foundation** (www.surfingheritage.com; 101 Calle Iglesia; admission by donation; ☺11am-5pm) exhibits surfboards ridden by the greats, from Duke Kahanamoku to Kelly Slater.

The Drive » Slingshot north on I-5, exiting onto Hwy 1 near Dana Point. Speed by the wealthy artists' colony of Laguna Beach, wild Crystal Cove State Park, Newport Beach's yacht harbor and 'Surf City USA' Huntington Beach (see p519, p520) and p521.

Turn west off Hwy 1 near Naples toward Long Beach, about 45 miles from San Clemente.

- - - - - - - - - - - - -

➌ Long Beach

In Long Beach, the biggest stars are the **Queen Mary** (www. queenmary.com; 1126 Queens Hwy; adult/child from $25/14; ☺10am-6pm Mon-Thu, to 7pm Fri-Sun), a grand (and allegedly haunted) British ocean liner permanently moored here, and the giant **Aquarium of the Pacific** (www.aquariumofpacific.org; 100 Aquarium Way; adult/child $26/15; ☺9am-6pm; 🅿), a high-tech romp through an underwater world in which sharks dart and jellyfish float. Often overlooked, the **Long Beach Museum of Art** (www.lbma.org; 2300 E Ocean Blvd; adult/child $7/free; ☺11am-5pm Fri-Sun, to 8pm Thu) focuses on California modernism and mixed media inside a 20th-century mansion by the ocean, while the urban **Museum of Latin American Art** (www.molaa. org; 628 Alamitos Ave; adult/child $9/free, all free Sun; ☺11am-5pm Wed & Fri-Sun, to 9pm Thu) shows off contemporary south-of-the-border art.

🛏 p500

The Drive » Wind slowly around the ruggedly scenic Palos Verdes Peninsula. Follow Hwy 1 north past the South Bay's primetime beaches. Curving around LAX airport and

Marina del Rey, Hwy 1 continues north to Venice, Santa Monica and all the way to Malibu, over 50 miles from Long Beach.

- - - - - - - - - - - - -

➍ Malibu

Leaving traffic-jammed LA behind, Hwy 1 breezes northwest of Santa Monica to Malibu. You'll feel like a movie star walking around on the public beaches, backing against gated compounds owned by Hollywood celebs. One mansion you can actually get a look inside is the **Getty Villa** (www. getty.edu; 17985 Pacific Coast Hwy; per car $15; ☺10am-5pm Wed-Mon), a hilltop showcase of Greek, Roman and Etruscan antiquities and manicured gardens (reservations required). Next to Malibu Lagoon State Beach, west of the surfers by Malibu Pier, **Adamson House** (www. adamsonhouse.org; 23200 Pacific Coast Hwy; adult/child $7/2; ☺11am-3pm Wed-Sat, last tour 2pm) is a Spanish-Moorish villa lavishly decorated with locally made hand-painted tiles. Motoring further west along the coast, where the Santa Monica Mountains plunge into the sea, take time out for a frolic on Malibu's mega-popular beaches like sandy Point Dume, Zuma or Leo Carrillo.

🍴 p500

The Drive » Hwy 1 crosses into Ventura County, winding alongside the ocean and windy Point Mugu. In Oxnard, join Hwy 101 northbound beyond Ventura, a jumping-off point for boat trips to Channel Islands, to Santa Barbara, just over 70 miles from Malibu Pier.

TRIP HIGHLIGHT

5 Santa Barbara

Seaside Santa Barbara has almost perfect weather and a string of idyllic beaches, where surfers, kite flyers, dog walkers and surfers mingle. Get a close-up of the city's iconic Mediterranean-style architecture along **State St** downtown or from the **county courthouse** (www.sbcourts.org; 1100 Anacapa St; admission free; ☺8:30am-4:45pm Mon-Fri, 10am-4:45pm Sat & Sun), its tower rising above the red-tiled rooftops.

Gaze south toward the busy harborfront and **Stearns Wharf** (www.stearnswharf.org; 👪) or north to the historic Spanish mission church. Santa Barbara's balmy climate is also perfect for growing grapes. A 45-minute drive northwest along Hwy 154, visit the Santa Ynez Valley wine country, made famous by the 2004 movie *Sideways*. Hit wine-tasting rooms in **Los Olivos**, then take Foxen Canyon Rd north past more wineries before rejoining Hwy 101.

🍴 🛏 p500

The Drive » Keep following fast Hwy 101 northbound or detour west onto slow Hwy 1, which squiggles along the Pacific coastline past Guadalupe, gateway to North America's largest sand dunes. Both highways meet up again in Pismo Beach, 100 miles northwest of Santa Barbara.

6 Pismo Beach

A classic California beach town, Pismo Beach has a long, lazy stretch of sand for swimming, surfing and strolling out onto the pier at sunset. After digging into bowls of clam chowder and baskets of fried seafood at surf-casual cafes, check out the retro family fun at the bowling alley, billiards halls and bars uphill from the beach, or dash 10 miles up Hwy 101 to the vintage **Sunset Drive-In** (www.fairoakstheatre.net; 255 Elks Lane, San Luis Obispo; adult/child $7/3; 👪), where you can put your feet up on the dash and munch on bottomless bags of popcorn while watching Hollywood blockbuster double-features.

🍴 p500

The Drive » Follow Hwy 101 north past San Luis Obispo, exiting onto Hwy 1 west to landmark Morro Rock in Morro Bay. North of Cayucos, Hwy 1 rolls through bucolic pasture lands, only swinging back to the coast at Cambria. Ten miles further north stands Hearst Castle, about 55 miles from Pismo Beach.

TRIP HIGHLIGHT

7 Around Hearst Castle

Hilltop **Hearst Castle** (☎reservations 800-444-4445; www.hearstcastle.org; tours adult/child from $25/12; ☺usually 9am-sunset) is California's most famous monument to wealth and ambition. William Randolph Hearst, the early-20th-century newspaper magnate, entertained Hollywood stars and royalty at this fantasy estate furnished with European antiques, accented by shimmering pools and surrounded by flowering gardens. Try to make tour reservations

---

TROUBLE-FREE ROAD TRIPPING

In coastal areas, thick fog may impede driving – slow down and if it's too soupy, get off the road. Along sea cliffs, watch out for falling rocks and mudslides that could damage or disable your car if struck. For current highway conditions, including road closures (which aren't uncommon during the rainy winter season) and construction updates, call ☎800-427-7623 or visit www.dot.ca.gov.

Classic Trip

LOCAL KNOWLEDGE
AMY STARBIN, LA
SCREENWRITER &
MOM

For a fun way to cool off when driving through LA along the coast, bring the family out to **Santa Monica Pier** (www.santamonicapier.org). Not only do you get a great view of the ocean, you can also get up close and personal with sea life at the **aquarium** (www.healthebay.org). Then head up top for a spin on the carousel used in *The Sting* or the solar-powered Ferris wheel.

Top: Pool, Hearst Castle.
Left: Lighthouse, Trinidad
Right: Redwoods

DAVID MUENCH / CORBIS ©

in advance, especially for living-history evening programs during the Christmas holiday season.

About 4.5 miles further north along Hwy 1, park at the signposted vista point and amble the boardwalk to view the enormous **elephant seal colony** that breeds, molts, sleeps, plays and fights on the beach. Seals haul out year-round, but the winter birthing and mating season peaks on Valentine's Day. Nearby, **Piedras Blancas Light Station** (www.piedrasblancas.org; tour adult/child $10/5; ☺ call for hr) is an outstandingly scenic spot.

✗ 🛏 p501

The Drive » Fill your car's gas tank before plunging north into the redwood forests of the remote Big Sur coast, where precipitous cliffs dominate the seascape, and tourist services are few and far between. Hwy 1 keeps curving north to the Monterey Peninsula, approximately a three-hour, 100-mile trip from Hearst Castle.

- - - - - - - - - -

❽ Monterey

As Big Sur loosens its condor's talons on the coastal highway, Hwy 1 rolls gently downhill towards Monterey Bay. The fishing community of Monterey is the heart of Steinbeck country, and although Cannery Row today is touristy claptrap, it's worth

Classic Trip

strolling down to step inside the mesmerizing **Monterey Bay Aquarium** (📞info 831-648-4800; tickets 866-963-9645; www.montereybayaquarium.org; 886 Cannery Row; adult/child $35/22; 🕙10am-5pm or 6pm daily, extended summer hr; 📶♿), inhabiting a converted sardine cannery on the shores of a national marine sanctuary. All kinds of aquatic denizens swim in giant tanks here, from sea stars to pot-bellied seahorses and comical sea otters. Afterwards, explore historic **Old Monterey**.

🍴 p501

The Drive » It's a relatively quick 45-mile trip north to Santa Cruz. Hwy 1 traces the crescent shoreline of Monterey Bay, passing Elkhorn Slough wildlife refuge near Moss Landing boat harbor, Watsonville's strawberry and artichoke farms, and a string of tiny beach towns in Santa Cruz County.

- - - - - - - - - - -

❾ Santa Cruz

Here, the flower power of the 1960s lives on, and bumper stickers on surfboard-laden woodies shout, 'Keep Santa Cruz weird.' Next to the ocean, **Santa Cruz Beach Boardwalk** (📞831-423-5590; www.beachboardwalk.com; 400 Beach St; admission free, rides $3-6; 🕙seasonal schedules vary, call for hr; ♿) has a glorious old-school Americana vibe and a 1911 Looff carousel. Its fun-for-all atmosphere is punctuated by squeals from nervous nellies on the stomach-turning Giant Dipper, a 1920s wooden roller coaster that's a national historic landmark, as seen in the vampire cult-classic movie *The Lost Boys*.

A kitschy, old-fashioned tourist trap, the **Mystery Spot** (📞831-423-8897; www.mysteryspot.com; 465 Mystery Spot Rd; admission $6, parking $5; 🕙daily, hr vary; ♿) makes compasses point crazily, while mysterious forces push you around and buildings lean at odd angles; call for directions, opening hours and tour reservations.

🛏 p501

The Drive » It's a blissful 75-mile coastal run from Santa Cruz up to San Francisco past Pescadero, Half Moon Bay and Pacifica, where Hwy 1 passes through the Devil's Slide twin tunnels. Merge with heavy freeway traffic in Daly City, staying on Hwy 1 north through the city into Golden Gate Park.

- - - - - - - - - - -

TRIP HIGHLIGHT

❿ San Francisco

Gridlock may shock your system after hundreds of lazy miles of wide-open, rolling coast. But don't despair. Hwy 1 runs straight through the city's biggest, most breathable green space: **Golden Gate Park** (www.golden-gate-park.com; admission free; ♿🎡). You could easily spend all day in the conservatory of flowers, arboretum and botanical gardens, perusing the **California**

DETOUR: POINT REYES

Start: ❿ San Francisco

A rough-hewn beauty, **Point Reyes National Seashore** (www.nps.gov/pore; admission free; ♿) lures marine mammals and birds, as well as scores of shipwrecks. It was here that Sir Francis Drake repaired his ship the *Golden Hind* in 1579 and, while he was at it, claimed the indigenous land for England. Follow Sir Francis Drake Blvd west out to the point's edge-of-the-world lighthouse, whipped by ferocious winds, where you can observe migrating whales in winter. The lighthouse is about 20 miles west of Point Reyes Station off Hwy 1 along the Marin County coast.

Academy of Sciences

(www.calacademy.org; 55 Music Concourse Dr; adult/child $35/25; ☉9:30am-5pm Mon-Sat, 11am-5pm Sun; 🍴) and the **de Young Museum** (http://deyoung.famsf.org; 50 Hagiwara Tea Garden Dr; adult/child $10/free; ☉9:30am-5:15pm Tue-Sun) of fine arts. Then follow Hwy 1 north over the **Golden Gate Bridge**. Guarding the entry to San Francisco Bay, this iconic bridge is named after the straits it spans, not for its 'International Orange' paint job. Park in the lot on the bridge's south or north side, then traipse out onto the pedestrian walkway for a photo.

 p501

The Drive » Past Sausalito, leave Hwy 101 in Marin City for slow-moving, wonderfully twisted Hwy 1 along the Marin County coast (see p545). Over the next 160 miles to Mendocino via Bodega Bay, revel in a remarkably uninterrupted stretch of coastal highway. En route, watch for the lighthouse road turnoff north of Point Arena town.

- - - - - - - - - - -

⑪ Around Point Arena

The fishing fleets of Bodega Bay and Jenner's harbor-seal colony are the last things you'll see before PCH dives into California's great rural northlands. Hwy 1 twists and turns past the Sonoma Coast's state parks packed with hiking trails, sand dunes and beaches, as well as underwater marine reserves, rhododendron groves and a 19th-century, Russian fur-trading fort. At Sea Ranch, don't let exclusive-looking vacation homes prevent you from following public-access trailhead signs and staircases down to empty beaches and across ocean bluffs. Further north, guarding an unbelievably windy point since 1908, **Point Arena Lighthouse** (www.pointarenalighthouse.com; 45500 Lighthouse Rd; adult/child $7.50/1; ☉10am-3:30pm, to 4:30pm late May-early Sep; 🍴) is the only lighthouse in California where you can actually climb to the top. Check in at the museum, then ascend the 115ft tower to inspect the Fresnel lens and panoramas of the sea and the jagged San Andreas Fault below.

🛏 p501

LOCAL KNOWLEDGE: GRIZZLY CREEK REDWOODS STATE PARK

To find the best hidden redwood groves, **Grizzly Creek Redwoods State Park** (www.parks.ca.gov; per car $8; ☉sunrise-sunset; 🍴) is the place to go. It's smaller than other parks, but so out of the way that it's pristine. Head to Cheatham Grove for lush sorrel carpets under the trees, then take a dip in summer swimming holes along the Van Duzen River. Bonus factoid: *Return of the Jedi* scenes were shot here. North of Scotia, exit Hwy 101 onto Hwy 36, then drive east for 17 miles.

Richard Stenger, retired park ranger

The Drive » It's an hour-long, 35-mile drive north along Hwy 1 from the Point Arena Lighthouse turnoff to Mendocino, crossing the Navarro, Little and Big Rivers. Feel free to stop and stretch at wind-tossed state beaches, parklands criss-crossed by hiking trails, and tiny coastal towns along the way.

- - - - - - - - - - -

⑫ Mendocino & Fort Bragg

Looking more like Cape Cod than California, the quaint maritime town of **Mendocino** has white picket fences surrounding New England–style cottages with blooming gardens and redwood-built water towers. Its dramatic headlands jutting into the Pacific, this yesteryear timber town and shipping port was 'discovered' by artists and bohemians in the 1950s and has served as a scenic backdrop in over 50 movies. Once you've browsed the souvenir shops and art galleries selling everything from driftwood carvings to homemade fruit jams, escape north to workaday **Fort Bragg**, with its simple fishing harbor and brewpub, stopping first for a short hike on the ecological staircase and pygmy forest trail at oceanfront **Jug Handle State Natural Reserve** (www.parks.ca.gov; Hwy 1; admission free; ☼sunrise-sunset; 🚹).

✕ 🛏 p501

The Drive » About 25 miles north of Mendocino, Westport is the last hamlet along this rugged stretch of Hwy 1. Rejoin Hwy 101 northbound at Leggett for another 90 miles to Eureka, detouring along the Avenue of the Giants and, if you have more time to spare, to the Lost Coast.

⑬ Eureka

Hwy 101 trundles alongside **Humboldt Bay National Wildlife Refuge** (www.fws.gov/refuge/humboldt_bay), a major stopover for migratory birds on the Pacific Flyway. Next comes the sleepy railroad town of Eureka. As you wander downtown, view the ornate **Carson Mansion** (143 M St), built in the 1880s by a timber baron and adorned with dizzying Victorian turrets, towers, gables and gingerbread details. Also a historical park, **Blue Ox Millworks** (www.blueoxmill.com; 1 X St; self-guided tour adult/child $7.50/3.50; ☼9am-5pm Mon-Fri, to 4pm Sat) still creates Victorian detailing by hand using traditional carpentry and 19th-century equipment. Back by Eureka's harborfront, climb aboard the blue-and-white 1910 **Madaket** (☎707-445-1910; www.humboldtbaymaritimemuseum.com; foot of C St; tour from $10; ☼mid-May–early Oct, call for hr). Sunset cocktail cruises serve from California's smallest licensed bar.

🛏 p501

The Drive » Follow Hwy 101 north past the Rastafarian-hippie college town of Arcata and turnoffs for Trinidad State Beach and Patrick's Point State Park. Hwy 101 drops out of the trees beside marshy Humboldt Lagoons State Park, rolling north towards Orick, just over 40 miles from Eureka.

TRIP HIGHLIGHT

⑭ Redwood National & State Parks

At last, you'll reach **Redwood National & State Parks** (www.nps.gov/redw, www.parks.ca.gov; state park day-use per car $8; 🚹). Get oriented to the tallest trees on earth at the coastal **Thoman H Kuchel Visitor Center** (☼9am-4pm, to 5pm Nov-Mar; 🚹), just south of Orick. Then commune with the coastal giants on their own mossy turf inside **Lady Bird Johnson Grove** or the majestic **Tall Trees Grove** (free drive-and-hike permit required). For more untouched redwood forests, wind along the 8-mile **Newton B Drury Scenic Parkway**, passing grassy meadows where Roosevelt elk roam, then follow Hwy 101 all the way north to Crescent City, the last pit-stop before the Oregon border.

Eureka Carson Mansion

Classic Trip

Eating & Sleeping

San Diego ❶

✕ C Level　　　　　Seafood $$
(☎619-298-6802; www.islandprime.com; 880 Harbor Island Dr; mains $15-30; ☺11am-late) Be mesmerized by bay views as you bite into carefully crafted salads, grilled seafood or the ultra-rich lobster sandwich on jalapeño-cheddar sourdough bread.

☕ Pearl Hotel　　　Boutique Hotel $$
(☎619-226-6100, 877-732-7573; www. thepearlsd.com; 1410 Rosecrans Ave, Point Loma; r $135-220; ❄☎☀) At this Mid-Century Modern motor lodge, rooms have soothing aquamarine hues, trippy surf motifs and fish bowls. With a lively pool scene, it's not for light sleepers.

Long Beach ❸

☕ Hotel Varden　　Boutique Hotel $$
(☎562-432-8950, 877-382-7336; www. thevardenhotel.com; 335 Pacific Ave; r $119-149; ❄@☎) Diminutive rooms at this historic art-deco hotel downtown have tiny sinks, cushy beds, white, white and more white. It's two blocks from Pine Ave's restaurant row.

Malibu ❹

✕ Neptune's Net　　Seafood $$
(www.neptunesnet.com; 42505 Pacific Coast Hwy; mains $6-20; ☺10:30am-8pm Mon-Thu, to 9pm Fri, to 8:30pm Sat & Sun; ♿☀) Order fish and chips at this 1950s roadhouse, where Harley riders and sand-covered kids chow down together at picnic tables.

Santa Barbara ❺

✕ Santa Barbara
Shellfish Company　　Seafood $$
(www.sbfishhouse.com; 230 Stearns Wharf; dishes $4-19; ☺11am-9pm) 'From sea to skillet to plate' best describes this end-of-the-wharf counter joint. Great lobster bisque, ocean views and the same location for 25 years.

☕ El Capitán
Canyon　　　Cabin, Campground $$$
(☎805-685-3887, 866-352-2729; www. elcapitancanyon.com; 11560 Calle Real, Goleta; safari tents $155-205, yurts $205, cabins $225-355; ☎☀♿) Go 'glamping' in this car-free zone near El Capitán State Beach, a 25-minute drive from downtown on Hwy 101. Creekside cabins come with heavenly mattresses, kitchenettes and outdoor fire pits.

☕ Hotel Indigo　　Boutique Hotel $$
(☎805-966-6586, 877-270-1392; www. indigosantabarbara.com; 121 State St; r $150-275; ❄@☎☀) Poised between downtown and the beach, this petite Euro-chic boutique hotel has all the right touches: curated contemporary-art displays, rooftop patios and ecofriendly green-design elements like the living-plant wall.

Pismo Beach ❻

✕ Splash Cafe　　　Seafood $
(www.splashcafe.com; 197 Pomeroy Ave; dishes $3-12; ☺8am-8:30pm Sun-Thu, to 9pm Fri & Sat; ♿) Uphill from the pier, lines go out the door and wrap around this scruffy hole-in-the-wall, famous for its clam chowder in fresh-baked sourdough-bread bowls.

Around Hearst Castle ⑦

✖ Sebastian's
General Store   Deli, Market **$**

(442 Slo San Simeon Rd, off I lwy 1; mains $6-12; ⏱11am-5pm Wed-Sun, deli till 4pm) Across Hwy 1 from Hearst Castle, this tiny historic market sells cold drinks, Hearst Ranch beef burgers and wines, giant deli sandwiches and salads for beach picnics at San Simeon Cove.

🛏 Blue Dolphin Inn   Hotel **$$**

(☎805-927-3300, 800-222-9157; www.cambriainns.com; 6470 Moonstone Beach Dr; d incl breakfast $179; 🛜👪🐾) Sand-colored, slate-sided, two-story building across from the ocean boardwalk has cozy rooms with romantic fireplaces.

Monterey ⑧

✖ Monterey's Fish House   Seafood **$$$**

(☎831-373-4647; 2114 Del Monte Ave, mains $12-35; ⏱11:30am-2:30pm Mon-Fri, 5-9:30pm daily; 👪) Watched over by photos of Sicilian fishermen, dig into dock-fresh seafood with some fusion twists. Try the barbecued oysters or the Mexican squid steak. The vibe is casual, but reservations are essential (it's *so* crowded).

Santa Cruz ⑨

🛏 Pelican Point Inn   Inn **$$**

(☎831-475-3381; www.pelicanpointinn-santacruz.com; 21345 E Cliff Dr; ste $109-199; 🛜👪🐾) Simple but roomy retro apartments near kid-friendly Twin Lakes State Beach come with everything you'll need for a coastal getaway, including kitchenettes. Expect some noise.

San Francisco ⑩

✖ Greens   Vegetarian **$$**

(☎415-771-6222; www.greensrestaurant.com; Fort Mason Center, Bldg A, 2 Marina Blvd; mains $11-24; ⏱11:45am-2:30pm Tue-Fri, 11am-2:30pm Sat & 10:30am-2pm Sun, plus 5:30-9pm Mon-Sat; �) In a converted army barracks, savor the Golden Gate Bridge views and meat-free, organic California cuisine, mostly sourced from a Zen Buddhist farm in Marin County.

🛏 Argonaut Hotel   Boutique Hotel **$$$**

(☎415-563-0800, 800-790-1415; www.argonauthotel.com; 495 Jefferson St; r from $300; ❄@🛜👪🐾) Inhabiting a converted cannery near Fisherman's Wharf, this nautical-themed hotel has century-old wooden beams, porthole-shaped mirrors and 'Tall Rooms' with extra-long beds.

Around Point Arena ⑪

🛏 Mar Vista Cottages   Cottage **$$**

(☎707-884-3522, 877-855-3522; www.marvistamendocino.com; 35101 S Hwy 1, Gualala; cottage $175-295; 🛜👪🐾) Stylishly renovated 1930s fishing cabins, south of Point Arena at Anchor Bay, make a perfectly relaxing coastal escape in a harmonious environment.

Mendocino & Fort Bragg ⑫

✖ North Coast
Brewing Co   Brewpub **$$$**

(www.northcoastbrewing.com; 444 N Main St; mains $17-31; ⏱4-9:30pm Wed-Thu & Sun, to 10pm Fri & Sat) Classic burgers and garlic waffle fries soak up locally handcrafted brews. Arrive early to get a table, or join the party in the bar.

🛏 Shoreline Cottages   Motel, Cottage **$$**

(☎707-964-2977; www.shoreline-cottage.com; 18725 Shoreline Hwy, Fort Bragg; d $120-165; 🛜👪🐾) Low-key rooms and cottages with kitchens surround a grassy lawn where dogs play. All are stocked with DVD players and complimentary snacks.

Eureka ⑬

🛏 Carter House Inns   Hotel, B&B **$$$**

(☎707-444-8062, 800-404-1930; www.carterhouse.com; 301 L St; r/ste incl breakfast from $189/295; 🛜) Hotel Carter's rooms are outfitted with top-quality linens and mod cons. Alternatively, reserve a romantic roost in a nearby historic home. Restaurant 301 is Eureka's top table for seasonal North Coast dinners with wine pairings.

Yosemite Falls *Triple-tiered, this waterfall is North America's tallest*

Classic Trip

Yosemite, Sequoia & Kings Canyon National Parks

40

Drive up into the lofty Sierra Nevada, where glacial valleys and ancient forests overfill the windshield scenery. Go climb a rock, pitch a tent or photograph wildflowers and wildlife.

TRIP HIGHLIGHTS

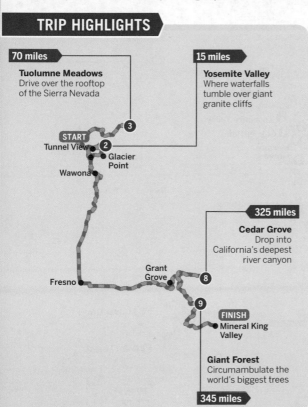

70 miles

Tuolumne Meadows
Drive over the rooftop of the Sierra Nevada

15 miles

Yosemite Valley
Where waterfalls tumble over giant granite cliffs

3

START
Tunnel View

2

Glacier Point

Wawona

325 miles

Cedar Grove
Drop into California's deepest river canyon

Grant Grove

Fresno

8

9

FINISH
Mineral King Valley

Giant Forest
Circumambulate the world's biggest trees

345 miles

5–7 DAYS
450 MILES/725KM

GREAT FOR...

BEST TIME TO GO
April and May for waterfalls; June to August for mountain highlands.

 ESSENTIAL PHOTO
Yosemite Valley from panoramic Tunnel View.

✓ **BEST SCENIC DRIVE**
Kings Canyon Scenic Byway to Cedar Grove.

Classic Trip

Yosemite, Sequoia & Kings Canyon National Parks

40

Glacier-carved valleys resting below dramatic peaks make Yosemite an all-ages playground. Here you can witness earth-shaking waterfalls, clamber up granite domes and camp out in high-country meadows where wildflowers bloom in summer. Home to one of the USA's deepest canyons and the biggest tree on the planet, Sequoia & Kings Canyon National Parks justify detouring further south into the Sierra Nevada, which conservationist John Muir called 'The Range of Light.'

❶ Tunnel View

Arriving in **Yosemite National Park** (📞209-372-0200; www.nps.gov/yose; 7-day pass per car $20; ♿) at the Arch Rock entrance station, follow Hwy 140 east. Pull over at **Tunnel View** for your first look into Yosemite Valley, which has inspired painters, poets, naturalists and adventurers for centuries. On the right, Bridalveil Fall swells with snowmelt in late spring, but by late summer, it's a mere whisper, often lifted and blown aloft by the wind. Spread below you are the pine forests and meadows of the valley floor, with the sheer face of El Capitan rising on the left, and in the distance straight ahead, iconic granite Half Dome.

The Drive » Merge carefully onto Wawona Rd, which continues downhill into Yosemite Valley, full of confusingly intersecting one-way roads. Drive east along the Merced River on Southside Dr past the Bridalveil Fall turnoff. Almost 6 miles from Tunnel View, turn left and drive across Sentinel Bridge to Yosemite Village's day-use parking lots. Ride free shuttle buses that circle the valley.

LINK YOUR TRIP

43 Eastern Sierra Scenic Byway

From Yosemite's Tuolumne Meadows, roll over high-elevation Tioga Pass and downhill towards Mono Lake, a 20-mile trip.

45 Highway 49 Through Gold Country

Pioneer ghost towns and swimming holes await just 45 miles northwest of Yosemite's Big Oak Flat via Hwy 120.

TRIP HIGHLIGHT

❷ Yosemite Valley

From the bottom looking up, this dramatic valley cut by the meandering Merced River is song-inspiring, and not just for birds: rippling meadow grasses; tall pines; cool, impassive pools reflecting granite monoliths; and cascading, glacier-cold whitewater ribbons. At busy **Yosemite Village**, start inside the **Yosemite Valley Visitor Center** (🕐10am-6pm late May-early Sep, 9am-5pm early Sep-late May; ♿), with its thought-provoking history and nature displays and free *Spirit of Yosemite* film screenings. At the nearby **Yosemite Museum** (🕐9am-5pm), Western landscape paintings are hung beside Native American baskets and beaded clothing.

The valley's famous waterfalls are thunderous cataracts in May, but mere trickles by late July. Triple-tiered **Yosemite Falls** is North America's tallest, while **Bridalveil Fall** is hardly less impressive. A strenuous, often slippery staircase beside **Vernal Fall** leads you, gasping, right to the top edge of the waterfall, where rainbows pop in clouds of mist. Keep hiking up the same Mist Trail to the top of **Nevada Fall** for a heady 6-mile round-trip trek.

In midsummer, you can rent a raft at Curry Village and float down the **Merced River**. The serene stretch between Stoneman Bridge and Sentinel Beach is gentle enough for kids. Or take the whole family to see the stuffed wildlife mounts at the hands-on **Nature Center at Happy Isles** (🕐usually 9:30am-5pm late May-Sep; ♿), east of Curry Village.

🍴🛏 p512

The Drive » From Yosemite Village, drive west on Northside Dr, passing Yosemite Falls and El Capitan. After 6 miles, turn right onto Big Oak Flat Rd/Hwy 120. For almost 10 miles, the road curves above the valley into the forest. Near Crane Flat gas station, turn right to follow Tioga Rd/Hwy 120 east (open summer and fall only). Continuing straight ahead, Big Oak Flat Rd/Hwy 120 west exits the park, leading past the turnoff to Hetch Hetchy (p512).

Classic Trip

- - - - - - - - - -
TRIP HIGHLIGHT

❸ Tuolumne Meadows

Leave the crushing crowds of Yosemite Valley behind and escape to the Sierra Nevada high country along Tioga Rd, which follows a 19th-century wagon road and Native American trading route. **Warning!** Completely closed by snow in winter, Tioga Rd is usually open *only* from May or June through October.

About 45 miles from Yosemite Valley, stop at **Olmsted Point**. Overlooking a lunar-type landscape of glaciated granite, gaze deeply down Tenaya Canyon to the backside of Half Dome. A few miles further east, a sandy half-moon beach wraps around **Tenaya Lake**, tempting you to brave some of the coldest swimming in the park. Sunbathers lie upon the rocks that rim the lake's northern shore.

About a 90-minute drive from Yosemite Valley, **Tuolumne Meadows** is the Sierra Nevada's largest subalpine meadow, with fields of wildflowers, bubbling streams, ragged granite peaks and cooler temperatures at an elevation of 8600ft. Hikers and climbers find a paradise of trails and granite domes to tackle, or unpack a picnic basket by the stream-fed meadows.

✕ 🛏 p512

The Drive » From Tuolumne Meadows, backtrack 50 miles to Yosemite Valley, turning left on El Portal Rd, then right on Northside Dr and right again on Wawona Rd. Follow narrow Wawona Rd/Hwy 41 up out of the valley. After 9 miles, turn

HIKING HALF DOME & AROUND YOSEMITE VALLEY

Over 800 miles of hiking trails in Yosemite National Park fit hikers of all abilities. Take an easy half-mile stroll on the valley floor or underneath giant sequoia trees, or venture out all day on a quest for viewpoints, waterfalls and lakes in the mountainous high country.

Some of the park's most popular hikes start right in Yosemite Valley, including to the top of **Half Dome** (17-mile round-trip), the most famous of all. It follows a section of the John Muir Trail and is strenuous, difficult and best tackled in two days with an overnight in Little Yosemite Valley. Reaching the top can only be done in summer after park rangers have installed fixed cables; depending on snow conditions, this may occur as early as late May or as late as July and the cables usually come down in October. To limit the cables' notorious human logjams, the park now requires permits for day hikers, but the route is still nerve-wracking as hikers must share the cables. **Advance permits** (☏877-444-6777; www.recreation.gov) go on sale by lottery in early spring, with a limited number available via another lottery two days in advance. Permit regulations and prices keep changing; check the park website (http://www.nps.gov/yose) for current details.

The less ambitious or physically fit will still have a ball following the **Mist Trail** as far as Vernal Fall (3-mile round-trip), the top of Nevada Fall (6-mile round-trip) or idyllic Little Yosemite Valley (8-mile round-trip). The **Four Mile Trail** (9-mile round-trip) up to Glacier Point is a strenuous but satisfying climb to a glorious viewpoint. If you've got the kids in tow, nice and easy **valley walks** include to Mirror Lake (2-mile round-trip) and viewpoints at the base of thundering Yosemite Falls (1-mile round-trip) and lacy Bridalveil Fall (0.5-mile round-trip).

WINTER WONDERLANDS

When the temperature drops and the white stuff falls, there are still tons of fun outdoor activities around the Sierra Nevada's national parks. In Yosemite, strap on some skis or a snowboard and go tubing downhill at Badger Pass; plod around Yosemite Valley or to Dewey Point on a ranger-led snowshoe tour; or just try to stay upright on ice skates at Curry Village. Further south in Sequoia & Kings Canyon National Parks, the whole family can go snowshoeing or cross-country skiing among groves of giant sequoias. Before embarking on a winter trip to the parks, check road conditions on the official park websites or by calling ahead. Don't forget to put snow tires on your car, and always carry tire chains, too.

left onto Glacier Point Rd at the Chinquapin intersection, driving 15 more miles to Glacier Point.

- - - - - - - - - - - -

❹ Glacier Point

In only an hour, you can zip from Yosemite Valley up to head-spinning Glacier Point. **Warning!** Glacier Point Rd is closed by snow in winter, usually not opening again until May. Between November and April, the road remains open as far as Badger Pass ski area, but snow tires and tire chains may be required.

Rising over 3000ft above the valley floor, dramatic **Glacier Point** (7214ft) practically puts you at eye level with Half Dome. Glimpse what John Muir and US President Teddy Roosevelt saw when they camped here in 1903: the waterfall-strewn Yosemite Valley below and the distant peaks ringing Tuolumne Meadows. To get away from the crowds, hike a little way down the Panorama Trail, just south of the crowded main viewpoint.

On your way back from Glacier Point, take time out for a 2-mile hike up **Sentinel Dome** or out to **Taft Point** for incredible 360-degree valley views.

🚶 p513

The Drive » Drive back downhill past Badger Pass, turning left at the Chinquapin intersection and winding south through thick forest on Wawona Rd/Hwy 41. After almost 13 curvy miles, you'll reach Wawona, with its hotel, visitor center, general store and gas station, all on your left.

- - - - - - - - - - - -

❺ Wawona

At Wawona, a 45-minute drive south of the valley, drop by the **Pioneer Yosemite History Center**, with its covered bridge, pioneer-era buildings and historic Wells Fargo office. In summer you can take a short, bumpy stagecoach ride and really feel like you're living in the past. Peek inside the **Wawona Visitor Center** (🕐8:30am-5pm mid-May–Oct) at 19th-century artist Thomas Hill's recreated studio, hung with romantic Sierra Nevada landscape paintings. On summer evenings, imbibe a civilized cocktail in the lobby lounge of the Wawona Hotel, where pianist Tom Bopp plays tunes from Yosemite's bygone days.

🛏 p513

The Drive » In summer, leave your car at Wawona and take a free shuttle bus to Mariposa Grove. By car, follow Wawona Rd/Hwy 41 south for 4.5 miles to the four-way stop by the park's south entrance. Continue straight ahead on Mariposa Rd (closed in winter) for 3.5 miles to the parking lot – when it's full, drivers are turned away.

- - - - - - - - - - - -

❻ Mariposa Grove

Wander giddily around the Mariposa Grove, home of the 1800-year-old Grizzly Giant and 500 other giant sequoias that tower above your head. Nature trails wind through this popular grove, but you can only hear yourself think above

Classic Trip

GALEN ROWELL / CORBIS ©

GALEN ROWELL / CORBIS ©

LOCAL KNOWLEDGE
SCHUYLER GREENLEAF, DIRECTOR OF PROJECTS FOR YOSEMITE CONSERVANCY

For a family-friendly hike (no little kids, though) off Tioga Rd, take the recently rehabilitated trail up Mt Hoffman. About 2.5 miles long, the trail takes you past May Lake, where you can take a dip either before or after your hike. When you're standing on top of Mt Hoffman, you're at the geographical center of Yosemite National Park with spectacular views all around, including of the Tuolumne River canyon.

Top: John Muir Trail, Yosemite Valley
Left: Tuolumne Meadows
Right: Woman standing in sequoia trunk, Sequoia National Park

the noise of vacationing crowds and motorized tram tours during the early morning or evening. Notwithstanding a cruel hack job back in 1895, the walk-through California Tunnel Tree continues to survive, so pose your family in front and snap away. If you've got the energy for a 5-mile round-trip hike to the upper grove, the **Mariposa Grove Museum** (⏰10am-4pm May-Sep) has displays about sequoia ecology inside a pioneer cabin.

The Drive » From Yosemite's south entrance station, it's a 120-mile, three-hour trip to Kings Canyon National Park. Follow Hwy 41 south 60 miles to Fresno, then slingshot east on Hwy 180 for another 50 miles, climbing out of the Central Valley back into the mountains. Keep left at the Hwy 198 intersection, staying on Hwy 180 towards Grant Grove.

- - - - - - - - - - - -

7 Grant Grove

Through **Sequoia & Kings Canyon National Parks** (📞559-565-3341; www.nps.gov/seki; 7-day pass per car $20; ♿), roads seem barely to scratch the surface of the twin parks' beauty. To see real treasures, you'll need to get out and stretch your legs. North of Big Stump entrance station in Grant Grove Village, turn left and wind downhill to **General Grant Grove**, where you'll see some of the park's landmark

CALIFORNIA TRIPS **40** YOSEMITE, SEQUOIA & KINGS CANYON NATIONAL PARKS

giant sequoia trees along a paved path. You can walk right through the Fallen Monarch, a massive, fire-hollowed trunk that's done duty as a cabin, hotel, saloon and horse stable. For views of Kings Canyon and the peaks of the Great Western Divide, follow a narrow, winding side road (closed in winter, no RVs or trailers) starting behind John Muir Lodge up to **Panoramic Point**.

p513

The Drive » Kings Canyon National Park's main visitor areas, Grant Grove and Cedar Grove, are linked by narrow, twisting Hwy 180, which dramatically descends into Kings Canyon. Expect spectacular views all along this

outstandingly scenic 30-mile drive. **Warning!** Hwy 180 from the Hume Lake turnoff to Cedar Grove is closed during winter (usually mid-November through mid-April).

TRIP HIGHLIGHT

8 Cedar Grove

Serpentining past chiseled rock walls laced with waterfalls, Hwy 180 plunges down to the Kings River, where roaring whitewater ricochets off the granite cliffs of one of North America's deepest canyons. Pull over partway down at **Junction View overlook** for an eyeful, then keep rolling along the river to **Cedar Grove Village**. East of the village, **Zumwalt Meadow** is the place for spotting birds, mule deer and black bears. If the day is hot and your suit is handy, stroll from Road's End to **Muir Rock**,

a large flat-top river boulder where John Muir once gave outdoor talks, now a popular summer swimming hole. Starting from Road's End, a very popular day hike climbs 4.5 miles each way to roaring **Mist Falls**.

p513

The Drive » Backtrack from Road's End nearly 30 miles up Hwy 180. Turn left onto Hume Lake Rd. Curve around the lake past swimming beaches, turning right onto 10 Mile Rd, which runs by US Forest Service (USFS) campgrounds. At Hwy 198, turn left and follow the Generals Hwy (sometimes closed in winter) south for about 23 miles to the Wolverton Rd turnoff on your left.

TRIP HIGHLIGHT

9 Giant Forest

We dare you to try hugging the trees in **Giant Forest**, a 3-sq-mile grove protecting the park's most gargantuan specimens. Park off Wolverton Rd and walk downhill to reach the world's biggest living tree, the **General Sherman Tree**, which towers 275ft into the sky. With sore arms and sticky sap fingers, you can lose the crowds on any of many forested trails nearby. The trail network stretches all the way south to Crescent Meadow, a 5-mile one-way ramble.

By car, drive 2.5 miles south along the Generals Hwy to get schooled on

DETOUR:
BUCK ROCK LOOKOUT

Start: 8 Cedar Grove

To climb one of California's most evocative fire lookouts, drive east of the Generals Hwy on Big Meadows Rd into the Sequoia National Forest between between Grant Grove and the Giant Forest. Follow the signs to staffed **Buck Rock Lookout** (www. buckrock.org; Forest Rd 13S04; admission free; ☺usually 9:30am-6pm Jul-Oct). Constructed in 1923, this active fire lookout allows panoramic views from a dollhouse-sized cab lording over the horizon from 8500ft atop a granite rise, reached by 172 spindly stairs. It's not for anyone with vertigo!

sequoia ecology and fire cycles at the **Giant Forest Museum** (⊙ usually 9am-4.30pm or 6pm mid-May–mid-Oct; ♿).

Starting outside the museum, Crescent Meadow Rd makes a 6-mile loop out through Giant Forest, passing right through the **Tunnel Log**. For 360-degree views of the Great Western Divide, climb the steep quarter-mile staircase up **Moro Rock**.

Warning! Crescent Meadow Rd is closed to traffic by winter snow; during summer, ride the free shuttle buses around the loop road and between the Giant Forest Museum and Wolverton Rd parking areas, rather than driving yourself.

 p513

The Drive » Narrowing, the Generals Hwy drops for almost 20 miles into the Sierra Nevada foothills, passing Amphitheater Point and exiting the park beyond Foothills Visitor Center. Before reaching the town of Three Rivers, turn left on Mineral King Rd, a dizzyingly scenic 25-mile road (partly unpaved, no trailers or RVs allowed) that switchbacks up to Mineral King Valley.

DETOUR: CRYSTAL CAVE

Start: ❾ Giant Forest

Off the Generals Hwy, about 2 miles south of the Giant Forest Museum, turn right onto twisting 6.5-mile-long Crystal Cave Rd for a fantastical walk inside 10,000-year-old **Crystal Cave** (www.sequoiahistory.org; tours adult/child from $15/8; ⊙ tours May-Nov, weather permitting; ♿), carved by an underground river. Stalactites hang like daggers from the ceiling, and 10,000-year-old milky-white marble formations take the shape of ethereal curtains, domes, columns and shields. Bring a light jacket – it's 50°F inside the cave. You must buy tour tickets in advance from the Lodgepole or Foothills Visitor Centers.

❿ Mineral King Valley

Navigating almost 700 hairpin turns, it's a winding 1½-hour drive up to glacially sculpted **Mineral King Valley** (7500ft), a 19th-century silver-mining camp and lumber settlement, and later a mountain retreat. Trailheads into the high country begin at the end of Mineral King Rd, where historic private cabins dot the valley floor flanked by massive mountains. Your final destination is just over

a mile past the ranger station, where the valley unfolds all of its hidden beauty, and hikes to granite peaks and alpine lakes beckon.

Warning! Mineral King Rd is typically open only from mid-May through late October. In early summer, marmots like to chew on parked cars, so wrap the undercarriage of your vehicle with a tarp or stake chicken-wire fencing (which can be rented from Silver City Resort) around the outside of your vehicle.

Eating & Sleeping

Yosemite Valley ❷

✖ Degnan's Deli   Deli $

(www.yosemitepark.com; Yosemite Village; mains $8-12; ⏰7am-5pm; ♿) Grab a custom-made deli sandwich and bag of chips before hitting the trail. Not far away, the Village Store sells groceries, snacks and camping supplies until 8pm or later.

✖ Mountain Room Restaurant   American $$$

(www.yosemitepark.com; Yosemite Lodge at the Falls; mains $18-35; ⏰5:30-9:30pm; ♿) Tuck into grass-fed steaks, river trout and organic veggies at this no-reservations dining room with waterfall views. A few steps away, the fireplace lounge serves microbrews and snacks.

🛏 Ahwahnee   Historic Hotel $$$

(☎209-372-1407, reservations 801-559-4884; www.yosemitepark.com; Ahwahnee Rd; r from $470; ❄@🛜♿♿) Charlie Chaplin, Eleanor Roosevelt and JFK have each slept at this 1927 National Historic Landmark. Sit a spell by the roaring fireplace beneath sugar-pine timbers. Skip the formal dining room (except at Sunday brunch) for cocktails in the lobby.

🛏 Curry Village & Housekeeping Camp   Cabin $$

(☎reservations 801-559-4884; www.yosemitepark.com; off Southside Dr; ♿♿) With a noisy summer-camp ambience, hundreds of helter-skelter tent cabins scatter beneath evergreens and beside the valley's Merced River.

🛏 Yosemite Bug Rustic Mountain Resort   Cabin, Hostel $

(☎209-966-6666, 866-826-7108; www.yosemitebug.com; 6979 Hwy 140; dm $23-26, tent cabins $45-75, r with shared/private bath from $65/75; @🛜✏♿🎮) In the forest about 30 miles west of Yosemite Valley, this mountain hostelry hosts globetrotters who dig the clean rooms, yoga studio, hot-tub spa, shared kitchen and vegetarian-friendly cafe (mains $5 to $18).

🛏 Yosemite Valley Campgrounds   Campground $

(☎reservations 877-444-6777; www.recreation.gov; campsites $20; ⏰most Apr-Oct, some year-round; ♿🎮) Comparatively quieter North Pines Campground offers some riverside sites, while Upper and Lower Pines Campgrounds are busy and crammed. Reserve campsites online up to five months in advance.

Hetch Hetchy

🛏 Evergreen Lodge   Cabin, Camping $$

(☎209-379-2606, 800-935-6343; www.evergreenlodge.com; 33160 Evergreen Rd; tents $80-120, cabins $210-380; @🛜✖♿) Outside Yosemite's northwest entrance near Hetch Hetchy Reservoir, this classic mountain resort foregoes roughing it for deluxe cabins and tents. Outdoor recreational activities abound. There's a general store, a tavern with a pool table and a restaurant (mains $10 to $30) serving three hearty meals a day.

Tuolumne Meadows ❸

✖ Tuolumne Meadows Grill   American $

(Tioga Rd; dishes $4-9; ⏰8am-5pm mid-Jun–mid-Sep) Scarf down burgers and grill items, breakfast sammiches and soft-serve ice cream at the picnic tables outside this summertime tent-topped eatery. The general store stays open till 8pm during summer.

🛏 Tuolumne Meadows & White Wolf Lodges   Cabin $$

(☎reservations 801-559-4884; www.yosemitepark.com; Tioga Rd; tent cabins from

$120; ⏰ mid-Jun–mid-Sep; 🏠) In the high country away from the hubbub of the valley, these canvas tent cabins without electricity (bring a flashlight!) are always in demand. Both camps offer breakfast, boxed lunches and dinner by reservation.

🛏 Tuolumne Meadows Campground   Campground $

(☎ reservations 877-444-6777; www.recreation. gov; Tioga Rd; campsites $20; ⏰ mid-Jul–late Sep; 🚻👨‍👩‍👧) At the park's biggest campground, 300-plus sites are decently spaced through the shady forest. Good news if you didn't book ahead: half are first-come, first-serve.

Glacier Point ❹

🛏 Bridalveil Creek Campground   Campground $

(www.nps.gov/yose; Glacier Point Rd; campsites $14; ⏰ mid-Jul–early Sep; 🚻👨‍👩‍👧) When the day ends, retreat to your own tent at this no-reservations campground shaded by pine forest. At 7200ft, nights can be chilly.

Wawona ❺

🛏 Wawona Hotel   Historic Hotel $$

(☎ 209-375-6556, reservations 801-559-4884; www.yosemitepark.com; Wawona Rd; r shared/ private bath incl breakfast from $155/225; ⏰ Apr-Nov & mid-Dec–early Jan; 🏠📶👨) Full of character, this Victorian-era throwback has wide porches with Adirondack chairs, manicured lawns and a golf course. Some of the thin-walled rooms, none of which have phones or TVs, share baths. A lamp-lit dining room serves classic American cooking (mains $12 to $34).

Grant Grove ❼

🛏 Grant Grove Campgrounds   Campground $

(www.nps.gov/seki; Hwy 180; campsites $10-18; ⏰ most May-Sep, some year-round; 🚻👨‍👩‍👧) All of Grant Grove's no-reservations campgrounds are shaded by evergreens. Crystal Springs is quieter than Sunset; Azalea stays open during winter.

🛏 John Muir Lodge & Grant Grove Cabins   Hotel, Cabin $$

(☎ 559-335-5500; www.sequoia-kingscanyon. com; Hwy 180; cabins with shared bath $65-95, r $120-190; 📶) This woodsy lodge has a cozy fireplace lobby with board games and wi-fi. Oddly assorted cabins range from thin-walled canvas tents to historical cottages. The pizza parlor and general store nearby will keep you from starving.

Cedar Grove ❽

🛏 Cedar Grove Campgrounds   Campground $

(www.nps.gov/seki; Hwy 180; campsites $18; ⏰ usually late Apr–mid-Oct; 🚻👨‍👩‍👧) Slumber creekside at Sheep Creek Campground or at Sentinel Campground next to the ranger station. Sunny campsites are further east at Moraine and tent-only Canyon View. No reservations.

🛏 Cedar Grove Lodge   Motel $$

(☎ 559-335-5500; www.sequoia-kingscanyon. com; Hwy 180; r $130-140; ⏰ mid-May–early Oct; ❄📶) This riverside lodge offers 21 rooms (no TVs), some with air-con, shady patios and kitchenettes. Check in downstairs at the market, next to the snack bar and grill (mains $6 to $12).

Giant Forest ❾

🍴 Lodgepole Market   Self-Catering, Deli $

(www.visitsequoia.com; Lodgepole Village; mains $6-10; ⏰ late May-early Oct, seasonal hr vary) Inside the general store selling groceries and camping supplies, a fast-food deli sells picnic fare like focaccia sandwiches and salads.

🛏 Lodgepole Campground   Campground $

(☎ 877-444-6777; www.recreation.gov; Lodgepole Village; campsites $20; ⏰ May-Nov; 🚻👨‍👩‍👧) On the Kaweah River, Sequoia's biggest and busiest campground shoehorns in tents and RVs.

🛏 Wuksachi Lodge   Hotel $$$

(☎ 559-565-4070; www.visitsequoia.com; 64740 Wuksachi Way, off Generals Hwy; r $225; 📶) Sequoia's most upscale lodging and dining option. The dining room (mains $8 to $40) has an inviting stone fireplace and forest views, but the motel-style rooms are charmless.

Laguna Beach *Dozens of beaches sprawl along a few miles of coastline*

Disneyland & Orange County Beaches

41

Let the kids loose at the 'Happiest Place on Earth,' then strike out for sunny SoCal beaches – as seen on TV and the silver screen. It's impossible not to have fun on this coastal getaway.

TRIP HIGHLIGHTS

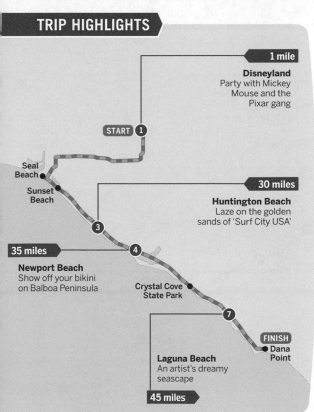

1 mile

Disneyland
Party with Mickey Mouse and the Pixar gang

START ①

Seal Beach

Sunset Beach

30 miles

Huntington Beach
Laze on the golden sands of 'Surf City USA'

③

④

35 miles

Newport Beach
Show off your bikini on Balboa Peninsula

Crystal Cove State Park

⑦

FINISH
● Dana Point

Laguna Beach
An artist's dreamy seascape

45 miles

2–4 DAYS
60 MILES/95KM

GREAT FOR...

BEST TIME TO GO
April to November to avoid winter rains.

ESSENTIAL PHOTO
Surfers at Huntington Beach Pier.

BEST FOR VIEWS
Corona del Mar's Lookout Point.

41 Disneyland & Orange County Beaches

It's true you'll find gorgeous sunsets, prime surfing breaks and just-off-the-boat seafood when road tripping down the OC's sun-kissed coastal Hwy 1. Yet it's the unexpected and serendipitous discoveries you'll remember long after you've left this blissful 42 miles of surf and sand behind. Top it all off with a day or two at Disneyland's theme parks, and let's call it a wrap for the perfect SoCal family vacation.

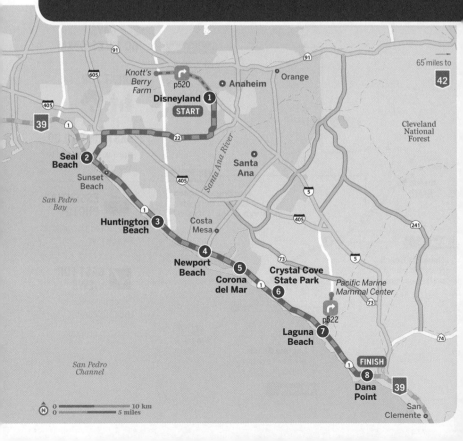

❶ Disneyland

No SoCal theme park welcomes more millions of visitors every year than **Disneyland** (📞714-781-4636; www.disneyland.com; 1313 S Harbor Blvd, Anaheim; 1-day single-park admission adult/child $92/86, 2-park day pass $137/131; ⬝). From the ghostly skeletons of *Pirates of the Caribbean* to the screeching monkeys of the *Indiana Jones* Adventure, there's magical detail everywhere. Retro-futuristic Tomorrowland is where the *Finding Nemo* Submarine Voyage

LINK YOUR TRIP

39 Pacific Coast Highways

Orange County is California's official section of the Pacific Coast Hwy (PCH), running along Hwy 1 between laidback Seal Beach and Dana Point.

42 Palm Springs & Joshua Tree Oases

Loving the SoCal sunshine? Go 110 miles further inland from Anaheim to find desert hot-springs resorts and all-natural parklands.

and *Star Wars*–themed Star Tours and Jedi Training Academy await. Use the Fastpass system and you'll be hurtling through Space Mountain – still the park's best adrenaline pumper – in no time. After dark, watch fireworks explode over Sleeping Beauty's Castle.

Any fear of heights? Then ditch the Twilight Zone Tower of Terror at **Disney's California Adventure** (DCA), Disneyland's newer neighbor. DCA's lightheartedly themed areas highlight the best of the Golden State, while plenty of adventures like Route 66–themed Cars Land don't involve losing your lunch. An exception is rockin' California Screamin' at Paradise Pier: this whip-fast coaster looks like an old-school carnival ride, but from the moment it blasts forward with a cannon-shot whoosh, this monster never lets go. Catch the enthusiasm of the Pixar Play Parade by day and World of Color special-effects show at night.

Just outside the parks, **Downtown Disney** pedestrian mall is packed with souvenir shops, family restaurants, after-dark bars and entertainment venues and, in summer, live musicians playing for the crowds.

🍴 🛏 p523

The Drive Follow Harbor Blvd south for 3 not-very-scenic miles, then take Hwy 22 west through inland Orange County, merging onto the I-405 north. After another mile or so, exit onto Seal Beach Blvd, which crawls 3 miles toward the coast. Turn left onto Hwy 1, also known as the Pacific Coast Hwy (PCH) throughout Orange County, then take a right onto Main St in Seal Beach.

❷ Seal Beach

In the SoCal beauty pageant for pint-sized beach towns, Seal Beach is the winner of the crown. Stop here and you'll discover it's a refreshingly unhurried alternative to the more crowded Orange County coast further south. Its three-block **Main St** is a stoplight-free zone that bustles with mom-and-pop restaurants and indie shops that are low on 'tude and high on nostalgia. Follow the path of barefoot surfers as they trot toward the beach to where Main St ends, then walk out onto **Seal Beach Pier**. The 1906 original first fell victim to winter storms in the 1930s, and since then it has been rebuilt three times with a splintery, wooden boardwalk. Down on the **beach**, you'll find families spread out on blankets, building sandcastles and playing in the water – all of them ignoring that hideous oil derrick offshore.

LOCAL KNOWLEDGE
VERONICA HILL,
'CALIFORNIA
TRAVEL TIPS'
YOUTUBE HOST

Want to get the most bang for your buck at Disneyland or Disney's California Adventure? If your kids are too young to ride, ask for the rider-switch pass. Grab it from a cast member as you enter the ride (while your partner watches the kids). Afterward, give the pass to your partner so they can whisk through the FastPass line. If you have an impatient teenager, send them through the single-rider line instead.

Top: Oceanfront homes, Newport Beach
Left: Restaurant, Newport Beach
Right: Competitor at US Open of Surfing, Huntington Beach Pier

The gentle waves make Seal Beach a great place to learn to surf. **M&M Surfing School** (☎714-846-7873; www.surfingschool.com; 1hr/3hr group lesson $50/65, wetsuit/surfboard rental $15/25; 👤) parks its van in the lot just north of the pier, off Ocean Ave at 8th St.

The Drive » Past a short bridge further south along Hwy 1, drivers drop onto a mile-long spit of land known as Sunset Beach, with its biker bars and harborside kayak and stand-up paddle boarding (SUP) rental shops. Keep cruising Hwy 1 south another 6 miles past Bolsa Chica State Beach and Ecological Reserve to Huntington Beach Pier.

- - - - - - - - - - - - -

TRIP HIGHLIGHT

❸ Huntington Beach

In 'Surf City USA,' SoCal obsession's with wave riding hits its frenzied peak. There's a statue of Hawaiian surfer Duke Kahanamoku at the intersection of Main St and PCH, and if you look down, you'll see names of legendary surfers in the sidewalk **Surfers' Hall of Fame** (www.hsssurf.com/shof/). A few blocks east, the **International Surfing Museum** (☎714-960-3483; www.surfingmuseum.org; 411 Olive Ave; suggested donation $2; ⏱noon-5pm Sun-Mon, to 9pm Tue, to 7pm Wed-Fri, 11am-7pm Sat) honors those same legends. Then join the crowds on the **Huntington Beach Pier**, where you

can catch up-close views of daredevils barreling through tubes. The surf here may not be the ideal place to test your newbie skills, however – locals can be territorial. In summer, the US Open of Surfing draws more than 600 world-class surfers and 400,000 spectators with a minivillage of concerts, motocross demos and skater jams. As for **Huntington City Beach** itself, it's wide and flat – a perfect place to snooze on the sand on a giant beach towel. Snag a fire pit just south of the pier to build an evening bonfire with friends.

 p523

The Drive » From the Huntington Beach Pier at the intersection of Main St, drive south on Hwy 1 (PCH) alongside the ocean for another 4 miles to Newport Beach. Turn right onto W Balboa Blvd, leading onto the Balboa Peninsula, squeezed between the ocean and Balboa Island, off Newport Harbor.

TRIP HIGHLIGHT

❹ Newport Beach

As seen on Bravo's *Real Housewives of Orange County* and Fox's *The OC* and *Arrested Development,* in glitzy Newport Beach wealthy socialites, glamorous teens and gorgeous beaches all share the spotlight. Bikini vixens strut down the sandy beach stretching between the peninsula's twin piers, while boogie boarders brave human-eating waves at the **Wedge**, and the ballet of yachts in the harbor makes you dream of being rich and famous. From the harbor, hop aboard a ferry over to old-fashioned **Balboa Island** or climb aboard the carousel by the landmark 1906 **Balboa Pavilion**. The Ferris wheel still spins at pint-sized **Balboa Fun Zone** (www.thebalboafunzone.com; 600 E Bay Ave; per ride $3; ⏱11am-9pm Sun-Thu, to 10pm Fri & Sat; ♿), nearby the marine-themed exhibits at **ExplorOcean** (☎949-675-8915; http://explorocean. org; 600 E Bay Ave; adult/child $4/2; ⏱11am-3pm Mon-Thu, to 6pm Fri & Sat, to 5pm Sun; ♿). Just inland, visit the cutting-edge contemporary **Orange County Museum of Art** (☎949-759-1122; www. ocma.net; 850 San Clemente Dr; adult/child $12/free; ⏱11am-5pm Wed-Sun, to 8pm Thu) to escape SoCal's vainglorious pop culture.

 p523

➤ **DETOUR: KNOTT'S BERRY FARM**

Start: ❶ Disneyland

Hear the screams? Got teens? Hello, **Knott's Berry Farm** (☎714-220-5200; www. knotts.com; 8039 Beach Blvd, Buena Park; adult/child $60/31; ⏱daily from 10am, closing time varies 6-11pm; ♿), America's first theme park, which opened in 1940. Today high-scream coasters lure fast-track fanatics. Look up as you enter to see the bare feet of riders who've removed their flip-flops for the Silver Bullet, the suspended coaster careening past overhead, famed for its corkscrew, double spiral and outside loop. In October, Knott's hosts SoCal's scariest after-dark Halloween party. Year-round, the *Peanuts* gang keeps moppets happy in Camp Snoopy, while the next-door water park **Soak City OC** (☎714-220-5200; www.soakcityoc.com; adult/child $35/25; ⏱10am-5pm, 6pm or 7pm mid-May–mid-Sep; ♿) keeps you cool on blazing-hot summer days. Knott's is a 20-minute drive from Disneyland via I-5 north to La Palma Ave west.

The Drive » South of Newport Beach, prime-time ocean views are just a short detour off Hwy 1. First drive south across the bridge over Newport Channel, then after 3 miles turn right onto Marguerite Ave in Corona del Mar. Once you reach the coast, take another right onto Ocean Blvd.

Dana Point Harbor

⑤ Corona del Mar

Savor some of SoCal's most celebrated ocean views from the bluffs of Corona del Mar, a chichi bedroom community south of Newport Channel. Several postcard beaches, rocky coves and child-friendly tidepools beckon along this idyllic stretch of coast. One of the best viewpoints is at breezy **Lookout Point** on Ocean Blvd near Heliotrope Ave. Below the rocky cliffs to the east is half-mile long Main Beach, officially **Corona del Mar State Beach** (☏949-644-3151; www.parks. ca.gov; per car $15; ☺6am-10pm), with fire rings and volleyball courts (arrive early on weekends to get a parking spot). Stairs lead down to Pirates Cove which has a great, waveless pocket beach for families – scenes from *Gilligan's Island* were shot here. Head east on Ocean Blvd to **Inspiration Point**, near the corner of Orchid Ave, for more vistas of surf, sand and sea.

The Drive » Follow Orchid Ave back north to Hwy 1, then turn right and drive southbound. Traffic thins out as ocean views become more wild and uncluttered by housing developments that head up into the hills on your left. It's just a couple of miles to the entrance of Crystal Cove State Park.

⑥ Crystal Cove State Park

With 3.5 miles of open beach and over 2300 acres of undeveloped woodland, **Crystal Cove State Park** (☏949-494-3539; www.parks.ca.gov, www. crystalcovestatepark.com; entry per car $15; ☺6am-sunset) lets you almost forget that you're in a crowded metro area. That is, once you get past the parking lot and stake out a place on the sand. Many visitors don't know it, but it's also an underwater park where scuba enthusiasts can check out the wreck of US Navy Corsair fighter plane that went down in 1949. Or just go tidepooling, fishing, kayaking and surfing along Crystal Cove's exhilaratingly wild, windy shoreline. On the inland side of Hwy 1, miles of hiking and mountain-biking trails wait for landlubbers.

✕ ⊨ p523

The Drive » Drive south on Hwy 1 for another 4 miles or so. As shops, restaurants, art galleries, motels and hotels start to crowd the highway once again, you've arrived in Laguna Beach. Downtown is a maze of one-way streets just southeast of the Laguna Canyon Rd (Hwy 133) intersection.

TRIP HIGHLIGHT

⑦ Laguna Beach

This early-20th-century artist colony's secluded coves, romantic-looking cliffs and Arts and

Crafts bungalows come as a relief after miles of suburban beige-box architecture. With joie de vivre, Laguna celebrates its bohemian roots with summer arts festivals, dozens of galleries and the acclaimed **Laguna Art Museum** (☎949-494-8971; http://lagunaartmuseum.org; 307 Cliff Dr; adult/child $7/free; ☻11am-5pm Fri-Tue, to 9pm Thu). In downtown's village, it's easy to while away an afternoon browsing the chic boutiques. Down on the shore, **Main Beach** is crowded with volleyball players and sunbathers. Just north atop the bluffs, **Heisler Park** winds past public art, palm trees, picnic tables and grand views of rocky shores and tidepools. Drop down to Divers Cove, a deep, protected inlet. Heading south, dozens of public beaches sprawl along just a few miles of coastline. Keep a sharp eye out for 'beach access' signs off Hwy 1, or pull into locals' favorite **Aliso Beach County Park** (http://ocparks.com/beaches/aliso; 31131 S Pacific Coast Hwy;

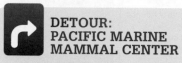

DETOUR: PACIFIC MARINE MAMMAL CENTER

Start: ❼ **Laguna Beach**

About 3 miles northeast of Laguna Beach is the heart-warming **Pacific Marine Mammal Center** (☎949-494-3050; www.pacificmmc.org; 20612 Laguna Canyon Rd; admission by donation; ☻10am-4pm; ♿), dedicated to rescuing and rehabilitating injured or ill marine mammals. This nonprofit center has a small staff and many volunteers who help nurse rescued pinnipeds (mostly sea lions and seals) back to health before releasing them into the wild. Stop by and take a self-guided facility tour to learn more about these marine mammals and to visit the 'patients' out back.

parking per hr $1; ☻6am-10pm).

✗ 🛏 p523

The Drive » Keep driving south of downtown Laguna Beach on Hwy 1 (PCH) for about 3 miles to Aliso Beach County Park, then another 4 miles into the town of Dana Point. Turn right onto Green Lantern St, then left onto Cove Rd, which winds past the state beach and Ocean Institute onto Dana Point Harbor Dr.

- - - - - - - - - -

❽ Dana Point

Last up is marina-flanked Dana Point, the namesake of 19th-century adventurer Richard Dana, who famously called the area 'the only romantic spot on the coast.' These days it's more about family

fun and sportfishing boats at **Dana Point Harbor**. Designed for kids, the **Ocean Institute** (☎949-496-2274; www.ocean-institute.org; 24200 Dana Pt Harbor Dr; adult/child $6.50/4.50; ☻10am-3pm Sat & Sun; ♿) owns replicas of historic tall ships, maritime-related exhibits and a floating research lab. East of the harbor, **Doheny State Beach** (☎949-496-6172; 25300 Dana Point Harbor Dr; www.parks.ca.gov, www.dohenystatebeach.org; entry per car $15; ☻6am-10pm daily; ♿) is where you'll find picnic tables, volleyball courts, an oceanfront bike path and a sandy beach for swimming, surfing, tidepooling and scuba diving.

Eating & Sleeping

Disneyland ❶

🛏 Candy Cane Inn
Motel $$

(☎714-774-5284, 800-345-7057; www.candycaneinn.net; 1747 S Harbor Blvd, Anaheim; r $95-189; ❄🤖📶🍴) Bright bursts of flowers, tidy grounds and a cobblestone drive welcome guests to this cute motel within walking distance of Disneyland.

🛏 Disney's Grand Californian Hotel
Hotel $$$

(☎714-635-2300; www.disneyland.com; 1600 S Disneyland Dr, Anaheim; r from $360; ❄@📶🍴) Timber beams soar above the fireplace lobby of this six-story homage to the Golden State's Arts and Crafts architectural movement. Rooms have cushy amenities.

Huntington Beach ❸

🍴 Sugar Shack
Cafe $

(www.hbsugarshack.com; 213 Main St; mains $6-10; ⏰6am-2pm Mon-Tue, to 8pm Wed, to 6pm Thu-Fri, to 4pm Sat-Sun; 🍴) Expect a wait at this HB institution with a bustling outdoor patio, or get here early when surfer dudes don their wetsuits. Breakfast served all day.

🛏 Shorebreak Hotel
Boutique Hotel $$$

(☎714-861-4470; www.shorebreakhotel.com; 500 Pacific Coast Hwy; r $189-495; ❄@📶) This hip hotel livens things up with a surf concierge, yoga studio, beanbag chairs in the lobby and geometric-patterned rooms. Knock back sunset cocktails on the upstairs deck.

Newport Beach ❹

🍴 Bear Flag Fish Company
Seafood $$

(☎949-673-3434; http://newport.bearflagfishco.com; 407 31st St; dishes $8-15; ⏰11am-9pm Tue-Sat, to 8pm Mon & Sun; 🍴) Seafood market that's *the* place for spankin' fresh oysters, fish tacos, Hawaiian-style *poke*

and more. Pick what you want from the ice-cold display cases.

🛏 Bay Shores Peninsula Hotel
Hotel $$$

(☎949-675-3463, 800-222-6675; www.thebestinn.com; 1800 W Balboa Blvd; r incl breakfast $190-325; ❄@📶🍴) This three-story hotel's beachy hospitality, surf murals, fresh-baked cookies, and boogie boards and beach chairs to borrow make up for its steep rates.

Crystal Cove State Park ❻

🍴 Ruby's Shake Shack
Fast Food $

(www.rubys.com; 7703 E Coast Hwy; dishes $5-10; ⏰7am-7pm Mon-Sat; 📶🍴👶) At this easy-to-miss roadside wooden shack, now run by the Ruby's Diner chain, the milkshakes and ocean views are as good as ever.

🛏 Crystal Cove Beach Cottages
Cottage $$

(☎800-444-7275 reservations; www.crystalcovebeachcottages.com, www.reserveamerica.com; r with shared bath $45-130, cottages $165-250; 🍴) To snag these historic oceanfront cottages, book on the first day of the month seven months before your intended stay – or look online for last-minute cancellations.

Laguna Beach ❼

🍴 The Stand
Health Food $

(238 Thalia St; dishes $5-10; ⏰7am-7pm; 🍴🍴) Tiny barn-shaped kitchen with a wooden patio reflects what's best about Laguna living. A long vegan-friendly menu includes veggie tamales, sunflower-sprout salads and banana-date shakes.

🛏 Laguna Cliffs Inn
Hotel $$$

(☎949-497-6645, 800-297-0007; www.lagunacliffsinn.com; 475 N Coast Hwy; r $179-329; ❄📶📺) Be it feng shui, friendly staff, comfy beds or proximity to the beach, something just feels right at this 36-room inn. Hit the outdoor hot tub as the sun drops over the ocean.

Joshua Tree National Park *A wonderland of rocks and sandy Joshua tree forests*

Palm Springs & Joshua Tree Oases

42

Southern California's deserts can be brutally hot, barren places – escape to Palm Springs and Joshua Tree National Park, where shady fan-palm oases and date gardens await.

TRIP HIGHLIGHTS

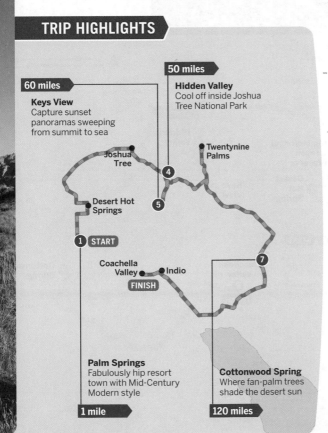

60 miles

Keys View
Capture sunset panoramas sweeping from summit to sea

50 miles

Hidden Valley
Cool off inside Joshua Tree National Park

Joshua Tree

Twentynine Palms

4

Desert Hot Springs

5

1 START

Coachella Valley ● **Indio**

FINISH

7

Palm Springs
Fabulously hip resort town with Mid-Century Modern style

1 mile

Cottonwood Spring
Where fan-palm trees shade the desert sun

120 miles

2–3 DAYS
185 MILES/300KM

GREAT FOR...

BEST TIME TO GO
February to April for wildflowers and cooler temperatures.

ESSENTIAL PHOTO
Sunset from Keys View.

BEST FOR SOLITUDE
Hike to the Lost Palms Oasis.

525

42 | Palm Springs & Joshua Tree Oases

Just a short drive from the chic resorts of Palm Springs, the vast Mojave and Sonoran Deserts are serenely spiritual places. You may find that what at first looked like desolate sands transform on foot into perfect beauty: shady palm tree and cactus gardens, tiny wildflowers pushing up from hard-baked soil in spring, natural hot-springs pools for soaking, and uncountable stars overhead in the inky dark.

TRIP HIGHLIGHT

❶ Palm Springs

Hollywood celebs have always counted on Palm Springs as a quick escape from LA. Today, this desert resort town shows off a trove of well-preserved Mid-Century Modern buildings. Stop at the **Palm Springs Visitor Center** (☏760-778-8418; www.visitpalmsprings.com; 2901 N Palm Canyon Dr, ⊗9am–5pm), inside a 1960s gas station by modernist Albert Frey, to pick up a self-guided

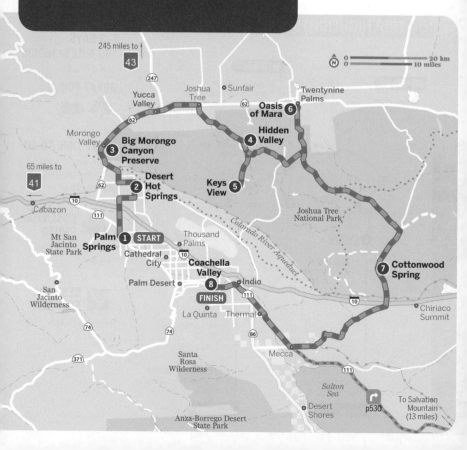

architectural tour map. Then drive uphill to clamber aboard the **Palm Springs Aerial Tramway** (📞888-515-8726; www. pstramway.com; 1 Tram Way; adult/child $24/17; ⏰10am-8pm Mon-Fri, 8am-8pm Sat & Sun, last tram down 9:45pm daily; 🚠), which climbs nearly 6000 vertical feet from the hot Sonoran Desert floor to the cool, even snowy San Jacinto Mountains in less than 15 minutes. Back down on the ground, drive south on Palm Canyon Dr, where you can hop between art galleries, cafes, cocktail bars and chic boutiques like fashionistas' find **Trina Turk** (www.trinaturk.com; 891 N Palm Canyon Dr; ⏰10am-5pm Mon-Fri, 10am-6pm Sat, 11am-5pm Sun).

LINK YOUR TRIP

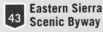

41 Disneyland & Orange County Beaches

Drive 110 miles west starting on I-10 to Disney's Magic Kingdom, then cruise the OC's bodacious beach towns.

43 Eastern Sierra Scenic Byway

Head northwest via I-10, I-15 and US 395 for 245 miles to Lone Pine, cinematically set beneath the majestic Sierra Nevada.

✕ 🛏 p531

The Drive ⟫ Drive north out of downtown Palm Springs along Indian Canyon Dr for 8 miles, passing over the I-10. Turn right onto Dillon Rd, then after 2.5 miles turn left onto Palm Dr, which heads north into central Desert Hot Springs.

❷ Desert Hot Springs

In 1774 Spanish explorer Juan Bautista de Anza was the first European to encounter the desert Cahuilla tribe. Afterward, the Spanish name Agua Caliente came to refer to both the indigenous people and the natural hot springs, which still flow restoratively today through the town of **Desert Hot Springs** (www.visitdeserthotsprings. com), where newly hip boutique hotels have appeared atop healing waters bubbling up from deep below. Imitate Tim Robbins in Robert Altman's film *The Player* and have a mud bath at **Two Bunch Palms Spa Resort** (📞800-472-4334; www.twobunchpalms.com; 67425 Two Bunch Palms Trail; ⏰by reservation only), which sits atop an actual oasis. Bounce between a variety of pools and sunbathing areas (including clothing-optional), but maintain the code of silence.

🛏 p531

The Drive ⟫ Head west on Pierson Blvd back to Indian Canyon Dr. Turn right and

drive northwest through the dusty outskirts of Desert Hot Springs. Turn right onto Hwy 62 eastbound toward Yucca Valley; after about 4 miles, turn right onto East Dr and look for signs for Big Morongo Canyon Preserve.

❸ Big Morongo Canyon Preserve

Another oasis hidden in the high desert, **Big Morongo Canyon Preserve** (📞760-363-7190; www.bigmorongo. org; admission by donation; 11055 East Dr, Yucca Valley; ⏰7:30am-sunset) is a bird-watching hotspot. Tucked into the Little San Bernardino Mountains, this stream-fed riparian habitat is flush with cottonwood and willow trees. Start from the educational kiosk by the parking lot, then tramp along wooden boardwalks through marshy woodlands as hummingbirds flutter atop flowers and woodpeckers hammer away.

The Drive ⟫ Rejoin Hwy 62 eastbound past Yucca Valley (p531), with its roadside antiques and vintage shops, art galleries and cafes, to the town of Joshua Tree 16 miles away, where you'll find places to sleep and eat (p531). At the intersection with Park Blvd, turn right and drive 5 miles to Joshua Tree National Park's west entrance. Make sure you've got a full tank of gas first.

❹ Hidden Valley

It's time to jump into **Joshua Tree National Park** (📞760-367-5500; www.nps.gov/jotr; 7-day entry permit per car $15; ⏲24hr; 🚻), a wonderland of jumbo rocks interspersed with sandy forests of Joshua trees. Related to agave plants, Joshua trees were named by Mormon settlers who thought the twisted, spiky arms resembled a prophet's arms stretching toward God. Revel in the scenery as you drive along the winding park

road for about 7 miles to Hidden Valley picnic area. Turn left and drive past the campground to the trailhead for **Barker Dam**. Here a kid-friendly nature trail loops for a mile past a pretty little artificial lake and a rock incised with Native American petroglyphs. If you enjoy history and Western lore, reserve ahead for a 90-minute guided walking tour of nearby **Keys Ranch** (📞760-367-5555; adult/child $5/2.50; ⏲usually 10am & 1pm Sep-May), where 19th-century pioneer homesteaders tried their hand at cattle ranching,

mining and desert farming.

🛏 p531

The Drive » Backtrack to Park Blvd, turn left and head south again past jumbled rock formations and fields of spiky Joshua trees. Take the well-signed right turn toward Keys View. You'll pass several trailheads and roadside interpretive exhibits over the next 5.5 miles leading up to the viewpoint.

❺ Keys View

Leave Hidden Valley at least an hour before sunset for the drive up to **Keys View**, where

Cottonwood Spring

panoramic views look into the Coachella Valley and reach as far south as the shimmering Salton Sea or, on an unusually clear day, Mexico's Mt Signal. Looming in front of you are Mt San Jacinto and Mt San Gorgonio, two of Southern California's highest peaks, often snow-dusted even in spring. Down below snakes the shaky San Andreas Fault.

The Drive » Head back downhill to Park Blvd. Turn right and wind through the park's Wonderland of Rocks, where boulders call out to scampering kids and serious rock jocks alike, passing more campgrounds.

After 10 miles, veer left to stay on Park Blvd and drive north for 7 miles toward the town of Twentynine Palms onto Utah Trail.

- - - - - - - - - - -

6 Oasis of Mara

Detour to the National Park Service (NPS) **Oasis Visitor Center** (www.nps. gov/jotr; 74485 National Park Dr, Twentynine Palms; ☺8am-5pm; ⑆) for its educational exhibits about Southern California's desert fan palms. These palms are often found growing along fault lines, where cracks in the earth's crust allow subterranean water to surface. Outside

the visitor center, a gentle half-mile nature trail leads around the **Oasis of Mara**, where Serrano tribespeoples once camped. Ask for directions to the trailhead off Hwy 62 for the 3-mile round-trip hike to **49 Palms Oasis**, where a sun-exposed dirt trail marches you over a ridge, then drops you into a rocky gorge, doggedly heading down past barrel cacti toward a distant speck of green.

🛏 p531

The Drive » Drive back south on Utah Trail and re-enter the park. Follow Park Blvd south,

DETOUR: SALTON SEA

Start ❼ : Cottonwood Spring

Driving along Hwy 111 southeast of Indio, it's a most unexpected sight: California's largest lake in the middle of its largest desert. In 1905 the Colorado River breached, giving birth to the Salton Sea. Marketed to mid-20th-century tourists as the 'California Riviera' with beachfront vacation homes, the Salton Sea has been mostly abandoned because of the stinky annual fish die-offs caused by chemical runoff from surrounding farmland. An even stranger sight is folk-art **Salvation Mountain** (www.salvationmountain.us), an artificial hill covered in acrylic paint and found objects and inscribed with Christian religious messages. It's in Niland, about 3 miles east of Hwy 111.

turning left at the first major junction onto Pinto Basin Rd for a winding 30-mile drive downhill to Cottonwood Spring.

TRIP HIGHLIGHT

❼ Cottonwood Spring

On your drive south to Cottonwood Spring, you'll pass from the high Mojave Desert into the lower Sonoran Desert. At the **Cholla Cactus Garden**, handily labeled specimens burst into bloom in spring, including unmistakable ocotillo plants, which look like green octopus tentacles adorned with flaming scarlet flowers. Turn left at the **Cottonwood Visitor Center** (www.nps.gov/jotr; off Cottonwood Springs Rd; ☺9am-4pm Mon-Fri, from 8am Sat & Sun) for a short drive east past the campground to **Cottonwood Spring**. Once used by the Cahuilla, who left behind archaeological evidence such as mortars and clay pots, the springs became a hotbed for gold mining in the late 19th century. The now-dry springs are the start of the moderately strenuous 7.2-mile round-trip trek out to **Lost Palms Oasis**, a fan-palm oasis blessed with solitude and scenery.

🛏 p531

The Drive » Head south from Cottonwood Springs and drive across the I-10 Fwy to pick up scenic Box Canyon Rd, which burrows a hole through the desert, twisting its way toward the Salton Sea. Take 66th Ave west to Mecca, then turn right onto Hwy 111 and drive northwest ('up valley') toward Indio.

------

❽ Coachella Valley

The hot but fertile Coachella Valley is the ideal place to find the date of your dreams – the kind that grows on trees, that is. Date farms let you sample exotic-sounding varieties like halawy, deglet noor and golden zahidi for free, but the signature taste of the valley is a rich date shake from certified-organic **Oasis Date Gardens** (www.oasisdate.com; 59-111 Grapefruit Blvd, Thermal; ☺9am-4pm) or the 1920s pioneer **Shields Date Garden** (www.shieldsdategarden.com; 80-225 Hwy 111, Indio; ☺9am-5pm).

Eating & Sleeping

Palm Springs ❶

✖ Cheeky's   Californian $$
(http://cheekysps.com; 622 N Palm Canyon Dr; mains $7-14; ☺8am-2pm Wed-Mon) Waits can be long, but this cafe's farm-to-table menu dazzles with witty inventiveness. Dishes change weekly, with chilaquile towers and bacon bar 'flights' making regular appearances.

✖ Sherman's   Deli, Bakery $$
(www.shermansdeli.com; 401 E Tahquitz Canyon Way; mains $8-18; ☺7am-9pm; 🖷) With a breezy sidewalk patio and Hollywood celebrity headshots hanging on the walls, this 1950s Jewish deli feeds an all-ages crowd on mile-high sandwich boards and homemade pies.

🛏 Horizon Hotel   Boutique Hotel $$
(☎760-323-1858, 800-377-7855; www. thehorizonhotel.com; 1050 E Palm Canyon Dr; r $129-295; ❄🐾🔁🛁) Designed by modernist architect William F Cody, this intimate retreat had Marilyn Monroe and Betty Grable lounging poolside back in the day. Adults only.

🛏 Parker Palm Springs   Resort $$$
(☎760-770-5000; www.theparkerpalmsprings. com; 4200 E Palm Canyon Dr; r from $249; ❄🔁🐾🛁) Once the star of a Bravo reality TV series, this posh full-service resort boasts whimsical decor by Jonathan Adler. Drop by the luxe spa or for cocktails at Mister Parker's steakhouse.

Desert Hot Springs ❷

🛏 El Morocco Inn & Spa   Boutique Hotel $$
(☎760-288-2527, 888-288-9905; www. elmoroccoinn.com; 66814 4th St; r incl breakfast $179-219; ❄🔁🐾) Heed the call of the kasbah in a drop-dead spa hideaway with 10 fantastically furnished rooms. Sip cocktails or homemade mint ice tea in the garden.

🛏 The Spring   Boutique Hotel $$
(☎760-251-6700; www.the-spring.com; 12699 Reposo Way; r incl breakfast $149-229; ❄🔁🐾) This 1950s motel has morphed into a chic, whisper-quiet spa retreat with natural hot-springs pools. The 10 blissful rooms are minimalist in design but not in amenities.

Yucca Valley

✖ Ma Rouge Coffee House   Cafe $
(www.marouge.net; 55844 Hwy 62; dishes $5-10; ☺7am-6pm; 🔁) At the corner of Pioneertown Rd, this locals' stop pours organic coffee and dishes up quiche, pastries, sandwiches and salads.

Joshua Tree

🛏 Hicksville Trailer Palace   Motel $$
(☎310-584-1086; www.hicksville.com; d $125-250; ❄🔁🐾) Eight outlandishly decorated vintage trailers are parked around a saltwater swimming pool. All but two share bathrooms. Reservations required; address given out only to guests.

🛏 Spin & Margie's Desert Hide-a-way   Inn $$
(☎760-366-9124; www.deserthideaway.com; ste $135-175; ❄🔁) This inn's five boldly colored suites are an eccentric symphony of corrugated tin, old license plates and cartoon art. Each has a kitchenette or kitchen. Reservations required.

Joshua Tree National Park ❹❻❼

🛏 NPS Campgrounds   Campground $
(☎877-444-6777 reservations; www.nps.gov/ jotr, www.recreation.gov; Joshua Tree National Park; campsites $10-15; 🖷🐾) Pitch a tent near Joshua Tree's jumbo rocks or in shady canyons at several designated campgrounds along the park's main roads. Most campgrounds don't accept reservations and sites fill up before noon on busy weekends during spring and fall.

Bodie State Historic Park *Time warp back to the Gold Rush era*

Eastern Sierra Scenic Byway

43

A straight shot north along California's arched geological backbone, Hwy 395 dazzles with high-altitude vistas, crumbling Old West ghost towns and limitless recreational distractions.

TRIP HIGHLIGHTS

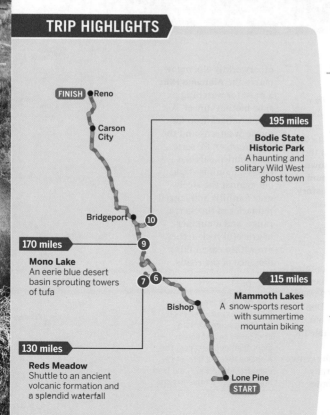

FINISH ● Reno

● Carson City

Bridgeport ● **10**

9

170 miles

Mono Lake
An eerie blue desert basin sprouting towers of tufa

7 **6**

Bishop ●

130 miles

Reds Meadow
Shuttle to an ancient volcanic formation and a splendid waterfall

195 miles

Bodie State Historic Park
A haunting and solitary Wild West ghost town

115 miles

Mammoth Lakes
A snow-sports resort with summertime mountain biking

● Lone Pine
START

3–5 DAYS
360 MILES/580KM

GREAT FOR...

BEST TIME TO GO

June to September for warm days and (mostly) snow-free mountain ramblings.

 ESSENTIAL PHOTO

Sunrise or sunset at Alabama Hills, framed by the snowy Sierra Nevada.

 BEST FOR OUTDOORS

Hike tranquil mountain trails and camp in Mammoth Lakes.

43 Eastern Sierra Scenic Byway

The gateway to California's largest expanse of wilderness, Hwy 395 – also called the Eastern Sierra Scenic Byway – borders towering mountain vistas, glistening blue lakes and the seemingly endless forests of the Eastern Sierra. A lifetime of outdoor activities beckon beyond the asphalt, and desolate ghost towns, unique geological formations and burbling natural hot springs await exploration.

1 Lone Pine

The diminutive town of Lone Pine stands as the southern gateway to the craggy jewels of the Eastern Sierra. In the southern end of town, drop by the **Museum of Lone Pine Film History** (☎760-876-9909; www.lonepinefilmhistorymuseum.org; 701 S Main St; adult/child $5/free; ⊗10am-6pm Mon-Wed, to 7pm Thu-Sat, to 4pm Sun), which contains exhibits of paraphernalia from the over 450 movies shot in the area. Don't miss the tricked-out Cadillac convertible in its foyer.

Just outside the center of town on Whitney Portal Rd, an orange otherworldly alpenglow makes the **Alabama Hills** a must for watching a slow-motion sunset. A frequent backdrop for movie Westerns and the *Lone Ranger* TV series, the rounded earthen-colored mounds stand out against the steely gray foothills and jagged pinnacles of the Sierra range, and a number of graceful rock arches are within easy hiking distance of the roads.

✕ p541

The Drive » From Lone Pine, the jagged incisors of the Sierra surge skyward in all their raw and fierce glory. Continue west past the Alabama Hills – a total of 13 miles from Hwy 395 – and then brace yourself for the dizzying

ascent to road's end. The White Mountains soar to the east, and the dramatic Owens Valley spreads below.

---

② Whitney Portal

At 14,505ft, the celestial granite giant of **Mt Whitney** (www.fs.usda.gov/inyo) stands as the loftiest peak in the Lower 48 and the obsession of thousands of high-country hikers every summer. Desperately coveted permits (assigned by advance lottery) are your only passport to the summit, though drop-in day-trippers can swan up the mountain as far as Lone Pine Lake – under 6 miles round-trip – to kick up some dust on the iconic Whitney Trail. Near the trailhead,

LINK YOUR TRIP

40 **Yosemite, Sequoia & Kings Canyon National Parks**

In Lee Vining, go west on Hwy 120 to enter Yosemite National Park via the 9945ft Tioga Pass.

42 **Palm Springs & Joshua Tree Oases**

From Lone Pine, it's a 245-mile drive southeast via Hwy 395, I-15 and I-10 to SoCal's desert playground.

stop by the cafe at the **Whitney Portal Store** (www.whitneyportalstore.com) for enormous burgers and plate-sized pancakes fit for ravenous hikers.

As you get a fix on this majestic megalith cradled by scores of smaller pinnacles, remember that the country's lowest point is only 80 miles (as the crow flies) east of here: Badwater in Death Valley.

The Drive › Double back to Lone Pine and drive 9 miles north on divided Hwy 395. Scrub brush and tumbleweed desert occupy the valley between the copper-colored foothills of the Sierra Nevada and the White Mountain range. Well-signed Manzanar sits along the west side of the highway.

- - - - - - - - - -

❸ Manzanar National Historic Site

A monument to one of the darkest chapters in US history, Manzanar unfolds across a barren and windy sweep of land cradled by snow-dipped peaks. During the height of WWII, the federal government interned more than 10,000 people of Japanese ancestry here following the attack on Pearl Harbor. Though little remains of the infamous war internment camp, the camp's former high-school auditorium houses a superb **interpretive center** (☎760-878-2194; www.nps.gov/manz; admission

free; ⊙9am-4:30pm daily). Watch the 22-minute documentary, then explore the thought-provoking exhibits chronicling the stories of the families that languished here yet built a vibrant community. Afterwards, take a self-guided, 3.2-mile driving tour around the grounds, which includes a recreated mess hall and barracks, vestiges of buildings and gardens, as well as the haunting camp cemetery.

Often mistaken for Mt Whitney, 14,375ft Mt Williamson looms above this flat, dusty plain, a lonely expanse that bursts with yellow wildflowers in spring.

The Drive › Continue north 6 miles on Hwy 395 to the small town of Independence. In the center of town, look for the columned Inyo County Courthouse and turn left onto W Center St. Drive six blocks through a residential area to the end of the road.

- - - - - - - - - -

❹ Independence

This sleepy highway town has been a county seat since 1866 and is home to the **Eastern California Museum** (☎760-878-0364;www.inyocounty.us/ecmsite; 155 N Grant St; donation requested; ⊙10am-5pm). An excellent archive of Eastern Sierra history and culture, it contains one of the most complete collections of Paiute and Shoshone

baskets in the country, as well as historic photographs of local rock climbers scaling Sierra peaks – including Mt Whitney – with huge packs and no harnesses. Other highlights include artifacts from Manzanar and an exhibit about the fight to keep the region's water supply from being diverted to Los Angeles.

Fans of Mary Austin (1868–1934), renowned author of *The Land of Little Rain* and vocal foe of the desertification of the Owens Valley, can follow signs leading east to her former house at **253 Market St**.

The Drive › Depart north along Hwy 395 as civilization again recedes amid a buffer of dreamy granite mountains, midsized foothills and (most of the year) an expanse of bright blue sky. Tuffs of blackened volcanic rock occasionally appear roadside. Pass through the blink-and-you-missed-it town of Big Pine, and enter Bishop approximately 40 miles from your starting point.

- - - - - - - - - -

❺ Bishop

The second-largest town in the Eastern Sierra and about a quarter of the way north from Lone Pine to Reno, Bishop is a major hub for hikers, cyclists, anglers and climbers. To see what draws them here, visit the **Mountain Light Gallery** (☎760-873-7700; http://mountainlight.com; 106 S Main St; admission free; ⊙10am-5pm Mon-Sat,

Mammoth Lakes Woman in hot springs

11am-4pm Sun), featuring the stunning outdoor photography of the late Galen Rowell, whose High Sierra images are some of the best in existence.

Where Hwy 395 swings west, continue northeast for 4.5 miles on Hwy 6 to reach the **Laws Railroad Museum & Historic Site** (760-873-5950; www. lawsmuseum.org; Silver Canyon Rd, Laws; donation $5; 10am-4pm;), a remnant of the narrow-gauge Carson and Colorado rail line that closed in 1960. Train buffs will hyperventilate over the collection of antique railcars, and kids love exploring the

1883 depot and clanging the brass bell. Dozens of historic buildings from the region are reassembled with period artifacts to create a time-capsule village.

The Drive » Back on Hwy 395, continue 38 miles north to Hwy 203, passing Crowley Lake and the southern reaches of the Long Valley Caldera seismic zone. On Hwy 203 before the center of town, stop in at the Mammoth Lakes Welcome Center for excellent local and regional information.

- - - - - - - - - - - -

TRIP HIGHLIGHT

6 Mammoth Lakes

Splendidly situated at a breathless 8000ft,

Mammoth Lakes is an active year-round outdoor-recreation town buffered by alpine wilderness and punctuated by its signature 11,053ft peak, **Mammoth Mountain** (800-626-6684; www. mammothmountain.com; winter lift ticket adult $99, child 7-12yr $30, child 13-18yr $77, 1-day bike pass adult/child 7-12yr $42/22;). This ever-burgeoning resort complex has 3100 vertical feet – enough to whet any snow-sports appetite – and an enviably long season that often lasts from November to June.

When the snow finally melts, the ski and snowboard resort does a quick costume change and becomes the massive Mammoth Mountain Bike Park, and with a slew of mountain-bikers decked out in body armor, it could be mistaken for a movie set of an apocalyptic *Mad Max* sequel. With more than 80 miles of well-tended single-track trails and a crazy terrain park, it draws those who know their knobby tires.

Open in winter and summer, a vertiginous **gondola** (adult/child 7-12yr $21/16) whisks sightseers to the apex for breathless views of snow-speckled mountaintops.

📖 p541

The Drive » Keep the car parked at Mammoth Mountain and catch the mandatory Reds Meadow shuttle bus from the Gondola Building. However, you may want to drive up 1.5 miles west on Hwy 203 as far as Minaret Vista to contemplate eye-popping views of the Ritter Range, the serrated Minarets and the remote reaches of Yosemite National Park.

- - - - - - - - - - - - -

TRIP HIGHLIGHT

⑦ Reds Meadow

One of the most beautiful and varied landscapes near Mammoth is the Reds Meadow Valley, west of Mammoth Mountain. The most fascinating attraction in Reds Meadow is the surreal 10,000-year-old volcanic formation of **Devils Postpile National Monument**. The 60ft curtains of near-vertical basalt columns formed when rivers of molten lava slowed, cooled and cracked with perplexing symmetry. This honeycomb design is best appreciated from atop the columns, reached by a short trail. The columns are an easy, half-mile hike from the **Devils Postpile Ranger Station** (☎760-934-2289; www.nps.gov/depo; ⏰9am-5pm mid-Jun–Oct).

From the monument, a 2.5-mile hike passing through fire-scarred forest leads to the spectacular **Rainbow Falls**, where the San Joaquin River gushes over a 101ft basalt cliff. Chances of actually seeing a rainbow forming in the billowing mist are greatest at midday. The falls can also be reached via an easy 1.5-mile walk from the Reds Meadow shuttle stop.

The Drive » Back on Hwy 395, continue north to Hwy 158

DETOUR:
ANCIENT BRISTLECONE PINE FOREST

Start: ④ Independence

For encounters with some of the earth's oldest living things, plan at least a half-day trip to the Ancient Bristlecone Pine Forest. These gnarled, otherworldly looking trees thrive above 10,000ft on the slopes of the seemingly inhospitable White Mountains, a parched and stark range that once stood even higher than the Sierra. The oldest tree – called Methuselah – is estimated to be over 4700 years old, beating even the Great Sphinx of Giza by about two centuries.

To reach the groves, take Hwy 168 east 13 miles from Big Pine to White Mountain Rd, then turn left (north) and climb the curvy road 10 miles to **Schulman Grove**, named for the scientist who first discovered the trees' biblical age in the 1950s. The entire trip takes about one hour one-way from Independence. There's access to self-guided trails, and a new solar-powered **visitors center** (☎760-873-2500; www.fs.usda. gov/inyo; per vehicle $6; ⏰usually 10am-5pm mid-May–Oct). White Mountain Rd is usually closed from sometime in November through mid-May.

and pull out the camera for the alpine lake and peak vistas of the June Lake Loop.

---

8 June Lake Loop

Under the shadow of massive Carson Peak (10,909ft), the stunning 16-mile June Lake Loop (Hwy 158) meanders through a picture-perfect horseshoe canyon, past the relaxed resort town of June Lake and four sparkling, fish-rich lakes: Grant, Silver, Gull and June. It's especially scenic in fall when the basin is ablaze with golden aspens, and hardy ice climbers scale its frozen waterfalls in winter.

June Lake is backed by the Ansel Adams Wilderness, which runs into Yosemite National Park. From Silver Lake, Gem and Agnew Lakes make spectacular day hikes, and boat rentals and horseback rides are available.

The Drive ❯❯ Rejoin Hwy 395 heading north, where the rounded Mono Craters dot the dry and scrubby eastern landscape and the Mono Lake Basin unfolds into view.

TRIP HIGHLIGHT

9 Mono Lake

North America's second-oldest lake is a quiet and mysterious expanse of deep blue water, whose glassy surface reflects jagged Sierra peaks, young volcanic cones and the unearthly tufa

HOT SPRINGS

Nestled between the White Mountains and the Sierra Nevada near Mammoth Lakes is a tantalizing slew of natural pools with snow-capped panoramic views. When the high-altitude summer nights turn chilly and the coyotes cry, you'll never want to towel off. About 9 miles southeast of town, Benton Crossing Rd juts east off Hwy 395, accessing a delicious bounty of hot springs. For detailed directions and maps, pick up Matt Bischoff's excellent *Touring California & Nevada Hot Springs* or see www.mammothweb.com/recreation/hottubbing.cfm for directions to a few.

(*too*-fah) towers that make the lake so distinctive. Protruding from the water like drip sand castles, tufas form when calcium bubbles up from subterranean springs and combines with carbonate in the alkaline lake waters.

The salinity and alkaline levels are unfortunately too high for a pleasant swim. Instead, paddle a kayak or canoe around the weathered towers of tufa, drink in wide-open views of the Mono Craters volcanic field, and discreetly spy on the ospreys and water birds that live in this unique habitat.

For area information, the **Mono Basin Scenic Area Visitors Center** (📞760-647-3044; www.fs.usda.gov/inyo; Hwy 395, 🕙8am-5pm Apr–Nov), a half a mile north of Lee Vining, has interpretive displays, a bookstore and

a 20-minute movie about Mono Lake.

🍽 🛏 p541

The Drive ❯❯ Ten miles north of Lee Vining, Hwy 395 arrives at its highest point, Conway Summit (8148ft). Pull off at the vista point for awe-inspiring panoramas of Mono Lake, backed by the Mono Craters and June and Mammoth Mountains. Continue approximately 8 miles north, and go 13 miles east on high desert Hwy 270; the last 3 miles are unpaved.

TRIP HIGHLIGHT

10 Bodie State Historic Park

For a time warp back to the Gold Rush era, swing by **Bodie** (📞760-647-6445; www.parks.ca.gov/bodie; Hwy 270; adult/child $7/5; 🕙9am-6pm mid-May–Oct, to 3pm Nov–mid-May), one of the West's most authentic and best-preserved ghost towns. Gold was discovered here in 1859, and the place grew from a bare-bones mining camp to a lawless

DETOUR:
VIRGINIA CITY

Start: ⑩ Bodie State Historic Park

During the 1860s gold rush, Virginia City was a high-flying, rip-roaring Wild West boomtown. It was the site of the legendary Comstock Lode, a massive silver bonanza that began in 1859 and stands as one of the world's richest strikes. Some of the silver barons went on to become major players in California history, and much of San Francisco was built with the treasure dug up from the soil beneath the town. Mark Twain spent time in this raucous place during its heyday, and his eyewitness descriptions of mining life were published in *Roughing It*.

The high-elevation town is a National Historic Landmark, with a main street of Victorian buildings, wooden sidewalks, wacky saloons and small museums ranging from hokey to intriguing. On the main drag, C street, you'll find the **visitors center** (📞800-718-7587; www.visitvirginiacitynv.com; 86 South C St; ⏰9am-5pm). To see how the mining elite lived, stop by the **Mackay Mansion** (129 D St) and the **Castle** (cnr Taylor & B Sts).

From Carson City, go east on Hwy 50, and then another 7 miles via Hwy 341 and Hwy 342. Continuing on to Reno, wind through a spectacular 13 miles of high desert along Hwy 341 to rejoin Hwy 395, with another 7 miles to reach Reno.

boomtown of 10,000. Fights and murders occurred almost daily, fueled by liquor from 65 saloons, some of which doubled as brothels, gambling halls or opium dens.

The hills disgorged some $35 million worth of gold and silver in the 1870s and '80s, but when production plummeted, Bodie was abandoned, and about 200 weather-beaten buildings now sit frozen in time in this cold, barren and windswept valley. Peering through dusty windows you'll see stocked stores, furnished homes, a schoolhouse with desks and books, the jail and many other buildings. The former Miners' Union Hall now houses a **museum** and **visitors center** (⏰seasonal hr vary), and rangers conduct free general tours.

The Drive » Retrace your way back to Hwy 395, where you'll soon come to the big sky settlement of Bridgeport. From there, it's over two hours to Reno along a lovely two-lane section of the highway that traces the bank of the snaking Walker River.

- - - - - - - - - - -

⑪ Reno

Nevada's second-largest city has steadily carved a noncasino niche as an all-season outdoor-recreation spot. The Truckee River bisects the heart of the high mountain-ringed city, and in the heat of summer, the **Truckee River Whitewater Park** teems with urban kayakers and swimmers bobbing along on inner tubes. Two kayak courses wrap around Wingfield Park, a small river island that hosts free concerts in summertime. **Tahoe Whitewater Tours** (📞775-787-5000; www.gowhitewater.com) and **Sierra Adventures** (📞866-323-8928; www.wildsierra.com) offer kayak trips and tube rentals.

🍴 🛏 p541

Eating & Sleeping

Lone Pine ❶

✗ Alabama Hills Café & Bakery   Diner $

(111 W Post St; mains $8-12; ☺6am-2pm Mon-Thu, 7am-2pm Fri-Sun; ✈) Swing by early in the morning to line up for lumberjack-sized breakfasts (think eggs with corned-beef hash, or whole-grain pancakes), then grab a deli sandwich stacked on home-baked bread for a trailside lunch or linger for the hearty soups and scratch-made fruit pies.

Mammoth Lakes ❻

🛏 Tamarack Lodge & Resort   Resort $$

(☎760-934-2442, 800-626-6684; www.tamaracklodge.com; lodge r $99-149, cabins $169-419; @ 🛜🐾) A charming year-round hideaway on the forested shore of Lower Twin Lake, this 1924 lodge building sports a dozen cozy homespun rooms with creaky floors, and the wood-beamed lobby is a spiffy setting for a nighttime book by the fireplace. Privacy-seekers can choose between cabins ranging from the very simple to simply deluxe.

🛏 USFS campgrounds   Campground $

(☎877-444-6777; www.recreation.gov; tent & RV sites $20-21; ☺Jun-Sep; 🐾) Sleep under the twinkling stars at one of the dozen or so 15 US Forest Service (USFS) campgrounds (see 'Recreation' at www.fs.usda.gov/inyo) scattered in and around Mammoth Lakes. Many sites are available on a first-come, first-served basis, and some are reservable; all have flush toilets but no showers.

Mono Lake ❾

✗ Whoa Nellie Deli   Deli $$

(www.whoanelliedeli.com; Tioga Gas Mart, 22 Vista Point Rd, Lee Vining; mains $7-20; ☺7am-9pm late Apr–early-Nov) Great food in a gas station? Come on... No, really, you gotta try this amazing kitchen where chef Matt 'Tioga' Toomey feeds delicious fish tacos, wild-buffalo meatloaf and other tasty morsels to locals and clued-in passersby. Portions are huge and the views from the outdoor patio are as great as the food.

🛏 Yosemite Gateway Motel   Motel $$

(☎760-647-6467; www.yosemitegatewaymotel.com; 51340 Hwy 395, Lee Vining; r $129-199; 🛜) Think vistas. This is the only motel on the east side of the highway, and the views from some of the rooms are phenomenal.

Reno ⓫

✗ Silver Peak
Restaurant & Brewery   Pub $$

(www.silverpeakbrewery.com; 124 Wonder St; mains lunch $9-11, dinner $10-22; ☺11am-midnight) Casual and pretense-free, this place hums with the chatter of happy locals settling in for a night of microbrews and great food, from pizza with roasted chicken to shrimp pasta and filet mignon.

🛏 Peppermill   Casino Hotel $$

(☎775-826-2121; www.peppermillreno.com; 2707 S Virginia St; r $59-199; ❄ @ 🛜🐾) Awash in Vegas-style opulence, the popular Peppermill boasts Tuscan-themed rooms in its newest 600-room tower, and has also recently completed a plush remodel of its older rooms. The three sparkling pools (one indoor) are dreamy, with a full spa on hand. Geothermal energy powers the resort's hot water and heat.

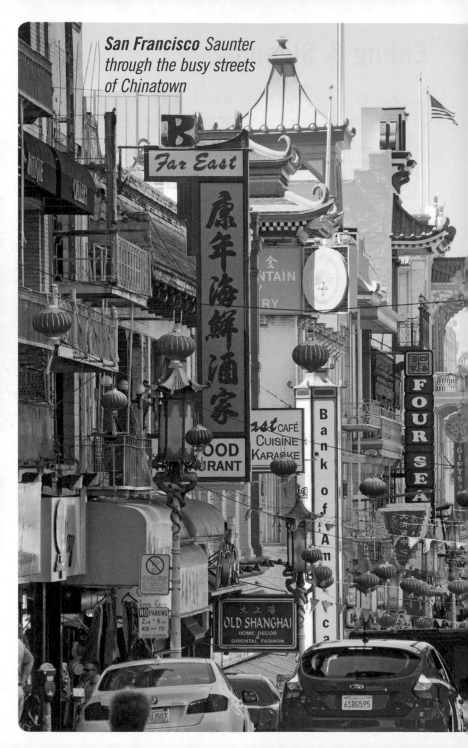

San Francisco Saunter through the busy streets of Chinatown

San Francisco, Marin & Napa Loop

44

Loop your way around the Bay Area, drinking in the sights of hilly San Francisco, the stunning wild vistas of Marin and the world-renowned wineries of Napa Valley and Sonoma County.

TRIP HIGHLIGHTS

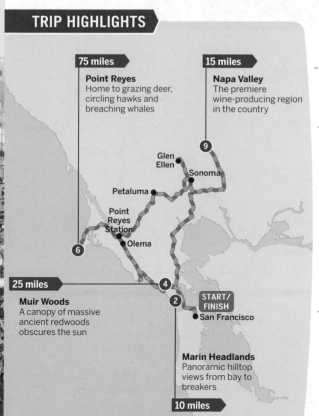

75 miles

Point Reyes
Home to grazing deer, circling hawks and breaching whales

15 miles

Napa Valley
The premiere wine-producing region in the country

Glen Ellen

Sonoma

⑨

Petaluma

Point Reyes Station

Olema

⑥

25 miles

Muir Woods
A canopy of massive ancient redwoods obscures the sun

④

②

START/ FINISH
San Francisco

Marin Headlands
Panoramic hilltop views from bay to breakers

10 miles

4–5 DAYS
240 MILES/385KM

GREAT FOR...

BEST TIME TO GO
April to October for dry and warmer days.

 ESSENTIAL PHOTO

Views of Alcatraz, the Pacific Ocean, the Golden Gate Bridge and shimmering San Francisco unfold from Conzelman Rd.

 BEST BIG TREES

Feel small under the rocketing redwoods of Muir Woods.

543

44 San Francisco, Marin & Napa Loop

Begin by exploring the heady sights of cosmopolitan San Francisco before crossing north on the windswept passageway of the Golden Gate Bridge. From here, the scenery turns untamed, and Marin County's undulating hills, redwood forest and crashing coastline prove a welcome respite from urban living. Continue north to Napa and Sonoma Valleys, basking in the warmer temperatures and tasting some of the best wines in the state.

❶ San Francisco

In two action-packed days, explore Golden Gate Park, spy on lolling sea lions at Fisherman's Wharf and saunter through the busy streets of Chinatown to the Italian sidewalk cafes in North Beach. Feast on an overstuffed burrito in the Mission District and then wander its mural-splashed alleys.

Queue up at Powell and Market Sts for a ride on a bell-clanging **cable car** (www.sfmta.com; ride $6), and then cruise to the

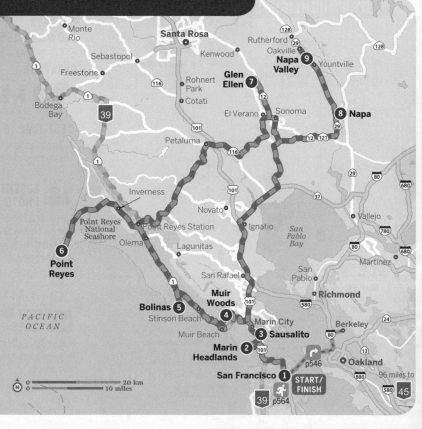

infamous prison island of **Alcatraz** (📞415-981-7625; www.alcatrazcruises.com, www.nps.gov/alcatraz; adult/child day $30/18, night $37/22; 🕑call center 8am-7pm, ferries depart Pier 33 every 30min 8:45am-3:50pm, plus 5:55pm & 6:30pm). In summer, book Alcatraz tickets online at least two weeks ahead.

At the foot of Market St, indulge your inner epicure at the **Ferry Building** (www.ferrybuildingmarketplace.com; Embarcadero; 🕑10am-6pm Mon-Fri, 9am-6pm Sat, 11am-5pm Sun) food stalls, and stop by its farmers market on Tuesday, Thursday and Saturday mornings year-round to wallow in the bounty of California-grown organic

produce and gourmet prepared foods.

At the historic **Castro Theatre** (📞415-621-6120; www.castrotheatre.com; 429 Castro St; adult/child $11/8.50), the crowd goes wild when the giant organ rises from the floor and pumps out show tunes until the movie starts, and the sumptuous chandeliered decor complements a repertory of silver-screen classics.

If you have extra time to cavort about town, see p564 for more ideas.

 p550

The Drive » Aim north over the turret-topped Golden Gate Bridge, pausing to stroll around the Marin-side Vista Point area. Exit at Alexander Ave and bear left before swinging back under the highway to ascend the bayview ridgeline of Conzelman Rd. It's 2 miles to Hawk Hill, located just before the road becomes one-way.

TRIP HIGHLIGHT

❷ Marin Headlands

Near echoey WWII battery tunnels, bird-watchers should make a mandatory stop to hike up **Hawk Hill**. Thousands of migrating birds of prey soar here from late summer to early fall, straddling a windy ridge with views of Rodeo Lagoon all the way to Alcatraz.

Stay west on Conzelman Rd until it ends in about 2 miles and then bear left

towards the bay. The third lighthouse built on the West Coast, **Point Bonita Lighthouse** (www.nps.gov/goga/pobo.htm; 🕑12:30-3:30pm Sat-Mon) was completed in 1855, but after complaints about its performance in fog, it was scooted down to the promontory about 20 years later. Three afternoons a week you can cross through a dark rock tunnel – carved out with hand tools only – and traverse a steep half-mile trail to inspect the lighthouse beacon. A bouncy suspension bridge delivers you to the Fresnel lens tower, and harbor seals sun themselves on the rocks below.

The Drive » Continue north along the oceanview bluffs of Field Rd, joining eastbound Bunker Rd (signed San Francisco) after passing the Marin Headlands Visitor Center. Pass through the timed one-way tunnel and turn left onto Alexander Ave towards Sausalito.

❸ Sausalito

Perfectly arranged on a secure little harbor on the bay, Sausalito's pretty houses tumble neatly down a green hillside into a well-heeled downtown, and much of the town affords uninterrupted views of San Francisco and Angel Island.

Just under the north tower of the Golden

LINK YOUR TRIP

39 Pacific Coast Highways

Marin County covers just a small stretch of scenic Hwy 1 along the California coast – there's so much more, both north and south.

45 Highway 49 Through Gold Country

Drive 60 miles northeast of Napa mostly via I-80 to Sacramento, the Golden State's historic capital.

Gate Bridge, at East Fort Baker, families should stop by the **Bay Area Discovery Museum** (www. baykidsmuseum.org; 557 McReynolds Rd; admission $11; ⊘9am-5pm Tue-Sun; 👶), an excellent hands-on activity museum specifically designed for children. Exhibits include a wave workshop, a small underwater tunnel and a large outdoor play area.

 p550

The Drive » Follow Hwy 101 north to Hwy 1, passing a stretch of Richardson Bay packed with funky houseboats. Ascend a mostly residential section of two-lane Hwy 1, and after 3 miles follow signs to Muir Woods via Panoramic Hwy.

GEOFF KUCHERA / ISTOCKPHOTO ©

TRIP HIGHLIGHT

❹ Muir Woods

Walking through an awesome stand of the world's tallest trees is an experience to be had only in Northern California and a small part of southern Oregon. The old-growth redwoods at **Muir Woods** (www.nps. gov/muwo; Muir Woods Rd, Mill Valley; adult/child $7/ free; ⊘8am-sunset) are the closest redwood stand to San Francisco. Logging plans were halted when congressman and naturalist William Kent bought a section of Redwood Creek, and in 1907 he donated 295 acres to the federal government. President Theodore Roosevelt made the site a national monument in 1908, the name honoring John Muir, naturalist and founder of the Sierra Club environmental organization.

Muir Woods can become quite crowded, especially on weekends. But even at busy times, a short hike will get you out of the densest crowds and onto trails with huge trees and stunning vistas. A lovely cafe serves local and organic goodies and hot drinks that hit the spot on foggy days.

The Drive » Head southwest on Muir Woods Dr (signed

DETOUR: CHEZ PANISSE

Start: ❶ San Francisco

The soul and anchor of Berkeley's 'Gourmet Ghetto,' Alice Waters' famed **Chez Panisse** (📞restaurant 510-548-5525, cafe 510-548-5049; www.chezpanisse.com; 1517 Shattuck Ave, Berkeley; restaurant meals $65-100, cafe mains $18-29; ⊘restaurant dinner Mon-Sat, cafe lunch & dinner Mon-Sat) gave birth to modern California cuisine and is a bucket-list destination for gourmands who prize fresh, local and organic ingredients. Upscale but unpretentious, its two dining rooms inhabit a welcoming Arts and Crafts house. The downstairs restaurant serves more formal prix-fixe meals, while the cafe upstairs is slightly less expensive. Reserve one month ahead.

Cross the Bay Bridge to I-80, exiting at University Ave. After 2 miles, turn left onto Shattuck Ave.

Sausalito

Muir Beach/Stinson Beach) and rejoin Hwy 1/Shoreline Hwy, winding north along this spectacularly scenic and curvy Pacific Ocean byway. Trace Bolinas Lagoon, where waterfowl prowl during low tide and harbor seals often frolic, and take the very first left after the lagoon. Go left onto Olema–Bolinas Rd into central Bolinas.

- - - - - - - - - - -

❺ Bolinas

Don't look for any signs directing you here. Residents from this famously private town tore the road sign down so many times that state highway officials finally gave in and stopped replacing it years ago.

Known as 'Jugville' during the Gold Rush days, the sleepy beachside community is home to writers, musicians and fisherfolk. Stroll along the sand from access points at Wharf Rd or Brighton Ave.

Hikers should veer off Olema–Bolinas Rd to Mesa Rd and follow it 5 miles to road's end at Palomarin Trailhead, the tromping-off point for coastal day hikes into the Point Reyes National Seashore. On a toasty day, pack some water and a towel and hightail it out from here to **Bass Lake**, a popular freshwater swimming

spot reached by way of a 3-mile hike skirting the coast. Another 1.5 miles of walking brings you to the a fantastic flume of **Alamere Falls**, which tumbles 50ft off a cliff to the beach below.

✖ p550

The Drive » Return to Hwy 1 and continue 11 miles north through Olema Valley. Just past Olema, drive 20 miles west on Sir Francis Drake Blvd (towards Inverness), following the 'lighthouse' signs. Raptors perch on fence posts of historic cattle ranches, and the road bumps over rolling hills as it twists towards the sea.

TRIP HIGHLIGHT

6 Point Reyes

At the very end of Sir Francis Drake Blvd, and jutting 10 miles out into the Pacific, this wild tip of land endures ferocious winds that can make it feel like the edge of the world. The **Point Reyes Lighthouse** (☎415-669-1534; www.nps.gov/pore; ⏱lens room 2:30-4pm Thu-Mon, visitor center & other chambers 10am-4:30pm Fri-Mon) sits below the headlands at the base of over 300 stairs. Not merely a beautiful beacon site, it's also one of the best whale-watching spots along the coast, as gray whales pass the shore during their annual migration from Alaska to Baja. Gray-whale sightings tend to peak in mid-January and mid-March, with the season lasting from about January through to April.

However, the occasional spout or spy-hop of humpbacks and minkes can occur year-round.

Note that on weekends and holidays from late December through to mid-April, the road to the lighthouse is closed to private vehicles, and visitors must take a shuttle (adult/child $5/free) from Drakes Beach.

✕ ⇤ p551

The Drive ≫ Retrace Sir Francis Drake Blvd to Hwy 1 north and through the tiny village of Point Reyes Station. Soon after, go right onto Point Reyes–Petaluma Rd for 18 miles to Petaluma, stopping en route to sample brie at Marin French Cheese. At the railroad crossing, go right on Lakeville St, which becomes Hwy 116. Drive east toward Sonoma, picking up Arnold Dr or Hwy 12 north.

7 Glen Ellen

In Sonoma Valley, picnic like a rock star at the perpetually busy **BR**

Cohn (www.brcohn.com; 15000 Sonoma Hwy; tasting $10 & applicable to purchase, bottles $22-55; ⏱10am-5pm), whose founder managed '70s superband the Doobie Brothers before moving on to make outstanding organic olive oils and fine wines – including excellent Cabernet Sauvignon. In autumn, he throws benefit concerts amid the olives.

The name **Little Vineyards** (www.littlevineyards.com; 15188 Sonoma Hwy; tastings $10, bottles $20-45; ⏱11am-4:30pm Thu-Mon;) fits at this family-owned small-scale winery. It's long on atmosphere, with a lazy dog to greet you and a weathered, cigarette-burned tasting bar, which Jack London drank at (before it was moved here). The tasting room is good for folks who dislike crowds, and there's good picnicking on the terrace with a vineyard view. The big reds include Syrah, Petite Sirah, Zinfandel, Cab and several blends.

✕ p551

The Drive ≫ Double back south on Hwy 12 and then east on Hwy 12/121. Make your way north on Hwy 29, exiting at Downtown Napa/First St. Follow the signs to the Oxbow Public Market.

WILDLIFE-WATCHING

Want to see marine wildlife in Marin? Here are a few choice spots suggested by Anne Bauer, Director of Education at the **Marine Mammal Center** (www.tmmc.org).

≫ Point Reyes National Seashore (Chimney Rock & Point Reyes Lighthouse) for gray whales

≫ Bolinas (Duxbury Reef, Bolinas Lagoon), Marin Headlands (around Point Bonita) and Point Reyes National Seashore (Limantour Estero) for harbor seals

≫ Point Reyes National Seashore (Sea Lion Overlook) for sea lions

8 Napa

Near the river in downtown Napa, the stands inside the **Oxbow Public Market** (www.oxbowpublicmarket.com; 610 & 644 First St; ⏰9am-7pm Mon-Sat, 10am-5pm Sun; 👶🅿) offer everything from fresh-roasted organic coffee to cranberry baguette sandwiches with pea shoots and fontina. Sample a beef frank at the counter of **Five Dot Ranch** (www.fivedotranch.com), an all-natural beef purveyor with a holistic, sustainable, open-pasture program combined with low-stress handling. The family has been raising California livestock for seven generations. Top it off a couple of stands over with the funky, creative and organic flavors of **Three Twins Ice Cream** (www.threetwinsicecream.com) – try the Strawberry Je Ne Sais Quoi, where the creaminess is cut with an unexpected dash of balsamic vinegar.

The Drive » Leaving Napa, take picturesque Hwy 29 (St Helena Hwy) 12 miles north to Oakville, driving past the Napa Valley foodie destination of Yountville.

WINE TASTING 101

Even if you know nothing about wine, you can enjoy it with gusto. Inhale the wine's aroma by burying your nose deep in the glass. Swirl it and look at its color before letting it hit every part of your tongue. It's OK not to drain every glass (in fact, it'll dull your taste buds if you do). Use the containers on the counter to empty your glass and prepare for your next taste. You won't be offending anyone!

TRIP HIGHLIGHT

9 Napa Valley

The huge, corporate-owned winery of **Robert Mondavi** (www.robertmondavi.com; 7801 Hwy 29, Oakville; tours $15-55, bottles $20-90; ⏰10am-5pm) draws oppressive crowds, but if you know nothing about wine, the worthwhile tours provide excellent insight into winemaking. Otherwise, skip it – unless you're here for one of the wonderful summer concerts, ranging from rock and jazz to R&B and Latin.

A half-mile south, just after the Oakville Grocery, take a left onto Oakville Cross Rd and drive 2.5 miles, passing through vineyards to Silverado Trail. For hilltop views and food-friendly wines,

head south another 2.5 miles to visit chef-owned **Robert Sinskey** (☎707-944-9090; www.robertsinskey.com; 6320 Silverado Trail, Napa; tasting $25, bottles $22-242; ⏰10am-4:30pm), whose discreetly dramatic tasting room of stone, redwood and teak resembles a small cathedral. The winery specializes in organically grown Pinot, Merlot and Cabernet, great Alsatian varietals, Vin Gris, and Cabernet Franc, and small bites accompany the vino.

🍴🛏 p551

The Drive » Continue south on Silverado Trail to Napa, picking up southbound Hwy 121 (Sonoma)/Hwy 29 (Vallejo) and turning right as it merges into westbound Hwy 12 (Sonoma). Stay on Hwy 121 until Hwy 37, and take it west. From Hwy 101, it's 20 miles back to San Francisco via the Golden Gate Bridge.

Eating & Sleeping

San Francisco ❶

✖ Bi-Rite Creamery — Ice Cream $

(www.biritecreamery.com; 3692 18th St; ice cream $3.50-7; ⊙11am-10pm Sun-Thu, to 11pm Fri & Sat) Velvet ropes at clubs seem pretentious in laid-back San Francisco, but at organic Bi-Rite Creamery they make perfect sense: lines wrap around the corner for legendary salted-caramel ice cream with housemade hot fudge.

✖ Cotogna — Italian $$$

(☎415-775-8508; www.cotognasf.com; 490 Pacific Ave; mains $17-28; ⊙11.30am-11pm Mon-Thu, to midnight Fri & Sat, 5-9pm Sun; 🐾) No wonder chef-owner Michael Tusk won the 2011 James Beard Award: his rustic Italian pastas and toothsome pizzas magically balance a few pristine, local flavors. Book ahead; the $24 prix-fixe (daily except Sunday) is among SF's best dining deals.

✖ Slanted Door — Vietnamese, Californian $$$

(☎415-861-8032; www.slanteddoor.com; 1 Ferry Bldg; mains $15-45, dinner mains $18-36; ⊙lunch & dinner 11am-2:30pm Mon-Sat, to 3pm Sun, also 5:30-10pm daily) California ingredients, Continental influences and Vietnamese flair with a sparkling bay outlook, from award-winning chef-owner Charles Phan. Reserve ahead or picnic on budget-friendly takeout from the Out the Door stall.

🛏 Galleria Park — Boutique Hotel $$$

(☎415-781-3060; www.jdvhotels.com; 191 Sutter St; r $200-475; ❄ @ 🛜 🛁) Exuberant staff greet you at this downtown boutique charmer, a 1911 hotel styled with contemporary art and handsome furnishings in soothing jewel tones. Some rooms (and bed sizes) run small, but include Frette linens, down pillows, high-end bath amenities, free evening wine hour and – most importantly – good service. Rooms on Sutter St are noisier, but get more light; interior rooms are quietest.

🛏 Good Hotel — Hotel $$

(☎415-621-7001, 800-544-5819; www.thegoodhotel.com; 112 7th St; r $135-225; @ 🛜 🛁) A revamped motor lodge attached to a restyled apartment hotel, Good Hotel places a premium on green, with reclaimed wood headboards, light fixtures of repurposed bottles, and fleece bedspreads made of recycled soda bottles and cast-off fabrics. The aesthetic is like a smartly decorated college dorm room: youthful and fun. The big drawbacks are a sometimes-sketchy neighborhood and street noise; book a room in the back. Also has bikes to borrow. The outdoor pool is across the street.

Sausalito ❸

✖ Avatar's — Indian $$

(www.enjoyavatars.com; 2656 Bridgeway Blvd; mains $10-17; ⊙11am-3pm & 5-9:30pm Mon-Sat; 🐾 👶) Boasting a cuisine of 'ethnic confusion,' the Indian fusion dishes here incorporate Mexican, Italian and Caribbean ingredients and will bowl you over with their flavor and creativity. Think Punjabi enchiladas with curried sweet potato or spinach and mushroom ravioli with mango and rose petal alfredo sauce. All diets (vegan, gluten-free etc) are graciously accommodated.

✖ Fish — Seafood $$

(www.331fish.com; 350 Harbor Dr; mains $13-25; ⊙11:30am-8:30pm; 👶) Chow down on seafood sandwiches, oysters and Dungeness crab rolls with organic local butter at redwood picnic tables facing Richardson Bay. A local leader in promoting fresh and sustainably caught fish, this place has wonderful wild salmon in season, and refuses to serve the farmed stuff. Cash only.

Bolinas ❺

✖ Bolinas People's Store — Market $

(14 Wharf Rd; ⊙8:30am-6:30pm; 🐾) An awesome little co-op grocery store hidden behind the community center, the People's Store serves Fair Trade coffee and sells organic produce, fresh soup and excellent tamales. Eat

at the tables in the shady courtyard, and have a rummage through the Free Box, a shed full of clothes and other waiting-to-be-reused items.

✕ Coast Café
American $$

(www.bolinascoastcafe.com; 46 Wharf Rd; mains $8-22; ☺lunch 11am-3pm Tue-Fri, brunch 8am-3pm Sat & Sun, dinner 5-8pm Tue-Thu & Sun, to 9pm Fri & Sat; 🖉🛗🔆) The only 'real' restaurant in town, so everyone jockeys for outdoor seats among the flower boxes for fish and chips, barbecued oysters, or buttermilk pancakes with damn good coffee.

Point Reyes ⑥

✕ Tomales Bay Foods & Cowgirl Creamery
Market $$

(www.cowgirlcreamery.com; 80 4th St, Point Reyes Station; sandwiches $6-12; ☺10am-6pm Wed-Sun; 🖉) A local market in an old barn selling picnic items, including gourmet cheeses and organic produce. All of the milk is local and organic, with vegetarian rennet in all its soft cheeses, and you can often watch cheese being made from a large window near the entryway.

🛏 Point Reyes Hostel
Hostel $

(☎415-663-8811; www.norcalhostels.org/reyes; dm $24, r $82-120, all with shared bath; @) This rustic HI property has bunkhouses with warm and cozy front rooms, big-view windows and outdoor areas with hill vistas, and an LEED-certified building with four private rooms. It's in a beautiful secluded valley 2 miles from the ocean and surrounded by lovely hiking trails, and the only lodging in the park.

Glen Ellen ⑦

✕ Vineyards Inn Bar & Grill
Spanish, Tapas $$$

(www.vineyardsinn.com; 8445 Hwy 12, Kenwood; shared plates $6-15, mains $11-30; ☺11:30am-9:30pm; 🖉) Though nothing fancy, this roadside tavern's food is terrific – succulent organic burgers, line-caught seafood, paella, ceviche and biodynamic produce from the chef's ranch. Full bar.

Napa Valley ⑨

✕ Ad Hoc
Californian $$$

(☎707-944-2487; www.adhocrestaurant.com; 6476 Washington St, Yountville; prix-fixe dinner from $52; ☺5pm-10pm Wed-Mon, also 10am-1pm Sun) A winning formula by Yountville's culinary oligarch, Thomas Keller, Ad Hoc serves the master's favorite American home-cooking in four-course family-style menus, with no variations except for dietary restrictions. There's also weekend lunchtime takeout behind the restaurant at Keller's latest venture, **Addendum** (lunch $17; ☺11am-2pm Thu-Sat, Mar-Oct), which also serves barbecue; get the daily menu online.

🛏 Hotel St Helena
Historic Hotel $$$

(☎707-963-4388; www.hotelsthelena.net; 1309 Main St, St Helena; r with shared/private bath from $195/275; 🔆🛜) Decorated with period furnishings, this frayed-at-the-edges 1881 hotel sits right in St Helena's downtown. Rooms are tiny, but good value, especially those with shared bathroom. No elevator.

🛏 Maison Fleurie
B&B $$$

(☎707-944-2056, 800-788-0369; www. maisonfleurienapa.com; 6529 Yount St, Yountville; r incl breakfast $150-295; 🔆🛜🐾) Rooms at this ivy-covered country inn are in a century-old home and carriage house, decorated in French-provincial style. There's a big breakfast, and afternoon wine and hors d'oeuvres. Hot tub.

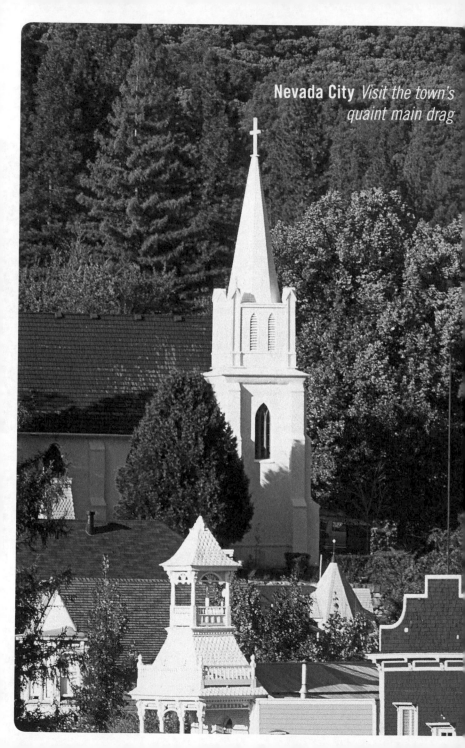

Nevada City *Visit the town's quaint main drag*

Highway 49 Through Gold Country

45

There's plenty to see on winding Hwy 49; a trip through Gold Country shows off California's early days, when hell-raising prospectors and ruffians rushed helter-skelter into the West.

TRIP HIGHLIGHTS

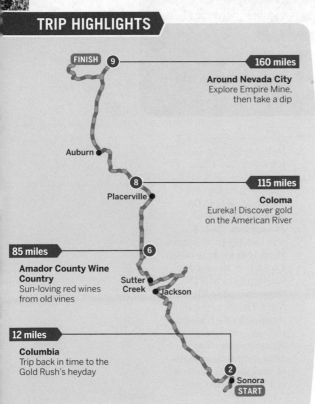

FINISH 9 — **160 miles**

Around Nevada City
Explore Empire Mine, then take a dip

Auburn

8

Placerville — **115 miles**

Coloma
Eureka! Discover gold on the American River

85 miles

6

Amador County Wine Country
Sun-loving red wines from old vines

Sutter Creek

Jackson

12 miles

Columbia
Trip back in time to the Gold Rush's heyday

2

Sonora
START

3–4 DAYS
175 MILES/280KM

GREAT FOR...

BEST TIME TO GO
April to October for sunny skies.

ESSENTIAL PHOTO
Sutter's Mill, California's original gold discovery site.

 BEST FOR SWIMMING
South Yuba River State Park.

45 Highway 49 Through Gold Country

When you roll into Gold Country on a sunny afternoon, the promise of adventure recalls the days when headlines screamed about gold discoveries and the Golden State was born. Today this rural region offers different cultural riches: exploring crumbling false-front saloons, rusting machines that once moved mountains and an endless parade of patinaed bronze historical markers along Hwy 49, one of California's most enchantingly scenic byways.

❶ Sonora

Settled in 1848 by Mexican miners, Sonora soon became a cosmopolitan center with ornate saloons for gamblers, drunkards and gold diggers. Its downtown district is so well preserved that it's frequently a location for Hollywood films such as Clint Eastwood's *Unforgiven*. Likewise, **Railtown 1897 State Historic Park** (📞209-984-3953; www.railtown1897.org, www.parks.ca.gov; 18115 5th

Ave, Jamestown; museum adult/child $5/3, incl train ride $15/8; ⊘9:30am-4:30pm Apr-Oct, 10am-3pm Nov-Mar, train rides 11am-3pm Sat & Sun Apr-Oct; 🚻) and the surrounding hills of **Jamestown**, about 4 miles southeast of Sonora along Hwy 49, have been a backdrop for over 200 Western films and TV shows including *High Noon*. There's a lyrical romance to the historical railway yard, where orange poppies bloom among the rusting shells of steel goliaths and you can board the narrow-

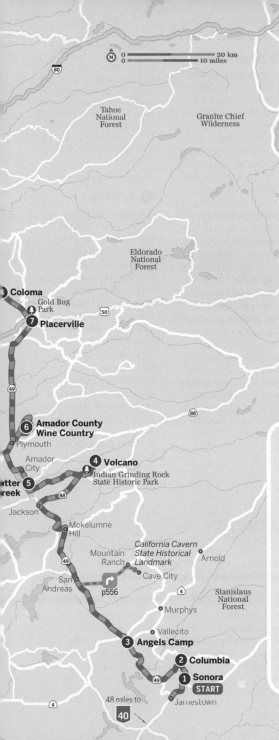

gauge railroad that once transported ore, lumber and miners.

 p561

The Drive » Follow Hwy 49 just over 2 miles north of Sonora, then turn right onto Parrots Ferry Rd at the sign for Columbia. The state historic park is 2 miles further along this two-lane country road.

TRIP HIGHLIGHT

② Columbia

Grab some suspenders and a floppy hat for **Columbia State Historic Park** (☎209-588-9128; www.parks.ca.gov/columbia; 11255 Jackson St; admission free; ⏱museum 9am-4:30pm Apr-Oct, 10am-4:30pm Nov-Mar; 🚻🎫), near the so-called 'Gem of the Southern Mines.' It's like a miniature Gold Rush Disneyland, but

🔗 LINK YOUR TRIP

40 **Yosemite, Sequoia & Kings Canyon National Parks**

Wind 45 miles southeast of Hwy 49 to Yosemite's Big Oak Flat entrance on Hwy 120.

44 **San Francisco, Marin & Napa Loop**

Drive 80 miles southeast on Hwy 108 over mountainous Sonora Pass (closed by snow in winter and spring) to Hwy 395.

with more authenticity and heart. Four blocks of town have been preserved, where volunteers perambulate in 19th-century dress and demonstrate gold panning. The blacksmith's shop, theater, hotels and saloon are all carefully framed windows into California's past. The yesteryear illusion of Main St is shaken only a bit by fudge shops and the occasional banjo-picker whose cell phone rings.

 p561

The Drive » Backtrack south on Parrots Ferry Rd, veering right and then turning right to stay on Springfield Rd for just over a mile. Rejoin Hwy 49 northbound, which crosses a long bridge over an artificial reservoir. After a dozen miles or so, Hwy 49 becomes Main St through Angels Camp.

❸ Angels Camp

On the southern stretch of Hwy 49, one literary giant looms over all other Western tall-tale tellers: Samuel Clemens, aka Mark Twain, who got his first big break with the short story *The Celebrated Jumping Frog of Calaveras County,* written and set in Angels Camp. With a mix of Victorian and art deco buildings that shelter antiques shops and cafes, this 19th-century mining camp makes the most of its Twain connection, hosting the **Jumping Frog Jubilee & Calaveras County Fair** (www.frogtown. org; Gun Club Rd; adult/child $10/6) on the third weekend in May. You could score $50 if your frog beats the world-record jump (over 21ft) set by 'Rosie the Ribeter' back in 1986.

The Drive » Hwy 49 heads north of Angels Camp through hillsides of farms and ranches. Past San Andreas, make a short detour through Mokelumne Hill, another historic mining town. In Jackson, turn right onto Hwy 88 east. After 9 miles, turn left on Pine Grove-Volcano Rd to reach Indian Grinding Rock State Historic Park.

❹ Volcano

Although the village of Volcano once yielded tons of gold and saw Civil War intrigue, today it slumbers away in solitude. Huge sandstone rocks lining Sutter Creek were blasted from the surrounding hills using a hydraulic process before being scraped clean of gold-bearing dirt. Hydraulic mining had dire environmental consequences, but at its peak, miners raked in nearly $100 a day. Less than a mile southeast of town, **Black Chasm** (☎888-762-2837; www.

DETOUR: CALIFORNIA CAVERN

Start: ❸ Angels Camp

A 25-minute drive east of San Andreas via Mountain Ranch Rd, off Hwy 49 about 12 miles north of Angels Camp, **California Cavern State Historical Landmark** (☎20 9-736-2708; www.caverntours.com; 9565 Cave City Rd, Mountain Ranch; tour adult/child from $15/8; ⊗10am-5pm daily Apr-Sep, 10am-4pm Sat & Sun Oct-Mar; 🚹) has the mother lode's most extensive system of natural underground caverns. John Muir described them as 'graceful flowing folds deeply placketed like stiff silken drapery.' Regular tours take 60 to 90 minutes, or reserve ahead for a five-hour 'Middle Earth Expedition' ($130), which includes some serious spelunking (no children under age 16 allowed). The Trail of Lakes walking tour, available only during the wet season, is magical.

caverntours.com; 15701 Pioneer Volcano Rd; tours adult/child from $15/8; ☺10am-4pm) has the whiff of a tourist trap, but one look at the helictite crystals – sparkling white formations resembling giant snowflakes – makes the crowds bearable. Two miles southwest of town at **Indian Grinding Rock State Historic Park** (☏20 9-296-7488; www.parks.ca.gov; 14881 Pine Grove-Volcano Rd; per car $8; ☺sunrise-sunset daily, museum 11am-2:30pm Fri-Mon; 🖐), a limestone outcrop is covered with petroglyphs and over 1000 mortar holes called *chaw'se* used for grinding acorns into meal. Learn more about the Sierra Nevada's indigenous tribes inside the park's museum, shaped like a Native American *hun'ge* (roundhouse).

🛏 p561

The Drive >> Backtrack along Pine Grove-Volcano Rd, turning right onto Hwy 88 for about half a mile, then turn right onto Ridge Rd, which winds through forests and past rural homesteads for 8 miles back to Hwy 49. Turn right and head north about a mile to Sutter Creek.

---

5 **Sutter Creek**

Perch on the balcony of one of Main St's gracefully restored buildings and view this gem of a Gold Country town, boasting raised, arcaded sidewalks and high-balconied, false-

---

---

fronted buildings that exemplify California's 19th-century frontier architecture. At the **visitor center** (☏209-267-1344; www.suttercreek.org; 71a Main St; ☺daily, hr vary) pick up self-guided walking and driving tour maps. Nearby **Monteverde General Store Museum** (☺209-267-0493; 11a Randolph St; admission free; ☺by appointment only) is a trip back in time, as is **Sutter Creek Theatre** (☏916-425-0077; www.suttercreektheater.com; 44 Main St), a 1919 brick building, now hosting live music, plays, films and cultural events.

🛏 p561

The Drive >> Follow Main St north of Sutter Creek for 3 miles through quaint Amador City. Back at Hwy 49, turn right and continue north another few miles to Drytown Cellars, south of the Hwy 16 junction.

TRIP HIGHLIGHT

6 **Amador County Wine Country**

Amador County might be something of an underdog among California's winemaking regions, but a welcoming circuit of family-owned wineries and local characters make for great sipping without any pretension. Planted with California's oldest surviving Zinfandel vines, the countryside has a lot in common with its most celebrated grape varietal – bold, richly colored and earthy. North of tiny Amador City, **Drytown Cellars** (www.drytowncellars.com; 16030 Hwy 49; ☺11am-5pm) has a gregarious host and an array of rich red blends and single-varietal wines. Drive further north to the one-horse town of Plymouth, then head east on Plymouth Shenandoah Rd, where rolling hills are covered with rocky rows of neatly pruned vines, soaking up gallons of sunshine. Turn left onto Steiner Rd towards **Renwood Winery** (www.renwoodwinery.com; 12225 Steiner Rd; ☺11am-6pm) and **Deaver Vineyards** (www.deavervineyards.com; 12455 Steiner Rd; ☺10:30am-

LOCAL KNOWLEDGE
JOHN SCOTT LAMB, COLUMBIA RESIDENT & FORMER CAVERN GUIDE

South of Vallecito and Hwy 49, there's a very short but memorable hike called Natural Bridges. The area has been a magnet for gold explorers and locals since the 1850s and it features two prominent caves where Coyote Creek flows through. In summertime, you can swim right through the upper cave – amazing! Look for the signed turnoff about 3 miles south of Moaning Cavern on Parrots Ferry Rd.

Top: Tepees, Marshall Gold Discovery State Historic Park
Left: Museum, Marshall Gold Discovery State Historic Park
Right: Main St, Jamestown

RICHARD CUMMINS / CORBIS ©

5pm), both crafting outstanding Zinfandels. Backtrack and continue straight across Plymouth Shenandoah Rd, bending south towards hilltop estate **Wilderotter Vineyard** (www.wilderottervineyard.com; 19890 Shenandoah School Rd; ⊙10:30am-5pm Wed-Mon), which pours dry, minerally whites and smoothly balanced reds.

✗ p561

The Drive » Follow Shenandoah School Rd another mile west until it ends. Turn left back onto Plymouth Shenandoah Rd for 1.5 miles, then turn right onto Hwy 49 northbound. Less then 20 miles later, after up-and-down roller-coaster stretches, you'll arrive in downtown Placerville, south of Hwy 50.

----

❼ Placerville

STEPHEN SAKS / GETTY IMAGES ©

Things get livelier in 'Old Hangtown,' a nickname Placerville earned for the vigilante-justice hangings that happened here in 1849. Most buildings along Placerville's Main St date from the 1850s. Poke around antiques shops and **Placerville Hardware** (441 Main St; ⊙8am-6pm Mon-Sat, 9am-5pm Sun), the oldest continuously operating hardware store west of the Mississippi River. Downtown dive bars open in the early morning, get an annual cleaning at Christmas and are great for knocking elbows with odd birds. Marked by a vintage neon sign and a dummy hanging in a noose outside, the **Hangman's Tree** (305 Main St) bar is built over the stump of the eponymous tree. For family-friendly shenanigans, head 1 mile north of town via Bedford Ave to **Gold Bug Park** ([📞]530-642-5207; www. goldbugpark.org; 2635 Gold Bug Lane; entry adult/child $5/3, gold panning per hr $2; [🕑]10am-4pm daily Apr-Oct, noon-4pm Sat & Sun Nov-Mar; [👶]), where hard-hatted visitors can descend into a 19th-century mine shaft, or try gold panning.

 p561

The Drive » Back on Hwy 49 northbound, you'll ride along one of the most scenic stretches of the Gold Country's historic route. Patched with shade from oak and pine trees, Hwy 49 drifts beside Sierra Nevada foothills for the next 9 miles to Coloma.

TRIP HIGHLIGHT

❽ Coloma

At pastoral, low-key **Marshall Gold Discovery State Historic Park** ([📞]530-622-3470; www.parks. ca.gov, www.marshallgold. org; 310 Back St; per car $8; [🕑]8am-5pm, to 7pm late May-early Sep, museum 10am-3pm Nov-Mar, to 4pm Apr-Oct; [👶🎒]), a simple dirt path leads to the place along the banks of the American River where James Marshall

made his famous discovery of gold flecks below Sutter's Mill on January 24, 1848. Today, several reconstructed and restored historical buildings are all within a short stroll along grassy trails that pass mining artifacts, a blacksmith's shop, pioneer emigrant houses and a historical museum. Panning for gold is always popular at **Bekeart's Gun Shop** (329 Hwy 49; per person $7; [🕑]10am-3pm Tue-Sun Apr-Oct). Opposite the pioneer cemetery, you can walk or drive up California's shortest state highway, Hwy 153, to where the **James Marshall Monument** marks Marshall's final resting place. Ironically, he died bankrupt, penniless and a ward of the state.

The Drive » Rolling northbound, Hwy 49 unfolds more of the region's historical beauty over the next 15 miles. In Auburn, drive across I-80 and stay on Hwy 49 north for another 22 miles, gaining elevation while heading toward Grass Valley. Exit onto Empire St, turning right to follow the signs for Empire Mine State Historic Park's visitor center.

TRIP HIGHLIGHT

❾ Around Nevada City

You've hit the biggest bonanza of the mother lode: **Empire Mine State Historic Park** ([📞]530-273-8522; www.empiremine.org,

www.parks.ca.gov; 10791 E Empire St, Grass Valley; adult/child $7/3, guided cottage tour $2; [🕑]10am-5pm; [👶]), where California's richest hard-rock mine produced 5.8 million ounces of gold between 1850 and 1956. The mine yard is littered with the massive mining equipment and buildings constructed from waste rock.

Backtrack west, then follow the Golden Chain Hwy (Hwy 49) four more miles north to Nevada City. On the town's quaint main drag, hilly Broad St, the **National Hotel** (211 Broad St) purports to be the oldest continuously operating hotel west of the Rockies. Mosey around the block to **Historic Firehouse No 1 Museum** (www.nevadacountyhistory. org; 215 Main St; admission free; [🕑]1-4pm Fri-Sun May-Oct), where Native American artifacts join displays about Chinese laborers and creepy Donner Party relics.

Last, cool off with a dip at **South Yuba River State Park** ([📞]530-432-2546; www.parks.ca.gov; 17660 Pleasant Valley Rd, Penn Valley; admission free; [🕑]sunrise-sunset; [👶🎒]), with hiking trails and swimming holes near the USA's longest covered wooden bridge. It's a 30-minute drive northwest of Nevada City or Grass Valley.

[🍴][🛏] p561

Eating & Sleeping

Sonora ❶

🍴 Diamondback Grill & Wine Bar   Californian $$
(📞209-532-6661; www.thediamondbackgrill.com; 93 S Washington St; mains $9-12; ⏱11am-9pm Mon-Thu, to 9:30pm Fri & Sat, to 8pm Sun) With exposed-brick walls and a long wooden bar, this contemporary cafe crafts sandwiches, salads, burgers and six daily specials.

🛏 Gunn House   B&B $
(📞209-532-3421; www.gunnhousehotel.com; 286 S Washington St; r incl breakfast $79-115; ❄🔣♨👷) A frilly, floral alternative to cookie-cutter chain hotels, with cozy rooms that feature period decor. Rocking chairs on wide porches overlook downtown's historic main drag.

Columbia ❷

🛏 City & Fallon Hotels   Historic Hotel $$
(📞209-532-1479; www.briggshospitalityllc.com; 22768 Main St & 11175 Washington St; r shared bath incl breakfast $80-150; ❄🔣) Hunt Gold Rush–era ghosts at these restored, but still rustic hotels. City Hotel's atmospheric What Cheer saloon, hung with oil paintings of 'soiled doves' and striped wallpaper, serves casual pub-grub lunches and dinners (mains $11 to $36).

Volcano ❹

🛏 Volcano Union Inn   Historic Hotel $$
(📞209-296-7711; www.volcanounion.com; 21375 Consolation St; r incl breakfast $119-149; ❄@🔣) Of four lovingly updated rooms with crooked floors and flat-screen TVs, two have street-facing balconies. Open Thursday through Monday, the Union Pub has a wine-country menu, (mains $10 to $20) dartboards and live music.

Sutter Creek ❺

🛏 Hanford House Inn   B&B $$
(📞209-267-0747; www.hanfordhouse.com; 61 Hanford St; d incl breakfast $99-259;

@🔣♿🔣) Nod off on platform beds in contemporary rooms or fireplace cottage suites. Chef-prepared breakfasts are harvested from the inn's garden, while evening brings out cheese-and-wine pairings.

Amador County Wine Country ❻

🍴 Taste   Californian $$$
(📞209-245-3463; www.restauranttaste.com; 9402 Main St, Plymouth; dinner mains $27-43; ⏱11:30am-2pm Sat & Sun,dinner from 5pm Thu & Mon, 4:30pm Fri & Sat; 🔣) Top-notch wines meld with artfully presented California fusion cooking. Pull on the oversized fork-shaped door handle and step inside the wine bar. Reservations recommended.

Placerville ❼

🍴 Cozmic Cafe   Cafe $
(www.ourcoz.com; 594 Main St; dishes $4-10; ⏱7am-6pm Tue, Wed & Sun, to 8pm or later Thu-Sat; 🔣🔣👷) With tables set in an underground mine shaft, this hippie-dippy spot's healthy menu is backed by fresh-fruit smoothies, organic coffee and tea. Live music most weekends.

Around Nevada City ❾

🍴 Ike's Quarter Cafe   Creole, Californian $$
(www.ikesquartercafe.com; 401 Commercial St, Nevada City; mains $6-16; ⏱8am-3pm Wed-Mon; 👷) Gigantic brunch plates are dished up on a N'awlins-style garden patio. Try the miners' classic 'Hangtown Fry' – cornmeal-crusted oysters, bacon, caramelized onions and spinach. Cash only.

🛏 Broad Street Inn   Inn $$
(📞530-265-2239; www.broadstreetinn.com; 517 W Broad St, Nevada City; r $110-120; ❄🔣👷) Forget about fussy B&Bs. This refreshingly simple, six-room Victorian inn has modern, brightly furnished rooms and sociable garden patios with fire pits and porch swings.

STRETCH YOUR LEGS
LOS ANGELES

Start/Finish Union Station

Distance 3.5 miles

Duration 4–5 hours

Nobody walks in LA? That's just not true in Downtown's historic core. Sample the jumbled sights, sounds and tastes of the city's Mexican, Asian and European heritage, with iconic architecture and famous TV and film locations, on this half-day ramble.

Take this walk on Trip

Union Station

This majestic 1939 **edifice** (www.amtrak. com; 800 N Alameda St; admission free; ⏱24hr) was the last of America's grand railway stations to be built. Walk into the waiting room, its glamorous interior glimpsed in dozens of movies and hit TV shows from *Speed* to *24*. Bordered by tall palm trees, the stately exterior is a uniquely Californian fusion of Mission revival and art deco streamline moderne styles.

The Walk » Walk a block up N Alameda St, cross over W Cesar E Chavez Ave and walk west a half block. Turn left down the passageway of Olvera St.

El Pueblo de Los Angeles

Compact, colorful and car-free, this historical district sits near the spot where LA's first Spanish colonists plunked down in 1781. Preserving some of the city's oldest buildings beside tiny museums and churches, El Pueblo is a microcosm of LA's multiethnic immigrant history. Join a free guided walking tour at the **visitors center** (☎213-628-1274; www.lasangelitas.org; Avila Adobe, 10 Olvera St; ⏱tours usually 10am, 11am & noon Tue-Sat).

The Walk » Northwest of the open-air bandstand, cross Main St. To your right is 'La Placita,' LA's oldest Catholic church (1822). After peeking inside, walk back down Main St a half block.

La Plaza de Cultura y Artes

Open since 2011, **La Plaza de Cultura y Artes** (☎213-542-6200; www.lapca.org; 501 N Main St; admission free; ⏱noon-7pm Wed-Mon) tells the whole truth about the Mexican American experience in LA, from Zoot Suit Riots to the Chicana movement. Calle Principal recreates Main Street in the 1920s. Rotating gallery exhibitions showcase Latino art, documentary films and oral history.

The Walk » Continue southwest along Main St, crossing over Hwy 101 toward LA's City Hall (1928). Turn left onto E Temple St, right onto N Los Angeles St and left onto E 1st St, entering Little Tokyo.

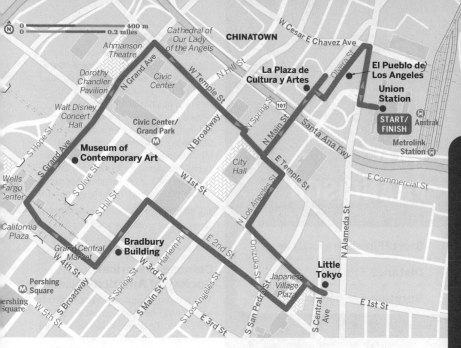

Little Tokyo

Walk past ramen shops and *izakaya* (gastropubs) over to the **Japanese American National Museum** (☏213-625-0414; www.janm.org; 100 N Central Ave; adult/child $9/5; ⊙11am-5pm Tue-Wed & Fri-Sun, noon-8pm Thu). The exhibits deal with WWII internment camps and life for immigrant families. Around the corner, the **Geffen Contemporary at MOCA** (☏213-626-6222; www.moca.org; 152 N Central Ave; adult/child $12/free; ⊙11am-5pm Mon & Fri, 11am-8pm Thu, 11am-6pm Sat & Sun) houses experimental art installations.

The Walk » West of Central Ave, turn left to walk through Japanese Village Plaza. Turn right onto E 2nd St, walk five blocks uphill to S Broadway, then turn left and walk a block southwest to W 3rd St.

Bradbury Building

A favorite of movie location scouts since *Blade Runner* was shot here, the 1893 **Bradbury Building** (www.laconservancy.org; 304 S Broadway; admission free; ⊙ usually 9am-5pm) is one of LA's architectural treasures. Its red-brick facade conceals a glass-roofed atrium with inky filigree grillwork, a rickety birdcage elevator and brick walls that look golden in the afternoon light.

The Walk » Opposite, walk through LA's Grand Central Market, with its multicultural food stalls. Ride Angels Flight railway (50¢) uphill to California Plaza. Walk northwest to Grand Ave. Turn right and walk a block northeast.

Museum of Contemporary Art

With collections from the 1940s to the present day, including works by Mark Rothko and Joseph Cornell, **MOCA** (☏213-626-6222; www.moca.org; 250 S Grand Ave; adult/child $12/free; ⊙11am-5pm Mon & Fri, to 8pm Thu, to 6pm Sat & Sun) inhabits a geometrically postmodern building designed by Arata Isozaki.

The Walk » Continue northeast up Grand Ave, passing Walt Disney Concert Hall. Turn right onto Temple St and roll downhill past the Cathedral of Our Lady of the Angels to City Hall, retracing your steps north through El Pueblo de Los Angeles back to Union Station.

STRETCH
YOUR LEGS
SAN
FRANCISCO

Start/Finish Dragon Gate

Distance 3 miles

Duration 4–5 hours

Limber up and look sharp: on this walk, you'll pass hidden architectural gems, navigate the winding alleys of Chinatown and catch shimmering views of the bay. Along the way, enjoy controversial art, savory street snacks and a flock of parrots.

Take this walk on Trips

Dragon Gate

The first steps of this tour are through the elaborate threshold of the **Dragon Gate** (cnr Bush St & Grant Ave), which was donated by Taiwan in 1969 and announces the entrance to Chinatown. The street, beyond the gate, was once a notorious red-light district, but forward-thinking Chinatown businessmen reinvented the area in the 1920s, hiring architects to create a signature 'Chinatown Deco' look. The jumble of glittering shops is the perfect place to pick up a cheap souvenir.

The Walk › Huff it uphill from Dragon Gate on Grant Ave, past gilded dragon lamps to Old St Mary's Square. Two blocks beyond Old St Mary's Cathedral (1854) take a left on Clay St.

Chinese Historical Society of America Museum

At this intimate museum, visitors picture what it was like to be Chinese during the Gold Rush, the transcontinental railroad construction and the Beat heyday. The **Chinese Historical Society of America Museum** (☎415-391-1188; www.chsa.org; 965 Clay St; adult/child $5/2, 1st Thu of month free; ☺noon-5pm Tue-Fri, 11am-4pm Sat) also hosts rotating exhibits across the courtyard, all inside a graceful building designed by Julia Morgan as Chinatown's YWCA in 1932.

The Walk › Backtrack past Stockton St and turn left down Spofford Alley where mah-jongg tiles click and Sun Yat-sen plotted the 1911 overthrow of China's last dynasty. At Washington St, take a right. Then go left on Ross Alley.

Golden Gate Fortune Cookie Factory

Ross Alley (sometimes marked as Old Chinatown Alley) might seem familiar to movie buffs; it has been the backdrop for flicks like *Karate Kid, Part II* and *Indiana Jones and the Temple of Doom*. The humble little warehouse at No 56 is where to get your fortune while it's hot, folded into warm cookies at the **Golden Gate Fortune Cookie Factory** (56 Ross Alley; admission free; ☺9am-6pm). For a small fee you can even print custom fortunes.

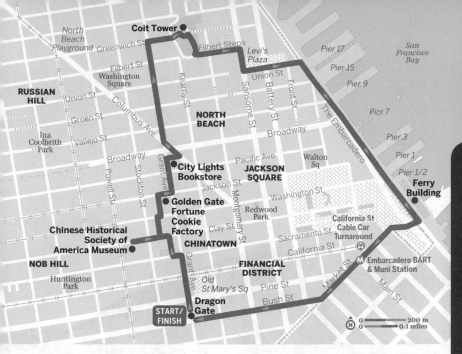

The Walk » Go right on Jackson St and left on Grant. You'll pass Chinese bakeries with piping hot *char siu bao* (BBQ pork buns). Take a shortcut through Jack Kerouac Alley, where the poetic vagabond once strolled.

City Lights Bookstore

Ever since clerk Shigeyoshi Murao and Beat poet Lawrence Ferlinghetti successfully defended their right to 'willfully and lewdly print' Allen Ginsberg's magnificent *Howl and Other Poems* in 1957, **City Lights Bookstore** (www.citylights.com; 261 Columbus Ave; ☺10am-midnight) has been a landmark. Snuggle into the Poet's Chair upstairs overlooking Jack Kerouac Alley or entertain radical ideas downstairs in the Muckracking and Stolen Continents sections. If reading makes you thirsty, grab a pint at Vesuvio next door.

The Walk » Leave City Lights' front door and go left on Columbus. Make a slight right on Grant Ave and walk for five blocks onto Greenwich St and hoof it up the steps to Coit Tower.

Coit Tower

Adding an exclamation mark to San Francisco's landscape, **Coit Tower** (☏415-362-0808; 1 Telegraph Hill Blvd; admission free, elevator ride adult/child $7/2; ☺10am-5:30pm Mar-Sep, 9am-4:30pm Oct-Feb) ends the walk up Telegraph Hill. This peculiar 210ft-projectile is a monument to San Francisco firefighters. To see more murals hidden inside Coit Tower's stairwell, take a free guided tour at 11am on Saturdays.

The Walk » Take the Filbert Steps downhill past wild parrots and hidden cottages to Levi's Plaza. Head right on Embarcadero to the Ferry Building.

Ferry Building

The historic **Ferry Building** is not just a hub for commuters. It has also transformed itself into a destination for foodies. Artisan food producers, organic produce and boutique suppliers make it a mouth-watering stop.

The Walk » Walk down Market St. Turn right on Bush St back to Chinatown's Dragon Gate.

Pacific Northwest Trips

GEOLOGICAL EVENTS OVER THOUSANDS OF YEARS HAVE DRAMATICALLY SHAPED THE PACIFIC NORTHWEST. Left behind are snowcapped mountain ranges, rocky islands, hundreds of waterfalls, natural hot springs and one particularly lovely gorge.

Because almost every drive in the Pacific Northwest is a scenic one, there's no better way to see it than by road trip. You can cruise along Oregon's epic coastline, explore the volcanic remnants of Crater Lake, go up the Inside Passage, or even travel in the footsteps of Lewis and Clark. We'll help you find all the great stops along the way, from historical sites to natural wonders to roadside attractions.

Wizard Island In Crater Lake (Trip 51)
ERIC FOLTZ / GETTY IMAGES ©

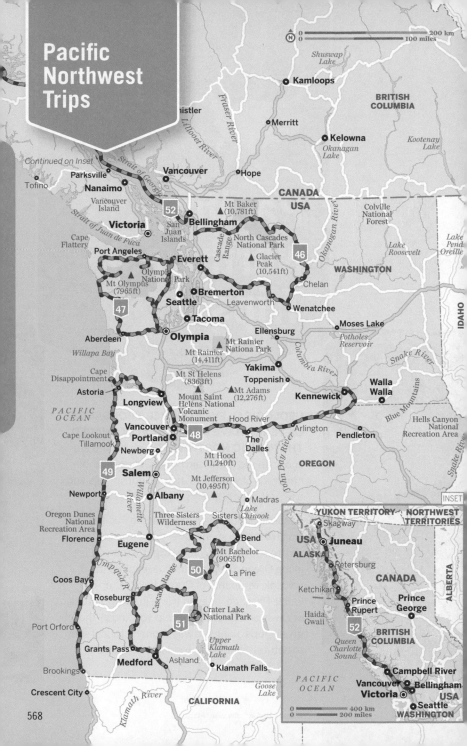

Pacific Northwest Trips

Shuswap Lake

Kamloops

BRITISH COLUMBIA

Merritt

Kelowna

Okanagan Lake

Kootenay Lake

Fraser River

Lillooet River

Whistler

Continued on Inset

Parksville

Tofino

Nanaimo

Vancouver Island

Strait of Georgia

52

Victoria

Cape Flattery

San Juan Islands

Vancouver

Hope

CANADA
USA

Mt Baker (10,781ft)

Bellingham

North Cascades National Park

Colville National Forest

Lake Pend Oreille

Lake Roosevelt

46

Okanogan River

Strait of Juan de Fuca

Port Angeles

Olympic National Park

Everett

Cascade Range

Glacier Peak (10,541ft)

Chelan

WASHINGTON

Mt Olympus (7965ft)

Seattle

Bremerton

Leavenworth

Wenatchee

Moses Lake

47

Tacoma

Olympia

Potholes Reservoir

Snake River

IDAHO

Aberdeen

Mt Rainier (14,411ft)

Mt Rainier Nationa Park

Ellensburg

Columbia River

Willapa Bay

Mt St Helens (8363ft)

Yakima

Toppenish

Cape Disappointment

Mount Saint Helens National Volcanic Monument

Mt Adams (12,276ft)

PACIFIC OCEAN

Astoria

Longview

Hood River

Kennewick

Walla Walla

Blue Mountains

Hells Canyon National Recreation Area

Cape Lookout Tillamook

Vancouver

Portland

48

Arlington

Pendleton

Newberg

The Dalles

John Day River

49

Salem

Mt Hood (11,240ft)

OREGON

Newport

Albany

Mt Jefferson (10,495ft)

Madras

Lake Chinook

INSET

Oregon Dunes National Recreation Area

Willamette River

Three Sisters Wilderness

Sisters

YUKON TERRITORY

NORTHWEST TERRITORIES

Florence

Eugene

Bend

Skagway

USA
ALASKA

Juneau

Coos Bay

50

Mt Bachelor (9065ft)

La Pine

Petersburg

CANADA

Roseburg

Cascade Range

Umpqua R

Ketchikan

Prince Rupert

Prince George

Port Orford

Crater Lake National Park

51

Haida Gwaii

52

BRITISH COLUMBIA

Grants Pass

Upper Klamath Lake

Queen Charlotte Sound

ALBERTA

Brookings

Medford

Ashland

Klamath Falls

Campbell River

Crescent City

Klamath River

Goose Lake

CALIFORNIA

PACIFIC OCEAN

Vancouver

Bellingham

Victoria

Seattle

USA

WASHINGTON

200 km
100 miles

400 km
200 miles

DON'T MISS

Cape Disappointment

Few leave Cape Disappointment disappointed, thanks to its spectacular, end-of-the-world setting. Check it out on Trip 48

Leavenworth

German theme towns rarely work in the US, but Leavenworth's alpine backdrop makes it look like the real deal in Trip 46

Cape Perpetua

The best view of the coast can't be seen from the highway; drive to the top of Cape Perpetua for gorgeous vistas on Trip 49

Ross Lake Resort

No wonder Kerouac loved this region with its cold, almost terrifying, beauty. Find this floating hotel on a wilderness lake with no road access on Trip 46

Proxy Falls

Oregon has waterfalls to spare, but one of the prettiest is Proxy Falls, accessed via an easy hike on Trip 50

North Cascades National Park
High-altitude scenery at its best

Classic Trip

Cascade Drive

46

Rugged and inaccessible for half the year, this brawny mountain drive is etched with the kind of monumental, Alaskan-style beauty that once inspired Jack Kerouac.

TRIP HIGHLIGHTS

276 miles

Diablo Lake Overlook
Staggering natural view of a man-made reservoir

250 miles

Rainy Pass
Towering, seasonally accessible road amid saw-toothed Cascade peaks

FINISH
Burlington

START
Everett

Steven's Pass

Chelan

Leavenworth
Bavarian 'theme' town blessed with an authentic alpine backdrop

100 miles

Sun Mountain Lodge
Simply the best place to stay in Washington state, period

215 miles

4–5 DAYS
350 MILES / 563KM

GREAT FOR...

BEST TIME TO GO
June to September when all roads are snow-free and passable.

ESSENTIAL PHOTO

View from the Sun Mountain Lodge over the Methow Valley.

BEST FOR HIKING

The Maple Pass Loop Trail from Rainy Pass.

571

46 Cascade Drive

Nature defies modern engineering in the North Cascades where high-altitude roads succumb to winter snow storms, and the names of the mountains — Mt Terror, Mt Fury, Forbidden Peak — whisper forebodingly. Less scary are the scattered settlements, small towns with esoteric distractions such as Bavarian Leavenworth and 'Wild West' Winthrop. Fill up the tank, put on your favorite Springsteen track and prepare for one of the rides of your life.

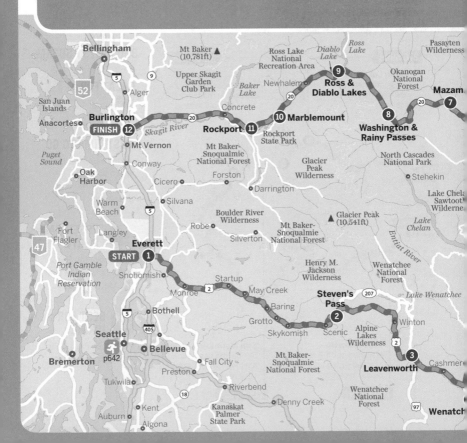

❶ Everett

This drive incorporates four-fifths of the popular 'Cascade Loop.' You'll find there's not much to detain you in Everett, the route's starting point 30 miles north of Seattle. Everett is known mainly for its Boeing connections and as the genesis for countless Seattle-region traffic jams. Head directly east and don't stop until Steven's Pass.

The Drive » The starting point of US-2, a 2579-mile cross-continental road that terminates in Maine, is in Everett. Crossing I-5, the route, which parallels the Great Northern Railway and Skykomish River for much of its journey, passes the small towns of Startup, Sultan and Index, climbing toward Steven's Pass. If you're thirsty, stop at one of the ubiquitous drive-through espresso huts en route.

❷ Steven's Pass

Accessible year round thanks to its day-use **ski area** (www.stevenspass.com), Steven's Pass was only 'discovered' by white settlers as recently as 1890. Despite its lofty vantage – at 4045ft it is more than 1000ft higher than Snoqualmie Pass – the Great Northern railroad chose it for their cross-cascade route. Notwithstanding, you won't see any train tracks here. Instead, the railway burrows underneath the pass via North America's longest rail tunnel, which stretches 7.8 miles. The long-distance **Pacific Crest Trail** also crosses the highway here. Tempted?

The Drive » From Steven's Pass the descent begins immediately, and you'll observe subtle changes in the vegetation; the cedars and hemlocks of the western slopes are gradually replaced with pine, larch and spruce. The road threads through the steep-sided Tumwater canyon alongside the turbulent Wenatchee River. Suddenly, you will see German-style houses start to appear against an eerily familiar alpine backdrop.

TRIP HIGHLIGHT

❸ Leavenworth

Blink hard and rub your eyes. This isn't some strange Germanic hallucination. This is Leavenworth, a former lumber town that underwent a Bavarian makeover in the 1960s after the re-routing of the cross-continental railway threatened to put it permanently out of business.

Swapping loggers for tourists, Leavenworth today has successfully reinvented itself as a traditional *Romantische Strasse* village, right

PACIFIC NORTHWEST TRIPS **46** CASCADE DRIVE

 LINK YOUR TRIP

47 Olympic Peninsula Loop

Drop down WA-20 and take the ferry over to Port Townsend to pick up the Olympic Peninsula Loop.

52 Up the Inside Passage

Head north on I-5 half an hour to Bellingham to take this journey north.

Classic Trip

down to the beer and sausages. The *Sound of Music*–style setting helps, as does the fact that Leavenworth serves as the main activity center for sorties into the nearby **Alpine Lakes Wilderness** and **Wenatchee National Forest**.

A surreal stroll through the gabled alpine houses of Leavenworth's Front St with its dirndl-wearing waitresses, wandering accordionists and European cheese-mongers is one of Washington state's oddest, but most endearing experiences. For white-water-rafting trips, call by **Osprey Rafting Co** (www.ospreyrafting.com; 4342 Icicle Rd), which offers excursions from $78.

 p579

The Drive » The 22 miles between Leavenworth and Wenatchee highlight one of the most abrupt scenery changes in the state. One minute you're in quasi-Bavaria surrounded by crenellated alpine peaks, the next you're in a sprawled couldn't-be-anywhere-but-America town amid bald hills and a Nile-like river valley. East of Leavenworth US-2 shares the road briefly with US-97.

❹ Wenatchee

Fruit stands start peppering the highway soon after you leave Leavenworth, paving your entry into Wenatchee, the self-proclaimed – and who's arguing? – Apple Capital of the World. Something of an ugly sister after cute Leavenworth, Wenatchee's a place to go local and taste the apples from the nearby orchards before swinging north. The best fruit stands enliven Hwy 2/97 on the way to Chelan. As an overture to your tasting experience, check out the **Washington Apple Commission Visitors Center** (☏509-663-9600; www.bestapples.com; 2900 Euclid Ave; ⏰8am-5pm Mon-Fri) on the way into town where you can bone up on the relative merits of a Gala versus a Braeburn over a surprisingly interesting video.

The Drive » Hwy 2/97 plies the east side of the Columbia River between Wenatchee and Chelan. This is one of the best places to 'shop' at impromptu seasonal fruit outlets run by enterprising local farmers who haul their freshly plucked produce from the nearby fields and orchards to sell roadside from semi-permanent stores, carts or just plain old boxes.

❺ Chelan

Lake Chelan shelters some of the nation's cleanest water and has consequently become one of Washington's premier water recreation areas. Not surprisingly, the place is cheek-to-jowl in summer, with all number of speedboats, jet-skis and power-craft battling it out for their own private slice of water. To avoid any high-speed collisions, try renting a kayak from **Lake Rider Sports** (www.lakeridersports.com; Lakeshore Waterfront Park, W Manson Hwy; single/double per day $50/70) and paddling up the lake to see some undiluted Cascadian nature firsthand.

There are public beaches at **Lakeside Park**, near the west side of Chelan town, and at **Lake Chelan State Park**, 9 miles west on S Lakeshore Rd.

If you have kids, don't even think they'll let you sneak past **Slidewaters Water Park** (www.slidewaters.com; 102 Waterslide Dr; day pass adult/child $18/15; ⏰10am-7pm May-Sep; 🖈) on a hill above the *Lady of the Lake* boat dock.

The Drive » Rejoin US-97 and follow it north through the grand coulees of the Columbia River Valley to the small town of Pateros. From here SR-153 aka the Methow Hwy tracks the younger, faster-flowing Methow River north to Twisp. At a junction with US-20 turn left, and continue on the highway into Winthrop.

6 Winthrop

Winthrop is – along with Leavenworth – one of two themed towns on this Cascade Drive. Once a struggling mining community, it avoided 'ghost town' status in the 1960s when it was madeover to look like a cowboy settlement out of the Wild West. Although on paper it sounds more like corny Hollywood than *Gun Fight at the OK Corral*, the Gary Cooper touches are surprisingly authentic. Winthrop's *High Noon* shopfronts hide a genuine frontier spirit (the road ends in winter not far beyond here), and some fantastic eating places and accommodations.

The facades of downtown Winthrop are so realistic it's easy to miss the collection of homesteader cabins that make up the **Shafer Museum** (www.shafermuseum.com; 285 Castle Ave; admission by donation; ⏱10am-5pm May-Sep). But best of all is the unmissable **Sun Mountain Lodge** (www.sunmountainlodge.com), a sporting and relaxation dreamscape 10 miles out of town overlooking the valley.

 p579

The Drive » SR-20 out of Winthrop enters the most bucolic and endearing stretch of the Methow Valley whose broad valley floor scattered with farms gives little hint of the jagged wilderness that lies beyond. If you thought Winthrop was small, don't blink in Mazama, a small cluster of wooden buildings reminiscent of a gunslinger movie.

7 Mazama

The last outpost before the raw, desolate, occasionally terrifying North Cascades, Mazama's half-dozen wooden abodes sit at the western end of the Methow Valley. Fuel up on brownies at the **Mazama Store** (50 Lost River Rd; ⏱7am-6pm Sun-Thu, to 7pm Fri & Sat), aka The Goat, an espresso bar for outdoorsy locals, but also a great place to pick up trail tips.

The Drive » You'll be working through your gears soon after leaving Mazama as the North Cascade Mountains start to close in. This part of US-20 is unlike any other trans-Cascade

LOCAL KNOWLEDGE: METHOW VALLEY TRAILS

The Methow's combination of powdery winter snow and abundant summer sunshine has transformed the valley into one of Washington's primary recreation areas. You can bike, hike and fish in the summer, and cross-country ski on the second-biggest snow-trail network in the US in the winter. The 125 miles of trails are maintained by a nonprofit organization, the **Methow Valley Sport Trails Association** (MVSTA; www.mvsta.com), and in the winter it provides the most comprehensive network of hut-to-hut (and hotel-to-hotel) skiing in North America.

road. Not only is the scenery more spectacular, but the road itself is a major engineering feat. Only completed in 1972, it still remains closed November to May due to snow blockage.

8 Washington & Rainy Passes

Venture less than 100yd from your car at the **Washington Pass overlook** (5477ft) and you'll be rewarded with fine views of the towering Liberty Bell and its Early Winter Spires, while the highway drops below you in ribbonlike loops. By the time the highway reaches **Rainy Pass** (5875ft) a couple of miles further west, the air has chilled and you're well into the high country, a hop and a skip from the drive's highest hiking trails. The 6.2-mile **Maple Pass Loop Trail** is a favorite, climbing 2150ft to aerial views

NIK WHEELER / CORBIS ©

LOCAL KNOWLEDGE
ARLENE WAGNER,
CURATOR,
NUTCRACKER
MUSEUM

Leavenworth is the most authentic German-flavored town in the US. The Bavarian theme was laid out in the 1960s and many German people came to live here later on. For souvenirs look for German clocks, German smokers (wood-carved incense burners), candle pyramids (ornate models where candle-heat turns a fan to rotate figurines and images) and nutcrackers. The Nutcracker Museum exhibits over 6000 nutcrackers, the oldest dating from 200 BC.

Top: Washington Pass
Left: Main St, Winthrop
Right: Leavenworth

over jewel-like Lake Ann. The epic **Pacific Crest Trail** also crosses Hwy 20 nearby, so keep an eye open for wide-eyed and bushy-bearded through-hikers popping out of the undergrowth. Perhaps the best choice to shake the crowds is the excellent climb up to **Easy Pass** (7.4 miles return), hardly 'easy,' but offering spectacular views of Mt Logan and the Fisher Basin below.

The Drive » Surrounded by Gothic peaks, the North Cascades Scenic Hwy makes a big swing north shadowing Granite Creek and then Ruby Creek where it swings back west and enters the Ross Lake National Recreation Area near Ruby Arm.

- - - - - - - - - - -

TRIP HIGHLIGHT

❾ Ross & Diablo Lakes

The odd thing about much of the landscape on this trip is that it's unnatural, born from the construction of three huge dams that still supply Seattle with much of its electricity. The wilderness that surrounds it, however, is as raw as you'll get outside Alaska. **Ross Lake** was formed in the 1930s after the building of the eponymous dam. It stretches north 23 miles into Canada. Soon after the **Ross Lake overlook** a path leads from the road to the dam. You'll see the

unique Ross Lake Resort floating on the other side.

A classic photo op comes a couple of miles later at the **Diablo Lake overlook**. The turquoise lake is the most popular part of the park, offering beaches, gorgeous views and a boat launch at **Colonial Creek campground**, with nearby hikes to Thunder Knob (3.6 miles return) and Thunder Creek.

🛏 p579

The Drive » From Diablo head west alongside the sinuous Gorge Reservoir on US-20. Pass through Newhalem (where you can stop at the North Cascades National Park Visitor Center). As the valley opens out and the damp west-coast air drifts in from the Pacific, you'll enter Marblemount.

- - - - - - - - - - - - - - - - -

⑩ Marblemount

Blink and you'll miss the town of Marblemount, but the thought of buffalo burgers may entice you to pull over at the **Buffalo Run Restaurant** (60084 Hwy 20; lunch $7-9, mains $15-20; ⏰noon-9pm Mon-Thu, 11am-10pm Fri & Sat, 11am-9pm Sun; 🖫), the first (or last) decent restaurant for miles and a friendly one at that, as long as you don't mind being greeted by the sight of several decoratively draped animal skins and a huge

KEROUAC AND THE VOID

A turnout at Mile 135 on US-20 offers the drive's only roadside views of **Desolation Peak**. The peak's lookout tower was famously home to Zen-influenced Beat writer Jack Kerouac who, in 1956, spent 63 days here in splendid isolation, honing his evolving Buddhist philosophy, raging at 'The Void' of nearby Hozomeen Mountain (also visible from the turnout) and penning drafts of *Desolation Angels*. It was the last time Kerouac would enjoy such anonymity; the following year saw the publication of *On the Road*, and his propulsion to the status of literary icon.

buffalo head mounted on the wall.

🛏 p579

The Drive » The Skagit River remains your constant companion as you motor the 8 miles from Marblemount to equally diminutive Rockport.

- - - - - - - - - - - - - - - - -

⑪ Rockport

As the valley widens further you'll touch down in Rockport where the miragelike appearance of an Indonesian-style Batak hut, aka the **Cascadian Home Farm** (www.cascadianfarm.com; Mile 100, Hwy 20; ⏰May-Oct; 🖫), begs you to stop for organic strawberries, delicious fruit shakes and life-saving espresso, which you can slurp down on a short self-guided tour of the farm.

Nearby, a 10-mile stretch of the Skagit River is a wintering ground for over 600 bald eagles who come here from November to early March to feast on spawning salmon. January

is the best time to view them, ideally on a winter float trip with **Skagit River Guide Service** (www.skagitriverfishingguide.com; Mt Vernon). Three-hour trips run early November to mid-February and cost $65.

The Drive » From Rockport head west on US-20 through the Cascade Mountain foothills and the ever-broadening Skagit River Valley to the small city of Burlington that sits just east of busy I-5.

- - - - - - - - - - - - - - - - -

⑫ Burlington

The drive's end, popularly known as the 'Hub City', is not a 'sight' in itself (unless you like looking at shopping malls), although the settlement's location in the heart of the Skagit River Valley means it acts as a hub for numerous nearby attractions including the tulip fields of La Conner, Chuckanut Drive (which officially ends here) and the San Juan Islands.

Eating & Sleeping

Leavenworth ③

✕ Pavz Cafe Bistro   European $$

(www.pavzcafe.com; 833 Front St; mains $15-25; 🕙11:30am-9pm Mon-Fri, from 9am Sat & Sun) The first culinary rule in Leavenworth is this: don't assume you have to dine on bratwurst. Pavz, nestled underneath the timbered gables of Front St, justifies its bistro tag with its signature crepes (savory and sweet) and some outstanding Mediterranean dishes with a northwestern twist. The scallops with pesto-doused angel-hair pasta are a highlight.

🛏 Enzian Inn   Hotel $$

(🖉509-548-5269; www.enzianinn.com; 590 Hwy 2; d/ste $120/250; P 🔊 🏊) Most hotels get by on one quirk, but the Enzian broadcasts at least a half-dozen, the most obscure of which is the sight of long-term owner, Bob Johnson, giving a morning blast on his famous alphorn before breakfast. If this doesn't grab you, look out for the free putting green, swimming pools, or the nightly pianist in the lobby.

Winthrop ⑥

✕ Duck Brand Cantina   Mexican $$

(www.methownet.com/duck; 248 Riverside Ave; mains $8-20; 🕙7am-9pm daily) No standard Mexican restaurant, the 'Duck' nonetheless serves quesadillas, enchiladas and tacos that could roast the socks off any authentic Monterey diner. Closer to home, the Wild West saloon–style cantina churns out a mean American breakfast. In the winter the hearty porridge will keep you skiing all day.

🛏 Sun Mountain Lodge   Hotel $$$

(🖉509-996-2211; www.sunmountainlodge.com; 604 Patterson Lake Rd; lodge d $155-365, cabin $185-485; ❄ 🔊 🏊 👨) Without a doubt one of the best places to stay in Washington, the Sun Mountain Lodge benefits from its incomparable natural setting perched like an eagle's nest high above the Methow Valley. Inside, the lodge and its assorted cabins manage to provide luxury without pretension, while the adjacent trail network could keep a hyperactive hiker/biker/skier occupied for weeks.

Ross & Diablo Lakes ⑨

🛏 Ross Lake Resort   Cabins $$

(🖉206-386-4437; www.rosslakeresort.com; d cabin $155-180; 🕙mid-Jun–Oct) The floating cabins at this secluded resort on Ross Lake were built in the 1930s for loggers. There's no road in – guests can either hike the 2-mile trail from Hwy 20 or take the resort's tugboat-taxi-and-truck shuttle from the parking area near Diablo Dam. Cabins vary in size and facilities, but all feature electricity, plumbing and kitchenettes. Bring food.

Marblemount ⑩

🛏 Buffalo Run Inn   Motel $

(🖉360-873-2103; www.buffaloruninn.com; 58179 Hwy 20; $59/89; ❄ 🔊) Situated on a sharp bend on Hwy 20, the buffalo doesn't look much from the outside. But within its wooden walls is a clean, scrubbed mix of modern motel (kitchenettes, TVs and comfy beds) and backcountry cabin (kitschy bear and buffalo paraphernalia). Five of the 15 rooms share baths and a sitting area upstairs. The Buffalo Run Restaurant is across the road.

Hoh Rainforest Dense, wet, green and intensely surreal

Olympic Peninsula Loop

47

Freakishly wet, fantastically green and chillingly remote, the Olympic Peninsula looks like it's been resurrected from a wilder, pre-civilized era.

TRIP HIGHLIGHTS

166 miles

Hall of Moss Trail
Short trail through moss-draped, old-growth forest

271 miles

Hurricane Ridge
Lofty viewpoint for weather-watching over the Olympic Mountains

Port Angeles

Port Townsend

Forks

6

4

3

2

START/ FINISH

Olympia

Ruby Beach
Blustery beach on Washington's wind-whipped, rain-lashed Pacific coast

134 miles

Lake Quinault Lodge
Historic accommodations with roaring fireplace and lakeside lawn

93 miles

4 DAYS
435 MILES / 700KM

GREAT FOR...

BEST TIME TO GO
June to September when your chances of getting drenched by continuous rain are slightly diminished.

 ESSENTIAL PHOTO

Hoh Rainforest to snap shades of green you haven't even seen yet.

 BEST FOR WILDLIFE

Hoh Rainforest offers rare glimpses of Roosevelt elk.

47 | Olympic Peninsula Loop

Imagine *Wuthering Heights* fused with an American Mt Olympus, with a topical slice of Stephanie Meyer's *Twilight* saga thrown in for good measure and you've got an approximation of what a drive around the Olympic Peninsula might look like. This is wilderness of the highest order where thick forest collides with an end-of-the-continent coastline that hasn't changed much since Juan de Fuca sailed by in 1592. Bring hiking boots – and an umbrella!

Olympia

Welcome to Olympia, city of weird contrasts, where streetside buskers belt out acoustic grunge, and stiff bureaucrats answer their ringtones on the lawns of the expansive state legislature. A quick circuit of the **Washington State Capitol** (admission free; ⏰7am-5pm Mon-Fri, 11am-4pm Sat & Sun), a huge Grecian temple of a building, will give you a last taste of civilization before you depart. Then load up the car and head swiftly for the exits.

✖ p587

The Drive » Your basic route is due west, initially on Hwy 101, then (briefly) on SR-8 before joining US-12 in Elma. In Gray's Harbor enter the twin cities of Aberdeen and Hoquiam, famous for producing William Boeing and the grunge group Nirvana. Here, you swing north on Hwy 101 (again!) to leafier climes at Lake Quinault.

 TRIP HIGHLIGHT

② Lake Quinault

Situated in the extreme southwest of the **Olympic National Park** (www.nps.gov/olym; vehicle $15), the thickly forested Quinault River Valley is one of the park's least-crowded corners. Clustered on the south shore of deep-blue glacial Lake Quinault is the tiny village of **Quinault**, complete with the luscious **Lake Quinault Lodge** (p587), a US Forest Service (USFS) office, plus a couple of stores.

A number of short **hiking trails** begin just below Lake Quinault Lodge; pick up a free map from the USFS office. The shortest of these is the **Quinault Rain Forest Nature Trail**, a half-mile walk through 500-year-old

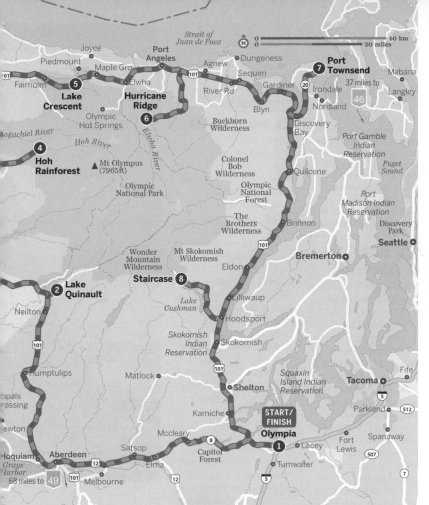

Douglas firs. This brief trail adjoins the 3-mile **Quinault Loop Trail**, which meanders through the rain forests before circling back to the lake. The Quinault region is renowned for its huge trees. Close to the village is a 191ft Sitka spruce tree (supposedly over 1000 years old), and nearby are

 LINK YOUR TRIP

46 **Cascade Drive**
From Port Townsend, take the ferry north then follow WA-20 to Burlington.

49 **Highway 101 Oregon Coast**
Take I-5 south then head west to the coastal town of Astoria, OR.

the world's largest red cedar, Douglas fir and mountain hemlock trees.

📖 p587

The Drive » West from Quinault Lake, Hwy 101 continues through the Quinault Indian Reservation before entering a thin strip of national park territory that protects the beaches around Kalaloch (*klay*-lock). This is some of the wildest coastal scenery in the US accessible by road. Various pullovers allow beach forays.

TRIP HIGHLIGHT

❸ Ruby Beach

Inhabiting a thin coastal strip that was added to the national park in 1953, Ruby Beach is accessed via a short 0.2-mile path that leads down to a large expanse of windswept coast embellished by polished black stones and wantonly strewn tree trunks. To the south toward Kalaloch, other accessible beachfronts are unimaginatively named Beach One through to Beach Six, all of which are popular with beachcombers. At low tide, rangers give talks on tidal-pool life at **Beach Four** and on the ecosystems of the Olympic coastal strip.

📖 p587

The Drive » North of Ruby Beach, Hwy 101 swings sharply northeast and inland, tracking the Hoh River. Turn right off 101 onto the Hoh River Rd to explore one of the national park's most popular inner sanctums. Suspend your excitement as the trees eerily close in as you (re-) enter the park.

TRIP HIGHLIGHT

❹ Hoh Rainforest

Count yourself lucky if you arrive on a day when it isn't raining! The most popular detour off Hwy 101 is the 19-mile paved road to the Hoh Valley, the densest, wettest, greenest and most intensely surreal temperate rainforest on planet earth. The essential hike here is the short but fascinating **Hall of Moss Trail**, an easy 0.75-mile loop through the kind of weird, ethereal scenery that even JRR Tolkien couldn't have invented. Old-man's beard drips from branches above you like corduroy fringe, while trailside licorice ferns and lettuce lichens overwhelm the massive fallen trunks of maple and Sitka spruce. Rangers lead interesting free guided walks here twice a day during summer and can help you spot some of the park's 5000-strong herd of Roosevelt elk.

The Drive » Rejoining Hwy 101, motor north to the small and relatively nondescript settlement of Forks. Press on through as Hwy 101 bends north then east through a large logging area before plunging back into the national park on the shores of wondrous Lake Crescent.

KEVIN SCHAFER / CORBIS ©

❺ Lake Crescent

Before you've even had time to erase the horror of teenage vampires from your head (see p586), the scenery shifts again as the road winds along the glittering pine-scented shores of glacial-carved Lake Crescent. The lake looks best from water level, on a rental kayak,

Ruby Beach This windswept coast is embellished by polished black stones

or from high above at its eastern edge on the **Storm King Mountain Trail** (named after the peak's wrathful spirit), accessible via a steep, 1.7-mile ascent that splits off the Barnes Creek Trail. For the less athletic, the **Marymere Falls Trail** is a 2-mile round-trip to a 90ft cascade that drops down over a basalt cliff. Both hikes leave from a parking lot to the right of SR 101 near the **Storm King Information Station** (🕐 summer only). The area is also the site of the Lake Crescent Lodge, the oldest of the park's trio of celebrated lodges that first opened in 1916.

🛏 p587

The Drive » From Lake Crescent take Hwy 101 east to the town of Port Angeles, a gateway to Victoria, Canada, which is reachable by ferry to the north. Starting in Race St, the 18-mile Hurricane Ridge Rd climbs up 5300ft toward extensive wildflower meadows and expansive mountain vistas often visible above the clouds.

- - - - - - - - - -

TRIP HIGHLIGHT

6 Hurricane Ridge

Up above the clouds, stormy Hurricane Ridge lives up to its name with

THE TWILIGHT ZONE

It would have been impossible to envisage a decade ago: diminutive Forks, a depressed lumber town full of hardnosed loggers, reborn as a pilgrimage site for 'tweenage' girls following in the ghostly footsteps of two fictional sweethearts named Bella and Edward. The reason for this weird metamorphosis is the *Twilight* saga, a four-part book series by US author Stephanie Meyer about love and vampires on the foggy Olympic Peninsula that in seven short years has shifted over 100 million books and spawned five Hollywood movies. With Forks acting as the book's main setting, the town has catapulted to international stardom. You can follow in Bella and Edward's footsteps with a Twilight Tour from **Team Forks** (360-374-5634; www.teamfoks.com; tickets $30-55), which takes you to most of the places mentioned in Meyer's books.

fickle weather and biting winds made slightly more bearable by the park's best high-altitude views. Its proximity to Port Angeles is another bonus; if you're heading up here be sure to call into the museum-like **Olympic National Park Visitor Center** (3002 Mt Angeles Rd, Port Angeles; park admission $15;) first. The smaller **Hurricane Ridge Visitor Center** (9:30am-5pm daily summer, Fri-Sun winter) has a snack bar, gift shop, toilets and is the starting point of various hikes. **Hurricane Hill Trail** (which begins at the end of the road), and the **Meadow Loop Trails** network are popular and moderately easy. The first half-mile of these trails is wheelchair-accessible.

The Drive » Wind back down the Hurricane Ridge Rd, kiss the suburbs of Port Angeles and press east through the retirement community of Sequim (pronounced 'squwim'). Turn north on SR-20 to reach another more attractive port, Port Townsend.

➐ Port Townsend

Leaving the park momentarily behind, ease back into civilization with the cultured Victorian comforts of Port Townsend, whose period charm dates from the railroad boom of the 1890s, when the town was earmarked to become the 'New York of the West.' That never happened but you can pick up a historic walking-tour map from the **Port Townsend visitors center** (www.enjoypt.com; 440 12th St; 9am-5pm Mon-Fri, 10am-4pm Sat, 11am-4pm Sun) and wander the waterfront's collection of shops, galleries and antique malls. Don't miss the old-time **Belmont Saloon** (Water St), the **Rose Theatre** (www.rosetheatre.com; 235 Taylor St), a gorgeously renovated theater that's been showing movies since 1908, and the fine Victorian mansions on the bluff above town, where several charming residences have been turned into B&Bs.

p587

The Drive » From Port Townsend retrace your steps to the junction of Hwy 101, but this time head south passing Quilcene, Brinnon, with its great diner (p587), and the Dosewallips park entrance. You get more unbroken water views here on the park's eastern side courtesy of the Hood Canal, a serene contrast to the wind-whipped waves of the open Pacific. Track the watery beauty to Hoodsport where signs point west (right) off Hwy 101 to Staircase.

➑ Staircase

It's drier on the park's eastern side and the mountains are closer. The Staircase park nexus, accessible via Hoodsport, has a ranger station, campground and a decent trail system that follows the drainage of the North Fork Skokomish River and is flanked by some of the most rugged peaks in the Olympics. Nearby **Lake Cushman** has a campground and water-sports opportunities.

Eating & Sleeping

Olympia ❶

✗ Spar Cafe
Pub, Diner $

(114 4th Ave E; breakfast $4-6, lunch $6-9; ⊙7am-midnight Sun-Thu, to 1am Fri & Sat) A long-established local cafe and eating joint now owned by Portland's McMenamin Brothers who have maintained its authentic wood-panel interior. You could spend hours here eating brunch, shooting pool, tasting the microbrews and listening to the buskers on 4th Ave outside.

Lake Quinault ❷

🛏 Lake Quinault Lodge
Lodge $$

(☎360-288-2900; www.olympicnationalparks. com; 345 S Shore Rd; d $150-289; ✱ ▨) Everything you could want in a historic national park lodge and more, the 'Quinault' has a huge, roaring fireplace, peek-a-boo lake views, a manicured cricket-pitch-quality lawn, huge comfy leather sofas, a regal reception area and – arguably – the finest eating experience on the whole peninsula. The latter is thanks to the memorable sweet-potato pancakes served up for breakfast.

Ruby Beach ❸

🛏 Kalaloch Lodge
Historic Hotel $$$

(☎360-962-2271; www.thekalalochlodge. com; 157151 US 101, Forks; d $165-311, cabins from $229; ✱) A little less grand than the Lake Quinault and Lake Crescent Lodges, the Kalaloch (built in 1953), nonetheless, enjoys an equally spectacular setting perched on a bluff overlooking the crashing Pacific.

Lake Crescent ❺

🛏 Lake Crescent Lodge
Historic Hotel $$

(☎360-928-3211; www.olympicnationalparks. com; 416 Lake Crescent Rd; d $168-278; ⊙May-Oct; ✱ 🛜) Built in 1915 as a fishing resort, this venerable shake-sided building is the oldest of the Olympic National Park lodges and, along with the Lake Quinault Lodge, leads the way in style and coziness. To add star appeal, President FD Roosevelt stayed here in 1937 – a year before he made the Olympics a national park.

Port Townsend ❼

✗ Waterfront Pizza
Pizza $$

(951 Water St; large pizzas $11-19; ⊙11am-9pm Sun-Thu, to 10pm Fri & Sat) Quite simply the best pizza in the state, this buy-by-the-slice outlet inspires huge local loyalty and will satisfy even the most querulous of Chicago-honed palates. The secret: crisp sourdough crusts and creative but not over-stacked toppings.

🛏 Palace Hotel
Hotel $

(☎360-385-0773; www.palacehotelpt.com; 1004 Water St; r $59-109; ✱ 🛜) Built in 1889, this beautiful Victorian building is a former brothel that was once run by the locally notorious Madame Marie, who did her dodgy business out of the 2nd-floor corner suite. Reincarnated as an attractive period hotel with antique furnishings and old-fashioned claw-foot baths, the Palace's seediness is now a thing of the past.

Brinnon

✗ Halfway House
Diner $

(☎360-796-4715; 41 Brinnon Lane; 7am-8pm Sun-Thu, to 9pm Fri & Sat) This is one of those 'great find' places that pepper the byways of rural America – an embellishment-free diner with friendly staff, lightning-quick service and crusty fruit pies that taste like they were made by someone's treasured grandma. It sits aside Hwy 101 in Brinnon, halfway between Port Townsend and Staircase.

Lewis & Clark monument, Seaside
America's greatest explorers

END OF THE TRAIL

On the Trail of Lewis & Clark

48

Follow the Columbia River on this historic drive that marks the climax of Lewis and Clark's cross-continental 1805 journey as they stumbled toward the Pacific and instant immortality.

TRIP HIGHLIGHTS

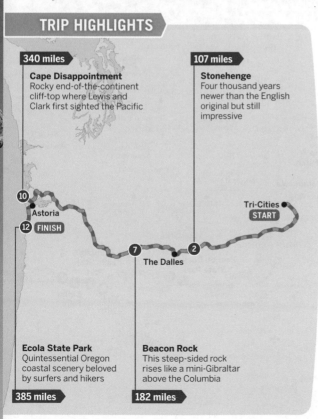

340 miles

Cape Disappointment
Rocky end-of-the-continent cliff-top where Lewis and Clark first sighted the Pacific

107 miles

Stonehenge
Four thousand years newer than the English original but still impressive

10 Astoria

12 FINISH

Tri-Cities
START

7

The Dalles

2

Ecola State Park
Quintessential Oregon coastal scenery beloved by surfers and hikers

385 miles

Beacon Rock
This steep-sided rock rises like a mini-Gibraltar above the Columbia

182 miles

3–4 DAYS
385 MILES / 620 KM

GREAT FOR...

BEST TIME TO GO
Year-round – if you don't mind frequent rain, the Columbia river valley is always open.

 ESSENTIAL PHOTO

Indian Beach, Ecola State Park; the Oregon coast personified.

 BEST FOR HISTORY

The Lewis & Clark Interpretive Center in Cape Disappointment State Park.

48 On the Trail of Lewis & Clark

It would take most people their combined annual leave to follow the Lewis and Clark trek in its entirety from St Louis, MO, to Cape Disappointment. Focusing on the final segment, this trip documents the contradictory mix of crippling exhaustion and building excitement that the two explorers felt as they struggled, car-less and weather-beaten, along the Columbia River on their way to completing the greatest overland trek in American history.

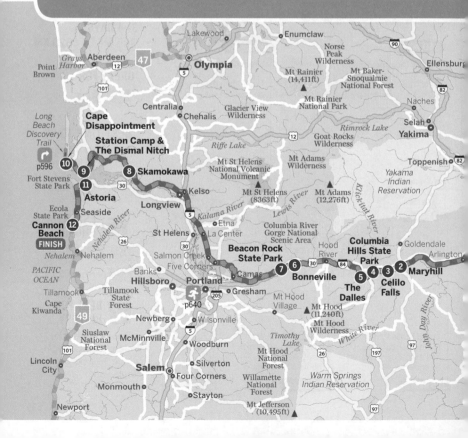

❶ Tri-Cities

This trip's start point has a weighty historical significance. The arrival of Lewis and Clark and the Corps of Discovery at the confluence of the Snake and Columbia Rivers on 16 October, 1805, marked a milestone achievement on their quest to map a river route to the Pacific. After a greeting by 200 Indians singing and drumming in a half-circle, the band camped at this spot for two days, trading clothing for dried

salmon. The **Sacajawea Interpretive Center** (☎509-545-2361; Sacajawea State Park, Pasco, WA; admission free; ◷10am-5pm late Mar-Nov 1; ♿), situated at the river confluence 5 miles southeast of present-day Pasco, relates the story of the expedition through the eyes of Sacajawea, the Shoshone Native American guide and interpreter the Corps had recruited in North Dakota.

✖ p597

The Drive » Head south on I-82 before switching east at the Columbia River on SR-14, aka the Lewis & Clark Hwy. Here, in dusty sagebrush country, you'll pass a couple of minor sites – Wallula Gap, where the Corps first spotted Mt Hood, and the volcanic bluff of Hat Rock, first named by William Clark.

❷ Maryhill

Conceived by great Northwest entrepreneur and road-builder Sam Hill, the **Maryhill Museum of Art** (www.maryhillmuseum.org; 35 Maryhill Museum Dr,

Goldendale, WA; adult/child/senior $9/3/8; ◷10am-5pm Mar 15-Nov 15) occupies a mansion atop a bluff overlooking the Columbia River. Its eclectic art collection is enhanced by a small Lewis and Clark display, while its peaceful gardens are perfect for a classy picnic punctuated by exotic peacock cries. Interpretive signs point you to fine views down the Columbia Gorge to the riverside spot (now a state park) where Meriwether Lewis and William Clark camped on 21 October, 1805. The park is just one of several along this trip where you can pitch a tent within a few hundred yards of the Corps' original camp.

Another of Hill's creations – a life-sized unruined replica of **Stonehenge** – lies 2 miles to the east.

The Drive » Continue west from Maryhill on SR-14 for 5 miles to the site of the now submerged Celilo Falls.

LINK YOUR TRIP

47 **Olympic Peninsula Loop**

From Astoria, take Hwy 101 north 78 miles to Aberdeen to join up with this loop.

49 **Highway 101 Oregon Coast**

At the end of this trip, head south down the coast starting in Astoria.

❸ Celilo Falls

A vivid imagination can be as important as sunscreen when following the 'Trail.' One example of this is the turnout 5 miles west of Maryhill that overlooks what was once the Indian salmon-fishing center of Celilo Falls. The explorers spent two days here in late October 1805, lowering their canoes down the crashing falls on elk-skin ropes. A century and a half later the rising waters of the dammed Columbia drowned the falls – which were the sixth-most voluminous in the world – destroying a centuries-old Native American fishing site and rendering much of Clark's description of the region unrecognizable.

The Drive » Head west on SR-14, paralleling the mighty Columbia, for another 15 miles.

❹ Columbia Hills State Park

Indian tribes including the Nez Perce, Clatsop and Walla Walla were essential to the success of the Lewis and Clark expedition, supplying them not only with food but also horses and guides. One of the best places to view tangible traces of the region's Native American heritage is the Temani Pesh-wa ('Written on Rocks') Trail at **Columbia Hills State Park** (www.parks.wa.gov; Hwy 14, Mile 85, WA; 6.30am-dusk Apr-Oct), which highlights the region's best petroglyphs. Reserve a spot in advance on the free **guided tours** (☏509-773-5007) on Friday and Saturday at 10am to view the famous but fragile pictograph of the god Tsagagalal (She Who Watches). The park is also a popular site for rock climbers and windsurfers.

The Drive » Two miles west of Horsethief Lake, turn south onto US-197, which takes you across the Columbia River into The Dalles in Oregon. Two miles upriver sits The Dalles Dam, which completely submerged the once-magnificent Celilo Falls and rapids on its completion in 1957.

❺ The Dalles

Once the urban neighbor of the formidable Celilo Falls, The Dalles' image is more mundane these days. The local economy focuses on cherry-growing, computer technology and outdoor recreation. Notwithstanding, the town hosts one of the best Lewis and Clark–related museums along this stretch of the Columbia, sited in the **Columbia Gorge Discovery Center** (www.gorgediscovery.org; 5000 Discovery Dr; adult/child/senior $9/5/7; ☻9am-5pm; ♿) on the western edge of the city. Displays detail the 30 tons of equipment the Corps dragged across the continent and the animals they had to kill to survive (including 190 dogs and a ferret). Kids will get a kick from dressing up in Lewis and Clark period costume.

✕ ﹝ p597

The Drive » You can continue west from The Dalles on either side of the Columbia (the expedition traveled straight down the middle by canoe) via SR-14 (Washington), or the slower, more scenic SR-30 (Oregon). En route, look for the views down to macabre Memaloose Island, once a burial site for Native Americans who left their dead here in canoes of cedar.

❻ Bonneville

There are two Bonnevilles: Bonneville, Oregon, and North Bonneville, Washington. At this stage in their trip, Lewis and Clark were flea-infested and half-starved from a diet of dog meat and starchy, potatolike wapto roots. Fortunately, 21st-century Bonneville – which is famous for its Depression-era dam completed in 1938 – has some tastier culinary offerings to contemplate.

﹝ p597

TRIP HIGHLIGHT

❼ Beacon Rock State Park

On November 2, 1805, a day after passing modern Bonneville, Clark wrote about a remarkable 848ft-tall monolith he called Beaten Rock, changing the name on his return to **Beacon Rock**. Just over a century later, Henry Biddle bought the rock for the bargain price of $1 (!) and you can still hike his snaking 1-mile trail to the top of the former lava plug in **Beacon Rock State Park** (www.parks.wa.gov; ⏱8am-dusk). As you enjoy the wonderful views, ponder the fact that you have effectively climbed up the *inside* of an ancient volcano. For the Corps, the rock brought a momentous discovery, for it was here that the excited duo first noticed the tide, proving at last that they were finally nearing their goal of crossing the American continent.

The Drive >> Your next stop along SR-14 should be the fantastic views of the flood-carved gorge and its impressive cascades from the Cape Horn overview. From here, it's a straight shot on I-5 to Kelso and then over the Lewis & Clark Bridge to parallel the Columbia River westward on SR-4.

HISTORIC PARK

The so-called **Lewis & Clark National & State Historical Parks** (www.nps.gov/lewi; admission $3; 9am-5pm) combines 10 different historical sites clustered around the mouth of the Columbia River, each of which relates to important facts about the Corps of Discovery and its historic mission to map the American West. It was formed through the amalgamation of various state parks and historic sites in 2004, and is run jointly by the National Park Service and the states of Washington and Oregon. Highlights include Cape Disappointment, Fort Clatsop and the 6.5-mile Fort to Sea trail linking Clatsop and the ocean at Sunset Beach.

❽ Skamokawa

For most of their trip down the Columbia River, Lewis and Clark traveled not on foot but by canoe. There's nowhere better to paddle in the Corps' canoe wake than at the **Skamokawa Center** (☎360-849-4016 www.skamokawakayak.com; 1391 Rte 4, Skamokawa, WA; tours $65-115), which offers one- or two-day kayak tours to Grays Bay or Pillar Rock, where Clark wrote 'Great joy in camp we are in view of the Ocian, this great Pacific Octean which we been So long anxious to See.'

The Drive >> Continue on SR-4 northwest out of Skamokawa. In Naselle, go southwest on SR-401.

❾ Station Camp & Dismal Nitch

Just east of the Astoria-Megler Bridge on the north bank of the Columbia River, a turnout marks Dismal Nitch, where the drenched duo were stuck in a pounding weeklong storm that Clark described as 'the most disagreeable time I have ever experienced.' The Corps finally managed to make camp at Station Camp, 3 miles further west, now an innocuous highway pullout, where they stayed for 10 days while the two leaders, no doubt sick of each other by now, separately explored the headlands around Cape Disappointment.

The Drive >> You're nearly there! Contain your excitement as you breeze the last few miles west along Hwy 101 to Ilwaco and the inappropriately named Cape Disappointment.

ON THE TRAIL OF LEWIS & CLARK
BRENDAN SAINSBURY, AUTHOR

This retracing of the Corps of Discovery's transcontinental wilderness odyssey is as close as it gets to an American pilgrimage. Lewis and Clark were, without doubt, America's greatest explorers and the nation wouldn't be the same today without them. Meticulous, curious, brave and groundbreaking, they also came in peace; only one small incident on their return journey with the Blackfeet Indians marred the charitable spirit of the Corps' grail-like quest.

Top: Cape Disappoinment
Left: Beacon Rock
Right: Fort Clatsop, Astoria

DANITA DELIMONT / GETTY IMAGES ©

GARY WEATHERS / GETTY IMAGES ©

TRIP HIGHLIGHT

❿ Cape Disappointment

Disappointment is probably the last thing you're likely to be feeling as you pull into blustery cliff-top **Cape Disappointment State Park** (Hwy 100; ⊘6:30am-dusk). Find time to make the short ascent of Mackenzie Hill in Clark's footprints and catch your first true sight of the Pacific. You can almost hear his protracted sigh of relief over two centuries later.

Located on a high bluff inside the park not far from the Washington town of Ilwaco, the sequentially laid-out **Lewis & Clark Interpretive Center** (☎360-642-3029; Hwy 100; adult/youth $5/2.50; ⊘10am-5pm) faithfully recounts the Corps of Discovery's cross-continental journey using a level of detail the journal-writing explorers would have been proud of. Anally retentive information includes everything from how to use an octant to what kind of underpants Lewis wore! A succinct 20-minute film backs up the permanent exhibits. Phone ahead and you can also tour the impressive end-of-continent **North Head Lighthouse** (tours $2.50) nearby.

RUSS BISHOP / ALAMY ©

DETOUR:
LONG BEACH DISCOVERY TRAIL

Start: ⑩ Cape Disappointment

Soon after arriving in 'Station Camp,' the indefatigable Clark, determined to find a better winter bivouac, set out with several companions to continue the hike west along a broad sandy peninsula, coming to a halt near present-day 26th St in Long Beach, where Clark dipped his toe in the Pacific and carved his name on a cedar tree for posterity. The route of this historic three-day trudge has been recreated in the Long Beach Discovery Trail, a footpath that runs from the small town of Ilwaco, adjacent to Cape Disappointment, to Clark's 26th St turnaround. Officially inaugurated in September 2009, the trail has incorporated some dramatic life-sized sculptures along its 8.2-mile length. One depicts a giant gray-whale skeleton, another recalls Clark's recorded sighting of a washed-up sea sturgeon, while a third recreates in bronze the original cedar tree (long since uprooted by a Pacific storm).

The Drive ≫ From Ilwaco, take Hwy 101 back east to the 4.1-mile long Astoria-Megler Bridge, the longest continuous truss bridge in the US. On the other side lies Astoria in Oregon, the oldest US-founded settlement west of the Mississippi.

- - - - - - - - - - - - - -

⑪ Astoria

After the first truly democratic ballot in US history (in which a woman and a black slave both voted), the party elected to make their winter bivouac across the Columbia River in present-day Oregon. A replica of the original **Fort Clatsop** (adult/child $3/free; ☺9am-6pm Jun-Aug, to 5pm Sep-May), where the Corps spent a miserable winter in 1805–06, lies 5 miles south of Astoria.

Also on-site are trails, a visitors center and buckskin-clad rangers who wander the camp between mid-June and Labor Day sewing moccasins (the Corps stockpiled an impressive 340 pairs for their return trip), tanning leather and firing their muskets.

✗ ⊨ p597

The Drive ≫ From Fort Clatsop, take Hwy 101, aka the Oregon Coast Hwy, south through the town of Seaside to Cannon Beach.

- - - - - - - - - - - - - -

TRIP HIGHLIGHT

⑫ Cannon Beach

Mission accomplished – or was it? Curiosity (and hunger) got the better of the Corps in early 1806 when news of a huge beached whale ('that monstrous fish') lured Clark and Sacagawea from a salt factory they had set up near the

present-day town of Seaside down through what is now Ecola State Park to Cannon Beach.

Ecola State Park is the Oregon you may have already visited in your dreams: sea stacks, crashing surf, hidden beaches and gorgeous pristine forest. Crisscrossed by paths, it lies 1.5 miles north of Cannon Beach, the high-end 'antiresort' resort so beloved by Portlanders.

Clark found the whale near **Haystack Rock**, a 295ft sea stack that's the most spectacular landmark on the Oregon coast and accessible from the beach. After bartering with the Tillamook tribe, he staggered away with 300lb of whale blubber – a feast for the half-starved Corps of Discovery.

✗ ⊨ p597

Eating & Sleeping

Tri-Cities ❶

✕ Atomic Ale Brewpub & Eatery   Pub $

(www.atomicalebrewpub.com; 1015 Lee Blvd; pizzas $13-17; ⏱11am-10pm Mon-Thu, to 11pm Fri & Sat, to 8pm Sun) Hanford-inspired 'gallows humor' pervades this cheery microbrewery, well known for its wood-fired specialty pizzas and locally crafted Atomic Amber. Real intellectuals grab an Oppenheimer Oatmeal Stout.

The Dalles ❺

✕ Baldwin Saloon   American $$

(☎541-296-5666; www.baldwinsaloon.com; 205 Court St; mains $9-25) The Baldwin is more about atmosphere than the food (burgers and decadent desserts). The saloon is a one-time bar, brothel, steamboat office and coffin storage warehouse that's been in business since 1876.

▤ Celilo Inn   Boutique Motel $$

(☎541-769-0001; www.celiloinn.com; 3550 East 2nd St; d from $99; ❄ 🛜 🏊) Overlooking The Dalles Dam on the Columbia River, the Celilo is a sort of upmarket motel whose plushness suggests regular refurbs.

Bonneville ❻

▤ Bonneville Hot Springs Resort & Spa   Hotel $$$

(☎866-459-1678; www.bonnevilleresort.com; 1252 E Cascade Dr, North Bonneville, WA; r $159-289) Recover from the rigors of the trail at this luxurious hotel, pool and spa complex a mile or two east of Beacon Rock. If this had been here in 1805, a knackered Lewis would have probably plumped for the restorative eucalyptus wrap.

Astoria ⓫

✕ T Paul's Urban Café   International $$

(www.tpaulsurbancafe.com; 1119 Commercial St; mains $9-16; ⏱11am-9pm Mon-Thu, to 10pm Fri & Sat) Cooks up formidable lunchtime quesadillas served with nachos and a homemade salsa dip.

✕ ▤ Commodore Hotel   Boutique Hotel $$

(☎503-325-4747; www.commodoreastoria. com; 258 14th St; d with shared/private bath from $79-109; @ 🛜) This early-20th-century wonder reopened in 2009 after 45 years as a pigeon coop. The birds and moths have been replaced by a stylish set of European-style rooms and suites. Don't miss the 14th Street Coffee House next door with its fine java and neo-industrial decor.

▤ Hotel Elliott   Historic Hotel $$

(☎503-325-2222; www.hotelelliott.com; 357 12th St; d/ste $99/189; ❄ 🛜) In the oldest part of the oldest town west in the Pacific Northwest is the elegant Elliot, a period piece that has clawed its way up to boutique standard without losing its historical significance.

Cannon Beach ⓬

✕ Newman's   French, Italian $$$

(☎503-436-1151; www.newmansat988.com; 988 S Hemlock St; mains $19-28; ⏱5:30-9pm daily, closed Mon Oct-Jun) Fuse the world's two greatest cuisines (Italian and French) to create a regionally lauded fine-dining experience in this historic beach house turned restaurant.

▤ Cannon Beach Hotel   Historic Hotel $$

(☎503-436-1392; www.cannonbeachhotel.com; 1116 S Hemlock St; d $99-189; @ 🛜) Classy joint with small but meticulously turned-out rooms in a historic wooden Craftsman-style building dating from 1914. A downstairs lounge and cafe-bistro add to the charm.

Cape Sebastian Wind past dramatic ocean views

Classic Trip

Highway 101 Oregon Coast

49

Routes like Highway 101 are the reason the road trip was invented. It meanders the length of the Oregon coast past sandy beaches, colorful tide pools and nearly a dozen lighthouses.

TRIP HIGHLIGHTS

START

1 ———— **1 mile**

Astoria
Cute Victorian town at the mouth of the Columbia

161 miles

Cape Perpetua
Hands-down the best views on the Oregon coast

Tillamook ●

9 ———— **134 miles**

Newport
Tide pools and two lighthouses make this a coastal favorite

11

● Florence

283 miles

Port Orford
Hike Humbug Mountain and meet some prehistoric creatures

● Coos Bay

17

● Brookings

FINISH

**7 DAYS
340 MILES / 547KM**

GREAT FOR...

BEST TIME TO GO
Visit July to October, when the weather is more cooperative.

 ESSENTIAL PHOTO

The life-size T-rex outside Prehistoric Gardens.

 BEST HIKING

Cape Perpetua offers several breathtaking hikes.

599

Classic Trip

49 Highway 101 Oregon Coast

Scenic, two-lane Highway 101 follows hundreds of miles of shoreline punctuated with charming seaside towns, exhilarating hikes and ocean views that remind you you're on the edge of the continent. In this trip, it's not about getting from point A to point B. Instead, the route itself is the destination. And everyone from nature lovers to gourmands to families can find their dream vacation along this exceptional coastal route.

TRIP HIGHLIGHT

① Astoria

We begin our coastal trek in the northwestern corner of the state, where the Columbia River meets the Pacific Ocean. Ever-so-slightly inland, Astoria doesn't rely on beach proximity for its character. It has a rich history, including being a stop on the Lewis and Clark trail (p589). Because of its location, it also has a unique maritime history, which you can explore at the **Columbia River Maritime Museum** (www.crmm.org; 1792 Marine Dr; adult/child $12/5; ◷9:30am-5pm).

Astoria has been the location of several Hollywood movies, making it a virtual Hollywood by the sea: it's best known as the setting for cult hit *The Goonies*. Fans can peek at the **Goonies House** (368 38th St) and the **Clatsop County Jail** (732 Duane St).

✕ ⮫ p610

The Drive » Head south on Hwy 101 for 14.5 miles to Gearhart.

② Gearhart

Check your tide table and head to the beach; Gearhart is famous for its razor clamming at low tide. All you need are boots, a shovel or a clam gun, a cut-resistant glove, a license (available in Gearhart) and a bucket for your catch. Watch your fingers – the name razor clam is well earned. Boiling up a batch will likely result in the most memorable meal of your trip. For information on where, when and how to clam, visit the **Oregon Department of Fish & Wildlife website** (www.dfw.state.or.us); it's a maze of a site, so just Google 'ODFW clamming.'

The Drive » Don't get too comfortable yet: Seaside is just 2.4 miles further down the coast.

③ Seaside

Oregon's biggest and busiest resort town delivers exactly what you'd expect from a town called Seaside, which is wholesome,

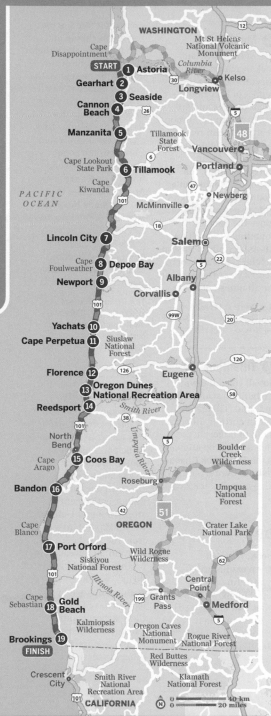

Coney Island-esque fun. The 2-mile boardwalk – known as 'the Prom' – is a kaleidoscope of seaside kitsch, with surrey rentals, video arcades, fudge, elephant ears, caramel apples, saltwater taffy and more. It's also where you'll find the **Seaside Aquarium** (www.seasideaquarium.com; 200 N Promenade; adult/child $8/4; ⊙9am-7pm; 🚻). Open since 1937, the privately owned aquarium isn't much more than a few fish tanks, a touch pool and a small indoor seal tank where you can feed the splashy critters, but it's a fun stop for inquisitive kids.

✖ p610

The Drive » Leave the beach behind for a bit as you veer inland for the 8.8-mile drive to Cannon Beach.

LINK YOUR TRIP

48 On the Trail of Lewis & Clark

Do the Hwy 101 trip backwards and you can pick up the trail of Lewis and Clark in Astoria.

51 Crater Lake Circuit

Continue south to Crescent City then take US-199 northeast to Grant's Pass.

❹ Cannon Beach

Charming Cannon Beach is one of the most popular beach resorts on the Oregon coast. The wide sandy beach stretches for miles, and you'll find great photo opportunities and tide-pooling possibilities at glorious **Haystack Rock**, the third-tallest sea stack in the world. (What's a sea stack, you might ask? It's a vertical rock formation – in this case, one that's shaped like a haystack.) For the area's best coastal hiking, head immediately north of town to **Ecola State Park** (www.oregonstateparks.org; day use $5), where you can hike to secluded beaches.

 p610

The Drive >> Follow the coast 14.4 miles through Oswald West State Park to reach your next stop.

❺ Manzanita

One of the more laid-back beach resorts on Oregon's coast is the hamlet of Manzanita – much smaller and far less hyped than Cannon Beach. You can relax on the white-sand beaches, or, if you're feeling more ambitious, hike on nearby **Neahkahnie Mountain**, where high cliffs rise dramatically above the Pacific's pounding waves. It's a 3.8-mile climb to the top, but the views are worth it: on a clear day, you can see 50 miles out to sea.

The Drive >> Drive 27 miles from Nehalem Bay to Tillamook Bay to reach inland Tillamook.

❻ Tillamook

Not all coastal towns are built on seafood and sand. Tillamook has an entirely different claim to fame: cheese. Thousands stop annually at the **Tillamook Cheese Visitors Center** (4175 N US 101; ⊘8am-6pm, to 8pm in summer) for free samples. You might choose to skip the dairy altogether and head to one of two interesting museums: the **Pioneer Museum** (www.tcpm.org; 2106 2nd St; adult/child $4/1; ⊘10am-4pm Tue-Sun) has antique toys, a great taxidermy room (check out the polar bear) and a basement full of pioneer artifacts. And just south of town, the **Tillamook Naval Air Museum** (www.tillamookair.com; 6030 Hangar Rd; adult/child $12/8; ⊘9am-5pm) has a large collection of fighter planes and a 7-acre blimp hangar.

The Drive >> South of Tillamook, Hwy 101 follows the Nestucca River through pastureland and logged-off mountains 44 miles to Lincoln City.

❼ Lincoln City

The sprawling modern beach resort of Lincoln City serves as the region's principal commercial center. In addition to gas and groceries, the town does offer a unique enticement to stop: from mid-October to late May volunteers from the Visitor & Convention Bureau hide brightly colored glass floats – which have been handblown by local artisans – along the beaches, making a memorable souvenir for the resourceful and diligent vacationer.

THREE CAPES LOOP

South of the town of Tillamook, Hwy 101 veers inland from the coast. An exhilarating alternative route is the slow, winding and sometimes bumpy Three Capes Loop, which hugs the shoreline for 30 miles and offers the chance to go clamming. En route you'll traverse Cape Meares, Cape Lookout and Cape Kiwanda – three stunning headlands that you'd otherwise miss entirely.

p610

The Drive » It's back to the coast for the 12-mile drive south to Depoe Bay.

8 Depoe Bay

Though edged by modern timeshare condominiums, Depoe Bay still retains some original coastal charm. It lays claim to having the 'world's smallest navigable harbor' and being the 'world's whale-watching capital' – pretty big talk for such a pint-sized town. Whale-watching and charter fishing are the main attractions in the area, though 5 miles south of town there is the **Devil's Punchbowl**, an impressive collapsed sea cave that churns with waves and offers good tide pools nearby.

The Drive » Another 12.8 miles brings you to the lively tourist city of Newport.

TRIP HIGHLIGHT

9 Newport

Don your marine-biologist cap and head to **Yaquina Head Outstanding Natural Area** (750 Lighthouse Dr; vehicle $7, bikes & pedestrians free; ☺dawn-dusk), a giant spit of land that protrudes nearly a mile into the ocean. This headland is home to some of the best touch pools on the Oregon coast. You'll also get a good look at

YAQUINA HEAD LIGHTHOUSE

If Yaquina Head Lighthouse in Newport, OR, seems a little creepier than a lighthouse ought to, that's because it was featured in the 2002 Naomi Watts film *The Ring*. Built in 1873, it was originally called Cape Foulweather Lighthouse, but in the movie it was known as the Moesko Island Lighthouse. (The lighthouse was also in the 1977 masterpiece *Nancy Drew: Pirate's Cove*.)

the tallest lighthouse in Oregon, **Yaquina Head Lighthouse** (not to be confused with **Yaquina Bay Lighthouse**, 3 miles south).

Also worth a stop: the cutting-edge **Oregon Coast Aquarium** (www.aquarium.org; 2820 SE Ferry Slip Rd; adult/child 3-12yr $19/12; ☺10am-5pm, 9am-6pm summer; 🚹). The seals and sea otters are cute as can be, and the jellyfish room is a near psychedelic experience. But what really knocks this place off the charts is the deep-sea exhibit that lets you walk through a Plexiglas tunnel through sharks, rays and other fish.

 p610

The Drive » Another 24 miles to Yachats along the edge of the Siuslaw National Forest.

10 Yachats

One of the Oregon coast's best-kept secrets is the friendly little town of Yachats (ya-*hots*), which kicks off about 20 miles of spectacular shoreline. This entire area was

once a series of volcanic intrusions that resisted the pummeling of the Pacific long enough to rise as oceanside peaks and promontories. Acres of tide pools are home to starfish, sea anemones and sea lions.

Fourteen miles south of town, picturesque **Heceta Head Lighthouse** (92072 Hwy 101, South Yachats) is one of the most photographed lighthouses on the Oregon coast. You can't see it from the highway, but you can park at **Heceta Head State Park** (day use $5) for great views from afar, as well as a trail leading past the former **lightkeeper's quarters** (now a B&B – see p611) and up to the lighthouse.

 p611

The Drive » Just 3 miles down the coast is dramatic Cape Perpetua.

TRIP HIGHLIGHT

11 Cape Perpetua

Whatever you do, don't miss the spectacular scenery of the **Cape Perpetua Scenic Area**

Classic Trip

(day use $5), just 3 miles south of Yachats. You could easily spend a day or two exploring trails that take you through moss-laden, old-growth forests to rocky beaches, tide pools and blasting marine geysers.

At the very least, drive up to the **Cape Perpetua Overlook** for a colossal coastal view from 800ft above sea level – the highest point on the coast. While you're up there, check out the historic **West Shelter** observation point built by the Civilian Conservation Corps in 1933.

If you have more time to spend, stop at the **visitors center** (⏰10am-5:30pm daily summer, 10am-4pm Wed-Mon off-season) to plan your day. High points include **Devil's Churn**, where waves shoot up a 30ft inlet to explode against the narrowing sides of the channel, and the **Giant Spruce Trail**, which leads to a 500-year-old Sitka spruce with a 10ft diameter.

The Drive ⟫ It's 22 miles to Florence, but only 12 miles to the Sea Lion Caves.

- - - - - - - - - - - -

⑫ Florence

Looking for a good, old-fashioned roadside attraction? North of Florence is the **Sea Lion Caves** (www.sealioncaves. com; adult/child/under 6yr $14/8/free; ⏰8:30am-6pm; ♿), an enormous sea grotto that's home to hundreds of groaning sea lions. Open to the public since the 1930s, the cave is accessed by an elevator that descends 208ft to the sea lions' stinky lair.

Here's the deal: it can be fascinating, but you might feel a little taken when you realize the view is exactly the same as what was on the monitor up in the gift shop – and there's not even free fudge samples down there. But if money's no object, you'll enjoy watching the sea lions cavort, especially if you have kids in tow.

✖ p611

The Drive ⟫ The Oregon Dunes start just south of Florence and continue for the next 50 miles.

WHY THIS IS A CLASSIC TRIP
MARIELLA KRAUSE, AUTHOR

Meandering your way down Oregon's coastline is the epitome of a carefree vacation. There are no major cities, no hustle, no bustle – just miles of ocean on one side of the road and miles of hiking on the other. My personal favorite part of the trip? Spending the night at Heceta Head Lighthouse and waking up to a seven-course breakfast, followed by hiking at Cape Perpetua.

Left: Heceta Head Lighthouse
Right: Elk at Ecola State Park

⑬ Oregon Dunes National Recreation Area

As you drive south you start to notice something altogether different: sand. Lots of it. Stretching 50 miles, the **Oregon Dunes** are the largest expanse of oceanfront sand dunes in the US. Sometimes topping heights of 500ft, these mountains of sand undulate inland up to 3 miles. Hikers and birdwatchers stick to the peaceful northern half of the dunes, and the southern half is dominated by dune buggies and dirt bikes.

At Mile 200.8, the **Oregon Dunes Overlook** is the easiest place to take a gander if you're just passing through. To learn more about trails and off-road vehicles, visit the **Oregon Dunes NRA Visitors Center** (855 Highway Ave,

Reedsport; 🕐8am-4:30pm). For the area's biggest dunes, the 6-mile **John Dellenbeck Trail** (at Mile 222.6) loops through a wilderness of massive sand peaks.

The Drive ⟫ Reedsport is about halfway into the dunes area, about 22 miles south of Florence.

⑭ Reedsport

Reedsport's location in the middle of the Oregon Dunes makes it an ideal base for exploring the region. Check out the **Umpqua Lighthouse State Park**, offering summer tours of a local 1894 **lighthouse** (adult/child $3/2; 🕐10am-4pm May-Oct, varies rest of year). Opposite is a whale-watching platform, and a nearby nature trail rings freshwater **Lake Marie**, which is popular for swimming.

Want to see how Oregon's largest land mammal spends its free time? Three miles east of town on Hwy 38, you can spy a herd of about 120 Roosevelt elk meandering about at the **Dean Creek Elk Viewing Area**.

WHALE-WATCHING

Each year, gray whales undertake one of the longest migrations of any animal on earth, swimming from the Bering Strait and Chukchi Sea to Baja California – and back. Look for them migrating south in winter (mid-December through mid-January) and north in spring (March through June).

The Drive ⟫ Enjoy the sand for another 27.5 miles, as you reach Coos Bay and the end of the dunes.

⑮ Coos Bay

The no-nonsense city of Coos Bay and its modest neighbor North Bend make up the largest urban area on the Oregon coast. Coos Bay was once the largest timber port in the world. The logs are long gone, but tourists are slowly taking their place.

In a historic art-deco building downtown, the **Coos Art Museum** (www.coosart.org; 235 Anderson Ave; adult/child $5/2; 🕐10am-4pm Tue-Fri, 1-4pm Sat) provides a hub for the region's art culture with rotating exhibits from the museum's permanent collection.

Cape Arago Hwy leads 14 miles southwest of town to **Cape Arago State Park** (www.oregonstateparks.org), where grassy picnic grounds make for great perches over a pounding sea. The park protects some of the best tide pools on the Oregon coast and is well worth the short detour.

The Drive ⟫ Hwy 101 heads inland for a bit then gets back to the coast 24 miles later at Bandon.

⑯ Bandon

Optimistically touted as Bandon-by-the-Sea, this little town sits happily at the bay of the Coquille River, with an Old Town district that's been gentrified into a picturesque harborside shopping location that offers pleasant strolling and window-shopping.

Along the beach, ledges of stone rise out of the surf to provide shelter for seals, sea lions and myriad forms of life in tide pools. One of the coast's most interesting rock formations is the much-photographed **Face Rock**, a huge monolith with some uncanny facial features that does indeed look like a woman with her head thrown back – giving rise to a requisite Native American legend.

The Drive » Follow the coastline another 24 miles south to Port Orford. This part of the drive isn't much to look at, but not to worry: there's more scenery to come.

TRIP HIGHLIGHT

⑰ Port Orford

Perched on a grassy headland, the hamlet of Port Orford is located in one of the most scenic stretches of coastal highway, and there are stellar views even from the center of town. If you're feeling ambitious, take the 3-mile trail up **Humbug Mountain** (38745 Hwy 101), which takes you up, up, up past streams and through prehistoric-looking landscapes to

---

TIDE-POOL ETIQUETTE

Tide pools are full of fascinating sea life such as anemones, purple shore crabs and sea stars. Normally flooded, their habitats are visible a couple of hours before and after low tide, when you can wander the rocks to explore their underwater world. The most important thing to remember is to watch where you step; stay on the bare rocks to avoid squishing the little creatures, and don't ever pick one up, no matter how tempting it may be. You can, however, gently touch them – just wet your hands first to keep from damaging them.

---

the top, where you'll be treated to dramatic views of Cape Sebastian and the Pacific.

Speaking of prehistoric scenery: your kids will scream at the sight of a tyrannosaurus rex 12 miles south of town in front of **Prehistoric Gardens** (36848 US 101; adult/child $10/8; ⊙9am-6pm; 🚻). Life-size replicas of the extinct beasties are set in a lush, first-growth temperate rainforest; the huge ferns and trees set the right mood for going back in time.

✗ 🛏 p611

The Drive » The scenery starts to pick up again, with unusual rock formations lining the 28-mile drive to Gold Beach.

---

⑱ Gold Beach

Next you'll pass through the tourist hub of Gold Beach, where you can take a jet-boat excursion up the scenic **Rogue River**. But the real treat

lies 13 miles south of town, when you enter the 12-mile stretch of coastal splendor known as the **Samuel Boardman State Scenic Corridor**, featuring giant stands of Sitka spruce, natural rock bridges, tide pools and loads of hiking trails.

Along the highway are well over a dozen roadside turnouts and picnic areas, with short trails leading to secluded beaches and dramatic viewpoints. A 30-second walk from the parking area to the viewing platform at **Natural Bridge Viewpoint** (Mile 346) offers a glorious photo op of rock arches – the remnants of collapsed sea caves – after which you can decide whether you want to commit to the hike down to **China Beach**.

✗ 🛏 p611

The Drive » It's just 34 miles to the California border, and 28 to Brookings.

Classic Trip

🔟 Brookings

Your last stop on
the Oregon coast
is Brookings. With
some of the warmest
temperatures on the
coast, Brookings is a
leader in Easter lily-bulb
production; in July, fields
south of town are filled
with bright colors and
a heavy scent. In May
and June you'll also find
magnificent displays of
flowers at the hilly, 30-
acre **Azalea Park** (Azalea
Park Rd).

History buffs take
note: Brookings has
the unique distinction
of being the location of
the only WWII aerial
bombing on the US
mainland. In 1942,
a Japanese seaplane
succeeded in bombing
nearby forests with the
intent to burn them, but
they failed to ignite. The
Japanese pilot, Nobuo
Fujita, returned to
Brookings 20 years later
and presented the city
with a peace offering:
his family's 400-year-old
samurai sword, which
is now displayed at the
**Chetco Community
Public Library**
(405 Alder St).

🍴 🛏 p611

Bandon Beach Rock formations at low tide

Classic Trip

Eating & Sleeping

Astoria ❶

✕ Wet Dog Café   Brewpub $$

(www.wetdogcafe.com; 144 11th St; mains $10-14;
⊙lunch & dinner, to 2am Fri & Sat) For casual
dining there's no beating this large, quirky pub,
which brews its own beer with names such as
Poop Deck Porter and Bitter Bitch IPA.

⌂ Hotel Elliott   Hotel $$

(📞503-325-2222; www.hotelelliott.com;
357 12th St; d $149-189; ⊛❋🛜) Standard
rooms have charming period elegance at this
historic hotel. For more space, get a suite (the
'presidential' boasts two bedrooms, two baths,
a grand piano and a rooftop deck).

Seaside ❸

✕ Bell Buoy   Seafood $$

(📞503-738-6348; 1800 S Roosevelt Dr; mains
$8-18; ⊙11:30am-7:30pm, closed Tue & Wed
winter) Best known as a seafood store, this
down-to-earth, family-run establishment
has an attached seafood restaurant serving
outstanding fish and chips, chowder and more.

Cannon Beach ❹

✕ Lumberyard   American $$

(📞503-436-0285; www.thelumberyardgrill.com;
264 3rd St; mains $11-20; ⊙ noon-10pm daily;
👶) This family-friendly eatery has something
for everyone, including seven kinds of burgers,
rotisserie specialties, pot pies, sandwiches,
pizzas and steaks.

⌂ Blue Gull Inn   Motel $$

(📞800-507-2714; www.haystacklodgings.
com; 487 S Hemlock St; d $69-229; ⊛🛜)
These are some of the more affordable rooms

in town, with comfortable atmosphere and
toned-down decor, except for the colorful
Mexican headboards and serapes on the beds.
Kitchenettes available.

Lincoln City ❼

✕ Blackfish Café   Northwestern $$$

(📞541-996-1007; www.blackfishcafe.com; 2733
NW US 101, mains $16-24; ⊙11:30am-9pm Wed-
Mon) This is one of the coast's best restaurants,
specializing in cutting-edge cuisine highlighting
fresh seafood and seasonal vegetables. Reserve
ahead for simple but delicious Northwest-
inspired dishes.

Newport ❾

✕ Rogue Ales Public House   Pub $$

(📞541-265-3188; www.rogue.com; 748 SW Bay
Blvd; mains $9-16; ⊙11am-midnight) Don't miss
out on microbrews, best quaffed at outdoor
tables or seated inside at the big wooden bar.
There's an expansive food menu, too.

⌂ Newport Belle   B&B $$

(📞541-867-6290; www.newportbelle.com;
South Beach Marina; d $150-165; ⊛) For a
unique stay there's no beating this sternwheeler
B&B – likely the only one of its kind. The five
small but shipshape rooms have private baths
and water views, while the common spaces are
wonderful for relaxing.

⌂ Beverly Beach
State Park   Campground $

(📞877-444-6777; www.oregonstateparks.
org; Hwy 101; tents $17-21, yurts $40) With
campsites, heated yurts and a long, wide beach
lying just across the highway, this is the perfect
base for ocean exploration. It's 7 miles north of
Newport.

Yachats ⑩

✗ Green Salmon
Coffee House   Coffeehouse $
(☎541-547-3077; 220 US 101; snacks under
$8; ⏰7:30am-2:30pm; 🖐) Queue up at the
counter for spectacularly tasty breakfast items
including pastries, lox bagels and fair-trade
coffee. This cafe is a popular local hangout, and
they earn bonus points for their focus on organic
ingredients and sustainable practices.

🛏 Heceta Head Lighthouse   B&B $$
(☎541-547-3416, 866-547-3696; www.
hecetalighthouse.com; 92072 Hwy 101 S; r
$133-315) Bunking in the former lightkeeper's
quarter is a treat – especially given this B&B's
exquisitely private setting. A seven-course
gourmet breakfast will leave you stuffed.

Florence ⑫

✗ Waterfront Depot   Northwestern $$
(☎541-902-9100; www.thewaterfrontdepot.com;
1252 Bay St; mains $8-15; ⏰4-10pm) Come early
to snag one of the few waterfront tables, then
enjoy your jambalaya pasta or crab-encrusted
halibut. There are excellent small plates too if
you want to try a bit of everything, and desserts
are spectacular. Reserve ahead.

Port Orford ⑰

✗ Red Fish   Northwestern $$
(☎541-336-2200; http://redfishportorford.wix.
com/redfish; 517 Jefferson St; lunch $8-12, dinner
$24-29; ⏰11am-9pm, from 9am Sat & Sun)
Turning Port Orford on its sleepy head is this slick
seaview restaurant that offers breakfast, lunch
and dinner. Prices are reasonable, despite the
fancy Northwest cuisine menu. Reserve ahead.

🛏 Wildspring
Guest Habitat   Luxury Cabins $$$
(☎866-333-9453; www.wildspring.com; 92978
Cemetery Loop; d $198-308; 😊@🛜) A few
acres of wooded serenity greet you at this
quiet retreat. Five luxury cabin suites, with
elegant furniture, radiant-floor heating and
slate showers, make for a very comfortable and
romantic getaway. Breakfast included.

🛏 Cape Blanco
State Park   Campground $
(☎541-332-6774, 800-452-5687; www.
oregonstateparks.org; tent & RV sites/cabins
$20/39) At the other end of the spectrum is this
campground located on a high, sheltered rocky
headland with beach access and great views of
the lighthouse. Showers, flush toilets and boat
ramp available.

Gold Beach ⑱

✗ Patti's Rollin 'n Dough
Bistro   American $$
(☎541-247-4438; 94257 N Bank Rogue Rd;
mains $9-15; ⏰9am-3pm Tue-Sat, to 2pm Sun)
This tiny bistro has a limited breakfast and
lunch menu, but what's there really counts.
Chef Patti Joyce has studied at the Culinary
Institute of America, and it shows. Reservations
recommended.

🛏 Ireland's Rustic
Lodges   Lodge, Cabins $$
(☎541-247-7718; www.irelandsrusticlodges.com;
29346 Ellensburg Ave; d $75-149; 🛜) A wide
variety of accommodations await you at this
woodsy place. There are suites, rustic cabins,
beach houses and even RV sites. A glorious
garden sits in front while beach views are out
back.

Brookings ⑲

✗ Mattie's Pancake &
Omelette   American $
(www.mattiespancakehouse.com; Hwy 101;
mains $7-13; ⏰6am-1:45pm daily) This casual
breakfast and lunch spot offers 20 kinds of
omelet along with pancakes (chocolate chip!)
– no surprise given its name. Sandwiches and
salads for lunch.

🛏 Harris Beach State Park   Camping $
(☎541-469-2021, 800-452-5687; www.
oregonstateparks.org; tents/yurts $20/39)
The area's best (make that only) coastal
camping. Camp beachside or sleep in a
yurt. Showers, flush toilets and coin laundry
available.

South Sister Stratovolcanoes tower over the landscape

Oregon Cascades Scenic Byways

50

Oregon's Central Cascades are a bonanza of natural wonder. Scenic byways pack in lush forests, thundering waterfalls, snowcapped mountains, high desert and lakes galore.

TRIP HIGHLIGHTS

178 miles

Terwilliger Hot Springs
A series of hot pools in a gorgeous natural setting

139 miles

Dee Wright Observatory
A Civilian Conservation Corps project offering spectacular views

Sisters

8

9

12

Bend

Mt Bachelor

START/ FINISH
Westfir

4

Salt Creek Falls
Right off the road is the second-highest waterfall in Oregon

26 miles

152 miles

Proxy Falls
Sheer veils of water tumble over columnar basalt

4 DAYS
240 MILES / 386KM

GREAT FOR...

BEST TIME TO GO
Go June through September to avoid seasonal road closures.

 ESSENTIAL PHOTO
Salt Creek Falls, the second-highest waterfall in Oregon.

 BEST HOT SPRINGS
Terwilliger Hot Springs at Cougar Reservoir.

50 Oregon Cascades Scenic Byways

The region around Oregon's Central Cascades is, without a doubt, some of the most spectacular terrain in the entire state. But one scenic byway just isn't enough to see it all. Here you have our version of an Oregon sampler platter: a loop that brings together several of the best roads to create a majestic route full of the state's best features.

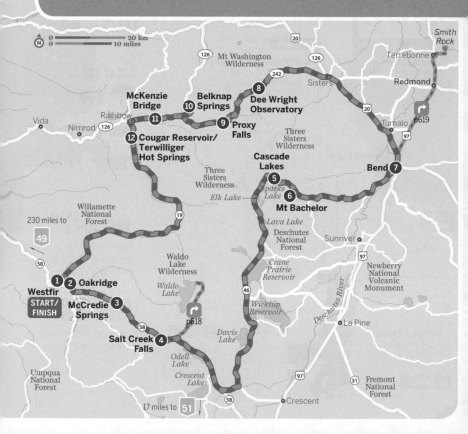

❶ Westfir

Before you spend several days enjoying abundant natural wonders, start with a quick photo op of an entirely man-made one: Oregon's longest covered bridge, the 180ft **Office Bridge**. Built in 1944, the bridge features a covered walkway to enable pedestrians to share the way with logging trucks crossing the Willamette River.

If you plan to do some exploring or mountain biking in the area, pick up a map of the Willamette National Forest at the **Middle Fork Ranger District** (46375 Hwy 58; ⏰8am-4:30pm Mon-Fri, plus Sat & Sun summer).

🛏 p621

LINK YOUR TRIP

49 **Highway 101 Oregon Coast**

Follow 58 NW to the I-5 and head north to Portland. From there, follow the US-30 along the south side of the Columbia River to Astoria.

51 **Crater Lake Circuit**

Crater Lake is a must-see, and it's just south of the Cascades. Take Hwy 97 south from Bend to join this route.

The Drive 》 Oakridge is just a few miles to the east on either Hwy 58 or Westfir–Oakridge Rd.

❷ Oakridge

Oakridge is one of Oregon's mountain-biking meccas. There are hundreds of miles of trails around town, ranging from short, easy loops to challenging single-track routes. For novice riders, the **Warrior Fitness Trail** is a mostly flat 12-mile loop. The **Larison Creek Trail** is a challenging ride through old-growth forests, and the 16-mile **Alpine Trail** is considered the 'crown jewel' of the local trails for its 7-mile downhill stretch. **Oregon Adventures** (☎541-968-5397; 47921 Hwy 58) offers shuttles to the top so you can skip the climb; they also offer bike-tour packages.

🛏 p621

The Drive 》 From Oakridge, Hwy 58 climbs steadily up the Cascade Range's densely forested western slope. Your next stop is about 10 miles east of Oakridge; park on the right just past Mile 45.

❸ McCredie Hot Springs

Because **McCredie Hot Springs** (admission free; ⏰dawn-dusk) lies just off the highway, it's a very popular spot for everyone, from mountain bikers fresh off the trails near Oakridge to truckers

plying Hwy 58. Despite this, it's worth a stop if only because it's the site of one of the largest – and hottest – thermal pools in Oregon. If you can hit it early in the morning or late in the evening midweek, you could have the place to yourself.

There are five pools in all: two upper pools that are often dangerously hot (as in don't-even-dip-your-foot-in hot), two warm riverside pools and one smaller, murkier but usually perfectly heated pool tucked back into the trees. **Salt Creek** rushes past only steps from the springs and is ideal for splashing down with icy water.

The Drive 》 Keep heading east another 12 miles and pull off the highway at the signed parking lot.

TRIP HIGHLIGHT

❹ Salt Creek Falls

At 286ft, this monster of a waterfall is Oregon's second highest. After a good snowmelt, this aqueous behemoth really roars, making for one of the most spectacular sights on the trip. Walk from the parking lot to the viewpoint and there below, in a massive basalt amphitheater hidden by the towering trees, 50,000 gallons of water pour every minute over a cliff into a giant, dark, tumultuous pool. Be sure to hike the short trail downhill

OREGON CASCADES
MARIELLA KRAUSE,
AUTHOR

This trip doesn't
promise something
for everyone; the Central Cascades'
appeal is intoxicatingly single-
minded. It epitomizes Oregon's
outdoorsy aesthetic, and it's
perfect for the road-tripper who
wants to hike for hours, find hidden
waterfalls, swim in crystal-clear
lakes, see entire forests whizzing by
the car window, and strip down at
the end of a long day to jump into a
natural hot spring.

Top: McKenzie River
Left: Dee Wright Observatory
Right: Salt Creek Falls

DOCBOMBAY / DREAMSTIME ©

toward the bottom of the falls. It's lined with rhododendrons that put on a colorful show in springtime, and the views of the falls on the way down are stunning.

Salt Creek Falls is also the starting point for some excellent short hikes, including a 1.5-mile jaunt to **Diamond Creek Falls** and a 4.75-mile hike to **Vivian Lake**.

The Drive » Continue along Hwy 58 until you reach the Cascade Lakes Scenic Byway (Hwy 46), which winds its way north through numerous tiny lakes and up to Mt Bachelor. This road is closed from November to May; as an alternative, follow Hwy 97 to Bend.

❺ Cascade Lakes

We could get all scientific and explain how lava from nearby volcanoes created the lakes around this area, or we could just tell you that Hwy 46 isn't called the Cascade Lakes Scenic Byway for nothing. The road winds past lake after beautiful lake – **Davis Lake**, **Crane Prairie Reservoir**, **Lava Lake**, **Elk Lake** – all worth a stop. Most have outstanding camping, trout fishing, boating and invigorating swimming ('invigorating' being a euphemism for *cold*).

We love **Sparks Lake** for its scenic beauty set against the backdrop of Mt Bachelor, and it's perfect for peaceful paddling. If you find

DETOUR: WALDO LAKE

Start: ❹ Salt Creek Falls

There's no shortage of lakes in the area, but lovely Waldo Lake stands out for its amazing clarity. Because it's at the crest of the Cascades, water doesn't flow into it from other sources; the only water that enters it is rainfall and snowfall, making it one of the purest bodies of water in the world. In fact, it's so clear that objects in the water are visible 100ft below the surface. You can swim in the summer months (it's too cold in the winter), and if you're feeling ambitious after playing 'I Spy' on the lakebed, you can hike the **Waldo Lake Trail**, a 22-mile loop that circumnavigates the lake.

yourself without a boat, **Wanderlust Tours** (☎800-862-2862; www. wanderlusttours.com; half-day tour $55) can hook you up with a guided canoe or kayak tour.

🛏 p621

The Drive ≫ Mt Bachelor is just a few miles past Sparks Lake. If Hwy 46 is closed for the season, you can backtrack from Bend to reach Mt Bachelor.

- - - - - - - - - - - - -

❻ Mt Bachelor

Glorious Mt Bachelor (9065ft) provides Oregon's best skiing. Here, Central Oregon's cold, continental air meets up with the warm, wet Pacific air. The result is tons of fairly dry snow and plenty of sunshine, and with 370in of snow a year, the season begins in November and can last until May.

At **Mt Bachelor Ski Resort** (www.mtbachelor. com; adult/child lift tickets $76/46), rentals are available at the base of the lifts. Mt Bachelor grooms about 35 miles of cross-country trails, though the day pass (weekends and holidays $17, weekdays $14) may prompt skiers to check out the free trails at **Dutchman Flat Sno-Park**, just past the turnoff for Mt Bachelor on Hwy 46.

The Drive ≫ Ready to add a little civilization to your rugged outdoor adventure? Head east to Bend, which is just 22 miles away.

- - - - - - - - - - - - -

❼ Bend

Sporting gear is *de rigueur* in a town where you can go rock climbing in the morning, hike through lava caves

in the afternoon, and stand-up paddleboard yourself into the sunset. Plus, you'll probably be enjoying all that activity in great weather, as the area gets more than 250 days of sunshine each year (don't forget the sunscreen!).

Find out what downtown has to offer, and be sure to check out the excellent **High Desert Museum** (www. highdesertmuseum.org; 59800 S US 97; adult/child $15/9; ◷9am-5pm, 10am-4pm winter; 🚹). It charts the exploration and settlement of the West, but it's no slog through history. The fascinating Native American exhibit shows off several wigwams worth of impressive artifacts, and live animal exhibits and living history are sure to be hits with the kids.

✕ 🛏 p621

The Drive ≫ Head north to Sisters, then drive northwest along Hwy 242. This is part of the McKenzie Pass–Santiam Pass Scenic Byway – closed during the winter months. Your next stop is 15 miles from Sisters.

- - - - - - - - - - - - -

TRIP HIGHLIGHT

❽ Dee Wright Observatory

Perched on a giant mound of lava rock, built entirely of lava rock, in the middle of a field of lava rock,

GREG VAUGHN / ALAMY ©

Newberry National Volcanic Monument

stands the historic Dee Wright Observatory. The structure, built in 1935 by Franklin D Roosevelt's Civilian Conservation Corps, offers spectacular views in all directions. The observatory windows, called 'lava tubes', were placed to highlight all the prominent Cascade peaks that can be seen from the summit, including Mt Washington, Mt Jefferson, North Sister, Middle Sister and a host of others.

The Drive » Head west on Hwy 242 to Mile 64 and look for the well-signed Proxy Falls trailhead.

TRIP HIGHLIGHT

❾ Proxy Falls

With all the waterfalls around the Central Cascades – hundreds of them in Oregon alone –

it's easy to feel like 'You've seen one, you've seen 'em all.' Not so fast. Grab your camera and see if you're not at least a little impressed by photogenic Proxy Falls. If there were a beauty contest for waterfalls, Proxy would certainly be in the running, scattering into sheer veils down a mossy wall of columnar basalt. It's not even like the falls make you work for it:

it's an easy 1.3-mile loop from the parking area. If you want to save the best for last, take the path in the opposite direction from what the sign suggests so you hit Upper Proxy Falls first and you can build up to the even better Lower Proxy Falls.

The Drive » Nine miles from the falls, turn right on Hwy 126 (McKenzie Hwy); Belknap is just 1.4 miles away.

DETOUR: SMITH ROCK

Start: ❼ Bend

Best known for its glorious rock climbing, **Smith Rock State Park** (www.oregonstateparks.org; 9241 NE Crooked River Dr, Terrebonne; day use $5) boasts rust-colored 800ft cliffs that tower over the pretty Crooked River, just 25 miles north of Bend. Nonclimbers can enjoy miles of hiking trails, some of which involve a little rock scrambling.

⑩ Belknap Hot Springs

Although nudity is the norm at most hot springs, Belknap is the sort of hot spring you can take your grandmother to and neither of you will feel out of place. Two giant swimming pools filled with 103°F (40°C) mineral water provide optimum soaking conditions in a family environment. The McKenzie River rushes by below, trees tower over everything and, as far as we could tell, everyone still has a good time. An excellent alternative to camping, the resort has rooms for nearly all budgets.

🛏 p621

The Drive >> Head southwest on Hwy 126 for 6 miles to get to your next stop.

⑪ McKenzie Bridge

Although from the road it looks like there is nothing but trees, there's actually plenty to do around here, including fishing on the McKenzie River and hiking on the nearby

BLAST FROM THE PAST

The Cascades are a region of immense volcanic importance. Lava fields can be seen from McKenzie Pass and along Hwy 46. Road cuts expose gray ash flows. Stratovolcanoes such as South Sister and Mt Bachelor and shield volcanoes such as Mt Washington tower over the landscape. Although it's not instantly obvious when you drive to the center of **Newberry National Volcanic Monument** (39 miles south of Bend), you're actually inside the caldera of a 500-sq-mile volcano. What could be stranger than that? It's still active.

McKenzie River National Recreation Trail. To learn more about all your recreational options, stop at the **McKenzie River Ranger Station** (57600 McKenzie Hwy, McKenzie Bridge; ⏰8am-4:30pm, reduced hr winter), about 2 miles east of town. The rangers are fonts of information, plus you can find anything you ever wanted to know about the McKenzie River trail, including maps and books.

🛏 p621

The Drive >> West of McKenzie Bridge, turn left on Hwy 19 (aka Aufderheide Memorial Drive) just past Rainbow. After almost 8 miles, you'll come to the parking lot from which you'll take a quarter-mile trail through old-growth forest.

TRIP HIGHLIGHT

⑫ Cougar Reservoir/Terwilliger Hot Springs

In a picturesque canyon in the Willamette National Forest is one of the state's most stunning hot springs. From a fern-shrouded hole, scorching water spills into a pool that maintains a steady minimum temperature of 108°F (42°C). The water then cascades into three successive pools, each one cooler than the one above it. Sitting there staring up at the trees is an utterly sublime experience. After hiking back to the car, you can even jump into Cougar Reservoir from the rocky shore below the parking lot.

The Drive >> Continue down Hwy 19 back to Westfir.

Eating & Sleeping

Westfir ❶

🛏 Westfir Lodge   B&B $

(📞541-782-3103; www.westfirlodge.com; 47365 1st St; r $75-90) Lovely B&B chock-full of antiques. Baths are private but most are outside the room. Full English breakfast included. Cheesecake served most evenings.

Oakridge ❷

🛏 Oakridge Motel   Motel $

(📞541-782-2432; http://oakridgemotel.net; 48197 Hwy 58; r $45-65) With a log exterior and wooden walls inside, this otherwise run-of-the-mill motel is slightly more interesting than some others.

Cascade Lakes ❺

🛏 Cultus Lake Resort   Motel $

(📞541-408-1560; www.cultuslakeresort.com; Hwy 46; cabins per night $85-155) Offers 23 homey cabins with a two-night minimum; week-only from July 4 to September 1. Book well ahead. There's a restaurant, too.

🛏 Sparks Lake Campground   Campground $

(Hwy 46; campsites free; 🕐Jul-Sep) It's one of the most scenically situated campgrounds on the entire route, with views of Mt Bachelor and meadows. Pit toilets available; no water.

Bend ❼

🍴 Blacksmith   Steakhouse $$$

(📞541-318-0588; www.bendblacksmith.com; 211 NW Greenwood Ave; mains $14-36; 🕐4:30-10pm) This renowned restaurant offers cowboy comfort food with a twist – such as gourmet meat loaf or grilled tenderloin with melted blue cheese – plus a full bar serving creative cocktails.

🍴 Victorian Café   Breakfast $$

(📞541-382-6411; www.victoriancafebend.com; 1404 NW Galveston Ave; mains $8-14; 🕐7am-2pm daily) One of Bend's best breakfast spots, Victorian Café is especially awesome for its eggs Benedict (nine kinds). It's also good for sandwiches, burgers and salads.

🍴 Deschutes Brewery   Brewpub $$

(📞541-382-9242; www.deschutesbrewery.com; 1044 NW Bond St; dinner mains $11-18; 🕐11am-11pm Mon-Thu, to midnight Fri & Sat, to 10pm Sun) Bend's first microbrewery gregariously serves up plenty of food and handcrafted beers.

🛏 McMenamins Old St Francis School   Hotel $$

(📞541-382-5174; www.mcmenamins.com; 700 NW Bond St; d $125-175; 🐾 ❄ 📶) The McMenamin brothers do it again with this old schoolhouse remodeled into a classy 19-room hotel. A restaurant-pub, three other bars and a movie theater keep you entertained.

Belknap Hot Springs ❿

🛏 Belknap Hot Springs Resort   Resort $$

(📞541-822-3512; www.belknaphotsprings. com; Hwy 126 near Hwy 242; tent sites $25-30, d $110-135, cabins $130-425, day use only $12) In addition to soaking, the resort boasts an 18-room lodge, 14 private cabins and 15 tent sites, so it's affordable for nearly all budgets.

McKenzie Bridge ⓫

🛏 Cedarwood Lodge   Cabins $$

(📞541-822-3351; www.cedarwoodlodge.com; 56535 McKenzie Hwy; cabins $95-185; 🕐closed winter) Ensconce yourself in one of eight rustic, comfortable, fully equipped cabins set above the McKenzie River.

Crater Lake *Still waters reflect mountains, like a giant mirror*

Crater Lake Circuit

51

Make it a day trip or stay a week – serene, mystical Crater Lake is one of Oregon's most enticing destinations. The best route takes you on a heavily forested, waterfall-studded loop.

TRIP HIGHLIGHTS

199 miles

Toketee Falls
Two tiers flow dramatically over columnar basalt

95 miles

Crater Lake
Clear, blue, serene – this famous lake is like no other

Roseburg

6

4

3

Medford

Ashland

START/ FINISH

Prospect
Take a short hike to the Avenue of Giant Boulders

57 miles

1–3 DAYS
365 MILES / 587KM

GREAT FOR...

BEST TIME TO GO
Late May to mid-October when all the roads are open.

ESSENTIAL PHOTO
No surprise here: Crater Lake.

BEST WATERFALL
Two-tiered Toketee Falls is our favorite.

623

Crater Lake Circuit

The star attraction of this trip is Crater Lake, considered by many to be the most beautiful spot in all of Oregon. The sight of the still, clear and ridiculously blue water that fills an ancient volcanic caldera is worth the trip alone, but the drive there is lined with beautiful hikes, dramatic waterfalls and natural hot springs, all right off the highway.

❶ Ashland

A favorite base for day trips to Crater Lake, Ashland is bursting at the seams with lovely places to sleep and eat (though you'll want to book your hotel rooms far in advance for the busy summer months). Home of the **Oregon Shakespeare Festival**, it has more culture than most towns its size, and is just far enough off the highway to resist becoming a chain-motel mecca.

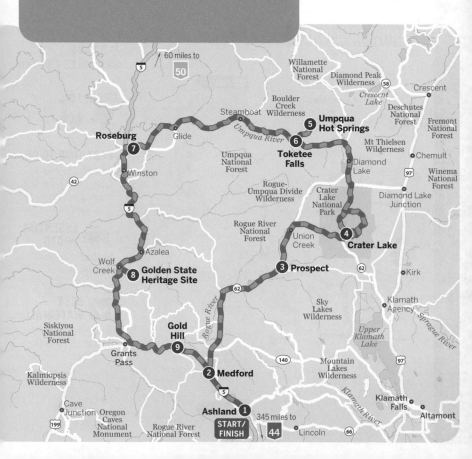

It's not just Shakespeare that makes Ashland the cultural heart of Southern Oregon. If you like contemporary art, check out the **Schneider Museum of Art** (www.sou.edu/sma; 1250 Siskiyou Blvd; suggested donation $5; ☺10am-4pm Mon-Sat).

Ashland's historic downtown and lovely **Lithia Park** make it a dandy place to spend some time before or after your journey to Crater Lake.

 p629

The Drive ❯❯ Medford is 13 miles north of Ashland on I-5.

➋ Medford

Southern Oregon's largest metropolis is where you hop off I-5 for your trek out to Crater Lake, and it can also serve as a suitable base of

LINK YOUR TRIP

44 San Francisco, Marin & Napa Loop

Head south on I-5 to the I-505 and take I-80 into San Fran to start your loop around the Bay Area.

50 Oregon Cascades Scenic Byways

From Roseburg head north on I-5 and then southeast towards Westfir on the 58.

operations if you want a cheap, convenient place to bunk down for the night.

On your way out, check out the **Table Rocks**, impressive 800ft mesas that speak of the area's volcanic past and are home to unique plant and animal species. Flowery spring is the best time for hiking to the flat tops, which were revered Native American sites. After TouVelle State Park, fork either left to reach the trailhead to Lower Table Rock (3.5-mile round-trip hike) or right for Upper Table Rock (2.5-mile round-trip hike).

 p629

The Drive ❯❯ The drive along Hwy 62 isn't much until after Shady Cove, when urban sprawl stops and forest begins. Your next stop is 45 miles northwest in Prospect.

TRIP HIGHLIGHT

➌ Prospect

No wonder they changed the name of Mill Creek Falls Scenic Area – that implies you're just going to see another waterfall (not that there's anything wrong with that). But the real treat at **Prospect State Scenic Viewpoint** is hiking down to the **Avenue of Giant Boulders**, where the Rogue River crashes dramatically through huge chunks of rock and a little bit of scrambling offers the most rewarding views.

Take the trail from the southernmost of two parking lots on Mill Creek Dr. Keep left to get to the boulders or right for a short hike to two viewpoints for **Mill Creek Falls** and **Barr Creek Falls**. If you've got one more falls-sighting left in you, take the short hike from the upper parking lot to the lovely **Pearsony Falls**.

The Drive ❯❯ Follow Hwy 62 for another 28 miles to get to the park turnoff at Munson Valley Rd.

TRIP HIGHLIGHT

➍ Crater Lake

This is it: the main highlight and reason for being of this entire trip is Oregon's most beautiful body of water, **Crater Lake** (www.nps.gov/crla; per vehicle for 7 days $10). This amazingly blue lake is filled with some of the clearest, purest water you can imagine – you can easily peer a hundred feet down – and sits inside a 6-mile-wide caldera created when Mt Mazama erupted nearly 8000 years ago. Protruding from the water and adding to the drama of the landscape is **Wizard Island**, a volcanic cinder cone topped by its own mini-crater called Witches Cauldron.

Get the overview with the 33-mile **Rim Drive** (☺Jun–mid-Oct), which offers over 30 viewpoints as it winds around the

edge of Crater Lake. The gloriously still waters reflect surrounding mountain peaks like a giant dark-blue mirror, making for spectacular photographs and breathtaking panoramas.

You can also camp, ski or hike in the surrounding old-growth forests. The popular and steep mile-long **Cleetwood Cove Trail**, at the north end of the crater, provides the only water access at the cove. Or get up close with a two-hour **boat tour** (📞 888-774-2728; adult/child $35/21; ⏰9:30am-3:30pm Jul–mid-Sep).

🍴 🛏 p629

The Drive ≫ Head north on Hwy 138 for 41 miles and turn right on Rd 34.

- - - - - - - - - -

⑤ Umpqua Hot Springs

Set on a mountainside overlooking the North Umpqua River, Umpqua Hot Springs is one of Oregon's most splendid hot springs, with a little bit of height-induced adrenaline thanks to the position atop a rocky bluff.

Toketee Falls

Springs are known for soothing weary muscles, so earn your soak at Umpqua by starting with a hike – it is in a national forest, after all – where you'll be treated to lush, old-growth forest and waterfalls punctuating the landscape. Half a mile from the parking lot is the scenic, 79-mile **North Umpqua Trail**.

The Drive » The turnout for Toketee Falls is right on Hwy 138, 2 miles past the Umpqua turnoff.

- - - - - - - - - - -

TRIP HIGHLIGHT

6 Toketee Falls

More than half a dozen waterfalls line this section of the Rogue-Umpqua Scenic Byway, but the one that truly demands a stop is the stunning, two-tiered Toketee Falls. The falls' first tier drops 40ft into an upper pool behind a cliff of columnar basalt, then crashes another 80ft down the rock columns into yet another gorgeous, green-blue pool below. One tiny disclaimer: although the hike is just 0.4 miles, there's a staircase of 200 steps down to the

TOP TIP:
VISITING CRATER LAKE

Crater Lake's popular south entrance is open year-round and provides access to Rim Village and Mazama Village, as well as the park headquarters at the Steel Visitors Center. In winter you can only go up to the lake's rim and back down the same way; no other roads are plowed. The north entrance is only open from early June to late October, depending on snowfall.

viewpoint, so climbing back up to your car is a bit of a workout.

The Drive » From here, the scenery tapers back down to normal as you leave the Umpqua National Forest, but it's just one more hour back to Roseburg.

❼ Roseburg

Sprawling Roseburg lies in a valley near the confluence of the South and North Umpqua Rivers. The city is mostly a cheap, modern sleepover for travelers headed elsewhere (such as Crater Lake), but it does have a cute, historic downtown area and is surrounded by award-winning wineries.

Don't miss the excellent **Douglas County Museum** (www. co.douglas.or.us/museum; I-5 exit 123; adult/child $5/ free; ⏰10am-5pm Tue-Sat; 🚻), which displays the area's cultural and natural histories.

Especially interesting are the railroad derailment photos and history of wine exhibit. Kids have an interactive area and live snakes to look at.

🍴 p629

The Drive » Go south on I-5 for 47 miles and take the Wolf Creek exit. Follow Old State Highway 99 to curve back under the interstate. Golden is 3.2 miles east on Coyote Creek Rd.

❽ Golden State Heritage Site

Not ready to return to civilization quite yet? Stop off in the ghost town of **Golden**, population zero. A former mining town that had over 100 residents in the mid-1800s, Golden was built on the banks of Coyote Creek when gold was discovered there.

A handful of structures remain, as well as some newfangled interpretive signs

that tell the tale of a curiously devout community that eschewed drinking and dancing, all giving a fascinating glimpse of what life was like back then. The weathered wooden buildings include a residence, the general store/post office, and a classic country church. Fun fact: the town was once used as a location for the long-running Western TV series *Gunsmoke*.

The Drive » Go south another 45 miles on I-5 and take exit 43. The Oregon Vortex is 4.2 miles north of the access road.

❾ Gold Hill

Just outside the town of Gold Hill lies the **Oregon Vortex** (www.oregonvortex. com; 4303 Sardine Creek L Fork Rd; adult/child/under 5yr $9.75/7/free; ⏰9am-4pm Mar-Oct) where the laws of physics don't seem to apply – or is it all just an optical illusion created by skewed buildings on steep hillsides? However you see it, the place is definitely bizarre: objects roll uphill, a person's height changes depending on where they stand, and brooms stand up on their own... or so it seems.

Eating & Sleeping

Ashland ❶

✗ Morning Glory   Cafe $
([☎]541-488-8636; 1149 Siskiyou Blvd; breakfast $9.50-14.50; [⏰]8am-1:30pm) There's bound to be something that will make you happy on their extensive menu full of creative dishes. Expect a long wait for weekend brunch.

✗ Dragonfly Cafe   Cafe $$
([☎]541-488-4855; www.dragonflyashland.com; 241 Hargadine St; dinner mains $13-21; [⏰]8am-3pm, dinner from 5pm) Tucked away on a side street, Dragonfly is an under-the-radar treat. They serve inventive, Latin-Asian fusion breakfast, lunch and dinner, and the twinkle-lit patio is lovely in summer.

🛏 Columbia Hotel   Hotel $$
([☎]541-482-3726, 800-718-2530; www.columbia hotel.com; 262-1/2 E Main St; d $79-149; [⏰][✳][@][📶]) The Columbia is a fabulously located 'European-style' hotel – which means most rooms share a bath. It's the best deal in downtown Ashland, with 24 quaint vintage rooms.

Medford ❷

✗ Organic Natural Cafe   American $
([☎]541-245-9802; 226 E Main St; mains under $10; [⏰]9am-4pm Mon-Sat; [✦]) The theme here is all about local, organic, vegan and gluten-free. In addition to panini-style sandwiches and burgers, there's a salad bar, fresh juices and fruit smoothies.

✗ Porters   American $$
([☎]541-857-1910; www.porterstrainstation.com; 147 N Front St; mains $11-30; [⏰]5-9pm Sun-Thu, to 9:30pm Fri & Sat) This gorgeous, Craftsman-style restaurant is decked out in dark-wood booths and boasts an awesome patio next to the train tracks. Steak, seafood and pasta dishes dominate the menu.

Crater Lake ❹

✗ Crater Lake Lodge
Dining Room   Northwestern $$$
([☎]541-594-2255/3217; mains $27-36; [⏰]7am-10pm) Try for a table with a lake view; either way, you'll feast on Northwest cuisine such as blue-cheese halibut and baked citrus duck. Dinner reservations recommended.

🛏 Crater Lake Lodge   Lodge $$$
([☎]541-594-2255, 888-774-2728; www.craterlakelodges.com; d $165-225; [⏰]) Open late May to mid-October, this grand old lodge has 71 simple but comfortable rooms (no TV or telephones) – but it's the common areas that are most impressive, with fireplaces, rustic leather sofas and a spectacular view of Crater Lake.

🛏 Cabins at Mazama Village   Cabin $$
([☎]541-830-8700, 888-774-2728; www.craterlakelodges.com; d $140, tent/RV site $21/$29; [⏰]) Also open late May to mid-October, these attractive four-plexes offer 40 additional in-park rooms. They're 7 miles from Crater Lake, with a small grocery store and gas pump nearby. There are also 200 campsites available mid-June through September.

Roseburg ❼

✗ McMenamins Roseburg
Station Pub   American $
([☎]541-672-1934; 700 SE Sheridan St; mains $10-14; [⏰]11am-11pm Mon-Thu, to midnight Fri & Sat, noon-10pm Sun) Pure McMenamins style, which means colorful, whimsical and fun. Burgers, sandwiches and salads (finished with a microbrew) are the rule at this cozy pub-restaurant.

Inside Passage Watch for whales in the Alaskan wild

Up the Inside Passage

52

Set sail on an Alaska Ferry from Bellingham, WA, tracing the lush Canadian coastline before slipping into the foggy emerald maze of Alaska's wild, remote Inside Passage.

TRIP HIGHLIGHTS

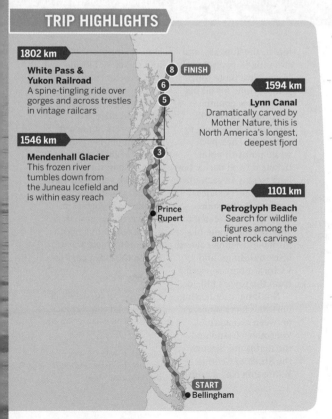

1802 km

White Pass & Yukon Railroad
A spine-tingling ride over gorges and across trestles in vintage railcars

1546 km

Mendenhall Glacier
This frozen river tumbles down from the Juneau Icefield and is within easy reach

8 FINISH
6
5

1594 km

Lynn Canal
Dramatically carved by Mother Nature, this is North America's longest, deepest fjord

3

1101 km

Petroglyph Beach
Search for wildlife figures among the ancient rock carvings

Prince Rupert

START
Bellingham

---

4 DAYS
1119 MILES /
1800KM

- - - - - - - -

GREAT FOR...

- - - - - - - -

BEST TIME TO GO
June to September – the snow has melted and wildflowers bloom.

- - - - - - - -

 ESSENTIAL PHOTO
Totem poles, tall pines and soaring eagles at Chief Shakes Island.

- - - - - - - -

 BEST FOR WILDLIFE
Bears, bald eagles, whales and sea lions – they're all out there waiting to be spotted.

52 Up the Inside Passage

Of the 27 All-American Roads, the Alaska Marine Hwy is the only one that takes to the water on a car ferry. Churning 3500 nautical miles from Bellingham and out to the far tendril of the Aleutian Chain, some of the highway's most dramatic scenes are pressed into the steep fjords, forests and waterlogged fishing towns of the Inside Passage. By land it takes 98 hours to reach Skagway from Bellingham, with lots of long, empty stretches where the forest seems to swallow you completely. By sea, it's a constant visual feast.

❶ Bellingham

In Bellingham, head to the brick-paved, historic **Fairhaven District**. Make sure to give yourself at least an afternoon to explore this city neighborhood, stamped onto several blocks and charmingly crammed with flower shops, cafes and bookstores. This is also where you board the **Alaska Ferry** (☎907-465-3941, 800-642-0066; www.alaska.gov/ferry; vehicle/adult/child/under 6yr to Skagway $820/363/200/free, to Ketchikan $515/239/120/free; ⊞); you can walk, bike, or drive onto the vessel. A three-day trip ends in Skagway, traveling through the US's largest national

forest, the Tongass, and stopping in several ports. If you have more time, your options for taking detours are countless. A through-ticket will give you a little time to explore in each port, while point-to-point tickets let you decide how long to stay in each town.

As the ferry slides out into **Bellingham Bay**, you'll be treated to views of meringue-like Mt Baker, sienna-colored brick buildings, and Victorian homes peering from the town's hillside.

Not long after leaving port, the ferry squeezes between Canada's Vancouver Island and the mainland through the Strait of Georgia. While this isn't a cruise

ship, it's comfortable and the mix of locals and travelers gives it the feeling of an authentic voyage. You'll find the solarium filled with adventurers hunkered down under heat lamps, while brightly colored tents flap in the wind on deck. The snack-bar fare is what you'd expect of public transportation, but warming up with a cup of coffee in a booth is a comfortable way to watch the coast pass by.

✕ ⨝ p639

The Drive » This is like autopilot in the extreme. Sit back and watch the amazing scenery pass by as you travel past lighthouse stations and between islands with wild coastlines, watching for eagles and even the occasional whale.

❷ Ketchikan

Thirty-eight hours after departing Bellingham, the ferry makes its first stop in Ketchikan. The ferry stays in port long enough for you to explore the historic, albeit touristy, **Creek Street**. Though this boardwalk is now safe for families, in Ketchikan's early boomtown years the street was a clatter of brothels and bars. Pop into **Dolly's House Museum** (www.dollyshouse. com; 24 Creek St; adult/child $5/free; ⏰8am-5pm), where you can get an insider's view of what was a working parlor. Namesake Dolly Arthur operated the brothel until prostitution was outlawed in 1953, and lived here until her death in the '70s.

For an introduction to a different kind of

LINK YOUR TRIP

46 Cascade Drive

From Bellingham, head south on I-5 to Burlington to begin your ride through the North Cascades.

47 Olympic Peninsula Loop

Take the I-5 south to Port Townsend to join up with this loop through the Olympic Peninsula.

wildlife, head to the **Southeast Alaska Discovery Center** (www.alaskacenters.gov/ketchikan.cfm; 50 Main St; adult/child $5/free; ⏰8am-3pm daily May-Sep, 10am-4pm Fri & Sat Oct-Apr; ♿). The center houses excellent exhibits on various aspects of the Southeast region (simply called 'Southeast' by locals), including ecosystems, artwork and Native Alaskan traditions, while downstairs a re-created rainforest looms. This is a great place to help you identify what you're seeing from the windows of the ferry.

✖ p639

The Drive » From Ketchikan, the ferry hums north through Clarence Strait to Wrangell.

3 Wrangell

Several hours after departing Ketchikan, you'll arrive at tiny, false-fronted Wrangell. You'll be greeted by the town's children, who set up folding tables (even in the rain) to sell their wares – deep-purple garnets that they've mined from the nearby Stikine River.

Wrangell practically spills over with historic, cultural and natural sights, including **Petroglyph Beach**. Less than a mile from the ferry terminal the beach is dotted with boulders depicting faces and figures that were carved thousands of years ago.

Lifelike whales and owls peer up at you, while some spirals eerily resemble crop circles. If you're just popping off the ferry during its quick stop, you can jog there and back for a speedy examination of the stones.

More recent Tlingit culture is showcased on the other side of town at **Chief Shakes Island & Tribal House**, an oddly peaceful site in the middle of the humming boat harbor. Here, six totem poles tower among pines, and eagles often congregate in the trees' branches. The island is always open for walking, though the tribal house usually only opens for cruise-ship groups.

Just after leaving Wrangell, the ferry enters the 22-mile long **Wrangell Narrows**. Too skinny and shallow for most large vessels, the Narrows (dubbed Pinball Alley) requires nearly 50 course corrections as boats thread between more than 70 channel markers. The ferry M/V *Columbia* is the largest boat to navigate the Narrows, as water depth can get as shallow as 24ft at low tide.

🛏 p639

The Drive » After maneuvering through the Narrows, the ferry continues northwest to Petersburg.

DETOUR: PRINCE OF WALES ISLAND

Start: 2 Ketchikan

The third-largest island in the US, mountainous Prince of Wales Island isn't a well-known mountain-biking destination, but that's due more to its remote location than its lack of spectacular terrain. Veined with over 1300 miles of mostly unpaved road and spotted with tiny villages, POW also has 21 public-use cabins scattered along its inlets and alpine lakes. There are dispiriting clear-cuts, but they're the reason for all those roads.

For an island guide, check out www.princeofwales coc.org. The **Inter-Island Ferry** (www.interislandferry.com) has services from Ketchikan, Wrangell and Petersburg. Adult/child fares from Ketchikan are CAN$37/18, vehicles from CAN$5 per foot.

DETOUR:
LECONTE GLACIER

Start: ❹ Petersburg

Complement a layover in Petersburg with a kayak tour to LeConte Glacier, at the head of serpentine LeConte Bay. Constantly calving, the glacier is somewhat infamous for icebergs that release under water and then shoot to the surface like icy torpedoes. If you're lucky you'll see one – from afar.

----

❹ Petersburg

At the end of the Narrows sits Petersburg, a fishing village with blond roots. Petersburg's thick Norwegian history is evident not just in the phonebook full of Scandinavian names, but also in the flowery rosemaling, a decorative Norwegian art form found on buildings throughout town. To really get into the heart of Petersburg, walk the docks of its **North Boat Harbor**. Here fisherfolk unload the day's catch from small purse seiners, distinguishable by the large nets piled in the sterns.

✕ p639

The Drive » From Petersburg, the ferry heads north alongside the densely forested Admiralty Island to the port of Juneau.

----

❺ Juneau

After brushing through quiet fishing towns, arriving in Juneau can be somewhat surprising. This is the only US capital with no road access, yet it still bustles with the importance of a government center. It's also postcard perfect, with massive green cliffs rising above the city center. Be sure to stroll past the **Governor's Mansion**, its assertive columns and landscaped shrubs a contrast to the usual rainforest-rotted cabins of Southeast.

If the political climate gets to be too much, head to the laid-back **Alaskan Brewing Company** (www.alaskanbeer.com; 5429 Shuane Dr; ☉11am-6pm May-Sep, 11am-5:30pm Tue-Sat Oct-Apr) for a tour and a sample of their beers. The brewery is in the same neighborhood as the massive **Mendenhall Glacier**, which tumbles down from the Juneau Icefield and is one of the few glaciers in Southeast you can drive up to. The visitor's center offers a movie about the glacier,

BC'S STAFFED LIGHTHOUSES

The misty stretch of Canada between Washington and Alaska is home to 40 lighthouses, more than half of which require keepers. Watch for **Addenbroke Island Lightstation**, an outpost called home by a family with three children. The ferry then glides by picturesque **Dryad Point Lightstation**, which features an old-school-style lighthouse perched on the northeastern tip of Campbell Island. Further north, **Boat Bluff Lightstation** is a simple aluminum skeleton, but the red-roofed outbuildings hug a small hillside and the keepers often emerge to wave to ferry passengers. After passing Prince Rupert, keep an eye out for **Triple Island Lightstation** where the lighthouse clings to the top of what appears to be more of a large rock than an island. This station has been kept since 1920 despite the lack of space or vegetation on the island. For an in-depth and often fascinating look at the history of the lighthouses, pick up a copy of *Lights of the Inside Passage* by Donald Graham (Harbour Publishing, 1987).

INSIDE PASSAGE
KORINA MILLER, AUTHOR

As the ferry enters the Inside Passage, you feel an undeniable spark of excitement. It's like following in the wake of the first European explorers. You appreciate the remoteness of it all. Catching a glimpse of a bear or a wolf on the shoreline, watching the bald eagles swoop overhead and stopping off at communities only accessible by water – quite quickly I realized this was no ordinary trip. The word 'remarkable' came to mind.

Top: Bears, Chilkoot River, Haines
Left: Mendenhall Glacier
Right: Petroglyph Beach, Wrangell

ROBERTA OLENICK / GETTY IMAGES ©

plus hiking trails and a salmon-viewing platform.

🛏 p639

The Drive » The route continues north, hugging the coastline into the Lynn Canal.

TRIP HIGHLIGHT

⑥ Lynn Canal

From Juneau, the ferry travels up the Lynn Canal, North America's longest (90 miles) and deepest (2000ft) fjord. Glaciers and waterfalls make the canal a visual feast. It was first mapped in 1794 and was later a major route to the boomtown of Skagway during the gold rush. This was also the scene of one of the worst maritime disasters in the Pacific Northwest: in 1918 a passenger ship grounded on a reef and sunk along with all of its 343 crew and passengers.

Because of the canal's high use, lighthouses were once scattered along the inlet; still standing are the octagonal **Eldred Rock Light** and the church-like **Sentinel Island Light**. The canal is now used less for freight and more by ferries, cruise lines and humpback whales.

The Drive » The trip north from Juneau via the Lynn Canal to Haines takes about 4½ hours.

⑦ Haines

Seventy-five miles from Juneau lies Haines,

ALASKA STOCK / ALAMY ©

where most passengers with cars disembark as the town is the main link to the Alaska Hwy. Haines has a laid-back vibe with almost extravagant scenery. You can't miss the huge hammer outside the **Hammer Museum** (www. hammermuseum.org; 108 Main St; adult/child $3/free; ☺10am-5pm Mon-Fri May-Sep), which displays 1500 versions of humanity's first tool and chronicles history through them. Not surprisingly, this is the world's first (and only) museum dedicated solely to the humble hammer.

Between September and December, Haines' population grows by over 3500 when thousands of migrating bald eagles descend on the area. This is the largest gathering of bald eagles in the world and the town celebrates with the mid-November **Alaska Bald Eagle Festival** (www.baldeagles. org/festival). If you arrive at the same time as these white-headed guys, you'll undoubtedly be wowed.

The Drive » A short one-hour trip north along the coast brings you to Skagway.

- - - - - - - - - - - -

TRIP HIGHLIGHT

❽ Skagway

At the turn of the 20th century, Skagway boomed with the

IN SEARCH OF AURORA BOREALIS

Glowing green and red across the sky like fluorescent curtains, the Northern Lights were named after Aurora, the Roman goddess of dawn, and Boreas, the Greek name for north wind. The Native Cree call them Dance of the Spirits.

The Northern Lights can be seen to some extent anywhere above N 60° latitude, within what is known as the aurora oval. However, you can sometimes catch a glimpse as far south as Juneau.

Sightings are hindered by the perpetual twilight that dominates the night skies from late April until September. The best time to see the Northern Lights is around the 22nd of September or March, on a new moon, late at night or very early in the morning. Head to the ferry deck and await the performance.

gold rush, when the population went from two to 10,000 in just a few years. Sandwiched between forested slopes, it now booms with tourism; if you want to see can-can girls or pan for gold, this is the place to do it. The ferry deposits you about 100yd from **Broadway Street**, where you'll find women dressed in feathered hats and bright satiny dresses. The rest is history.

Since Skagway is likely your last ferry stop, it's worth boarding the **White Pass & Yukon Railroad** (www.wpyr.com; depot at 231 2nd Ave; Yukon Adventure adult/child return $249/119.50, White Pass Summit Excursion $115/57.50), a narrated sightseeing tour aboard vintage parlor cars. This

dramatic ride rumbles through Glacier Gorge and over White Pass (a 2885ft climb).

Whether you end your trip in Skagway or another port, you'll need to backtrack on the ferry, or fly south, to get home. There are few commercial flights from smaller towns, and to catch a major airline flight to Seattle you'll first need to fly to Juneau, Ketchikan or Sitka. Unless you brought your car on board, in which case you're in for a scenic road trip home. A one-way ticket from Skagway to Juneau with **Wings of Alaska** (www.wingsofalaska. com) is about $120 and takes just under an hour.

🛏 p639

Eating & Sleeping

Bellingham ❶

✗ Colophon Café & Deli — Cafe $

(📞360-647-0092; 1208 11th St; mains $7-14; ⏱9am-9pm Mon-Sat, 10am-8pm Sun) Renowned for its rotating menu of 35 soups (from African peanut soup to New England clam chowder) as well as for its peanut-butter pie, this cafe – with a welcoming garden – is the perfect place to make yourself at home.

⊨ Fairhaven Village Inn — Hotel $$$

(📞360-733-1311, 877-733-1100; www.fairhavenvillageinn.com; 1200 10th St; r $179-229) A vintage hotel that's perfectly located in the Fairhaven District and a class above the standard motel experience. Enjoy wonderfully comfortable beds and views over the sea or a park.

Ketchikan ❷

✗ Bar Habor Restaurant — Seafood $$$

(📞907-225-2813; 2813 Tongass Ave; mains $20-34; ⏱5pm-9pm Mon-Sat) A cozy place with a covered outdoor deck, between downtown and the ferry terminal. Yeah, they serve seafood here – who doesn't in Southeast? – but the signature dish is Ketchikan's best prime rib.

Wrangell ❸

⊨ Alaskan Sourdough Lodge — Motel $$

(📞907-874-3613, 800-874-3613; www.akgetaway.com; 1104 Peninsula St; s/d $114-124) For an overnight stay – and Wrangell is certainly worth it – this family-owned lodge has 16 basic but spotless rooms, a sauna and a steam room. It's a good place to thaw out if you've been exploring in the cold. They also offer a free shuttle from the ferry, and home-cooked evening meals served family-style.

Petersburg ❹

✗ Coastal Cold Storage — Seafood $

(306 N Nordic Dr; breakfast $4-8, lunch $8-12; ⏱6am-6pm Mon-Sat, 7am-2pm Sun) The local speciality is halibut beer bits, and this place serves the best ones in this seafood town.

Juneau ❺

⊨ Silverbow Inn — Hotel $$

(📞907-586-4146; www.silverbowinn.com; 120 2nd St; r $89-229) If your trip calls for a night in town, cozy up at the artsy, six-room Silverbow Inn where the smell of fresh bread from the bakery downstairs will wake you in the morning. Amenities at this historic hotel include a rooftop hot tub, full breakfast and a bottomless cookie jar.

Skagway ❽

⊨ At the White House — Hotel $$

(📞907-983-9000; www.atthewhitehouse.com; 475 8th Ave; r $125-155) A small, 10-room inn that retains its 1902 character with details such as hand-crafted quilts. All rooms have a private bath, and in the morning you wake up to a breakfast of fresh baked goods and fruit.

STRETCH YOUR LEGS **PORTLAND**

Start/Finish Stumptown Coffee

Distance 2 miles

Duration 3 hours

With green spaces galore, the world's largest independent bookstore, art, handcrafted beer, a vibrant food culture and a livability rating that's off the charts, Portland is made for walking. This route takes you to the highlights of downtown.

Coffee & Doughnuts

Start with coffee at **Stumptown Coffee** (128 SW 3rd Ave; 🕑6am-7pm Mon-Fri, from 7am Sat & Sun), roasting its own beans since 1999. A minute's walk away is **Voodoo Doughnut** (www.voodoodoughnut.com; 22 SW 3rd Ave; 🕑24hr), which bakes quirky treats – go for the bacon maple bar or the 'voodoo doll' filled with raspberry jelly 'blood.'

The Walk » Head toward the waterfront on pedestrian-only SW Ankeny St.

Saturday Market & Tom McCall Waterfront Park

Victorian-era architecture and the lovely **Skidmore Fountain** give the area beneath the Burnside Bridge near-European flair. Hit it on a weekend to catch the chaotic **Saturday Market** (www.portlandsaturdaymarket.com; SW Ankeny St & Naito Pkwy; 🕑10am-5pm Sat, 11am-4:30pm Sun Mar-Dec), an outdoor crafts fair with yummy food carts. From here you can explore the Tom McCall Waterfront Park along the Willamette River.

The Walk » Walk north under the Burnside Bridge through the park, then turn left on NW Couch St and right into NW 3rd Ave.

Chinatown

The ornate **Chinatown Gates** (cnr NW 4th Ave & W Burnside St) define the southern edge of Portland's so-called Chinatown, but you'll be lucky to find any Chinese people here at all. The main attraction is the **Lan Su Chinese Gardens** (www.lansugarden.org; NW 3rd Ave & NW Everett St; adult/student/child under 5yr $9.50/7/free; 🕑10am-6pm, to 5pm Nov-Mar), a one-block haven of tranquility, ponds and manicured greenery.

The Walk » Make your way west on NW Davis St to NW 8th Ave.

Museum of Contemporary Craft

The **Museum of Contemporary Craft** (www.museumofcontemporarycraft.org; 724

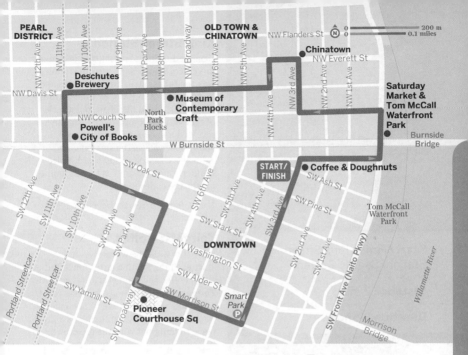

NW Davis St; adult/child under 12yr $4/free; ⊘11am-6pm Tue-Sat; 🚹) hosts some of the best exhibits you'll find anywhere in Portland, generally featuring fine crafts from artists throughout the Pacific Northwest. Several other top-notch galleries can be found on this block.

The Walk » Continue up NW Davis St to NW 11th Ave.

Deschutes Brewery

Since walking makes you thirsty and you're in Beervana (a group is lobbying to make this Portland's official name), it's high time for a pint and/or lunch. Grab a table under the arches framing the restaurant at **Deschutes Brewery** (www.deschutesbrewery.com; 210 NW 11th Ave; ⊘11am-11pm Mon-Thu, to midnight Fri & Sat).

The Walk » Walk west on NW 11th Ave one block to find yourself in the Pearl District's upmarket shopping area.

Powell's City of Books

Powell's City of Books (📞503-228-4651; www.powells.com; 1005 W Burnside St; ⊘9am-11pm; 🚹) is, until someone proves otherwise, the world's largest independent bookstore. Find a whole, awe-inspiring city block of new and used titles and prepare to get lost.

The Walk » Cross W Burnside St then turn left on SW Stark St and right on SW Broadway St to SW Morrison St.

Pioneer Courthouse Square

End your walk in the heart of downtown Portland. This brick plaza is nicknamed 'Portland's living room' and is the most visited public space in the city. When it isn't full of hacky-sack players, sunbathers or office workers lunching, the square hosts concerts, festivals, rallies, farmers markets – and even summer Friday-night movies, **Flicks on the Bricks** (www.thesquarepdx. org). Around the square is an endless array of shopping, restaurants and food carts.

The Walk » Head east one block down SW Morrison St, turn left on SW 3rd Ave and in five blocks you'll be back at Stumptown Coffee.

STRETCH YOUR LEGS
SEATTLE

Start/Finish King Street Station/Seattle Center

Distance 2 miles

Duration 3½ hours

Successive mayors have tried hard to alleviate Seattle's car chaos, and – hills and drizzly rain aside – this is now a good city for walking. Strategically placed coffee bars provide liquid fuel for urban hikers.

Take this walk on Trip

King Street Station

Designed to imitate St Mark's bell tower in Venice, Seattle's main train station was the tallest structure in Seattle upon its completion in 1906. By the late 1900s it had fallen into disrepair, but a series of renovations completed in 2013 have revealed a once-grandiose interior. Today, it serves as the start and end of Amtrak's Coast Starlight and Empire Builder routes, as well as the midpoint for the Cascades route.

The Walk >> From the station entrance, head quite literally around the corner onto S Jackson St.

Zeitgeist Coffee

Start this walk the way Seattleites start each day: with a latte. You'll find chain coffee shops on every corner, but **Zeitgeist Coffee** (www.zeitgeistcoffee.com; 171 S Jackson St; ☺6am-7pm Mon-Fri, 8am-7pm Sat-Sun), in a converted warehouse, is a great place to hang out with the hip crowd.

The Walk >> Go west on S Jackson St and right on 1st Ave S, admiring the red-brick Victorian buildings.

Pioneer Square

Seattle was born in the muddy shores of Elliott Bay and reborn here post the catastrophic 1889 fire. The handsome red-brick buildings remain, built in a style known as Richardson Romanesque in the 1890s. Yesler Way was America's original 'Skid Row,' so named as they used to skid logs down the thoroughfare toward the harbor.

The Walk >> Walk north on 1st Ave into the modern downtown core.

Seattle Art Museum

Seattle isn't just a meeting ground for Gore-Tex-wearing adventurers planning sorties into the surrounding mountains. There's culture here too. The **Seattle Art Museum** (www.seattleartmuseum.org; 1300 1st Ave; adult/student/child $17/11/free; ☺10am-5pm Wed-Sun, to 9pm Thu & Fri) is the best place to start. The collections span multiple genres from modern Warhol to Northwestern totem poles.

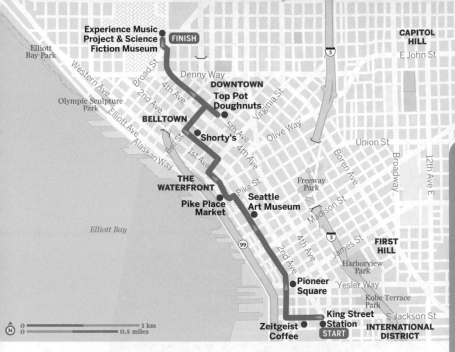

The Walk ›› Continue north on 1st Ave two blocks to Pike Place Market.

Pike Place Market

The soul of the city is encased in 105-year-old **Pike Place Market** (www.pikeplacemarket.org; 1501 Pike Pl). You'll need an early start if you want to spend more time dodging flying fish and less time dodging hordes of people. Locals love it for its fresh flowers, produce and seafood; for out-of-towners, its big neon sign is a quintessential Seattle photo op.

The Walk ›› Exit the north end of Pike Pl and you're in Belltown.

Shorty's

An early pulpit for grunge music, Belltown, north of downtown, has gone upscale since the 1990s with new condo developments and huddles of restaurants. A standout is **Shorty's** (www.shortydog.com; 2222 2nd Ave; ☺noon-2am daily), a cross between a pinball arcade and a dive bar.

The Walk ›› Turn right on Bell St and right again on 5th Ave.

Top Pot Doughnuts

Inhabiting an old car showroom, **Top Pot Doughnuts** (2124 5th Ave; ☺6am-7pm Mon-Fri, 7am-7pm Sat & Sun) has done for doughnuts what champagne did for wine. The coffee isn't bad either.

The Walk ›› Walk along 5th Ave to the intersection with Denny Way. Hang a left and you'll see the Seattle Center and Space Needle in front of you.

Experience Music Project & Science Fiction Museum

It's hard to miss the huge, crazily colorful building at the foot of the Space Needle. That would be the **Experience Music Project & Science Fiction Museum** (www.empmuseum.org; 325 5th Ave N; adult/child $20/14; ☺10am-7pm), a fun place to immerse yourself in rock and roll and/or sci-fi for one admission price.

The Walk ›› To get back to the start simply catch bus 131 ($2.25) from Broad St and 2nd Ave which drops you in South Jackson St near King Street Station.

ROAD TRIP ESSENTIALS

USA Driving Guide

With a comprehensive network of interstate highways, enthusiastic car culture and jaw-dropping scenery, the USA is an ideal road-tripping destination.

DRIVER'S LICENSE & DOCUMENTS

All US drivers must carry a valid driving license from their home state, proof of vehicle insurance and their vehicle's registration papers or a copy of their vehicle-rental contract.

Foreign drivers can legally drive in the USA for 12 months using their home driver's license. An International Driving Permit (IDP) isn't required, but will have more credibility with traffic police and will simplify the car-rental process, especially if your home license isn't written in English and/or doesn't have a photo. International automobile associations issue IDPs, valid for one year, for a fee. Always carry your home license with your IDP.

The American Automobile Association (AAA) has reciprocal agreements with some international auto clubs (eg Canada's CAA, AA in the UK). Bring your membership card from home.

INSURANCE

Liability insurance is legally required for all vehicles, although minimum coverage varies by state. When renting a car, check your home auto-insurance policy and, if applicable, your travel-insurance policy to see if rental cars are already covered. If not, expect to pay about $15 a day for rental-car liability insurance.

Insurance against damage to the car, called Collision Damage Waiver (CDW) or Loss Damage Waiver (LDW), adds another $15 to $20 per day for rental cars. Even with a CDW/LDW, you may be required to

Driving Fast Facts

➡ **Right or left?** Drive on the right
➡ **Legal driving age** 16
➡ **Top speed limit** 70mph on some highways.
➡ **Best bumper sticker** 'Where the heck is Wall Drug?'
➡ **Best radio station** National Public Radio (NPR)

pay up to the first $500 for any repairs. If you decline CDW/LDW, you will be held liable for damages up to the car's full value.

Some credit cards cover CDW/LDW if you charge the entire cost of the car rental to that card. If you have an accident, you may be required to pay the car-rental company first, then seek reimbursement from the credit-card issuer. Most credit-card coverage isn't valid for rentals over 15 days or 'exotic' models (eg convertibles, 4WD Jeeps).

RENTING A VEHICLE

To rent your own wheels, you'll usually need to be at least 25 years old, hold a valid driver's license and have a major credit card, *not* a check or debit card.

Cars

Rental car rates generally include unlimited mileage, but expect surcharges for additional drivers and one-way rentals. Airport locations may have cheaper base

Road Trip Websites

AUTO CLUBS

American Automobile Association (www.aaa.com) Roadside assistance, travel discounts, trip planning and maps for members.

Better World Club (www.betterworldclub.com) Ecofriendly alternative to AAA.

MAPS

America's Byways (http://byways.org) Inspiring itineraries, maps and directions for scenic drives.

Google Maps (http://maps.google.com) Turn-by-turn driving directions with estimated traffic delays.

ROAD CONDITIONS & CLOSURES

US Department of Transportation (www.fhwa.dot.gov/trafficinfo) Links to state and local road conditions, traffic and weather.

---

rates but higher add-on fees. If you get a fly-drive package, local taxes may be extra when you pick up the car. Child and infant safety seats are legally required; reserve them (around $10 per day, or $50 per trip) when booking your car.

Some major car-rental companies offer 'green' fleets of hybrid or alternative-fuel rental cars, but they're in short supply. Make reservations far in advance and expect to pay significantly more for these models. Many companies rent vans with wheelchair lifts and hand-controlled vehicles at no extra cost, but you must also reserve these well in advance.

International car-rental companies with hundreds of branches nationwide include:

Alamo (www.alamo.com)

Avis (www.avis.com)

Budget (www.budget.com)

Dollar (www.dollar.com)

Enterprise (www.enterprise.com)

Fox (www.foxrentacar.com)

Hertz (www.hertz.com)

National (www.nationalcar.com)

Thrifty (www.thrifty.com)

To find local and independent car-rental companies, check:

Car Rental Express (www.carrentalexpress.com) Search for independent car-rental companies and specialty cars (eg hybrids).

Rent-a-Wreck (www.rentawreck.com) Often rents to younger drivers (over-18s) and those without credit cards; ask about long-term rentals.

Wheelchair Getaways (www.wheelchairgetaways.com) Rents wheelchair-accessible vans across the country.

Zipcar (www.zipcar.com) Car-sharing club in dozens of cities; some foreign drivers are eligible for membership.

If you don't mind no-cancellation policies or which company you rent from, you may find better deals on car rentals through online travel discounters such as **Priceline** (www.priceline.com) and **Hotwire** (www.hotwire.com).

Motorcycles

Motorcycle rentals and insurance are very expensive, with steep surcharges for one-way rentals. Discounts may be available for three-day and weekly rentals.

National rental outfitters include:

Eagle Rider (www.eaglerider.com) Motorcycle rentals and tours in more than 25 states.

Harley-Davidson (www.harley-davidson.com) Links to scores of local motorcycle shops that rent Harleys.

RVs & Campervans

Popular with road-trippers, recreational vehicles (RVs, also called motorhomes) are cumbersome to drive and burn fuel at an alarming rate. However, they do solve transportation, accommodation and self-catering kitchen needs in one fell swoop. Even so, there are many places in national parks and scenic areas (eg narrow mountain roads) that they can't be driven.

Make reservations for RVs and smaller campervans as far in advance as possible.

Rental costs vary by size and model; basic rates often don't include mileage, bedding or kitchen kits, vehicle prep and cleaning or additional taxes and fees. If bringing pets is allowed, a surcharge may apply.

National rental agencies include:

Cruise America (www.cruiseamerica.com) With 125 RV rental locations nationwide.

El Monte RV (www.elmonterv.com) RV rentals in more than 25 states.

Happy Travel Campers (www.camperusa.com) Rents campervans in Los Angeles, San Francisco, Las Vegas and Denver.

Jucy Rentals (www.jucyrentals.com) Campervan rentals in Los Angeles, San Francisco and Las Vegas.

BORDER CROSSING

Citizens of Canada and Mexico who are driving across the border should be sure to bring their vehicle's registration papers, proof of liability insurance valid for driving in the USA and their home driving license. An International Driving Permit (IDP) isn't required, but may be helpful. Only some rental-car companies allow their vehicles to be driven across international borders.

MAPS

Tourist information offices and visitor centers distribute free but often very basic maps. GPS navigation can't be relied upon everywhere, notably in thick forests

Road Distances (miles)

	Atlanta	Boston	Chicago	Dallas	Denver	El Paso	Houston	Las Vegas	Los Angeles	Miami	New Orleans	New York	Oklahoma City	Phoenix	Portland	Salt Lake City	San Francisco	Seattle	St Louis
Boston	1100																		
Chicago	720	1005																	
Dallas	790	1770	935																
Denver	1405	2005	1010	785															
El Paso	1425	2405	1490	635	700														
Houston	800	1860	1090	240	1030	750													
Las Vegas	1990	2755	1760	1225	750	725	1475												
Los Angeles	2210	3025	2035	1445	1025	815	1560	275											
Miami	660	1510	1380	1320	2070	1940	1190	2545	2750										
New Orleans	475	1530	930	525	1305	1100	350	1740	1915	860									
New York	870	215	800	1565	1800	2200	1655	2550	2820	1290	1310								
Oklahoma City	865	1690	790	210	675	695	450	1125	1345	1500	725	1470							
Phoenix	1860	2690	1800	1070	825	430	1185	285	375	2370	1535	2480	1010						
Portland	2605	3120	2130	2030	1260	1630	2270	1020	965	3265	2555	2925	1925	1335					
Salt Lake City	1880	2395	1405	1265	535	865	1505	420	690	2545	1785	2190	1205	655	765				
San Francisco	2510	3100	2145	1750	1270	1190	1940	570	380	3130	2295	2930	1645	750	635	745			
Seattle	2675	3070	2065	2105	1330	1725	2345	1165	1150	3335	2630	2865	2000	1490	175	840	810		
St Louis	555	1190	295	630	855	1195	840	1615	1840	1215	680	955	500	1505	2050	1325	2065	2120	
Washington DC	635	440	700	1330	1690	1965	1415	2460	2690	1055	1090	230	1345	2350	2820	2095	2835	2770	845

Driving Problem-Buster

What should I do if my car breaks down? Put on your hazard lights (flashers) and carefully pull over to the side of the road. Call the roadside emergency assistance number for your auto club or rental-car company. Otherwise, call information (411) for the number of the nearest towing service or auto-repair shop.

What if I have an accident? If you're safely able to do so, move your vehicle out of traffic and onto the road's shoulder. For minor collisions with no major property damage or bodily injuries, be sure to exchange driver's license and auto-insurance information with the other driver, then file a report with your insurance provider or notify your car-rental company as soon as possible. For major accidents, call 911 and wait for the police and emergency services to arrive.

What should I do if I'm stopped by the police? Don't get out of the car unless asked. Keep your hands where the officer can see them (ie on the steering wheel). Always be courteous. Most fines for traffic or parking violations can be handled by mail or online within a 30-day period.

What happens if my car gets towed? Call the local non-emergency police number and ask where to pick up your car. Towing and vehicle storage fees accumulate quickly, up to hundreds of dollars for just a few hours or a day, so act promptly.

and remote mountain, desert and canyon areas. If you're planning on doing a lot of driving, you may want a more detailed fold-out road map or map atlas, such as those published by **Rand McNally** (www. randmcnally.com). Members of the American Automobile Association (AAA) and its international auto-club affiliates (bring your membership card from home) can pick up free maps at AAA branch offices nationwide.

Drunk Driving

The maximum legal blood-alcohol concentration for drivers is 0.08%. Penalties for 'DUI' (driving under the influence of alcohol or drugs) are severe, including heavy fines, driver's license suspension, court appearances and/or jail time. Police may give roadside sobriety checks to assess if you've been drinking or using drugs. If you fail, they'll require you to take a breath, urine or blood test to determine the level of drugs and alcohol in your body. Refusing to be tested is treated the same as if you'd taken the test and failed.

ROADS & CONDITIONS

The USA's highways are not always perfect ribbons of unblemished asphalt. Common road hazards include potholes, rockfalls, mudslides, flooding, fog, free-ranging livestock and wildlife, commuter traffic jams on weekday mornings and afternoons, and drivers distracted by technology, kids and pets or blinded by road rage.

In places where winter driving is an issue, snow tires and tire chains may be necessary, especially in the mountains. Ideally, carry your own chains and learn how to use them before you hit the road. Driving off-road or on dirt roads is often forbidden by rental-car contracts, and it can be very dangerous in wet weather.

Major highways, expressways and bridges in some urban areas require paying tolls. Sometimes tolls can be paid using cash (bills or coins), but occasionally an electronic toll-payment sensor is required. If you don't have one, your vehicle's license plate will likely be photographed and you'll be billed later, usually at a higher rate. Ask about this when picking up your rental vehicle to avoid surprising surcharges on your final bill after you've returned the car.

ROAD RULES

➜ Drive on the right-hand side of the road.

➜ Talking or texting on a cell (mobile) phone while driving is illegal in most states.

➜ The use of seat belts and infant and child safety seats is legally required nationwide, although exact regulations vary by state.

➜ Wearing motorcycle helmets is mandatory in many states, and always a good idea.

➜ High-occupancy vehicle (HOV) lanes marked with a diamond symbol are reserved for cars with multiple occupants, but sometimes only during specific signposted hours.

➜ Unless otherwise posted, the speed limit is generally 55mph or 65mph on highways, 25mph to 35mph in cities and towns and as low as 15mph in school zones. It's illegal to pass a school bus when its lights are flashing.

➜ Except where signs prohibit doing so, turning right at a red light after coming to a full stop is usually permitted (one notable exception is New York City). Intersecting cross-traffic still has the right of way, however.

➜ At four-way stop signs, cars proceed in order of arrival. If two cars arrive simultaneously, the one on the right goes first. When in doubt, politely wave the other driver ahead.

➜ At intersections, U-turns may be legal unless otherwise posted, but this varies by state – don't do it in Oregon and Illinois, for example.

➜ When emergency vehicles approach from either direction, carefully pull over to the side of the road.

➜ In many states, it's illegal to carry open containers of alcohol (even if they're empty) inside a vehicle. Unless the containers are full and still sealed, put them in the trunk instead.

➜ Most states have strict anti-littering laws; throwing trash from a vehicle may incur a $1000 fine. Besides, it's bad for the environment.

➜ Hitchhiking is illegal in some states, and restricted in others.

PARKING

Free parking is plentiful in small towns and rural areas, but scarce and often expensive in cities. Municipal parking meters and centralized pay stations usually accept coins and credit or debit cards. Parking at broken meters is often prohibited; where allowed, the posted time limit still applies.

USA Playlist

(Get Your Kicks on) Route 66 Bobby Troup, as recorded by Nat King Cole

I've Been Everywhere Johnny Cash

This Land Is Your Land Woody Guthrie

Born to Be Wild Steppenwolf

Runnin' Down a Dream Tom Petty & the Heartbreakers

Life Is a Highway Tom Cochrane

When parking on the street, carefully read all posted regulations and restrictions (eg 30-minute maximum, no parking during scheduled street-cleaning hours) and pay attention to colored curbs, or you may be ticketed and towed. In many towns and cities, overnight street parking is prohibited downtown and in designated areas reserved for local residents with permits.

At city parking garages and lots, expect to pay at least $2 per hour and $10 to $45 for all-day or overnight parking. For valet parking at hotels, restaurants, nightclubs etc, a flat fee of $5 to $40 is typically charged. Tip the valet attendant at least $2 when your keys are handed back to you.

FUEL

Gas stations are everywhere, except in national parks, rural areas and remote regions (eg mountains, deserts). Most gas stations are self-service, except in Oregon and New Jersey, where drivers are not legally allowed to pump their own gas.

Gas is sold in gallons (one US gallon equals 3.78L). The average price for regular-grade gas averages $3.15 to $4.25 across the country.

SAFETY

Vehicle theft, break-ins and vandalism are a problem mostly in urban areas. Be sure to lock your vehicle's doors, leave the windows rolled up and use any anti-theft devices that have been installed (eg car alarm, steering-wheel lock). Do not leave any valuables visible inside your vehicle; instead, stow them in the trunk before arriving at your destination, or else take them with you once you've parked.

USA Travel Guide

GETTING THERE & AWAY

Every visitor entering the USA from abroad needs a passport. Your passport must be valid for at least six months longer than your intended stay in the USA. Also, if your passport does not meet current US standards, you'll be turned back at the border.

Canadian and Mexican citizens arriving in the USA by air or overland will need to show either a valid passport or another pre-approved identification card for 'trusted travelers' who cross the border frequently. Check the **Western Hemisphere Travel Initiative (WHTI)** website (www.getyouhome.gov) for more information.

For visa requirements for entering the USA, see the visa information in the Directory. Remember that no matter what your visa says, US immigration officers have an absolute authority to refuse admission. They will ask about your travel plans and whether you have sufficient funds. It's a good idea to list an itinerary, produce an onward or round-trip ticket and have at least one major credit card.

AIR

Major international gateway and domestic hub airports across the USA include:

Charlotte-Douglas International Airport (CLT; www.charlotteairport.com) In Charlotte, NC.

Chicago O'Hare International Airport (ORD; www.flychicago.com)

Dallas/Fort Worth International Airport (DFW; www.dfwairport.com)

Denver International Airport (DEN; www.flydenver.com)

Dulles International Airport (IAD; www.metwashairports.com) Near Washington, DC.

George Bush Intercontinental Airport (IAH; www.fly2houston.com) In Houston, TX.

Hartsfield-Jackson Atlanta International Airport (ATL; www.atlanta-airport.com)

John F Kennedy International Airport (JFK; www.panynj.gov/airports) In NYC.

Los Angeles International Airport (LAX; www.lawa.org)

McCarran International Airport (LAS; www.mccarran.com) In Las Vegas, NV.

Miami International Airport (MIA; www.miami-airport.com)

Newark Liberty International Airport (EWR; www.panynj.gov/airports/newark-liberty.html) Near NYC.

Phoenix Sky Harbor International Airport (PHX; http://skyharbor.com)

San Francisco International Airport (SFO; www.flysfo.com)

Seattle-Tacoma International Airport (SEA; www.portseattle.org/Sea-Tac)

If you are flying to the US, the first airport that you land in is where you must go through immigration and customs, even if you are continuing on the flight to another destination. Upon arrival, all international visitors must register with the Department of Homeland Security, which involves having your fingerprints scanned and a digital photo taken.

Most mid-sized and larger US airports have car-rental counters staffed by major international agencies in the arrivals area near baggage claim. Courtesy shuttles usually wait curbside to transport rental-car customers to each company's on- or off-site parking lot.

Always make airport car-rental reservations in advance to ensure a car is available,

Practicalities

Smoking The majority of states prohibit smoking inside all public buildings, including airports, hotels, restaurants and bars.

Time The continental USA has four time zones: Eastern (GMT/UTC -5), Central (GMT/UTC -6), Mountain (GMT/UTC -7) and Pacific (GMT/UTC -8). Daylight Saving Time (DST), when clocks move one hour ahead (except in parts of Indiana and Arizona), applies from the second Sunday in March through to the first Sunday in November.

TV & DVD PBS (Public Broadcasting Service); major cable stations: ESPN (sports), HBO (movies), Weather Channel. DVDs coded region 1 (USA and Canada only).

Weights & Measures Imperial system used, except 1 US gallon = 0.83 imperial gallons.

as well as to lock in the lowest rental rates and minimize wait times. You may also save time and money by signing up in advance for the rental company's rewards program; membership is usually free, and could entitle you to perks such as priority check-in, free upgrades etc.

CAR & MOTORCYCLE

On weekends and holidays, especially during summer, traffic at the main border crossings between the USA and its neighboring countries Canada and Mexico can be heavy and waits long. Check current border-crossing wait times online with **US Customs & Border Protection** (http://apps.cbp.gov/bwt).

Be sure to bring all necessary documentation with you, including your vehicle's registration papers, proof of liability insurance valid for driving in the USA and your home driving license. Occasionally law-enforcement and customs authorities from the USA, Canada or Mexico will decide to search a car very thoroughly for contraband or undeclared dutiable items.

TRAIN

For Canadians living near the US border, taking the train can be an economical option. It also eliminates the hassle of driving a car across the border, which some rental companies do not allow. Instead, you can just rent a car upon arrival in the USA, then return it before leaving.

The USA's national passenger railway, **Amtrak** (www.amtrak.com), operates cross-border trains, including to and from Toronto, ON; Montréal, QC; and Vancouver, BC. Immigration and customs inspections at the US–Canada border can delay trains by an unpredictable amount of time.

Rental car pick-ups are available at some bigger Amtrak train stations in the USA, but usually only with advance bookings. Expect your choice of rental-car companies to be more limited than at airports.

DIRECTORY A–Z

ACCOMMODATIONS

Budget-conscious options for road-trippers include campgrounds, hostels and motels. Motels are ubiquitous on both highways and byways, while hostels are only common in cities and some popular vacation destinations. A variety of camping options exist, from free, bare-bones wilderness tent sites to full-service RV parks with wi-fi and cable-TV hookups.

At midrange motels and hotels, expect clean, decently sized rooms with a private bathroom, direct-dial telephone, cable TV and perhaps a coffeemaker, mini fridge and microwave. If it's included, breakfast might be just stale donuts and weak coffee, or a full hot-and-cold breakfast buffet. Wi-fi (🛜) is usually free, but sometimes slow or with a weak signal. A shared internet computer (@)for guests to use may be available, usually in the lobby.

Top-end hotels and luxury resorts offer many more amenities (eg swimming pool, fitness room, business center, restaurants and bars) and sometimes a scenic location or edgy contemporary design. Additional parking, internet and 'resort' fees may add $10 to $50 or more per day. Air-conditioning (❄) is standard in most rooms, with the exception of some historical hotels and coastal or mountain resorts.

Smaller and more intimate, B&Bs and inns offer widely varying amenities. Although their idiosyncratic design can be a relief from cookie-cutter chains, B&B rooms may lack phones, TVs, internet and private bathrooms. Breakfast is not always served, regardless of what the name 'bed-and-breakfast' implies. Some properties close during the off-season, many do not allow children or pets, and almost all require advance reservations.

Rates & Reservations

Generally, midweek rates are lower, except at business-oriented hotels in cities, where weekend leisure rates may be cheaper. Rates quoted in this book usually apply for high season, which means summer (June to August) across much of the country. At ski resorts and sunny winter-escape destinations, rates peak from Thanksgiving in late November through spring break in March or April.

Demand and prices also skyrocket around major holidays and special events, when some properties require multi-night stays. Reservations are recommended for holidays, festivals and weekends year-round, and also on weekdays in high season. If you reserve by phone, ask about the cancellation policy up front and get a booking confirmation number.

If you plan to arrive late in the evening, you may want to call ahead on the day of your stay to ask the front desk to hold your room. Hotels commonly overbook, but if you've guaranteed your reservation with a credit card, they should accommodate you regardless. At off-peak times, polite bargaining may be possible for walk-in guests without reservations.

Even if motels or hotels advertise that 'children sleep free,' this may be true only if kids use existing bedding in their parents' room. Requesting a rollaway bed or cot may cost extra.

Helpful Resources

Airbnb (www.airbnb.com) Nightly vacation rentals, sublet apartments and private rooms of varying quality; use at your own risk.

BedandBreakfast.com (www.bedand-breakfast.com) Online directory of B&Bs and inns with user reviews and professionally inspected 'Diamond Collection.'

Hostelling International USA (www.hiusa.org) Operates more than 50 hostels scattered across the country (nightly surcharge for non-members $3).

Hostelz.com (www.hostelz.com) Search engine, online bookings and reviews for independent hostels nationwide.

Hotel Coupons (www.hotelcoupons.com) Website and mobile app for the same motel and hotel discounts available in free booklets at tourist offices and highway rest areas.

Kampgrounds of America (www.koa.com) Network of more than 400 private RV parks and campgrounds across the country.

Recreation.gov (www.recreation.gov) Reservations for federal recreation-area campgrounds and cabins, including in national parks and forests.

ReserveAmerica (www.reserveamerica.com) Reservations for public campgrounds and cabins, including at many state parks.

Vacation Rentals by Owner (www.vrbo.com) Vacation rental houses, apartments, condos and more lodging options, most privately owned and operated.

FOOD

At most restaurants, lunch is more casual and generally cheaper, sometimes half the price of dinner. Some diners and cafes serve breakfast all day, and a few stay open 24 hours. Weekend brunch is typically available from mid-morning until early afternoon on Saturdays and Sundays.

Dress codes rarely apply except at top-end restaurants, where a collared shirt and possibly a jacket may be required for men. More often than not, smoking is illegal indoors at restaurants; ask first or look around for an ashtray before lighting up on an outdoor patio or at sidewalk tables.

Sleeping Price Ranges

The following price ranges refer to a private room with bathroom in high season excluding tax, unless otherwise stated.

$	less than $100
$$	$100-200
$$$	more than $200

Eating Price Ranges

The following price ranges refer to a main course excluding taxes and tip, unless otherwise stated.

$	less than $10
$$	$10-20
$$$	more than $20

Don't expect your neighbors to be happy about inhaling secondhand smoke.

You can bring your own wine (BYOB) at many restaurants, although a 'corkage' fee of $10 to $30 may be charged. If two diners share one main course, there's sometimes a split-plate surcharge. Vegetarians and travelers with food allergies or other dietary restrictions can usually be accommodated, especially in urban areas and at popular vacation destinations.

It's perfectly fine to bring kids along to casual restaurants, where high chairs, booster seats, special kids' menus, crayons and paper placemats for drawing are often available. Look for the family-friendly icon (🖼) included with listings throughout this book.

GAY & LESBIAN TRAVELERS

Most US cities have a visible and open LGBTQ community that is easy to connect with. The level of everyday acceptance varies nationwide. In some places there is no tolerance whatsoever, while in others acceptance is predicated on one's sexual preference and identity being downplayed or hidden. In conservative enclaves, some people follow a 'don't ask, don't tell' policy.

Although anti-hate crime legislation has been enacted across the country and popular attitudes are increasingly tolerant, bigotry still exists. Verbal harassment and occasional violence against lesbians, gay men, bisexuals and transgender people still occurs in both urban and rural areas, but most travelers are unlikely to experience anything seriously threatening.

Helpful Resources

Advocate (www.advocate.com) Gay-oriented newspaper covering politics, events, travel, arts and entertainment.

Damron (www.damron.com) Publishes annual advertiser-driven gay travel guides and a 'Gay Scout' mobile app.

GLBT National Help Center (888-843-4564; www.glnh.org; 1pm-9pm PST Mon-Fri, 9am-2pm PST Sat) National hotline for counseling, information and referrals.

OutTraveler (www.outtraveler.com) Free online magazine, destination guides, travel tips and an e-newsletter.

Purple Roofs (www.purpleroofs.com) Online directory of gay-owned and queer-friendly accommodations and tour operators.

HEALTH

Medical treatment in the USA is high-caliber, but the expense could kill you. Many health-care professionals demand payment at the time of service, especially from out-of-towners and international tourists.

Except for medical emergencies (in which case call 911 or go to the nearest 24-hour hospital emergency room, or ER), phone around to find an urgent-care or walk-in clinic or doctor's office that will accept your insurance.

Keep all receipts and documentation for billing and insurance claims, and later reimbursement. Some health-insurance (eg HMOs) and travel-insurance policies with medical benefits require you to get pre-authorization for treatment over the phone before seeking help.

Pharmacies are abundantly supplied, but you may find that some medications available over the counter in your home country will require a prescription in the USA, and without US health insurance, prescriptions can be shockingly expensive. Bring a signed, dated letter from your doctor describing all medications (including their generic names) that you regularly take.

INTERNET ACCESS

Travelers will have few problems staying connected in the tech-savvy USA.

This guide uses an internet icon (@) when a place has an online computer terminal for public use and the wi-fi icon (📶) wherever wireless internet is available. Either may be for free, sometimes only for paying guests or customers. Otherwise,

Tipping Guide
- -

Tipping is *not* optional. Only withhold tips in cases of outrageously bad service.

Airport skycaps & hotel porters $2 per bag, minimum per cart $5

Bartenders 10-15% per round, minimum per drink $1

Hotel concierges Nothing for simple information, up to $20 for securing last-minute restaurant reservations, sold-out show tickets etc

Hotel housekeepers $2-5 per night, left with the card provided; more if you're messy

Restaurant servers 15-20% of total bill, unless a gratuity is already charged

Taxi drivers 10-15% of metered fare, rounded up to next dollar

Valet parking attendants At least $2 when handed back the keys

expect to pay around $6 to $12 per hour for internet use, and $10 or more per day for unlimited wi-fi access.

Cities have a few cybercafes, as well as copy centers such as **FedEx Office** (www.fedex.com/us/office) with self-service online computer terminals and digital photo printing and CD-burning stations. Public libraries often provide online computers and wi-fi for free; internet terminals may require advance sign-up, and non-residents may have to pay a small surcharge.

Sniff out public wi-fi hotspots (free or fee-based) at airports, coffee shops, shopping malls (including Apple retail stores), tourist information offices and visitor centers, hotels and motels, museums, restaurants (including McDonald's), bars and some national, state and city parks.

- - - - - - - - - - - - - - - - - - -
MONEY

Prices in this book are quoted in US dollars and exclude state and local taxes, unless otherwise noted. Most locals don't carry large amounts of cash for everyday use, instead relying on credit cards, ATMs and debit or check cards. Smaller businesses may refuse to accept bills in denominations larger than $20 or traveler's checks.

ATMs are available 24/7 at banks, shopping malls, airports and grocery and convenience stores. Expect a transaction surcharge of at least $2, in addition to any fees charged by your home bank. Withdrawing cash from an ATM using your

credit card requires a four-digit PIN and usually incurs a significant fee; check with your credit-card company first.

Credit cards are almost universally accepted, and are typically required for making reservations online or over the phone. Visa, MasterCard and American Express are the most widely accepted issuers. If you use a debit or check card for transactions, large holds may be placed on your account, which will inconveniently freeze some or all available funds.

International exchange rates for withdrawals at ATMs are usually as good as you'll get at major banks, airport moneychangers and currency-exchange offices such as **American Express** (www.americanexpress.com). Outside cities and larger towns, exchanging foreign currency may be a problem, so make sure you have a credit card and sufficient cash on hand.

Traveler's checks are becoming obsolete, except as a trustworthy back-up. If you do carry them, purchase them in US dollars. Visa or American Express are the most widely accepted issuers.

- - - - - - - - - - - - - - - - - - -
OPENING HOURS

Full opening hours are usually included with all listings in this book. Hours may be shorter during winter or the off-season.

With regional variations, standard opening hours in the USA are as follows:

Banks 8:30am-4:30pm Mon-Fri, some to 6pm Fri & 9am-12:30pm Sat

Bars Noon or 5pm-midnight Sun-Thu, some to 2am Fri & Sat

Businesses & government offices 9am-5pm Mon-Fri

Nightclubs 10pm-2am or 4am Thu-Sat

Restaurants 7am-10:30am, 11:30am-2:30pm & 5-9pm daily, some later Fri & Sat

Shops 10am-6pm Mon-Sat, noon-5pm Sun (malls close later)

Supermarkets 8am-8pm daily, some 24hr

PUBLIC HOLIDAYS

On the following national holidays, banks, schools and government offices (including post offices) are closed, and museums, transportation and other services operate on a Sunday schedule. Holidays falling on a weekend are usually observed the following Monday.

New Year's Day January 1

Martin Luther King Jr Day Third Monday in January

Presidents' Day Third Monday in February

Memorial Day Last Monday in May

Independence Day July 4

Labor Day First Monday in September

Columbus Day Second Monday in October

Veterans Day November 11

Thanksgiving Fourth Thursday in November

Christmas December 25

During spring break, falling sometime around the Easter holiday in March or April, students get a week or two off from school, and families and throngs of party-ing college undergrads overrun beach resorts. School summer vacation runs from June through August, which are the USA's busiest travel months.

SAFE TRAVEL

Despite its seemingly apocalyptic list of dangers – guns, violent crime, riots, earth-quakes, tornadoes, hurricanes, wildfires – the USA is a reasonably safe place to visit. The greatest danger to visitors is traffic accidents (buckle up – it's the law).

For travelers, petty theft is the biggest concern, not violent crime. Wherever possible, withdraw money from ATMs during the day or in well-lit, busy areas at night.

When driving, secure valuables in the trunk of your car before arriving at your destination and don't leave valuables in your car overnight. Many hotels provide in-room wall safes, some of which can fit a tablet or laptop computer.

TELEPHONE

Cell (Mobile) Phones

You'll need a multiband GSM phone in order to make calls in the USA. Popping in a US prepaid rechargeable SIM card, which will give you a local phone number and voicemail, is usually cheaper than using your home network, on which international roaming charges may add up quickly.

Telecommunications and electronic stores such as Best Buy sell SIM cards and inexpensive, no-contract (prepaid) cell phones with some airtime included. You can also buy rechargeable SIM cards and rent cell phones from international-terminal shops at major US gateway airports.

Dialing Codes

➡ US phone numbers consist of a three-digit area code followed by a seven-digit local number.

➡ When dialing a number within the same area code, usually you'll need to dial just the seven-digit number. If that doesn't work, try dialing all 10 digits.

➡ If you are making a long-distance call to another area code, dial 1 plus the area code, plus the local phone number.

Important Numbers

Country code ☏1

Emergency (police, fire, ambulance) ☏911

International access code ☏011

International operator ☏00

Local directory assistance ☏411

Local operator ☏0

Toll-free directory assistance ☏800-555-1212

➜ Toll-free numbers beginning with 800, 866, 877 and 888 must be preceded by 1 when dialing.

➜ To make a direct international call, dial 011 then the country code, plus area code, plus local number.

➜ If calling from abroad, the country code for the USA is 1 (the same as for Canada, but international rates apply for calls between the two countries).

Phonecards

Avoid making long-distance calls on an in-room hotel or motel phone or at a public payphone without a phonecard. Prepaid phonecards are sold at convenience shops, supermarkets, newsstands and electronics and big-box stores. Be sure to read the fine print for hidden costs such as 'activation fees,' per-call 'connection fees' and payphone surcharges. **AT&T** (www. att.com) sells a reliable phonecard that's widely available in the USA.

TOURIST INFORMATION

The USA's official tourism website, **Discover America** (www.discoveramerica. com), is of limited use for trip-planning purposes. More helpful are the comprehensive tourism websites maintained by each US state, links to all of which can be easily found with a simple web search.

Any regional or local tourist office worth contacting has a website with downloadable travel guides. They also field phone calls and some can help book accommodations or have lists of last-minute lodging availability. All tourist offices, including state-run highway welcome centers, have racks of tourist brochures with discount coupons and sometimes free driving maps.

Many cities have an official convention and visitors bureau (CVB) that doubles as a tourist office, but these are less helpful to independent travelers because their primary focus is on drawing the business trade. In popular vacation destinations, privately run 'tourist information centers' are usually just fronts for travel agents selling hotel rooms, activities and tours on commission.

TRAVELERS WITH DISABILITIES

The USA is reasonably well equipped for travelers with mobility issues or other physical disabilities, although this varies by region. Some local tourist offices and visitor centers helpfully publish detailed accessibility guides. At national parks, US citizens or permanent residents with permanent disabilities are entitled to a free 'America the Beautiful' Access Pass (visit http://store.usgs.gov/pass for more information).

The Americans with Disabilities Act (ADA) requires all public transit and public buildings built after 1993 to be wheelchair-accessible, including restrooms. However, it's a good idea to call ahead and check, especially at historical or private buildings, for which there are no accessibility guarantees. Most intersections in cities have dropped curbs and audible crossing signals.

All major airlines, Greyhound buses and Amtrak trains and buses can accommodate people with disabilities with at least 48 hours of advance notice. Local buses, trains and subways are usually equipped with wheelchair lifts and ramps. City taxi companies typically have at least one wheelchair-accessible van, but you'll have to call for one and probably wait a while. For hand-controlled car and wheelchair-accessible van rentals, see the Driving in the USA chapter.

Service animals (ie guide dogs) are allowed to accompany passengers on public transit and in public buildings; bring documentation and make sure your animal wears its identifying vest. Most banks offer ATMs with instructions in Braille and earphone jacks. Telephone companies provide relay operators (dial 711) for hearing-impaired customers.

VISAS

Warning: All of the following information is highly subject to change. US entry requirements keep evolving as national security regulations change. Double-check visa and passport requirements *before* coming to the USA.

The **US Department of State** (http://travel.state.gov/visa) provides the most comprehensive visa information, with downloadable application forms, lists of US consulates abroad and visa wait times by country.

Currently, under the US Visa Waiver Program (VWP), visas are not required for stays of up to 90 days (no extensions) for citizens of 37 countries, as long as your passport meets current US standards. Citizens of VWP countries must still register with the **Electronic System for Travel Authorization** (https://esta.cbp.dhs.gov) at least 72 hours before traveling. Once approved, ESTA registration ($14) is usually valid for up to two years or until your passport expires, whichever comes first.

Most Canadian citizens with passports that meet current US standards do not need a visa for short-term visits to the USA. Citizens of Mexico usually need to get a non-immigrant or border-crossing 'laser' visa in advance. For details, check the **Western Hemisphere Travel Initiative (WHTI)** website (www.getyouhome.gov).

Citizens of all other countries or whose passports don't meet current US requirements will need to apply for a temporary visitor visa. Best done in your home country, the process costs a nonrefundable fee (minimum $160), involves a personal interview and can take several weeks, so apply early.

BEHIND THE SCENES

SEND US YOUR FEEDBACK

We love to hear from travellers – your comments help make our books better. We read every word, and we guarantee that your feedback goes straight to the authors. Visit **lonelyplanet. com/contact** to submit your updates and suggestions.

Note: We may edit, reproduce and incorporate your comments in Lonely Planet products such as guidebooks, websites and digital products, so let us know if you don't want your comments reproduced or your name acknowledged. For a copy of our privacy policy visit lonelyplanet.com/privacy.

OUR READERS

Many thanks to the travelers who used the last edition and wrote to us with helpful hints, useful advice and interesting anecdotes: Debra Janis, Fergus & Lorraine Maclagan, Jaye Albright, Julie Homer.

AUTHOR THANKS

SARA BENSON

Thanks to everyone at Lonely Planet for making this book happen, to all of my co-authors for all of their help and to everyone I met on the road who generously shared their local expertise. Big thanks to my Golden State friends and family, especially the Picketts, Starbins and Boyles.

CAROLYN MCCARTHY

I'm indebted to the good people of the Rocky Mountains. Special thanks to Lance and his Ouray friends for the bed and BBQ. Many thanks go out to the talented Rachel Dowd and virtual beers go out to all my colleagues for being the best to work with.

RYAN VER BERKMOES

Serious thanks to my parents who believed in the value of road trips and my sister who always sided with demanding the motel pool have a slide. Endless gratitude for fruitful support and golden advice from Alexis during my journeys near and far.

KARLA ZIMMERMAN

Many thanks to Lisa Beran, Lisa DiChiera, Jim DuFresne and Susan Hayes Stephan. Bucketloads of appreciation to Lonely Planeteers Sara Benson, Amy Balfour and Ryan Ver Berkmoes for the help. Thanks most to Eric Markowitz, the world's best partner-for-life, who indulges all my harebrained, pie-filled road trips. Sorry about the bug bites.

PUBLISHER THANKS

Climate map data adapted from Peel MC, Finlayson BL & McMahon TA (2007) 'Updated World Map of the Köppen-Geiger Climate Classification', *Hydrology and Earth System Sciences*, 11, 1633–44.

Cover photographs
Front Top: Mount Rushmore National Memorial, nagelestock. com/Alamy; Front Bottom Left: classic cars in Lenoir City, Tennessee, Jim West/ Alamy; Front Bottom Right: historic Route 66 sign near Amboy, California, Michael DeFreitas /Alamy; Back: farm in Woodstock, Vermont, Bob Krist /Corbis.

THIS BOOK

This 2nd edition of Lonely Planet's *USA's Best Trips* guidebook was researched and written by Sara Benson, Amy Balfour, Michael Benanav, Greg Benchwick, Lisa Dunford, Michael Grosberg, Adam Karlin, Mariella Krause, Carolyn McCarthy, Christopher Pitts, Adam Skolnick, Ryan Ver Berkmoes, Mara Vorhees and Karla Zimmerman. The previous edition was written by Sara Benson, Alison Bing, Becca Blond, Jennifer Denniston, Lisa Dunford, Alex Leviton, David Ozanich, Danny Palmerlee, Brandon Presser and Karla Zimmerman. This guidebook was commissioned in Lonely Planet's Oakland office, and produced by the following:

Commissioning Editors Jennye Garibaldi, Suki Gear, Joe Bindloss

Coordinating Editor Anne Mason

Senior Cartographer Alison Lyall

Coordinating Cartographer Gabriel Lindquist

Coordinating Layout Designer Mazzy Prinsep

Managing Editors Bruce Evans, Angela Tinson

Managing Layout Designer Jane Hart

Assisting Editors Elin Berglund, Helen Koehne, Kate Mathews, Katie O'Connell, Kate Whitfield

Assisting Layout Designers Adrian Blackburn, Carol Jackson

Cover Research Naomi Parker

Internal Image Research Kylie McLaughlin

Thanks to Anita Banh, Jeff Cameron, Ryan Evans, Larissa Frost, Genesys India, Jouve India, Catherine Naghten, Trent Paton, Saralinder Turner, Gerard Walker

INDEX